HARDWARE SECURITY

Design, Threats, and Safeguards

HARDWARE SECURITY

Design, Threats, and Safeguards

Debdeep Mukhopadhyay

Rajat Subhra Chakraborty

Indian Institute of Technology Kharagpur
West Bengal, India

CRC Press
Taylor & Francis Group
Boca Raton   London   New York

CRC Press is an imprint of the
Taylor & Francis Group, an **Informa** business

A CHAPMAN & HALL BOOK

CRC Press
Taylor & Francis Group
6000 Broken Sound Parkway NW, Suite 300
Boca Raton, FL 33487-2742

© 2015 by Taylor & Francis Group, LLC
CRC Press is an imprint of Taylor & Francis Group, an Informa business

No claim to original U.S. Government works

Version Date: 20140908

ISBN 13: 13: 978-1-4398-9583-2

Visit the Taylor & Francis Web site at
http://www.taylorandfrancis.com

and the CRC Press Web site at
http://www.crcpress.com

Contents

VI Physically Unclonable Functions 473

Foreword

In the past decade, the field of hardware security has grown into a major research topic, attracting intense interest from academics, industry, and governments alike. Indeed, electronic information technology now controls, documents, and supports virtually every aspect of our life. Be it electronic money, ID-cards, car electronics, industrial controllers, or Internet routers, this world is governed by bits as much as it is governed by physical resources. Hardware security addresses multiple key requirements in this information landscape: the need to securely handle and store electronic information any time, anywhere; and the need to do it very efficiently in terms of resource cost and energy cost.

Hardware security collects a rich field of research which combines multiple knowledge domains including, among others, discrete math, algorithm design and transformations, digital architecture design with analog twists, and controlled production technologies. Hardware security puts traditional notions of hardware design on their head. Examples are the beneficial use of noise to produce random numbers and to feed security protocols, and the design of hardware that has a constant, rather than minimal, power dissipation, to avoid side-channel leakage.

The origins of hardware security lie within cryptographic engineering, a field young enough to have new artifacts and methods still carry the inventor's last name. Indeed, although cryptography has been around for centuries, it's only since the last 50 years that it has established itself as a field of science that enables participation of a broad community. Cryptography is now a fundamental part of information technology. Cryptographic Engineering is concerned with design and implementation aspects of cryptography. It is a vibrant area with established conference venues such as CHES attracting hundreds of participants. New ideas in cryptography, such as privacy-friendly subscriptions and multi-party computation, provide a continuous influx of new design challenges to the hardware security engineer.

Besides a continuous innovation at the level of applications, secure hardware has also benefited, and is still benefiting, from tremendous improvements in technology. Although the impeding end-of-the-road for traditional CMOS has been predicted many years, the technology has propelled secure hardware into applications that would have been unthinkable just a decade ago. In fact, the 'Things' in the Internet of Things would be impossible without secure hardware, and this secure hardware would be impossible without the dense integration and high efficiencies offered by technology.

A fourth factor that makes secure hardware an exciting field of research is in its role as last-line-of-defense. Traditional software-based cyber-security has been plagued by security issues for many years, and hardware has been touted as a safe haven for our private electronic information. However, secure hardware is under attack, as well. Adversaries have learned to pick up side-channel information from secure processing using low-cost, simple measurement equipment; they have learned how faults can reveal the inner workings of algorithms that are conceived as a black box by cryptographers. Adversaries have even learned to interfere with the IC design flow itself, subverting the design with a Trojan and making the IC do something different than it was conceived for.

It is with great excitement that I see this book on 'Hardware Security Design' published.

In recent years, many schools have started graduate courses on this topic, often relying on advanced research papers. There is a clear need for a general, comprehensive text that can be used as the basis for a course. Furthermore, there is a great need for a reference text that will help designers and practitioners in the field to understand the main issues. This text stands out among others in that it has been written by a team of just two authors. They have not only done an admirable effort, but they have also ensured a consistent presentation and discussion.

The authors have done an excellent job at systematically introducing the field of hardware security. They start with the fundamentals, touch upon practical aspects of hardware design, discuss the mapping of symmetric-key and public-key algorithms, and finally provide an in-depth treatment of the last-line-of-defense aspects of secure hardware. The book is supported by an extensive collection of references, testifying to the intensive level of research ongoing in this exciting, innovative field. I hope the book will encourage new researchers and practitioners to join the effort in building the fundamentals of secure information technology that our future calls for.

Patrick Schaumont
Blacksburg, August 2014

Preface

With the ever-increasing proliferation of e-business practices, great volumes of secure business transactions and data transmissions are routinely carried out in an encrypted form in devices ranging in scale from personal smartcards to business servers. These cryptographic algorithms are often computationally intensive and are designed in hardware and embedded systems to meet the real-time requirements. Developing expertise in this field of *hardware security* requires background in a wide range of topics. On one end is understanding of the mathematical principles behind the cryptographic algorithms and the underlying theory behind their working. These principles are necessary to innovate in the process of developing efficient implementations, which is central to this discourse. This also needs to be backed by exposure in the field of Very Large Scale Integration (VLSI) and embedded systems. Understanding the platforms on which the designs are developed is needed to develop high performance and compact solutions to the cryptographic algorithms. On the other end are the threats which arise from the hardware implementations. History has taught us that strong cryptographic algorithms and their efficient designs are just the beginning. Naïve optimizations to develop efficient hardware devices can lead to embarrassing attacks which can have catastrophic implications. Often these attacks are based on exploitation of *side-channels*, which are covert channels leaking information which the designers of the cryptographic algorithms or the conventional hardware engineer will be unaware of. Further, the complexity of hardware designs also makes it increasingly difficult to detect bugs and modifications. These modifications can be malicious, as they can be the seat of *hardware Trojans*, which when triggered can lead to disastrous system failures and/or security breaches. Another pressing issue in the world of cyber-security arises from the threats of counterfeit integrated circuits (ICs). Detecting and protecting against these vulnerabilities requires "unclonable" novel hardware security primitives, which can act as *fingerprint generators* for the manufactured IC instances.

This book thus attempts to bring on a single platform a treatment of all these aspects of hardware security which we believe are quite challenging and unique. The book is targeted for a senior undergraduate or post-graduate course on hardware security. The book is suitable for students from not only CS and EE backgrounds, but also from mathematics. The book is also suitable for self-study of the practising professional who requires an exposure to state-of-the-art research on hardware security. Although we have strived to provide a contemporary overview on the design, threats and safeguards required for assurance in hardware security, we believe that the work, because of its constant evolution, will always be dynamic. However having said that, the fundamentals, which we have attempted to bring out, should stand out in the mind of the reader, assisting in future developments and research.

As mentioned, the content of the book covers modern day hardware security issues, along with fundamental aspects which are imperative for a comprehensive understanding. We briefly describe these aspects:

- **Mathematical Background and Cryptographic Algorithms:** Modern-day cryptographic systems rely heavily on field theory. Understanding of field arithmetic techniques, definitions, constructions, and inter-relations of several fields are required to develop efficient crypto-designs. Modern ciphers come in wide-ranging variety, from symmetric algorithms like *Advanced Encryption Standard* (AES), to asymmetric algorithms like *Elliptic Curve Cryptography* (ECC). As we will see in the book, the internal structures of the algorithms and suitable manipulations can lead to facts which can be exploited in efficient implementations.

- **Modern Hardware Design:** A designer has to develop a thorough understanding of the hardware platforms on which the implementations are to be developed. In this book we focus on Field Programmable Gate Arrays (FPGAs), which are fast, programmable and low cost. With the rapid development of FPGA technology, they have become high-performance, and are suitable test beds for cryptographic engineering research and development. With their in-house nature they provide excellent test beds for learning the trade secrets of hardware security, while also providing avenues for developing complete end products. While depending on various algorithms the architecture of the designs vary, a systematic approach can lead to a suitable design with proper separation of the control and data-path. The Look-up-Table (LUT)-based structure of an FPGA also allows suitable modeling of the critical path and LUT, which enables the exploration of the design alternatives.

- **Hardware Design of Cryptographic Algorithms and Arithmetic Units in FPGAs:** It is a challenging task to transform the cryptographic algorithms into efficient implementations on a hardware platform. Further, FPGAs because of their underlying Lookup Table (LUT)-based structures provide new design challenges, which the architecture should be capable of leveraging. In these parts of the book, we study several algorithmic and architectural optimizations for arithmetic circuits useful in the cryptographic domain, like field multipliers, inverses and also for various ciphers, like AES and ECC.

- **Side Channel Analysis:** As discussed, naïve implementations and optimizations can lead to vulnerabilities in crypto-implementations through several information leakage channels, which are commonly referred to as *side-channels*. The book first attempts to present an overview on some of the common side channels and their usage in attacking ciphers. Side channels range from timing, power, behavior under faults, performance on platforms enabled with cache memories, and also Design-for-Testability (DFT) features. Subsequently, we deal in depth on each of the side-channels to understand the working principles of the attacks. How to protect against these attacks is a related question, which we also address with respect to each of the attacks.

- **Hardware Intellectual Property Protection:** Modern electronic design regularly employs high-performance, pre-verified hardware *intellectual property* (IP) cores to meet aggressive time-to-market demands. While this practice improves design quality and decreases design cost and time, this also exposes the IP vendor to IP piracy, thereby causing large loss of revenue. We develop a systematic design approach for hardware IP protection, based on the principle of *design obfuscation*. This technique is applicable for hardware IPs at both the *gate-level* and *Register Transfer Level* (RTL).

- **Hardware Trojans:** Modern semiconductor manufacturing follows a "horizontal" business model, where several external agencies are involved in the design and manufacturing phase. The resources and services procured from external agents include hardware IP cores (mentioned previously), *computer-aided design* (CAD) software tools, *standard cell libraries*, fabrication and testing services, etc. However, such practices decrease the amount of control that the design house used to traditionally exercise over their own products, thus making them vulnerable to malicious, hard-to-detect, design modifications, commonly termed as *Hardware Trojan Horses* ("Hardware Trojans" in short). If undetected, these hardware Trojans can cause irreparable loss to critical infrastructure, human life and property. Traditional post-manufacturing testing methods are often unable to detect hardware Trojans. We explore the unique threat posed by hardware Trojans, and novel logic and side-channel analysis-based testing techniques to detect them. We also explore a design obfuscation based technique to resist hardware Trojan insertion, and to make inserted hardware Trojans more detectable.

- **Physically Unclonable Functions:** The threat posed by counterfeit and cloned ICs has become a major global issue, and is a consequence of the practice of remote fabrication of ICs. Silicon *Physically Unclonable Functions* (PUFs), proposed in recent years, constitute a class of hardware security primitives, which hold great promise in solving the problem of IC authentication. However, design of silicon PUFs comes with its unique set of challenges. It has also been shown that PUFs are vulnerable to the so-called *model-building attacks*. We explore PUF designs, metrics to judge the quality of a designed PUF, and state-of-the-art model building attacks on PUFs.

Acknowledgements: This preface would be incomplete without a mention of the people who made this effort possible. The authors would like to express their sincere gratitude to the Computer Science and Engineering Department of IIT Kharagpur, which provides an ideal environment for research on hardware security. The students of the *Secure Embedded Architecture Laboratory* (SEAL) in the CSE department of IIT Kharagpur read initial versions of the draft, and gave constructive criticisms. The authors appreciate the staff at CRC Press, especially Ms. Aastha Sharma, for their encouragement and understanding, in spite of missing several deadlines.

Debdeep Mukhopadhyay would like to thank all his former and present students for serving as a motivation and also window to this evolving subject. He would like also to thank all his colleagues, collaborators and funding agencies without whose support this work would not have been possible. Special thanks to Dr Chester Rebeiro (Columbia University), Dr Subidh Ali (NYU-Abu Dhabi), Sujoy Sinha Roy (K.U. Leuven), Dr Xiaofei (Rex) Guo (NYU-Poly), Dr Bodhisatwa Mazumdar (NYU-Abu Dhabi), Suvadeep Hajra (IIT Kharagpur), Prof Abhijit Das (IIT Kharagpur), Prof Dipanwita Roy Chowdhury (IIT Kharagpur), Prof Indranil Sengupta (IIT Kharagpur), Prof Partha Pratim Chakrabarti (IIT Kharagpur), Prof Ramesh Karri (NYU-Poly), Prof Ingrid Verbauwhede (K.U.Leuven), Prof C. Pandurangan (IIT Madras), Prof V. Kamakoti (IIT Madras), Dr Sanjay Burman (CAIR, DRDO), Dr P. K. Saxena (SAG, DRDO), Prof Bimal Roy (ISI Kolkata), Prof Sylvain Guilley (Telecom Paris Tech), Dr Junko Takahashi (NTT Labs), Dr Toshinori Fukunaga (NTT Labs), for their contributions and encouragement in various stages of the book. He would like to say a thanks to his brother Rajdeep for being a constant companion and for emphasizing the importance of working with choice. He would like to take this occasion to express gratitude to family members for their constant support, prayers and encouragement. He would like to specially mention his father-in-law, Anup Chatterjee for his constant enquiry on the status of the book, which helped to get back to the book after the occasional gaps. This book would not have been possible without the *silent* support of his wife Ayantika through several highs and lows in life, and most importantly to help him dream big. Her help to provide a home after a tiring day to collect himself for a new challenge has been instrumental in this long journey. He would also like to take this moment to remember his Grand Mother, who passed away in the final moments of compiling this text, and pray for her soul's eternal peace. Finally, he would like to thank *God* for being kind to gift with a lovely daughter, *Debanti* in the final phases of writing the book, to inspire him for his future endeavours. Debdeep would like to dedicate the book to his parents, Niharendu and Dipa Mukhopadhyay, without whom nothing would be possible.

Rajat Subhra Chakraborty would like to thank his family members, especially his wife Munmun, for their love, patience and understanding, and for allowing him to concentrate on the book during the weekends and vacations. Rajat would like to dedicate this book to the memory of his father, Pratyush Kumar Chakraborty, who passed away while this book was being written. Rest in peace, *Baba*.

List of Figures

List of Tables

Part I

Background

Chapter 1

Mathematical Background

"Mathematics is the language with which God wrote the universe."

Galileo Galilei

1.1 Introduction

Mathematics is often referred to as the *mother of all sciences*. It is every where, and without it no scienctific study would have progressed. Mathematics defines not only the laws of the universe, but also gives us insight to solutions to many unsolved mysteries around us. Frankly, mathematical discoveries have often given rise to many questions, a large share of which are *unknown* to our present knowledge. These unproven results often are the backbone of science. To quote Vonn Neumann, *In mathematics you don't understand things. You just get used to them.* However, we start from these results and discover by logical deduction results, which are used in several discourses. The study of any *engineering* discipline, thus relies on the applications of these mathematical principles to solve practical problems for the benefit of mankind.

The study of *hardware security*, like many other engineering subjects, relies heavily on mathematics. To start with, it involves the implementation of complex cryptographic algorithms on various platforms in an efficient manner. By the term efficiency, we often imply resource utilization and the time required by a hardware circuit. Although there are other measures, like power consumption, just restricting ourselves to these two classical objectives of hardware circuits poses several challenges, solutions to which are often obtained in the tricks in mathematics. The choice of a suitable algorithm for a specific purpose implies one has to be aware of the contemporary algorithms in the crypto literature. But these algorithms often are based on deep theories in mathematics: number theory, field theory, and the like. Hence to obtain a proper understanding and ,most importantly, to compare the algorithms, one needs to develop a grasp of these topics. Once an algorithm is chosen, the underlying primitives must be understood: for example, a given algorithm may employ a multiplication step, more specifically a *finite field* multiplier. So the question is which multiplier should be chosen? Each design has their positives and negatives, thus a designer equipped with proper mathematical training and algorithm analysis prowess can make the choices in a prudent manner, which leads to efficient architectures. Today hardware designs of cryptographic algorithms are threatened with attacks, that exploit the properties of the implementations rather than the algorithms themselves. These attacks, commonly referred to as *side channel attacks* rely heaviliy on *statistics*. Thus in order to develop suitable defenses against these attacks, the designer also needs to understand these statistical methods. Knowledge of these methods shall help the designer not only to improve the existing attacks, but finally develop sound counter-measures. In short, design of *efficient* and *secured* implementations of cryptographic algorithms needs not only prudent engineering practices and architectural knowledge, but also understanding of the underlying mathematical principles.

In this chapter, we present an overview of some of the important mathematical concepts that are often useful for the understanding of hardware security designs.

1.2   Modular Arithmetic

Modular arithmetic is central to the discussion of ciphering algorithms. Starting from prehistoric classical ciphers to the present-day cryptographic algorithms, modular arithmetic is heavily used.

Also from the point of view of devices performing these ciphering operations, the underlying operations need to be done with finite numbers. An 8-bit computer bus, for example, can store only 256 numbers. The question is can we define arithmetic as we are used to with real numbers. Can we define *addition, subtraction, multiplication, division* on a finite space of numbers? Here is the beauty of mathematics, that we can have our own rules!

Consider, the set of numbers, $\mathbb{S} = \{0, \ldots, 5\}$. Suppose we consider the two operations (later we define these notions more formally), addition (denoted by $+$) and multiplication (denoted by $*$). We obtain sums and products, such as shown in the **Tables 1.1** and **1.2**.

The above results show that we can define the laws of addition and multiplication, just as we have over the set of real numbers. Closer investigation shows that all the numbers in the set have additive inverse, that is another number which if added with it gives the number 0, commonly referred to as the *additive identity*. Similarly, all numbers except zero have

TABLE 1.1: Addition on the set $\mathbb{S}$

+	0	1	2	3	4
0	0	1	2	3	4
1	1	2	3	4	0
2	2	3	4	1	0
3	3	4	0	1	2
4	4	0	1	2	3

TABLE 1.2: Multiplication on the set $\mathbb{S}$

*	0	1	2	3	4
0	0	0	0	0	0
1	0	1	2	3	4
2	0	2	4	1	3
3	0	3	1	4	2
4	0	4	3	2	1

multiplicative inverse, that is another number which multiplied with it gives the number 1, known as the *multiplicative identity*. Since, we can define arithmetic on a finite set, we can envisage to develop ciphering algorithms on these numbers. For this we have to generalize this observation, in particular answer questions, like is there any speciality of the number 5 that we chose. It turns out that the primality of the number 5 has a very significant role in the theory that follows. We gradually develop the results subsequently. It may be kept in mind that we shall often state important results without formal proofs, which can be found in more details in textbooks on number theory and algebra.

We first state some definitions in the following:

Definition 1.2.1 *An integer a is said to be congruent to an integer b modulo m, when m divides $b - a$ and is denoted as $a \equiv b \bmod m$.*

Congruence modulo m is an equivalence relation on the integers.

- (**Reflexivity**): any integer is congruent to itself modulo m.

- (**Symmetricity**): $a \equiv b \bmod m \Rightarrow b \equiv a \bmod m$.

- (**Transitivity**): $(a \equiv b \bmod m) \wedge (b \equiv c \bmod m) \Rightarrow a \equiv c \bmod m$.

The expression $a \equiv b \bmod m$ can also be written as $\exists k \in \mathbb{Z}, st.a = b + km$. Equivalently, when divided by m, both a and b leave the same remainder.

Definition 1.2.2 *The equivalence class of a mod m consists of all integers that are obtained by adding a with integral multiples of m. This class is also called the residue class of a mod m.*

Example 1 *Residue class of 1 mod 4 is the set $\{1, 1 \pm 4, 1 \pm 2 * 4, 1 \pm 3 * 4, \ldots\}$*

The residue classes mod m is denoted by the symbol $\mathbb{Z}/m\mathbb{Z}$. Each class has a representative element, $0, 1 \ldots, m - 1$. The equivalence class for a representative element, say 0, is denoted by [0]. The set $\{0, 1, \ldots, m - 1\}$ formed of the m incongruent residues is also called a *complete system*.

Example 2 *Complete systems for a given modulo m is not unique. For example for $m = 5$, the sets $\{0, 1, 2, 3, 4\}$ and $\{-12, -15, 82, -1, 31\}$ are both complete systems.*

The following theorem is straightforward and is stated without any proof.

Theorem 1 *$a \equiv b \bmod m$ and $c \equiv d \bmod m$, implies that $-a \equiv -b \bmod m$, $a + c \equiv b + d \bmod m$, and $a * c \equiv b * d \bmod m$, $\forall a, b, c, d, m \in \mathbb{Z}$.*

This result is particularly useful as it shows that operations in modular arithmetic can be made much easier by performing intermediate modular reduction. The following example illustrates this point.

Example 3 *Prove that $2^{2^5} + 1$ is divisible by 641.*

We note that $641 = 640 + 1 = 5 * 2^7 + 1$. Thus,

$$
\begin{aligned}
5 * 2^7 &\equiv -1 \bmod 641 \\
\Rightarrow (5 * 2^7)^4 &\equiv (-1)^4 \bmod 641 \\
\Rightarrow 5^4 * 2^{28} &\equiv 1 \bmod 641 \\
\Rightarrow (625 \bmod 641) * 2^{28} &\equiv 1 \bmod 641 \\
\Rightarrow (-2^4) * 2^{28} &\equiv 1 \bmod 641 \\
\Rightarrow 2^{32} &\equiv -1 \bmod 641
\end{aligned}
$$

This example shows that the complicated computation can be simplified by performing modular reductions and subsequently carrying on the computations. This fact holds true for all the ciphering operations which work on finite sets of data that we shall subsequently study.

1.3   Groups, Rings, and Fields

Next we develop the concepts of groups and fields, which are central to the study of ciphers. We browse through a series of definitions in order to build up the concept.

Definition 1.3.1 *If X is a set, a map $\circ: X \times X \to X$, which transforms an element (x_1, x_2) to the element $x_1 \circ x_2$ is called an operation.*

Example 4 *The sum of the residue classes $a + m\mathbb{Z}$ and $b + m\mathbb{Z}$ is $(a + b) + m\mathbb{Z}$.*

Example 5 *The product of the residue classes $a + m\mathbb{Z}$ and $b + m\mathbb{Z}$ is $(a * b) + m\mathbb{Z}$.*

Definition 1.3.2 *An operation $\circ$ on X is associative if $(a \circ b) \circ c = a \circ (b \circ c)$, for all $a, b, c \in X$.*

Definition 1.3.3 *A pair $(H, \circ)$ consisting of a set H and an associative operation $\circ$ on H is called a semigroup. The semigroup is called abelian or commutative if the operation is also commutative.*

Example 6 *The pairs $(\mathbb{Z}, +)$, $(\mathbb{Z}, *)$, $(\mathbb{Z}/m\mathbb{Z}, +)$, $(\mathbb{Z}/m\mathbb{Z}, *)$ are abelian semigroups.*

Definition 1.3.4 *An identity element of the semigroup $(H, \circ)$ is an element $e \in H$, which satisfies $e \circ a = a \circ e = a$, $\forall a \in H$.*

Definition 1.3.5 *If the semigroup contains an identity element it is called a monoid.*

It can be easily seen that the semigroup can have at most one identity element. This is so, if there are two identities, e and e', we have $e \circ e' = e = e'$.

Definition 1.3.6 *If $e \in H$ is an identity element of the semigroup $(H, \circ)$ (i,e it is a monoid), then $b \in H$ is called an inverse of $a \in H$ if $a \circ b = b \circ a = e$.*

If a has an inverse it is called invertible in the semigroup H. In a monoid, each element can have at most one inverse. To see this, assume that an element $a \in H$ has two inverses, b and b' and let e be the identity element. Thus from the definition, $a \circ b = b \circ a = a \circ b' = b' \circ a = e \Rightarrow b' = b' \circ e = b' \circ (a \circ b) = (b' \circ a) \circ b = e \circ b = b$.

Example 7 $(\mathbb{Z}, +)$ *has an identity element 0, and inverse $-a$. $(\mathbb{Z}, *)$ has an identity element 1, while the only invertible elements are $+1$ and -1. $(\mathbb{Z}/m\mathbb{Z}, +)$ has as identity element, $m\mathbb{Z}$. The inverse is $-a + m\mathbb{Z}$. This monoid is often referred to as $\mathbb{Z}_m$. $(\mathbb{Z}/m\mathbb{Z}, *)$ has as identity element $1 + m\mathbb{Z}$. The invertible elements of $\mathbb{Z}$ are $t \in \mathbb{Z}$, st. $\gcd(t, m) = 1$, i.e., if and only if t and m are mutually co-prime. The invertible elements of this monoid is a set denoted by $\mathbb{Z}_m^*$.*

Definition 1.3.7 *A group is a monoid in which every element is invertible. The group is commutative or abelian if the monoid is commutative.*

Example 8 $(\mathbb{Z}, +)$ *and $(\mathbb{Z}/m\mathbb{Z}, +)$ are abelian groups. However, $(\mathbb{Z}, *)$ is not an abelian group. $((\mathbb{Z}/m\mathbb{Z})\backslash\{0\}, *)$ is an abelian group if and only if m is prime.*

Definition 1.3.8 *A ring is a triplet $(R, +, *)$ such that $(R, +)$ is an abelian group, $(R, *)$ is a monoid and the operation * distributes over the operation +, i.e. $\forall x, y, z \in R, x * (y + z) = (x * y) + (x * z)$. The ring is called commutative if the monoid $(R, *)$ is commutative.*

Definition 1.3.9 *A field is a commutative ring $(R, +, *)$ in which every element in the monoid $(R, *)$ is invertible.*

Example 9 *The set of integers is not a field. The set of real and complex numbers form a field. The residue class modulo a prime number, except the element 0, is a field.*

Thus summarizing the above concepts, the definition of groups, rings, and fields are rewritten below:

Definition 1.3.10 *A group denoted by $\{\mathbb{G}, \cdot\}$, is a set of elements $\mathbb{G}$ with a binary operation '$\cdot$', such that for each ordered pair (a, b) of elements in $\mathbb{G}$, the following axioms are obeyed [122][369]:*

- Closure: *If $a, b \in \mathbb{G}$, then $a \cdot b \in \mathbb{G}$.*

- Associative: *$a \cdot (b \cdot c) = (a \cdot b) \cdot c$ for all $a, b, c \in \mathbb{G}$.*

- Identity element: *There is a unique element $e \in \mathbb{G}$ such that $a \cdot e = e \cdot a = a$ for all $a \in \mathbb{G}$.*

- Inverse element: *For each $a \in \mathbb{G}$, there is an element $a' \in \mathbb{G}$ such that $a \cdot a' = a' \cdot a = e$*

If the group also satisfies $a \cdot b = b \cdot a$ for all $a, b \in \mathbb{G}$ then it is known as a *commutative* or an *abelian group*.

Definition 1.3.11 *A* ring *denoted by* $\{\mathbb{R}, +, *\}$ *or simply* $\mathbb{R}$ *is a set of elements with two binary operations called addition and multiplication, such that for all $a, b, c \in \mathbb{R}$ the following are satisfied:*

- $\mathbb{R}$ *is an abelian group under addition.*

- *The closure property of* $\mathbb{R}$ *is satisfied under multiplication.*

- *The associativity property of* $\mathbb{R}$ *is satisfied under multiplication.*

- *There exists a multiplicative identity element denoted by* 1 *such that for every* $a \in \mathbb{F}$, $a * 1 = 1 * a = 1$.

- Distributive Law : *For all* $a, b, c \in \mathbb{R}$, $a*(b+c) = a*b+a*c$ *and* $(a+b)*c = a*c+b*c$.

The set of integers, rational numbers, real numbers, and complex numbers are all rings. A ring is said to be commutative if the commutative property under multiplication holds. That is, for all $a, b \in \mathbb{R}, a * b = b * a$.

Definition 1.3.12 *A* field *denoted by* $\{\mathbb{F}, +, *\}$ *or simply* $\mathbb{F}$ *is a commutative ring which satisfies the following properties*

- Multiplicative inverse : *For every element* $a \in \mathbb{F}$ *except* 0, *there exists a unique element* a^{-1} *such that* $a \cdot (a^{-1}) = (a^{-1}) \cdot a = 1$. a^{-1} *is called the multiplicative inverse of the element* a.

- No zero divisors : *If* $a, b \in \mathbb{F}$ *and* $a \cdot b = 0$, *then either* $a = 0$ *or* $b = 0$.

As we have seen the set of rational numbers, real numbers and complex number are examples of fields, while the set of integers is not. This is because the multiplicative inverse property does not hold in the case of integers.

Definition 1.3.13 *The* characteristic *of a field* $\mathbb{F}$ *is the minimal value of the integer* k, *such that for any element* $a \in \mathbb{F}$, $a + \ldots + a(k\ times) = k.a = 0$, *where* $0 \in \mathbb{F}$, *is the additive identity of the field* $\mathbb{F}$. *Since the inverse* a^{-1} *exists, an alternative way of defining is by the equation,* $k.1 = 0$, *where* 1 *is the multiplicative identity of the field* $\mathbb{F}$.

The characteristic of a field is a prime number. If k is not prime, one can factor $k = k_1 k_2$, $1 < k_1, k_2 < k$. Thus, for $1 \in \mathbb{F}$, $k.1 = (k_1.1).(k_2.1) = 0$. Since in a field there are no zero-divisors, either $k_1.1 = 0$, or $k_2.1 = 0$. Since k is the smallest positive integer such that $k.1 = 0$, k has to be prime.

The residue class $\mathbb{Z}/\ p\mathbb{Z}$ is of extreme importance to cryptography. Each element in the set, a has a multiplicative inverse if and only if $gcd(a, p) = 1$. This happens if and only if p is prime. Thus,

Theorem 2 *The residue class* $\mathbb{Z}/\ p\mathbb{Z}$ *is a field if and only if* p *is prime.*

1.4   Greatest Common Divisors and Multiplicative Inverse

Computing multiplicative inverse is a central topic of number theory and finite fields. This operation is at the heart of cryptography, and is central to several important public

---

Algorithm 1.1: Euclidean Algorithm for computing gcd

Input: $a, b, a > b$

Output: $d = gcd(a, b)$

1   $r_0 = a$

2   $r_1 = b$

3   $m = 1$

4   **while** $r_m \neq 0$ **do**

5      $q_m = \left\lfloor \frac{r_{m-1}}{r_m} \right\rfloor$

6      $r_{m+1} = r_{m-1} - q_m r_m$

7      $m = m + 1$

8   **end**

9   **return** r_{m-1}

---

key algorithms. While there are several techniques for computing multiplicative inverses, Euclidean algorithm is one of the most well known techniques. The original Euclidean algorithm computes the greatest common divisor of two integers (elements).

1.4.1   Euclidean Algorithm

In this section, we present a discussion on greatest common divisor (gcd) of two integers. For simplicity, we restrict the discussion to positive integers. A non-zero integer has a finite number of divisors because the divisors must lie between 0 and n. An integer d is called a common divisor of a and b if it divides both a and b; that is $d \mid a$ and $d \mid b$.

Definition 1.4.1 *If a and b are integers that are not both zero, then the greatest common divisor d of a and b is the largest of the common divisors of a and b. We denote this as:* $d = gcd(a, b)$.

Because every number divides 0, there is strictly no greatest common divisor of 0 and 0; for convenience we set $gcd(0, 0) = 0$. Further, it may be easy to observe that $gcd(a, a) = a$ and $gcd(a, 0) = a$. The following facts are useful for computing the gcd of two integers:

Theorem 3 *If a, b, and k are integers, then*

$$gcd(a, b) \quad = \quad gcd(a + kb, b)$$

This follows from the fact that the set of common divisors of a and b is the same set as the common divisors of $a + kb$ and b. Thus we have the following useful corollary:

Corollary 1 *If a and b are positive integers, then $gcd(a, b) = gcd(a \bmod b, b) = gcd(b, a \bmod b)$.*

The proof of correctness of the above algorithm is easy to verify. It follows because of the following sequence of equations:

$$
\begin{aligned}
gcd(a,b) &= gcd(r_0, r_1) \\
&= gcd(q_1 r_1 + r_2, r_1) \\
&= gcd(r_2, r_1) \\
&= gcd(r_1, r_2) \\
&= \ldots \\
&= gcd(r_{m-1}, r_m) \\
&= r_m
\end{aligned}
$$

Thus the Euclidean algorithm can be used to check the gcd of two positive integers. It can also be used for checking for the existence of inverse of an element, a modulo another element n. An extended version of this algorithm can also be used for the computation of the inverse, $a^{-1} \bmod n$ and is explained in the next subsection.

1.4.2   Extended Euclidean Algorithm

Let us start this section, with an example to compute the inverse of 28 mod 75. If we apply the Euclidean Algorithm (EA) to compute the $gcd(28, 75)$, the following steps are performed:

$$
\begin{aligned}
75 &= 2 \times 28 + 19 \\
28 &= 1 \times 19 + 9 \\
19 &= 2 \times 9 + 1 \\
9 &= 9 \times 1
\end{aligned}
$$

The algorithm terminates at this point and we obtain that the gcd is 1. As stated previously, this implies the existence of the inverse of 28 mod 75. The inverse can be easily obtained by observing the sequence of numbers generated while applying the EA above. In order to compute the inverse, we first express the gcd as a linear combination of the numbers, 28 and 75. This can be easily done as:

$$
\begin{aligned}
19 &= 75 - 2 \times 28 \\
9 &= 28 - 19 = 28 - (75 - 2 \times 28) = -75 + 3 \times 28 \\
1 &= 19 - 2 \times 9 = (75 - 2 \times 28) - 2 \times (-75 + 3 \times 28) = 3 \times 75 - 8 \times 28
\end{aligned}
$$

It may be observed that the linear expression: $1 = 3 \times 75 - 8 \times 28$ is unique. Thus the inverse of 28 mod 75 can be easily obtained by taking modulo 75 to the above expression, and we observe that $-8 \times 28 \equiv 1 \bmod 75$. This shows that $28^{-1} \bmod 75 \equiv -8 = 67$.

Thus if the inverse of an integer $a \bmod n$ exists (ie. $gcd(a, n) = 1$), one applies the Euclidean Algorithm on a and n and generates a sequence of remainders. These remainders can be expressed as unique linear combinations of the integers a and n. The Extended Euclidean Algorithm (EEA) is a systematic method for generating the coefficients of these linear combinations.

The coefficients are generated by EEA as two series: s and t, and the final $gcd(a, b) = sa + tn$. The series elements, $s_0, s_1, \ldots, s_m = s$, and $t_0, t_1, \ldots, t_m = t$, are generated along with the remainders. The above series are obtained through the following recurrences:

Algorithm 1.2: Extended Euclidean Algorithm for computing inverse

---

Input: $a, n, a < n, gcd(a, n) = 1$
Output: $r = gcd(a, n), s \equiv a^{-1} \bmod n$

1 $r_0 = n$
2 $r_1 = a$
3 $s_0 = 1$
4 $s_1 = 0$
5 $m = 1$
6 **while** $r_m > 0$ **do**
7    $q_m = \lfloor \frac{r_{m-1}}{r_m} \rfloor$
8    $r_{m+1} = r_{m-1} - q_m r_m$
9    $s_{m+1} = s_{m-1} - q_m s_m$
10   $m = m + 1$
11 **end**
12 $r = r_{m-1}, s = s_{m-1}$
13 **return** r, s

$$s_j = \begin{cases} 1 & \text{if } j = 0 \\ 0 & \text{if } j = 1 \\ s_{j-2} - q_{j-1}s_{j-1} & \text{if } j \geq 2 \end{cases} \tag{1.1}$$

$$t_j = \begin{cases} 0 & \text{if } j = 0 \\ 1 & \text{if } j = 1 \\ t_{j-2} - q_{j-1}t_{j-1} & \text{if } j \geq 2 \end{cases} \tag{1.2}$$

For $0 \leq j \leq m$, we have that $r_j = s_j r_0 + t_j r_1$, where the r_js are defined in the EA, and the s_js and t_js are as defined in the above recurrences. Note that the final remainder, $r = gcd(a, n) = 1$ is expressed as $sa + tn$, and hence, $1 \equiv sa \bmod n$. Thus $s \equiv a^{-1} \bmod n$. Thus while computing the inverse the computations of the t-series is not required and can be omitted.

The operations are summarized in algorithm 1.2.

In the next section, we present another application of the Euclidean Algorithm (EA), called the Chinese Remainder Theorem (CRT). This theorem is often useful in development of some implementations of the RSA algorithm.

1.4.3 Chinese Remainder Theorem

Consider there are t integers $m_1, m_2, \ldots, m_t$, which are relatively prime in pairs, i.e. $gcd(m_i, m_j) = 1$ for any distinct i and j where $1 \leq i, j \leq t$.

Let $a_1, a_2, \ldots, a_t$ be any t integers. The Chinese Remainder Theorem says, then there is a *unique* number x, which satisfies the property:

$$x \equiv a_i(\bmod m_i), i = 1, 2, \ldots, t$$

The uniqueness of x is defined in the following sense: Let M be the product $m_1 m_2 \ldots m_t$, and let y satisfy the above system of congruences. Then $y \equiv x(\bmod M)$.

The uniqueness can be proved in the following inductive manner on the variable t. For $t = 1$, it suffices to take $x = a_1$. The uniqueness is straight forward.

Let us assume that the result holds for $t = k$. We prove the result (that such an x exists and is unique in the sense asserted) for $t = k + 1$. Consider the system of congruences:

$$x \equiv a_1 (\text{mod } m_1)$$
$$\vdots$$
$$x \equiv a_k (\text{mod } m_k)$$
$$x \equiv a_{k+1} (\text{mod } m_{k+1})$$

The moduli are relatively prime in pairs. From the inductive hypothesis, there is a number x' satisfying the first k congruences.

It is easy to check that the product of the first k integers, $m_1 m_2 \ldots m_k$ are relatively prime to the integer m_{k+1}. Hence from Extended Euclidean Algorithm, there are unique integers, u and v, such that:

$$u m_1 m_2 \ldots m_k + v m_{k+1} = 1$$

Multiplying both sides by $(a_{k+1} - x')$, we obtain;

$$u(a_{k+1} - x') m_1 m_2 \ldots m_k + v(a_{k+1} - x') m_{k+1} = (a_{k+1} - x')$$

This can be written as:

$$x' + u'' m_1 m_2 \ldots m_k = a_{k+1} + v'' m_{k+1}$$

Here we have, $u'' = u(a_{k+1} - x')$ and $v'' = -v(a_{k+1} - x')$.
Thus, denoting $x'' = x' + u'' m_1 m_2 \ldots m_k$, we have:

$$x'' \equiv a_{k+1} (\text{mod } m_{k+1})$$

On the other hand,

$$x'' \equiv x' \equiv a_i (\text{mod } m_i), i = 1, \ldots, k$$

This proves the existence of a solution.

The uniqueness can be observed as follows: From the induction hypothesis, x' is a unique solution to the first k congruences mod $m = m_1 \ldots m_k$. Consider for $k + 1$ congruences, there are two distinct solutions x and x_1. However since these values also are a solution for the first k congruences, we have by the induction hypothesis: $x \equiv x_1 \bmod m$. Further since both satisfy the last congruence: $x \equiv x_1 \bmod m_{k+1}$. Note that m and m_{k+1} are relatively prime. Thus, $x \equiv x_1 \bmod mm_{k+1}$. This proves that $x \equiv x' \bmod M$, where $M = mm_{k+1} = m_1 \ldots m_k m_{k+1}$. Hence, $x'' \equiv x' \bmod M$. This completes the proof.

The above theorem, though it gives a hint on how to obtain the solution, is not constructive. Next we present a solution to the above problem, called as the Chinese Remainder Algorithm (CRA). The above algorithm occurred for the first time in the mathematical classic of Sun Zi, a mathematician in ancient China.

The Chinese Remainder Theorem (CRT) is a classic example of expressing the whole in parts. The complete information is expressed as subparts, and the problem is to recover the original information from the parts. As can be understood, there can be several applications like secret sharing schemes, efficient implementations as the parts are often smaller numbers.

The CRT problem is to find the original x from the parts, a_i, where:

$$x \equiv a_i \bmod m_i, i = 0, 1, \ldots, n - 1 \tag{1.3}$$

where m_i are pairwise relatively primes, and a_i are integers. In order to solve Equations 1.3 we compute the values, $s_0, s_1, \ldots, s_{n-1}$ satisfying:

$$s_i \equiv 1 \bmod m_i, \qquad s_i \equiv 0 \bmod m_j, \text{for } i \neq j \tag{1.4}$$

Then $x = \sum_{i=0}^{n-1} a_i s_i \bmod m$ is the smallest non-negative integer congruent modulo m, where $m = m_0 m_1 \ldots m_{n-1}$, which is a solution to Equation 1.3.

Let $M_i = m/m_i$. Then the above congruence is equivalent to solve:

$$M_i y_i \equiv 1 \bmod m_i \tag{1.5}$$

It may be noted that y_i is the multiplicative inverse of M_i modulo m_i. Further it may be observed that the inverse exists, as M_i and m_i are relatively prime. The inverse can be computed using the Extended Euclidean Algorithm.

It can be easily seen then the congruence of Equation 1.4 can be solved by setting $s_i = M_i y_i$, as then $s_i \equiv 1 \bmod m_i$, and $s_i \equiv 0 \bmod m_j$, for $i \neq j$.

We discuss the above in the following theorem, called the **Chinese Remainder Theorem**.

Theorem 4 *Suppose $m_0, m_1, \ldots, m_{n-1}$ are pairwise relatively prime positive integers, and suppose $a_0, a_1, \ldots, a_{n-1}$ are integers. Then the system of congruences $x \equiv a_i \bmod m_i, 0 \leq i < n$ has a unique solution modulo $m = m_0 \times m_1 \cdots \times m_{n-1}$, $x = \sum_{i=0}^{n-1} a_i M_i y_i \bmod m$, where $M_i = m/m_i$, and $y_i = M_i^{-1} \bmod m_i$, for $0 \leq i < n - 1$.*

1.5 Subgroups, Subrings, and Extensions

Groups and rings give a nice theory of subgroups and subrings, which may be extended to fields as well. The theory of subrings (subfields) gives a very useful concept of equivalent rings (subrings), which are technically called isomorphic subrings (subfields), which are often useful for efficient implementations.

We first define subgroups and then subrings:

Definition 1.5.1 *Let $\mathbb{R}$ be a group under the operation $+$. Let $\mathbb{S}$ be a subset of $\mathbb{R}$. $\mathbb{S}$ is called a subgroup of $\mathbb{R}$ if and only if:*

- $a \in \mathbb{S}$ *and* $b \in \mathbb{S} \Rightarrow a + b$ *belong to* $\mathbb{S}$.

- $a \in \mathbb{S} \Rightarrow -a \in \mathbb{S}$, *that is the additive inverse of* $\mathbb{S}$ *also belongs to* $\mathbb{S}$.

A subring is an extension of the concept of subgroups, reminding that a ring is defined wrt. two operations, say $+$ and $*$.

Definition 1.5.2 *Let $\mathbb{R}$ be a ring under the operations $+$ and $*$. Let $\mathbb{S}$ be a subset of $\mathbb{R}$. $\mathbb{S}$ is called a subring of $\mathbb{R}$ if and only if:*

- $\mathbb{S}$ *is a subgroup of* $\mathbb{R}$.

- $\mathbb{S}$ *is closed under the operation* $*$, *called as multiplication.*

TABLE 1.3: Addition on the set $\mathbb{S}$

+	0	3	6	9
0	0	3	6	9
3	3	6	9	0
6	6	9	0	3
9	9	0	3	6

TABLE 1.4: Additive inverse operation on the set $\mathbb{S}$

-	0	3	6	9
	0	9	6	3

TABLE 1.5: Multiplication on the set $\mathbb{S}$

*	0	3	6	9
0	0	0	0	0
3	0	9	6	3
6	0	6	0	6
9	0	3	6	9

Every ring has two trivial subrings: itself and the set $\{0\}$.

Example 10 *Consider the set $\mathbb{R} = \mathbb{Z}/12\mathbb{Z}$. Consider the subset $\mathbb{S} = \{0, 3, 6, 9\}$. The following Tables (Tables 1.3,1.4,1.5 confirm that it is a subring).*

It may be noted that the set $\mathbb{S}$ does not form a group wrt. multiplication. Further although the set $\mathbb{R} = \mathbb{Z}/12\mathbb{Z}$ posseses a multiplicative identity, $\mathbb{S}$ does not. It may be interesting to note that it may also be possible for $\mathbb{S}$ to have a multiplicative identity, but not $\mathbb{R}$. The two sets can also have same or different identities wrt. multiplication. However as per our definition for rings, we impose the further condition that $\mathbb{S}$ has to be a ring for it to qualify as a subring. Thus the subring also has to have a *multiplicative identity*. When $\mathbb{S}$ is the subring of $\mathbb{R}$, the later is called as the ring extension of the former. When both $\mathbb{S}$ and $\mathbb{R}$ are fields, the later is called as the field extension of the former. Equivalently, one also says that $\mathbb{S} \subseteq \mathbb{R}$ is a field extension or $\mathbb{R}$ is a field extension over $\mathbb{S}$.

1.6   Groups, Rings, and Field Isomorphisms

Often a group, ring or a field can be expressed in several equivalent forms. For two groups, G_1 and G_2, a surjective function $f : G_1 \to G_2$ is said to be a homomorphism if and only if: $f(x \circ y) = f(x) \dagger f(y)$. Note that the group operations on the left need not be the same as on the right. Thus the homomorphism is a function which not only transforms the elements, but also transforms the operators. For simplicity, we state $f(x.y) = f(x).f(y)$, though the operators on the left and right are defined over different groups.

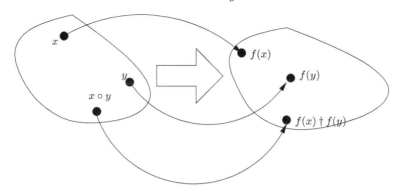

FIGURE 1.1: Homomorphism

The following theorems state two important properties for homomorphisms on groups.

Theorem 5 *If $f : G_1 \to G_2$ is a group homomorphism then $f(e_1) = e_2$, where e_1 is the identity of G_1 and e_2 is the identity of G_2.*

Let x be an element of G_1. Thus $f(x)$ is an element of G_2. Thus, $f(x) = f(x.e_1) = f(x).f(e_1) \Rightarrow f(x).e_2 = f(x).f(e_1)$. Thus, $f(e_1) = e_1$. It may be noted that the cancellation is allowed, owing to the existence of the multiplicative inverse, $[f(x)]^{-1}$ and associativity of the groups.

Theorem 6 *If $f : G_1 \to G_2$ is a group homomorphism then for every $x \in G_1$, $f(x^{-1}) = (f(x))^{-1}$.*

We have $f(x.x^{-1}) = f(e_1) = e_2$. Also, $f(x.x^{-1}) = f(x).f(x^{-1})$. Hence, we have $f(x^{-1}) = (f(x))^{-1}$

Example 11 *Let G_1 be the group of all real numbers under multiplication, and G_2 be the group of all real numbers under addition. The function defined as $f : G_1 \to G_2$, where $f(x) = log_e(x) = ln(x)$, is a group homomorphism.*

An injective (one-to-one) homomorphism is called an isomorphism.

The idea of homomorphism and hence isomorphism can be extended to rings and fields in a similar fashion. In these extensions the only difference is from the fact that a ring and a field are defined wrt. two operations, denoted by $+$ and $\circ$.

Let R_1 and R_2 be rings and consider a surjective function, $f : R_1 \to R_2$. It is called a ring isomorphism if and only if:

1. $f(a + b) = f(a) + f(b)$ for every a and b in R_1

2. $f(a \circ b) = f(a) \circ f(b)$ for every a and b in R_1

An obvious extension of the previous two theorems to the rings R_1 and R_2, is $f(0) = 0$, and $f(-x) = -f(x)$, for every $x \in R_1$. If R_1 has a multiplicative identity denoted by 1, and R_2 has a multiplicative identity denoted by $1'$, we have $f(1) = 1'$.

Further, if x is a unit in the ring R_1, then $f(x)$ is a unit in the ring R_2, and $f(x^{-1}) = [f(x)]^{-1}$. These properties also holds for fields. The property of isomorphisms have been found to be useful for developing efficient implementations for finite field-based algorithms. The fact of isomorphism is utilized to transform a given field into another isomorphic field, perform operations in this field, and then transform back the solutions. The advantage in such implementations occurs from the fact that the operations in the newer field are more efficient to implement than the initial field.

1.7 Polynomials and Fields

Elements of a field are often represented in the form of polynomials. Let $\mathbb{R}$ be a commutative ring, with unit element 1. A polynomial in the variable $X \in \mathbb{R}$, is an expression:

$$f(X) \quad = \quad a_n X^n + a_{n-1} X^{n-1} + \ldots + a_1 X + a_0,$$

where X is the variable and the coefficients $a_0, \ldots, a_n$ of the polynomial are elements of $\mathbb{R}$. The set of all polynomials over $\mathbb{R}$ in the variable X is denoted by $\mathbb{R}[X]$.

If the *leading coefficient* of the polynomial f, denoted by a_n is nonzero, then the degree of the polynomial is said to be n. A *monomial* is a polynomial whose all co-efficients except the leading one are zero.

If the value of a polynomial vanishes for a particular value of the variable, $r \in \mathbb{R}$: ie. $f(r) = 0$, then r is called a *root* or *zero* of f.

Consider two polynomials, $f(x) = \sum_{i=0}^{n} a_i X^i$, and $g(x) = \sum_{i=0}^{m} b_i X^i$, defined over R, and suppose $n \geq m$. Then the sum of the polynomials is defined by $(f + g)(X) = \sum_{i=0}^{m}(a_i + b_i)X^i + \sum_{i=(m+1)}^{n} a_i X^i$. The number of operations needed is $O(n+1)$.

The product of the polynomials f and g is $(fg)(X) = \sum_{k=0}^{n+m} c_k X^k$, where $c_k = \sum_{i=0}^{k} a_i b_{k-i}$, $0 \leq k \leq n + m$. The coefficients, a_i and b_i which are not defined are set to 0. The multiplication requires $O(nm)$ computations, considering the products and additions.

Example 12 *The set $\mathbb{Z}/3\mathbb{Z}$ contains the elements, 0, 1 and 2. Consider the polynomials, $f(X) = X^2 + X + 1$, and $g(X) = X^3 + 2X^2 + X \in (\mathbb{Z}/3\mathbb{Z})[X]$. It can be checked that the first polynomial has a zero at 1, while the later has at 2.*

The sum of the polynomials, is $(f+g)(X) = X^3 + (1+2)X^2 + (1+1)X + 1 = X^3 + 2X + 1$. The product of the polynomials is denoted by $fg(X) = X^5 + (1 + 2)X^4 + (1 + 2 + 1)X^3 + (2 + 1)X^2 + X = X^5 + X^3 + X$.

The set of polynomials, $\mathbb{R}[\mathbb{X}]$ forms a commutative ring with the operations, addition and multiplication. If $\mathbb{K}$ is a field, then the ring $\mathbb{K}[X]$ of polynomials over $\mathbb{K}$ contains no zero divisors, that there does not exist two non-zero polynomials, $a(X)$ and $b(X)$ st. $a(X)b(X) = 0$, the zero polynomial.

The following theorem is stated without proof but can be followed from any classic text of number theory:

Theorem 7 *Let $f(X), g(X) \in \mathbb{K}[X], g(X) \neq 0$. Then there are uniquely determined polynomials $q(X), r(X) \in \mathbb{K}[X]$, with $f(X) = q(X)g(X) + r(X)$ and $r(X) = 0$ or $\deg r(X) < \deg g(X)$. The polynomials $q(X)$ and $r(X)$ are referred to as the quotient and remainder polynomials.*

Example 13 *Let, $g(X) = X^2 + X + 1$, and $f(X) = X^3 + 2X^2 + X \in (\mathbb{Z}/3\mathbb{Z})[X]$. The polynomials, $q(X) = X + 1$ and $r(X) = 2X + 2$ are unique and satisfies the property, $\deg r(X) < \deg g(X)$.*

An important observation based on the above result, which is often called the *division algorithm* on polynomials, is that if $b \in \mathbb{K}$ is the root of a polynomial $f(X) \in \mathbb{K}[X]$, then $(X-b)$ divides the polynomial $f(X)$. It can be followed quite easily, as we have by polynomial division of $f(X)$ by $(X - b)$, polynomials $q(X)$ and $r(X)$, st. $\deg(r(X)) < \deg(X - b) = 1$ and $f(X) = (X-b)q(X)+r(X)$. Thus we have $r(X)$ a constant, and we denote it by $r \in \mathbb{K}$.

Substituting, $X = b$, since b is a root of $f(X)$ we have $f(b) = r = 0$. This shows that the remainder constant is zero, and thus $(X - b)$ divides the polynomial $f(X)$.

The above result shows that *modular arithmetic* can be defined over the ring of polynomials, in the same way as it can be done over integers.

Definition 1.7.1 *Let $a(x), b(x)$, and $f(x)$ be polynomials in $\mathbb{R}[X]$. Then $a(x)$ and $b(x)$ are* **congruent modulo** *$m(x)$ if $a(x) - b(x) = m(x)k(x)$ for some polynomial $k(x) \in \mathbb{R}[X]$. We write this as:*

$$a(x) \equiv b(x) \; mod m(x)$$

Likewise for two polynomials $f(X)$ and $g(X) \in \mathbb{K}[X]$, we can define the greatest common divisor of the two polynomials. However, the greatest common divisor (gcd) of two non-zero polynomials implicitly refers to the monic polynomial. This makes the gcd of two polynomials unique. From *Theorem 7*, we have $f(X) \equiv r(X) \; mod g(X)$. This gives rise to the following result, which can be used to determine the gcd of two polynomials and, later as we shall see, to compute the inverse of a polynomial defined in a field.

Theorem 8 *Let $f(X), g(X) \in \mathbb{K}[X]$, both of which are not zero. The (monic) gcd of $f(X)$ and $g(X)$ is denoted by $d(X)$. Then, there are polynomials $u(X)$ and $v(X) \in \mathbb{K}[X]$, st. $d(X) = u(X)f(X) + v(X)g(X)$. Further, if $f(X)$ and $g(X)$ are non-zero and not both constants, then $u(X)$ and $v(X)$ can be chosen st. $degree(u(X)) < degree(g(X))$ and $degree(v(X)) < degree(f(X))$.*

This theorem forms the basis of the famous Euclidean algorithm for computing the greatest common divisors for two polynomials. An extension of the algorithm, referred to as the Extended Euclidean algorithm is used for computing the inverse of a polynomial defined in a field.

1.8 Construction of Galois Field

Fields with a finite number of elements are called *Finite Fields*, often called *Galois Fields* and abbreviated as GF. We know that when p is prime, the residue class $\mathbb{Z}/p\mathbb{Z}$ is a field. This field is often abbreviated as $GF(p)$, and commonly referred to as the *prime field*. The characteristic of this field is p. When $p = 2$, this field $GF(2)$ is called the binary field and is popular for fast and efficient implementations.

The field $GF(p)$ is often extended to a larger field, which has p^n elements for any positive integer n. The field is represented by the symbol $GF(p^n)$. The construction of the extension field is detailed underneath and is due to *Kronecker*.

Let p be a prime number and let f be a polynomial in $\mathbb{Z}/p\mathbb{Z}$, of degree n, where n is a positive integer. The polynomial is irreducible, implying that it cannot be factored into polynomials, g and h which are polynomials in $(\mathbb{Z}/p\mathbb{Z})[X]$ of positive degree, i.e., neither of the polynomials is a constant. As an analogy, the irreducible polynomials can be imagined to correspond to prime numbers in the domain of integers.

Example 14 *The polynomial $f(X) = X^2 + X + 1$ is irreducible in $(\mathbb{Z}/2\mathbb{Z})[X]$. This can be checked easily, as if the polynomial is reducible (not irreducible), one can factor $f(X) = g(X)h(X)$, and both $g(X)$ and $h(X)$ are degree one polynomials in $(\mathbb{Z}/2\mathbb{Z})[X]$. This follows from the fact, that since $g(X), h(X) \neq 0$, $degree(f(X)) = degree(h(X)) + degree((g(X))$. Thus, $f(X)$ must have a zero in $(\mathbb{Z}/2\mathbb{Z})[X]$, i.e., either 0 or 1 is a zero or root of $f(X)$. But both $f(0)$ and $f(1)$ are non-zero. Hence, the polynomial $f(X)$ is irreducible.*

The finite field is constructed much similar to what we do in the context of modular arithmetic. We define residue classes modulo $f(X)$, ie. we generate the set of polynomials modulo $f(X)$ and place them in separate classes. Thus the set consists of all polynomials of *degree* $<$ *degree* $f(X)$. Each of these polynomials has representative elements of all the polynomials in the corresponding residue class. The residue class represented by the polynomial $h(X)$ is denoted as:

$$g(X) + f(\mathbb{Z}/p\mathbb{Z})[X] \quad = \quad \{g(X) + h(X)f(X) : h(X) \in (\mathbb{Z}/p\mathbb{Z})[X]\}$$

In other words, the polynomials $g(X)$ and the elements of the residue class are *congruent* modulo $f(X)$. It is easy to see that the representative elements, denoted by $(\mathbb{Z}/p\mathbb{Z})[X]/\langle f(X) \rangle$ form a ring under the standard operations of addition and multiplications, they form a field if and only if the polynomial $f(X)$ is irreducible.

Below we state a theorem which states that the above fact.

Theorem 9 *For a non-constant polynomials $f(X) \in (\mathbb{Z}/p\mathbb{Z})[X]$, the ring $(\mathbb{Z}/p\mathbb{Z})[X]/\langle f(X) \rangle$ is a field if and only if $f(X)$ is irreducible in $(\mathbb{Z}/p\mathbb{Z})[X]$.*

The proof is quite straightfoward. If, $f(X)$ is reducible over $(\mathbb{Z}/p\mathbb{Z})[X]$, we have $g(X), h(X)$, st. $f(X) = g(X)h(X)$ and $1 \le degree(g(X)), degree(h(X)) < degree(f(X))$.

Then both $g(X)$ and $h(X)$ are non-zero elements in $(\mathbb{Z}/p\mathbb{Z})[X]$ whose product is zero modulo $f(X)$. Thus, the ring $(\mathbb{Z}/p\mathbb{Z})[X]$ contains non-zero zero divisors.

If $f(X)$ is irreducible over $(\mathbb{Z}/p\mathbb{Z})[X]$ and $g(X)$ is a non-zero polynomial, st. $degree(g(X)) < degree(f(X))$, then $gcd(f(X), g(X)) = 1$. Thus from Euclidean algorithm $\exists$ polynomials $u(X), v(X) \in (\mathbb{Z}/p\mathbb{Z})[X]$, $u(X)f(X) + v(X)g(X) = 1$, and $degree(v(X)) < degree(f(X))$.

Thus, $v(X)g(X) \equiv 1(mod(f(X)))$, i.e., $g(X)$ has a multiplicative inverse in the ring $(\mathbb{Z}/p\mathbb{Z})[X]/\langle f(X) \rangle$, which hence qualifies as a field.

1.9 Extensions of Fields

The above idea of extending the field $GF(p)$ to $GF(p^n)$ can be generalized. Consider a field K and $f(X)$ irreducible over K. Define, $L = K[X]/\langle f(X) \rangle$ is a field extension. We denote this by stating $K \subseteq L$.

We use $f(X)$ to construct the congruence class modulo $f(X)$. Let θ be the equivalence class of the polynomial X in L. It is also denoted as $[X]$. Clearly, $f(\theta) = 0$.

Example 15 *Consider the field $GF(2^2)$, as an extension field of $GF(2)$. Thus define $GF(2^2)[X] = GF(2)[X]/\langle f(X) \rangle$, where $f(X) = X^2 + X + 1$ is an irreducible polynomial in $GF(2)[X]$. It is clear that the polynomials are of the form $aX + b$, where $a, b \in GF(2)$.*

The four equivalence classes are $0, 1, X, X + 1$, which are obtained by reducing the polynomial of $GF(2)[X]$ by the irreducible polynomial $X^2 + X + 1$.

If θ denotes the equivalence class of the polynomial $X \in GF(2^2)$, the classes can be represented as $0, 1, \theta, \theta + 1$.

Notice, that setting $\theta^2 = \theta + 1$, (ie. $f(\theta) = \theta^2 + \theta + 1 = 0$), reduces any polynomial $f(\theta) \in GF(2)[\theta]$ modulo $(\theta^2 + \theta + 1)$.

If $f(X)$ is not irreducible, then $f(X)$ has a factor $f_1(X) \in K[X]$, st. $1 \le deg(f_1(X)) < deg(f(X))$. Either, $f_1(X)$ is irreducible, or $f_1(X)$ has a factor $f_2(X)$, such that $1 \le$

$deg(f_2(X)) < deg(f_1(X))$. Eventually, we will have an irreducible polynomial $q(X)$, which can be used to define the extension field. Even then, $f(\theta) = 0$, because $q(X)$ is a factor of $f(X)$ in $K[X]$.

The number of elements in a field is defined as the *order*. Thus if the order of the field K is p, the elements of the extension field, $K' = K/\langle f(X)\rangle$, where $f(X)$ is an irreducible polynomial of degree m, can be represented as: $a(X) = a_0 + a_1(X) + \ldots + a_{m-1}X^{m-1}$.

Since there are exactly p choices for each of the coefficients, there are p^m values in the field. Thus the order of the extension field is p^m.

Thus summarizing every non-constant polynomial over a field has a root in some extension field.

Theorem 10 *Let $f(X)$ be a non-constant polynomial with coefficients in a field K. Then there is a field L containing K that also contains a root of $f(X)$.*

We can apply the above result repeatedly to obtain further extensions of a given field, and finally arrive at a bigger field. Consider a field K with order p. Let us start with the polynomial $f(X) = X^{p^n} - X$ over a field K. It can be extended to K^1, where a root θ_1 of f lies. In turn the field K^1 can be extended to the field K^2, where a root θ_2 lies. Thus continuing we can write:

$$X^{p^n} - X = (X - \theta_1)\ldots(X - \theta_{p^n})$$

The set of roots, $\theta_1, \theta_2, \ldots, \theta_{p^n}$ itself forms a field and are called a splitting field of $f(X)$. In other words, a splitting field of a polynomial with coefficients in a field is the smallest field extension of that field over which the polynomial splits or decomposes into linear factors.

Next we introduce another important class of polynomials which are called minimal polynomials.

Definition 1.9.1 *Let $K \subseteq L$ be a field extension, and θ an element of L. The minimal polynomial of θ over K is the monic polynomial $m(X) \in K[X]$ of smallest degree st. $m(\theta) = 0$.*

The minimal polynomial divides any polynomial that has θ as a root. It is easy to follow, since dividing $f(X)$ by $m(X)$ gives the quotient $q(X)$ and the remainder $r(X)$, st. $deg(r(X)) < deg(m(X))$. Thus we have, $f(X) = q(X)m(X) + r(X)$. Substituting, θ we have $f(\theta) = r(\theta) = 0$, since $f(\theta) = 0$. Since, $deg(r(X)) < deg(m(X))$ and $m(X)$ is the minimal polynomial, we have $r(X) = 0$. Thus, the minimal polynomial $m(X)$ of θ divides any polynomial which has θ as its root.

1.10 Cyclic Groups of Group Elements

The concept of cyclic groups is central to the study of cryptographic algorithms. The theory of cyclic groups gives an alternative representation of the group elements, which can be often handy for performing certain operations.

If G is a group wrt. a binary operation indicated by simple juxtaposition. G is said to be cyclic if there exists an element $g \in G$, st. every element of G can be written as g^m for some integer m. The elements in the group are enumerated as $\{g^0, g^1, \ldots, g^r, g^{r+1}, \ldots\}$. The convention is $g^{-m} = (g^{-1})^m$, and $g^0 = 1$.

The non-zero elements of a field form a commutative group under multiplication. The group is called the multiplicatve group of the field F, and is denoted bt F^*.

Let a be a finite element of a finite group G, and consider the list of powers of a, $\{a^1, a^2, \ldots, \}$. As G is finite the list will eventually have duplicates, so there are positive integers $j < k$, st. $a^j = a^k$.

Thus, we have $1 = a^{k-j}$ (multiplying both sides by $(a^{-1})^j$).

So, $\exists$ a positive integer $t = k - j$, st. $a^t = 1$. The smallest such positive integer is called the order of a, and is denoted by $ord(a)$. Thus, whenever we have an integer n, st. $a^n = 1$, we have $ord(a)$ divides n.

The subset $S = \{a, a^2, \ldots, a^{ord(a)} = 1\}$ is itself a group and thus qualifies as a subgroup. If G is a finite group, order of the group G is defined as the number of elements in G.

Let S be a subgroup of a finite group G. For each element $a \in G$, the set $aS = \{as | s \in S\}$ has the same number of elements as S. If $a, b \in G$, and $a \neq b$, then aS and bS are either disjoint or equal. Thus the group G can be partitioned into m units, denoted by $a_1 S, a_2 S, \ldots, a_m S$, so that $G = a_1 S \cup \ldots \cup a_m S$, and $a_i S \cap a_j S = \phi$, $\forall i \neq j$.

Thus, we have $ord(G) = m \times ord(S)$. Hence, the order of a subgroup divides the order of the group G.

Thus we have the following theorem known as Lagrange's Theorem.

Theorem 11 *If S is a subgroup of the finite group G, then the order of S divides the order of G.*

In particular, there is an element α such that every non-zero element can be written in the form of α^k. Such an element α is called the generator of the multiplicative group, and is often referred to as the primitive element.

Specifically consider the field $GF(p^n)$, where p is a prime number. The primitive element of the field is defined as follows:

Definition 1.10.1 *A generator of the multiplicative group of $GF(p^n)$ is called a primitive element.*

The minimal polynomial of the primitive element is given a special name, primitive polynomials.

Definition 1.10.2 *A polynomial of degree n over $GF(p)$ is a primitive polynomial if it is the minimal polynomial of a primitive element in $GF(p^n)$.*

The concepts of irreducibility, minimality and primitivity of polynomials play a central role in the theory of fields. It can be seen that there are several interesting interrelations and properties of these concepts. We state a few in the following sequel:

Theorem 12 *The minimal polynomial of an element of $GF(p^n)$ is irreducible.*

Further, a minimal polynomial over $GF(p)$ of any primitive element of $GF(p^n)$ is an irreducible polynomial of degree n. Thus, a primitive polynomial is irreducible, but not the vice versa. A primitive polynomial must have a non-zero constant term, for otherwise it will be divisible by x. Over the field $GF(2)$, $x + 1$ is a primitive polynomial and all other primitive polynomials have odd number of terms, since any polynomial mod 2 with an even number of terms is divisible by $x + 1$.

If $f(X)$ is an irreducible polynomial of degree n over $GF(p)$, then $f(X)$ divides $g(X) = X^{p^n} - X$. The argument for the above is from the fact, that from the theory of extension of fields, there is a field of order p^n that contains an element θ st. $f(\theta) = 0$. Since, $f(X)$ is irreducible it should be a minimal polynomial as well. Also, the polynomial $g(X) = X^{p^n} - X$ vanishes at $X = \theta$. Thus, $g(X) = f(X)q(X) + r(X)$, where $degree(r(X)) < degree(f(X))$, then $r(\theta) = 0$. Since, $f(X)$ is a minimal polynomial of θ, $r(X) = 0$.

Thus, we have an alternative definition of primitive polynomials, which are nothing but minimal polynomials of the primitive polynomials.

Definition 1.10.3 *An irreducible polynomial of degree n, $f(X)$ over $GF(p)$ for prime p, is a primitive polynomial if the smallest positive integer m such that $f(X)$ divides $x^m - 1$ is $m = p^n - 1$.*

Over $GF(p^n)$ there are exactly $\phi(p^n - 1)/n$ primitive polynomials, where ϕ is Euler's Totient function. The roots of a primitive polynomial all have order $p^n - 1$. Thus the roots of a primitive polynomial can be used to generate and represent the elements of a field.

We conclude this section, with the comment that all fields of the order p^n are essentially the same. Hence, we can define isomorphism between the elements of the field. We explain a specific case in the context of binary fields in a following section.

1.11 Efficient Galois Fields

In cryptography, *finite fields* play an important role. A finite field is also known as *Galois field* and is denoted by $GF(p^m)$. Here, p is a prime called the *characteristic* of the field, while m is a positive integer. The *order* of the finite field, that is, the number of elements in the field is p^m. When $m = 1$, the resulting field is called a *prime field* and contains the *residue classes* modulo p[122].

In cryptography, two of the most studied fields are finite fields of characteristic two and prime fields. Finite fields of characteristic two, denoted by $GF(2^m)$, is also known as *binary extension finite fields* or simply *binary finite fields*. They have several advantages when compared to prime fields. Most important is the fact that modern computer systems are built on the binary number system. With m bits all possible elements of $GF(2^m)$ can be represented. This is not possible with prime fields (with $p \neq 2$). For example a $GF(2^2)$ field would require 2 bits for representation and use all possible numbers generated by the 2 bits. A $GF(3)$ field would also require 2 bits for representing the three elements in the field. This leaves one of the four possible numbers generated by 2 bits unused leading to an inefficient representation. Another advantage of binary extension fields is the simple hardware required for computation of some of the commonly used arithmetic operations such as addition and squaring. Addition in binary extension fields can be easily performed by a simple XOR. There is no carry generated. Squaring in this field is a linear operation and can also be done using XOR circuits. These circuits are much simpler than the addition and squaring circuits of a $GF(p)$ field.

1.11.1 Binary Finite Fields

A polynomial of the form $a(x) = a_m x^m + a_{m-1} x^{m-1} + \cdots + a_1 x + a_0$ is said to be a *polynomial over $GF(2)$* if the coefficients a_m, a_{m-1}, $\cdots$, a_1, a_0 are in $GF(2)$. Further, the polynomial is said to be *irreducible* over $GF(2)$ if $a(x)$ is divisible only by c or by $c \cdot a(x)$ where $c \in GF(2)$ [286]. An irreducible polynomial of degree m with coefficients in $GF(2)$ can be used to construct the extension field $G(2^m)$. All elements of the extension field can be represented by polynomials of degree $m - 1$ over $GF(2)$.

Binary finite fields are generally represented using two types of bases. These are the *polynomial* and *normal base* representations.

Definition 1.11.1 *Let $p(x)$ be an irreducible polynomial over $GF(2^m)$ and let α be the root of $p(x)$. Then the set*
$$\{1, \alpha, \alpha^2, \cdots, \alpha^{m-1}\}$$

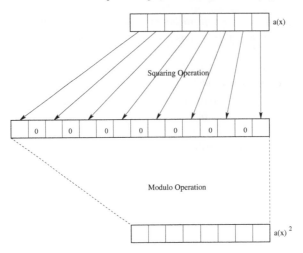

FIGURE 1.2: Squaring Circuit

is called the polynomial base.

Definition 1.11.2 *Let $p(x)$ be an irreducible polynomial over $GF(2^m)$, and let α be the root of $p(x)$, then the set*

$$\{\alpha,\ \alpha^2,\ \alpha^{2^2},\ \cdots,\ \alpha^{2^{(m-1))}}\}$$

is called the normal base *if the m elements are linearly independent.*

The normal bases representation is useful for arithmetic circuits, as squaring an element is accomplished by cyclic shifts. More generally, for any field $GF(p^m)$, the basis vector is $\{b^{p^0}, b^{p^1}, \ldots, b^{p^{m-1}}\}$, where b is chosen such that they are linearly independent.

Any element in the field $GF(2^m)$ can be represented in terms of its bases as shown below.

$$a(x) = a_{m-1}\alpha^{m-1} + \cdots + a_1\alpha + a_0$$

Alternatively, the element $a(x)$ can be represented as a binary string $(a_{m-1}, \cdots, a_1, a_0)$ making it suited for representation on computer systems. For example, the polynomial $x^4 + x^3 + x + 1$ in the field $GF(2^8)$ is represented as $(00011011)_2$.

Various arithmetic operations such as addition, subtraction, multiplication, squaring and inversion are carried out on binary fields. *Addition* and *subtraction* operations are identical and are performed by XOR operations.

Let $a(x)$, $b(x) \in GF(2^m)$ be denoted by

$$a(x) = \sum_{i=0}^{m-1} a_i x^i \qquad b(x) = \sum_{i=0}^{m-1} b_i x^i$$

then the *addition* (or *subtraction*) of $a(x)$ and $b(x)$ is given by

$$a(x) + b(x) = \sum_{i=0}^{m-1} (a_i + b_i)x^i \qquad (1.6)$$

here the $+$ between a_i and b_i denotes a XOR operation.

The *squaring* operation on binary finite fields is as easy as addition. The square of the polynomial $a(x) \in GF(2^m)$ is given by

$$a(x)^2 = \sum_{i=0}^{m-1} a_i x^{2i} \bmod p(x) \qquad (1.7)$$

The squaring essentially spreads out the input bits by inserting zeroes in between two bits as shown in **Fig. 1.2**.

Multiplication is not as trivial as addition or squaring. The product of the two polynomials $a(x)$ and $b(x)$ is given by

$$a(x) \cdot b(x) = \Big(\sum_{i=0}^{n-1} b(x) a_i x^i \Big) \bmod p(x) \qquad (1.8)$$

Most multiplication algorithms are $O(n^2)$.

Inversion is the most complex of all field operations. Even the best technique to implement inversion is several times more complex than multiplication. Hence, algorithms which use finite field arithmetic generally try to reduce the number of inversions at the cost of increasing the number of multiplications.

The multiplication and squaring operation require a *modular operation* to be done. The modular operation is the remainder produced when divided by the field's irreducible polynomial. If a certain class of irreducible polynomials is used, the modular operation can be easily done. Consider the irreducible trinomial $x^m + x^n + 1$, having a root α and

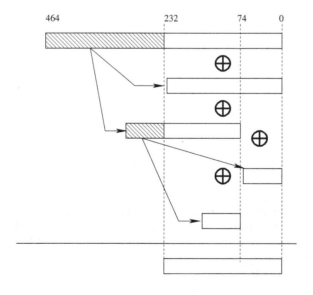

FIGURE 1.3: Modular Reduction with Trinomial $x^{233} + x^{74} + 1$

$1 < n < m/2$. Therefore, $\alpha^m + \alpha^n + 1 = 0$. Therefore,

$$\alpha^m = 1 + \alpha^n$$
$$\alpha^{m+1} = \alpha + \alpha^{n+1}$$
$$\vdots \qquad\qquad (1.9)$$
$$\alpha^{2m-3} = \alpha^{m-3} + \alpha^{m+n-3}$$
$$\alpha^{2m-2} = \alpha^{m-2} + \alpha^{m+n-2}$$

For example, consider the irreducible trinomial $x^{233} + x^{74} + 1$. The multiplication or squaring of the polynomial results in a polynomial of degree at most 464. This can be reduced as shown in **Fig. 1.3**. The higher-order terms 233 to 464 are reduced by using Equation 1.9.

1.12 Mapping between Binary and Composite Fields

In this section, we define two extension fields of $GF(2)$, one of them called as the composite fields.

Definition 1.12.1 *The pair of the fields $GF(2^n)$ and $GF(2^n)^m$ are called a composite field, if there exists irreducible polynomials, $Q(Y)$ of degree n and $P(X)$ of degree m, which are used to extend $GF(2)$ to $GF(2^n)$, and $GF((2^n)^m)$ from $GF(2^n)$.*

Composite fields are denoted by $GF(2^n)^m$. A composite field is isomorphic to the field, $GF(2^k)$, where $k = m \times n$. However, it is interesting to note that the underlying field operations in both the fields have different complexity, and varies with the exact values of n, m and the polynomials used to the construct the fields.

Below we provide an example.

Example 16 *Consider the fields $GF(2^4)$, elements of which are the following 16 polynomials with binary coefficients:*

0	z^2	z^3	$z^3 + z^2$
1	$z^2 + 1$	$z^3 + 1$	$z^3 + z^2 + 1$
z	$z^2 + z$	$z^3 + z$	$z^3 + z^2 + z$
$z + 1$	$z^2 + z + 1$	$z^3 + z + 1$	$z^3 + z^2 + z + 1$

There are 3 irreducible polynomials of degree 4, which can be used to construct the fields: $f_1(z) = z^4 + z + 1$, $f_2(z) = z^4 + z^3 + 1$, $f_3(z) = z^4 + z^3 + z^2 + z + 1$.

The resulting fields, F_1, F_2, F_3 all have the same elements, ie. the above 16 polynomials.

However, the operations are different: like the same operation, $z.z^3$ would result in $z + 1, z^3 + 1, z^3 + z^2 + z + 1$ in the three fields F_1, F_2, and F_3, respectively.

The fields are isomorphic and one can establish between the fields, say F_1 and F_2 a mapping, by computing $c \in F_2$, st. $f_1(c) \equiv 0 (\text{mod } f_2)$ The map $z \to c$ is thus used to construct an isomorphism $\mathbb{T} : F_1 \to F_2$.

The choices of c are $z^2 + z$, $z^2 + z + 1$, $z^3 + z^2$, and $z^3 + z^2 + 1$. One can verify that $c = z^2 + z \Rightarrow f_1(c) = (z^2 + z)^4 + (z^2 + z) + 1 = z^8 + z^4 + z^2 + z + 1 \equiv 0 (\text{mod } f_2)$. The modulo f_2 can be performed by substituting, z^4 by $z^3 + 1$, ie. $f_2(z) = 0$.

The homomorphism property of the mapping wrt. to the multiplication operation can easily be observed. Mathematically we check that, $T(e_1 \times e_2 \bmod f_1) \equiv (T(e_1) \times T(e_2)) \bmod f_2$

Let us consider two elements, $e_1 = z^2 + z$ and $e_2 = z^3 + z$. The product of the elements in the field F_1 are: $(z^2 + z)(z^3 + z) \bmod (z^4 + z + 1) = z^3 + 1$. The above reduction, uses the fact that in the field E_1 $f_1(z) = 0 \Rightarrow z^4 = z + 1$.

The same operation can also be performed in the field, F_2. That is $\mathbb{T}(e_1) = (z^2 + z)^2 + (z^2 + z) \bmod (z^4 + z^3 + 1) = z^3 + z + 1$. This uses the fact that the mapping, $\mathbb{T}$ maps, $z \in F_1$ to $z^2 + z \in F_2$. Reduction modulo f_2 is performed by setting $f_2(z) = 0 \Rightarrow z^4 = z^3 + 1$.

Likewise, $\mathbb{T}(e_2) = (z^2 + z)^3 + (z^2 + z) = z + 1$.

Multiplying the two mapped elements results in $(z+1)(z^3+z+1) \equiv z^2 \bmod (z^4 + z^3 = 1)$. This can be seen as same as $\mathbb{T}(z^3 + 1)$.

We present next an algorithm based on this same idea to construct an isomorphism between the composite fields.

1.12.1 Constructing Isomorphisms between Composite Fields

Let the polynomial used to construct, $GF(2^n)$ be denoted by $Q(Y)$ and the polynomial used to construct the polynomial $GF(2^n)^m$ by $P(X)$. Assuming both the polynomials as primitive, the roots of $Q(Y)$ and $P(X)$, denoted as ω and α can be used to generate the fields. The field elements of $GF(2^n)$ are thus represented by $\{0, 1, \omega, \omega^2, \ldots, \omega^{2^n - 2}\}$, while the elements of the composite field are represented by $\{0, 1, \alpha, \alpha^2, \ldots, \alpha^{2^{nm} - 2}\}$.

Arithmetic in the field $GF(2^k)$, $k = nm$ can be performed by modulo the polynomial $R(z) = z^k + r_{k-1}z^{k-1} + \ldots + 1$, $r_i \in GF(2)$. If γ is a root of the polynomial $R(z)$, $B_2 = (\gamma^{k-1}, \gamma^{k-2}, \ldots, \gamma, 1)$ is the standard basis with which the elements in $GF(2^k)$ are represented. Each element of the field can thus be visualized as a binary vector of dimension, k, and each element can be expressed as a linear combination of the basis elements.

The elements of the composite field $GF(2^n)^m$ are likewise represented as m-bit vectors, where each element is an element of $GF(2^n)$. The operations are performed modulo the two field generator polynomials $Q(Y) = Y^n + q_{n-1}Y^{n-1} + \ldots + q_1 Y + 1$ and $P(X) = X^m + p_{m-1}X^{m-1} + \ldots + p_1 X + p_0$.

The primitive elements of the field $GF(2^n)^m$ is denoted by α, while that of $GF(2^k)$ is denoted by γ.

We first present the basic idea for the conversion between the two fields in the following section.

1.12.1.1 Mapping from $GF(2^k)$ to $GF(2^n)^m$, where $k = nm$

A simple method to obtain such a conversion is to find the primitive element of both the fields, $GF(2^k)$ and $GF(2^n)^m$. The primitive elements are denoted by γ and α respectively. One checks that $R(\gamma)$ and $R(\alpha)$ are both zero, and thus we establish the mapping $GF(2^k) \to GF(2^n)^m : \gamma \to \alpha$. If the roots do not satisfy the polynomial R, we find the next primitive element and repeat the test.

The subsequent mappings are easy to obtain, by raising the respective primitive elements to their power and establishing the mappings. Thus, the mappings are obtained as: $GF(2^k) \to GF(2^n)^m : \gamma^i \to \alpha^i$, for $0 \le i \le 2^k - 2$, where $R(\alpha) \equiv 0 \bmod Q(Y), P(X)$. It may be noted that $R(\gamma) \equiv 0 \bmod R(Z)$, as γ is primitive.

The above is stated in algorithm 1.3.

Example 17 *Consider $GF(2^4)$ with primitive polynomial $R(Z) = Z^4 + Z + 1$, $GF(2^2)$ with primitive polynomials $Q(Y) = Y^2 + Y + 1$, and $GF(2^2)^2$ with primitive polynomials $P(X) = X^2 + X + \{2\}$, where $\{2\} \in GF(2^2)$.*

Algorithm 1.3: Determining Composite Field Mapping Using Primitive Roots

Input: $n, m, Q(Y), P(X), R(Z)$
Output: Mapping: $GF(2^k) \to GF(2^n)^m$, where $k = nm$

1   Find Primitive Element of $GF(2^k)$: denoted as γ
2   **for** *($\alpha = 1; \alpha < 2^{nm} - 1;$)* **do**
3   **if** *IsPrimitive(α) & $R(\alpha)$* **then**
4   break;
5   **end**
6   **end**
7   **for** *($i = 0; i < 2^{nm} - 1; i++$)* **do**
8      $a_1 = \alpha^i \bmod P(X), Q(Y)$
9      $b_1 = \gamma^i \bmod R(Z)$
10   Map: $a_1 \to b_1$
11   **end**

$GF(2^4) \to GF(2^2)^2$	$GF(2^4) \to GF(2^2)^2$
$\{02\} \to \{04\}$	$\{04\} \to \{06\}$
$\{08\} \to \{0e\}$	$\{03\} \to \{05\}$
$\{06\} \to \{02\}$	$\{0c\} \to \{08\}$
$\{0b\} \to \{0b\}$	$\{05\} \to \{07\}$
$\{0a\} \to \{0a\}$	$\{07\} \to \{03\}$
$\{0e\} \to \{0c\}$	$\{0f\} \to \{0d\}$
$\{0d\} \to \{09\}$	$\{09\} \to \{0f\}$
$\{01\} \to \{01\}$	$\{00\} \to \{00\}$

TABLE 1.6: An Example Isomorphic Mapping between the field $GF(2^4)$ and $GF(2^2)^2$

The first primitive element $\gamma \in GF(2^4)$ is 2. It can be checked that raising higher powers of 2, modulo $Z^4 + Z + 1$ all the non-zero elements of $GF(2^4)$ can be generated. Likewise, the first primitive element of $GF(2^2)^2$, such that $R(Z) \equiv 0$ modulo $Q(Y)$ and $P(X)$ is 4. Hence, we establish the mapping $\{02\} \to \{04\}$.

The complete mapping obtained by raising the above elements to their higher powers is written in Table 1.6. It may be noted that for completeness, we specify that 0 is mapped to 0 in the table.

The above algorithm can be made more efficient, by using suitable tests for primitivity and also storages. One such algorithm is presented in the following subsection.

1.12.1.2   An Efficient Conversion Algorithm

Next we present an algorithm to determine the mapping between a binary to a composite field representation. That is the algorithm takes two fields, $GF(2^k)$ and $GF(2^n)^m$), with $k = nm$ and returns a binary matrix of dimension $k \times k$, denoted by T, which performs an isomorphic mapping from the field $GF(2^k)$ to $GF(2^n)^m$). The inverse matrix, T^{-1} can be used to perform the mapping in the reverse direction.

Thus in order to construct the mapping you need to develop the relationship between the k elements of the two fields, $GF(2^k)$ and $GF(2^n)^m$, where $k = mn$.

The unity element in $GF(2^k)$ is mapped to the unity element in the composite field. The primitive element, γ is mapped to the element α^t, the base element γ^2 is mapped to

α^{2t}. Thus continuing similarly we have:

$$\mathbb{T}\gamma^i \quad = \quad \alpha^{it}, i = 0, 1, \dots, k-1$$

It may be noted that the choice of t cannot be arbitrary; it has to be done such that the homomorphism is established. wrt. addition and multiplications. For this we use the property discussed before:

$$R(\alpha^t) \quad = \quad 0, \text{ mod } Q(Y), P(X) \tag{1.10}$$

There will be exactly k primitive elements which will satisfy the condition, namely α^t and α^{t2^j}, $j = 1, 2, \dots, k-1$, where the exponents are computed modulo $2^k - 1$.

We summarize the above in algorithm 1.4.

Algorithm 1.4: Determining Composite Field Mappings, Isomorphic Mapping

---

Input: $n, m, Q(Y), P(X), R(Z)$

Output: Transformation $\mathbb{T}$

1   α is the primitive element in $GF(2^n)^m$ for which $P(\alpha) = 0$.
2   $t = 1$
3   Initialize a list $S[1 : 2^k - 1]$ with $2^k - 1$ addresses and one bit amount of information is stored in each address location.
4   Initialize a $k \times k$ matrix $\mathbb{T}$ with each column being indicated by $\mathbb{T}[i]$, where $1 \leq i \leq k$.
5   Set, $\mathbb{T}[k] = (0, 0, \dots, 1)$.
6   **while** $(R(\alpha^t)! = 0)$ **do**
7   **for** $(j = 0; j \leq k - 1; j + +)$ **do**
8         $S[t2^j \text{ mod } (2^k - 1)] = 0$
9   **end**
10     $t = t + 1$
11   **while** $(S[t] == 0 \text{ or } gcd(t, 2^k - 1) > 1)$ **do**
12        $t = t + 1$
13   **end**
14 **end**
15 **for** $(j = 2; j \leq k; j + +)$ **do**
16     $T[j] = \text{binary}(\alpha^{(j-1)t})$
17 **end**

The algorithm can be explained as follows: Line 5 of the algorithm ensures that the identity element in the field $GF(2^k)$ is mapped to the identity element in $GF(2^n)^m$. Both the identity elements are represented by the polynomial 1. Line 6 checks for the equality of $R(\alpha^t)$ to zero, which if true indicates that t is found. If α^t is not the element to which β is mapped, then α^{t2^j} are also not primitive elements, where $1 < j < k - 1$. Hence we set the corresponding elements in the array, S to 0, and proceed by incrementing t by 1.

In line 10 and 11, we continue the search for the appropriate t by checking whether the corresponding entry in the S array has been set to 0 (indicating it was found unsuitable during a previous run of the while loop of line 6), or if not previously marked by checking the primitivity of α^t by computing the gcd of t and $2^k - 1$. If the gcd is found to be greater than 1, it indicates that α^t is not primitive, hence, we increment t.

When the correct value of t is obtained, the matrix T is populated columnwise from the right by the binary representations of α^{jt}, where $2 \leq j \leq k$.

1.13   Conclusions

In this chapter, we developed several mathematical concepts, which form the foundations of modern cryptography. The chapter presented discussions on modular arithmetic and defined the concepts of mathematical groups, rings, and fields. Useful operations like the Euclidean algorithm, its extensions to evaluate the greatest common divisor, and the multiplicative inverse were elaborated. We also discussed the Chinese Remainder Theorem, which is a useful tool to develop efficient designs for RSA-like algorithms and also to perform attacks on them. The chapter subsequently developed the important concept of subfields and shows how to construct extension fields from a field. As modern cryptographic algorithm relies heavily on Galois (finite) fields, the chapter presents a special attention to them, efficient representation of elements in the Galois fields, and their various properties, like formation of cyclic group, etc. The chapter also elaborated with examples on how to define isomorphic mapping between several equivalent fields, often technically referred to as the composite fields. All these concepts and techniques built on them have useful impact in efficient (hardware) designs and attacks. We show several such applications in the following chapters.

Chapter 2

Overview of Modern Cryptography

"Maunam Caivasmi Guhyanam Jnanam"

(Of Secrecy I am Silence)

Bhagavad Gita

Vibhuti-yoga, Sloka 38

2.1   Introduction

The art of keeping messages secret is cryptography, while cryptanalysis is the study attempted to defeat cryptographic techniques. *Cryptography* is used to protect information from illegal access. It largely encompasses the art of building schemes (*ciphers*) which allow secret data exchange over insecure channels [351]. The need of secured information exchange is as old as civilization itself. It is believed that the oldest use of cryptography was found in non-standard hieroglyphics carved into monuments from Egypt's Old Kingdom. In 5 B.C. the Spartans developed a cryptographic device, called *scytale* to send and receive secret messages. The code was the basis of transposition ciphers, in which the letters remained the same but the order is changed. This is still the basis for many modern day ciphers. The other major ingredient of many modern-day ciphers is substitution ciphers, which was used by Julius Caesar and is popularly known as Caesar's shift cipher. In this cipher, each plaintext character was replaced by the character 3 places to the right in the alphabet set modulo 26. However, in the last three decades cryptography has grown beyond designing ciphers to encompass also other activities like design of signature schemes for signing digital contracts. Also the design of cryptographic protocols for securely proving one's identity has been an important aspect of cryptography of the modern age. Yet the construction of encryption schemes remains, and is likely to remain, a central enterprise of cryptography [134]. The primitive operation of cryptography is hence *encryption*. The inverse operation of obtaining the original message from the encrypted data is known as *decryption*. Encryption transforms messages into representation that is meaningless for all parties other than the intended receiver. Almost all cryptosystems rely upon the difficulty of reversing the encryption transformation in order to provide security to communication [353]. *Cryptanalysis* is the art and science of breaking the encrypted message. The branch of science encompassing both cryptography and cryptanalysis is cryptology and its practitioners are cryptologists. One of the greatest triumph of cryptanalysis over cryptography was the breaking of a ciphering machine named Enigma and used during Worldwar II. In short cryptology evolves from the long-lasting tussle between the cryptographer and cryptanalyst.

For many years, many fundamental developments in cryptology outpoured from military organizations around the world. One of the most influential cryptanalytic papers of the twentieth century was William F. Friedman's monograph [123] entitled *The Index of Coincidence and its Applications in Cryptography*. For the next fifty years, research in cryptography was predominantly done in a secret fashion, with few exceptions like the revolutionary contribution of Claude Shannon's paper "*The Communication Theory of Secrecy Systems*", which appeared in the *Bell System Technical Journal* in 1949 [359].

However, after the world wars cryptography became a science of interest to the research community. The *Code Breakers* by David Kahn produced the remarkable history of cryptography [171]. The significance of this classic text was that it raised the public awareness of cryptography. The subsequent development of communication and hence the need of privacy in message exchange also increased the impetus on research in this field. A large number of cryptographers from various fields of study began to contribute leading to the rebirth of this field. Horst Fiestel [119] began the development of the US Data Encryption Standard (DES) and laid the foundation of a class of ciphers called as private or symmetric key algorithms. The structure of these ciphers became popular as the Fiestel Networks in general. Symmetric key algorithms use a single key to both encrypt and decrypt. In order to establish the key between the sender and the receiver they required to meet once to decide the key. This problem commonly known as the key exchange problem was solved by Martin Hellman and Whitfield Diffie [111] in 1976 in their ground-breaking paper *New Directions in Cryptography.* The developed protocol allows two users to exchange a secret key over an insecure medium without any prior secrets. The work not only solved the problem of key exchange but also provided the foundation of a new class of cryptography, known as the public key cryptography. As a result of this work the RSA algorithm, named after the inventors Ron Rivest, Adi Shamir, and Leonard Adleman, was developed [307]. The security of the protocol was based on the computational task in factoring the product of large prime numbers.

Cryptology has evolved further with the growing importance of communications and the development in both processor speeds and hardware. Modern-day cryptographers have thus more work than merely jumbling up messages. They have to look into the application areas in which the cryptographic algorithms have to work. The transistor has become more powerful. The development of the VLSI technology (now in submicrons) have made the once cumbersome computers faster and smaller. The more powerful computers and devices will allow the complicated encryption algorithm run faster. The same computing power is also available to the cryptanalysts who will now try to break the ciphers with both straight forward brute force analysis, as well as by leveraging the growth in cryptanalysis. The world has thus changed since the DES was adopted as the standard cryptographic algorithm and DES was feeling its age. Large public literature on ciphers and the development of tools for cryptanalysis urged the importance of a new standard. The National Institute for Standards and Technology (NIST) organized a contest for the new Advanced Encryption Standard (AES) in 1997. The block cipher Rijndael emerged as the winner in October 2000 because of its features of security, elegance in implementations and principled design approach. Simultaneously Rijndael was evaluated by cryptanalysts and a lot of interesting works were reported. Cryptosystems are inherently computationally complex and in order to satisfy the high throughput requirements of many applications, they are often implemented by means of either VLSI devices or highly optimized software routines. In recent years such cryptographic implementations have been attacked using a class of attacks which exploits leaking of information through side-channels like power, timing, intrusion of faults etc. In short as technology progresses new efficient encryption algorithms and their implementations will be invented, which in turn shall be cryptanalyzed in unconventional ways. Without doubt cryptology promises to remain an interesting field of research both from theoretical and application point of view.

2.2 Cryptography: Some Technical Details

The aim of the cryptographer is to find methods to secure and authenticate messages. The original message is called the plaintext and the encrypted output is called the ciphertext. A secret key is employed to generate the ciphertext from the plaintext. The process of converting the plaintext to the cipher text is called encryption and the vice versa is called decryption. The cryptographer tries to keep the messages secret from the attacker or intruder. A cryptosystem is a communication system encompassing a message source, an encryptor, an insecure channel, a decryptor, a message destination and a secure key transfer mechanism. The scenario of a cryptographic communication is illustrated in **Fig. 2.1**. The encryptor uses a key K_a and the decryptor used a key K_b, where depending on the equality of K_a and K_b there are two important classes of cryptographic algorithms.

The sender and the receiver are often given the names of **Alice** and **Bob**, while the untrusted channel is being observed by an adversary whom we name as **Mallory**. She has access to the ciphertexts, and is aware of the encryption and decryption algorithm. The goal of the attacker Mallory is to ascertain the value of the decryption key K_b, thus obtaining the information which he is not supposed to know. The attacker or cryptanalyst is a powerful

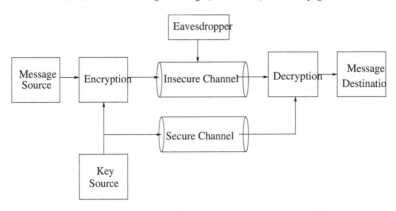

FIGURE 2.1: Secret Key Cryptosystem Model

entity who studies the cipher and uses algebraic and statistical techniques to attack a cryptographic scheme. A cryptanalytic attack is a procedure through which the cryptanalyst gains information about the secret decryption key. Attacks are classified according to the level of a-priori knowledge available to the cryptanalyst.

A **Ciphertext-only attack** is an attack where the cryptanalyst has access to ciphertexts generated using a given key but has no access to the corresponding plaintexts or the key. A **Known-plaintext attack** is an attack where the cryptanalyst has access to both ciphertexts and the corresponding plaintexts, but not the key.

A **Chosen-plaintext attack** (CPA) is an attack where the cryptanalyst can choose plaintexts to be encrypted and has access to the resulting ciphertexts, again their purpose being to determine the key.

A **Chosen-ciphertext attack** (CCA) is an attack in which the cryptanalyst can choose ciphertexts, apart from the challenge ciphertext and can obtain the corresponding plaintext. The attacker has access to the decryption device.

In case of CPA and CCA, adversaries can make a bounded number of queries to its encryption or decryption device. The encryption device is often called as oracle: meaning it is like a black-box without details like in an algorithm of how an input is transformed or used to obtain the output. Although this may seem a bit hypothetical, but there are enough real life instances where such encryption and decryption oracles can be obtained. Thus security analysis with the existence of such oracles is imperative.

The attacks are measured against a worst case referred to as the brute-force method. The method is a trial-and-error approach, whereby every possible key is tried until the correct one is found. Any attack that permits the discovery of the correct key faster than the brute-force method, on average, is considered successful. An important principle known as the *Kerckhoff's principle* states that the secrecy of a cipher must reside entirely in the key. Thus an enemy will have a complete knowledge of the cipher but shall not know the key. A secured cryptographic scheme should withstand the attack of such a well-informed adversary.

Formal definition of a cryptosystem is stated below for the sake of completeness:

Definition 1 *A cryptosystem is a five-tuple* (P, C, K, E, D), *where the following are satisfied:*

1. *P is a finite set of possible plaintexts*

2. *C is a finite set of possible ciphertexts*

3. K, the key space, is a finite set of possible keys

4. $\forall K_a, K_b \in K$, there is an encryption rule $e_{K_a} \in E$ and a corresponding decryption rule $d_{K_b} \in D$. Each chosen pair $e_{K_a} : P \to C$ and $d_{K_b} : C \to P$ are invertible functions, ie. $\forall x \in P$, $d_{K_b}(e_{K_a}(x)) = x$.

Example 18 *Let $P = C = Z_{26}$. Let $K_a = K_b = k \in Z_{26}$. We can define a cryptosystem as follows $\forall x, y \in Z_{26}$:*

$$e_k(x) = (x + k) \bmod 26 \quad d_k(x) = (y - k) \bmod 26$$

Example 19 *Let $P = C = \{0,1\}^{128}$. Let $K_a = K_b = k \in \{0,1\}^{128}$. We can define a cryptosystem as follows $\forall x, y \in \{0,1\}^{128}$:*

$$e_K(x) = (x \oplus k) \quad d_K(x) = (y \oplus k)$$

Here the operator $\oplus$ is a bitwise operation and is a self-invertible operation. Not all ciphers have K_a and K_b same. In fact, depending on their equality we have two important dichotomy of ciphers which are explained next:

- Private-key (or symmetric) ciphers: These ciphers have the same key shared between the sender and the receiver. Thus, referring to **Fig. 2.1** $K_a = K_b$.

- Public-key (or asymmetric) ciphers: In these ciphers we have $K_a \neq K_b$. The encryption key and the decryption keys are different.

These types differ mainly in the manner in which keys are shared. In symmetric-key or private-key cryptography both the encryptor and decryptor use the same key. Thus, the key must somehow be securely exchanged before secret key communication can begin (through a secured channel, **Fig. 2.1**). In public key cryptography the encryption and decryption keys are different.

In such algorithms we have a key-pair, consisting of:

- Public key, which can be freely distributed and is used to encrypt messages. In the **Fig. 2.1**, this is denoted by the key K_a.

- Private key, which must be kept secret and is used to decrypt messages. The decryption key is denoted by K_b in the **Fig. 2.1**.

In the public key or asymmetric ciphers, the two parties –namely Alice and Bob–are communicating with each other and have their own key pair. They distribute their public keys freely. Mallory has the knowledge of not only the encryption function, the decryption function, and the ciphertext, but also has the capability to encrypt the messages using Bob's public key. However, he is unaware of the secret decryption key, which is the private key of the algorithm. The security of these classes of algorithms rely on the assumption that it is mathematically hard or complex to obtain the private key from the public informations. Doing so would imply that the adversary solves a mathematical problem which is widely believed to be difficult. It may be noted that we do not have any proofs for their hardness, however we are unaware of any efficient techniques to solve them. The elegance of constructing these ciphers lies in the fact that the public keys and private keys still have to be related in the sense, that they perform the invertible operations to obtain the message back. This is achieved through a class of magical functions, which are called *one-way* functions. These functions are easy to compute in one direction, while computing the inverse from the output is believed to be a difficult problem. We shall discuss this in more details in a following section. However, first let us see an example for this class of ciphers.

Example 20 *This cipher is called the famous RSA algorithm (Rivest Shamir Adleman). Let $n = pq$, where p and q are properly chosen and large prime numbers. Here the proper choice of p and q are to ensure that factorization of n is mathematically complex. The plaintexts and ciphertexts are $P = C = Z_n$, the keys are $K_a = \{n, a\}$ and $K_b = \{b, p, q\}$, st $ab \equiv 1 \bmod \phi(n)$. The encryption and decryption functions are defined as, $\forall x \in P$, $e_{K_a}(x) = y = x^a \bmod n$ and $d_{K_b}(y) = y^b \bmod n$.*

The proof of correctness of the above algorithm follows from the combination of the Fermat's little theorem and the Chinese Remainder Theorem (CRT). The algorithm is correct if $\forall x \in P$, we have:

$$x^{ab} \equiv x \bmod n$$

It suffices to show that:

$$x^{ab} \equiv x \bmod p \quad x^{ab} \equiv x \bmod q \tag{2.1}$$

It may be observed that since $gcd(p, q) = 1$ we have from the Extended Euclidean Algorithm (EEA) $1 = (q^{-1} \bmod p)q + (p^{-1} \bmod q)p$. Thus, from Equation 2.1 applying CRT we have $x^{ab} \equiv x((q^{-1} \bmod p)q + (p^{-1} \bmod q)p) \bmod n = x$.

If $x \equiv 0 \bmod p$, then it is trivial that $x^{ab} \equiv x \bmod p$.

Otherwise if $x \not\equiv 0 \bmod p$, $x^{p-1} \equiv 1 \bmod p$. Also, since $ab \equiv 1 \bmod \phi(n)$ and $\phi(n) = (p-1)(q-1)$ we have $ab = 1 + k(p-1)(q-1)$ for some integer k.

Thus we have, $x^{ab} = x.x^{k(p-1)(q-1)} \equiv x \bmod p$. Likewise, we have $x^{ab} \equiv x \bmod q$. Combining the two facts, by CRT we have that $x^{ab} \equiv x \bmod n$. This shows the correctness of the RSA cipher.

It may be observed that the knowledge of the factors of p and q help to ascertain the value of the decryption key K_b from the encryption key K_a. Likewise, if the decryption key K_b is leaked, then the value of n can be factored using a probabilistic algorithm with probability of success at least 0.5.

Another kind of public key ciphers is the ElGamal cryptosystem, which is based on another hard problem which is called the *Discrete Log Problem* (DLP).

Consider a finite mathematical group $(G, .)$. For an element $\alpha \in G$ of order n, let:

$$< \alpha > = \{\alpha^i : 0 \le i \le n - 1\}$$

The DLP problem is to find the unique integer i st. $\alpha^i = \beta$, $0 \le i \le n - 1$. We denote this number as $i = log_\alpha \beta$ and is referred as the *Discrete Log*.

Computing Discrete Log, is thus the inverse computation of a modular exponentiation operation. We have efficient algorithms for computing the modular exponentiation, by the square and multiply algorithm, however it is generally difficult to compute the DLP for properly chosen groups. Thus, the modular exponentiation is a potential one-way function having applications in public key cryptography.

We define one such cryptosystem, known as the ElGamal cipher.

Example 21 *Let p be a prime, st. computing DLP in $(Z_p^*, .)$ is hard. Let $\alpha \in Z_p^*$ be a primitive element, and define the plaintext set as $P = Z_p^*$ and the ciphertext set as $C = Z_p^* \times Z_p^*$. The key set is defined as $K = (p, \alpha, a, \beta) : \alpha^a \equiv \beta \bmod p$.*

For a given $k \in K$, $x \in P$, $c \in C$ and for a secret number $r \in Z_{p-1}$, define $c = e_k(x, r) = (y_1, y_2)$, where $y_1 = \alpha^r \bmod p$, and $y_2 = x\beta^r \bmod p$. This cryptosystem is called as the ElGamal cryptosystem. The decryption is straightforward: for a given ciphertext, $c = (y_1, y_2)$, where $y_1, y_2 \in Z_p^*$, we have $x = (y_1^a)^{-1}(y_2)$.

The plaintext x is thus masked by multiplying it by β^r in the second part of the cipher-text, y_2. The hint to decrypt is transmitted in the first part of the ciphertext in the form of α^r. It is assumed that only the receiver who has the secret key a can compute β^r by raising α^r to the power of a, as $\beta \equiv \alpha^a \bmod p$. Then decrypting and obtaining back x as one just needs to multiply the multiplicative inverse of β^r with y_2.

Thus one can observe that the ElGamal cipher is randomized, and one can for the same plaintext x obtain $p-1$ ciphertexts, depending on the choice of r.

An interesting point to note about the hardness of the DLP is that the difficulty arises from the modular operation. As otherwise, α^i would have been monotonically increasing, and one can apply a binary search technique to obtain the value of i from a given value of α and $\beta = \alpha^i$. However, as the operations are performed modular p, there is no ordering among the powers, a higher value of i can give a lower value of the α^i. Thus in the worst case, one has to do brute force search among all the possible $p-1$ values of i to obtain the exact value (note that there is a unique value of i). Hence the time complexity is $O(p)$. One can try to use some storage and perform a time-memory trade-off.

An attacker can pre-compute and store all possible values of (i, α^i), and then sort the table based on the second field using an efficient sorting method. Thus the total storage required is $O(p)$ and the time to sort is $O(p\log p)$. Given a value of β, now the time to search is $O(\log p)$. Sometimes for complexity analysis of DLP, we neglect the value of $\log$, and then thus in this case the time complexity is reduced to $O(1)$ while the memory complexity is increased to $O(p)$. However there are developments in cryptanalysis which allows us to solve the DLP in time-memory product of $O(\sqrt{p})$, but the study of these algorithms is beyond the scope of this text.

Public (or asymmetric) and Private (or symmetric) key algorithms have complementary advantages and disadvantages. They have their specific application areas. Symmetric key ciphers have higher data throughput but the key must remain secret at both the ends. Thus in a large network there are many key pairs that should be managed. Sound cryptographic practice dictates that the key should be changed frequently for each communication session. The throughputs of the most popular public-key encryption methods are several orders of magnitude slower than the best known symmetric key schemes. In a large network the number of keys required are considerably smaller and needs to be changed less frequently. In practice thus public-key cryptography is used for efficient key management while symmetric key algorithms are used for bulk data encryption.

In the next subsection, we highlight an application of public key systems to achieve key-exchanges between two parties. The famous protocol known as the Diffie-Hellman key-exchange is based on another hard problem related closely with the DLP. This is called as the Diffie-Hellman Problem (DHP) and the key-exchange is called as the Diffie Hellman (DH) key-exchange.

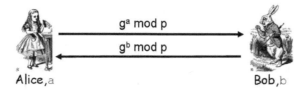

FIGURE 2.2: The Diffie Hellman Key Exchange

In this exchange, Alice and Bob (see **Fig. 2.2**) agree upon two public elements, p and g. Alice has a secret element a, and Bob has a secret element b, where $a, b \in Z_{p-1}$.

Alice computes $x_1 \equiv g^a \bmod p$, while Bob computes $x_2 \equiv g^b \bmod p$ and then exchanges these informations over the network. Then Alice computes $x_2^a \bmod p$, while Bob computes $x_1^b \bmod p$, both of which are the same. Apart from the agreement (which is quite evident), the most important question is of the secrecy of the agreed key, i.e. the untrusted third party should not be able to compute the agreed key, which is numerically $x_1^b \equiv x_2^a \equiv g^{ab} \bmod p$.

Thus the eavesdropper has to compute this value from the public information of g and p and the exchanged information of $x_1 \equiv g^a \bmod p$ and $x_2 \equiv g^b \bmod p$. This problem is known as the *Computational Diffie Hellman Problem* (CDH). As can be observed this problem is related to the DLP: if one can solve the DLP he can obtain the values of a or b and can solve the CDH problem as well. The other direction is however not so straightforward and is beyond the current discussion.

The classical DH key-exchange can be subjected to simple man-in-the-middle (MiM) attacks. As an interceptor *Eve* can modify the value x_1 from Alice to Bob and hand over Bob a modified value of $x_1' \equiv g^t \bmod p$, for some arbitrarily chosen $t \in Z_{p-1}$. Similarly, she also modifies x_2 received from Bob into $x_2' = x_1' \equiv g^t \bmod p$. However, Alice and Bob are unaware of this attack scenario and goes ahead with the DH key-exchange and computes the keys as $g^{ta} \bmod p$ and $g^{tb} \bmod p$, respectively. They use these keys to communicate with each other. However, the future messages that are encrypted with these keys can all be deciphered by Eve as she also can compute these keys using the exchanged values of x_1 and x_2 and the public values g and p. This simple attack obviates the use of other reinforcements to the classical DH Key-exchange, like encrypting the exchanged messages by symmetric or asymmetric ciphers. Thus for an end-to-end security interplay of symmetric and asymmetric ciphers is very important. However, the objective of this text is to understand the design challenges of these primitives on hardware.

One of the important class of symmetric algorithms is block ciphers, which are used for bulk data encryption. In the next section, we present an overview of block cipher structures. As an important example, we present the Advanced Encryption Standard (AES), which is the current standard block cipher. The AES algorithm uses finite field arithmetic and the underlying field is of the form $GF(2^8)$. Subsequently in a later section, we describe a present-day public key cipher, namely elliptic curve cryptosystem. These ciphers rely on the arithmetic on elliptic curves which can be defined over finite fields over characteristic 2 and primes.

2.3   Block Ciphers

Block ciphers are encryption algorithms that encrypt n bits of plaintext using an m bits of the key (m and n may be different) and produces an n bits of the ciphertext. **Fig. 2.3** shows a top-level diagram of a block cipher. As can be observed that the plaintext is divided into the Block Length, which is a block of size n bits. Each block is transformed by the encryption algorithm to result in an n bits of the ciphertext. The plaintext block P_i is thus processed by the key K, resulting in the ciphertext block $C_i = E_K(P_i)$.

The encryption algorithm is used in several modes to obtain the ciphertext blocks. The most naïve way of doing the operation is called Electronic Code Book (ECB). In this mode, as shown in **Fig. 2.4**, each block P_i gets encrypted independent of another block P_j, where $i \neq j$.

However, this is not a secured form of encryption and is not used for most applications. A popular and secured mode of encryption is called as the Cipher Block Chaining (CBC).

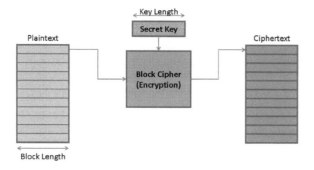

FIGURE 2.3: Block Cipher: Encryption

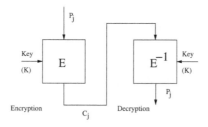

FIGURE 2.4: Electronic Code Book

In this mode, as shown in **Fig. 2.5** the cipher of a block, C_{j-1} is XORed with the next plaintext block, P_j. Thus the ciphertext for the next block is $C_j = E_K(P_j \oplus C_{j-1})$. This indicates that the output of the jth instance depends on the output of the previous step. Thus although, as we shall see in the following sections, that the block ciphers have an iterated structure, there is no benefit from pipelining. More precisely, the reason is that the next block encryption cannot start unless the encryption of the previous block is completed. However, there are other modes of ciphers, like **counter mode** and *Output Feedback* (OFB) where pipelining provides advantage.

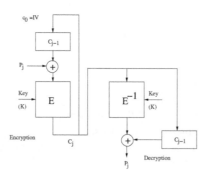

FIGURE 2.5: Cipher Block Chaining

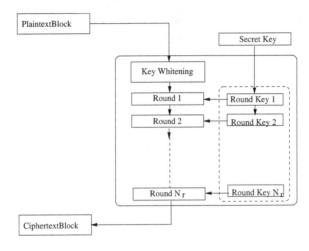

FIGURE 2.6: Structure of a Block Cipher

2.3.1   Inner Structures of a Block Cipher

In order to understand the design aspects of a block cipher, it is important to know what they are comprised of.

The block ciphers of the present day have typically blocks of size 128 bits, while the keys are of size $128, 192$, or 256 bits. For lightweight applications, there are some ciphers which have keys of length 80 bits. The choice of the key size is very important for security against brute force attacks, and is referred to as the security margin of the cipher. However, the longer the key implies that the cipher design has a larger overhead, in terms of hardware area, time, power. Further it may be noted that a cipher with a large key size is not necessarily more secured. For example, it is widely believed that AES-128 is the most secured among its other variants with key sizes 192 and 256 bits.

The block cipher is typically made of further subdivisions or transformations. The transformations are often called *rounds* of the cipher (refer **Fig. 2.6**). A block cipher has, say, N_r number of rounds. The input key, which is the *secret key* is transformed by the *key-scheduling algorithm*, to generate the N_r round keys. The input key is often used as the *whitening key* and is mixed with the plaintext block, P_i. Typically the key mixing is performed through bit-wise XOR between the plaintext block and the input key. Subsequently, each round operates on the message, and the message *state* gets updated due to each transformation. The transformations of a round is achieved by further sub-operations, which make up the rounds. The round keys, computed by the key-scheduling algorithm also are mixed with the present state of the message, typically through bit-wise *XOR*. After the N_r rounds, the final state is returned as the ciphertext.

The round of a cipher is made of further components which provide the cipher much needed **confusion** and **diffusion**. Classically, diffusion hides the relation between the ciphertext and the plaintext. On the other hand, confusion obscures the relation between the ciphertext and the key. The objective of both the steps are to make the task of the cryptanalyst harder.

The round comprises of three distinct operations:

1. **Addition with Round Key**: The message state is typically XORed with the round key.

2. **D-box**: It is a key-less transformation called as the diffusion box, or D-box. It provides

diffusion to the cipher. This step is typically a linear transformation wrt. the XOR operation. Hence it can be expressed in terms of the input using only *XOR* gates. Thus often they are easy to implement and hence can be applied on larger block lengths as the resource requirement typically is less.

3. **S-Box**: It is generally a key-less transformation, commonly referred to as the substitution box, or S-Box. It provides the much needed confusion to the cipher as it makes the algebraic relations of the ciphertext bits in terms of the message state bits and the key bits more complex. The S-Boxes are typically non-linear wrt. the XOR operations. These transformations require both **XOR** and also **AND** gates. These transformations are mathematically complex and pose a large over-head. Hence they are often performed in smaller chunks. The hardware required also grows fast with the input size and thus requires special techniques for implementation.

The rounds combine the diffusion and the substitution layers suitably for achieving security. In the following section we present the design of the AES algorithm, to illustrate the construction of a block cipher.

2.3.2 The Advanced Encryption Standard

In 1997 the National Institute of Standards and Technology (NIST) initiated the selection for the next generation standard block cipher after DES. One of the primary reasons being the shorter key size of DES (56 bits for encryption) was becoming more and more inadequate for providing security. Efforts to extend DES by cascading instances of DES also was not successful owing to the existence of *meet-in-the-mddle* attacks. Thus 3-DES was evaluated to provide security corresponding to 2 rounds of DES (112 bits), as opposed to the expected security provided by a 168-bit key. Moreover, DES was not very efficient for implementations because of its rather unexplained S-Box design. On November 26, 2011 a cipher designed by Belgian inventors, Rijmen and Daemen, was selected as the Advanced Encryption Standard (AES).

AES is thus a block cipher which works on $GF(2^8)$. Although Rijndael was originally designed to support plaintext blocks and the key blocks of $128, 192$, or 256 bits, the adopted AES cipher has a restricted plaintext block of side 128 bits.

The AES algorithm receives a plaintext block as input and produces the ciphertext block after several rounds of the cipher. The cipher algorithm explains the input plaintext, the intermediate blocks and the final ciphertext blocks as states, denoted by matrices with elements in $GF(2^8)$. We next explain some of the notations that have been used in the subsequent exposition:

The state matrix of the Rijndael cipher has Nb 32-bit words, $4 \leq Nb \leq 8$, thus the block length is $32Nb$. For AES, as stated before the block length is 128, thus $Nb = 4$. The key block is parameterized by Nk, which denotes the number of columns of size 32 bits. The range of Nk is $4 \leq Nk \leq 8$. For AES the key length can be either $128, 192$, or 256, thus $Nk = 4, 6,$ or 8. The number of rounds of the cipher is denoted by Nr, which varies with the size of the key.

The state matrix for AES is as follows:

$$\mathbb{S} = \begin{pmatrix} b_{0,0} & b_{0,1} & b_{1,0} & b_{1,1} \\ b_{1,0} & b_{1,1} & b_{1,2} & b_{1,3} \\ b_{2,0} & b_{2,1} & b_{2,2} & b_{2,3} \\ b_{3,0} & b_{3,1} & b_{3,2} & b_{3,3} \end{pmatrix}$$

The state $\mathbb{S}$ comprises of 16 bytes, indicated by $b_{i,j}$, where $0 \leq i, j \leq 15$. Each of the bytes are elements of $GF(2^8)$.

Algorithm 2.1: The AES function **Cipher**

Input: byte in[4,Nb], word w[Nb(Nr+1)]
Output: byte out[4,Nb]

1 byte state[4,Nb]
2 state = in
3 AddRoundKey(state, w[0:Nb-1])
4 **for** round = 1 to Nr-1 **do**
5   SubBytes(state)
6   ShiftRows(state)
7   MixColumns(state)
8   AddRoundKey(state, w[round*Nb:(round+1)*Nb-1])
9 **end**
10 SubBytes(state)
11 ShiftRows(state)
12 AddRoundKey(state, w[Nr*Nb:(Nr+1)*Nb-1])
13 out=state

The state matrices of AES undergo transformations through the rounds of the cipher. The plaintext is of 128 bits and are arranged in the state matrix, so that each of the 16 bytes are elements of the state matrix. The AES key can also be arranged in a similar fashion, comprising of Nk words of length 4 bytes each. The input key is expanded by a **Key-Scheduling** algorithm to an expanded key w. The plaintext state matrix (denoted by in), is transformed by the round keys which are extracted from the expanded key w. The final cipher (denoted by out) is the result of applying the encryption algorithm, Cipher on the plaintext, in. In the next two sections, we present the round functions and the key scheduling algorithm respectively.

2.3.3   The AES Round Transformations

The AES Cipher receives as an input the plaintext, denoted by the byte in[4,Nb], while the output is denoted by out[4,Nb]. The plaintext is stored in the state matrix, denoted by the byte array state. The key is stored in a key matrix, w which is mixed with the plaintext by XORing. This step is often referred to as the key whitening. The plaintext is subsequently transformed by Nr rounds. Each of the first $Nr - 1$ rounds have round transformations, namely **SubBytes**, **ShiftRows**, **MixColumns**, and **AddRoundKey**. In the last round only the transformations SubBytes, ShiftRows, and AddRoundKey are present. Each of the $Nr + 1$ rounds thus require a share of the key which is stored in the key w[Nb(Nr+1)], generated via the key-scheduling algorithm.

The bytes of the state matrix are elements of $GF(2^8)$ and are often written in hexadecimal notation. For example an element, $a(x) = x^7 + x + 1$, can be encoded in binary as 10000011, where the ones denote the corresponding coefficient in $GF(2)$. The element in hexadecimal is denoted as {13}. Likewise, an element in $GF(2^8)$ encoded as 10110011 is expressed as {F3}. As described before, the field is generated by using the following irreducible poynomial as the reduction polynomial:

$$m(X) \;=\; X^8 + X^4 + X^3 + X + 1$$

Thus the extension field $GF(2^8)$ is created and the elements of the field are expressible as polynomials $\in GF(2)[X]/\langle m(X)\rangle$. Each non-zero element has a multiplicative inverse, which can be computed by the Euclidean inverse algorithm. This forms the basis of what is known as the SubBytes step of the algorithm.

2.3.3.1 SubBytes

The **SubBytes** step is a non-linear byte-wise function. It acts on the bytes of the state and subsequently applies an affine transformation on the cipher (**Fig. 2.7**). The step is based on the computation of finite field inverse, which is as follows:

$$x' = \begin{cases} x^{-1} & \text{if } x \neq 0 \\ 0 & \text{otherwise} \end{cases}$$

The final output is computed as $y = A(x') + B$, where A and B are fixed matrices defined as follows:

$$\mathbf{A} = \begin{pmatrix} 1 & 0 & 0 & 0 & 1 & 1 & 1 & 1 \\ 1 & 1 & 0 & 0 & 0 & 1 & 1 & 1 \\ 1 & 1 & 1 & 0 & 0 & 0 & 1 & 1 \\ 1 & 1 & 1 & 1 & 0 & 0 & 0 & 1 \\ 1 & 1 & 1 & 1 & 1 & 0 & 0 & 0 \\ 0 & 1 & 1 & 1 & 1 & 1 & 0 & 0 \\ 0 & 0 & 1 & 1 & 1 & 1 & 1 & 0 \\ 0 & 0 & 0 & 1 & 1 & 1 & 1 & 1 \end{pmatrix} \tag{2.2}$$

and the value of B vector is :

$$(\mathbf{B})^{\mathbf{t}} = \begin{pmatrix} 0 & 1 & 1 & 0 & 0 & 0 & 1 & 1 \end{pmatrix} \tag{2.3}$$

Here, $(B)^t$ represents the transpose of B, and the left most bit is the LSB.

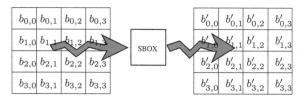

FIGURE 2.7: SubBytes Transformation

The **InvSubBytes** step operates upon the bytes in the reverse order. It is defined as :

$$X = Y^{-1}A^{-1} + D \tag{2.4}$$

where D is an 8×1 vector-matrix. The matrix A^{-1} is defined as [103]:

$$\mathbf{A}^{-1} = \begin{pmatrix} 0 & 0 & 1 & 0 & 0 & 1 & 0 & 1 \\ 1 & 0 & 0 & 1 & 0 & 0 & 1 & 0 \\ 0 & 1 & 0 & 0 & 1 & 0 & 0 & 1 \\ 1 & 0 & 1 & 0 & 0 & 1 & 0 & 0 \\ 0 & 1 & 0 & 1 & 0 & 0 & 1 & 0 \\ 0 & 0 & 1 & 0 & 1 & 0 & 0 & 1 \\ 1 & 0 & 0 & 1 & 0 & 1 & 0 & 0 \\ 0 & 1 & 0 & 0 & 1 & 0 & 1 & 0 \end{pmatrix} \tag{2.5}$$

and the value of D vector is :

$$(\mathbf{D})^t = \begin{pmatrix} 0 & 0 & 0 & 0 & 0 & 1 & 0 & 1 \end{pmatrix} \tag{2.6}$$

Here, $(D)^t$ represents the transpose of D, and the left most bit is the LSB.

The SubBytes is the only non-linear layer of the cipher. The other two operations ShiftRows and MixColumns are linear and provide fast diffusion of disturbances in the cipher [103].

2.3.3.2   ShiftRows

In the operation **ShiftRows**, the rows of the State are cyclically left shifted over different offsets. We denote the number of shifts of the 4 rows by c_0, c_1, c_2 and c_3. The shift offsets c_0, c_1, c_2 and c_3 depend on N_b. The different values of the shift offsets are specified in Table 2.1 [103].

TABLE 2.1: Shift offsets for different block lengths

N_b	c_0	c_1	c_2	c_3
4	0	1	2	3
5	0	1	2	3
6	0	1	2	3
7	0	1	2	4
8	0	1	3	4

The **InvShiftRows** operation performs circular shift in the opposite direction. The offset values for InvShiftRows are the same as ShiftRows (Table 2.1). ShiftRows implementations do not require any resource as they can be implemented by rewiring.

2.3.3.3   MixColumns

The **MixColumns** transformation operates on each column of State (X) individually. Each column of the state matrix can be imagined as the extension field $GF(2^8)^4$. For $0 \le j \le Nb$ a column of the state matrix S is denoted by the polynomial:

$$s_j(X) = s_{3,j}X^3 + s_{2,j}X^2 + s_{1,j}X + s_{0,j} \in GF(2^8)[X]$$

The transformation for MixColumns is denoted by the polynomial:

$$m(X) = \{03\}X^3 + \{01\}X^2 + \{01\}X + \{02\} \in GF(2^8)[X]$$

The output of the MixColumns operation is obtained by taking the product of the above two polynomials, $s_j(X)$ and $m(X)$ over the field $GF(2^8)^4$, with the reduction polynomial being $X^4 + 1$.

Thus the output can be expressed as a modified column, computed as follows:

$$s'_j(X) = (s_j(X) * m(X)) \bmod (X^4 + 1), 0 \le j < Nb$$

The transformation can also be viewed as a linear transformation in $GF(2^8)^4$ as follows:

$$\begin{bmatrix} s'_{0,j} \\ s'_{1,j} \\ s'_{2,j} \\ s'_{3,j} \end{bmatrix} = \begin{bmatrix} \{02\} & \{03\} & \{01\} & \{01\} \\ \{01\} & \{02\} & \{03\} & \{01\} \\ \{01\} & \{01\} & \{02\} & \{03\} \\ \{03\} & \{01\} & \{01\} & \{02\} \end{bmatrix} \begin{bmatrix} s_{0,j} \\ s_{1,j} \\ s_{2,j} \\ s_{3,j} \end{bmatrix} \tag{2.7}$$

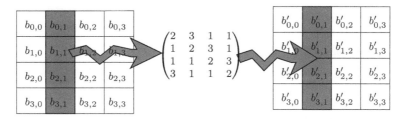

FIGURE 2.8: MixColumn Transformation

In case of **InvMixColumns**, the inverse of the same polynomial is used. If $m^{-1}(X)$ is defined as a function of the transformation of InvMixColumns that operates on State X, then

In matrix form the InvMixColumns transformation can be expressed as :

$$
\begin{bmatrix} s''_{0,j} \\ s''_{1,j} \\ s''_{2,j} \\ s''_{3,j} \end{bmatrix} = \begin{bmatrix} \{0E\} & \{0B\} & \{0D\} & \{09\} \\ \{09\} & \{0E\} & \{0B\} & \{0D\} \\ \{0D\} & \{09\} & \{0E\} & \{0B\} \\ \{0B\} & \{0D\} & \{09\} & \{0E\} \end{bmatrix} \begin{bmatrix} s_{0,j} \\ s_{1,j} \\ s_{2,j} \\ s_{3,j} \end{bmatrix} \tag{2.8}
$$

2.3.3.4 AddRoundKey

Let the input state of a particular round of the cipher round be denoted by s. The columns of the state are denoted by $s_0, s_1, \ldots, s_{Nb-1}$. The function **AddRoundKey(state, w[round*Nb,(round+1)*Nb-1])** is denoted as:

$$
s_j = s_j \oplus w[round * Nb + j], 0 \le j < Nb
$$

Here $\oplus$ is bit-wise XOR operation. Thus the words of the round key are combined with the state through a mod 2 addition (bitwise XOR). The objective of the key mixing step is to make every round states after the key mixing independent of the previous rounds, assuming that the round keys are generated by an efficient key-scheduling algorithm, which is detailed next.

2.3.4 Key-Scheduling in AES

The algorithm **Key-Scheduling** or **Key-Expansion** takes a Rijndael key key and generates the round keys of the ciphers. The input key is a byte-array of length $4Nk$, while the expanded key is a word array of length $Nb(Nr + 1)$. The round keys are mixed in the cipher via application of XOR.

The pseudocode presented in Algorithm 6 explains the generation of the round keys from the input key in AES. The pseudocode uses the functions, **word, SubWord** and **RotWord**.

The function Word just concatenates its arguments. The input to SubWord is a word, which is transformed by the SubBytes transformations. Consider the input to SubWord is the word (b_0, b_1, b_2, b_3), where each of the $b_i s$ are bytes. Each byte, b_i is transformed by the SubBytes transformation, thus resulting in $d_i = SubBytes(b_i)$. Thus the output of the SubWord is (d_0, d_1, d_2, d_3), after the application of the SubBytes transformation on each of the bytes.

Algorithm 2.2: The AES KeyExpansion function, KeyExpansion

Input: Nk, byte key[4,Nk]
Output: word word w[Nb(Nr+1)]

1   word temp
2   i=0
3   **while** *(i<Nk)* **do**
4   w[i]=word(key[4*i],key[4*i+1],key[4*i+2],key[4*i+3])
5   i=i+1
6   **end**
7   i=Nk
8   **while** *(i < Nb*(Nr+1))* **do**
9   temp=w[i-1]
10   **if** *(i mod Nk=0)* **then**
11   temp=SubWord(RotWord(temp)) XOR Rcon[i/Nk]
12   **end**
13   **else if** *(Nk>6 and i mod Nk = 4)* **then**
14   temp = SubWord(temp)
15   **end**
16   w[i]=w[i-Nk] XOR temp
17   i=i+1
18   **end**

The input to the RotWord is also a word (b_0, b_1, b_2, b_3). The output is (b_1, b_2, b_3, b_0), which is nothing but the bytewise left cyclic rotation applied on the input word.

Finally, the round constant, abbreviated as $\mathsf{Rcon}[n] = (\{02\}^n, \{00\}, \{00\}, \{00\})$. The round constants are added to the round keys to provided asymmetry to the key expansion algorithm and protect against certain class of attacks.

2.4   Rijndael in Composite Field

Rijndael involves arithmetic in $GF(2^8)$ elements. As discussed in *Section 1.12* the operations can be expressed in composite fields, exploiting isomporphism properties.

A wide variety of techniques have evolved for implementing the AES algorithm with various objectives. Isomorphism properties and use of subfield arithmetic helps to obtain compact circuits for the AES operations. The techniques proposed in [326] presents a method of efficiently expressing the inverse in $GF(2^8)$ using inverse computations in the subfield $GF(2^4)$.

2.4.1   Expressing an Element of $GF(2^8)$ in Subfield

The AES algorithm uses the particular Galois field of 8-bit bytes, where the bits are coefficients of a polynomial. The multiplications are performed modulo an irreducible polynomial $q(X) = X^8 + X^4 + X^3 + X + 1$, while the additions of the coefficients are performed using modulo 2 arithmetic. This representation, as described earlier is called the polynomial representation. If A is a root of the polynomial then the standard polynomial basis of the field is denoted by $1, A, A^2, \cdots, A^7$. Following the notations as introduced in [71], we use uppercase Roman letters for specific elements of $GF(2^8)$ or its isomorphic field $GF(2^4)^2$. Lowercase Greek letters are used for the subfield $GF(2^4)$.

An element in $GF(2^8)$ is mapped to an element in the composite field $GF(2^4)^2$. The converted element is expressed as a linear polynomial in y over $GF(2^4)$. Thus, $G \in GF(2^4)^2$ is expressed as $G = \gamma_1 Y + \gamma_0$. The multiplications are defined modulo an irreducible polynomial $r(Y) = Y^2 + \tau Y + \mu$. All the coefficients are in the field $GF(2^4)$ and the pair (γ_1, γ_0) represents G in terms of a polynomial basis $(y, 1)$ where y is one root of $r(Y)$.

Alternately, one can use the normal basis also for $GF(2^4)^2$, which is (y, y^{16}) using the roots of $r(Y)$. Note that $r(Y) = Y^2 + \tau Y + \mu = (Y + y)(Y + y^{16})$. Here, $\tau = y + y^{16}$ is the trace, while $\mu = (y)(y^{16})$ is the norm of Y. [1]

2.4.2 Inversion of an Element in Composite Field

The most complex operation is the finite field inverse, which forms the basis of the AES S-Box. Direct computation of the inverse of an eight degree polynomial modulo the irreducible eight degree polynomial is difficult. However, an efficient technique was proposed in [326]. As outlined previously, the inverse of a $GF(2^8)$ element is computed by converting it into an isomorphic composite field $GF(2^4)^2$. The element in the composite field is expressed as a polynomial of the first degree with coefficients from $GF(2^4)$ [325].

Let us assume that the element in $GF(2^4)^2$ whose multiplicative inverse is to be computed is denoted as $\gamma_1 Y + \gamma_0$. The operations are performed modulo the polynomial $r(Y) = Y^2 + \tau Y + \mu$.

The multiplication modulo $Y^2 + \tau Y + \mu$ is:

$$
\begin{aligned}
(\gamma_1 Y + \gamma_0)(\delta_1 Y + \delta_0) &= \gamma_1 \delta_1 Y^2 + (\gamma_1 \delta_0 + \gamma_0 \delta_1)Y + \gamma_0 \delta_0 \\
&= \gamma_1 \delta_1 (\tau Y + \mu) + (\gamma_1 \delta_0 + \gamma_0 \delta_1)Y + \gamma_0 \delta_0 \\
&= (\gamma_1 \delta_0 + \gamma_0 \delta_1 + \gamma_1 \delta_1 \tau)Y + (\gamma_0 \delta_0 + \gamma_1 \delta_1 \mu)
\end{aligned}
$$

Let, $(\gamma_1 Y + \gamma_0)^{-1} = (\delta_1 Y + \delta_0) \bmod (Y^2 + \tau Y + \mu)$. Rearranging we have $(\gamma_1 Y + \gamma_0)(\delta_1 Y + \delta_0) \equiv 1 \bmod (Y^2 + \tau Y + \mu)$. Thus, using the product and equating to 1 by matching the coefficients we can write the following simultaneous equation:

$$
\begin{aligned}
\gamma_1 \delta_0 + \gamma_0 \delta_1 + \gamma_1 \delta_1 \tau &= 0 \\
\gamma_0 \delta_0 + \gamma_1 \delta_1 \mu &= 1
\end{aligned}
$$

We solve the above equations to compute the values of δ_0 and δ_1:

$$
\begin{aligned}
\delta_0 &= (\gamma_0 + \gamma_1 \tau)(\gamma_0^2 + \gamma_0 \gamma_1 \tau + \gamma_1^2 \mu)^{-1} \\
\delta_1 &= \gamma_1 (\gamma_0^2 + \gamma_0 \gamma_1 \tau + \gamma_1^2 \mu)^{-1}
\end{aligned}
$$

---

[1] In order to map an element in $GF(2^8)$ to an element in the composite field $GF((2^4)^2)$, as discussed in *section 1.12.1* the element is multiplied with a transformation matrix, T.

One such matrix T is as follows [4],

$$
\mathbf{T} = \begin{pmatrix}
1 & 0 & 1 & 0 & 0 & 0 & 0 & 0 \\
1 & 0 & 1 & 0 & 1 & 1 & 0 & 0 \\
1 & 1 & 0 & 1 & 0 & 0 & 1 & 0 \\
0 & 1 & 1 & 1 & 0 & 0 & 0 & 0 \\
1 & 1 & 0 & 0 & 0 & 1 & 1 & 0 \\
0 & 1 & 0 & 1 & 0 & 0 & 1 & 0 \\
0 & 0 & 0 & 0 & 1 & 0 & 1 & 0 \\
1 & 1 & 0 & 1 & 1 & 1 & 0 & 1
\end{pmatrix}
$$

However, other transformations are also possible depending on the corresponding irreducible polynomials of the fields $GF(2^8), GF(2^4), GF(2^4)^2$.

The computations can also be similarly reworked if the basis is normal. Considering the normal basis of (Y, Y^{16}). Since both the elements of the basis are roots of the polynomial $Y^2 + \tau Y + \mu = 0$, we have the following identities which we use in the equations of the multiplication and inverse of the elements in the composite field:

$$\begin{aligned}
Y^2 &= \tau Y + \mu \\
1 &= \tau^{-1}(Y^{16} + Y) \\
\mu &= (Y^{16})Y
\end{aligned}$$

Thus the multiplication modulo $Y^2 + \tau Y + \mu$ in the normal basis is:

$$\begin{aligned}
(\gamma_1 Y^{16} + \gamma_0 Y)(\delta_1 Y^{16} + \delta_0 Y) &= \gamma_1 \delta_1 Y^{32} + (\gamma_1 \delta_0 + \gamma_0 \delta_1)(Y^{16}Y) + \gamma_0 \delta_0 Y^2 \\
&= \gamma_1 \delta_1 (\tau^2 + Y^2) + \mu(\gamma_1 \delta_0 + \gamma_0 \delta_1) + \gamma_0 \delta_0 Y^2 \\
&= Y^2(\gamma_1 \delta_1 + \gamma_0 \delta_0) + [\gamma_1 \delta_1 \tau^2 + \mu(\gamma_1 \delta_0 + \gamma_0 \delta_1)] \\
&= (\tau Y + \mu \tau^{-1}(Y^{16} + Y))(\gamma_1 \delta_1 + \gamma_0 \delta_0) + \\
&\quad [\gamma_1 \delta_1 \tau^2 + \mu(\gamma_1 \delta_0 + \gamma_0 \delta_1)](\tau^{-1}(Y^{16} + Y)) \\
&= [\gamma_1 \delta_1 \tau + \theta]Y^{16} + [\gamma_0 \delta_0 \tau + \theta]Y,
\end{aligned}$$

where $\theta = (\gamma_1 + \gamma_0)(\delta_1 + \delta_0)\mu \tau^{-1}$

Thus, if $(\gamma_1 Y^{16} + \gamma_0 Y)$ and $(\delta_1 Y^{16} + \delta_0 Y)$ are inverses of each other, then we can equate the above product to $1 = \tau^{-1}(Y^{16} + Y)$. Equating the coefficients we have:

$$\begin{aligned}
\delta_0 &= [\gamma_1 \gamma_0 \tau^2 + (\gamma_1^2 + \gamma_0^2)\mu]^{-1} \gamma_1 \\
\delta_1 &= [\gamma_1 \gamma_0 \tau^2 + (\gamma_1^2 + \gamma_0^2)\mu]^{-1} \gamma_0
\end{aligned}$$

These equations show that the inverse in the field $GF(2^8)$ can be reduced to the inverse in the smaller field $GF(2^4)$ along with several additional operations, like addition, multiplication, and squaring in the subfield. The inverse in the subfield can be stored in a smaller table (as compared to a table to store the inverses of $GF(2^8)$). The operations in $GF(2^4)$ can be in turn expressed in the sub-subfield $GF(2^2)$. The inverses in the sub-subfield $GF(2^2)$ is the same as squaring.

Depending on the choices of the irreducible polynomials, the level of decompositions and the choices of the basis of the fields, the complexity of the computations differ and is a subject of significant research. In the subsequent chapter on implementation of the AES algorithm, we shall discuss this aspect and the performances achieved.

2.4.3   The Round of AES in Composite Fields

Like the SubByte, the entire round of AES (and the entire AES algorithm) can be expressed in the composite fields. In [4], the authors develop the entire round of AES in composite fields. It must be kept in mind that though there is a gain in terms of compact representations and efficient computations in the subfield and sub-subfields, for further decompositions, there is an accompanied cost involved. The cost comes from the transformation of the elements between the various field representations. Hence, it is the designer's job to study these transformations and decide a final architecture which optimizes this trade-off efficiently.

The above point also implies that performing the inverse in composite fields for computing the S-Box operation, imply a continuous overhead of the transformation of the elements from $GF(2^8)$ to $GF(2^4)^2$, and vice versa. Hence, it is worth-while to explore techniques to represent the entire AES in the composite field representation. This minimizes the overhead in the transformations among the different field representations, being performed once at the beginning and finally at the end.

The Rijndael round transformations in subfield are defined as follows Consider the transformation T maps an element from $GF(2^8)$ to $GF(2^4)^2$. The T, as discussed before represents a transformation matrix an 8×8 binary matrix, which operates on each byte of the 4×4 state matrix of AES. Denote the AES state by S, where each element is denoted by b_{ij}, where $0 \leq i, j \leq 3$. Thus, an element in $x \in GF(2^8)$ is mapped to $T(x) \in GF(2^4)^2$. Now let us consider each of the round transformations one by one:

1. **SubBytes Transformation**: This operation has two steps:

   (a) **Inverse**: $b'_{i,j} = (b_{ij})^{-1}$. In the composite field, we have $\mathsf{T}(b'_{i,j}) = (\mathsf{T}(b_{ij}))^{-1}$. Note that the inverse on the RHS of the above equation is in $GF(2^4)^2$. The computation of the inverse is as explained above in section 2.4.1.

   (b) **Affine**: $b''_{i,j} = \mathsf{A}(b'_{i,j}) + B$. Here A and B are fixed matrices as discussed in section 2.3.3.1. In the composite field, $T(b''_{i,j}) = T(\mathsf{A}(b'_{i,j})) + T(B) = TAT^{-1}(T((b'_{i,j}))) + T(B)$. Thus the matrices of the SubBytes operations needs to be changed by applying the transformation matrix T.

2. **ShiftRows**: This step remains the same as this is a mere transposition of bytes and the field transformation to the composite field is localized inside a byte.

3. **MixColumns**: This step essentially involves multiplication of a column of the state matrix with a row of the Mix Column matrix. As can be observed from Equation 2.6, all the rows of the Mix Column matrix are permutations of $(\{01\}, \{01\}, \{02\}, \{03\})$. If we denote the ith row of this matrix as (m_0, m_1, m_2, m_3), and the jth column of the state matrix as $(s_{0,j}, s_{1,j}, s_{2,j}, s_{3,j})$, then the $(i, j)^{th}$ element of the state matrix corresponding to the output of the Mix Column is:

$$s'_{i,j} = m_0 s_{0,j} + m_1 s_{1,j} + m_2 s_{2,j} + m_3 s_{3,j}$$

Thus in the composite field the above transformation is,

$$T(s'_{i,j}) = T(m_0)T(s_{0,j}) + T(m_1)T(s_{1,j}) + T(m_2)T(s_{2,j}) + T(m_3)T(s_{3,j})$$

Here the additions in either the original field or the composite field are all in characteristic-2 field, they are bitwise XORs in both the representations.

4. **Add Round Key**: The operation is $s'_{i,j} = s_{i,j} + k_{i,j}$, where $k_{i,j}$ is a particular byte of the round key. In the composite field, thus this transformation is $T(s'_{i,j}) = T(s_{i,j}) + T(k_{i,j})$. Again the addition is a bitwise XOR.

   This implies that the round keys also need to be computed in the composite field. Hence, similar transformations also needs to be performed on the key-scheduling algorithm.

We shall discuss about these transformations and the effect of them in realizing an efficient and compact AES design in Chapter 4. In the next section, we present an overview on a popular public key encryption algorithm, known as **Elliptic Curve Cryprography** (ECC), which leads to much efficient implementations compared to the older generation algorithms like RSA, ElGamal etc.

2.5   Elliptic Curves

Let us start with a puzzle: What is the number of balls that may be piled as a square pyramid and also rearranged into a square array? The number is more than one.

The answer to this simple question can be solved by assuming that the height of the pyramid is denoted by the integer x and the dimension of the sides of the rearranged square is denoted by the integer y.

Since the number of balls in both the arrangements are the same, we have the following equation:

$$y^2 = 1^2 + 2^2 + \cdots + x^2$$
$$= \frac{x(x+1)(2x+1)}{6}$$

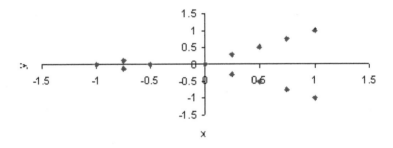

FIGURE 2.9: Plot of y vs x

Some discrete values of y are plotted wrt. x and is depicted in **Fig. 2.9**. Curves of this nature are commonly called **Elliptic Curves**: these are curves which are quadratic wrt. y and cubic wrt. x. It may be observed that the curve has two distinct regions or lobes, as it is often referred to as curves of genus 2. Also since, the curve is quadratic wrt. y, the curve is symmetric over the x-axis.

We next present a method by Diophantus of Alexandria, who lived around 200 A.D. to determine non-trivial points on the curve. This method uses a set of known points to find an unknown point on the curve. Let us start with two trivial points: (0,0) and (1,1). Clearly, both these two points do not indicate a solution to the puzzle.

Now the equation of a straight line between these two points is: $y = x$. Since the equation of the curve is cubic wrt. x, the straight line must intersect the curve on a third point (the points may not be distinct though!). In order to obtain the third point, we substitute $y = x$ in the equation of the curve, $y^2 = x(x+1)(2x+1)/6$, and we obtain:

$$x^3 - \frac{3}{2}x^2 + \frac{1}{2}x = 0$$

We know that $x = 0$ and 1 are two roots of the equation. From the theory of equations, thus if the third root of the equation is $x = \alpha$, we have $0 + 1 + \alpha = \frac{3}{2} \Rightarrow \alpha = \frac{1}{2}$. Since the point on the curve is $y = x$, we have $y = \frac{1}{2}$.

Thus $(\frac{1}{2}, \frac{1}{2})$ is a point on the curve. Since the curve is symmetric over the x-axis, $(\frac{1}{2}, -\frac{1}{2})$ is also another point on the curve. However these points also do not provide a solution as they are not integral.

Now, consider a straight line through $(\frac{1}{2}, -\frac{1}{2})$ and $(1,1)$. The equation of this line is $y = 3x - 2$, and intersecting with the curve we have:

$$x^3 - \frac{51}{2}x^2 + \cdots + = 0$$

Thus, again the third root $x = \beta$ can be obtained from $1 + \frac{1}{2} + \beta = \frac{51}{2} \Rightarrow \beta = 24$. The corresponding y value is 70, and so we have a non-trivial solution of the puzzle as 4900.

Through this seemingly simple puzzle, we have observed an interesting *geometric* method to solve an *algebraic* problem. This technique forms the base of the geometric techniques (the chord-and-tangent rule) in Elliptic Curves.

An Elliptic curve over a field K is a cubic curve in two variables, denoted as $f(x,y) = 0$, along with a rational point, which is referred to as the point at infinity. The field K is usually taken to be the complex numbers, reals, rationals, algebraic extensions of rationals, p-adic numbers, or a finite field. Elliptic curves groups for cryptography are examined with the underlying fields of F_p (where $p > 3$ is a prime) and F_{2^m} (a binary representation with 2^m elements).

A general form of the curve is introduced next. However the curve equation used for implementation is often transformed forms of this curve using the properties of the underlying field K.

Definition 2.5.1 *An elliptic curve E over the field K is given by the Weierstraß equation mentioned in Equation 2.9. The generalized Weierstraß equation is :*

$$E : y^2 + a_1 xy + a_3 y = x^3 + a_2 x^2 + a_4 x + a_6 \tag{2.9}$$

with the constant coefficients $a_1, a_2, a_3, a_4, a_6 \in K$ and $\Delta \neq 0$, where Δ is the discriminant of E and is defined as:

$$
\begin{aligned}
\Delta &= -d_2^2 d_8 - 8d_4^3 - 27d_6^2 + 9d_2 d_4 d_6 \\
d_2 &= a_1^2 + 4a_2 \\
d_4 &= 2a_4 + a_1 a_3 \\
d_6 &= a_3^2 + 4a_6 \\
d_8 &= a_1^2 a_6 + 4a_2 a_6 - a_1 a_3 a_4 + a_2 a_3^2 - a_4^2
\end{aligned}
$$

This equation, known as the generalized *Weierstraß* equation defines the Elliptic Curve E over the field K. It may be noted that if E is defined over K, it is also defined over any extension of the field K. If L is any extension of K, then the set of L-rational points on E is defined as:

$$E(L) = \{(x,y) \in L \times L : y^2 + a_1 xy + a_3 y = x^3 + a_2 x^2 + a_4 x + a_6 = 0\} \cup \{\infty\}$$

where ∞ is the point of infinity.

Point at ∞ is a point at the top of the y-axis, and is also at the bottom of the y-axis. We conceptualize this by thinking that the ends of the y-axis are wrapped around and meet in the back. However when working with finite fields, there is no meaningful ordering of the points. Thus the point at ∞ is also conceptualized as the intersecting point of two vertical lines. By symmetry, if they meet at the top they also meet in the bottom. Also from another sense, two parallel lines intersect at only one point, thus implying that the top point at ∞ is the same as that in the bottom.

2.5.1   Simplification of the Weierstraß Equation

Two elliptic curves E_1 and E_2 defined over K are said to be *isomorphic* over K if change of variables transform one form to the other. However the change of variables should be *admissible* depending on the underlying field.

More precisely, consider two elliptic curve equations:

$$
\begin{aligned}
E_1 : y^2 + a_1 xy + a_3 y &= x^3 + a_2 x^2 + a_4 x + a_6 \\
E_2 : y^2 + a_1' xy + a_3' y &= x^3 + a_2' x^2 + a_4' x + a_6'
\end{aligned}
$$

If there exists $u, r, s, t \in K$, $u \neq 0$, such that the change of variables:

$$
(x, y) \quad \rightarrow \quad (u^2 x + r, u^3 y + u^2 s x + t)
$$

transform equation E_1 into equation E_2. We next present those simplifications for different characteristics for K.

Characteristic of K is neither 2 nor 3: The admissible change of variables are

$$
(x, y) \rightarrow (\frac{x - 3a_1^2 - 12a_2}{36}, \frac{y - 3a_1 x}{216} - \frac{a_1^3 + 4a_1 a_2 - 12a_3}{24})
$$

transforms E to the curve:

$$
y^2 = x^3 + ax + b
$$

where $a, b \in K$. The discriminant of the curve is $\Delta = -16(4a^3 + 27b^2)$.

Characteristic of K is 2: If $a_1 \neq 0$, then the admissible change of variables are:

$$
(x, y) \rightarrow (a_1^2 x + \frac{a_3}{a_1}, a_1^3 y + \frac{a_1^2 a_4 + a_3^2}{a_1^3})
$$

transforms the curve E to the form:

$$
y^2 + xy = x^3 + ax^2 + b
$$

where a and $b \in K$. The discriminant of the curve is $\Delta = b$.

If $a_1 = 0$, then the admissible change of variables are as follows:

$$
(x, y) \quad \rightarrow \quad (x + a_2, y)
$$

This transforms the curve E to the form:

$$
y^2 + cy = x^3 + ax + b
$$

where $a, b, c \in K$. The discriminant of the curve is $\Delta = c^4$.

Characteristic of K is 3:

Similar simplification of the curve can be done for curves of characteristic 3 also using the admissible change of variables:

$$
(x, y) \rightarrow (x + \frac{d_4}{d_2}, y + a_1 x + a_1 \frac{d_4}{d_2} + a_3)
$$

where $d_2 = a_1^2 + a_2$ and $d_4 = a_4 - a_1 a_3$, transforms E to the curve:

$$
y^2 = x^3 + ax^2 + b
$$

where $a, b, c \in K$. The discriminant of the curve is $\Delta = -a^3 b$. If $a_1^2 = -a_2$, then the admissible change of variables:

$$(x, y) \rightarrow (x, y + a_1 x + a_3)$$

transforms E to the curve:

$$y^2 = x^3 + ax + b$$

where $a, b, c \in K$. The discriminant of the curve is $\Delta = -a^3$.

2.5.2 Singularity of Curves

For an elliptic curve defined as $y^2 = f(x)$ defined over some K, singularity is the point (x_0, y_0) where there are multiple roots. This can be alternately stated by defining $F(x, y) = y^2 - f(x)$ and evaluating when the partial derivatives vanish wrt. both x and y.

$$\frac{\delta F}{\delta x}(x_0, y_0) = \frac{\delta F}{\delta y}(x_0, y_0) = 0$$
$$or, -f'(x_0) = 2y_0 = 0$$
$$or, f(x_0) = f'(x_0) = 0$$

Thus f has a double root at the point (x_0, y_0). Usually we assume that Elliptic Curves do not have singular points. Let us find the condition for the curve defined as $y^2 = x^3 + Ax + B$, defined over a field K with appropriate characteristics.

Thus, we have:

$$3x^2 + A = 0 \quad \Rightarrow x^2 = -A/3$$

Also we have,

$$x^3 + Ax + B = 0 \Rightarrow x^4 + Ax^2 + Bx = 0$$
$$\Rightarrow (-A/3)^2 + A(-A/3) + Bx = 0 \Rightarrow x = -\frac{2A^2}{9B}$$
$$\Rightarrow 3(\frac{2A^2}{9B})^2 + A = 0 \Rightarrow 4A^3 + 27B^2 = 0$$

Thus, the criteria for non-singularity of the curve is $\Delta = 4A^3 + 27B^2 \neq 0$. For elliptic curve cryptography usually the curves do not have singularity.

2.5.3 The Abelian Group and the Group Laws

In this section we show that addition laws can be defined on the points of the elliptic curve so that they satisfy the conditions required for a mathematical group. As discussed in Chapter 1, the essential requirements for a group operation is that the operations have to be associative, there should be a neutral or identity element, and every element should have an inverse on the elliptic curve. The rules are commonly called as chord-and-tangent rules (useful to conceptualize when the elliptic curve is defined over real numbers), also known as the **double** and **add** rules. Further the group is abelian, implying that the operations are commutative. The operation of addition is realized by two distinct operations (unlike over a finite field where a single operation is used): addition when the two points are distinct, and doubling when the points are same.

We summarize the properties of the addition operations (doubling is a special case of the addition operation when the two points are same). The addition is denoted by the symbol $+$ below for an elliptic curve $E(K)$, where K is some underlying field.

Given two points $P, Q \in E(K)$, there is a third point, denoted by $P + Q \in E(K)$, and the following relations hold for all $P, Q, R \in E(K)$

- $P + Q = Q + P$ (commutative)

- $(P + Q) + R = P + (Q + R)$ (associativity)

- $\exists \mathcal{O}$, such that $P + \mathcal{O} = \mathcal{O} + P = P$ (existence of an identity element, $\mathcal{O}$)

- $\exists (-P)$ such that $-P + P = P + (-P) = \mathcal{O}$ (existence of inverses)

For cryptography, the points on the elliptic curve are chosen from a large finite field. The set of points on the elliptic curve form a *group* under the addition rule. The point at infinity, denoted by $\mathcal{O}$, is the identity element of the group. The operations on the elliptic curve, i.e., the group operations are *point addition*, *point doubling* and *point inverse*. Given a point $P = (x, y)$ on the elliptic curve, and a positive integer n, *scalar multiplication* is defined as

$$nP = P + P + P + \cdots P (n \text{ times}) \qquad (2.10)$$

The *order* of the point P is the smallest positive integer n such that $nP = \mathcal{O}$. The points $\{\mathcal{O}, P, 2P, 3P, \cdots (n-1)P\}$ form a group generated by P. The group is denoted as $< P >$.

The security of ECC is provided by the Elliptic Curve Discrete Logarithm problem (ECDLP), which is defined as follows : *Given a point P on the elliptic curve and another point $Q \in < P >$, determine an integer k ($0 \le k \le n$) such that $Q = kP$*. The difficulty of ECDLP is to calculate the value of the scalar k given the points P and Q. k is called the discrete logarithm of Q to the base P. P is the generator of the elliptic curve and is called the basepoint.

The ECDLP forms the base on which asymmetric key algorithms are built. These algorithms include the elliptic curve Diffie-Hellman key exchange, elliptic curve ElGamal public key encryption and the elliptic curve digital signature algorithm.

Next we define the above operations and the underlying computations for elliptic curves of characteristic 2, which is the object of focus of this textbook.

2.5.4   Elliptic Curves with Characteristic 2

For elliptic curves defined on characteristic 2 fields we have the alternate definition as follows:

Definition 2.5.2 *An elliptic curve E over the field $GF(2^m)$ is given by the simplified form of the Weierstraß equation mentioned in Equation 2.9. The simplified Weierstraß equation is :*

$$y^2 + xy = x^3 + ax^2 + b \qquad (2.11)$$

with the coefficients a and b in $GF(2^m)$ and $b \neq 0$.

Equation 2.11 can be rewritten as

$$F(x, y) : y^2 + x^3 + xy + ax^2 + b = 0 \qquad (2.12)$$

The partial derivatives of this equation are

$$\frac{\delta F}{dy} = x$$
$$\frac{\delta F}{dx} = x^2 + y \tag{2.13}$$

If we consider the curve given in Equation 2.11, with $b = 0$, then the point $(0, 0)$ lies on the curve. At this point $\delta F/dy = \delta F/dx = 0$. This forms a *singular point* and cannot be included in the elliptic curve group, therefore an additional condition of $b \neq 0$ is required on the elliptic curve of Equation 2.11. This condition ensures that the curve is *non singular*. Hence for the rest of the text we will assume $b \neq 0$, ie. the curve in Equation 2.11 is a *non-singular curve*.

The set of points on the elliptic curve along with a special point $\mathcal{O}$, called the *point at infinity*, form a group under addition. The identity element of the group is the point at infinity ($\mathcal{O}$). The arithmetic operations permitted on the group are point inversion, point addition and point doubling which are described as follows.

Point Inversion: Let P be a point on the curve with coordinates (x_1, y_1), then the inverse of P is the point $-P$ with coordinates $(x_1, x_1 + y_1)$. The point $-P$ is obtained by drawing a vertical line through P. The point at which the line intersects the curve is the inverse of P.

Let $P = (x_1, y_1)$ be a point on the elliptic curve of Equation 2.11. To find the inverse of point P, a vertical line is drawn passing through P. The equation of this line is $x = x_1$. The point at which this line intersects the curve is the inverse $-P$. The coordinates of $-P$ is (x_1, y_1'). To find y_1', the point of intersection between the line and the curve must be found. Equation 2.12 is represented in terms of its roots p and q as shown below.

$$(y - A)(y - B) = y^2 - (p + q)y + pq \tag{2.14}$$

The coefficients of y is the sum of the roots. Equating the coefficients of y in Equations 2.12 and 2.14.

$$p + q = x_1$$

One of the roots is $q = y_1$, therefore the other root p is given by

$$p = x_1 + y_1$$

This is the y coordinate of the inverse. The inverse of the point P is therefore given by $(x_1, x_1 + y_1)$.

Point Addition: Let P and Q be two points on the curve with coordinates (x_1, y_1) and (x_2, y_2). Also, let $P \neq \pm Q$, then adding the two points results in a third point $R = (P + Q)$. The addition is performed by drawing a line through P and Q as shown in **Fig. 2.10**. The point at which the line intersects the curve is $-(P + Q)$. The inverse of this is $R = (P + Q)$. Let the coordinates of R be (x_3, y_3), then the equations for x_3 and y_3 is

$$x_3 = \lambda^2 + \lambda + x_1 + x_2 + a$$
$$y_3 = \lambda(x_1 + x_3) + x_3 + y_1 \tag{2.15}$$

where $\lambda = (y_1 + y_2)/(x_1 + x_2)$. If $P = -Q$, then $P + (-P)$ is $\mathcal{O}$.

The derivation of the co-ordinates can be done from simple principles of co-ordinate geometry. Let $P = (x_1, y_1)$ and $Q = (x_2, y_2)$ be two points on the elliptic curve. To add the

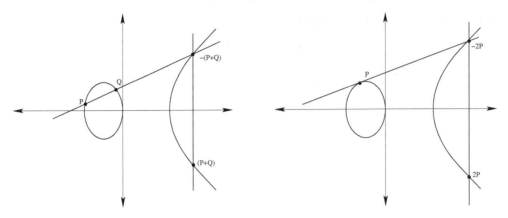

FIGURE 2.10: Point Addition　　　　　FIGURE 2.11: Point Doubling

two points, a line (l) is drawn through P and Q. If $P \neq \pm Q$, the line intersects the curve of Equation 2.11 at the point $-R = (x_3, y_3')$. The inverse of the point $-R$ is $R = (P + Q)$ having coordinates (x_3, y_3).

The slope of the line l passing through P and Q is given by

$$\lambda = \frac{y_2 - y_1}{x_2 - x_1}$$

Equation of the line l is

$$y - y_1 = \lambda(x - x_1)$$
$$y = \lambda(x - x_1) + y_1 \tag{2.16}$$

Substituting y from 2.16 in the elliptic curve Equation 2.11 we get,

$$(\lambda(x - x_1) + y_1)^2 + x(\lambda(x - x_1) + y_1) = x^3 + ax^2 + b$$

This can be rewritten as

$$x^3 + (\lambda^2 + \lambda + a)x^2 + \cdots = 0 \tag{2.17}$$

Equation 2.17 is a cubic equation having three roots. Let the roots be p, q, and r. These roots represent the x coordinates of the points on the line that intersect the curve (the point P, Q and $-R$). Equation 2.17 can be also represented in terms of its roots as

$$(x - p)(x - q)(x - r) = 0$$
$$x^3 - (p + q + r)x^2 \cdots = 0 \tag{2.18}$$

Equating the x^2 coefficients of Equations 2.18 and 2.17 we get,

$$p + q + r = \lambda^2 + \lambda + a \tag{2.19}$$

Since $P = (x_1, y_1)$ and $Q = (x_2, y_2)$ lie on the line l, therefore two roots of Equation 2.17 are x_1 and x_2. Substituting $p = x_1$ and $q = x_2$ in Equation 2.19 we get the third root, this is the x coordinate of the third point on the line which intersects the curve(i.e., $-R$). This point is denoted by x_3, and it also represents the x coordinate of R.

$$x_3 = \lambda^2 + \lambda + x_1 + x_2 + a \tag{2.20}$$

The y coordinate of $-R$ can be obtained by substituting $x = x_3$ in Equation 2.16. This point is denoted as y_3'.

$$y_3' = \lambda(x_3 + x_1) + y_1 \tag{2.21}$$

Reflecting this point about the x axis is done by substituting $y_3' = x_3 + y_3$. This gives the y coordinate of R, denoted by y_3.

$$y_3 = \lambda(x_3 + x_1) + y_1 + x_3 \tag{2.22}$$

Since we are working with binary finite fields, subtraction is the same as addition. Therefore,

$$\begin{aligned} x_3 &= \lambda^2 + \lambda + x_1 + x_2 + a \\ y_3 &= \lambda(x_3 + x_1) + y_1 + x_3 \\ \lambda &= \frac{y_2 + y_1}{x_2 + x_1} \end{aligned} \tag{2.23}$$

Point Doubling : Let P be a point on the curve with coordinates (x_1, y_1) and $P \neq -P$. The double of P is the point $2 \cdot P = (x_3, y_3)$ obtained by drawing a tangent to the curve through P. The inverse of the point at which the tangent intersects the curve is the double of P (**Fig. 2.11**). The equation for computing $2 \cdot P$ is given as

$$\begin{aligned} x_3 &= \lambda^2 + \lambda + a = {x_1}^2 + \frac{b}{{x_1}^2} \\ y_3 &= {x_1}^2 + \lambda x_3 + x_3 \end{aligned} \tag{2.24}$$

where $\lambda = x_1 + (y_1/x_1)$.

Let $P = (x_1, y_1)$ be a point on the elliptic curve. The double of P, ie. $2P$, is found by drawing a tangent t through P. This tangent intersects the curve at the point $-2P = (x_3, y_3')$. Taking the reflection of the point $-2P$ about the X axis gives $2P = (x_3, y_3)$.

First, let us look at the tangent t through P. The slope of the tangent t is obtained by differentiation of Equation 2.11.

$$2y\frac{dy}{dx} + x\frac{dy}{dx} + y = 3x^2 + 2ax$$

Since we are using modular 2 arithmetic,

$$x\frac{dy}{dx} + y = x^2$$

The slope dy/dx of the line t passing through the point P is given by

$$\lambda = \frac{{x_1}^2 + y_1}{x_1} \tag{2.25}$$

The equation of the line t can be represented by the following.

$$y + y_1 = \lambda(x + x_1) \tag{2.26}$$

This gives,

$$\begin{aligned} y &= \lambda(x + x_1) + y_1 \\ y &= \lambda x + c \text{ for some constant } c \end{aligned}$$

To find x_3 (the x coordinate of $-2P$), substitute for y in Equation 2.11.

$$(\lambda x + c)^2 + x(\lambda x + c) = x^3 + ax + b$$

This equation can be rewritten as

$$0 = x^3 + (\lambda^2 + \lambda + a)x + \cdots \tag{2.27}$$

This equation is cubic and has three roots. Of these three roots, two roots must be equal since the line intersects the curve at exactly two points. The two equal roots are represented by p. The sum of the three roots is $(\lambda^2 + \lambda + a)$, similar to Equation 2.18. Therefore,

$$p + p + r = \lambda^2 + \lambda + a$$
$$r = \lambda^2 + \lambda + a$$

The dissimilar root is r. This root corresponds to the x coordinate of $-2P$ ie. x_3. Therefore,

$$x_3 = \lambda^2 + \lambda + a$$

To find the y coordinate of $-2P$, ie. y_3', substitute x_3 in Equation 2.26. This gives,

$$y_3' = \lambda x_3 + \lambda x_1 + y_1$$
$$y_3' = \lambda x_3 + x_1{}^2$$

To find y_3, the y coordinate of $2P$, the point y_3' is reflected on the x axis. From the point inverse equation

$$y_3 = \lambda x_3 + x_1{}^2 + x_3$$

To summarize, the coordinates of the double are given by Equation 2.28

$$x_3 = \lambda^2 + \lambda + a$$
$$y_3 = x_1{}^2 + \lambda x_3 + x_3 \tag{2.28}$$
$$\lambda = x_1 + \frac{y_1}{x_1}$$

The fundamental algorithm for ECC is the *scalar multiplication*, which can be obtained using the basic double and add computations as shown in Algorithm 2.3. The input to the algorithm is a *basepoint* P and a m bit scalar k. The result is the scalar product kP, which is equivalent to adding the point P k times.

As an example of how Algorithm 2.3 works, consider $k = 22$. The binary equivalent of this is $(10110)_2$. Table 2.2 below shows how $22P$ is computed.

Each iteration of i does a doubling on Q if k_i is 0 or a doubling followed by an addition if k_i is 1. The underlying operations in the addition and doubling equations use the finite field arithmetic discussed in the previous section. Both point doubling and point addition have 1 inversion (I) and 2 multiplications (M) each (from Equations 2.15 and 2.24), neglecting squaring operations which are free in characterstic 2. From this, the entire scalar multiplier for the m bit scalar k will have $m(1I+2M)$ doublings and $\frac{m}{2}(1I+2M)$ additions (assuming k has approximately $m/2$ ones on an average). The overall expected running time of the scalar multiplier is therefore obtained as

$$t_a \approx (3M + \frac{3}{2}I)m \tag{2.29}$$

For this expected running time, finite field addition and squaring operations have been neglected as they are simple operations and can be considered to have no overhead to the run time.

Algorithm 2.3: Double and Add algorithm for scalar multiplication

---

Input: Basepoint $P = (x, y)$ and Scalar $k = (k_{m-1}, k_{m-2} \cdots k_0)_2$, where $k_{m-1} = 1$
Output: Point on the curve $Q = kP$

1 $Q = P$
2 **for** $i = m - 2$ **to** 0 **do**
3      $Q = 2 \cdot Q$
4   **if** $k_i = 1$ **then**
5          $Q = Q + P$
6   **end**
7 **end**
8 **return** Q

TABLE 2.2: Scalar Multiplication using Double and Add to find $22P$

i	k_i	Operation	Q
3	0	Double only	$2P$
2	1	Double and Add	$5P$
1	1	Double and Add	$11P$
0	0	Double only	**22P**

2.5.5 Projective Coordinate Representation

The complexity of a finite field inversion is typically eight times that of a finite field multiplier in the same field [331]. Therefore, there is a huge motivation for an alternate point representation which would require lesser inversions. The two point coordinate system (x, y) used in Equations 2.11, 2.15, and 2.24 discussed in the previous section is called *affine representation*. It has been shown that each affine point on the elliptic curve has a one to one correspondence with a unique equivalence class in which each point is represented by three coordinates (X, Y, Z). The three point coordinate system is called the *projective representation* [249]. In the projective representation, inversions are replaced by multiplications. The projective form of the Weierstraßequation can be obtained by replacing x with X/Z^c and y by Y/Z^d. There are several projective coordinates systems proposed. The most commonly used projective coordinate system are the *standard* where $c = 1$ and $d = 1$, the *Jacobian* with $c = 2$ and $d = 3$ and the *López-Dahab (LD) coordinates*[249] which has $c = 1$ and $d = 2$. The LD coordinate system [227] allows point addition using *mixed coordinates*, i.e., one point in affine while the other in projective.

Replacing x by X/Z and y by Y/Z^2 in Equation 2.11 results in the LD projective form of the Weierstraß equation.

$$Y^2 + XYZ = X^3 + aX^2Z^2 + bZ^4 \qquad (2.30)$$

Let $P = (X_1, Y_1, Z_1)$ be an LD projective point on the elliptic curve, then the inverse of point P is given by $-P = (X_1, X_1Z_1 + Y_1, Z_1)$. Also, $P + (-P) = \mathcal{O}$, where $\mathcal{O}$ is the point at infinity. In LD projective coordinates $\mathcal{O}$ is represented as $(1, 0, 0)$.

The equation for doubling the point P in LD projective coordinates [227] results in the point $2P = (X_3, Y_3, Z_3)$. This is given by the following equation.

$$
\begin{aligned}
Z_3 &= X_1^2 \cdot Z_1^2 \\
X_3 &= X_1^4 + b \cdot Z_1^4 \\
Y_3 &= b \cdot Z_1^4 \cdot Z_3 + X_3 \cdot (a \cdot Z_3 + Y_1^2 + b \cdot Z_1^4)
\end{aligned}
\tag{2.31}
$$

The equations for doubling require 5 finite field multiplications and zero inversions.

The equation in LD coordinates for adding the affine point $Q = (x_2, y_2)$ to P, where $Q \neq \pm P$, is shown in Equation 2.32. The resulting point is $P + Q = (X_3, Y_3, Z_3)$.

$$
\begin{aligned}
A &= y_2 \cdot Z_1^2 + Y_1 \\
B &= x_2 \cdot Z_1 + X_1 \\
C &= Z_1 \cdot B \\
D &= B^2 \cdot (C + a \cdot Z_1^2) \\
Z_3 &= C^2 \\
E &= A \cdot C \\
X_3 &= A^2 + D + E \\
F &= X_3 + x_2 \cdot Z_3 \\
G &= (x_2 + y_2) \cdot Z_3^2 \\
Y_3 &= (E + Z_3) \cdot F + G
\end{aligned}
\tag{2.32}
$$

Point addition in LD coordinates thus requires 9 finite field multiplications and zero inversions. For an m bit scalar with approximately half the bits one, the running time expected is given by Equation 2.33. One inversion and 2 multiplications are required at the end to convert the result from projective coordinates back into affine.

$$
\begin{aligned}
t_{ld} &\approx m(5M + \frac{9M}{2}) + 2M + 1I \\
&= (9.5m + 2)M + 1I
\end{aligned}
\tag{2.33}
$$

The LD coordinates require several multiplications to be done but have the advantage of requiring just one inversion. To be beneficial, the extra multiplications should have a lower complexity than the inversions removed.

2.6   Scalar Multiplications: LSB First and MSB First Approaches

The scalar multiplication algorithm is at the heart of the ECC systems. Several optimization techniques have been evolved to implement this operation efficiently. In this section, we compare a simple but interesting and effective variation of the scalar multiplication algorithms. Consider the algorithm stated in Algorithm 2.3 for performing scalar multiplication using double and add. The algorithm parses the scalar bits from the left, and is often referred to as the MSB first algorithm. For an m-bit length scalar, this algorithm requires m-doubling operations and on an average $(m-1)/2$ additions. However in the following we consider a variation of the algorithm where the scalar is read from the LSB.

Algorithm 2.4: Double and Add algorithm for scalar multiplication (LSB First)

Input: Basepoint $P = (x, y)$ and Scalar $k = (k_{m-1}, k_{m-2} \cdots k_0)_2$, where $k_{m-1} = 1$
Output: Point on the curve $Q = kP$

1 $Q = 0, R = P$
2 **for** $i = 0$ **to** $m - 1$ **do**
3   **if** $k_i = 1$ **then**
4         $Q = Q + R$
5   **end**
6     $R = 2R$
7 **end**
8 **return** Q

The working of the algorithm is self evident. However we can observe that compared to the Algorithm 2.4, the LSB first algorithm has the opportunity of parallelism. However it requires two variables R and Q. In the following section, we present another trick called as the Montgomery's ladder for efficient implementation of the scalar multiplications. The algorithm also has consequences in the **side channel analysis** of the hardware implementations derived from these algorithms.

2.7 Montgomery's Algorithm for Scalar Multiplication

Let $P = (x_1, y_1)$ be a point on the curve: $y^2 + xy = x^3 + ax^2 + b$, where $(x, y) \in GF(2^m) \times GF(2^m)$. It is evident that $-P = (x_1, x_1 + y_1)$. We restate the equations for $R = P + Q = (x_3, y_3)$ as follows:

$$x_3 = \begin{cases} (\frac{y_1+y_2}{x_1+x_2})^2 + (\frac{y_1+y_2}{x_1+x_2}) + x_1 + x_2 + a & \text{if } P \neq Q; \\ x_1^2 + \frac{b}{x_1^2} & \text{if } P = Q. \end{cases}$$

$$y_3 = \begin{cases} (\frac{y_1+y_2}{x_1+x_2})(x_1 + x_3) + x_3 + y_1 & \text{if } P \neq Q; \\ x_1^2 + (x_1 + \frac{y_1}{x_1})x_3 + x_3 & \text{if } P = Q. \end{cases}$$

Neglecting squaring and addition operations, as they are cheap, point addition and doubling each has one inversion and two multiplication operations. It is interesting to note that the x-coordinate of the doubling operation is devoid of any y-coordinate, it works only using x-coordinates. However, the x-cordinate of the addition operation naïvely needs the y-coordinate. If both the operations, namely addition and doubling can be performed with only one coordinate, say the x-coordinate, then the entire scalar multiplication can be performed without storing one of the coordinates. This can lead to a compact hardware implementation, and each of these coordinates is quite a large value and typically stored in a register.

Before explaining how we can perform the addition without the y-cordinate we present a technique for performing the scalar multiplication, which is referred to as the Montgomery's Ladder.

2.7.1　Montgomery's Ladder

Algorithm 2.5 presents the Montgomery's ladder for performing point multiplication. In this algorithm, like the LSB first algorithm, there are two variables. The variables are initialized with the values $P_1 = P$ and $P_2 = 2P$. The algorithm parses the key bits from the MSB; depending on the present key bit being one point addition is performed on P_1, and point doubling is performed on P_2. On the contrary, if the key bit is zero, point addition is performed on P_2, while point doubling is performed on P_1. Thus at every iteration, both addition and doubling are performed, making the operations uniform. This helps to prevent simple side channel analysis, like simple power attacks (SPA).

Algorithm 2.5: Montgomery's Ladder for scalar multiplication

Input: Basepoint $P = (x, y)$ and Scalar $k = (k_{m-1}, k_{m-2} \cdots k_0)_2$, where $k_{m-1} = 1$
Output: Point on the curve $Q = kP$

1　$P_1 = P, P_2 = 2P$
2　**for** $i = m - 2$ **to** 0 **do**
3　　　**if** $k_i = 1$ **then**
4　　　　　$P_1 = P_1 + P_2, P_2 = 2P_2$
5　　　**end**
6　　　**else**
7　　　　　$P_2 = P_1 + P_2, P_1 = 2P_1$
8　　　**end**
9　**end**
10　**return** P_1

Apart from this, we also an interesting property: the difference between $P_2 - P_1 = P$ throughout the scalar multiplication. The invariance property was found to very useful in designing fast scalar multiplication circuits without any pre-computations.

2.7.2　Faster Multiplication on EC without Pre-computations

We have previously seen that the x-coordinate of the double of a point P can be performed without the y-coordinate. The x-coordinate of the addition of two points P_1 and P_2 can also be similarly performed using only the x-coordinate, using the invariance property: $P = P_2 - P_1$ throughout the scalar multiplication in Algorithm 2.5. The following results help us to understand the technique to do so.

Theorem 13 *Let $P_1 = (x_1, y_1)$ and $P_2 = (x_2, y_2)$ be points on the ECC curve, $y^2 + xy = x^3 + ax^2 + b$, where $(x, y) \in GF(2^m) \times GF(2^m)$. Then the x-coordinate of $P_1 + P_2$, x_3 can be computed as:*

$$x_3 = \frac{x_1 y_2 + x_2 y_1 + x_1 x_2^2 + x_2 x_1^2}{(x_1 + x_2)^2}$$

The result is based on the fact that the characteristic of the underlying field is 2, and that the points P_1 and P_2 are on the curve.

The next theorem expresses the x-coordinates of the $P_1 + P_2$ in terms of only the x-coordinates of the P_1, P_2 and that of $P = P_2 - P_1$.

Theorem 14 *Let $P = (x, y)$, $P_1 = (x_1, y_1)$ and $P_2 = (x_2, y_2)$ be elliptic points. Let $P =$*

$P_2 - P_1$ be an invariant. Then the x-coordinate of $P_1 + P_2$, x_3 can be computed in terms of the x-coordinates as:

$$x_3 = x + \left(\frac{x_1}{x_1 + x_2}\right)^2 + \left(\frac{x_1}{x_1 + x_2}\right)$$

Thus the x-coordinates of both the sum and doubling can be computed storing only the x-coordinates of the respective points. The next theorem shows how to observe the y-coordinates after the computation of the scalar product.

Theorem 15 *Let* $P = (x, y)$, $P_1 = (x_1, y_1)$ *and* $P_2 = (x_2, y_2)$ *be elliptic points. Assume that* $P_2 - P_1 = P$ *and* x *is not 0. Then the* y*-coordinates of* P_1 *can be expressed in terms of* P, *and the* x*-coordinates of* P_1 *and* P_2 *as follows:*

$$y_1 = (x_1 + x)\frac{(x_1 + x)(x_2 + x) + x^2 + y}{x} + y$$

Using these theorems, one can develop Algorithm 2.6 for performing scalar multiplications. Note that the algorithm uses only the x*-coordinates of the points* P_1 *and* P_2, *and the coordinate of the point* P, *which is an invariant.*

Algorithm 2.6: Detailed working of Montgomery's Ladder for scalar multiplication

---

Input: Basepoint $P = (x, y)$ and Scalar $k = (k_{m-1}, k_{m-2} \cdots k_0)_2$, where $k_{m-1} = 1$
Output: Point on the curve $Q = kP$

1 **if** $k = 0$ *or* $x = 0$ **then**
2   **return** $(0, 0)$
3 **end**
4 $x_1 = x$, $x_2 = x^2 + \frac{b}{x^2}$
5 **for** $i = m - 2$ **to** 0 **do**
6      $t = \frac{x_1}{(x_1 + x_2)}$
7   **if** $k_i = 1$ **then**
8          $x_1 = x + t^2 + t, x_2 = x_2^2 + \frac{b}{x_2^2}$
9   **end**
10   **else**
11          $x_2 = x + t^2 + t, x_1 = x_2^2 + \frac{b}{x_2^2}$
12   **end**
13 **end**
14 $r_1 = x_1 + x; r_2 = x_2 + x$
15 $y_1 = \frac{r_1(r_1 r_2 + x^2 + y)}{x} + y$
16 **return** (x_1, y_1)

The number of operations required in the scalar multiplication can be observed by counting the number of multiplications, inversions, squaring, and additions required. As can be observed that each of the loops require two multiplications and two inversions, thus accounting for $2(m - 2)$ multiplications and inversions. Further, each of the loops also requires 4 additions, and 2 squaring operations. This accounts for $4(m - 2)$ additions and $2(m - 2)$ squarings to be performed. Outside the loop also there are some computations to be performed. There is one inverse, four multiplications, six additions, and two squarings to be performed. It may be pointed out that since the inverse is a costly operation in finite fields, we minimize them at the cost of other operations. Like in the Montgomery's ladder, we compute the inverse of x, and then evaluate the inverse of x^2 by squaring x^{-1} rather than paying the cost of another field inversion. This simple trick helps to obtain efficient architectures!

2.7.3 Using Projective co-ordinates to Reduce the Number of Inversions

The number of inversions can be reduced by using Projective Co-ordinates as discussed in section 2.5.5. Using the projective co-ordinates the transformed equations are:

$$X_3 = \begin{cases} (xZ_2 + (X_1 Z_2)(X_2 Z_1) & \text{if } P \neq Q; \\ X_1^4 + bZ_1^4 & \text{if } P = Q. \end{cases}$$

$$Z_3 = \begin{cases} (X_1 Z_2 + X_2 Z_1)^2 & \text{if } P \neq Q; \\ (Z_1^2 X_1^2) & \text{if } P = Q. \end{cases}$$

Each of the above steps thus require, no inversions, four multiplications, three additions, and five squaring operations.

The final conversion from projective to affine coordinates however requires inversions and can be performed using the following equations:

$$x_3 = X_1/Z_1$$
$$y_3 = (x + X_1/Z_1)[(X_1 + xZ_2) + (x^2 + y)(Z_1 Z_2)](xZ_1 Z_2)^{-1} + y$$

This step reduces the number of inversions, by computing $(xZ_1 Z_2)^{-1}$, and then obtaining Z_1^{-1} by multiplying with xZ_2. The required number of multiplication is thus ten, however the inversions required is only one.

In table 2.3, we present a summary of the two design techniques that we have studied: namely affine vs projective coordinates for implementation of the scalar multiplication using Montgomery's ladder. In Chapter 6, we present a description of a high performance pipelined design of a ECC processor on random curves on an FPGA technology. However before going into the design, we shall develop some other ideas on hardware designs on FPGAs.

TABLE 2.3: Computations for performing ECC scalar multiplication (projective vs affine coordinates)

Computations	Affine Coordinates	Projective Coordinates
Addition	$4k + 6$	$3k + 7$
Squaring	$2k + 2$	$5k + 3$
Multiplication	$2k + 4$	$6k + 10$
Inversion	$2k + 1$	1

2.8 Conclusions

The chapter presents an overview on modern cryptography. It starts with the classification of ciphers, presenting the concepts of symmetric and asymmetric key cryptosystems. The chapter details the inner compositions of block ciphers, with a special attention to the AES algorithm. The composite field representation of the Advanced Encryption Standard

(AES) algorithm is used in several efficient implementations of the block cipher, hence the present chapter develops the background theory. The chapter subsequently develops the underlying mathematics of the growingly popular asymmetric key algorithm, the Elliptic Curve Cryptosystems (ECC). The chapter discusses several concepts for efficient implementations of the ECC scalar multiplication, like LSB first and MSB first algorithms, the Montgomery ladder. These techniques are used in the subsequent chapters for developing efficient hardware designs for both AES and ECC.

Chapter 3

Modern Hardware Design Practices

"Design can be art. Design can be aesthetics. Design is so simple, that's why it is so complicated."

Paul Rand, American Graphic Designer, 1914-1996

3.1   Introduction

With the growth of electronics, there has been tremendous growth in the applications requiring security. Mobile communications, automatic teller machines (ATMs), digital signatures, and online banking are some probable applications requiring cryptographic principles. However, the real-time processing required in these applications obviates the necessity of optimized and high performance implementations of the ciphers.

There has been lot of research in the design of cryptographic algorithms, both on software platforms as well as dedicated hardware environments. While conventional software platforms are limited by their parallelisms, dedicated hardware provides significant opportunities for speed up due to their parallelism. However they are costly, and often require off-shore fabrication facilities. Further, the design cycle for such Application Specific Integrated Circuits (ASICs) are lengthy and complex. On the contrary, the Field Programmable Gate Arrays (FPGAs) are reconfigurable platforms to build hardware. They combine the advantages of both hardware: (in extracting parallelism, and achieving better performance); and software: (in terms of programmability). Thus these resources are excellent low cost, high performance devices for performing design exploration and even in the final prototyping for many applications. However, designing in FPGAs is tricky, and as what works for ASIC libraries does not necessarily work for FPGAs. FPGAs have a different architecture, with fixed units in the name of Look-up-Tables (LUTs) to realize the basic operations, along with larger inter-connect delays. Thus, the designs need to be carefully analyzed to ensure that the utilizations of the FPGAs are enhanced, and the timing constraints are met. In the next section, we provide an outline of the FPGA architecture.

3.1.1   FPGA Architecture

FPGAs are reconfigurable devices offering parallelism and flexibility, on one hand, while being low cost and easy to use on the other. Moreover, they have much shorter design cycle times compared to ASICs. FPGAs were initially used as prototyping device and in high performance scientific applications, but the short time-to-market and on site reconfigurability features have expanded their application space. These devices can now be found in various consumer electronic devices, high performance networking applications, medical electronics and space applications. The reconfigurability aspect of FPGAs also makes them suited for cryptographic applications. Reconfigurability results in flexible implementations allowing operating modes, encryption algorithms and curve constants etc. to be configured from software. FPGAs do not require sophisticated equipment for production, they can be programmed in house. This is a distinct advantage for cryptography as no third party is involved, thus increasing trust in the hardware circuit (reducing chances of IP theft, IC cloning, counterfeiting, insertion of Trojans etc.).

There are two main parts of the FPGA chip [89] : the input/output (I/O) blocks and the core. The I/O blocks are located around the periphery of the chip, and are used to provide programmable connectivity to the chip. The core of the chip consists of programmable logic blocks and programmable routing architectures. A popular architecture for the core called island style architecture is shown in **Fig. 3.1**. *Logic blocks*, also called *configurable logic blocks* (CLB), consists of logic circuitry for implementing logic. Each CLB is surrounded by routing channels connected through switch blocks and connection blocks. A *switch block* connects wires in adjacent channels through programmable switches. A *connection block* connects the wire segments around a logic block to its inputs and outputs, also through programmable switches. Each logic block further contains a group of *basic logic elements* (BLE). Each BLE has a *look up table* (LUT), a storage element and combinational logic as shown in **Fig. 3.2**. The storage element can be configured as a edge triggered D-flipflop or as level-sensitive latches. The combinational logic generally contains logic for carry and control signal generation.

The LUTs can be configured to be used in logic circuitry. If there are m inputs to the LUT then any m variable Boolean function can be implemented. The LUT mainly contains memory to store truth tables of Boolean functions, and multiplexers to select the values of memories. There have been several studies on the best configuration for the LUT. A larger LUT would result in more logic fitted into a single LUT, and hence lesser critical delay. However, a larger LUT would also indicate larger memory and bigger multiplexers, hence larger area. Most studies show that a 4-input LUT provides the best area-delay product, though there have been few applications where a 3-input LUT [152] and 6-input LUT [158] is more beneficial. Most FPGA manufacturers, including Xilinx[1] and Altera[2] have an

---

[1] http://www.xilinx.com
[2] http://www.altera.com

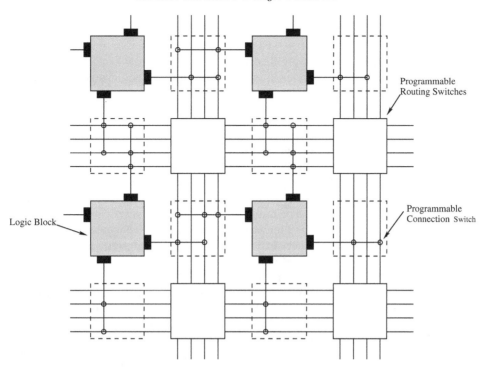

FIGURE 3.1: FPGA island-style architecture

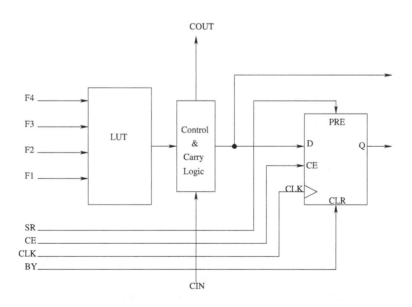

FIGURE 3.2: FPGA Logic Block

increasing number of inputs, namely 4 and 6. However, for a given device the number of inputs are fixed.

3.1.2   The FPGA Design Flow

The Field Programmable Gate Arrays (FPGAs) are programmable devices which can be configured through a design flow as entailed next. The design flow is a semi-automated or automated sequence of steps that translates the conception of the design to an actual hardware realization on a target platform, in our case an FPGA device. The sequence of steps starts with the hardware description of the design using a *Hardware Description Language* (HDL). We describe the inputs to the design flow subsequently:

1. **HDL description:** The design is described through an HDL specification. The most commonly known languages are Verilog and VHDL. Today, even higher-level languages are used like SystemC, MatLab, or Simulink to make the design faster and easier. The HDL describes the design at what is known at the *Register Transfer Level* (RTL), which describes the flow of signals or data between hardware registers and the operations that are performed on them. The hardware registers are conceptually the lowest level of abstraction to the designer, in this case. The HDL design can be designed in two alternative styles, *behavorial* and *structural*. The former style is using more high-level constructions, and based on the manner or behavior in which the described hardware functions. The latter style is based on the actual instantiations of hardware elements or sub-blocks. Thus a structural style requires an architectural knowledge of the designer, and is often preferred for architectural exploration for design trade-offs, performance etc. In real life, the HDL codes are developed in a mixed fashion. For example, in verilog the designs are modeled as encapsulations called as *modules*. The entire design is in reality a hierarchy of these modules and can be depicted often in the form of a tree-like structure. The root node of the tree, is the top-level of the design, which can be thought of to be made of sub-modules, which can be in turn broken into submodules. Finally, the design hierarchy terminates at the leaf levels, which are often simple descriptions, like shifters, flip-flops etc. A popular way of developing the design, is to make the leaf-level behavorial, while as we go up the tree the HDLs become more structural, the top-level being entirely structural. Such an approach improves the programmability, readibilty, and testability of the design, and often helps in an efficient design exploration for better performance.

2. **Constraints:** The HDLs described above are mapped into actual hardware through a sequence of automated steps, namely synthesis, mapping, translation, and routing. However, along with the HDLs the designer also provides some *constraints* to the CAD tools which convert the HDL to an actual hardware. The constraints are typically the desired clock frequency (f_{clk}), and various delays which characterize a given design. The delays could be the following:

   - **Input delay:** This delay is from the input pad[3] to the register, which holds the input signal.

   - **Register to Register Delay:** The synthesis tool assumes that all combinational paths in the design are to be performed in a single clock period. Thus this component of the delay, which describes the delay of a combinational path between two registers, help to compute the critical path of the design. The critical path of the design gives an upper bound to the value of f_{clk}, hence the delay specifications should be carefully provided. Following are some important delay constraints which needs special mention:

     (a) **Set-up time:** It is the minimum time that the synchronous data must arrive before the active clock edge in a sequential circuit.

---

[3]Pads are dedicated terminals through which the design communiciates with the external world.

(b) **Hold Time:** It is the minimum time that the synchronous data should be stable after the active clock edge.

(c) **False Path:** The analyzer considers all combinational paths that are to be performed in a single clock cycle. However in the circuits there be paths that are never activated. Consider **Fig. 3.3** consisting of two sub-circuits separated by the dashed line. First consider the portion on the right-side of the dashed line and the signal transitions showing how the path (the critical path), $g1 \rightarrow g2 \rightarrow g3 \rightarrow g4 \rightarrow g5$ can get sensitized. Next consider the other portion of the circuit and note that due to the presence of the gates $g6$ and $g7$, this path becomes a false path as no input condition can trigger this path. In the example shown, the inverter ($g6$) and the NAND gate ($g7$) ensure that an input of logic one to the inverter, results in the NAND gate producing an output logic one, thus making the output of the circuit logic one much earlier. When the input to the inverter is logic zero, the mentioned path is again false. Thus to obtain a proper estimate of f_{clk}, the designer or the CAD tool should properly identify these false paths.

(d) **Multi-cycle Path:** There are some paths in a design which are intentionally designed to require more than one clock signals to become stable. Thus the set-up and hold-time violation analysis for the overall circuit should be done by taking care of such paths, else the timing reports will be wrongly generated. Consider the **Fig. 3.4**, showing an encryption hardware circuit. The selection of the two multiplexers, MUX-A and MUX-B are the output of a 3-stage circular shifter made of 3-DFFs (D-Flip Flop) as shown in the diagram. The shifter is initially loaded with the value $(1, 0, 0)$, which in 3 clock cycles makes the following transitions: $(1, 0, 0) \rightarrow (0, 1, 0) \rightarrow (0, 0, 1) \rightarrow (1, 0, 0)$. Thus at the start the input multiplexer (MUX-A) selects the plaintext input and passes the result to the DFF. The DFF subsequently latches the data, while the encryption hardware performs the transformation on the data. The output multiplexer (MUX-B) passes the output of the encryption hardware to the DFF as the ciphertext, when the select becomes one in the third clock cycle, i.e., two clock cycles after the encryption starts. Meanwhile it latches the previous ciphertext, which gets updated every two clock cycles. Thus the encryption circuit has two clock cycles to finish its encryption operation. This is an example of a multi-cycle path, as the combinational delay of the circuit is supposed to be performed in more than one clock cycles. This constraint also should be detected and properly kept in mind for a proper estimation of the clock frequency.

The other important design choices are the type of FPGA device, with different cost, performance and power consumptions. Generally, the designer starts with the lower end FPGAs and iteratively depending on the complexity of the design chooses higher end platforms.

Fig. 3.5 depicts the typical design flow for FPGA design. As may be observed that the design flow is top-down starting from the RTL design, RTL elaboration, Architecture Independent Optimizations, Technology Mapping (Architecture Dependent Optimizations), Placement, Placement Driven Optimizations, Routing and Bit Stream Generation. In the design world along with this flow, the verification flow also goes on hand in hand. However it may be noted that the verification flow proceeds in the opposite direction: answering queries like is the RTL elaboration equivalent to the RTL design? In the following description we describe the individual steps in the flow in more details.

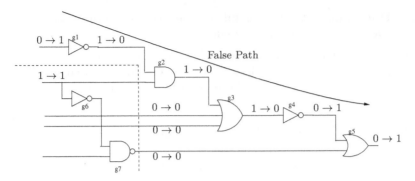

FIGURE 3.3: False path in a circuit

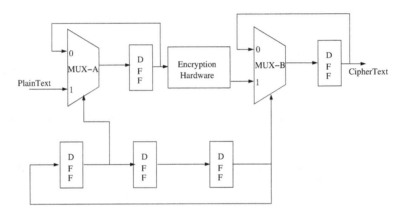

FIGURE 3.4: Multi-cycle path in a circuit

1. **RTL Design:** This step involves the description of the design in a HDL language, like verilog. The step involves the architecture planning for the design into sub-modules, understanding the data-path and control-path of the design and in developing the RTL codes for the sub-modules. This step also involves the integration of the sub-modules to realize the complete design. Testing individual sub-modules and the complete design via test-benches, also written in a high-level language, often verilog, system verilog etc. is also an integral part of this step.

2. **RTL Elaboration:** This step involves the inferring of data-path to be realized by special components internal to the FPGA, like adders with dedicated fast-carry chains, specially designed multipliers, etc. The control-path elements on the other hand get elaborated into state machines, or Boolean equations.

3. **Architecture Independent Optimization:** This step involves various optimization methods which are not related to the underlying architecture of the FPGA platform. For data-path optimization constant propagation, strength reduction, operation sharing, and expression optimization are some popular techniques. On the other hand for control-path optimizations, finite state machine encoding and state minimization are some well known methods. The combinational circuits are optimized exploiting don't-care logic present in the circuit.

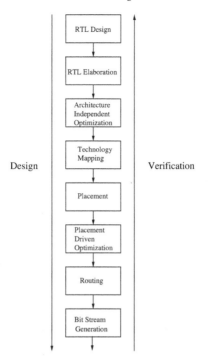

FIGURE 3.5: The FPGA Design Flow

4. **Technology Mapping:** In this step, the various elements of the design are optimally assigned to the resources of the FPGAs. Hence this step is specific to the FPGA device, and depends on the underlying architecture. Depending on the platform the data-path elements get inferred to adders, multipliers, memory elements embedded in the device. The control-path elements and the elements in the control-path, which are not inferred to special embedded elements are realized in the FPGA logic block. The performance of the implemented design, both area and delay, depends on the architecture of the LUTs of the FPGA logic block. We shall discuss later, that the number of inputs to the LUTs can be suitably used to advantage to have high-performance implementations. Thus these optimizations are specific to the underlying architecture and depends on the type of the FPGAs being used.

5. **Placement:** Placement in FPGA decides the physical locations and inter connections of each logic block in the circuit design, which becomes the bottleneck of the circuit performance. A bad placement can increase the interconnects which leads to significant reduction in performance.

6. **Placement-Driven Optimization:** In order to reduce the interconnect delay, and to improve the performance of the design, the initial placement is incrementally updated through logic restructuring, rewiring, duplication etc.

7. **Routing:** Global and detailed routing are performed to connect the signal nets using restricted routing resources which are predesigned. The routing resources used are programmable switches, wire segments which are available for routing, and multiplexers.

8. **Bit-stream Generation:** This is the final step of the design flow. It takes the routed design as input, and produces the bit-stream to program the logic and interconnects to implement the design on the FPGA device.

3.2   Mapping an Algorithm to Hardware: Components of a Hardware Architecture

The conversion of an algorithm to an efficient hardware is a challenging task. While functional correctness of the hardware is important, the main reason for designing a hardware is performance. Thus, one needs to consider all opportunities for a high-performance design: namely by reducing the critical path of the circuit, by making it more compact, thus ensuring that the resources of the FPGA platform are used efficiently. Hence, in order to develop an efficient implementation, one needs to look into the components of a hardware and understand the *architecture* of the design. **Fig. 3.6** describes the important components of a digital hardware design. As can be observed, the three most important parts of the architecture are the data-path elements, the control-path block, and the memory unit.

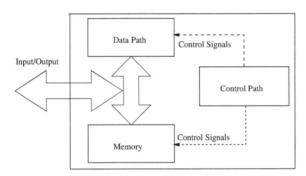

FIGURE 3.6: Important Components of an Architecture

- The *data-path* elements are the computational units of the design. The data-paths are central to the performance of a given circuit, and have a dominating effect on the overall performance. Thus the data-path elements need to be properly optimized and carefully designed. However it is not trivial, as there are numerous equivalent circuit topologies and various designs have different effect on the delay, area and power consumption of the device. Also one has to decide whether the data-path elements will be combinational or sequential units, depending on the underlying application and its constraints. Examples of common data-path elements are registers, adders, shifters etc. These data-path elements often form the components of the Arithmetic Logic Unit (ALU) of a given design.

- The *control-path* elements, on the other hand, sequences the data flow through the data-path elements. Hence the input data is processed or transformed by the data-path elements, which are typically combinational. On the other hand, the data is switched and cycled through the data-path elements by the control unit, which is typically a

---

Algorithm 3.1: Binary gcd Algorithm

Input: Integers u and v
Output: Greatest Common Divisor of u and v: $z = gcd(u, v)$

1 **while** *(u!=v)* **do**
2   **if** *u and v are even* **then**
3       $z = 2gcd(u/2, v/2)$
4   **end**
5   **else if** *(u is odd and v is even)* **then**
6       $z = gcd(u, v/2)$
7   **end**
8   **else if** *(u is even and v is odd)* **then**
9       $z = gcd(u/2, v)$
10   **end**
11   **else**
12   **if** *(u ≥ v)* **then**
13          $z = gcd((u - v)/2, v)$
14   **end**
15   **else**
16          $z = gcd(u, (v - u)/2)$
17   **end**
18   **end**
19 **end**

---

sequential design. The control signals generated by the sequential controller are often dependent on the states, or sometimes on both the state or partial outputs from the datapath. The former form of controller is known as the **Moore** machine, while the latter as the **Mealy** machine.

Whatever be the design type of the controller, a key to a good design is to comprehend the effective split between the data-path and control-path elements. We illustrate this concept with the help of a case study in the next section.

3.3   Case study: Binary gcd Processor

Consider the following algorithm (algorithm 11) for computing the greatest common divisor (gcd) of two given integers. The algorithm is commonly known as the binary Euclidean gcd algorithm, and is an improvement on the classical school book Euclidean algorithm for computing gcd.

In order to illustrate the development of a separate data and control paths, we shall take the example of the above gcd algorithm. The objective of the present exercise is to develop a special-purpose hardware that computes the greatest common divisor of two positive integers, X and Y. We assume that $gcd(0, 0) = 0$. We shall present a step by step approach to realize the hardware.

1. **Identification of the states of the algorithm**: The pseudo-code of the algorithm is expressed in an HDL-like language in (algorithm 12). The pseudo-code identifies

---

Algorithm 3.2: HDL like description of the Binary gcd Algorithm

---

Input: Integers u and v
Output: Greatest Common Divisor of u and v: $z = gcd(u, v)$

```
1  register XR, YR;
2  XR = u; YR = v; count = 0;                              /* State 0 */
3  while (XR != YR) do
4      if (XR[0] = 0 and YR[0] = 0) then                   /* State 1 */
5          XR = right shift(XR)
6          YR = right shift(YR)
7          count = count + 1
8      end
9      else if (XR[0] = 1 and YR[0] = 1) then              /* State 2 */
10         YR = right shift(YR)
11     end
12     else if (XR[0] = 0 and YR[0] = 1) then              /* State 3 */
13         XR = right shift(XR)
14     end
15     else                                                /* State 4 */
16         if (XR ≥ YR) then
17             XR = right shift(XR − YR)
18         end
19         else
20             YR = right shift(YR − XR)
21         end
22  end
23  while (count > 0) do                                   /* State 5 */
24      XR = left shift(XR)
25      count = count − 1
26  end
```

---

the essential states or simple stages of the algorithm. It may be noted that in each state, the intended hardware is expected to perform certain computations, which are realized by the computation or data path elements. The pseudo-code shows that there are six states of the design, denoted by S_0 to S_5.

2. **Identification of the data path elements**: As evident from the pseudo-code, the data path elements required for the gcd computation are *subtracter, complementer, right shifter, left shifter* and *counter*. The other very common data path element is the *multiplexer* which are required in large numbers for the switching necessary for the computations done in the datapath. The *selection* lines of the multiplexers are configured by the control circuitry, which is essentially a state machine.

3. **Identification of the state machine of the control path**: The control path is a sequential design, which comprises of the state machine. In this example, there is a six state machine, which receives inputs from the computations performed in the data path elements, and accordingly performs the state transitions. It also produces output signals which configures or switches the data path elements.

4. **Design of the data path architecture**: The data path of the gcd processor is

depicted in **Fig. 3.7**. The diagram shows the two distinct parts: data path and control path for the design. The data-path stores the values of X_R and Y_R (as mentioned in the HDL-like code) in two registers. The registers are loadable, which means they are updated by an input when they are enabled by an appropriate control signal (e.g., *load_X_R* for the register X_R). The values of the inputs u and v are initially loaded into the registers X_R and Y_R through the input *multiplexer*, using the control signals *load_uv*. The least bits of X_R and Y_R are passed to the controller to indicate whether the present values of X_R and Y_R are even or not. The next iteration values of X_R and Y_R are updated, by feeding back the register values (after necessary computations) through the input *multiplexer* and this is controlled by the signals *update_X_R* and *update_Y_R*. The computations on the registers X_R and Y_R are division by 2, which is performed easily by the two *right-shifters*, and subtraction and comparison for equality, both of which are performed by a *subtracter*. The values stored in X_R and Y_R are compared using a subtracter, which indicates to the controller the events ($X_R! = Y_R$) and ($X_R \geq Y_R$) by raising appropriate flag signals. In the case, when $X_R < Y_R$ and the subtraction $Y_R - X_R$ is to be performed, the result is complemented. The next iteration values of X_R and Y_R are loaded either after the subtraction or directly, which is controlled by the signals *load_X_R_after_sub* and *load_Y_R_after_sub*. The circuit also includes an *up down counter*, which is incremented whenever both X_R and Y_R are even values. Finally, when $X_R = Y_R$ the result is obtained by computing $2^{count}(X_R)$, which is obtained by using a *left-shifter* and shifting the value of X_R, until the value of *count* becomes zero.

5. **Design of the state machine for the controller**: The state machine of the controller is depicted in table 3.3. As discussed there are six states of the controller, and the controller receives four inputs from the data path computations, namely ($X_R! = Y_R$), $X_R[0]$, $Y_R[0]$, and $X_R \geq Y_R$ respectively. The state transitions are self-explanatory and can be easily followed by relating the table and the data path diagram of **Fig. 3.7**. The state machine is an example of a Mealy machine.

TABLE 3.1: State Transition Matrix of the Controller

Present State	Next State					Output Signals										
	0	100	110	101	111	load uv	update X_R	update Y_R	load X_R	load Y_R	load_X_R after_sub	load_Y_R after_sub	Update counter	Inc /Dec	left shift	count zero
S_0	S_5	S_1	S_2	S_3	S_4	1	0	0	1	1	0	0	0	_	_	_
S_1	S_5	S_1	S_2	S_3	S_4	0	1	1	1	1	0	0	1	1	_	_
S_2	S_5	S_1	S_2	S_3	S_4	0	0	1	0	1	0	0	0	_	_	_
S_3	S_5	S_1	S_2	S_3	S_4	0	1	0	1	0	0	0	0	_	_	_
S_4 ($X_R \geq Y_R$)	S_5	S_1	S_2	S_3	S_4	0	1	0	1	0	1	0	0	_	_	_
S_4 ($X_R < Y_R$)	S_5	S_1	S_2	S_3	S_4	0	0	1	0	1	0	1	0	_	_	_
S_5	S_5	S_5	S_5	S_5	S_5	0	0	0	0	0	0	0	1	0	1	0

3.4 Enhancing the Performance of a Hardware Design

One of the primary goals of developing a hardware architecture is *performance*. But the term performance has several implications, depending on the application at hand. For

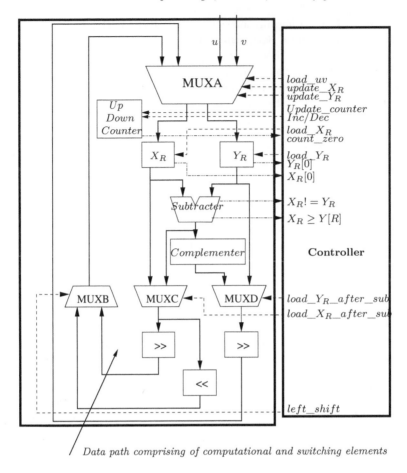

Data path comprising of computational and switching elements

FIGURE 3.7: Data Path of a gcd Processor

certain applications, speed may be of utmost importance, while for others it may be the area budget of the design is of primary concern.

In general, if any standard book of computer architecture is referred to we obtain several definitions of performance. We revise certain definitions here and consider some more variants of these. To start with, the performance of a hardware design is often stated through its critical path, as that limits the clock frequency. In a combinational circuit, the critical path is of primary concern and a circuit which has a better optimized critical path, ie. a smaller critical delay is faster. On the other hand for a sequential circuit, it is also important to know the number of clock cycles necessary to complete a computation. Like in the previous example of the gcd processor, the number of clock cycles needed is proportional to the number of bits in the larger argument. However, the number of clock cycles required is not a constant, and varies with the inputs. Thus one may consider the average number of clock cycles needed to perform the computation. Let the fastest clock frequency be denoted by f_{max} and the average number of clock cycles is say denoted by cc_{avg}, then the total computation time for the gcd processor is obtained by $t_c = \frac{cc_{avg}}{f_{max}}$. Another important metric is the throughput of the hardware, denoted by $\tau = N_b/t_c = \frac{N_b f_{max}}{cc_{avg}}$, where N_b is the number of bytes of data being simultaneously processed.

The other important aspect of hardware designs is the resource consumed. In context to FPGAs the resources largely comprise of slices, which are made of LUTs and flipflops. As discussed, the LUTs have typically fixed number of inputs. In order to improve the performance of a hardware design, it requires to customize the design for the target architecture to ensure that the resource used is minimized. The smallest programmable entity on an FPGA is the lookup table (Section 3.1.1). As an example, Virtex-4 FPGAs have LUTs with four inputs and can be configured for any logic function having a maximum of four inputs. The LUT can also be used to implement logic functions having less than four inputs, two for example. In this case, only half the LUT is utilized the remaining part is not utilized. Such a LUT having less than four inputs is an *under-utilized LUT*. For example, the logic function $y = x_1 + x_2$ under utilizes the LUT as it has only two inputs. Most compact implementations are obtained when the utilization of each LUT is maximized. From the above fact it may be derived that the minimum number of LUTs required for a q bit combinational circuit is given by Equation 3.1.

$$\#LUT(q) = \begin{cases} 0 & \text{if } q = 1 \\ 1 & \text{if } 1 < q \leq 4 \\ \lceil q/3 \rceil & \text{if } q > 4 \text{ and } q \bmod 3 = 2 \\ \lfloor q/3 \rfloor & \text{if } q > 4 \text{ and } q \bmod 3 \neq 2 \end{cases} \tag{3.1}$$

The delay of the q bit combinational circuit in terms of LUTs is given by Equation 3.2, where D_{LUT} is the delay of one LUT.

$$DELAY(q) = \lceil log_4(q) \rceil * D_{LUT} \tag{3.2}$$

The percentage of under-utilized LUTs in a design is determined using Equation 3.3. Here, LUT_k signifies that k inputs out of 4 are used by the design block realized by the LUT. So, LUT_2 and LUT_3 are under utilized LUTs, while LUT_4 is fully utilized.

$$\%UnderUtilizedLUTs = \frac{LUT_2 + LUT_3}{LUT_2 + LUT_3 + LUT_4} * 100 \tag{3.3}$$

It may be stressed that the above formulation provides minimum number of LUTs required and not an exact count. As an example, consider $y = x_5x_6x_1 + x_5x_6x_2 + x_1x_2x_3 + x_2x_3x_4 + x_1x_3x_5$. Observe that the number of LUTs required is 3, and the formula says that the minimum is 2-LUTs. Our analysis and experiments, show that the above formulation although provides a lower bound, matches quite closely with the actual results. Most importantly the formulation helps us to perform design exploration much faster, which is the prime objective of such a formulation.

The number of LUTs required to implement a Boolean function is the measure of the area of a function. The above formulation can also be generalized for any k-input LUT. A k input LUT (k-LUT) can be considered a black box that can perform any functionality of a maximum of k variables. If there is a single variable, then no LUT is required. If there are more than k variables, then more than one k−LUTs are required to implement the functionality. The lower bound of the total number of k input LUTs for a function with x variables can thus be similarly expressed as,

$$lut(x) = \begin{cases} 0 & \text{if } x \leq 1 \\ 1 & \text{if } 1 < x \leq k \\ \lfloor \frac{x-k}{k-1} \rfloor + 2 & \text{if } x > k \text{ and } (k-1) \nmid (x-k) \\ \frac{x-k}{k-1} + 1 & \text{if } x > k \text{ and } (k-1)|(x-k) \end{cases} \tag{3.4}$$

Delay in FPGAs comprises of LUT delays and routing delays. Analyzing the delay of

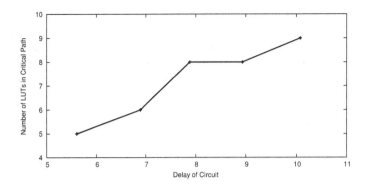

FIGURE 3.8: LUTs in Critical Path vs. Delay for a Combinational Multiplier

a circuit on FPGA platform is much more complex than the area analysis. By experimentation we have found that for designs having combinational components, the delay of the design varies linearly with the number of LUTs present in the critical path. **Fig. 3.8** shows this linear relationship between the number of LUTs in the critical path and the delay in multipliers of different sizes. Due to such linear relationship, we can consider that the number of LUTs in the critical path is a measure of actual delay. From now onwards, we use the term LUT delay to mean the number of $k-$LUTs present in the critical path.

For an x variable Boolean function, number of $k-$LUTs in the critical path is denoted by the function $maxlutpath(x)$ and is thus expressed as:

$$maxlutpath(x) = \lceil log_k(x) \rceil. \tag{3.5}$$

We will use Equation 3.4 and 3.5 for estimating area and delay of the architecture proposed in **Fig. 3.7**. In the following section, we present gradually the estimation of the hardware blocks as required in the data-path.

3.5 Modelling of the Computational Elements of the gcd Processor

The important datapath elements as shown in the **Fig. 3.7** are *multiplexers* and *subtracter*.

3.5.1 Modeling of an Adder

In the architecture as depicted in **Fig. 3.7**, the most important components to influence the delay are the integer adders/subtracters. As on hardware platforms, both adder and subtracters have same area and delay, we consider a general structure. The carry propagation is a major challenge in designing efficient integer adders on hardware platforms. There are several methods for realizing fast adder topologies. On FPGA platforms, carry chain based adders are very popular due to their low-cost and optimized carry propagation techniques. Here in this discussion, we consider such a carry chain–based integer adder available in most common FPGAs.

Internal diagram of such an adder is shown in **Fig. 3.9**. For fast carry propagation, a dedicated chain of MUXCY is provided in FPGAs. For an m bit adder, the carry propagates through m number of cascaded MUXCY. Dedicated carry chains are much faster than generic LUT based fabric in FPGA, hence carry propagation delay is small. Since these MUXCY are used only for fast carry propagation, and other blocks present are constructed of LUTs, we need to scale the delay of MUXCY circuits for comparing delay of an adder with any other primitive. Let us consider that delay of a MUXCY is s times lesser than that of a LUT. This scaling factor s depends on device technology. For Xilinx Virtex IV FPGAs, $s \approx 17$. So, for an m bit adder, we can say that the LUT delay of the carry chain is $\lceil m/s \rceil$. Since the delay of the adder is determined by the delay of the carry chain, we can consider that the delay of the adder

$$D_{add} = \lceil m/s \rceil. \tag{3.6}$$

Likewise the delay of a subtracter can also be approximated similarly as:

$$D_{sub} = \lceil m/s \rceil. \tag{3.7}$$

The architecture of the gcd circuit also requires a complementer, which is obtained in the usual 2's complement sense. This requires also a subtracter, and hence has similar area and delay requirements as above.

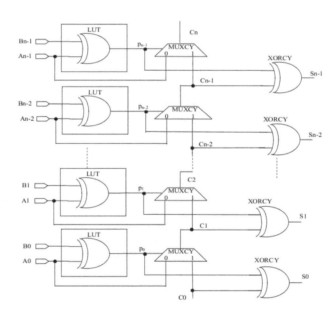

FIGURE 3.9: Adder with Carry Chain

3.5.2 Modeling of a Multiplexer

For a $2^t : 1$ MUX, there are t selection lines, thus the output of a 2^t input MUX is a function of $2^t + t$ variables. So the total LUT requirements to implement the output functionality is $lut(2^t + t)$. For $GF(2^m)$, each input line to the MUX has m bits and the output has m bits. Thus the total LUT requirement for a 2^s input MUX, is given by

$$\#LUT_{MUX} = m \times lut(2^t + t). \tag{3.8}$$

Delay of the MUX in terms of LUTs is equal to the *maxlutpath* of $2^t + t$ variables and is given by,

$$D_{MUX} = maxlutpath(2^t + t). \tag{3.9}$$

If $2^{t-1} <$ *number of inputs* $< 2^t$, then estimations in Equations (3.8) and (3.9) for 2^t inputs give an upper bound. Practically, the values in this case are slightly lesser than the values for 2^t inputs in Equations (3.8) and (3.9), and the difference can be neglected.

3.5.3   Total LUT Estimate of the gcd Processor

From **Fig. 3.7**, we can observe that the total number of LUTs in the gcd processor is the sum of the LUTs in the multiplexers, namely MUX_A, MUX_B, MUX_C and MUX_D, and the subtracter along with the complementer, which is also another subtracter. The state machine (control block in **Fig. 3.7**) consumes very few LUTs and is not considered in the overall LUT count. Thus the total number of $k-$LUTs in the entire circuit is,

$$\#LUT_{gcd} = 2LUT_{Subtractor} + LUT_{MUX_A} + LUT_{MUX_B} + LUT_{MUX_C} + LUT_{MUX_D}$$

3.5.4   Delay Estimate of the gcd Processor

In **Fig. 3.7** we can observe that the critical path of the design goes through the path: subtracter $\rightarrow$ complementer $\rightarrow MUX_D \rightarrow MUX_B \rightarrow MUX_A$. Hence the total delay using Equations 3.7, 3.9, and 3.6 can be approximated as:

$$\begin{aligned} D_{PATH} &= 2D_{sub} + D_{MUX_D} + D_{MUX_B} + D_{MUX_A} \\ &\approx 2\lceil m/s \rceil + 1 + 1 + 1 \\ nonumber &\approx 3 + 2\lceil m/s \rceil \end{aligned}$$

Note that the last part of the equation, namely the delay of MUX_A comes from the fact that the multiplexer is made of two smaller 2-input multiplexers in parallel: one input writing into the register X_R and the other into the register Y_R.

3.6   Experimental Results

The above design was synthesized using Xilinx ISE tools and targeted on a Virtex-4 FPGA. The objective of the experiments was to study the above dependence on the LUT utilization and to estimate the critical path delay for the circuit. It may be noted that while the estimation of the LUT utilization matches quite closely, the objective of the delay is to observe the trend, as an exact delay optimization is not aimed at. We vary the bit length of the gcd processor and repeat the experiments to study the scalability of the design. The estimations help in design exploration as we are able to estimate the dependence and thus tweak the architecture in a more planned manner and most importantly before actually implementing the hardware.

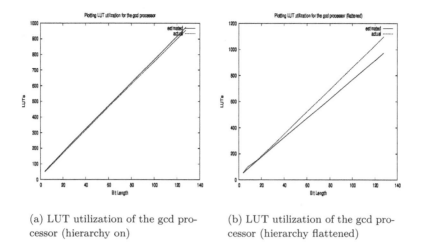

(a) LUT utilization of the gcd processor (hierarchy on)

(b) LUT utilization of the gcd processor (hierarchy flattened)

FIGURE 3.10: LUT utilization of the gcd processor (both theoretical and actual)

3.6.1　LUT utilization of the gcd processor

Fig. 3.10 shows the plots for the LUT utilization of the gcd processor designed as described in the previous section. The results are furnished with two settings of the FPGA tool: one with the hierarchy on (**Fig. 3.10(a)**) and the other flattened (**Fig. 3.10(b)**). It may be observed that the theoretical estimates and the actual resource utilization match quite closely.

3.6.2　Delay Estimates for the gcd Processor

Fig. 3.11 shows the plots for the critical path delays for the gcd processor with varying bit sizes. The plots are shown for both for hierarchy on and hierarchy off, as shown in **Fig. 3.11(a)** and **Fig. 3.11(b)**, respectively.

3.7　Conclusions

Both the estimates for the LUTs and the critical path show that the designer can make estimates of the performance ahead of the design. Thus, the theoretical model may be used as a guideline for design exploration. Again it may be noted that the estimates are not exact, and provides approximations to the exact requirements but nevertheless, can be used for design explorations in an analytic way. We show subsequently in the design of finite field circuits and an Elliptic Curve Crypto-processor how to leverage these models and framework for designing efficient architectures.

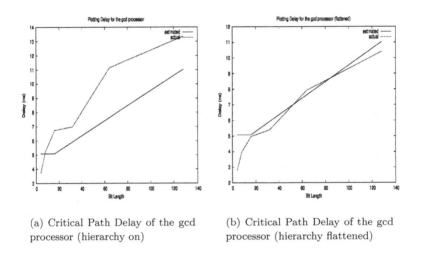

(a) Critical Path Delay of the gcd   (b) Critical Path Delay of the gcd
processor (hierarchy on)   processor (hierarchy flattened)

FIGURE 3.11: Delay Modeling of the gcd processor (both theoretical and actual)

Part II

Hardware Design of Cryptographic Algorithms

Chapter 4

Hardware Design of the Advanced Encryption Standard (AES)

"Everything should be made as simple as possible, but not simpler."

(Albert Einstein)

4.1 Introduction

Advanced Encryption Standard (AES) is the de facto standard worldwide for the Ever since 2001, the National Institute for Standard and Technology (NIST) selected the Rijndael block cipher as the new AES. This lead to several applications requiring encryption starting to adopt this algorithm into their products. Due to the high-performance requirement of these applications, namely in the form of high speed, less latency, less area footprint, and even less power, several approaches for software and hardware designs for AES have been studied even since its inception. Requirements of throughput, power and compactness have made design of Rijndael quite challenging. Various approaches have been developed. Often these approaches have been found to be conflicting, implying proper understanding of design rationales.

In this chapter, we focus to aim at understanding the key principles of developing a hardware design of AES, the scopes that the algorithm provides etc. We shall also be using FPGAs as a validating platform, though most of the discussions are valid for ASICs as well.

4.2 Algorithmic and Architectural Optimizations for AES Design

In this section, we outline the optimization methods employed in hardware designs for AES. The techniques for optimization can be broadly categorized as follows:

1. **Algorithmic optimizations:** AES is based on finite field operations. Hence suitable choices of representation of finite fields, composite fields, use of suitable isomorphisms help to develop compact and efficient designs. Further, the round description of AES has some interesting properties, enabling to design the encryption and decryption hardwares in a similar fashion, thus helping in providing both encryption and decryptions in the same hardware. Also, the underlying platform like FPGAs provide some unique opportunities for efficient implementations of some round transformations.

2. **Architectural optimizations:** Standard architectural techniques such as pipelining have also been applied for improving the throughputs of hardware designs of AES. Systematic design approaches for separating the data-path and control-paths of the design, design of suitable key-schedule architecture helps in developing efficient reconfigurable AES designs, which can support all the three versions of AES, namely 128, 192, and 256 bits.

4.3 Circuit for the AES S-Box

Among the round operations of AES, the S-Box which is obtained using the SubBytes step is the only non-linear transformation and is challenging to implement. The remaining steps, namely ShiftRows, MixColumns, and AddRoundKey are linear, in the sense that the output bits are expressible by modulo-2 addition, ie. XOR operations in terms of the input bits. On the contrary, the S-Boxes i.e., the SubBytes are non-linear, hence requiring AND gates, in addition to the XOR gates required to process the input. The core step in the SubBytes is the finite field inversion defined over the field $GF(2^8)$. This is a complex operation, and a naive implementation would require large number of AND gates because of the good cryptographic properties of the transformation. Thus many software designs use table look-ups, which are fast and efficient. They are essentially stored in tables, and the input is used as an address to obtain the resultant output. However, this technique has the drawback of large resource utilization when implemented in hardware. Each copy of the table requires 256 bytes, and since each round has 16 parallel S-Box look-ups, for a high-performance design, one would require 16 copies of this table. Further, if the AES hardware is to be pipelined and unrolled for further high throughput applications, like counter-mode of ciphers, they require separate copies for each of the 10 rounds for AES-128. For the other versions of AES, the cost is even more. To reduce this large resource allocation for a combinational logical representation of the SubBytes, composite field representation have been found to lead to compact and efficient designs.

4.3.1 Subfield Mappings

A very popular technique to implement the AES SubBytes is by hierarchically expressing the field elements in $GF(2^8)$ in terms of elements in the subfields. As discussed in Chapter 2, we first define an isomorphic mapping of an element in $GF(2^8)$ to the composite field $GF(2^4)^2$. Then the inverse in the larger field is performed by expressing the inverses in the subfield. Let us recall the equations for the inverse computation in the composite field, which is the main step of the SubBytes transformation in AES.

One of the most compact implementation of the AES S-Box was presented in the work of [71]. The field $GF(2^8)$ is isomorphic to $GF(2^4)^2$, and hence translated to the composite field through a mapping. The mapping varies depending on the choice of the basis: polynomial or normal. The field $GF(2^4)^2$ operations are performed modulo an irreducible polynomial over $GF(2^4)$. Let the polynomial be $r(Y) = Y^2 + \tau Y + \mu$. Here for implementation efficiency we take $\tau = 1$, simply because it is used more often in the subfield equations which are realized by hardware circuit to perform the computations. Both μ and τ cannot be 1 as then we get the irreducible polynomial for $GF(2^2)$, which is a subfield of $GF(2^4)$. The choice of μ is such that the polynomial $r(Y) = Y^2 + Y + \mu$ is irreducible over $GF(2^4)$. The variable $\mu \in GF(2^4)$ can thus take eight possible values: roots of the irreducible polynomials in $GF(2^4)$, namely $x^4 + x^3 + 1$ and $x^4 + x^3 + x^2 + x + 1$.

The decomposition is continued in a hierarchical fashion. The field computations in $GF(2^4)$ are performed by expressing the elements in the composite field $GF(2^2)^2$. Thus the operations are modulo a polynomial $s(Z) = Z^2 + TZ + N$ irreducible over $GF(2^2)$. Again we take the value of $T = 1$, and the value of N is chosen such that it is a root of the irreducible polynomial $x^2 + x + 1$ over $GF(2^2)$. Thus N can take two values.

The equations leading to the circuits evaluating the inverse using this technique can thus lead to several configurations based on the choices of the coefficients in the irreducible polynomials $r(Y)$ and $s(Z)$.

Further, the choices of the basis also leads to different circuits. For each choice of the variable, say μ, there are two roots, the roots of the polynomial $r(Y)$: any one of which can be used for circuits using polynomial basis, while both of these are used for the normal basis. Thus for the choice of μ, there are three basis choices for the decomposition of the $GF(2^8)$ computation in terms of $GF(2^4)$. Likewise, for every step there are three basis choices. Hence overall the total number of circuit configurations are: $(8 \times 3) \times (2 \times 3) \times (1 \times 3) = 432$ possible cases.

In [71] it was shown that a particular configuration can be arrived which can lead to the most compact realization of the AES S-Box: the S-Box was implemented using only 195 gates. Combined with the affine mapping the SubBytes step required around 253 gates. In the following, we present the circuit description using polynomial and normal basis, though the most compact realization reported was due to normal basis.

4.3.2 Circuit Optimizations in the Polynomial Basis

Let the irreducible polynomial of an element in $GF(2^4)^2$ be $r(Y) = Y^2 + \tau Y + \mu$, and let an element in the composite field be $\gamma = (\gamma_1 Y + \gamma_0)$. Let us denote: $\delta = (\gamma_1 Y + \gamma_0)^{-1} =$

$(\delta_1 Y + \delta_0) \mod (Y^2 + \tau Y + \mu)$. Thus, the inverse of the element is expressed by the following equations:

$$\begin{aligned} \delta_0 &= (\gamma_0 + \gamma_1 \tau)(\gamma_0^2 + \gamma_0 \gamma_1 \tau + \gamma_1^2 \mu)^{-1} \\ \delta_1 &= \gamma_1 (\gamma_0^2 + \gamma_0 \gamma_1 \tau + \gamma_1^2 \mu)^{-1} \end{aligned} \qquad (4.1)$$

The above equations can be used to realize a hardware circuit. As τ appears in two equations, we make $\tau = 1$ for compact realization. Note as earlier stated we cannot make $\mu = 1$. Thus with the above choices, Equation 4.1 can be rewritten as:

$$\begin{aligned} \delta_0 &= (\gamma_0 + \gamma_1)(\gamma_0(\gamma_0 + \gamma_1) + \mu\gamma_1^2)^{-1} \\ \delta_1 &= \gamma_1(\gamma_0(\gamma_0 + \gamma_1) + \mu\gamma_1^2)^{-1} \end{aligned} \qquad (4.2)$$

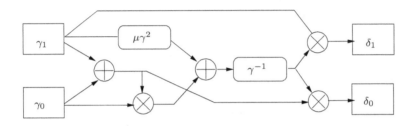

FIGURE 4.1: Polynomial $GF(2^8)$ Inverter

The corresponding circuit is depicted in **Fig. 4.1**. The circuit shows that the 8 bit computation is performed in terms of 4 bit computations: namely additions, multiplications, squarings and inverses. The addition is the simple XOR, while the multiplication is performed in $GF(2^4)$. When one of the inputs to the multiplier is a constant, or when a squaring is performed, a specialized circuit is used rather than using a general multiplier. In the paper of [71], the multiplication with a constant is given a special name as *scaling*.

The polynomial $GF(2^4)$ multiplier can also be obtained by similarly expressing the elements as polynomials with coefficients in $GF(2^2)$. Consider the product of two elements in $GF(2^4)$, being mapped to $GF(2^2)^2$ and denoted by $\gamma = \Gamma_1 Z + \Gamma_0$, and $\delta = \Delta_1 Z + \Delta_0$. Using the irreducible polynomial $s(Z) = Z^2 + Z + N$, we have:

$$(\Gamma_1 Z + \Gamma_0)(\Delta_1 Z + \Delta_0) = Z(\Gamma_0 \Delta_0 + (\Gamma_1 + \Gamma_0)(\Delta_1 + \Delta_0)) + (\Gamma_0 \Delta_0 + N\Gamma_1 \Delta_1)$$

For *scaling*, proper choices of the constant μ can lead to some scopes for optimization. Like for $\mu = \Delta_1 Z + \Delta_0$, we set $\Delta_0 = 0$. Note that $\Delta_1 \neq 0$, as then μ cannot make the polynomial $r(Y)$ irreducible over $GF(2^4)$. Further, choosing $N = \Delta_1^{-1}$ we can further simplify the scaling operation.

As discussed, the choice of N makes the polynomial $s(Z) = Z^2 + Z + N$ irreducible over $GF(2^2)$. Thus N is the root of $t(W) = W^2 + W + 1$, and the roots cannot be 0, 1. They are denoted by N and $N + 1$ (note that the sum of the roots is 1). Depending on the root chosen for the polynomial basis $(W, 1)$, either $N = W$, or $N^2 = N + 1 = W$. Also note $N^{-1} = N^2 = N + 1$.

This leads to further improvement by combining the squaring operation with the scaling operation. For completeness we state the following equation, leaving the details to the reader:

$$\begin{aligned}
\mu\gamma^2 &= \mu(\Gamma_1 Z + \Gamma_0)^2 \\
&= \mu(\Gamma_1^2 Z + (\Gamma_0^2 + N\Gamma_1^2))
\end{aligned}$$

Using the above choices for $\mu = N^2 Z$ for suitably optimizing the scaling operation we have:

$$\begin{aligned}
\mu\gamma^2 &= [(N^2)(\Gamma_1^2 + (\Gamma_0^2 + N\Gamma_1^2))Z + \Gamma_1^2 \\
&= [N^2\Gamma_1^2 + N^2\Gamma_0^2 + (N+1)N\Gamma_1^2]Z + \Gamma_1^2 \\
&= [N^2\Gamma_0^2 + N\Gamma_1^2]Z + \Gamma_1^2
\end{aligned}$$

Similarly, the element in $GF(2^4)$ can also be converted to an element in $GF(2^2)^2$ and the inverse can be computed in the subfield $GF(2^2)$. The irreducible polynomial of $GF(2^2)^2$ is denoted as $s(Z) = Z^2 + TZ + N$, where all coefficients are in $GF(2^2)$.

The inverse of an element in $GF(2^2)^2$ is $\Gamma = (\Gamma_1 Z + \Gamma_0)$ and let its inverse $\Delta = (\Gamma_1 Z + \Gamma_0)^{-1} = (\Delta_1 Z + \Delta_0)\bmod (Z^2 + TZ + N)$.

We have likewise the following equations:

$$\begin{aligned}
\Delta_0 &= (\Gamma_0 + \Gamma_1 T)(\Gamma_0^2 + \Gamma_0\Gamma_1 T + \Gamma_1^2 N)^{-1} \\
\Delta_1 &= \Gamma_1(\Gamma_0^2 + \Gamma_0\Gamma_1 T + \Gamma_1^2 N)^{-1}
\end{aligned} \tag{4.3}$$

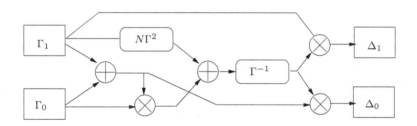

FIGURE 4.2: Polynomial $GF(2^4)$ Inverter

The corresponding circuit is shown in **Fig 4.2**. The underlying operations are likewise to **Fig 4.1**, scaling and squaring in $GF(2^2)$, multiplication and inversion in the subfield.

The multiplications in $GF(2^2)$, the product $\Gamma\Delta$ can be similarly obtained by reducing with the polynomial $t(W) = W^2 + W + 1$. Thus we have for $\Gamma = g_1 W + g_0$ and $\Delta = d_1 W + d_0$,

$$(g_1 W + g_0)(d_1 W + d_0) = W(g_0 d_0 + (g_1 + g_0)(d_1 + d_0)) + (g_0 d_0 + g_1 d_1)$$

Here the multiplications and additions are in $GF(2)$ and are thus equivalent to AND and XOR gates respectively.

The scaling operation to compute $N\Gamma$, can be computed using the fact that $N = W$ or $N^2 = W$. In the combined squaring and scaling operation, we need scaling in $GF(2^2)$ for both N and N^2. Assuming $N = W$, thus we need a W-scaler and W^2-scaler circuit.

Thus we have:

$$\begin{aligned}
W(g_1 W + g_0) &= W(g_1 + g_0) + g_1 \\
W^2(g_1 W + g_0) &= g_0 W + (g_1 + g_0)
\end{aligned}$$

Like before, we can also combine the squaring and multiplication operation for efficiency. Thus assuming $N = w$, squaring and scaling with N can be computed as:

$$
\begin{aligned}
W\Gamma^2 &= W(g_1 W + g_0)^2 \\
&= W(g_1 W + (g_1 + g_0)) \\
&= (g_1 + (g_1 + g_0))W + g_1 \\
&= g_0 W + g_1
\end{aligned}
$$

Thus we see that the squaring and multiplication are *free*! One can obtain it by simply swapping the inputs.

Using this fact, one can further optimize the square and scale architecture in $GF(2^4)$. When $N = W$ we can further simplify $\mu\gamma^2$ as follows:

$$
\mu\gamma^2 = (\{N\Gamma_1^2\} + N\{N\Gamma_0^2\})Z + (N^2\{N\Gamma_1^2\})
$$

Observe that the entire operation can now be performed with one addition and two scaling operations, as the square and scale operations in $GF(2^2)$ denoted in $\{\ \}$ are free. Note that we have used the fact that for any non-zero element $\Gamma = (g_1 W + g_0) \in GF(2^2)$, $\Gamma^3 = 1$. Thus $\Gamma^{-1} = \Gamma^2$. Hence, an inverter in $GF(2^2)$ is same as squarer: $\Gamma^2 = g_1 W + (g_1 + g_0)$.

We can also verify the inversion in $GF(2^2)$ in a similar fashion as for the fields $GF(2^8)$ and $GF(2^4)$. Let the inverse of an element in $GF(2^2)$, say $G = g_1 W + g_0$ is $D = d_1 W + d_0$, where the coefficients belong to $GF(2)$. The irreducible polynomial is $t(W) = W^2 + W + 1$.

Thus, we have:

$$
\begin{aligned}
d_0 &= (g_0 + g_1)(g_0^2 + g_0 g_1 + g_0^2)^{-1} \\
d_1 &= g_1(g_0^2 + g_0 g_1 + g_1^2)^{-1}
\end{aligned}
$$

Since, for an element $g \in GF(2)$, we have $g^2 = g^{-1} = g$, one can further simplify the above equations to:

$$
\begin{aligned}
d_0 &= (g_0 + g_1)(g_0 + g_0 g_1 + g_0) = (g_1 + g_0) \\
d_1 &= g_1(g_0 + g_0 g_1 + g_1) = g_1
\end{aligned}
\tag{4.4}
$$

It should be observed that in all the above equations, a zero input is converted into an all zero output. Thus the special case is handled by the equations implicitly.

All the above equations can be used together to derive a compact inversion circuit for an element in $GF(2^8)$. The steps are summarized as follows:

1. Obtain a field isomorphism mapping of an element in $GF(2^8)$ to $GF((2^2)^2)^2$.

2. For a given element in $GF(2^8)$, we map it to $GF((2^2)^2)^2$.

3. We apply the Equations 4.1, 4.3, and 4.4 to obtain the complete inverse.

The field isomorphism can be obtained using Algorithm 1.3 presented in section 1.12.1. Another way of obtaining the mappings is explained below.

Say an element $g \in GF(2^8)$, which is the standard representation of an element of the state matrix of AES be denoted by the byte: $(g_7 g_6 g_5 g_4 g_3 g_2 g_1 g_0)$. The polynomial representing the byte is $g_7 X^7 + g_6 X^6 + g_5 X^5 + g_4 X^4 + g_3 X^3 + g_2 X^2 + g_1 X + g_0$. We map the element to a new element $(b_7 b_6 b_5 b_4 b_3 b_2 b_1 b_0)$ in a new basis. In polynomial basis, thus for $g \in GF(2^8)/GF(2^4)$ we have $g = \gamma_1 Y + \gamma_0$, where for each element $\gamma \in GF(2^4)/GF(2^2)$, $\gamma = \Gamma_1 Z + \Gamma_0$. Further each element $\Gamma \in GF(2^2)$ can be viewed as $(b_1 W + b_0)$, and can be represented as a pair of bits, $(b_1 b_0)$. Thus the relation between the two byte representations of g is as follows:

$$g_7 X^7 + g_6 X^6 + g_5 X^5 + g_4 X^4 + g_3 X^3 + g_2 X^2 + g_1 X + g_0$$
$$= [(b_7 W + b_6)Z + (b_5 W + b_4)]Y + [(b_3 W + b_2)Z + (b_1 W + b_0)]$$
$$= b_7(WZY) + b_6(ZY) + b_5(WY) + b_4(Y) + b_3(WZ) + b_2(Z) + b_1(W) + b_0$$

Thus the map is decided for a choice of the basis denoted by (Y, Z, W). As discussed these values are fixed by the choices of the parameters μ and N which fixes the polynomials $r(Y)$ and $s(Z)$. As an example, consider μ=0xEC and N=0xBC, then the basis choices are Y=0xFF, Z=0x5C, W=0xBD. Using this we have, WZY=0x60, ZY=0xBE, WY=0x49, Y=0xFF, WZ=0xEC, Z=0x5C, W=0xBD. The mapping can be represented in the form of a matrix:

$$\begin{pmatrix} g_7 \\ g_6 \\ g_5 \\ g_4 \\ g_3 \\ g_2 \\ g_1 \\ g_0 \end{pmatrix} = \begin{pmatrix} 0 & 1 & 0 & 1 & 1 & 0 & 1 & 0 \\ 1 & 0 & 1 & 1 & 1 & 1 & 0 & 0 \\ 1 & 1 & 0 & 1 & 1 & 0 & 1 & 0 \\ 0 & 1 & 0 & 1 & 0 & 1 & 1 & 0 \\ 0 & 1 & 1 & 1 & 1 & 1 & 1 & 0 \\ 0 & 1 & 0 & 1 & 1 & 1 & 1 & 0 \\ 0 & 1 & 0 & 1 & 0 & 0 & 0 & 0 \\ 0 & 0 & 1 & 1 & 0 & 0 & 1 & 1 \end{pmatrix} \begin{pmatrix} b_7 \\ b_6 \\ b_5 \\ b_4 \\ b_3 \\ b_2 \\ b_1 \\ b_0 \end{pmatrix}$$

The above matrix, denoted by X thus converts an element from $GF((2^2)^2)^2$ to $GF(2^8)$. The inverse mapping X^{-1} can be obtained by computing the inverse of the above matrix modulo 2.

Thus to compute the S-Box output for a given byte, we apply the transformation X^{-1}, then utilize the discussed circuitry to compute the inverse, finally we apply the transformation X to get the inverse. The affine mapping of the AES S-Box is applied to get the result. One can further experiment by combining the fixed linear transformation A of the affine map of the AES SubBytes with the transformation X. That is, we apply AX to the output inverse computed in the composite field. We leave the details of obtaining the corresponding matrices as an exercise to the reader.

As mentioned, the inversion circuit can also be developed in normal basis, which we discuss next.

4.3.3   Circuit Optimizations in the Normal Basis

For normal basis, the derivations of the inverse circuit is similar, except that the representation of the polynomial is slightly different. The most compact representation of the AES S-Box reported by [71] is where normal basis has been applied at all the three decomposition levels. We detail the derivations, and optimizations next.

In $GF(2^8)/GF(2^4)$ an element can be represented in the normal base (Y^{16}, Y) as $g = \gamma_1 Y^{16} + \gamma_0 Y$. If the corresponding inverse modulo $Y^2 + \tau Y + \mu$ is expressed as $(\delta_1 Y^{16} + \delta_0 Y)$, then we can equate the above product to $1 = \tau^{-1}(Y^{16} + Y)$ (refer Chapter 2). Equating the coefficients we have:

$$\delta_0 = [\gamma_1 \gamma_0 \tau^2 + (\gamma_1^2 + \gamma_0^2)\mu]^{-1}\gamma_1$$
$$\delta_1 = [\gamma_1 \gamma_0 \tau^2 + (\gamma_1^2 + \gamma_0^2)\mu]^{-1}\gamma_0$$

Analogously, an element in $GF(2^4)/GF(2^2)$ is expressed using the normal basis (Z^4, Z).

Let the inverse of an element in $GF(2^4)$, denoted as $\gamma = \Gamma_1 Z^4 + \Gamma_0 Z$, modulo $Z^2 + TZ + N$, is expressed as $\delta = \Delta_1 Z^4 + \Delta_0 Z$. Then we have the following relation:

$$\Delta_0 = [\gamma_1 \gamma_0 \tau^2 + (\gamma_1^2 + \gamma_0^2)N]^{-1}\Gamma_1$$
$$\Delta_1 = [\Gamma_1 \Gamma_0 T^2 + (\Gamma_1^2 + \Gamma_0^2)N]^{-1}\Gamma_0$$

Thus continuing, the inverse of an element of $GF(2^2)/GF(2)$ denoted as $g_1 W^2 + g_0 W$, modulo $W^2 + W + 1$ (basis is (W^2, W)), can be represented as $d_1 W^2 + d_0 W$. Thus we have the following equations, using similar simplifications used before for $GF(2)$ in case of polynomial basis.

$$d_0 = [g_1 g_0 + g_1 + g_0]g_1 = g_1$$
$$d_1 = [g_1 g_0 + g_1 + g_0]g_0 = g_0$$

The above equations lead to several optimizations and, like for the polynomial basis, can be simplified with prudent choices of the coefficients in the irreducible polynomials $r(Y)$ and $s(Z)$. It appears that setting $T = \tau = 1$ gives efficient circuits also for the normal basis. Likewise, the value of μ and N are selected as discussed before.

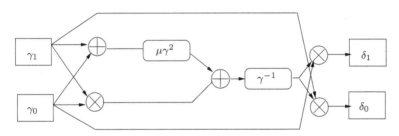

FIGURE 4.3: Normal $GF(2^8)$ Inverter

With the choice of $\tau = 1$, the circuit for the $GF(2^8)$ normal multiplier is depicted in **Fig 4.3**. The important blocks in the architecture are the scaling and squarer block, the $GF(2^4)$ inverse and the $GF(2^4)$ multipliers, all implemented in the normal basis.

Consider the multiplication of two elements $\gamma = \Gamma_1 Z^4 + \Gamma_0 Z$ and $\delta = \Delta_1 Z^4 + \Delta_0 Z$ in $GF(2^4)$. Since, the basis elements (Z^4, Z) are both roots of $s(Z)$, we have the following identities:

$$Z^2 = Z + N$$
$$Z^4 + Z = 1$$
$$Z(Z^4) = N$$

Using the above identities we can express the product $\gamma\delta$ as follows:

$$
\begin{aligned}
\gamma\delta &= \Gamma_1 \Delta_1 (Z^8) + Z^4 Z(\Gamma_1 \Delta_0 + \Delta_0 \Gamma_1) + \Gamma_0 \Delta_0 (Z^2) \\
&= \Gamma_1 \Delta_1 (Z^2 + 1) + N(\Gamma_1 \Delta_0 + \Gamma_0 \Delta_1) + \Gamma_0 \Delta_0 Z^2 \\
&= (Z + N)(\Gamma_1 \Delta_1 + \Gamma_0 \Delta_0) + (\Gamma_1 \Delta_1 + N(\Gamma_1 \Delta_0 + \Gamma_0 \Delta_1)) \\
&= Z(\Gamma_1 \Delta_1 + \Gamma_0 \Delta_0) + (N(\Gamma_1 \Delta_1 + \Gamma_0 \Delta_0) + (\Gamma_1 \Delta_1 + N(\Gamma_1 \Delta_0 + \Gamma_0 \Delta_1)))(Z^4 + Z) \\
&= Z^4(\Gamma_1 \Delta_1 + N(\Gamma_1 + \Gamma_0)(\Delta_1 + \Delta_0)) + Z(\Gamma_0 \Delta_0 + N(\Gamma_1 + \Gamma_0)(\Delta_1 + \Delta_0))
\end{aligned}
$$

The product thus has several multiplications in the subfield $GF(2^2)$. The subfield product $\Gamma\Delta = (g_1 W^2 + g_0 W)(d_1 W^2 + d_0)$ can be obtained as:

$$\Gamma\Delta = ((g_1 + g_0)(d_1 + d_0) + g_1 d_1)W^2 + ((g_1 + g_0)(d_1 + d_0) + g_0 d_0)W$$

The other important component in **Fig. 4.3** is the scaling of squaring of $\gamma = \Gamma_1 Z^4 + \Gamma_0 Z$, by $\mu = \Delta_1 Z^4 + \Delta_0 Z$. Thus we have:

$$\gamma^2 \;=\; (\Gamma_1^2 + N(\Gamma_1^2 + \Gamma_0^2))Z^4 + (\Gamma_0^2 + N(\Gamma_1^2 + \Gamma_0^2))Z$$

Thus the combination of scaling and squaring can be derived as:

$$
\begin{aligned}
\mu\gamma^2 \;&=\; (\Delta_1 Z^4 + \Delta_0 Z)(\Gamma_1^2 + N(\Gamma_1^2 + \Gamma_0^2))Z^4 + (\Gamma_0^2 + N(\Gamma_1^2 + \Gamma_0^2))Z \\
&=\; (\Gamma_1^2(\Delta_1 + N\Delta_0) + \Gamma_0^2(N\Delta_0))Z^4 + (\Gamma_1^2(N\Delta_1) + \Gamma_0^2(\Delta_0 + N\Delta_1))Z
\end{aligned}
$$

For further optimization we choose μ such that $\Delta_1 = N\Delta_0$, then we have:

$$
\begin{aligned}
\mu\gamma^2 \;&=\; (\Gamma_0^2(N\Delta_0))Z^4 + (\Gamma_1^2(N^2\Delta_0) + \Gamma_0^2(\Delta_0 + N^2\Delta_0))Z \\
&=\; (\Gamma_0^2(N\Delta_0))Z^4 + (\Gamma_1^2(N^2\Delta_0) + \Gamma_0^2(\Delta_0(1 + N^2)))Z \\
&=\; (\Gamma_0^2(N\Delta_0))Z^4 + (\Gamma_1^2(N^2\Delta_0) + \Gamma_0^2(N\Delta_0))Z
\end{aligned}
$$

Thus the squaring and scaling operation can be done by two scalings and one addition. Note that the squaring operations in the above equations are in $GF(2^2)$ and are free! To see, we assume the basis as (W^2, W) and use the fact that for any non-zero $W \in GF(2^2)$ $W^4 = W$. Thus the squaring operation in $GF(2^2)$ in normal basis can be expressed as $(g_1 W^2 + g_0 W)^2 = g_0 W^2 + g_1 W$ which is just the swap of the input.

Likewise, for a choice of $T = 1$, the inversion circuit in the subfield $GF(2^4)$ is shown in **Fig. 4.4**. This consists of operations like multiplication and squaring and scaling in the subfield $GF(2^2)$.

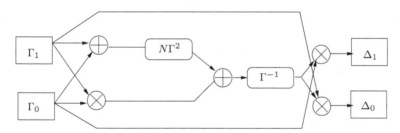

FIGURE 4.4: Normal $GF(2^4)$ Inverter

The circuit for squaring and scaling in $GF(2^2)$ can be simplified by assuming the choices of N which can be W or W^2. In any case, we need both a W-scaler and W^2-scaler in the circuit of squaring and scaling in $GF(2^2)$. Hence we have:

$$
\begin{aligned}
W(g_1 W^2 + g_0 W) \;&=\; (g_1 + g_0)W^2 + g_1 W \\
W^2(g_1 W^2 + g_0 W) \;&=\; g_0 W^2 + (g_1 + g_0)W
\end{aligned}
$$

The change in basis from the polynomial representation of AES to a normal basis representation can be obtained as when we converted to the polynomial basis.

Consider an element $g \in GF(2^8)$, which is an element of the state matrix of AES, and represented in the standard way. Let it be denoted by the byte: $(g_7 g_6 g_5 g_4 g_3 g_2 g_1 g_0)$. The polynomial representing the byte is $g_7 X^7 + g_6 X^6 + g_5 X^5 + g_4 X^4 + g_3 X^3 + g_2 X^2 + g_1 X + g_0$. We map the element to a new element $(b_7 b_6 b_5 b_4 b_3 b_2 b_1 b_0)$ in a new basis. In normal basis, thus for $g \in GF(2^8)/GF(2^4)$ we have $g = \gamma_1 Y^{16} + \gamma_0 Y$, where for each element $\gamma \in GF(2^4)/GF(2^2)$, $\gamma = \Gamma_1 Z^4 + \Gamma_0 Z$. Further each element $\Gamma \in GF(2^2)$ can be viewed as $(b_1 W^2 + b_0 W)$, and can be represented as a pair of bits, $(b_1 b_0)$. Thus the relation between the two byte representations of g is as follows:

$$
\begin{aligned}
& g_7 X^7 + g_6 X^6 + g_5 X^5 + g_4 X^4 + g_3 X^3 + g_2 X^2 + g_1 X + g_0 \\
= & [(b_7 W^2 + b_6 W) Z^4 + (b_5 W^2 + b_4 W)] Y^{16} + [(b_3 W^2 + b_2 W) Z^4 + (b_1 W^2 + b_0 W) Z] \\
= & b_7 (W^2 Z^4 Y^{16}) + b_6 (W Z^4 Y^{16}) + b_5 (W^2 Z Y^{16}) + b_4 (W Z Y^{16}) + b_3 (W^2 Z^4 Y) \\
& + b_2 (W Z^4 Y) + b_1 (W^2 Z Y) + b_0 (W Z Y)
\end{aligned}
$$

Thus the map is decided for a choice of the basis denoted by (Y, Z, W). As before for polynomial basis the basis values are chosen by fixing Y=0xFF, Z=0x5C, W=0xBD (note here, $N = W^2$). Using this we have, $W^2 Z^4 Y^{16}$=0x64, $W Z^4 Y^{16}$=0x78, $W^2 Z Y^{16}$=0x6E, $W Z Y^{16}$=0x8C, $W^2 Z^4 Y$=0x68, $W Z^4 Y$=0x29, $W^2 Z Y$=0xDE, $W Z Y$=0x60.

The mapping can be represented in the form of a matrix:

$$
\begin{pmatrix} g_7 \\ g_6 \\ g_5 \\ g_4 \\ g_3 \\ g_2 \\ g_1 \\ g_0 \end{pmatrix} =
\begin{pmatrix}
0 & 0 & 0 & 1 & 0 & 0 & 1 & 0 \\
1 & 1 & 1 & 0 & 1 & 0 & 1 & 1 \\
1 & 1 & 1 & 0 & 1 & 1 & 0 & 1 \\
0 & 1 & 0 & 0 & 0 & 0 & 1 & 0 \\
0 & 1 & 1 & 1 & 1 & 1 & 1 & 0 \\
1 & 0 & 1 & 1 & 0 & 0 & 1 & 0 \\
0 & 0 & 1 & 0 & 0 & 0 & 1 & 0 \\
0 & 0 & 0 & 0 & 0 & 1 & 0 & 0
\end{pmatrix}
\begin{pmatrix} b_7 \\ b_6 \\ b_5 \\ b_4 \\ b_3 \\ b_2 \\ b_1 \\ b_0 \end{pmatrix}
$$

The above transformation denoted by the basis change matrix T can be inverted to obtain the matrix T^{-1} which converts an element from $GF(2^8)$ to $GF((2^2)^2)^2$ in normal basis at each level of the decomposition. The inverse is then computed by the above circuits, the result is finally multiplied with T to obtain the result in the standard polynomial basis of AES. The affine transformation matrix A can be combined with T to allow further optimizations.

4.3.4 Most Compact Realization: Polynomial vs. Normal basis

It may be observed from the above discussions that with most of the optimization tricks, both polynomial and normal basis offers the same level of compactness. The inverter circuits of $GF(2^8)$ require the same number of components: 2 adders, 3 multiplications, 1 squarer and scaler, 1 inversion circuit in the subfield $GF(2^4)$. The same is true for the internal fields.

Both the polynomial and normal basis offer opportunities for very efficient computations. As discussed before, in the field $GF(2^2)$ the squaring and scaling is free in the polynomial basis, while the square is free in normal basis. The main difference between the two bases occurs in the combined squarer and scaling operation in the field $GF(2^4)$. As mentioned in [71] we summarize the discussions in Table 4.1 and Table 4.2. The first two columns shows the values of μ which as discussed before has 8 values. The corresponding computations for performing squaring and scaling is also detailed for both the bases. The corresponding number of XOR gates is also detailed. As can be observed that the number of XOR gates varies depending on the basis of the underlying field $GF(2^2)$ and the value of w. To explain consider the case when $\mu = N^2 Z + 1$, assuming a polynomial basis for the field $GF(2^4)$. Thus, as $N \in GF(2^2)$, we have $N^3 = 1$. Further, the basis Z is the root of $Z^2 + Z + N = 0$, where $N^2 + N + 1 = 0$. Using this fact, $\mu^4 = N^2 Z^2 + N^2$, $\mu^3 = N^2 Z^2 + Z + 1$, $\mu^2 = NZ^2 + 1$. Thus, $\mu^4 + \mu^3 + \mu^2 + \mu + 1 = N^2 + Z(1 + N^2) + NZ^2 = N^2 + N(Z + Z^2) = 0$, thus showing that μ is a root of the irreducible polynomial $x^4 + x^3 + x^2 + x + 1$. Thus, the square and scale operation is equal to $[(N^4 + 1)A^2 + N^2 B^2]Z + [(N^2 + 1)NA^2 + B^2] = N^2(A + B)^2 Z + [N^2(A + B)^2 + NB^2]$. The underlying operations are in $GF(2^2)$.

When the underlying field operations are performed in normal basis, squaring is free and squaring and scaling with $N = W$ and $N = W^2$ both requires one XOR. Thus to sum up, the computation of $A + B$ requires 2 XORs, the two scalings with N and N^2 each require one XOR, and the sum $N^2(A + B)^2 + NB^2$ requires 2 XORs, thus totalling 6 XORs.

When the underlying field uses polynomial basis, and $W = N$, the underlying operations are squaring and scaling and additions. The squaring and scaling is with $N = W$ and $N^2 = W^2$. The squaring and scaling with $N = W$ is free in the polynomial basis, while that for $N^2 = W^2$ requires 1 XOR. The sum $A + B$ and $N^2(A + B)^2 + NB^2$ requires 2 XORs each, thus requiring 5 XORs in total. Similarly, when the underlying polynomial basis is such that $W = N^2$, we have the squaring and scaling with N free, while that with N^2 requiring 1 XOR. This does not change the total number of XOR operations, and keeps it 5.

An important point to address at this juncture, is the number of XOR gates required in the $GF(2^4)$ inverter for the above basis choices. It may be recollected that for the polynomial basis $GF(2^4)$ inverter, the main underlying operations are a squaring and scaling with N and an inverse in $GF(2^2)$. When the underlying field $GF(2^2)$ is implemented with normal basis, the inverse is free (being equivalent to the square in $GF(2^2)$) and the scaling and squaring requires always 1 XOR, irrespective of whether the scaling and squaring is with N or N^2. However, when the underlying fields are in polynomial basis, the inversion requires 1 XOR. But the scaling and squarer is free when $N = W$, while it requires 1 XOR when $N = W^2$.

Coefficients and Operations in $GF(2^2)$			XOR Gates		
$\mu =$		$\mu(AZ + B)^2 =$	polynomial $GF(2^2)$		normal
$CZ + D$		$(CN^2 + D)A^2 + CB^2]Z + [(C + D)NA^2 + DB^2]$	$w = N$	$w = N^2$	$GF(2^2)$
N	0	$A^2 + NB^2$	$N^2 A^2$	4	4	4
N^2	0	$NA^2 + N^2 B^2$	A^2	4	4	4
N	N	$N^2 A^2 + NB^2$	NB^2	3	3	4
N^2	N^2	$A^2 + N^2 B^2$	$N^2 B^2$	4	3	3
N	1	NB^2	$(A + B)^2$	3	3	3
N^2	N	$N^2 B^2$	$N(A + B)^2$	3	3	4
N	N^2	$N(A + B)^2$	$N(A + B)^2 + B^2$	5	6	5
N^2	1	$N^2(A + B)^2$	$N^2(A + B)^2 + NB^2$	5	5	6

TABLE 4.1: XOR count of Square and Scaling circuit for $GF(2^4)$ Polynomial Basis

From the above tables, we observe that the choice of the basis plays a crucial role in determining the overall number of gates of the AES S-Box, which is based on the finite field inverse in $GF(2^8)$. However, it may be also noted that the difference in the largest and smallest inversion is only 4 XORs (considering the above optimizations in the square and scaling, and the inversion in the field $GF(2^2)$). Hence, the other optimizations for

Coefficients and Operations in $GF(2^2)$				XOR Gates		
$\mu =$		$\mu(AZ^4+BZ)^2 =$		polynomial $GF(2^2)$		normal
CZ^4+DZ		$(CN^2+D)A^2+CB^2]Z^4+[(C+D)NA^2+DB^2]Z$		$w=N$	$w=N^2$	$GF(2^2)$
N	0	NA^2	$N^2(A+B)^2$	3	3	4
0	N	$N^2(A+B)^2$	NB^2	3	3	4
N^2	0	N^2A^2	$(A+B)^2$	4	3	3
0	N^2	$(A+B)^2$	N^2B^2	4	3	3
N	1	NB^2	$N^2A^2+NB^2$	3	3	4
1	N	$NA^2+N^2B^2$	NA^2	3	3	4
N^2	1	A^2+NB^2	A^2	3	4	3
1	N^2	B^2	NA^2+B^2	3	4	3

TABLE 4.2: XOR count of Square and Scaling circuit for $GF(2^4)$ Normal Basis

implementing the change in representations (basis) at the input and output of the inverter, the affine transformations needs to be done carefully.

The authors in [71] shows further optimizations, some of which are generic for any hardware platform, others which are more specific to ASIC libraries. We highlight two generic techniques in the following.

4.3.5　Common Subexpressions

There are further scopes of optimizations when the circuit is observed as a hierarchical structure, and not composed of isolated blocks. To highlight, consider the $GF(2^4)$ multiplier architecture in the polynomial basis. As shown in **Fig. 4.5**, if two multipliers share a 4-bit input or factor (one of the terms being multiplied), then as each multiplier requires the sum of the high and low halves of each factor, one of the XORs can be shared.

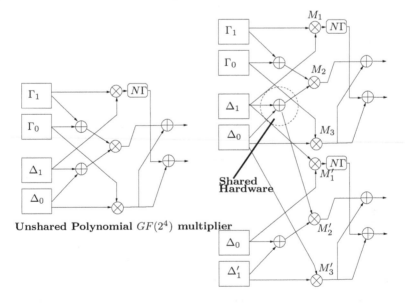

FIGURE 4.5: Polynomial $GF(2^4)$ Multiplier Sharing a Common Input

Further, it can be observed that the multipliers have three smaller multipliers in $GF(2^2)$

which share inputs in $GF(2^2)$. For example, the pair of multipliers which share an input are labeled as (M_1, M_1'), (M_2, M_2'), (M_3, M_3'). These multipliers using the same logic, can each share a 2-bit XOR. Thus we have a total saving of 5 XORs. The same saving is obtained in the context of a multiplier in $GF(2^4)$ in normal basis and sharing a common input.

Now consider the effect of these optimizations in the $GF(2^8)$ and $GF(2^4)$ inverters in the polynomial and normal basis. Refer to the **Fig. 4.1** for the polynomial $GF(2^8)$ inversion circuit. We observe that the three multipliers has two sharings of a common input. However there is a pairing of the multipliers for which there is no sharing. The same fact holds for the polynomial inversion circuit for $GF(2^4)$ as well. However, if we observe the circuit diagram for **Fig. 4.4**, we observe that the three multipliers pairwise have a common input, which leads to an additional saving of 5 XORs, for the previously mentioned reason. This leads to a significant saving, and makes the normal basis an ideal choice for a compact realization of the AES S-Box.

4.3.6 Merging of Basis Change Matrix and Affine Mapping

The architecture heavily employs basis changes and transformation among three isomorphic fields, using two different basis choices, namely polynomial and normal. We focus on the normal basis representation for the above mentioned reasons. As discussed, the basis transformation can be obtained through the matrix multiplication, T^{-1}. The converted elements are then inverted using the above mentioned circuits, and then again brought back to the field $GF(2^8)$ in the AES representation by applying the matrix T. Subsequently, we perform the affine mapping by the matrices A and the vector B to complete the S-Box computation. Let us denote the inversion circuit in normal basis by f_{norm}. For an input byte $x \in GF(2^8)$, we summarize the steps as follows:

$$x' = T^{-1}(x) \tag{4.5}$$
$$x'' = f_{norm}(x') \tag{4.6}$$
$$x''' = T(x'') \tag{4.7}$$
$$y = A(x''') + B \tag{4.8}$$

Thus, we can combine the last two steps by performing the two matrix multiplications in a merged step, (AT). Likewise for the inverse S-Box computation, one can merge the steps as $(AT)^{-1}$.

Each such matrix multiplication operating on constant 0-1 matrices gives further scopes of sharing hardware. If we are able to find out combinations of input bits that are shared between different output bits, we can combine the common inputs and then use the output as a temporary input to generate the other output bits. This can lead to further saving in area. One can apply search techniques to find out the minimal circuit. The greedy method, as the name suggests will involve finding out at each stage two inputs, which are shared by maximum number of common outputs. Then a temporary signal is derived using the XOR of the chosen inputs. This temporary signal is used as a new input and the process is repeated. It must be noted that though the greedy approach is easy to implement, may not lead to the minimal circuit. More sophisticated search techniques can be employed to derive the most compact circuit.

4.3.7 Merged S-Box and Inverse S-Box

It is often to have both the S-Box and the inverse to be implemented in the same hardware. The above technique for sharing hardware during the transformations can be employed for compactness. Thus, given an input x, $T^{-1}(x)$ for encryption and $(AT)^{-1}(x+B)$ for decryption are computed. The output byte y is then processed by $(AT)y + B$ or Ty for encryption or decryption respectively. With this merging, thus one can optimize both the basis change matrices, namely T^{-1} and (AT) together as a 16×8 matrices. These bigger matrices provides further scope of optimizations because larger the number of rows, more the chance of finding commonalities for optimizations.

In [71], there are further optimizations suggested for ASIC designs. For modern technolgies, like $0.13~\mu$ CMOS cell libraries, a NAND gate is smaller than an AND gate. Since the AND gates are always involved in the $GF(2^2)$ multiplier and are combined by the XOR gates, in the following form: $[(aANDb)XOR(cANDd)]$, the AND gates can be combined by using the $[(aNANDb)XOR(cNANDd)]$. Further in the library if we find the XNOR to be of the same size as an XOR, then when in the affine transformation the vector B has ones, then using the XNOR saves the extra NOT gate. However when the matrix A is such that only one input bit affects the output bit, then the NOT gate is used. In the inverter circuit, whenever the XORs are combined using the following combination: $a \oplus b \oplus (ab)$, then can replace them by the equivalent OR gate. If the NAND gate is used, as mentioned before we have the NOR gates, which is even more compact than the OR gate. Multiplexors are used to implement the selection function needed to implement both the S-Box and the inverse S-Box.

Combining all these techniques, the complete merged S-Box and the inverse circuit is equivalent to 234 NAND gate. Stand-alone S-Box takes 180 gates, while the inverse takes 182 gates. According to [71], the optimizations lead to a 20% saving of resources. This makes the design suitable for area-limited hardware implementations, including smart cards.

In the following section, we describe implementation aspects of the remaining transformations of the AES hardware. We first consider the MixColumns transformation.

4.4   Implementation of the MixColumns Transformation

The MixColumns transformation comprises of pre-multiplying a column of the state matrix, denoted by $(a, b, c, d)^T$ with the matrix:

$$M = \begin{pmatrix} 2 & 3 & 1 & 1 \\ 1 & 2 & 3 & 1 \\ 1 & 1 & 2 & 3 \\ 3 & 1 & 1 & 2 \end{pmatrix}$$

The corresponding output column $(A, B, C, D)^T$ is thus computed as:

$$
\begin{aligned}
A &= 2a + 3b + c + d \\
B &= a + 2b + 3c + d \\
C &= a + b + 2c + 3d \\
D &= 3a + b + c + 2d
\end{aligned}
$$

The previous computation is quite advantageous as multiplication by 2, can be performed as:

$$
2x = \begin{cases} x \ll 2 & \text{if MSB}(x) = 0 \\ (x \ll 2)\&(1B)_{16} & \text{else if MSB}(x) = 1 \end{cases}
\tag{4.9}
$$

Multiplication by 3 can be performed easily by multiplying by 2, and then adding to itself. The overall architecture is depicted in **Fig. 4.6**. Note that the key mixing (XORing) has been combined with the final XORings. Considering the fact that all modern FPGAs are four input LUTs this saves using additional LUTs.

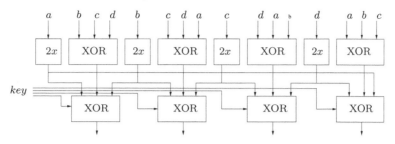

FIGURE 4.6: MixColumns and Key XORing Combined to Save LUTs

4.4.1 The AES S-Box and MixColumns

As discussed before, a very effective way of obtaining a compact AES S-Box hardware is to use the concept of composite fields. Often the input byte is transformed to the composite fields, the S-Box is computed in the subfield and the result is brought back to the field $GF(2^8)$ as specified in the AES documentation. However such a transformation also incurs delay in the computations. Hence there are some published documents which convert the entire AES description to the subfield. In such designs, even the MixColumns needs to be transformed into the subfield.

Say, the hardware performs all its operations in the field $GF(2^4)^2$. Let the matrix T transforming an element in $GF(2^8)$ to $GF(2^4)^2$ be:

$$T = \begin{pmatrix} 1 & 0 & 1 & 0 & 0 & 0 & 0 & 0 \\ 1 & 0 & 1 & 0 & 1 & 1 & 0 & 0 \\ 1 & 1 & 0 & 1 & 0 & 0 & 1 & 0 \\ 0 & 1 & 1 & 1 & 0 & 0 & 0 & 0 \\ 1 & 1 & 0 & 0 & 0 & 1 & 1 & 0 \\ 0 & 1 & 0 & 1 & 0 & 0 & 1 & 0 \\ 0 & 0 & 0 & 0 & 1 & 0 & 1 & 0 \\ 1 & 1 & 0 & 1 & 1 & 1 & 0 & 1 \end{pmatrix}$$

The entire MixColumns matrix is thus transformed with this mapping. Hence the transformed MixColumns matrix is denoted as:

$$M = \begin{pmatrix} T(2) & T(3) & T(1) & T(1) \\ T(1) & T(2) & T(3) & T(1) \\ T(1) & T(1) & T(2) & T(3) \\ T(3) & T(1) & T(1) & T(2) \end{pmatrix}$$

In order to compute the output of this transformed MixColumns matrix, it is thus needed to compute the products of the input bytes and $T(2)$ and $T(3)$. It may be noted that due to the transformations the matrix elements becomes less amenable to efficient designs, than the original values, namely 2 and 3. However one can obtain a compact design in the following way.

Let the irreducible polynomial for the field $GF(2^4)^2$ be denoted by $x^2 + x + \alpha^{14}$, where α is the primitive element of $GF(2^4)$. One can check that $T(2) = 00101110 = (\alpha^{11} + x\alpha)$. Let an input byte be represented as $(a_0 + a_1 x)$.

Thus we have using $\alpha^{15} = 1$:

$$
\begin{aligned}
T(2)(a_0 + a_1 x) &= a_0 x \alpha + a_1 x^2 \alpha + a_0 \alpha^{11} + a_1 x \alpha^{11} \\
&= a_0 x \alpha + a_1 (x + \alpha^{14}) \alpha + a_0 \alpha^{11} + a_1 x \alpha^{11} \\
&= [(\alpha(a_1 + a_0)) + a_1 \alpha^{11}]x + [a_1 + \alpha^{11} a_0] \\
T(3)(a_0 + a_1 x) &= T(2)(a_0 + a_1 x) + T(1)(a_0 + a_1 x) \\
&= [a_1 + \alpha^{11} a_0 + a_0] + x[(\alpha(a_1 + a_0)) + \alpha^{11} a_1 + a_1]
\end{aligned}
$$

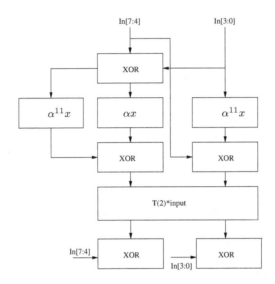

FIGURE 4.7: The MixColumns architecture in a composite field

4.4.2   Implementing the Inverse MixColumns

The inverse MixColumns matrix is obtained by finding the inverse of the matrix M, of course the operations being in the field $GF(2^8)$ and $x^8 + x^4 + x^3 + x + 1$ as the irreducible polynomial. The inverse matrix is:

$$
M-1 = \begin{pmatrix} 0E & 0B & 0D & 09 \\ 09 & 0E & 0B & 0D \\ 0D & 09 & 0E & 0B \\ 0B & 0D & 09 & 0E \end{pmatrix}
$$

As may be observed that the elements of the inverse MixColumns matrix have larger Hamming weights than the elements of the MixColumns matrix. However one can obtain an efficient deisgn using the following observation [332].

$$
\begin{pmatrix} 0E & 0B & 0D & 09 \\ 09 & 0E & 0B & 0D \\ 0D & 09 & 0E & 0B \\ 0B & 0D & 09 & 0E \end{pmatrix} = \begin{pmatrix} 02 & 03 & 01 & 01 \\ 01 & 02 & 03 & 01 \\ 01 & 01 & 02 & 03 \\ 03 & 01 & 01 & 02 \end{pmatrix} \begin{pmatrix} 05 & 00 & 04 & 00 \\ 00 & 05 & 00 & 04 \\ 04 & 00 & 05 & 00 \\ 00 & 04 & 00 & 05 \end{pmatrix}
$$

The above equation is useful as we reuse the output of the MixColumns transformation. This is quite handy when the same hardware supports both encryption and decryption.

Also note that the elements of the second matrix above are more easy to multiply as the Hamming weights of them are smaller compared to the original elements of the inverse MixColumns matrix.

As discussed earlier, for an implementation where the entire operation is performed in the subfield, the elements are transformed by the conversion matrix T, and subsequently multiplied with the input byte. As an example, consider the element $0e$, which is transformed to $T(0e) = 24$. Thus,

$$
\begin{aligned}
(2x + 4)(ax + b) &= 2ax^2 + x(2b + 4a) + 4b \\
&= 2a(x + \alpha^{14}) + x(2b + 4a) + 4b \\
&= 2ax + a((\alpha)(\alpha^{14}) + x(2b + 4a) + 4b, \text{ since } \alpha = 02 \\
&= x(2a + 2b + 4a) + (a + 4b) \\
&= x(2b + 6a) + (a + 4b).
\end{aligned}
$$

4.5 An Example Reconfigurable Design for the Rijndael Cryptosystem

In this section, the above techniques are used to design a reconfigurable design for the Rijndael-AES cryptosystem, supporting all the three versions for the data as well as the three key sizes, namely 128, 192, and 256 bits [25]. The reconfigurable architecture of the AES cryptosystem is capable of handling all possible combinations of the data and key bits, and thus imposes challenge to reduce the hardware resource of the design. The fully rolled inner-pipelined architecture ensures lesser hardware complexity. Additionally we stress on the iterated architecture as opposed to a pipelined architecture, as the later is unable to lead to any improvement in throughput when the block cipher is used for a desirable Cipher Block Chain (CBC) mode. It may be recalled that the AES specification is only for 128 bit datapath, but in this section by AES we shall refer to the original Rijndael algorithm which supports also the other two sizes of data block.

The design is developed using the above concepts of efficient and compact AES design, using the concepts of hardware design ensuring that the datapath and controlpath are properly separated. The datapath comprises of the AES round transformations in a composite field $GF(2^4)^2$. Thus the S-Box and the MixColumns are all described in the subfield. The complete design uses combinational logic, thus eliminating any requirement for internal memory to store the S-Box elements. The controller has been designed using the concepts of finite state machines, and reconfigures efficiently the hardware for AES using different key lengths.

4.5.1 Overview of the Design

Fig. 4.8 provides a top-level overview on the architecture of the design. The design has an 8-bit interface, and comprises of the *DataScheduler* block which converts an 8-bit input element in $GF(2^8)$ to an element in $GF((2^4)^2)$ using an isomorphic function δ. The *Data-Converter* does the reverse mapping (**Fig. 4.8**). The crux of the design is the *Encryption unit*, the *Key-Scheduler*, ,and the *Control Unit*. Both the Encryption and the Key-Scheduler has been designed ensuring that the hardware is shared and rolling of architecture is done

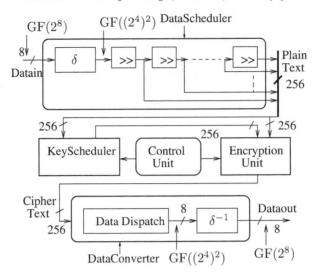

FIGURE 4.8: Top-Level Architecture [25]

to save area resources. All computations involving the S-Box, MixColumns have been performed using logic gates, removing completely any memory elements.

4.5.1.1   Encryption Unit

During encryption, the data are organized conceptually in an 4×8 matrix of bytes. This organization is used for data block sizes of 256 bits. For smaller data block sizes (128 or 192 bits), the leftmost columns of the matrix are unused. The encryption unit is fully rolled which ensures a reduction in hardware. It has been implemented with inner pipelining technique for reduction of the combinational path delay. Pipelining and Serializing are two different design styles which are adopted by designers for achieving various levels of performance. We discuss them briefly.

4.5.1.2   Pipelining and Serializing in FPGAs

Pipelining have been used by several designs of block ciphers, owing to their iterative nature. Block ciphers are typically implemented as shown in the basic architecture of **Fig. 4.9**. The multiplexer and the combinational logic implementing the round is separated by a register stage, which helps to store temporary data as well as ensures that the critical path of the design is shorter. This helps to achieve a high operating frequency of the clock.

The clock frequency can be further improved by introducing inner pipeline stages. These are further register stages placed inside a round. Optimal placement of these registers is crucial to ensure that the critical path is divided into fragments of equal length. This helps to obtain a further speed up in the clock frequency. Moreover the register stages could be placed in between the rounds also, the concept called as outer pipelining. It may be kept in mind that all these stages introduces further area requirements in the hardware. However the FPGAs are composed of slices, which are made of LUTs and flip-flops. Hence when the combinational logic utilizes the LUTs, the flip-flops can be occupied by the register stages. This implies that larger pipeline stages does not necessarily bloat the design, if properly monitored. The above stages of pipelines can also provide parallelism to the modes of encryption which support them, like countermode, Output Feedback Mode (OFB). However the Cipher Block Chaining (CBC) does not gain any advantage owing to the parallelism,

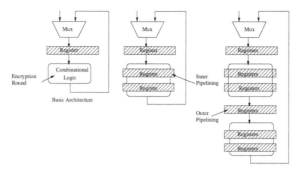

FIGURE 4.9: Pipelining of the Encryption Unit

as the algorithm is inherently not capable to taking advantage of this feature. Hence, one can obtain nice performance if the above alternatives, design choices, and the application are considered while architecting a hardware for an encryption unit.

4.5.1.3 Back to the Design

The encryption data path is detailed in **Fig. 4.10**. It processes 32-byte block in parallel. A complete round transformation executes in two clock cycles. Each transformation is optimized appropriately for maximal performance. The data flow through various parts of the unit are controlled by three control signals, namely *Data_enable*, *Addkey_enable* and *Last_round*, that are generated by the control unit. Due to its rolling technique the design can support all standard modes of encryption operation including CBC, OFB etc.

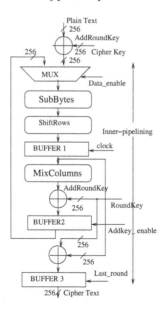

FIGURE 4.10: The Encryption Unit

The central blocks of the design are the SubBytes and the MixColumns transformations. The major computation inside S-Box is to find out the multiplicative inverse of an element in the finite field $GF(2^8)$. As discussed before using composite fields several authors attempted to reduce the area requirement of the S-Box [348, 410, 150]. Significant research and several techniques as presented in the compact designs of [71] were also proposed to realize compact AES S-Box.

A simple three-stage strategy is used as shown in **Fig. 4.11** to realize the AES S-Box [25, 4]:

- Map the element X $\in GF(2^8)$ to a composite field $F \in GF(2^4)^2)$ using an isomorphic function δ [347].

- Compute the multiplicative inverse over the field $F \in GF(2^4)^2)$.

- Finally map the computation result back to the original field using the inverse function δ^{-1}.

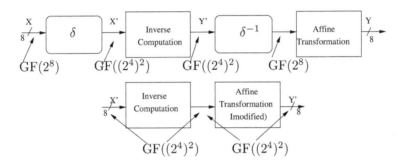

FIGURE 4.11: Structure of Different S-Boxes

For processing the entire 128-bit data in *SubBytes* operations, we can use 32 isomorphic functions (δ and δ^{-1}) parallely, 16 for mapping $GF(2^8)$ elements to $GF((2^4)^2)$ elements and 16 for reverse conversion. On the contrary, we use only two isomorphic functions δ and δ^{-1}: one in the *DataScheduler* and another in the *DataConverter* (**Fig. 4.8**). The idea to reduce the number of isomorphic mappings to one at the start of encryption and the reverse at the end of it was applied to designs in [266, 4].

The function δ converts an element x in $GF(2^8)$ to an element in $GF((2^4)^2)$ (refer Section 2.4.1). The function δ is defined as $\delta(x) = $ T.x, where T is the transformation matrix. The inverse mapping is performed by the function δ^{-1}. We have not used any transformation function (δ or δ^{-1}) in the S-Box operation (**Fig. 4.11**).

The elements of the standard affine matrix of AES is transformed and is defined over the composite field $GF((2^4)^2)$.

As discussed in Section 2.3.3.1, Y $= $ A$X^{-1} + $ B. In the composite field,

$$Y' = \delta(Y) \quad = \quad \delta(AX^{-1}) + \delta(B) \tag{4.10}$$
$$= \quad \delta(A\delta^{-1}(\delta(X^{-1}))) + \delta(B) \tag{4.11}$$
$$= \quad A'X' + B' \tag{4.12}$$

where $A' = \delta A \delta^{-1}$, $B' = \delta(B)$, and $X' = \delta(X^{-1})$.

Now, because of the isomorphism established by the mapping δ, we have the following for any $X \in GF(2^8)$:

$$\delta^{-1}(\delta(X))^{-1} = X^{-1}$$

Thus, $X' = (\delta(X))^{-1}$, and hence the equation $Y' = A'(X') + B'$ is exactly like the affine transformation of the SubBytes operation in the description of AES. Only here the computation is performed on X' which is the result of the inverse computed in the composite field $GF(2^4)$. The matrices A' and B' can be computed using the above transformations.

The *SubBytes* (S-Box) transformation is carried out in our design over the composite field $GF((2^4)^2)$ using the technique suggested in section 2.4.2. We summarize here for convenience.

Every $X \in GF((2^4)^2)$ can be represented as $(ax + b)$. As discussed before, the multiplicative inverse for an arbitrary polynomial $(ax + b)$ is given by: $(ax + b)^{-1} = a(a^2\lambda + ab + b^2)^{-1}x + (a+b)(a^2\lambda + ab + b^2)^{-1}$, where λ is a primitive element of $GF(2^4)$.

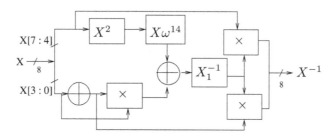

FIGURE 4.12: Structure of Inversion Calculation

Fig. 4.12 depicts the corresponding block-diagram of the three stage inverse circuit. The field polynomial used for the computations in $GF(2^4)$ is $(x^4 + x + 1)$. The multiplication employs modulo arithmetic of an irreducible polynomial $(x^2 + x + \lambda)$, where λ is a primitive in $GF(2^4)$. There are various polynomials, out of which we choose the one with $\lambda = \omega^{14}$, where $\omega = (0010)_2$ is an element in $GF(2^4)$ [4]. The above circuit can be realized in standard cell using 273 gates.

A key point to be kept in mind is that depending on the values of λ, the values of the matrix T can change. Further, the number of ones in the Affine transformation matrix also should be noted. For example, with the above transformation to the composite field, the matrix A is transformed to A' where:

$$
\mathbf{A}' = \begin{pmatrix}
0 & 0 & 1 & 0 & 1 & 0 & 0 & 0 \\
0 & 1 & 0 & 1 & 0 & 0 & 0 & 1 \\
0 & 0 & 1 & 0 & 0 & 1 & 0 & 0 \\
0 & 0 & 0 & 0 & 0 & 0 & 0 & 1 \\
1 & 0 & 1 & 0 & 0 & 1 & 0 & 0 \\
0 & 1 & 0 & 0 & 0 & 1 & 0 & 1 \\
0 & 0 & 1 & 0 & 1 & 0 & 1 & 0 \\
0 & 0 & 0 & 1 & 0 & 0 & 0 & 0
\end{pmatrix}
\tag{4.13}
$$

The total number of 1-entries in the fixed affine matrix A is equal to 40 (refer section 2.3.3.1). The total number of 1-entries in the new affine matrix A' is equal to 18. Implementing the matrices in a straightforward way, the number of XORs would be equal to the number of 1-entries minus the number of rows in the matrices. This would lead to an XOR gate count of 10, which results in a reduction of 22 XOR gates.

The implementation of the MixColumns is performed as discussed in Section 4.4.1. The other important component in the design of the AES architecture is the Key-Schedule, which we discuss next.

4.5.2   Key-Schedule Optimization

The Key-Schedule algorithm as described in section 2.3.3.4, supports key expansion for 128, 192, and 256 bits. In the following we present an architecture for the key scheduling or expansion algorithm, where all the computations occur wordwise ie. on 32-bits. Let N_k denotes the length of the key divided by 32 and N_b denotes the length of the data block divided by 32. Let W[0],...,W[N_k-1] be the N_k columns of the original key. These N_k columns can be iteratively expanded to obtain $N_k \times N_r$ more columns (RoundKey), where N_r is the number of rounds. The values of N_r are determined from the Table 4.3.

TABLE 4.3: Numbers of rounds (N_r) as a function of the block and key length

N_r	N_b=4	N_b=6	N_b=8
N_k=4	10	12	14
N_k=6	12	12	14
N_k=8	14	14	14

Recalling algorithm 6, suppose that all columns up to W[i-1] have been expanded. The next column W[i] can be constructed as follows:

$$W[i] = \begin{cases} W[i\text{-}N_k]\oplus T(W[i\text{-}1]) & \text{if } i \bmod N_k =4 (N_k = 8) \\ W[i\text{-}N_k]\oplus T(W[i\text{-}1],\text{Rcon}) & \text{if } i \bmod N_k = 0 \\ W[i\text{-}N_k]\oplus W[i\text{-}1]) & \text{otherwise} \end{cases}$$

Here T(W[i-1],Rcon) is a non-linear transformation based on the application of the S-Box to the four bytes of the column, and the addition of a round constant (Rcon) for symmetry elimination (refer Algorithm 6). T(W[i-1]) represents the same without addition of Rcon.

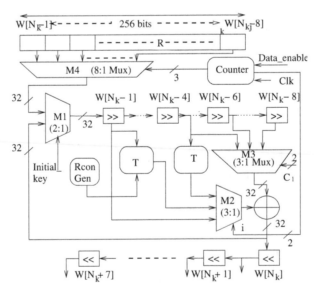

FIGURE 4.13: Key-Scheduler

The Key-Scheduler architecture is presented in **Fig. 4.13**. The figure shows the datapath components in the key expansion block. R is a 256-bit register to store initial key and the *W*'s are the 32-bit shift registers for storing intermediate round keys. The *Data_enable* signal is set when data blocks are ready to be processed (refer **Fig. 4.10**). The *Data_enable* signal sets the value of the running index i, which is generated from an 8-bit counter, to value 1. When *Data_enable* signal is set, a single word (32 bits) among the 8 words goes through the shift registers $W[N_k\text{-}8],...,W[N_k\text{-}1]$ at every clock. The corresponding word to be shifted in is selected by a 3 bits control signal generated by the counter. After N_k cycles all registers $W[N_k\text{-}8],...,W[N_k\text{-}1]$ are occupied by the initial key stored at register R. These intermediate registers are processed by the transformation T as detailed above. The user input C_1 is used to multiplex out one of $W[N_k\text{-}4]$, $W[N_k\text{-}6]$, or $W[N_k\text{-}8]$ (refer Algorithm 6) to be XORed with $W[N_k\text{-}1]$, $T(W[N_k\text{-}1])$ or $T(W[N_k\text{-}4],\text{Rcon})$. Now at every clock cycle, one word of the **RoundKey** is generated, which is shitfted to another set of 32-bit shift registers, namely $W[N_k],...,W[N_k\text{+}7]$ as the round key. Each round key is generated in N_b clock cycles. The generated word of the round key is fed back to the register $W[N_k\text{-}1]$ through the multiplexer M1 for generating the next round key.

4.5.3   The Control Unit

As discussed in Chapter 3, the design of an efficient controller is essential to the efficiency of a hardware design. The datapath of the Key-Scheduler architecure can be suitably controlled by an FSM based control circuitry. The Finite State Machine with Data-path (FSMD) provides an area efficient architecture for providing all the 9 options of the key scheduling algorithm of Rijndael through a single architecture.

In **Fig. 4.14**, $\{S_0, S_1, S_2, S_3, \ldots, S_{86}\}$ are the set of control states, S_0 is the reset or initial state, $\{clock, reset, C_2C_1\}$ are the input signals, $\{O_0, O_1, O_2, O_3, O_4, O_5\}$ are the output signals. Here $O_0 = Key\_enable$, $O_1 = Data\_enable$, $O_2 = Initial\_key$, $O_3 = Addkey\_enable$, $O_4 = First\_round$ and $O_5 = Last\_round$. C_2C_1 is a 4-bit control signal specified by the user, depending on the key and block length. The lower 2-bit C_1 specifies the key length and the higher 2-bit C_2 specifies the block length. The *Key_enable* signal loads the initial key into the register R shown in **Fig. 4.13**.

Data_enable signal selects 256 bits block among two 256 bits blocks, one coming from Plain Text and other generated as intermediate cipher shown in **Fig. 4.10**. This signal is also used to initiate the value of the *Counter*, as shown in **Fig. 4.13**. **Fig. 4.10** has a one-stage inner pipeline, thus it takes two clock cycles to complete a single round. The intermediate values of the cipher round are stored in three buffers, BUFFER1-3. The critical path is divided into two parts: the SubBytes and the ShifRow in one, and the MixColumns and the AddRoundKey in the other. BUFFER1 is enabled by clock, and hence gets written at the positive edge of the clock. The *Key-Scheduler* (**Fig. 4.13**) takes a minimum of 4 cycles for generating single round key. The *Addkey_enable* signal is used as an enable signal of BUFFER2 to get valid data from XOR operation (**Fig. 4.10**). Similarly, *Last_round* signal is used as an enable signal for BUFFER3 to get valid Cipher Text. The *First_round* signal is used to start the counting of the number of rounds.

The state transitions shown in **Fig. 6.13** takes place at every clock cycle. The transitions make several branches depending upon the control signal C_2C_1. Values of C_2C_1 for different values of key and data length are shown in Table 4.4.

We provide below an example to illustrate the generation of round keys for the case, 128 bit data and 128 bit key ($N_b = N_k = 4$, $N_r = 10$). It may be noted that the IO is 8 bits (refer **Fig. 4.8**), thus the initial loading of the input key to the register R takes $4 \times N_k = 16$ clocks.

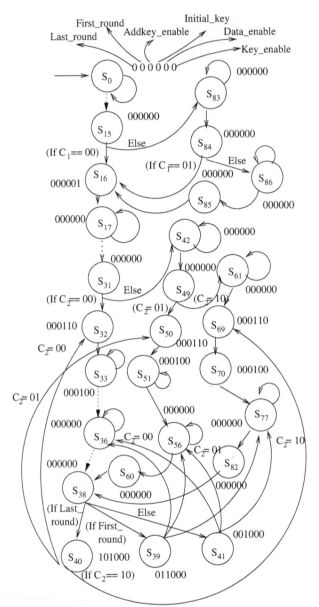

FIGURE 4.14: FSMD of Control Unit

Example: In the example let us take 128 bits data and 128 bits key (i.e $C_2C_1 = 0000$).

- The controller starts at S_0 with the positive edge of reset. The consecutive 15 clock cycles states $\{S_0, S_1, \ldots S_{15}\}$ have same status and in those cases all outputs are 0.

- At the next state S_{16} (16th cycle) *Key_enable* signal becomes 1 and rest are 0. It signifies that 128 bits data are stored in register R as initial key.

- In next cycle (state S_{17}) all output signals are set to 0. Similarly after 15 cycles at state S_{32} *Data_enable* and *Initial_key* are set to 1. In consecutive 4 cycles *Initial_key* signal sets to 1. At these stages, Mux M1 selects 4 words from R (**Fig. 4.13**), and

TABLE 4.4: C_2C_1 for different Key and Data

C_2C_1		Key		
		128	192	256
Data	128	0000	0100	1000
	192	0001	0101	1001
	256	0010	0110	1010

those words are stored in shift registers $W[N_k-4]$,...,$W[N_k-1]$, i.e., $W[0]$,...,$W[3]$. Now the words of the key are ready to be expanded.

- In the next 4 cycles 128 bits the next round key is made. At S_{38} there are three branches, S_{39}, S_{40} and S_{41}. Those branching take place depending upon the signals *Last_round* and *First_round*.
- All those states except S_{40} comes back to S_{36} in the next cycle, signifying that the expansion of next round keys can start. State S_{40} comes back to S_{32}. It signifies that all 10 rounds key generation are completed and ready to store initial keys from register R to the shift registers $W[N_k-4]$,...,$W[N_k-1]$, i.e, $W[0]$,...,$W[3]$ to generate the next 10 round keys.

4.6 Experimental Results

TABLE 4.5: Throughput in FPGA

Clock Frequency = 37.73 MHz			
Throughput (Mb/s)	N_b=4	N_b=6	N_b=8
N_k=4	120.74	100.61	86.24
N_k=6	100.61	100.61	86.24
N_k=8	86.24	86.24	86.24

TABLE 4.6: Throughput in ASIC

Clock Frequency = 120 MHz			
Throughput (Mb/s)	N_b=4	N_b=6	N_b=8
N_k=4	384	320	274.28
N_k=6	320	320	274.28
N_k=8	274.28	274.28	274.28

The proposed design has been implemented on Xilinx XCV1000 device and simulated by ModelSim8.1i. The design is also implemented in 0.18 μ CMOS technology using Synopsys Design Compiler tools. The throughput of the design, $\tau = (\beta \times f)/(\psi)$, where β, f and

ψ stand for block length, clock frequency and number of clock cycle, respectively. In our approach $N_b \times N_r$ clock cycles are needed to generate a block of cipher text. Thus, $\tau = (N_b \times 32 \times f)/(N_b \times N_r) = (32 \times f)/N_r$. The performances (throughput and frequency) for FPGAs and ASICs are shown in Table 4.5 and Table 4.6. We present a comparision of the present design with some other AES cores in Table 4.7. Note that we do not compare with implementations of AES which uses pipelining as they are not useful for several modes like CBC [266] as they give greater throughput at the expense of larger area. The comparisions show that while the present design is superior in terms of throughput per kilo gates, other applications may require designs with throughput or area as the primary concern.

TABLE 4.7: Performances of Compared Cores

	Frequency (MHz)	Throughput (Mb/s)	Gate (K)	Throughput per kilo gates
[120]	80	9.9	3.4	2.91
[304]	50	70	7	10
[396]	125	2290	173	13.23
[358]	132	2400	149	16.17
This work **[25]**	**120**	**384**	**21**	**18.21**

Finally, the present design shows the datapath for only the encryption operation. There may be applications requiring both encryption and decryption. In the next section, we provide a snapshot of such a shared datapath.

4.7   Single Chip Encryptor/Decryptor

The AES hardware provides several scopes of developing an efficient single chip encryptor/decryptor core. The objective is to reutilize blocks and ensure that hardware is shared in encryption and decryption datapaths as much as possible.

The decryption structure can be derived by inverting the encryption structure directly. However, the sequence of the subunits operations will be different from that in encryption (see **Fig. 4.15**). This feature prohibits resource sharing between the encryptor and decryptor. To increase the resource sharing we need some sort of rearrangements of the subunit operations.

It can be observed from the operations involved in the decryption transformations that the inverse ShiftRows (InvShiftRows) and the InvSubBytes can be exchanged without affecting the decryption process. The InvMixColumns can be moved before the *AddRoundKey*, provided that InvMixColumns is also applied to the roundkeys before it is added. This follows easily because of the linearity of the InvMixColumns wrt. the XOR operation in the *AddRoundKey* operation. Taking these into consideration, an equivalent decryption structure can be used (**Fig. 4.16(b)**). In this figure, the *MixRoundkey* is the modified roundkey resulted from applying InvMixColumns to the *AddRoundKey*. The equivalent decryption structure has the same sequence of transformations as that in the encryption structure, and thus, resource sharing between encryptor and decryptor are possible. **Fig. 4.17** shows the block diagram of Encryption/Decryption core in a single chip. The encryption or decryption

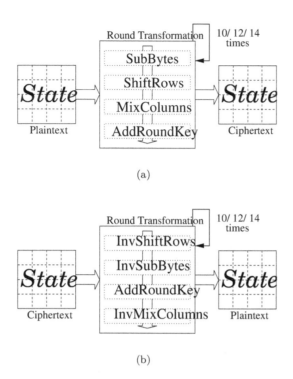

FIGURE 4.15: Different Data-Flow of (a) Encryption and (b) Decryption Datapath

functionality is selected by the user defined control signal called *Mode*. In the figures *REG1 and REG2* are used for sub-pipelined S-Box or InvS-Box implementations (further levels of inner pipelining).

4.8   Conclusions

In this chapter, we presented several design strategies for efficient implementations of the AES cipher. The S-Box is the most hardware intensive component of the AES structure. However, isomorphism of the finite field $GF(2^8)$ and various other composite fields, helps to express the design in terms of smaller field computations. This leads to several compact designs of the S-Box of AES. Further, we presented design strategies of the MixColumns transformation, the other important round component. A state machine based area efficient key schedule is described to ensure support for all the 9 modes of the Rijndael algorithm. Finally, most of the design tricks are combined to present a complete design of AES. The rich properties of the AES structure and its underlying characteristic 2 computations indeed help designers to develop high-performance and compact designs of the cipher.

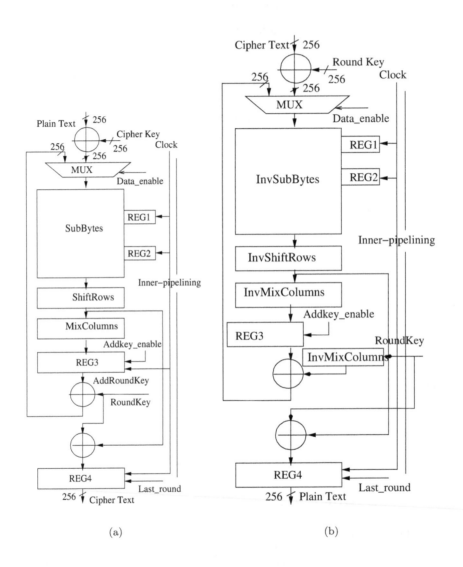

FIGURE 4.16: (a) Architecture of Encryption Datapath, (b) Architecture of Decryption Datapath

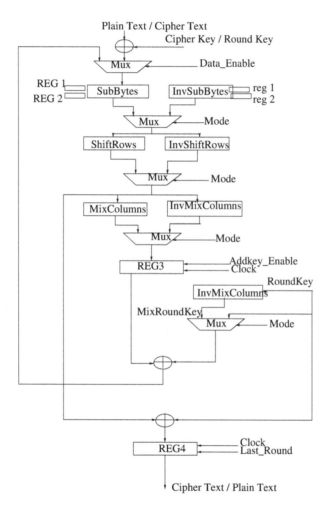

FIGURE 4.17: Single Chip Encryptor/Decryptor Core Design

Chapter 5

Efficient Design of Finite Field Arithmetic on FPGAs

"The loftiest edifices need the deepest foundations."

(George Santayana)

5.1   Introduction

We have seen in the previous chapter, that efficient designs of cryptographic algorithms require proper understanding of underlying finite field primitives. Like the AES, most ciphers are developed using complex mathematical operations, relying largely on finite fields. The Elliptic Curve Cryptosystems are the current generation choice for public key ciphers. As discussed in Chapter 2, they also rely heaviliy on finite fields. These are somewhat more complex, as they operate on larger bit sizes as the primitives required in AES. Further, unlike AES, the bit-sizes of these designs vary, and thus have to be scalable.

The implementation of elliptic curve crypto systems constitutes a complex interdisciplinary research field involving mathematics, computer science and electrical engineering [3]. Elliptic curve crypto systems have a layered hierarchy as shown in **Fig. 5.1**. The bottom layer constituting the arithmetic on the underlying finite field most prominently influences the area and critical delay of the overall implementation. The group operations on the elliptic curve and the scalar multiplication influences the number of clock cycles required for encryption.

To be usable in real-world applications, the crypto system implementation must be efficient, scalable and reusable. Applications such as smart cards and mobile phones require implementations where the amount of resources used and the power consumed is critical. Such implementations should be compact and designed for low power. The computation speed is a secondary criteria. Also, the degree of reconfigurability of the device can be kept minimum [409]. This is because, such devices have a short lifetime and are generally configured only once. On the other side of the spectrum, high-performance systems such as network servers, data base systems, etc. require high speed implementations of ECC. The crypto algorithm should not be the bottleneck on the application's performance. These implementations must also be highly flexible. Operating parameters such as algorithm constants, etc. should be reconfigurable. Reconfiguration can easily be done in software, however software implementations do not always scale to the performance demanded by the application. Such systems require use of dedicated hardware to speedup computations. When using such hardware accelerators, the clock cycles required, frequency of operation, and area are important design criteria. The clock cycles and frequency should be high so that the overall latency of the hardware is less. The area is important because smaller area implies more parallelism can be implemented on the same hardware, thus increasing the device's throughput.

In the next sections, we gradually develop the underlying finite field operations. We also focus on ensuring that the architectures utilize the underlying resources, namely the FPGAs efficiently. We first start with the architecture for a finite field multiplier.

5.2   Finite Field Multiplier

The finite field multiplier forms the most important component in the elliptic curve crypto processor (ECCP). It occupies the most area on the device and also has the longest latency. The multiplier affects most the performance of the ECCP. Finite field multiplication of two elements in the field $GF(2^m)$ is defined as

$$C(x) = A(x) \cdot B(x) \, mod \, P(x) \tag{5.1}$$

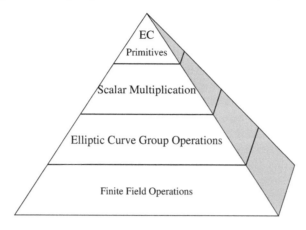

FIGURE 5.1: Elliptic Curve Pyramid

where $C(x)$, $A(x)$, and $B(x)$ are in $GF(2^m)$ and $P(x)$ is the irreducible polynomial that generates the field $GF(2^m)$. Implementing the multiplication requires two steps. First, the polynomial product $C'(x) = A(x) \cdot B(x)$ is determined, then the modulo operation is done on $C'(x)$. This chapter deals with polynomial multiplication.

5.3   Finite Field Multipliers for High Performance Applications

The *school book* method to multiply two polynomials requires m^2 AND gates to generate the partial products. The final product is formed by adding the partial products. Since we deal with binary fields, addition is easily done using XOR gates without any carries being propagated, thus $(m-1)^2$ XOR gates are required to do the additions.

The *Massey-Omura* multiplier operates in normal basis representations of the field elements. With this representation, the structure of the multiplication becomes highly uniform resulting in efficient hardware architecture. The architecture takes a parallel input but the result is produced serially [24].

Another multiplier based on normal basis is the *Sunar-Koç* [74] multiplier. The multiplier requires lesser hardware compared to the Massey-Omura multiplier but has similar timing requirements.

In [75], the *Montgomery multiplier* is adapted to binary finite fields. The multiplication in Equation 5.1 is represented by the following equation

$$C(x) = A(x) \cdot B(x) \cdot R(x)^{-1} mod P(x) \tag{5.2}$$

where, $R(x)$ is of the form x^k and is an element in the field. Also, $gcd(R(x), P(x)) = 1$. The division by $R(x)$ reduces the complexity of the modular operation. For binary finite fields, $R(x)$ has the form 2^k therefore division by $R(x)$ can be easily accomplished on a computer. This multiplier is best suited for low resource environments where speed of operation is not so important [331].

The *Karatsuba multiplier* [176] uses a divide and conquer approach to multiply $A(x)$ and $B(x)$. The m term polynomials are recursively split into two. With each split the size of the multiplication required reduces by half. This leads to a reduction in the number of AND gates required at the cost of an increase in XOR gates. This also results in the multiplier having a space complexity of $O(m^{log_2 3})$ for polynomial representations of finite fields. A comparison of all available multipliers show that only the Karatsuba multiplier has a complexity which is of sub quadratic order. All other multipliers have a complexity which is quadratic. Besides this, it has been shown in [331] and [136] that the Karatsuba multiplier if designed properly is also the fastest.

For a high-performance elliptic curve crypto processor, the finite field multiplier with the smallest delay and the least number of clock cycles is best suited. Karatsuba multiplier, if properly designed, attains the above speed requirements and at the same time has a sub-quadratic space complexity. This makes the Karatsuba multiplier the best choice for high-performance applications.

5.4   Karatsuba Multiplication

In the Karatsuba multiplier, the m bit multiplicands $A(x)$ and $B(x)$ represented in polynomial basis are split as shown in Equation 5.3. For brevity, the equations that follow represent the polynomials $A_h(x)$, $A_l(x)$, $B_h(x)$, and $B_l(x)$ by A_h, A_l, B_h, and B_l respectively.

$$
\begin{aligned}
A(x) &= A_h x^{m/2} + A_l \\
B(x) &= B_h x^{m/2} + B_l
\end{aligned}
\tag{5.3}
$$

The multiplication is then done using three $m/2$ bit multiplications as shown in Equation 5.4.

$$
\begin{aligned}
C'(x) &= (A_h x^{m/2} + A_l)(B_h x^{m/2} + B_l) \\
&= A_h B_h x^m + (A_h B_l + A_l B_h) x^{m/2} + A_l B_l \\
&= A_h B_h x^m \\
&\quad + ((A_h + A_l)(B_h + B_l) + A_h B_h + A_l B_l) x^{m/2} \\
&\quad + A_l B_l
\end{aligned}
\tag{5.4}
$$

The Karatsuba multiplier can be applied recursively to each $m/2$ bit multiplication in Equation 5.4. Ideally this multiplier is best suited when m is a power of 2, this allows the multiplicands to be broken down until they reach 2 bits. The final recursion consisting of 2 bit multiplications can be achieved by AND gates. Such a multiplier with m a power of 2 is called the *basic Karatsuba multiplier*.

5.5   Karatsuba Multipliers for Elliptic Curves

The basic recursive Karatsuba multiplier cannot be applied directly to ECC because the binary extension fields used in standards such as [393] have a prime degree. There have been several published works which implement a modified Karatsuba algorithm for use in elliptic curves. There are two main design approaches followed. The first approach is a sequential circuit having less hardware and latency but requiring several clock cycles to produce the result. Generally at every clock cycle the outputs are fed-back into the circuit thus reusing the hardware. The advantage of this approach is that it can be pipelined. Examples of implementations following this approach can be found in[136][115][397][299]. The second approach is a combinational circuit having large area and delay but is capable of generating the result in one clock cycle. Examples of this approach can found in [287][329][253][404]. Our proposed Karatsuba multiplier follows the second approach. Therefore, in the remaining part of this section we analyze the combinational circuits for Karatsuba multipliers.

The easiest method to modify the Karatsuba algorithm for elliptic curves is by padding. The *padded Karatsuba multiplier* extends the m bit multiplicands to $2^{\lceil log_2 m \rceil}$ bits by padding the most significant bits with zeroes. This allows the use of the basic recursive Karatsuba algorithm. The obvious drawback of this method is the extra arithmetic introduced due to the padding.

In [329], a *binary Karatsuba multiplier* was proposed to handle multiplications in any field of the form $GF(2^m)$, where $m = 2^k + d$ and k is the largest integer such that $2^k < m$. The binary Karatsuba multiplier splits the m bit multiplicands ($A(x)$ and $B(x)$) into two terms. The lower terms (A_l and B_l) have 2^k bits while the higher terms (A_h and B_h) have d bits. Two 2^k bit multipliers are required to obtain the partial products $A_l B_l$ and $(A_h + A_l)(B_h + B_l)$. For the latter multiplication, the A_h and B_h terms have to be padded with $2^k - d$ bits. $A_h B_h$ product is determined using a d bit binary Karatsuba multiplier.

The *simple Karatsuba multiplier* [404] is the basic recursive Karatsuba multiplier with a small modification. If an m bit multiplication is needed to be done, m being any integer, it is split into two polynomials as in Equation 5.3. The A_l and B_l terms have $\lceil m/2 \rceil$ bits and the A_h and B_h terms have $\lfloor m/2 \rfloor$ bits. The Karatsuba multiplication can then be done with two $\lceil m/2 \rceil$ bit multiplications and one $\lfloor m/2 \rfloor$ bit multiplication. The upper bound for the number of AND gates and XOR gates required for the simple Karatsuba multiplier is the same as that of a $2^{\lceil log_2 m \rceil}$ bit basic recursive Karatsuba multiplier. The maximum number of gates required and the time delay for an m bit simple Karatsuba multiplier is given below.

$$\#ANDgates: 3^{\lceil log_2 m \rceil}$$

$$\#XORgates: \sum_{r=0}^{\lceil log_2 m \rceil} 3^r \left(4\lceil m/2^r \rceil - 4\right) \tag{5.5}$$

In the *general Karatsuba multiplier* [404], the multiplicands are split into more than two terms. For example an m term multiplier is split into m different terms. The number of gates required is given below.

$$\#ANDgates: m(m+1)/2$$

$$\#XORgates: \frac{5}{2}m^2 - \frac{7}{2}m + 1 \tag{5.6}$$

5.6 Designing for the FPGA Architecture

Maximizing the performance of a hardware design requires the design to be customized for the target architecture. The smallest programmable entity on an FPGA is the lookup table (Section 3.1.1). A LUT generally has four inputs and can be configured for any logic function having a maximum of four inputs. The LUT can also be used to implement logic functions having less than four inputs, two for example. In this case, only half the LUT is utilized the remaining part is not utilized. Such a LUT having less than four inputs is an *under-utilized LUT*. For example, the logic function $y = x_1 + x_2$ under utilizes the LUT as it has only two inputs. *Most compact implementations are obtained when the utilization of each LUT is maximized.* From the above fact it may be derived that the minimum number of LUTs required for a q bit combinational circuit is given by Equation 5.7.

$$\#LUT(q) = \begin{cases} 0 & \text{if } q = 1 \\ 1 & \text{if } 1 < q \leq 4 \\ \lceil q/3 \rceil & \text{if } q > 4 \text{ and } q \bmod 3 = 2 \\ \lfloor q/3 \rfloor & \text{if } q > 4 \text{ and } q \bmod 3 \neq 2 \end{cases} \tag{5.7}$$

The delay of the q bit combinational circuit in terms of LUTs is given by Equation 5.8, where D_{LUT} is the delay of one LUT.

$$DELAY(q) = \lceil log_4(q) \rceil * D_{LUT} \tag{5.8}$$

The percentage of under utilized LUTs in a design is determined using Equation 5.9. Here, LUT_k signifies that k inputs out of 4 are used by the design block realized by the LUT. So, LUT_2 and LUT_3 are under-utilized LUTs, while LUT_4 is fully utilized.

$$\%UnderUtilizedLUTs = \frac{LUT_2 + LUT_3}{LUT_2 + LUT_3 + LUT_4} * 100 \tag{5.9}$$

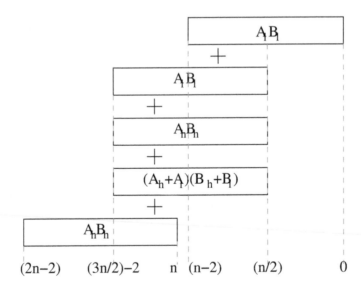

FIGURE 5.2: Combining the Partial Products in a Karatsuba Multiplier

5.7 Analyzing Karatsuba Multipliers on FPGA Platforms

In this section, we discuss the mapping of various Karatsuba algorithms on an FPGA. We estimate the amount of FPGA resources that is required for the implementations.

Recursive Karatsuba Multiplier: In an m ($= 2^k$) bit recursive Karatsuba multiplier the basic Karatsuba algorithm of [176] is applied recursively. Each recursion reduces the size of the input by half while tripling the number of multiplications required. At each recursion, except the final, only *XOR* operations are involved. Let $n = 2^{(log_2 m)-k}$ be the size of the inputs (A and B) for the kth recursion of the m bit multiplier. There are 3^k such n bit multipliers required. The A and B inputs are split into two: A_h, A_l and B_h, B_l respectively with each term having $n/2$ bits. $n/2$ two input XORs are required for the computation of $A_h + A_l$ and $B_h + B_l$, respectively (Equation 5.4). Each two input XOR requires one LUT on the FPGA, thus in total there are n LUTs required. Combining the partial products as shown in **Fig. 5.2** is the last step of the recursion. Determining the output bits $n - 2$ to $n/2$ and $3n/2 - 2$ to n requires $3(n/2 - 1)$ two input XORs each. The output bit $n - 1$ requires 2 two input XORs. In all $(3n - 4)$ two input *XORs* are required to add the partial products. The number of LUTs required to combine the partial products is much lower. This is because each LUT implements a four input *XOR*. Each output bit $n/2$ to $3n/2 - 2$ requires one LUT, therefore $(n - 1)$ LUTs are required for the purpose. In total, $2n - 1$ LUTs are required for each recursion on the FPGA. The final recursion has $3^{(log_2 m)-1}$ two-bit Karatsuba multipliers. The equation for the two bit Karatsuba multiplier is shown in Equation 5.10.

$$
\begin{aligned}
C_0 &= A_0 B_0 \\
C_1 &= A_0 B_0 + A_1 B_1 + (A_0 + A_1)(B_0 + B_1) \\
C_2 &= A_1 B_1
\end{aligned}
\tag{5.10}
$$

This requires three LUTs on the FPGA: one for each of the output bits (C_0, C_1, C_2).

The total number of LUTs required for the m bit recursive Karatsuba multiplication is given by Equation 5.11.

$$
\begin{aligned}
\#LUTS_R(m) &= 3 * 3^{log_2 m - 1} + \sum_{k=0}^{log_2 m - 2} 3^k (2 * 2^{log_2 m - k} - 1) \\
&= \sum_{k=0}^{log_2 m - 1} 3^k (2^{log_2 m - k + 1} - 1)
\end{aligned}
\tag{5.11}
$$

The delay of the recursive Karatsuba multiplier in terms of LUTs is given by Equation 5.12. The first $log_2(m) - 1$ recursions have a delay of $2LUTs$. The last recursion has a delay of $1LUT$.

$$
\begin{aligned}
DELAY_R(m) &= (2(log_2(m) - 1) + 1)D_{LUT} \\
&= (2log_2(m) - 1)D_{LUT}
\end{aligned}
\tag{5.12}
$$

When m is not necessarily a power of 2, the number of recursions of an m bit simple Karatsuba multiplier is equivalent to that of a $2^{\lceil log_2 m \rceil}$ recursive Karatsuba multiplier, therefore Equations 5.11 and 5.12 form the upper bound for the number of LUTs and delay of a simple Karatsuba multiplier [404] (Equations 5.13 and 5.14).

$$
\#LUTS_S(m) \leq \#LUTS_R(2^{\lceil log_2 m \rceil})
\tag{5.13}
$$

$$
DELAY_S(m) \leq DELAY_R(2^{\lceil log_2 m \rceil})
\tag{5.14}
$$

General Karatsuba Multiplier: The m bit general Karatsuba algorithm [404] is shown in Algorithm 5.1. Each iteration of i computes two output bits C_i and C_{2m-2-i}. Computing the two output bits require same amount of resources on the FPGA. The lines 6 and 7 in the algorithm is executed once for every even iteration of i and is not executed for odd iterations of i. The term $M_j + M_{i-j} + M_{(j,i-j)}$ is computed with the four inputs A_j, A_{i-j}, B_j and B_{i-j}, therefore, on the FPGA, computing the term would require one LUT. For an odd i, C_i would have $\lceil i/2 \rceil$ such LUTs whose outputs have to be added. The number of LUTs required for this is obtained from Equation 5.7. An even value of i would have two additional inputs corresponding to $M_{i/2}$ that have to be added. The number of LUTs required for computing C_i ($0 \leq i \leq m-1$) is given by Equation 5.15.

$$\#LUT_{c_i} = \begin{cases} 1 & \text{if } i = 0 \\ \lceil i/2 \rceil + \#LUT(\lceil i/2 \rceil) & \text{if } i \text{ is odd} \\ i/2 + \#LUT(i/2 + 2) & \text{if } i \text{ is even} \end{cases} \qquad (5.15)$$

Algorithm 5.1: gkmul *(General Karatsuba Multiplier)*

Input: A, B are multiplicands of m bits
Output: C of length $2m - 1$ bits

```
   /* Define : Mₓ → AₓBₓ                                              */
   /* Define : M₍ₓ,ᵧ₎ → (Aₓ + Aᵧ)(Bₓ + Bᵧ)                            */
 1 begin
 2    for i = 0 to m − 2 do
 3       Cᵢ = C₂ₘ₋₂₋ᵢ = 0
 4       for j = 0 to ⌊i/2⌋ do
 5          if i = 2j then
 6             Cᵢ = Cᵢ + Mⱼ
 7             C₂ₘ₋₂₋ᵢ = C₂ₘ₋₂₋ᵢ + Mₘ₋₁₋ⱼ
 8          else
 9             Cᵢ = Cᵢ + Mⱼ + Mᵢ₋ⱼ + M₍ⱼ,ᵢ₋ⱼ₎
10             C₂ₘ₋₂₋ᵢ = C₂ₘ₋₂₋ᵢ + Mₘ₋₁₋ⱼ
11                +Mₘ₋₁₋ᵢ₊ⱼ + M₍ₘ₋₁₋ⱼ,ₘ₋₁₋ᵢ₊ⱼ₎
12          end
13       end
14    end
15    Cₘ₋₁ = 0
16    for j = 0 to ⌊(m − 1)/2⌋ do
17       if m − 1 = 2j then
18          Cₘ₋₁ = Cₘ₋₁ + Mⱼ
19       else
20          Cₘ₋₁ = Cₘ₋₁ + Mⱼ + Mₘ₋₁₋ⱼ + M₍ⱼ,ₘ₋₁₋ⱼ₎
21       end
22    end
23 end
```

The total number of LUTs required for the general Karatsuba multiplier is given by Equation 5.16.

$$\#LUTS_G(m) = 2\left(\sum_{i=0}^{m-2} \#LUT_{C_i} \right) + \#LUT_{C_{m-1}} \qquad (5.16)$$

When implemented in hardware, all output bits are computed simultaneously. The delay of the general Karatsuba multiplier (Equation 5.17) is equal to the delay of the output bit with the most terms. This is the output bit C_{m-1} (lines 15 to 22 in the Algorithm 5.1). Equation 5.17 is obtained from Equation 5.15 with $i = m - 1$. The $\lceil i/2 \rceil$ computations are done with a delay of one LUT (D_{LUT}). Equation 5.8 is used to compute the second term of Equation 5.17.

TABLE 5.1: Comparison of LUT Utilization in Multipliers

m	General			Simple		
	Gates	LUTs	LUTs Under Utilized	Gates	LUTs	LUTs Under Utilized
2	7	3	66.6%	7	3	66.6%
4	37	11	45.5%	33	16	68.7%
8	169	53	20.7%	127	63	66.6%
16	721	188	17.0%	441	220	65.0%
29	2437	670	10.7%	1339	669	65.4%
32	2977	799	11.3%	1447	723	63.9%

$$DELAY_G(m) = \begin{cases} D_{LUT} + DELAY(\lceil (m-1)/2 \rceil) & \text{if } m-1 \text{ is odd} \\ D_{LUT} + DELAY((m-1)/2 + 2) & \text{if } m-1 \text{ is even} \end{cases} \qquad (5.17)$$

5.7.1 The Hybrid Karatsuba Multiplier

In this section we present our proposed multiplier called the *hybrid Karatsuba multiplier* which was proposed in [315]. We show how we combine techniques to maximize utilization of LUTs resulting in minimum area.

Table 5.1 compares the general and simple Karatsuba algorithms for gate counts (two input XOR and AND gates), LUTs required on a *Xilinx Virtex 4 FPGA* and the percentage of LUTs under-utilized (Equation 5.9).

The simple Karatsuba multiplier alone is not efficient for FPGA platforms as the number of under-utilized LUTs is about 65%. For an m bit simple Karatsuba multiplier the two bit multipliers take up approximately a third of the area (for $m = 256$). In a two bit multiplier, two out of three LUTs required, are under utilized (In Equation 5.10, C_0 and C_2 result in under-utilized LUTs). In addition to this, around half the LUTs used for each recursion is under utilized. The under utilized LUTs results in a bloated area requirement on the FPGA.

The m-term general Karatsuba is more efficient on the FPGA for small values on m (Table 5.1) even though the gate count is significantly higher. This is because a large number of operations can be grouped in fours which fully utilizes the LUT. For small values of m ($m < 29$) the compactness obtained by the fully utilized LUTs is more prominent than the large gate count, resulting in low footprints on the FPGA. For $m \geq 29$, the gate count far exceeds the efficiency obtained by the fully utilized LUTs, resulting in larger footprints with respect to the simple Karatsuba implementation.

In our proposed hybrid Karatsuba multiplier, shown in Algorithm 5.2, the m bit multiplicands are split into two parts when the number of bits is greater than or equal to the threshold 29. The higher term has $\lfloor m/2 \rfloor$ bits while the lower term has $\lceil m/2 \rceil$ bits. If the number of bits of the multiplicand is less than 29 the general Karatsuba algorithm is invoked. The general Karatsuba algorithm ensures maximum utilization of the LUTs for the smaller bit multiplications, while the simple Karatsuba algorithm ensures least gate count for the larger bit multiplications. For a 233-bit hybrid Karatsuba multiplier (**Fig. 5.3**), the multiplicands are split into two terms with A_h and B_h of 116 bits and A_l and B_l of 117 bits. The 116-bit multiplication is implemented using three 58-bit multipliers, while the 117-bit multiplier is implemented using two 59-bit multipliers and a 58-bit multiplier. The 58 and

---

Algorithm 5.2: hmul *(Hybrid Karatsuba Multiplier)*

Input: The multiplicands A, B and their length m
Output: C of length $2m - 1$ bits

1 **begin**
2   **if** $m < 29$ **then**
3   **return** $gkmul(A, B, m)$
4   **else**
5         $l = \lceil m/2 \rceil$
6         $A' = A_{[m-1\cdots l]} + A_{[l-1\cdots 0]}$
7         $B' = B_{[m-1\cdots l]} + B_{[l-1\cdots 0]}$
8         $C_{p1} = hmul(A_{[l-1\cdots 0]}, B_{[l-1\cdots 0]}, l)$
9         $C_{p2} = hmul(A', B', l)$
10        $C_{p3} = hmul(A_{[m-1\cdots l]}, B_{[m-1\cdots l]}, m - l)$
11   **return** $(C_{p3} << 2l) + (C_{p1} + C_{p2} + C_{p3}) << l + C_{p1}$
        ;   /* $<<$ *indicates left shift* */
12
13   **end**
14 **end**

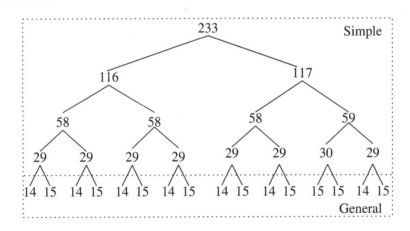

FIGURE 5.3: 233-Bit Hybrid Karatsuba Multiplier [315]

59 bit multiplications are implemented with 29 and 30-bit multipliers, the 29 and 30-bit multiplications are done using 14 and 15 bit general Karatsuba multipliers.

The number of recursions in the hybrid Karatsuba multiplier is given by

$$r = \lceil log_2 \left(\frac{m}{29} \right) \rceil + 1 \tag{5.18}$$

The ith recursion $(0 < i < r)$ of the m-bit multiplier has 3^i multiplications. The multipliers in this recursion have bit lengths $\lceil m/2^i \rceil$ and $\lfloor m/2^i \rfloor$. For simplicity we assume the number of gates required for the $\lfloor m/2^i \rfloor$ bit multiplier is equal to that of the $\lceil m/2^i \rceil$ bit multiplier. The total number of AND gates required is the AND gates for the multiplier in the final recursion (i.e. $\lceil m/2^{r-1} \rceil$ bit multiplier) times the number of $\lceil m/2^{r-1} \rceil$ multipliers present. Using Equation 5.6,

$$\#AND = \frac{3^{r-1}}{2} \lceil \frac{m}{2^{r-1}} \rceil \left(\lceil \frac{m}{2^{r-1}} \rceil + 1 \right) \tag{5.19}$$

The number of XOR gates required for the ith recursion is given by $4\lceil\frac{m}{2^i}\rceil - 4$. The total number of two input $XORs$ is the sum of the $XORs$ required for last recursion, $\#XOR_{g_{r-1}}$, and the $XORs$ required for the other recursions, $\#XOR_{s_i}$. Using Equations 5.5 and 5.6,

$$\#XOR = 3^{r-1}\#XOR_{g_{r-1}} + \sum_{i=1}^{r-2} 3^i \#XOR_{s_i}$$
$$= 3^{r-1}\left(10\lceil\frac{m}{2^r}\rceil^2 - 7\lceil\frac{m}{2^r}\rceil + 1\right) + \sum_{i=1}^{r-2} 3^i\left(4\lceil\frac{m}{2^i}\rceil - 4\right) \tag{5.20}$$

The delay of the hybrid Karatsuba multiplier (Equation 5.21) is obtained by subtracting the delay of a $\lceil m/2^{r-1}\rceil$ bit simple Karatsuba multiplier from the delay of an m bit simple Karatsuba multiplier, and adding the delay of a $\lceil m/2^{r-1}\rceil$ bit general Karatsuba multiplier.

$$DELAY_H(m) = DELAY_S(m)$$
$$- DELAY_S(\lceil m/2^{r-1}\rceil) + DELAY_G(\lceil m/2^{r-1}\rceil) \tag{5.21}$$

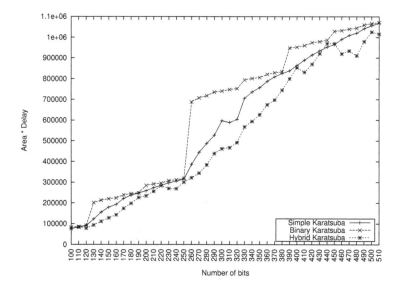

FIGURE 5.4: m-Bit Multiplication vs. Area $\times$ Time [315]

TABLE 5.2: Comparison of the Hybrid Karatsuba Multiplier with Reported FPGA Implementations

Multiplier	Platform	Field	Slices	Delay (ns)	Clock Cycles	Computation Time(ns)	Performance AT (μs)
Grabbe [136] [397]	XC2V6000	240	1660	12.12	54	655	1087
Gathen [397]	XC2V6000	240	1480	12.6	30	378	559
This work [315]	XC4V140	233	10434	16	1	16	154
	XC2VP100	233	12107	19.9	1	19.9	241

5.8 Performance Evaluation

The graph in **Fig. 5.4** compares the area time product for the hybrid Karatsuba multiplier with the simple Karatsuba multiplier and the binary Karatsuba multipliers for increasing values of m. The simple and binary Karatsuba multipliers were reimplemented and scaled for different field sizes. The results were obtained by synthesizing using *Xilinx's ISE* for a *Virtex 4* FPGA. The area was determined by the number of LUTs required for the multiplier, and the time in nano-seconds includes the I/O pad delay. The graph shows that the area time product for the hybrid Karatsuba multiplier is lesser compared to the other multipliers.

Table 5.2 compares the hybrid Karatsuba with reported FPGA implementations of Karatsuba variants. The implementations of [136] and [397] are sequential and hence require multiple clock cycles, thus they are not suited for high performance ECC. In order to alleviate this, we proposed a combinational Karatsuba multiplier. However to ensure that the design operates at a high clock frequency, we perform hardware replication. For example, in a 233-bit multiplier, 14-bit and 15-bit general Karatsuba multipliers are replicated, since the general Karatsuba multipliers utilize LUTs efficiently. This gain is reflected in Table 5.2.

5.9 High-Performance Finite Field Inversion Architecture for FPGAs

For any nonzero element $a \in GF(2^m)$, the inverse is the element $a^{-1} \in GF(2^m)$ such that $a \cdot a^{-1} = a^{-1} \cdot a = 1$. Of all arithmetic operations used in ECC, finite field inversion is the most complex. Commonly used algorithms for computing inverse in binary fields are *extended Euclidean algorithm* (EEA), *binary Euclidean algorithm* (BEA), *Montgomery inversion algorithm* [173] and *Itoh-Tsujii algorithm* (ITA) [160]. On hardware platforms, ITA is faster than other inversion algorithms [331]. However, standalone implementation of ITA has more area due requirement of field multiplier. For hardware implementation of ECC, where field multiplier is essential, ITA is the most efficient inversion technique [331]. The field multiplier which is used for elliptic curve point addition and doubling operations during scalar multiplication, can be reused by the ITA for inverse computation. Hence, the large area overhead of ITA due to requirement of field multiplier is not an issue for elliptic curve cryptosystems.

The ITA computes the inverse by a series of multiplications and exponentiations along an addition chain. The performance of ITA architecture on FPGA platform depends on several configurable design parameters such as the choice of addition chain, exponentiation circuits, and the number of replicated circuits. These parameters have to be selected appropriately to achieve best performance. While the selection of the addition chain is straight forward [337], selection of the other configuration parameters are not. In the current FPGA design scenario, the only way to find best performing architecture is to experimentally evaluate every possible design configurations and then select the best configuration parameters. This results in long design cycles.

This chapter presents a theoretical approach to find the best design parameters for any architecture on $k \geq 4$ input LUT based FPGAs, thus reducing the design cycle time.

A theoretical model is used for the ITA design to analyze how various design strategies affect the area, delay, and clock cycle requirements on FPGA platforms. For a given field $GF(2^m)$, size of an LUT in the FPGA (k), and addition chain, our model predicts the best exponentiation circuit 2^n and the ideal number of replicated circuits which would give peak performance. The theoretical results are experimentally validated on 4 and 6 input LUT-based FPGAs over binary fields specifed in NIST's Digital Signature Standard[393].

5.10 Itoh-Tsujii Inversion Algorithm

According to Fermat's little theorem, the inverse of any nonzero element $a \in GF(2^m)$ can be computed using Equation 5.22.

$$a^{-1} = a^{2^m - 2} \tag{5.22}$$

The naive method for computing inverse using the above equation requires $m - 1$ squarings and $m - 2$ field multiplications. Since field multiplications are costly, the naive approach is not efficient. Itoh-Tsujii algorithm [160] reduces the number of field multiplications required by using an addition chain for $m - 1$. An addition chain for a positive integer n is a sequence of natural numbers $U = (u_0, u_1, \cdots, u_l)$, such that the following properties are satisfied.

- $u_0 = 1$

- $u_l = n$

- $u_i = u_j + u_k$ for $i = j + k$ and $u_j, u_k \in U$

An example of addition chain for 162 is $U = (1, 2, 4, 5, 10, 20, 40, 80, 81, 162)$.

Brauer chains are a special class of addition chains in which $j = i - 1$. An *optimal chain* for n is the smallest addition chain for n.

The Itoh-Tsujii inversion algorithm was initially proposed for computing inverse using normal basis representations. Later in [141], ITA was modified for polynomial basis representations.

The ITA works as follows: For $a \in GF(2^m)$, let $\beta_k(a) = a^{2^k - 1}$ and $k \in N$. Using Equation 5.22 we get, $a^{-1} = \beta_{m-1}(a)^2$. For simplicity, we denote $\beta_k(a)$ by β_k. In [333], the following recursive sequence is used with an addition chain for $m - 1$ to compute β_{m-1}.

$$\beta_{k+j}(a) = (\beta_j)^{2^k} \beta_k = (\beta_k)^{2^j} \beta_j \tag{5.23}$$

Here k, j and $k + j$ are integers and are members of an addition chain for $m - 1$. As an example, computing the inverse of a nonzero element $a \in GF(2^{163})$ requires computation of $\beta_{162}(a) = a^{2^{162} - 1}$. Finally a squaring is performed to get $a^{-1} = [\beta_{162}(a)]^2$. The recursive steps followed in computing β_{162} are shown in Table 5.4.

As a further example, consider finding the inverse of an element $a \in GF(2^{233})$. This requires computing $\beta_{232}(a) = a^{2^{232} - 1}$ and then doing a squaring (i.e. $[\beta_{232}(a)]^2 = a^{-1}$). A Brauer chain for 232 is as shown below.

$$U_1 = (\quad 1 \quad 2 \quad 3 \quad 6 \quad 7 \quad 14 \quad 28 \quad 29 \quad 58 \quad 116 \quad 232 \quad) \tag{5.24}$$

Computing $\beta_{232}(a)$ is done in 10 steps with 231 squarings and 10 multiplications as shown in Table 5.4.

TABLE 5.3: Inverse of $a \in GF(2^{163})$ using ITA

	$\beta_{u_i}(a)$	$\beta_{u_j+u_k}(a)$	Exponentiation
1	$\beta_1(a)$		a
2	$\beta_2(a)$	$\beta_{1+1}(a)$	$(\beta_1)^{2^1}\beta_1 = a^{2^2-1}$
3	$\beta_4(a)$	$\beta_{2+2}(a)$	$(\beta_2)^{2^2}\beta_2 = a^{2^4-1}$
4	$\beta_5(a)$	$\beta_{4+1}(a)$	$(\beta_4)^{2^1}\beta_1 = a^{2^5-1}$
5	$\beta_{10}(a)$	$\beta_{5+5}(a)$	$(\beta_5)^{2^5}\beta_5 = a^{2^{10}-1}$
6	$\beta_{20}(a)$	$\beta_{10+10}(a)$	$(\beta_{10})^{2^{10}}\beta_{10} = a^{2^{20}-1}$
7	$\beta_{40}(a)$	$\beta_{20+20}(a)$	$(\beta_{20})^{2^{20}}\beta_{20} = a^{2^{40}-1}$
8	$\beta_{80}(a)$	$\beta_{40+40}(a)$	$(\beta_{40})^{2^{40}}\beta_{40} = a^{2^{80}-1}$
9	$\beta_{81}(a)$	$\beta_{80+1}(a)$	$(\beta_{80})^{2^1}\beta_1 = a^{2^{81}-1}$
10	$\beta_{162}(a)$	$\beta_{81+81}(a)$	$(\beta_{81})^{2^{81}}\beta_{81} = a^{2^{161}-1}$

TABLE 5.4: Inverse of $a \in GF(2^{233})$ using generic ITA

	$\beta_{u_i}(a)$	$\beta_{u_j+u_k}(a)$	Exponentiation
1	$\beta_1(a)$		a
2	$\beta_2(a)$	$\beta_{1+1}(a)$	$(\beta_1)^{2^1}\beta_1 = a^{2^2-1}$
3	$\beta_3(a)$	$\beta_{2+1}(a)$	$(\beta_2)^{2^1}\beta_1 = a^{2^3-1}$
4	$\beta_6(a)$	$\beta_{3+3}(a)$	$(\beta_3)^{2^3}\beta_3 = a^{2^6-1}$
5	$\beta_7(a)$	$\beta_{6+1}(a)$	$(\beta_6)^{2^1}\beta_1 = a^{2^7-1}$
6	$\beta_{14}(a)$	$\beta_{7+7}(a)$	$(\beta_7)^{2^7}\beta_7 = a^{2^{14}-1}$
7	$\beta_{28}(a)$	$\beta_{14+14}(a)$	$(\beta_{14})^{2^{14}}\beta_{14} = a^{2^{28}-1}$
8	$\beta_{29}(a)$	$\beta_{28+1}(a)$	$(\beta_{28})^{2^1}\beta_1 = a^{2^{29}-1}$
9	$\beta_{58}(a)$	$\beta_{29+29}(a)$	$(\beta_{29})^{2^{29}}\beta_{29} = a^{2^{58}-1}$
10	$\beta_{116}(a)$	$\beta_{58+58}(a)$	$(\beta_{58})^{2^{58}}\beta_{58} = a^{2^{116}-1}$
11	$\beta_{232}(a)$	$\beta_{116+116}(a)$	$(\beta_{116})^{2^{116}}\beta_{116} = a^{2^{232}-1}$

In general if l is the length of the addition chain, finding the inverse of an element in $GF(2^m)$, requires $l-1$ multiplications and $m-1$ squarings. The length of the addition chain is related to m by the equation $l \leq \lfloor log_2 m \rfloor$ [201], therefore the number of multiplications required by the ITA is much lesser than that of the naive method.

5.11   The Quad ITA Algorithm

In [314] and [337], a variant of ITA uses 2^2 (*quad*) circuits as exponentiation circuits to achieve acceleration. Quad circuit based ITA requires addition chain for $(m-1)/2$ and thus has lesser computational steps compared to squaring based ITA. Additionally, for any trinomial generated field both the quad and squarer circuits have same delay, while the area of quad circuit is just 1.5 times the size of the squarer (instead of twice).

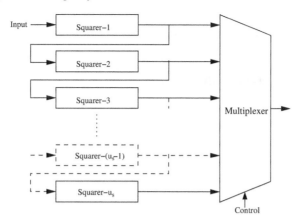

FIGURE 5.5: Circuit to Raise the Input to the Power of 2^k

We estimate the clock cycles required in an ITA architecture, and subsequently show the gains for performing the ITA computation in higher powers on a LUT based FPGA.

5.11.1 Clock Cycles for the ITA

In the ITA for field $GF(2^m)$, the number of squarings required is as high as m. Further from Table 5.4, it may be noted that most of the squarings required is towards the end of the addition chain. The maximum number of squarings at any particular step could be as high as $u_i/2$. Although the circuit for a squarer is relatively simple, the large number of squarings required hampers the performance of the ITA. A straightforward way of implement the squarings would require $u_i/2$ clock cycles at each step. The technique used in [333] and [330] cascades u_s (where u_s is an element in the addition chain) squarers (**Fig. 5.5**) so that the output of one squarer is fed to the input of the next. If the number of squarings required is less than u_s, a multiplexer is used to tap out interim outputs. In this case the output can be obtained in one clock cycle. If the number of squarings required is greater than u_s, the output of the squaring block is fed back to get squares which are a multiple of u_s. For example, if u_i ($u_i > u_s$) squarings are needed, the output of the squarer block would be fed back $\lceil u_i/u_s \rceil$ times. This would also require $\lceil u_i/u_s \rceil$ clock cycles.

In addition to the squarings, each step in the ITA has exactly one multiplication requiring one clock cycle. The total number of clock cycles required for this design, assuming a Brauer chain, is given by Equation 5.25. The summation in the equation is the clock cycles for the squarings at each step of the algorithm. The $(l-1)$ term is due to the $(l-1)$ multiplications. The extra clock cycle is for the final squaring.

$$
\begin{aligned}
\#ClockCycles &= 1 + (l-1) + \sum_{i=2}^{l} \lceil \frac{u_i - u_{i-1}}{u_s} \rceil \\
&= l + \sum_{i=2}^{l} \lceil \frac{u_i - u_{i-1}}{u_s} \rceil
\end{aligned}
\tag{5.25}
$$

In order to reduce the clock cycles a parallel architecture was proposed in [330]. The reduced clock cycles is achieved at the cost of increased hardware. In the remaining part of this section we propose a novel ITA designed for the FPGA architecture. The proposed design, though sequential, requires the same number of clock cycles as the parallel architecture of [330] but has better area×time product.

5.11.2   The Quad ITA Generalization

The equation for the square of an element $a \in GF(2^m)$ is given by Equation 5.26, where $p(x)$ is the irreducible polynomial

$$a(x)^2 = \sum_{i=0}^{m-1} a_i x^{2i} \bmod p(x) \tag{5.26}$$

This is a linear equation and hence can be represented in the form of a matrix (T) as shown in the equation below.

$$a^2 = T \cdot a$$

The matrix depends on the finite field $GF(2^m)$ and the irreducible polynomial of the field. Exponentiation in the ITA is done with squarer circuits. We extend the ITA so that the exponentiation can be done with any 2^n circuit and not just squarers. Raising a to the power of 2^n is also linear and can be represented in the form of a matrix as shown below.

$$a^{2^n} = T^n(a) = T'a$$

For any $a \in GF(2^m)$ and $k \in \mathbb{N}$, Define,

$$\alpha_k(a) = a^{2^{nk}-1} \tag{5.27}$$

Theorem 5.11.1 *If* $a \in GF(2^m)$ *,* $\alpha_{k_1}(a) = a^{2^{nk_1}-1}$*, and* $\alpha_{k_2}(a) = a^{2^{nk_2}-1}$ *then*

$$\alpha_{k_1+k_2}(a) = (\alpha_{k_1}(a))^{2^{nk_2}} \alpha_{k_2}(a)$$

where k_1*,* k_2*, and* $n \in \mathbb{N}$

Proof 1

$$\begin{aligned}
RHS &= (\alpha_{k_1}(a))^{2^{nk_2}} \alpha_{k_2}(a) \\
&= (a^{2^{nk_1}-1})^{2^{nk_2}} (a^{2^{nk_2}-1}) \\
&= (a^{2^{n(k_1+k_2)}-2^{nk_2}+2^{nk_2}-1}) \\
&= (a^{2^{n(k_1+k_2)}-1}) \\
&= \alpha_{k_1+k_2}(a) \\
&= LHS
\end{aligned}$$

Theorem 5.11.2 *The inverse of an element* $a \in GF(2^m)$ *is given by*

$$a^{-1} = \begin{cases} \left[\alpha_{\frac{m-1}{n}}(a)\right]^2 & when\ n \mid (m-1) \\ \left[(\alpha_q(a))^{2^r}\beta_r(a)\right]^2 & when\ n \nmid (m-1) \end{cases}$$

where $nq + r = m - 1$ *and* n*,* q*, and* $r \in \mathbb{N}$

TABLE 5.5: Comparison of LUTs Required for a Squarer and Quad Circuit for $GF(2^9)$

Output bit	Squarer Circuit		Quad Circuit	
	$b(x)^2$	#LUTs	$b(x)^4$	#LUTs
0	b_0	0	b_0	0
1	b_5	0	b_7	0
2	$b_1 + b_5$	1	$b_5 + b_7$	1
3	b_6	0	$b_3 + b_7$	1
4	$b_2 + b_6$	1	$b_1 + b_3 + b_5 + b_7$	1
5	b_7	0	b_8	0
6	$b_3 + b_8$	1	$b_6 + b_8$	1
7	b_8	0	$b_4 + b_8$	1
8	$b_4 + b_8$	1	$b_2 + b_4 + b_6 + b_8$	1
Total LUTs		4		6

Proof 2 *When* $n \mid (m-1)$

$$\left[\alpha_{\frac{m-1}{n}}(a)\right]^2 = \left[a^{2^{n(\frac{m-1}{n})}-1}\right]^2$$
$$= \left[a^{2^{m-1}-1}\right]^2$$
$$= a^{-1}$$

When $n \nmid (m-1)$

$$\left[(\alpha_q(a))^{2^r}\beta_r(a)\right]^2 = \left[(a^{2^{nq}-1})^{2^r}(a^{2^r-1})\right]^2$$
$$= \left[a^{2^{nq+r}-1}\right]^2$$
$$= \left[a^{2^{m-1}-1}\right]^2$$
$$= a^{-1}$$

We note that elliptic curves over the field $GF(2^m)$ used for cryptographic purposes [393] have an odd m, therefore we discuss with respect to such values of m, although the results are valid for all m. In particular, we consider the case when $n = 2$; such that

$$\alpha_k(a) = a^{4^k-1}$$

To implement this we require *quad* circuits. To show the benefits of using a quad circuit on an FPGA instead of the conventional squarer, consider the equations for a squarer and a quad for an element $b(x) \in GF(2^9)$ (Table 5.5). The irreducible polynomial for the field is $x^9 + x + 1$. In the table, $b_0 \cdots b_8$ are the coefficients of $b(x)$. The #LUTs column shows the number of LUTs required for obtaining the particular output bit.

We would expect the LUTs required by the quad circuit be twice that of the squarer. However this is not the case. The quad circuit's LUT requirement is only 1.5 times that of the squarer. This is because the quad circuit has a lower percentage of *under utilized LUTs* (Equation 5.9). For example, from Table 5.5 we note that output bit 4 requires three *XOR* gates in the quad circuit and only one in the squarer. However, both circuits require only 1

TABLE 5.6: Comparison of Squarer and Quad Circuits on Xilinx Virtex 4 FPGA

Field	Squarer Circuit		Quad Circuit		Size ratio $\frac{\#LUT_q}{2(\#LUT_s)}$
	$\#LUT_s$	Delay (ns)	$\#LUT_q$	Delay (ns)	
$GF(2^{193})$	96	1.48	145	1.48	0.75
$GF(2^{233})$	153	1.48	230	1.48	0.75

Algorithm 5.3: qitmia *(Quad-ITA)*

Input: The element $a \in GF(2^m)$ and the Brauer chain $U = \{1, 2, \cdots, \frac{m-1}{2}, m-1\}$

Output: The multiplicative inverse a^{-1}

1 **begin**

2      $l = \text{length}(U)$

3      $a^2 = \text{hmul}(a, a)$;   /* hmul: hybrid Karatsuba multiplier */

     ;   /* proposed in Algorithm 5.2 */

4      $\alpha_{u_1} = a^3 = a^2 \cdot a$

5   **foreach** $u_i \in U (2 \leq i \leq l - 1)$ **do**

6          $p = u_{i-1}$

7          $q = u_i - u_{i-1}$

8          $\alpha_{u_i} = \text{hmul}(\alpha_p^{4^q}, \alpha_q)$

9   **end**

10      $a^{-1} = \text{hmul}(\alpha_{u_{l-1}}, \alpha_{u_{1-1}})$

11 **end**

LUT. This is also the case with output bit 8. This shows that the quad circuit is better at utilizing FPGA resources compared to the squarer. Moreover, both circuits have the same delay of one LUT. If we generate the fourth power by cascading two squarer circuits (i.e., $(b(x)^2)^2$), the resulting circuit would have twice the delay and require 25% more hardware resources than a single quad circuit.

These observations are scalable to larger fields as shown in Table 5.6. The circuits for the finite fields $GF(2^{233})$ and $GF(2^{193})$ use the irreducible polynomials $x^{233} + x^{74} + 1$ and $x^{193} + x^{15} + 1$, respectively. They were synthesized for a *Xilinx Virtex 4* FPGA. The table shows that the area saved even for large fields is about 25%. While the combinational delay of a single squarer is equal to that of the quad.

Based on this observation we propose a *quad-ITA* using quad exponentiation circuits instead of squarers. The procedure for obtaining the inverse for an odd m using the quad-ITA is shown in Algorithm 5.3. The algorithm assumes a Brauer addition chain.

The overhead of the quad-ITA is the need to precompute a^3. Since we do not have a squarer this has to be done by the multiplication block, which is present in the architecture. Using the multiplication unit, cubing is accomplished in two clock cycles without any additional hardware requirements. Similarly, the final squaring can be done in one clock cycle by the multiplier with no additional hardware required.

Consider the example of finding the multiplicative inverse of an element $a \in GF(2^{233})$ using the quad-ITA. From Theorem 5.11.2, setting $n = 2$ and $m = 233$, $a^{-1} = [\alpha_{\frac{232}{2}}(a)]^2 = [\alpha_{116}(a)]^2$. This requires computation of $\alpha_{116}(a) = a^{2^{2 \cdot 116} - 1} = a^{4^{116} - 1}$ and then doing a squaring, $a^{-1} = (\alpha_{116}(a))^2$. We use the same Brauer chain (Equation 5.24) as we did in the previous example. Excluding the precomputation step, computing $\alpha_{116}(a)$ requires 9 steps. The total number of quad operations to compute $\alpha_{116}(a)$ is 115 and the number of multiplications is 9. The precomputation step requires 2 clock cycles and the final squaring takes one clock cycle. In all, **12** multiplications are required for the inverse operation. In general for an addition chain for $m - 1$ of length l, the quad-ITA requires two additional multiplications compared to the ITA implementation of [330].

$$\#Multiplications : l + 1 \qquad (5.28)$$

The number of quad operations required is given by

$$\#QuadPowers : \frac{(m-1)}{2} - 1 \qquad (5.29)$$

The number of clock cycles required is given by the Equation 5.30. The summation in the equation is the clock cycles required for the quadblock, while $l + 1$ is the clock cycles of the multiplier.

$$\#ClockCycles = (l+1) + \sum_{i=2}^{l-1} \lceil \frac{u_i - u_{i-1}}{u_s} \rceil \qquad (5.30)$$

The difference in the clock cycles between the ITA of [330] (Equation 5.25) and the quad-ITA (Equation 5.30) is

$$\lceil \frac{u_l - u_{l-1}}{u_s} - 1 \rceil \qquad (5.31)$$

In general for addition chains used in ECC, the value of $u_l - u_{l-1}$ is as large as $(m-1)/2$ and much greater than u_s, therefore the clock cycles saved is significant.

5.11.3 Hardware Architecture of Quad ITA

To compare the proposed quad-ITA with other reported inverse implementations we develop a dedicated processor shown in **Fig. 5.6** that generates the inverse of the input $a \in GF(2^{233})$. Generating the inverse requires the computation of the steps in Table 5.7 followed by a squaring. The main components of the architecture is a finite field multiplier and a quadblock. The multiplier is an implementation of the hybrid Karatsuba algorithm (Section 5.7.1). The quadblock (**Fig. 5.7**) consists of 14 cascaded circuits, each circuit

TABLE 5.7: Inverse of $a \in GF(2^{233})$ using Quad-ITA

	$\alpha_{u_i}(\mathbf{a})$	$\alpha_{u_j+u_k}(\mathbf{a})$	Exponentiation
1	$\alpha_1(a)$		a^3
2	$\alpha_2(a)$	$\alpha_{1+1}(a)$	$(\alpha_1)^{4^1}\alpha_1 = a^{4^2-1}$
3	$\alpha_3(a)$	$\alpha_{2+1}(a)$	$(\alpha_2)^{4^1}\alpha_1 = a^{4^3-1}$
4	$\alpha_6(a)$	$\alpha_{3+3}(a)$	$(\alpha_3)^{4^3}\alpha_3 = a^{4^6-1}$
5	$\alpha_7(a)$	$\alpha_{6+1}(a)$	$(\alpha_6)^{4^1}\alpha_1 = a^{4^7-1}$
6	$\alpha_{14}(a)$	$\alpha_{7+7}(a)$	$(\alpha_7)^{4^7}\alpha_7 = a^{4^{14}-1}$
7	$\alpha_{28}(a)$	$\alpha_{14+14}(a)$	$(\alpha_{14})^{4^{14}}\alpha_{14} = a^{4^{28}-1}$
8	$\alpha_{29}(a)$	$\alpha_{28+1}(a)$	$(\alpha_{28})^{4^1}\alpha_1 = a^{4^{29}-1}$
9	$\alpha_{58}(a)$	$\alpha_{29+29}(a)$	$(\alpha_{29})^{4^{29}}\alpha_{29} = a^{4^{58}-1}$
10	$\alpha_{116}(a)$	$\alpha_{58+58}(a)$	$(\alpha_{58})^{4^{58}}\alpha_{58} = a^{4^{116}-1}$

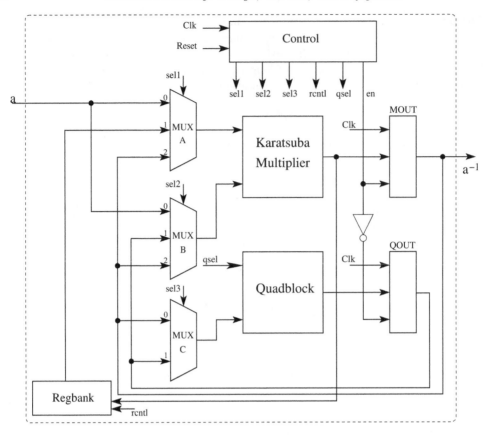

FIGURE 5.6: Quad-ITA Architecture for $GF(2^{233})$ with the Addition Chain 5.24

generating the fourth power of its input. If qin is the input to the quadblock, the powers of qin generated are qin^4, qin^{4^2}, $qin^{4^3} \cdots qin^{4^{14}}$. A multiplexer in the quadblock, controlled

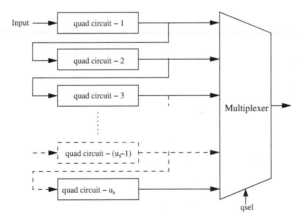

FIGURE 5.7: Quadblock Design: Raises the Input to the Power of 4^k

TABLE 5.8: Control Word for $GF(2^{233})$ Quad-ITA for Table 5.7

Step	Clock	sel1	sel2	sel3	qsel	en
$\alpha_1(a)$	1	0	0	$\times$	$\times$	1
	2	0	2	$\times$	$\times$	1
$\alpha_2(a)$	3	$\times$	$\times$	0	1	0
	4	1	1	$\times$	$\times$	1
$\alpha_3(a)$	5	$\times$	$\times$	0	1	0
	6	1	1	$\times$	$\times$	1
$\alpha_6(a)$	7	$\times$	$\times$	0	3	0
	8	2	1	$\times$	$\times$	1
$\alpha_7(a)$	9	$\times$	$\times$	0	1	0
	10	1	1	$\times$	$\times$	1
$\alpha_{14}(a)$	11	$\times$	$\times$	0	7	0
	12	2	1	$\times$	$\times$	1
$\alpha_{28}(a)$	13	$\times$	$\times$	0	14	0
	14	2	1	$\times$	$\times$	1
$\alpha_{29}(a)$	15	$\times$	$\times$	0	1	0
	16	1	1	$\times$	$\times$	1
$\alpha_{58}(a)$	17	$\times$	$\times$	0	14	0
	18	$\times$	$\times$	1	14	0
	19	$\times$	$\times$	1	1	0
	20	2	1	$\times$	$\times$	1
$\alpha_{116}(a)$	21	$\times$	$\times$	0	14	0
	22	$\times$	$\times$	1	14	0
	23	$\times$	$\times$	1	14	0
	24	$\times$	$\times$	1	14	0
	25	$\times$	$\times$	1	2	0
	26	2	1	$\times$	$\times$	1
$FinalSquare$	27	2	2	$\times$	$\times$	1

by the select lines $qsel$, determines which of the 14 powers gets passed on to the output. The output of the quadblock can be represented as $qin^{4^{qsel}}$.

Two buffers $MOUT$ and $QOUT$ store the output of the multiplier and the quadblock respectively. At every clock cycle, either the multiplier or the quadblock (but not both) is active (The *en* signal if 1 enables either the $MOUT$, otherwise the $QOUT$ buffer). A register bank may be used to store results of each step (α_{u_i}) of Algorithm 5.3. A result is stored only if it is required for later computations.

The controller is a state machine designed based on the adder chain and the number of cascaded quad circuits in the quadblock. At every clock cycle, control signals are generated for the multiplexer selection lines, enables to the buffers and access signals to the register bank. As an example, consider the computations of Table 5.7. The corresponding control signals generated by the controller is as shown in Table 5.8. The first step in the computation of a^{-1} is the determination of a^3. This takes two clock cycles. In the first clock, a is fed to both inputs of the multiplier. This is done by controlling the appropriate select lines of the multiplexers. The result, a^2, is used in the following clock along with a to produce a^3. This is stored in the register bank. The second step is the computation of $\alpha_2(a)$. This too requires two clock cycles. The first clock uses a^3 as the input to the quadblock to compute

$(\alpha_1)^{4^1}$. In the next clock, this is multiplied with a^3 to produce the required output. In general, computing any step $\alpha_{u_i}(a) = \alpha_{u_j + u_k}(a)$ takes $1 + \lceil \frac{u_j}{14} \rceil$ clock cycles. Of this, $\lceil \frac{u_j}{14} \rceil$ clock cycles are used by the quadblock, while the multiplier requires a single clock cycle. At the end of a step, the result is present in $MOUT$.

5.11.3.1   Addition Chain Selection Criteria

The length of the addition chain influences the number of clock cycles required to compute the inverse (Equations 5.25 and 5.30), hence proper selection of the addition chain is critical to the design. For a given m, there could be several optimal addition chains. It is required to select one chain from available optimal chains. The amount of memory required by the addition chain can be used as a secondary selection criteria. The memory utilized by an addition chain is the registers required for storage of the results from intermediate steps. The result of step $\alpha_i(a)$ is stored only if it is required to be used in any other step $\alpha_j(a)$ and $j > i + 1$. Consider the addition chain in 5.32.

$$U_2 = (\quad 1 \quad 2 \quad 3 \quad 5 \quad 6 \quad 12 \quad 17 \quad 29 \quad 58 \quad 116 \quad 232 \quad) \tag{5.32}$$

Computing $\alpha_5(a) = \alpha_{2+3}(a)$ requires $\alpha_2(a)$, therefore $\alpha_2(a)$ needs to be stored. Similarly, $\alpha_1(a)$, $\alpha_5(a)$ and $\alpha_{12}(a)$ needs to be stored to compute $\alpha_3(a)$, $\alpha_{17}(a)$ and $\alpha_{29}(a)$ respectively. In all four registers are required. Minimizing the number of registers is important because, for cryptographic applications m is generally large, therefore each register's size is significant.

Using Brauer chains has the advantage that for every step (except the first), at least one input is read from the output of the previous step. The output of the previous step is stored in $MOUT$, therefore need not be read from any register and no storage is required. The second input to the step would ideally be a doubling. For example, computing $\alpha_{116}(a)$ requires only $\alpha_{58}(a)$. Since $\alpha_{58}(a)$ is the result from the previous step, it is stored in $MOUT$. Therefore, computing $\alpha_{116}(a)$ does not require any stored values.

5.11.3.2   Design of the Quadblock

The number of quad circuits cascaded (u_s) has an influence on the clock cycles, frequency and area requirements of the quad-ITA. Increasing the number of cascaded blocks would reduce the number of clock cycles (Equation 5.25) required at the cost of an increase in area and delay.

Let a single quad circuit require l_p LUTs and have a combinational delay of t_p. For this analysis we assume that t_p includes the gate delay as well as the path delay. We also assume that the path delay is constant. The values of l_p and t_p depend on the finite field $GF(2^m)$ and the irreducible polynomial. A cascade of u_s quad circuits would require $u_s \cdot l_p$ LUTs and have a delay of $u_s \cdot t_p$.

In order that the quadblock not alter the frequency of operation, u_s should be selected such that $u_s \cdot t_p$ is less than the maximum combinational delay of the entire design. In the quad-ITA hardware, the maximum delay is from the Karatsuba multiplier, therefore we select u_s such that the delay of the quadblock is less than the delay of the multiplier.

$$u_s \cdot t_p \leq \text{Delay of multiplier}$$

However, reducing u_s would increase the clock cycles required. Therefore, we select u_s so that the quadblock delay is close to the multiplier delay.

The graph in **Fig. 5.8** plots the computation delay (clock period in nanoseconds × the clock cycles) required versus the number of quads in the quad-ITA for the field $GF(2^{233})$. For small values of u_s, the delay is mainly decided by the multiplier, while the clock cycles

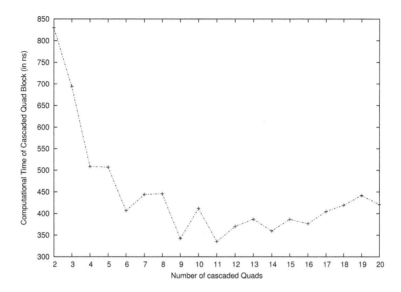

FIGURE 5.8: Clock Cycles of Computation Time versus Number of Quads in Quadblock on a Xilinx Virtex 4 FPGA for $GF(2^{233})$

required is large. For large number of cascades, the delay of the quadblock exceeds that of the multiplier, therefore the delay of the circuit is now decided by the quadblock. Lowest computation time is obtained with around 11 cascaded quads. For this, the delay of the quadblock is slightly lower than the multiplier. Therefore, the critical delay is the path through the multiplier, while the clock cycles required is around 30. Therefore for the quad-ITA in a field $GF(2^{233})$, 11 cascaded quads result in least computation time. However, in order to make the clock cycles required to compute the finite field inverse in $GF(2^{233})$ equal to the parallel implementation of [330], 14 cascaded quads are used even though this causes a marginal increase in the computation time (which is still quite lesser than the parallel implementation at 0.55 μsec).

5.12   Experimental Results

In this section we compare our work with reported finite field inverse results. We also test our design for scalability over several fields.

The graph in **Fig. 5.9** shows the scalability of the quad-ITA and compares it with a squarer-ITA. The design of the squarer-ITA is similar to that of the quad-ITA (**Fig. 5.6**) except for the quadblock. The quad circuits in the quadblock is replaced by squarer circuits. Both the quadblock and squarer block have the same number of cascaded circuits. The platform used for generating the graph is a *Xilinx Virtex 4 FPGA*. The X axis has increasing field sizes (see the Appendix for list of finite fields), and the Y axis has the performance metric shown below.

$$Performance = \frac{Frequency}{Slices \times ClockCycles} \tag{5.33}$$

The *slices* is the number of slices required on the FPGA as reported by Xilinx's ISE

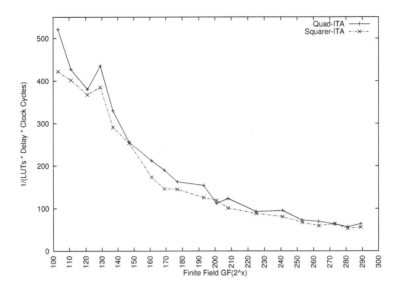

FIGURE 5.9: Performance of Quad-ITA vs Squarer-ITA Implementation for Different Fields on a Xilinx Virtex 4 FPGA

TABLE 5.9: Comparison for Inversion on Xilinx Virtex E

Implementation	Algorithm	Platform	Field	Slices	Frequency (MHz) (f)	Clock Cycle (c)	Computation Time (c/f)	Performance (Equation 5.33)
Dormale [108]	Montgomery	XCV2000E	160	890	50	-	$9.71\mu sec$	115.7
		XCV2000E	256	1390	41	-	$18.7\mu sec$	38.4
Crowe [102]	Montgomery	XCV2000E	160	1094	51	-	$6.28\mu sec$	145.5
		XCV2000E	256	1722	39	-	$13.17\mu sec$	44.1
Henriquez [333]	ITA	XCV3200E	193	10065	21.2	27	$1.33\mu sec$	78
Henriquez [330]	Parallel ITA	XCV3200E	193	11081	21.2	20	$0.94\mu sec$	95.7
This work	quad-ITA	XCV3200E	193	11911	36.2	20	$0.55\mu sec$	152.1

synthesis tool. The graph shows that the quad-ITA has better performance compared to the squarer-ITA for most fields.

Table 5.9 compares the quad-ITA with the best reported ITA and Montgomery inverse algorithms available. The FPGA used in all designs is the *Xilinx Virtex E*. The quad-ITA has the best computation time and performance compared to the other implementations. It may be noted that the larger area compared to [333] and [330] of the quad-ITA is because it uses distributed RAM [418] for registers, while [333] and [330] use block RAM [417]. The distributed RAM requires additional CLB resources while block RAM does not.

Other higher order exponentiation circuits can also be used in ITA [321]. In the next section, we show a generalization of ITA that uses exponentiation by 2^n to compute inverse.

5.13   Generalization of the ITA for 2^n Circuit

Theorems 16 and 17 show that the ITA algorithm can be extended to use any 2^n circuit and not just squarers or quads [141]. For any $a \in GF(2^m)$ and natural number k, define

$\alpha_k(a) = a^{2^{nk}-1}$.

Theorem 16 *If $a \in GF(2^m)$, $\alpha_{k_1}(a) = a^{2^{nk_1}-1}$ and $\alpha_{k_2}(a) = a^{2^{nk_2}-1}$ then*

$$\alpha_{k_1+k_2}(a) = [\alpha_{k_1}(a)]^{2^{nk_2}} \cdot \alpha_{k_2}(a)$$

where k_1, k_2 and $n \in \mathbb{N}$.

Theorem 17 *The inverse of an element $a \in GF(2^m)$ is*

$$a^{-1} = \begin{cases} \{\alpha_{\frac{m-1}{n}}(a)\}^2 & \text{if } n \mid (m-1); \\ \{(\alpha_q(a))^{2^r}\beta_r(a)\}^2 & \text{if } n \nmid (m-1). \end{cases}$$

where $nq + r = m - 1$ and n, q, and $r \in \mathbb{N}$.

Addition chain for $(m-1)/n$ is used when $n|(m-1)$, while addition chain for q is used for the other case. The working principle of ITA using 2^n exponentiation circuit is presented in Algorithm 5.4.

Algorithm 5.4: genita (2^n ITA)

Input: An element $a \in GF(2^m)$ and addition chain $U = \{u_i\}$ for $q = \lfloor \frac{m-1}{n} \rfloor$

$$U = \{1, 2, \ldots, q\} \text{ where } q = \lfloor \frac{m-1}{n} \rfloor$$

Output: $a^{-1} \in GF(2^m)$ such that $a^{-1} \cdot a = 1$
1 **begin**
2     $l = length \ of \ U$
3     $\alpha_{u_1} = a^{2^n-1}$
4     $\beta_r = a^{2^r-1}$
5   **for** $i = 2$ **to** l **do**
6         $k_1 = u_{i-1}$
7         $k_2 = u_i - u_{i-1}$
8         $\alpha_{u_i} = \alpha_{k_1}^{2^{nk_2}} * \alpha_{k_2}$
9   **end**
10     $\alpha_{u_l} = \alpha_{u_l}^{2^r} \cdot \beta_r$
11     $a^{-1} = \alpha_{u_l} * \alpha_{u_l}$
12 **end**

Algorithm 5.4 starts with the precomputation of $\alpha_1 = a^{2^n-1} = a \cdot a^2 \cdot a^{2^2} \cdots a^{2^{n-1}}$. The precomputation can be done efficiently using an addition chain for $2^n - 1$. For the case $n \nmid (m-1)$ computation of $\beta_r(a) = a^{2^r-1}$ is required. Since $1 \leq r \leq (n-1)$, the computation cost of $\beta_r(a)$ can be reduced by using an addition chain for $2^n - 1$ which contains r. When such an addition chain is used, $\beta_r(a)$ becomes an intermediate value during the computation of α_1. The iteration in line 5 of the algorithm is used for computation of the recursive relation shown in Theorem 16. After computation of α_{u_l}, a final squaring is required to get the inverse for the case $n|(m-1)$, while small amount of extra computation (line number 10 of Algorithm 5.4) is required for the case $n \nmid (m-1)$.

The next section describes a generic hardware architecture for the generalized ITA.

5.14   Hardware Architecture for 2^n Circuit Based ITA

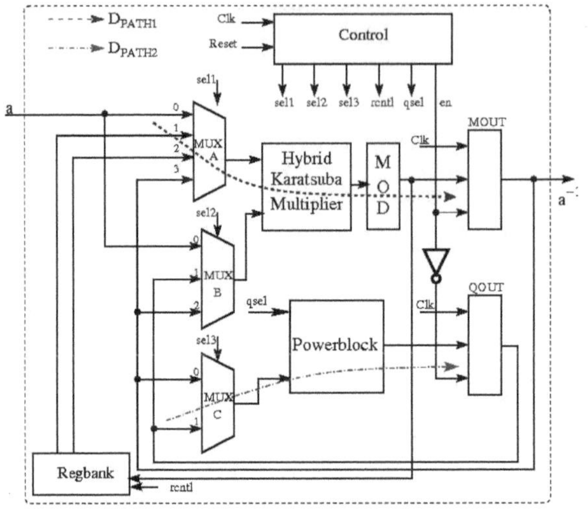

FIGURE 5.10: FPGA Architecture for 2^n ITA

A hardware architecture for generalized ITA is presented in **Fig. 5.10**. The finite field multiplier is used to perform field multiplications required in Algorithm 5.4. The multiplier is of combinational type and follows the *hybrid Karatsuba algorithm*. Buffer $MOUT$ is used to latch output from the multiplier.

Computing α_{u_i}, $2 \le i \le l$ in line 8 of Algorithm 5.4 requires exponentiation of α_{k_1} by 2^{nk_2}. Exponentiations are performed by the *Powerblock* in **Fig. 5.10** which contains 2^n exponentiation circuits. Output from the Powerblock is latched in buffer $QOUT$. If a single 2^n circuit is used, it will take k_2 number of clock cycles to compute $\alpha_{k_1}^{2^{nk_2}}$. To reduce the number of clock cycles required for repeated exponentiations, u_s number of cascaded 2^n circuits are kept in the Powerblock. An explored diagram of the Powerblock is shown in **Fig. 5.11**. In a single clock cycle, the Powerblock can raise an element a to a maximum of $a^{2^{nu_s}}$. The multiplexer in the Powerblock is used to tap out interim outputs when the number of repeated exponentiations k_2 is less than u_s. The control signal for the Powerblock is *qsel*. For the case $k_2 > u_s$, more than one clock cycles are required and buffer $QOUT$ works as a feedback for the Powerblock.

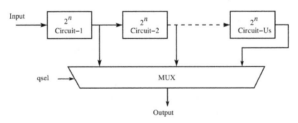

FIGURE 5.11: Powerblock Design with Cascaded 2^n Circuits

Control signal *en* is used in each clock cycle to latch the output of either the multiplier or the Powerblock (but not both). Any intermediate result that is required in a later step for the recursive sequence, is stored in a register bank *Regbank*. The *Control* block generates all the control signals that drive a Finite State Machine (FSM).

The performance of the architecture as a function of the area, delay, and number of clock cycles required, mainly depends on the multiplier and the Powerblock. For a given field, the multiplier architecture is fixed, while the exponentiation circuit (n) and the number of such circuits (u_s) are variable. In order to achieve optimal performance, these design parameters have to be tuned. Later in Section 5.15, a formal approach is presented which models the area and delay requirement of the generalized ITA architecture for various values of n and u_s, and tries to estimate the ideal values for these two design parameters for any given field $GF(2^m)$ on k-LUT based FPGAs. The next few lines of this section present an analysis for the number of clock cycles required to compute inverse using the 2^n ITA architecture over field $GF(2^m)$.

Clock Cycle Requirement for the 2^n ITA Architecture: Computing $\alpha_{k_1}^{2^{nk_2}}$ in line 8 of Algorithm 5.4 requires $k_2 = u_i - u_{i-1}$ number of repeated exponentiations, where u_i and u_{i-1} are elements in the addition chain for q. Considering u_s number of cascaded 2^n circuits, $\lceil \frac{u_i - u_{i-1}}{u_s} \rceil$ number of clock cycles are required for computing $\alpha_{k_1}^{2^{nk_2}}$. For the multiplication with α_{k_2}, a single clock cycle is required (assuming a combinational multiplier). Additionally, $l' - 1$ clock cycles are required to compute α_1, where l' is the length of the addition chain for $2^n - 1$. The final squaring requires a clock cycle, and an extra clock cycle is used to indicate completion of the field inversion. In all, the total number of clock cycles required when $n \mid (m-1)$ is

$$\#ClockCycles = l' + l + \sum_{i=2}^{l} \left\lceil \frac{u_i - u_{i-1}}{u_s} \right\rceil \tag{5.34}$$

When $n \nmid (m-1)$, r additional clock cycles are required for $(\alpha_q(a))^{2^r}$ calculation and one clock cycle for $(\alpha_q(a))^{2^r} \beta_r(a)$ calculation (line 10 in Algorithm 5.4). Thus, the total clock-cycle requirement for $n \nmid (m-1)$ is

$$\#ClockCycles = l' + l + 1 + r + \sum_{i=2}^{l} \left\lceil \frac{u_i - u_{i-1}}{u_s} \right\rceil \tag{5.35}$$

5.15 Area and Delay Estimations for the 2^n ITA

In this section, we propose a theoretical approach to estimate the number of LUTs required to implement a Boolean function with x number of input variables on k-LUT based FPGAs. The theoretical model also estimates the number of k-LUTs present in the critical path of the Boolean function. With the help of the theoretical model, we estimate area and delay requirement of the ITA architecture for various configurations. Later we will show how such estimations can be used to find optimal configurations for the ITA architecture.

5.15.1 Area and Delay of a x Variable Boolean Function

The number of LUTs required to implement a Boolean function is the measure of the area of a function. A k input LUT (k-LUT) can be considered a black box that can perform any functionality of a maximum of k variables. If there is a single variable, then no LUT is required. If there are more than k variables, then more than one k-LUTs are required to implement the functionality. The total number of k input LUTs for a function with x variables can be expressed as,

$$lut(x) = \begin{cases} 0 & \text{if } x \leq 1 \\ 1 & \text{if } 1 < x \leq k \\ \lfloor \frac{x-k}{k-1} \rfloor + 2 & \text{if } x > k \text{ and } (k-1) \nmid (x-k) \\ \frac{x-k}{k-1} + 1 & \text{if } x > k \text{ and } (k-1)|(x-k) \end{cases} \tag{5.36}$$

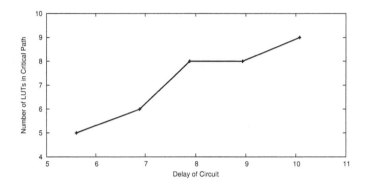

FIGURE 5.12: LUTs in Critical Path vs Delay for a Combinational Multiplier

Delay in FPGAs is comprised of LUT delays and routing delays. Analyzing the delay of a circuit on FPGA platform is much more complex than area analysis. By experimentation we have found that for designs having combinational components, the delay of the design varies linearly with the number of LUTs present in the critical path. **Fig. 5.12** shows this linear relationship between the number of LUTs in the critical path and the delay in multipliers of different sizes. Due to such linear relationship, we can consider that the number of LUTs in the critical path is a measure of actual delay. From now onwards we use the term *lut delay* to mean the number of k-LUTs present in the critical path.

For a x variable Boolean function, number of k-LUTs in the critical path is denoted by the function $maxlutpath(x)$ and is

$$maxlutpath(x) = \lceil log_k(x) \rceil. \tag{5.37}$$

We will use Equation 5.36 and 5.37 for estimating area and delay of different finite field primitives used in the generalized ITA architecture.

5.15.2 Area and LUT Delay Estimates for the Field Multiplier

Multiplication in binary finite fields involves a polynomial multiplication followed by a modular reduction. Multipliers are categorized into different configurations based on the scope of the parallelism in them. Three common architectures are serial multipliers, word-parallel multipliers, and bit-parallel multipliers. Serial multipliers and word-parallel multipliers use less area and have less delays but require several clock cycles. A bit-parallel multiplier is one in which all the computed output bits are available in the same clock cycle. Bit-parallel multipliers are fast, but comes with an enormous area overhead, and has large delays. For fast ECC architectures, number of clock cycles is an important factor affecting the performance and thus bit-parallel multipliers are preferred.

Several algorithms for bit-parallel finite field multiplication exist in literature. Of these the Karatsuba multiplier is the only one with sub-quadratic space and time complexity. In a Karatsuba multiplier, the m degree polynomial operands a and b are split into half as shown:

$$a = a_h x^{\lfloor \frac{m}{2} \rfloor} + a_l \qquad b = b_h x^{\lfloor \frac{m}{2} \rfloor} + b_l$$

If m is odd, a_h and b_h are padded with a bit to make all terms equal size. The m bit multiplication is given by

$$a \cdot b = (a_h \cdot b_h)x^m + [(a_h + a_l) \cdot (b_h + b_l) + a_h \cdot b_h + a_l \cdot b_l]x^{m/2} + (a_l \cdot b_l) \qquad (5.38)$$

The Karatsuba algorithm is applied recursively for the three $m/2$ bit multiplications: $(a_h \cdot b_h)$, $(a_l \cdot b_l)$, and $(a_h + a_l) \cdot (b_h + b_l)$. Each recursion reduces the size of the input by half while tripling the number of multiplications required.

A fully recursive Karatsuba multiplier is inefficient due to two reasons. First, for small sized multiplications, the percentage of under utilized LUTs is high causing a bloated area requirement. Second, in the Karatsuba algorithm the number of multiplications triple with every recursion. So there are several instances of small multipliers. Thus the bloated size of the small multipliers affects the overall area.

For small operands, other quadratic complexity multiplication algorithms out-perform the Karatsuba algorithm. There exists a threshold (τ) in the operand size, above which the Karatsuba algorithm performs better. The multiplier uses the Simple Karatsuba algorithm when the size of the multiplicands is above the threshold and a general Karatsuba algorithm [404] for multiplications smaller than the threshold. Our field multiplier is designed in the similar way described in Section 5.7.1, but uses the classical polynomial multiplier instead of the general Karatsuba multiplier for multiplications below the threshold τ. We have found that classical multipliers deliver better results compared to general Karatsuba multipliers when used in threshold level.

For the multiplication $a \cdot b$, the operands a and b are recursively split into smaller operands until the size of each operand reaches the threshold. Classical multiplications are performed at the threshold level and then output from threshold multipliers are recursively combined and the final multiplication result is obtained after modular reduction. Thus, the entire bit-parallel Karatsuba multiplier consists of four stages (**Fig. 5.13**): the first stage splits the input operands to produce threshold operands; the second stage consists of threshold level multipliers; the third stage recursively combines the outputs from threshold level multipliers; and final stage does modular reduction.

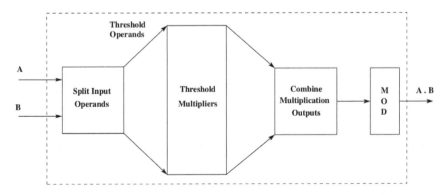

FIGURE 5.13: Three Stages of a Combinational Hybrid Karatsuba Multiplier

Here we present an analysis for estimating the number of LUTs required for the field multiplier. In Equation 5.38, it can be seen that the splitting of a and b introduces several smaller operands, out of which $(a_h + a_l)$ and $(b_h + b_l)$ requires addition operations (bitwise exclusive-or) and thus requires LUTs. We call such operands as *overlapped operands*. We consider the LUT size k is not less than 4. For a m bit Karatsuba multiplier where $m > \tau$, the splitting of the m bit operands requires $2 \cdot \lceil \frac{m}{2} \rceil$ number of LUTs, while the combination stage has an area requirement of $2m - 1$ LUTs. The total LUT requirement for the recursive Karatsuba multiplier of size $m > \tau$ is given by the recursive formula:

$$
\begin{aligned}
\#LUT_{hkmul}(m) &= 2 \cdot LUT_{hkmul}(\lceil \tfrac{m}{2} \rceil) + LUT_{hkmul}(\lfloor \tfrac{m}{2} \rfloor) \\
&\quad + 2 \cdot \lceil \tfrac{m}{2} \rceil + 2m - 1
\end{aligned}
\tag{5.39}
$$

When the multiplication size reaches τ, classical multipliers are used. The total number of LUTs for a τ bit classical multiplier is given by the following formula:

$$
\#LUT_{sbmul} = 2 \sum_{i=1}^{\tau-1} lut(2i) + lut(2\tau)
\tag{5.40}
$$

Now we present an analysis for delay of the combinational bit-parallel hybrid Karatsuba multiplier. As the splitting is recursive, a chain of overlapped operands are generated. The critical delay path of the splitting stage is through the longest chain of overlapped operands. **Fig. 5.14** shows the first two steps of recursive splitting of overlapped operands for a 256-bit input operand. After first round, the overlapped operand size reduces to 128 bits and each bit is sum of two input bits. Similarly, after second round of splitting, size of overlapped operands become 64 bits and each bit of the new overlapped operand is sum of four input bits. If the threshold operand size τ bits, then after $r = log_2 \lceil \frac{256}{\tau} \rceil$ rounds, the operand will reduce to a size of τ and each bit of the threshold overlapped operand will be sum of 2^r input bits. Thus, from Equation 5.37, the maximum LUT delay of the splitting stage is $D_{sp} = \lceil log_k(2^r) \rceil = \lceil log_k \frac{m}{\tau} \rceil$.

The threshold multipliers follow classical multiplication algorithm and has LUT delay given below

$$
D_{th} = maxlutpath(2\tau) = \lceil log_k(2\tau) \rceil
\tag{5.41}
$$

The *Combine Multiplication Outputs* block in the **Fig. 5.13** has $\lceil log_2(\frac{m}{\tau}) \rceil$ levels and each level has one LUT delay for $k \geq 4$. So, the delay of this stage is $D_{com} = \lceil log_2(\frac{m}{\tau}) \rceil$.

After the polynomial multiplication, the modular reduction circuit is used to reduce the $2m - 2$ bit output of the multiplier to m bits. The delay of the reduction circuit D_{mod} depends on the irreducible polynomials. D_{mod} is 1 for trinomials and 2 for pentanomials considering $4 \leq k \leq 6$.

The delay for the entire hybrid Karatsuba multiplier is given by the following equation.

$$
\begin{aligned}
D_{mul}(m) &= D_{sp} + D_{th} + D_{com} + D_{Mod} \tag{5.42} \\
&= \lceil log_k(\tfrac{m}{\tau}) \rceil + \lceil log_k(2\tau) \rceil + \lceil log_2(\tfrac{m}{\tau}) \rceil + D_{Mod}
\end{aligned}
$$

The delay reduces in a logarithm fashion with increase in τ (Equation 5.42). For example, it can be seen that for the field $GF(2^{163})$, $\tau = 10$ and $\tau = 30$ result in same LUT delay on 4−LUT based FPGAs. Since the threshold multipliers have quadratic complexity, the area requirement of the multiplier increases significantly with increase in τ. **Fig. 5.15** shows the area requirements of a $GF(2^{163})$ multiplier on a 4−LUT based FPGA for different threshold values. For $11 \leq \tau \leq 19$, minimum area is used, thus for $GF(2^{163})$ a threshold between 11 and 19 is optimal.

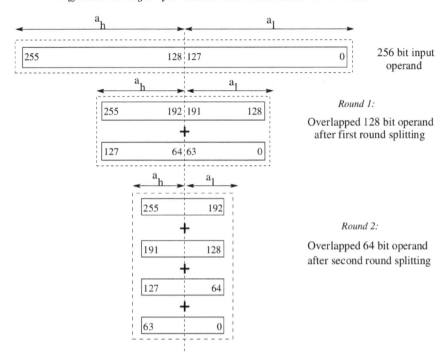

FIGURE 5.14: Generation of Overlapped Operands During Recursive Splitting of Inputs

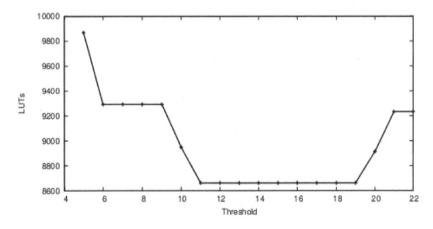

FIGURE 5.15: Threshold vs LUT Requirements for $GF(2^{163})$ Multiplier

5.15.3 Area and LUT Delay Estimates for the Reduction Circuit

The output of an m bit multiplier has $2m - 1$ bits and is fed to a modular reduction circuit to convert it into an m bit output. We denote the total number of LUTs in the modular reduction circuit by LUT_{Mod} and delay in terms of LUTs by D_{Mod}. For fields generated by irreducible trinomials, total number of k−LUTs for this reduction circuit is almost equal to the field size m (considering $k \geq 4$) and the *maxlutpath* is 1. For fields generated by irreducible pentanomials, total number of k−LUTs of the reduction circuit is almost twice the field size m for $4 \le k < 6$ and is almost equal to m for $k \ge 6$, while the *maxlutpath* is 2.

5.15.4   Area and LUT Delay Estimates of a 2^n Circuit

The output of a squarer circuit in $GF(2^m)$ is given by $d = A \cdot a$, where A is an $m \times m$ binary square matrix and a is the input column matrix $[a_0 \; a_1 \; \cdots \; a_{m-1}]^T$. Output d is the column matrix $[d_0 \; d_1 \; \cdots \; d_{m-1}]^T$. The matrix A depends on the irreducible polynomial and m. Similarly, the output of a 2^n circuit which raises an input $a \in GF(2^m)$ to a^{2^n}, can be expressed as $d = A^n \cdot a$ [141]. A particular output bit d_i is the XOR of some of the elements in the column matrix a. We use a program to get equations of all the m output bits for the 2^n circuit and then using Equation 5.36, we obtain the total LUT requirement per output bit d_i for $0 \le i \le m - 1$. The total LUT requirement of the entire 2^n circuit is given by,

$$\#LUT_{2^n} = \sum_{i=0}^{m-1} lut(d_i)$$

Similarly, Equation 5.37 gives the delay per output bit d_i in terms of LUTs. Since all output bits are computed in parallel, the delay of the 2^n circuit is the maximum LUT delays of all the d_i output bits and is given by,

$$\#D_{2^n} = Max(LUT \; delay \; of \; d_i) \quad for \; 0 \le i \le m - 1$$

5.15.5   Area and LUT Delay Estimates of a Multiplexer

For a $2^s : 1$ MUX, there are s selection lines, thus the output of a 2^s input MUX is a function of $2^s + s$ variables. So the total LUT requirements to implement the output functionality is $lut(2^s + s)$. For $GF(2^m)$, each input line to the MUX has m bits and the output has m bits. Thus the total LUT requirement for a 2^s input MUX, is given by

$$\#LUT_{MUX} = m \times lut(2^s + s) \tag{5.43}$$

Delay of the MUX in terms of LUTs is equal to the *maxlutpath* of $2^s + s$ variables and is given by,

$$\#D_{MUX} = maxlutpath(2^s + s) \tag{5.44}$$

If $2^{s-1} < number \; of \; inputs < 2^s$, then estimations in (5.43) and (5.44) for 2^s inputs give an upper bound. Practically, the values in this case are slightly lesser than the values for 2^s inputs in (5.43) and (5.44), and therefore the difference can be neglected.

5.15.6   Area and LUT Delay Estimates for the Powerblock

Let the Powerblock contain u_s number of cascaded 2^n circuits and the multiplexer MUX_P. The multiplexer is controlled by r number of selection lines where $2^{r-1} < u_s \le 2^r$. Thus number of k-LUTs in MUX_P is given by,

$$\#LUT_{MUX_P} = m \times lut(2^r + r)$$

Total number of LUTs in the Powerblock is,

$$\#LUT_{Powblk} = u_s \times LUT_{2^n} + LUT_{MUX_P}$$

Using Equations 5.37 and 5.44, delay of MUX_P in terms of LUTs is,

$$\#D_{MUX_P} = \lceil log_k(u_s + log_2 u_s) \rceil \tag{5.45}$$

Since, there are u_s number of cascaded 2^n circuits, the delay of the entire cascade is u_s times the delay of a single 2^n circuit. The delay of the multiplexer in the Powerblock is added to this delay to get the total delay of the Powerblock.

$$\begin{aligned} \#D_{Powblk} &= u_s \times D_{2^n} + D_{MUX_P} \\ &= u_s \times D_{2^n} + \lceil log_k(u_s + log_2 u_s) \rceil. \end{aligned} \tag{5.46}$$

5.15.7 Area Estimate for the Entire ITA Architecture

From **Fig. 5.10**, it can be seen that the total number of LUTs in the ITA architecture is the sum of the LUTs in the multiplier, reduction block, Powerblock, MUX_A, MUX_B, and MUX_C. The state machine (control block in **Fig. 5.10**) consumes very few LUTs and is not considered in the overall LUT count. Thus the total number of k-LUTs in the entire ITA is,

$$\#LUT_{ITA} = LUT_{Multiplier} + LUT_{Mod} + LUT_{Powblk} + LUT_{MUX_A} + LUT_{MUX_B} + LUT_{MUX_C}$$

5.15.8 LUT Delay Estimate for the Entire ITA Architecture

In **Fig. 5.10**, there are two parallel critical paths. The lut delay of the first path (D_{PATH1}) is through MUX_A, multiplier, and reduction block. The lut delay of second path (D_{PATH2}) is through MUX_C and the *Powerblock*. The delay of the entire ITA architecture is equal to the maximum of D_{PATH1} and D_{PATH2}. Using Equations 5.42 and 5.44, D_{PATH1} can be approximated in terms of LUTs as

$$D_{PATH1} \approx \lceil \frac{6}{k} \rceil + \lceil log_k(\frac{m}{\tau}) \rceil + \lceil log_2(\frac{m}{\tau}) \rceil + \lceil log_k(2\tau) \rceil + D_{Mod}$$

,where D_{Mod} has values of 1 and 2 for trinomials and pentanomials respectively. Similarly, D_{PATH2} can be approximated using Equation 5.44 as

$$\begin{aligned} D_{PATH2} &= D_{MUX_C} + D_{Powblk} \\ &\approx 1 + u_s \times D_{2^n} + \lceil log_k(u_s + log_2(u_s)) \rceil \end{aligned}$$

A finite state machine drives the control signals. Each control signal depends only on the value of the state variable and nothing else. Therefore it can be assumed that the delay in generating the control signals depends on the number of bits in the *state* register. The *state* variable increments up to the value of $\#ClockCycles$. Assuming a binary counter, the number of bits in the *state* variable is $log_2(\#ClockCycles)$. The delay in the control signals is

$$D_{Cntrl} = maxlutpath(log_2(\#ClockCycles))$$

This delay is added to the path delay. The total delay in the ITA in terms of LUTs is

$$\#D_{ITA} = Max(D_{PATH1}, D_{PATH2}) + D_{Cntrl} \tag{5.47}$$

5.16   Obtaining the Optimal Performing ITA Architecture

We measure the performance of the ITA hardware by the metric

$$Performance = \frac{1}{(LUT_{ITA} \times D_{ITA} \times ClockCycles)}$$

For a given field $GF(2^m)$ and k-LUT based FPGA, the Powerblock can be configured with different exponentiation circuits (2^n) and number of cascades (u_s). An increase in u_s, decreases the clock cycles required at the cost of an increase in area and delay through the Powerblock. To get maximum performance, u_s should be chosen in such a way that it minimizes clock cycles without increasing the delay (D_{ITA}) and area (LUT_{ITA}) significantly. D_{PATH1} is not dependent on n or u_s and is constant. From Equation 5.47, it follows that D_{ITA} is minimum when

$$D_{PATH1} \approx D_{PATH2}. \tag{5.48}$$

When Equation 5.48 is satisfied, we can assume that D_{ITA} in Equation 5.47 is

$$\#D_{ITA} = D_{PATH1} + D_{Cntrl}.$$

D_{Cntrl} has a small value and is less dependent on n and u_s. Since D_{PATH1} is constant, D_{ITA} can be considered to be a constant when Equation 5.48 is satisfied.

In Equation of LUT_{ITA}, the multiplier consumes a significant portion of total area. The area of a 2^n circuit is small. So, variation of n and u_s under Equation 5.48 causes negligible variation in total area. Thus, we can assume that LUT_{ITA} remains almost unaffected when Equation 5.48 is satisfied.

The $\#ClockCycles$ changes significantly with n and u_s. Clock cycle requirement in Equations 5.34 and 6.7 can be approximated as ,

$$Clock\tilde{C}ycles \approx (2n - 1) + l + r + \lceil \frac{m-1}{nu_s} \rceil \tag{5.49}$$

where $2n - 1$ is the clock cycle requirement for α_1 computation and l is the length of addition chain for $\lfloor \frac{m-1}{n} \rfloor$. From Equation 5.49, it can be seen that with increase in n, α_1 computation increases linearly with n, but the term $\lceil \frac{m-1}{nu_s} \rceil$ reduces. When n is small, $\lceil \frac{m-1}{nu_s} \rceil$ is significant compared to $2n - 1$. So, $Clock\hat{C}ycles$ reduces significantly with increase in n. For large values of n, the term $(2n - 1)$ dominates the term $\lceil \frac{m-1}{nu_s} \rceil$. So, $Clock\tilde{C}ycles$ increases monotonically with n. This implies that we could restrict n to those values for which we get savings in $\#ClockCycles$. This effect of increase in n on clock cycles for α_1 computation and on $\#ClockCycles$ is shown in **Fig. 5.16** for the field $GF(2^{233})$.

Minimization of $\#ClockCycles$ without increasing the D_{ITA} leads to maximum performance. The following algorithm is used to obtain best design parameters.

1. Starting from the squarer ($n = 1$) circuits, estimate u_s so that Equation 5.48 is achieved. Plug in the values of n and u_s in Equation 5.49 and get $Clock\tilde{C}ycles$. For $n = 1$, we call it $Clock\tilde{C}ycles_1$.

2. Now, for a higher value of n say $n_i = i$, where $i > 1$, the number of cascades u_{s_i} is determined as in Step 1 and the corresponding value of $Clock\tilde{C}ycles$ (say $Clock\tilde{C}ycles_i$ is obtained.

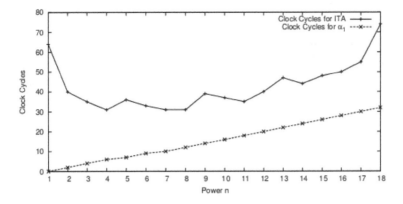

FIGURE 5.16: Number of Clock Cycles vs. n

3. The second step is repeated for incremental values of n_i until $Clock\tilde{C}ycles_i$ increases monotonically (as per the previous discussion) as n_i increases.

The best design strategy for the Powerblock is the configuration $(\hat{n}, \hat{u}_s)$ which gives the minimum $Clock\tilde{C}ycles$. For example, when $m = 233$ and $k = 4$, $(2, 8)$ and $(4, 5)$ give minimum value of $Clock\tilde{C}ycles$ and satisfy Equation 5.48 closely. In the next section we support our theoretical estimates with experimental results.

5.17   Validation of Theoretical Estimations

For validation of the theoretical estimates, experiments were done on Xilinx Virtex IV and Virtex V FPGAs using ISE version 10.1. Our estimation model used *maxlutpath* to estimate delays. In FPGAs, the delays are difficult to characterize. The delay of an LUT and routing delay depends on the device technology and CAD tool. To estimate FPGA delay of any ITA architecture for a field $GF(2^m)$, we do the following. We first synthesize a squarer based ITA architecture (which we call *reference architecture*) and obtain its delay. We denote this delay as *reference delay*. Using our estimation model, we estimate the *maxlutpath* of the reference architecture (which we call *reference maxlutpath*). It was found experimentally that the FPGA delay of the ITA architecture varies proportionally with the *maxlutpath*. Therefore, for ITA designs in the same field as the reference architecture, we can consider the variation in FPGA delay to be proportional to *maxlutpath* variation. This is given by

$$reference\ \ delay + \mathcal{C} \times (maxlutpath - reference\ maxlutpath)$$

Here $\mathcal{C}$ is a constant which depends on the device technology. In our experiments we used *4vlx80ff1148-11* and *xc5vlx220-2-ff1760* FPGAs, which have 4-LUT and 6-LUT respectively. For the 4-LUT FPGA, we experimentally found $\mathcal{C} = 0.2$, while the 6-LUT had $\mathcal{C} = 0.1$.

Table 5.10 shows comparisons between the theoretical and experimental results for quad based ITA in $GF(2^{233})$ with different number of cascaded quad blocks for 4-LUT based FPGAs. The table (5.10) shows that our estimation for number of cascades $\hat{u}_s = 8$ gives best performance for $\hat{n} = 2$. Graphs in **Fig. 5.17** and **Fig. 5.18** show performance variations with exponentiations on 4 and 6−LUT based FPGAs for the trinomial field $GF(2^{233})$ and pentanomial fields $GF(2^{163})$ and $GF(2^{283})$ [393]. In the graphs Ex implies performance

N	Theoretical estimation					Experimental values			
	Clock Cycle	LUT	LUT Delay	Total Delay (ns)	P	Clock Cycle	LUT	Total Delay (ns)	P
7	35	19523	13	13.3	110	35	21049	13.5	100
8	32	19753	14	13.5	117	32	21291	13.47	109
10	30	20912	16	13.9	114	30	23926	13.72	102
12	29	21372	18	14.3	113	29	24220	14.28	100

TABLE 5.10: Theoretical and Experimental Comparison for Different Number of Cascades of a 2^2 based ITA in the field $GF(2^{233})$

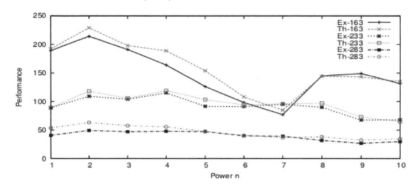

FIGURE 5.17: Performance Variation with n in 4-LUT-based FPGA

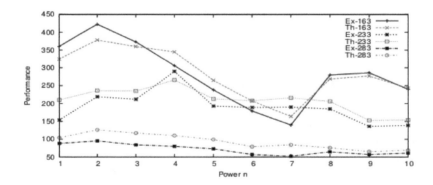

FIGURE 5.18: Performance Variation with n in 6-LUT-based FPGA

obtained by experiments and *Th* implies theoretical estimates. From the graphs, it can be seen that experimental and theoretical performances follow the same trend. The small differences occur due to unpredictablity of FPGA routing.

Table 5.11 shows the best performing configurations for some of the NIST recommended binary fields [393] and $GF(2^{193})$. The exponentiation circuit used (ITA type) and the number of cascades in the table result in best performance for the respective field. It can be seen that in most cases exponentiations higher than quad give best results.

Experimental and theoretical results show that performance of the ITA architecture increases significantly in 6-LUT based FPGAs compared to 4-LUT based FPGAs. This happens due to lesser LUT requirement and better routing in 6-LUT based FPGAs.

Table 5.12 shows a comparison of performances with existing ITA architectures for the field $GF(2^{193})$. All results are taken on the same Xilinx Virtex E platform. Our design is a 2^3 (octet) based ITA with 8 exponentiation circuits, since for $GF(2^{193})$ on Virtex E, our

Experimental Results in Virtex IV						
Field	ITA Type	Number of Cascades	Total LUT	Total Delay (*ns*)	Clock Cycle	Performance
163	2^2	7	12260	13.58	28	214
193	2^3	6	15043	12.9	26	198
233	2^4	5	21464	13.57	30	114
283	2^3	6	31802	14.82	43	49
Experimental Results in Virtex V						
Field	ITA Type	Number of Cascades	Total LUT	Total Delay (*ns*)	Clock Cycle	Performance
163	2^2	5	8692	8.79	31	422
193	2^3	8	11254	8.91	22	453
233	2^4	7	13962	9.16	27	290
283	2^2	8	27509	10.09	38	95

TABLE 5.11: Experimental Performance of ITA for Different Fields

Implementation	Resources Utilized (Slices, Brams)	Freq (MHz) (f)	Clock Cycle (c)	Time *μsec* (c/f)	Performance
Sequential [333]	10065, 12	21.2	28	1.32	75.2
Parallel [330]	11081, 12	21.2	20	0.94	95.7
Quad-ITA [337]	10420, 0	35	21	0.60	160
Octate-ITA (our design)	8401, 0	31.9	22	0.69	172

TABLE 5.12: Comparison for inversion in $GF(2^{193})$ on $XCV3200efg1156$

estimation model found ($\hat{n} = 3, \hat{u}_s = 8$). It is clear from Table 5.12 that 2^3 (octet) based ITA gives the best performance.

5.18 Conclusions

In this chapter, we study some design approaches for implementing basic finite field operations, namely multipliers and inversions. We focus on the Karatsuba multiplier and the Itoh-Tsujii inversion algorithms for their speeds. Various design challenges are discussed, keeping in mind the underlying LUT structure of the FPGAs. We observe that for Karatsuba multipliers, proper thresholding, selection of suitable algorithms help in obtaining efficient designs. In context with the Itoh-Tsujii inversion circuit, we observe that higher powers often give circuits which utilize the LUTs in a better way; however, there is a limiting condition beyond which the advantage is lost. In the next chapter, we discuss on design of an efficient Elliptic Curve Cryptosystem using the above underlying primitives.

Chapter 6

High-Speed Implementation of Elliptic Curve Scalar Multiplication on FPGAs

"If people do not believe that mathematics is simple, it is only because they do not realize how complicated life is."

(Tobias Dantzig)

6.1   Introduction

This chapter presents the construction of an *elliptic curve crypto processor* (ECCP) for the NIST specified curve [393] given in Equation 6.1 over the binary finite field $GF(2^{233})$.

$$y^2 + xy = x^3 + ax^2 + b \tag{6.1}$$

The processor implements the double and add scalar multiplication algorithm described in Algorithm 2.3. The processor (**Fig. 6.1**), is capable of doing the elliptic curve operations of point addition and point doubling. Point doubling is done at every iteration of the loop in Algorithm 2.3, while point addition is done for every bit set to one in the binary expansion of the scalar input k. The output produced as a result of the scalar multiplication is the product kP. Here, P is the basepoint of the curve and is stored in the ROM in its affine form. At every clock cycle, the register bank (*regbank*) containing dual ported registers feed the *arithmetic unit* (AU) through five buses ($A0$, $A1$, $A2$, $A3$, and Qin). At the end of the clock cycle, results of the computation are stored in registers through buses $C0$, $C1$ and $Qout$. There can be at most two results produced at every clock. Control signals ($c[0] \cdots c[32]$) generated every clock cycle depending on the elliptic curve operation control the data flow and the computation done. Details about the processor, the flow of data on the buses, the computations done, etc. are elaborated on in following sections.

The scalar multiplication implemented in the processor of**Fig. 6.1** is done using the *López-Dahab (LD) projective coordinate* system. The LD coordinate form of the elliptic curve over binary finite fields is

$$Y^2 + XYZ = X^3 + aX^2Z^2 + bZ^4 \tag{6.2}$$

In the ECCP, a is taken as 1, while b is stored in the ROM along with the basepoint P. Equations for point doubling and point addition in LD coordinates are shown in Equations 2.31 and 2.32, respectively.

During the initialization phase the curve constant b and the basepoint P are loaded from the ROM into the registers after which there are two computational phases. The first phase multiplies the scalar k to the basepoint P. The result produced by this phase is in projective coordinates. The second phase of the computation converts the projective point result of the first phase into the affine point kP. The second phase mainly involves an inverse computation. The inverse is computed using the *quad Itoh-Tsujii inverse algorithm*, which is a special case for the generalized Itoh-Tsujii proposed in Algorithm 5.4, with $n = 2$.

The next section describes in detail the ECCP. Section 6.3 describes the implementation

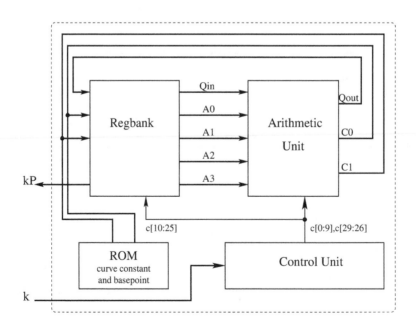

FIGURE 6.1: Block Diagram of the Elliptic Curve Crypto Processor

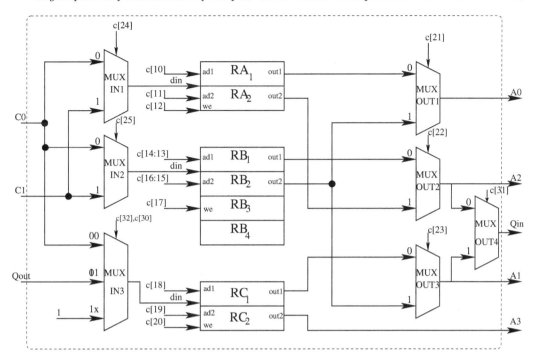

FIGURE 6.2: Register File for Elliptic Curve Crypto Processor

of the elliptic curve operations in the processor. Section 6.4 presents the finite state machine that implements Algorithm 2.3. Section 6.5 has the performance results, while the final section has the conclusion.

6.2 The Elliptic Curve Cryptoprocessor

This section describes in detail the register file, arithmetic unit and the control unit of the elliptic curve crypto processor.

6.2.1 Register Bank

The heart of the register file (**Fig. 6.2**) are eight registers, each of size 233 bits. The registers are used to store the results of the computations done at every clock cycle. The registers are dual ported and arranged in three banks, RA, RB, and RC. The dual ported RAM allows asynchronous reads on the lines *out1* and *out2* corresponding to the address on the address lines *ad1* and *ad2* respectively. A synchronous write of the data on *din* is done to the location addressed by *ad1*. The *we* signal enables the write. On the FPGA, the registers are implemented as distributed RAM[418]. At every clock cycle, the register file is capable of delivering five operands (on buses $A0$, $A1$, $A2$, $A3$ and Qin) to the arithmetic unit and able to store three results (from buses $C0$, $C1$, and $Qout$). The inputs to the

TABLE 6.1: Utility of Registers in the Register Bank

Register	Description
RA_1	1. During initialization it is loaded with P_x.
	2. Stores the x coordinate of the result.
	3. Also used for temporary storage.
RA_2	Stores P_x.
RB_1	1. During initialization it is loaded with P_y.
	2. Stores the y coordinate of the result.
	3. Also used for temporary storage.
RB_2	Stores P_y.
RB_3	Used for temporary storage.
RB_4	Stores the curve constant b.
RC_1	1. During initialization it is set to 1.
	2. Store z coordinate of the projective result.
	3. Also used for temporary storage.
RC_2	Used for temporary storage.

register file is either the arithmetic unit outputs, the curve constant (b of Equation 6.2), or the basepoint $P = (P_x, P_y)$.

Multiplexers $MUXIN1$, $MUXIN2$, and $MUXIN3$ determine which of the three inputs gets stored into the register banks. Further, bits in the control word select a register, or enable or disable a write operation to a particular register bank. Multiplexers $MUXOUT1$, $MUXOUT2$, $MUXOUT3$, and $MUXOUT4$ determine which output of a register bank get driven on the output buses. Table 6.1 shows how the each register in the bank is utilized.

6.2.2   Finite Field Arithmetic Unit

The arithmetic unit (**Fig. 6.3**) is built using finite field arithmetic circuits and organized for efficient implementation of point addition (Equation 2.32) and point doubling (Equation 2.31) in LD coordinates. The AU has 5 inputs ($A0$ to $A3$ and Qin) and 3 outputs ($C0$, $C1$ and $Qout$). The main components of the AU is a quadblock and a multiplier. The multiplier is based on the *hybrid Karatsuba algorithm* (Section 5.7.1). It is used in both phases (during the scalar multiplication phase and conversion to affine coordinate phase) of the computation. The *quadblock* is designed according to **Fig. 5.10**. Here, the quadblock consists of 14 cascaded quad circuits (refer to **Fig. 5.11**) and is capable of generating the output $Qout = Qin^{4^{c[29]\cdots c[26]}}$. The quadblock is used only for inversion which is done during the final phase of the computation. The AU has several adders and squarer circuits. These circuits are small compared to the multiplier and the quadblock and therefore contribute marginally to the overall area and latency of the processor.

6.2.3   Control Unit

At every clock cycle the control unit produces a control word. Control words are produced in a sequence depending on the type of elliptic curve operation being done. The control word signals control the flow of data and also decide the operations performed on the data. There are 33 control signals ($c[0]$ to $c[32]$) that are generated by the control unit. The signals $c[0]$ to $c[9]$ control the inputs to the finite field multiplier and the outputs $C0$ and $C1$ of the

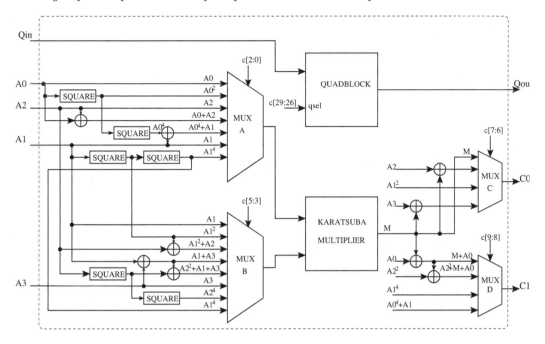

FIGURE 6.3: Finite Field Arithmetic Unit

AU. The control lines $c[26]$ to $c[29]$ are used for the select lines to the multiplexer in the quadblock (**Fig. 5.11**). The remaining control bits are used in the register file to read and write data to the registers. Section 6.4 has the detailed list of all control words generated.

6.3 Point Arithmetic on the ECCP

This section presents the implementation of LD point addition and doubling equations on the ECCP.

6.3.1 Point Doubling

The equation for doubling the point P in LD projective coordinates was shown in Equation 2.31 and is repeated here (Equation 6.3). [227]. The input required for doubling is the point $P = (X_1, Y_1, Z_1)$ and the output is its double $2P = (X_3, Y_3, Z_3)$. The equation show that four multiplications are required (assuming $a = 1$). The ECCP has just one multiplier, which is capable of doing one multiplication per clock cycle. Hence, the ECCP would require at least four clock cycles for computing the double.

$$
\begin{aligned}
Z_3 &= X_1^2 \cdot Z_1^2 \\
X_3 &= X_1^4 + b \cdot Z_1^4 \\
Y_3 &= b \cdot Z_1^4 \cdot Z_3 + X_3 \cdot (a \cdot Z_3 + Y_1^2 + b \cdot Z_1^4)
\end{aligned}
\tag{6.3}
$$

This doubling operation is mapped to the elliptic curve hardware using Algorithm 6.1.

Algorithm 6.1: Hardware Implementation of Doubling on ECCP

Input: LD Point P=(X_1, Y_1, Z_1) present in registers (RA_1, RB_1, RC_1), respectively.
The curve constant b is present in register RB_4

Output: LD Point 2P=(X_3, Y_3, Z_3) present in registers (RA_1, RB_1, RC_1),
respectively.

1 $RB_3 = RB_4 \cdot RC_1^4$
2 $RC_1 = RA_1^2 \cdot RC_1^2$
3 $RA_1 = RA_1^4 + RB_3$
4 $RB_1 = RB_3 \cdot RC_1 + RA_1 \cdot (RC_1 + RB_1^2 + RB_3)$

TABLE 6.2: Parallel LD Point Doubling on the ECCP

Clock	Operation 1 ($C0$)	Operation 2($C1$)
1	$RC_1 = RA_1^2 \cdot RC_1^2$	$RB_3 = RC_1^4$
2	$RB_3 = RB_3 \cdot RB_4$	
3	$RC_2 = (RA_1^4 + RB_3) \cdot (RC_1 + RB_1^2 + RB_3)$	$RA_1 = (RA_1^4 + RB_3)$
4	$RB_1 = RB_3 \cdot RC_1 + RC_2$	

TABLE 6.3: Inputs and Outputs of the Register File for Point Doubling

Clock	A0	A1	A2	A3	C0	C1
1	RA_1	RC_1	-	-	RC_1	RB_3
2	-	RB_4	RB_3	-	RB_3	
3	RA_1	RB_3	RB_1	RC_1	RC_2	RA_1
4	RB_3	RC_1	-	RC_2	RB_1	-

On the ECCP, the LD doubling algorithm can be parallelized to complete in four clock cycles as shown in Table 6.2 [328]. The parallelization is based on the fact that the multiplier is several times more complex than the squarer and adder circuits used. So, in every clock cycle the multiplier is used and it produces one of the outputs of the AU. The other AU output is produced by additions or squaring operations alone.

Table 6.3 shows the data held on the buses at every clock cycle. It also shows where the results are stored. For example, in clock cycle 1, the contents of the registers RA_1 and RC_1 are placed on the bus $A0$ and $A1$, respectively. Control lines in $MUXA$ and $MUXB$ of the AU are set such that $A0^2$ and $A1$ are fed to the multiplier. The output multiplexers $MUXC$ and $MUXD$ are set such that M and $A1^4$ are sent on the buses $C0$ and $C1$. These are stored in registers RC_1 and RB_3, respectively. Effectively, the computation done by the AU are $RC_1 = RA_1^2 \cdot RC_1^2$ and $RB_3 = RC_1^4$. Similarly the subsequent operations required for doubling as stated in 6.2 are performed.

$$A = y_2 \cdot Z_1^2 + Y_1$$
$$B = x_2 \cdot Z_1 + X_1$$
$$C = Z_1 \cdot B$$
$$D = B^2 \cdot (C + a \cdot Z_1^2)$$
$$Z_3 = C^2$$
$$E = A \cdot C \tag{6.4}$$
$$X_3 = A^2 + D + E$$
$$F = X_3 + x_2 \cdot Z_3$$
$$G = (x_2 + y_2) \cdot Z_3^2$$
$$Y_3 = (E + Z_3) \cdot F + G$$

6.3.2 Point Addition

The equation for adding an affine point to a point in LD projective coordinates was shown in Equation 2.32 and repeated here in Equation 6.4. The equation adds two points $P = (X_1, Y_1, Z_1)$ and $Q = (x_2, y_2)$ where $Q \neq \pm P$. The resulting point is $P + Q = (X_3, Y_3, Z_3)$.

Algorithm 6.2: Hardware Implementation of Addition on ECCP

Input: LD Point P=(X_1, Y_1, Z_1) present in registers (RA_1, RB_1, RC_1) respectively
and Affine Point Q=(x_2, y_2) present in registers (RA_2, RB_2) respectively
Output: LD Point P+Q=(X_3, Y_3, Z_3) present in registers (RA_1, RB_1, RC_1)
respectively

1 $RB_1 = RB_2 \cdot RC_1^2 + RB_1$;   /* A */
2 $RA_1 = RA_2 \cdot RC_1 + RA_1$;   /* B */
3 $RB_3 = RC_1 \cdot RA_1$;   /* C */
4 $RA_1 = RA_1^2 \cdot (RB_3 + RC_1^2)$;   /* D */
5 $RC_1 = RB_3^2$;   /* Z_3 */
6 $RC_2 = RB_1 \cdot RB_3$;   /* E */
7 $RA_1 = RB_1^2 + RA_1 + RC_2$;   /* X_3 */
8 $RB_3 = RA_1 + RA_2 \cdot RC_1^2$;   /* F */
9 $RB_1 = (RA_2 + RB_2) \cdot RC_1^2$;   /* G */
10 $RB_1 = (RC_2 + RC_1) \cdot RB_3 + RB_1$;   /* Y_3 */

The addition operation is mapped to the elliptic curve hardware using Algorithm 6.2. Note, a is taken as 1. On the ECCP the operations in Algorithm 6.2 are scheduled efficiently to complete in eight clock cycles [328]. The scheduled operations for point addition is shown in Table 6.4, and the inputs and outputs of the registers at each clock cycle is shown in Table 6.5.

TABLE 6.4: Parallel LD Point Addition on the ECCP

Clock	Operation 1 (C_0)	Operation 2(C_1)
1	$RB_1 = RB_2 \cdot RC_1^2 + RB_1$	-
2	$RA_1 = RA_2 \cdot RC_1 + RA_1$	-
3	$RB_3 = RC_1 \cdot RA_1$	-
4	$RA_1 = RA_1^2 \cdot (RB_3 + RC_1^2)$	-
5	$RC_2 = RB_1 \cdot RB_3$	$RA_1 = RB_1^2 + RA_1 + RB_1 \cdot RB_3$
6	$RC_1 = RB_3^2$	$RB_3 = RA_1 + RA_2 \cdot RB_3^2$
7	$RB_1 = (RA_2 + RB_2) \cdot RC_1^2$	-
8	$RB_1 = (RC_2 + RC_1) \cdot RB_3 + RB_1$	-

TABLE 6.5: Inputs and Outputs of the Register Bank for Point Addition

Clock	A0	A1	A2	A3	C0	C1
1	RB_2	RC_1	RB_1	-	RB_1	-
2	RA_1	RC_1	RA_2	-	RA_1	-
3	RA_1	-	-	RC_1	RB_3	-
4	RA_1	RC_1	RB_3	-	RA_1	-
5	RA_1	RB_3	RB_1	-	RC_2	RA_1
6	RA_1	RB_3	RA_2	-	RC_1	RB_3
7	RB_2	RC_1	RA_2	-	RB_1	-
8	RB_3	RC_1	RB_1	RC_2	RB_1	-

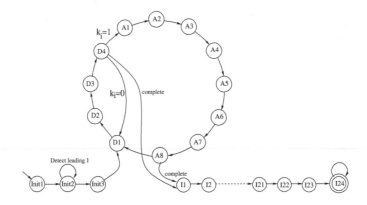

FIGURE 6.4: The ECCP Finite State Machine

6.4   The Finite State Machine (FSM)

The three phases of computation done by the ECCP, namely the initialization, scalar multiplication and projective to affine conversion phase are implemented using the FSM shown in **Fig. 6.4**. The first three states of the FSM do the initialization. In these states

TABLE 6.6: Inputs and Outputs of Regbank for Every State

State	Regbank Outputs					Regbank Inputs
	$A0$	$A1$	$A2$	$A3$	Qin	
Init1	-	-	-	-	-	$\textbf{C0}: RA_1 = P_x$; $\textbf{C1}: RB_1 = P_y$; $RC_1 = 1$
Init2	-	-	-	-	-	$\textbf{C0}: RA_2 = P_x$; $\textbf{C1}: RB_2 = P_y$
Init3	-	-	-	-	-	$\textbf{C1}: RB_4 = b$
D1	RA_1	RC_1	-	-	-	$\textbf{C0}: RC_1 = RA_1^2 \cdot RC_1^2$; $\textbf{C1}: RB_3 = RC_1^4$
D2	-	RB_4	RB_3	-	-	$\textbf{C0}: RB_3 = RB_3 \cdot RB_4$
D3	RA_1	RB_3	RB_1	RC_1	-	$\textbf{C0}: RC_2 = (RA_1^4 + RB_3) \cdot (RC_1 + RB_1^2 + RB_3)$; $\textbf{C1}: RA_1 = (RA_1^4 + RB_3)$
D4	RB_3	RC_1	-	RC_2	-	$\textbf{C0}: RB_1 = RB_3 \cdot RC_1 + RC_2$
A1	RB_2	RC_1	RB_1	-	-	$\textbf{C0}: RB_1 = RB_2 \cdot RC_1^2 + RB_1$
A2	RA_1	RC_1	RA_2	-	-	$\textbf{C0}: RA_1 = RA_2 \cdot RC_1^2 + RA_1$
A3	RA_1	-	-	RC_1	-	$\textbf{C0}: RB_3 = RC_1 \cdot RA_1$
A4	RA_1	RC_1	RB_3	-	-	$\textbf{C0}: RA_1 = RA_1^2 \cdot (RB_3 + RC_1^2)$
A5	RA_1	RB_3	RB_1	-	-	$\textbf{C0}: RC_2 = RB_1 \cdot RB_3$; $\textbf{C1}: RA_1 = RB_1^2 + RA_1 + RB_1 \cdot RB_3$
A6	RA_1	RB_3	RA_2	-	-	$\textbf{C0}: RC_1 = RB_3^2$; $\textbf{C1}: RB_3 = RA_1 + RA_2 \cdot RB_3^2$
A7	RB_2	RC_1	RA_2	-	-	$\textbf{C0}: RB_1 = (RA_2 + RB_2) \cdot RC_1^2$
A8	RB_3	RC_1	RB_1	RC_2	-	$\textbf{C0}: RB_1 = (RC_2 + RC_1) \cdot RB_3 + RB_1$
I1	-	RC_1	-	-	-	$\textbf{C0}: RC_1 = RC_1^2 \cdot RC_1$
I2	-	RC_1	-	-	-	$\textbf{C0}: RB_3 = RC_1^4 \cdot RC_1$
I3	-	RC_1	RB_3	-	-	$\textbf{C0}: RB_3 = RB_3^4 \cdot RC_1$
I4	-	-	-	-	RB_3	$\textbf{Qout}: RC_2 = RB_3^3$
I5	-	RC_2	RB_3	-	-	$\textbf{C0}: RB_3 = RC_2 \cdot RB_3$
I6	-	RC_1	RB_3	-	-	$\textbf{C0}: RB_3 = RB_3^4 \cdot RC_1$
I7	-	-	-	-	RB_3	$\textbf{Qout}: RC_2 = RB_3^7$
I8	-	RC_2	RB_3	-	-	$\textbf{C0}: RB_3 = RC_2 \cdot RB_3$
I9	-	-	-	-	RB_3	$\textbf{Qout}: RC_2 = RB_3^{14}$
I10	-	RC_2	RB_3	-	-	$\textbf{C0}: RB_3 = RC_2 \cdot RB_3$
I11	-	RC_1	RB_3	-	-	$\textbf{C0}: RB_3 = RB_3^4 \cdot RC_1$
I12	-	-	-	-	RB_3	$\textbf{Qout}: RC_2 = RB_3^{14}$
I13	-	-	-	-	RC_2	$\textbf{Qout}: RC_2 = RC_2^{14}$
I14	-	RC_2	RB_3	-	-	$\textbf{C0}: RB_3 = RC_2^4 \cdot RB_3$
I15	-	-	-	-	RB_3	$\textbf{Qout}: RC_2 = RB_3^{14}$
I16	-	-	-	-	RC_2	$\textbf{Qout}: RC_2 = RC_2^{14}$
I17	-	-	-	-	RC_2	$\textbf{Qout}: RC_2 = RC_2^{14}$
I18	-	-	-	-	RC_2	$\textbf{Qout}: RC_2 = RC_2^{14}$
I19	-	-	-	-	RC_2	$\textbf{Qout}: RC_2 = RC_2^2$
I20	-	RC_2	RB_3	-	-	$\textbf{C0}: RB_3 = RC_2 \cdot RB_3$
I21	-	RB_3	-	-	-	$\textbf{C0}: RC_1 = RB_3^2$
I22	RA_1	RC_1	-	-	-	$\textbf{C0}: RA_1 = RA_1 \cdot RC_1$
I23	RB_1	RC_1	-	-	-	$\textbf{C0}: RB_1 = RB_1 \cdot RC_1^2$

TABLE 6.7: Control Words for ECCP

State	Quadblock $c_{29}\cdots c_{26}$	Regfile MUXIN $c_{32}c_{30}c_{25}c_{24}$	Regfile MUXOUT $c_{31}c_{23}c_{22}c_{21}$	Regbank signals $c_{20}\cdots c_{10}$	AU Mux C and D $c_9\cdots c_6$	AU Mux A and B $c_5\cdots c_0$
Init1	x x x x	1 0 1 0	0 0 x x	1 x 0 1 x x 0 0 1 x 0	0 0 0 0	0 0 0 0 0 0
Init2	x x x x	1 0 1 0	0 0 x x	0 x x 1 x x 0 1 1 x 1	x x x x	x x x x x x
Init3	x x x x	1 x x x	x x x x	0 x x 1 x x 1 1 0 x x	x x x x	x x x x x x
D1	x x x x	0 0 1 x	0 0 x 0	1 x 0 1 x x 1 0 0 x 0	1 0 0 0	0 0 1 0 0 1
D2	x x x x	0 0 0 x	x 1 0 x	0 x x 1 1 1 1 0 0 x x	x x 0 0	0 0 0 0 1 0
D3	x x x x	0 0 x 1	0 1 0 0	1 0 1 0 1 0 0 0 1 x 0	1 1 0 0	1 0 0 1 0 0
D4	x x x x	0 0 0 x	0 0 x 1	0 1 0 1 1 0 0 0 0 x x	x x 1 1	0 0 0 0 0 0
A1	x x x x	0 0 0 x	0 0 0 1	0 x 0 1 0 1 0 0 0 x x	x x 0 1	0 0 1 0 0 0
A2	x x x x	0 0 x 1	0 0 1 0	0 x 0 0 x x 0 0 1 1 0	0 0 x x	0 0 0 0 1 0
A3	x x x x	0 0 x x	0 0 x 0	0 0 x 1 x x 1 0 0 x 0	x x 0 0	1 0 1 0 0 0
A4	x x x x	0 0 x 0	0 0 0 0	0 1 0 0 x x 1 0 1 x 0	x x 0 0	0 1 0 0 0 1
A5	x x x x	0 0 x 1	0 1 0 0	1 x 1 0 1 0 0 0 1 x 0	0 1 0 0	0 0 0 0 1 0
A6	x x x x	0 0 1 x	0 1 1 0	1 x 0 1 1 0 1 0 0 1 0	0 0 1 0	0 0 1 0 1 0
A7	x x x x	0 0 0 x	0 0 1 1	0 x 0 1 0 1 0 0 0 1 x	x x 0 0	0 0 1 0 1 1
A8	x x x x	0 0 0 x	0 0 0 1	0 1 0 1 1 0 0 0 0 x x	x x 0 1	0 1 1 0 0 0
I1	x x x x	0 0 x x	0 0 x x	1 x 0 x x x x x 0 x x	x x 0 0	0 0 1 1 0 1
I2	x x x x	0 0 0 x	0 0 0 x	0 x 0 1 x x 1 0 0 x x	x x 0 0	0 0 0 1 1 0
I3	x x x x	0 0 0 x	0 0 0 x	x x 0 1 x x 1 0 0 x x	x x 0 0	1 1 0 1 0 1
I4	0 0 1 1	0 1 x x	0 0 0 x	1 x 1 0 x x 1 0 0 x x	x x x x	x x x x x x
I5	x x x x	0 0 0 x	0 0 0 x	0 x 1 1 x x 1 0 0 x x	x x 0 0	0 0 0 0 1 0
I6	x x x x	0 0 0 x	0 0 0 x	0 x 0 1 x x 1 0 0 x x	x x 0 0	1 1 0 1 0 1
I7	0 1 1 1	0 1 x x	0 0 0 x	1 x 1 0 x x 1 0 0 x x	x x x x	x x x x x x
I8	x x x x	0 0 0 x	0 0 x x	0 x 1 1 x x 1 0 0 x x	x x 0 0	0 0 0 0 1 0
I9	1 1 1 0	0 1 x x	0 0 0 x	1 x 1 0 x x 1 0 0 x x	x x x x	x x x x x x
I10	x x x x	0 0 0 x	0 0 x x	0 x 1 1 x x 1 0 0 x x	x x 0 0	0 0 0 0 1 0
I11	x x x x	0 0 0 x	0 0 0 x	0 x 0 1 x x 1 0 0 x x	x x 0 0	1 1 0 1 0 1
I12	1 1 1 0	0 1 x x	0 0 0 x	1 x 1 0 x x 1 0 0 x x	x x x x	x x x x x x
I13	1 1 1 0	0 1 x x	1 0 0 x	1 x 1 0 x x x x 0 x x	x x x x	x x x x x x
I14	x x x x	0 0 0 x	0 0 0 x	0 x 1 1 x x 1 0 0 x x	x x 0 0	1 1 1 0 1 0
I15	1 1 1 0	0 1 x x	0 0 0 x	1 x 1 0 x x 1 0 0 x x	x x x x	x x x x x x
I16	1 1 1 0	0 1 x x	1 0 0 x	1 x 1 0 x x x x 0 x x	x x x x	x x x x x x
I17	1 1 1 0	0 1 x x	1 0 0 x	1 x 1 0 x x x x 0 x x	x x x x	x x x x x x
I18	1 1 1 0	0 1 x x	1 0 0 x	1 x 1 0 x x x x 0 x x	x x x x	x x x x x x
I19	0 0 1 0	0 1 x x	1 0 0 x	1 x 1 0 x x x x 0 x x	x x x x	x x x x x x
I20	x x x x	0 0 0 x	0 0 0 x	0 x 1 1 x x 1 0 0 x x	x x 0 0	0 0 0 0 1 0
I21	x x x x	0 0 0 x	0 1 x x	1 x 0 0 1 0 x x 0 x x	x x 1 0	x x x x x x
I22	x x x x	0 0 x 0	0 0 x 0	0 x 0 0 x x x x 1 x 0	x x 0 0	0 0 0 0 0 0
I23	x x x x	0 0 0 x	0 0 x 1	0 x 0 1 0 0 x x 0 x x	x x 0 0	0 0 1 0 0 0
I24	x x x x	0 0 0 x	0 0 0 0	0 x x 0 x x 0 0 0 x 0	x x x x	x x x x x x

the curve constant and basepoint coordinates are loaded from ROM into the registers (Table 6.6). These states also detect the leading MSB in the scalar key k.

After initialization, the scalar multiplication is done. This consists of 4 states for doubling and 8 for the point addition. The states that do the doubling are $D1\cdots D4$. In state $D4$, a decision is made depending on the key bit k_i (i is a loop counter initially set to the position of the leading one in the key, and k_i is the ith bit of the key k). If $k_i = 1$ then a point addition is done and state $A1$ is entered. If $k_i = 0$, the addition is not done and the next key bit (corresponding to $i-1$) is considered. If $k_i = 0$ and there are no more key bits to be considered then the *complete* signal is issued and it marks the end of the scalar multiplication phase. The states that do the addition are $A1\cdots A8$. At the end of the addition (state $A8$) state $D1$ is entered and the key bit k_{i-1} is considered. If there are no more key bits remaining the complete signal is asserted. Table 6.7 shows the control words generated at every state.

At the end of the scalar multiplication phase, the result obtained is in projective coordinates and the X, Y and Z coordinates are stored in the registers RA_1, RB_1 and RC_1, respectively. To convert the projective point to affine, the following equation is used.

$$x = X \cdot Z^{-1}$$
$$y = Y \cdot (Z^{-1})^2 \tag{6.5}$$

The inverse of Z is obtained using the *quad-ITA* discussed in Algorithm 5.3. The addition chain used is the Brauer chain in Equation 5.24. The processor implements the steps given in Table 5.7. Each step in Table 5.7 gets mapped into one or more states from $I1$ to $I21$. The number of clock cycles required to find the inverse is 21. This is lesser than the clock cycles estimated by Equation 5.30. This is because, inverse can be implemented more efficiently in the ECCP by utilizing the squarers present in the AU.

At the end of state $I21$, the inverse of Z is present in the register RC_1. The states $I22$ and $I23$ compute the affine coordinates x and y, respectively.

The number of clock cycles required for the ECCP to produce the output is computed as follows. Let the scalar k has length l and hamming weight h, then the clock cycles required to produce the output is given by the following equation.

$$\#ClockCycles = 3 + 12(h-1) + 4(l-h) + 24$$
$$= 15 + 8h + 4l \tag{6.6}$$

Three clock cycles are added for the initial states, 24 clock cycles are required for the final projective to affine conversion. $12(h-1)$ cycles are required to handle the 1's in k. Note that the MSB of k does not need to be considered. $4(l-h)$ cycles are required for the 0's in k.

6.5   Performance Evaluation

In this section we evaluate the above elliptic curve crypto processors implemented on FPGA platforms. The ECCP was synthesized using *Xilinx's ISE* for *Virtex 4* and *Virtex E* platforms. The design takes 20917 slices and has a latency of 0.029 ms. The area-time product is 606, which may be compared to some state-of-the-art designs as proposed in [87], where the product is 894 for similar bit sizes.

In the above section, we studied the development of the ECC processor from the previously developed finite field arithmetic blocks. However one can further improve the performance of the above ECC processor using Mongomery's ladder (algorithmic optimization) and suitable pipeline stages (architectural optimization) in the design.

6.6   Further Acceleration Techniques of the ECC Processor

High speeds are achieved by boosting the operating clock frequency while at the same time reducing the number of clock cycles required to do a scalar multiplication. To increase clock frequency further, the design uses pipelining. However the pipelined stages required is carefully computed to maximize the benefit. To reduce clock cycles, a scheduling scheme is presented that allows overlapped processing of scalar bits.

The speed of a hardware design is dictated by two parameters: the frequency of the clock and the number of clock cycles required to perform the computation. One method to boost the maximum operable clock frequency is by reducing area. Smaller area generally implies lesser routing delay, which in turn implies higher operable clock frequencies. Another method to increase clock frequency is by pipelining. Chelton and Benaissa [87] extensively rely on this in order to achieve high speeds. However extensive pipelining in the design is likely to increase the clock cycles required for the computation. Clock cycles can be reduced by parallelization, efficient scheduling, and advanced pipeline techniques such as data-forwarding. Parallelization by replication of computing units was used in [37] to achieve high speeds. The drawback of parallelization however is the large area requirements.

We now discuss a design, which is an improvement of the prior design. The objectives are to obtain high-speed by: *(1)* reducing area, *(2)* appropriate usage of FPGA hardware resources, *(3)* optimal pipelining enhanced with data-forwarding, *(4)* and efficient scheduling mechanisms.

6.7   Pipelining Strategies for the Scalar Multiplier

Algorithm 6.3: *Montgomery Point Multiplication*

Input: Base point P and scalar $s = \{s_{t-1}s_{t-2}\dots s_0\}_2$ with $s_{t-1} = 1$

Output: Point on the curve $Q = sP$

1   **begin**
2      $P_1(X_1, Z_1) \leftarrow P(X, Z); \; P_2(X_2, Z_2) \leftarrow 2P(X, Z)$
3   **for** $k = t - 2 \; to \; 0$ **do**
4   **if** $s_k = 1$ **then**
5             $P_1 \leftarrow P_1 + P_2$
6             $P_2 \leftarrow 2P_2$
7   **end**
8   **else**
9             $P_2 \leftarrow P_1 + P_2$
10            $P_1 \leftarrow 2P_1$
11   **end**
12   **end**
13   **return** $Q \leftarrow Projective2Affine(P_1, P_2)$
14 **end**

The functionality of the developed architecure, named as *ECM* is to execute Algorithm 19. It comprises of 2 units: the register bank and the arithmetic unit as seen in **Fig. 6.5**. In each clock cycle, control signals are generated according to the value of the bit s_k, which reads operands from the register bank, performs the computation in the arithmetic unit, and finally write back the results.

There are six registers in the register bank, each capable of storing a field element. Five of the registers are used for the computations in Algorithm 19 and detailed later in Equation 6.9, while one is used for field inversion. There are three ways in which the registers can be implemented in FPGAs. The first approach, using *block RAM*, is slow due to constraints in routing. The two other alternatives are *distributed RAM* and Flip-Flops. Distributed RAM allows the FPGA's LUTs to be configured as RAM. Each bit of the 6 registers will share the same LUT. However, each register is used for a different purpose therefore the centralization effect of distributed RAM will cause long routes, leading to lowering of clock frequencies. Additionally, there is an impact on the area requirements. Flip-flops on the other hand allow decentralization of the registers, there by allowing registers to be placed in locations close to their usage, thus routing is easier. Further, each slice in the FPGA has equal number of LUTs and Flip-Flops. The *ECM* is an LUT intensive design, because several of the Flip-Flops in the slice remain unutilized. By configuring the registers

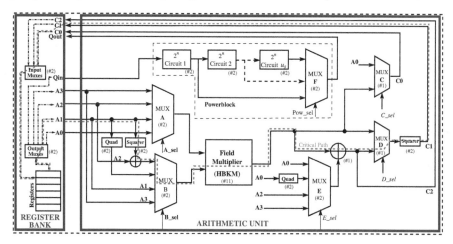

FIGURE 6.5: Block Diagram of the Processor Organization showing the critical path

to use these Flip-Flops, no additional area (in terms of the number of slices) is required. These available Flip-Flops provide opportunity for improving the performance of the design through pipelining.

In this section, we discuss the piplelining strategy for this datapath in a proper fashion to increase the clock frequency. Ideally, an L-stage pipeline can boost the clock frequency up to L times. In order to achieve the maximum effectiveness of the pipelines, the design should be partitioned into L equal stages. That is, each stage of the pipeline should have the same delay. However to date the only means of achieving this is by trial-and-error. Here we use the theoretical model for FPGA designs developed in Chapter 3, to show how to estimate the delay in the critical path and there by find the ideal pipelining. As L increases, there is likely to be more data dependencies in the computations, thus resulting in more stalls (*bubbles*) in the pipeline. Thus suitable scheduling strategies for the Montgomery scalar multiplication algorithm is required developing an efficient method for pipelining the processor [249].

All combinational data paths in the *ECM* start from the register bank output and end at the register bank input. The maximum operable frequency of the *ECM* is dictated by the longest combinational path, known as the *critical path*. There can be several critical paths, one such example is highlighted through the dashed line in **Fig. 6.5**.

Estimating Delays in the *ECM* : Let t_{cp}^* be the delay of the critical paths and $f_1^* = \frac{1}{t_{cp}^*}$ the maximum operable frequency of the *ECM* prior to pipelining. Consider the case of pipelining the *ECM* into L stages, then the maximum operable frequency can be increased to at-most $f_L^* = L \times f_1^*$. This *ideal frequency* can be achieved if and only if the following two conditions are satisfied.

1. Every critical path in the design should be split into L stages with each stage having a delay of exactly $\frac{t_{cp}^*}{L}$.

2. All other paths in the design should be split so that any stage in these paths should have a delay which is less than or equal to $\frac{t_{cp}^*}{L}$.

While it is not always possible to exactly obtain f_L^*, we can achieve close to the ideal clock frequency by making a theoretical estimation of t_{cp}^* and then identifying the locations in the architecture where the pipeline stages have to be inserted. We denote this theoretical

FIGURE 6.6: Different Stages in the HBKM

estimate of delay by $t_{cp}^{\#}$. The theoretical analysis is based on the following prepositions[338]. These facts were stated in the above discussions on the inversion circuits in the context of designing high-speed inversion circuits.

Fact 1 *For circuits which are implemented using LUTs, the delay of a path in the circuit is proportional to the number of LUTs in the path.*

Fact 2 *The number of LUTs in the critical path of an n variable Boolean function having the form $y = g_n(x_1, x_2, \cdots, x_n)$ is given by $\lceil log_k(n) \rceil$, where k is the number of inputs to the LUTs (k − LUT).*

Using these two facts it is possible to analyze the delay of various combinational circuit components in terms of LUTs: namely the adder, multiplexers, exponentiation circuit, Powerblock, Modular Reduction, and the hybrid bit-parallel Karatsuba multiplier (denoted as *HBKM*). The *field multiplier* is the central part of the arithmetic unit. We choose to use a *hybrid bit-parallel Karatsuba field multiplier* (*HBKM*), which was first introduced in [316] and then used in [314]. The advantage of the *HBKM* is the sub-quadratic complexity of the Karatsuba algorithm coupled with efficient utilization of the FPGA's LUT resources. Further, the bit-parallel scheme requires lesser clock cycles compared to digit level multipliers used in [37]. The *HBKM* recursively splits the input operands until a threshold (τ) is reached, then threshold (school-book) multipliers are applied. The outputs of the threshold multipliers are combined and then reduced (**Fig. 6.6**).

Field inversion is performed by a generalization of the Itoh-Tsujii inversion algorithm for FPGA platforms [338]. The generalization requires a cascade of 2^n exponentiation circuits (implemented as the *Powerblock* in **Fig. 6.5**), where $1 \leq n \leq m - 1$. The ideal choice for n depends on the field and the FPGA platform. For example, in $GF(2^{163})$ and FPGAs having 4 input LUTs (such as Xilinx Virtex 4), the optimal choice for n is 2. More details on choosing n can be found in [164]. The number of cascades, u_s, depends on the critical delay of the *ECM* and will be discussed in Section 6.7. Further, an addition chain for $\lfloor \frac{m-1}{n} \rfloor$ is required. Therefore, for $GF(2^{163})$ and $n = 2$, an addition chain for 81 is needed. The number of clock cycles required for inversion, assuming a Brauer chain, is given by Equation 6.7, where the addition chain has the form $(u_1, u_2, \cdots, u_l)$, and L is the number of pipeline stages in the *ECM* [69].

$$cc_{ita} = L(l+1) + \sum_{i=2}^{l} \left\lceil \frac{u_i - u_{i-1}}{u_s} \right\rceil \tag{6.7}$$

The *LUT delays* of relevant combinational components are summarized in Table 6.8. The reader is referred to [338] for detailed analysis of the LUT delays. The LUT delays of all components in **Fig. 6.5** are shown in parenthesis for k = 4. Note that the analysis also considers optimizations by the synthesis tool (such as the merging of the squarer and adder before Mux B (**Fig. 6.5**), which reduces the delay from 3 to 2).

Pipelining Paths in the *ECM*: Table 6.8 can be used to determine the LUT delays of any path in the *ECM*. For the example critical path, (the dashed line in **Fig. 6.5**),

TABLE 6.8: LUT delays of Various Combinational Circuit Components

Component	$k - LUT$ **Delay for** $k \geq 4$	$m = 163, k = 4$
m bit field adder	1	1
m bit $n : 1$ Mux $(D_{n:1}(m))$	$\lceil log_k(n + log_2 n) \rceil$	2 (for $n = 4$) 1 (for $n = 2$)
Exponentiation Circuit $(D_{2^n}(m))$	$max(LUTDelay(d_i))$, where d_i is the ith output bit of the exponentiation circuit	2 (for $n = 1$) 2 (for $n = 2$)
Powerblock $(D_{powerblk}(m))$	$u_s \times D_{2^n}(m) + D_{u_s:1}(m)$	4 (for $u_s = 2$)
Modular Reduction (D_{mod})	1 for irreducible trinomials 2 for pentanomials	2 (for pentanomials)
HBKM $(D_{HBKM}(m))$	As seen in **Fig. 6.6**, this can be written as $D_{split} + D_{threshold} + D_{combine} + D_{mod}$ $= \lceil log_k(\frac{m}{\tau}) \rceil + \lceil log_k(2\tau) \rceil$ $+ \lceil log_2(\frac{m}{\tau}) \rceil + D_{mod}$	11 (for $\tau = 11$)

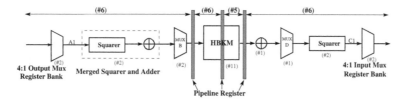

FIGURE 6.7: Example Critical Path (with $L = 4$ and k $= 4$)

the estimate for t_{cp}^* is the sum of the LUT delays of each component in the path. This evaluates to $t_{cp}^\# = 23$. **Fig. 6.7** gives a detailed view of this path. Pipelining the paths in the *ECM* require pipeline registers to be introduced in between the LUTs. The following fact determines how the pipeline registers have to be inserted in a path in order to achieve the maximum operable frequency $(f_L^\#)$ as close to the ideal (f_L^*) as possible (Note that $f_L^\# \leq f_L^*$).

Fact 3 *If $t_{cp}^\#$ is the LUT delay of the critical paths, and L is the desired number of stages in the pipeline, then the best clock frequency $(f_L^\#)$ is achieved only if no path has delay more than $\lceil \frac{t_{cp}^\#}{L} \rceil$.*

For example for $L = 4$, no path should have a LUT delay more than $\lceil \frac{23}{4} \rceil$. This identifies the exact locations in the paths where pipeline registers have to be inserted. **Fig. 6.7** shows the positions of the pipeline register for $L = 4$ for the critical path.

On the Pipelining of the Powerblock: The powerblock is used only once during the computation; at the end of the scalar multiplication. There are two choices with regard to implementing the powerblock, either pipeline the powerblock as per Proposition 3 or reduce the number of 2^n circuits in the cascade so that the following LUT delay condition is satisfied (refer Table 6.8),

$$D_{powerblock}(m) \leq \lceil \frac{t_{cp}^\#}{L} \rceil - 1 \qquad (6.8)$$

,where -1 is due to the output mux in the register bank. However the sequential nature of

TABLE 6.9: Scheduling Instructions for the ECM

$e_1^k : X_i \leftarrow X_i \cdot Z_j$	$e_4^k : Z_j \leftarrow (T \cdot Z_j)^2$
$e_2^k : Z_i \leftarrow X_j \cdot Z_i$	$e_5^k : T \leftarrow X_i \cdot Z_i; \; Z_i \leftarrow (X_i + Z_i)^2$
$e_3^k : T \leftarrow X_j; \; X_j \leftarrow X_j^4 + b \cdot Z_j^4$	$e_6^k : X_i \leftarrow x \cdot Z_i + T$

the Itoh-Tsujii algorithm [160] ensures that the result of one step is used in the next. Due to the data dependencies which arise the algorithm is not suited for pipelining and hence the latter strategy is favored. For $k = 4$ and $m = 163$, the optimal exponentiation circuit is $n = 2$ having an LUT delay of 2 [338]. Thus a cascade of two 2^2 circuits would best satisfy the inequality in (6.8).

In the following portion of the chapter, we outline the efficient scheduling of the Montgomery algorithm for performing the point multiplication.

6.8 Scheduling of the Montgomery Algorithm

For a given point P on the curve (called the *base point*) and a scalar s, *scalar multiplication* is the computation of the scalar product sP. Algorithm 19 depicts the Montgomery algorithm [226, 252] for computing sP. For each bit in s, a point addition followed by a point doubling is done (lines 5,6 and 9,10). In these operations (listed in Equation 6.9) only the X and Z coordinates of the points are used.

$$X_i \leftarrow X_i \cdot Z_j \; ; \; Z_i \leftarrow X_j \cdot Z_i \; ; \; T \leftarrow X_j \; ; \; X_j \leftarrow X_j^4 + b \cdot Z_j^4$$
$$Z_j \leftarrow (T \cdot Z_j)^2 \; ; \; T \leftarrow X_i \cdot Z_i \; ; \; Z_i \leftarrow (X_i + Z_i)^2 \; ; \; X_i \leftarrow x \cdot Z_i + T \tag{6.9}$$

Depending on the value of the bit s_k, operand and destination registers for the point operations vary. When $s_k = 1$ then $i = 1$ and $j = 2$, and when $s_k = 0$ then $i = 2$ and $j = 1$. The final step in the algorithm, $Projective2Affine(\cdot)$, converts the 3 coordinate scalar product in to the acceptable 2 coordinate affine form. This step involves a finite field inversion along with 9 other multiplications [249].

For each bit in the scalar (s_k), the eight operations in Equation 6.9 are computed. In this architecture we consider a situation where only one finite field multiplier. This can be compared with architectures in literature where two field multipliers are used, like [37]. There are other architectures proposed in literature like [87] which uses a single multiplier; we follow the later approach in the discussed design. This restriction makes the field multiplier the most critical resource in the ECM as Equation 6.9 involves six field multiplications, which have to be done sequentially. The remaining operations comprise of additions, squarings, and data transfers can be done in parallel with the multiplications. Equation 6.9 can be rewritten as in Table 6.8 using 6 instructions, with each instruction capable of executing simultaneously in the ECM.

Proper scheduling of the 6 instructions is required to minimize the impact of data dependencies, thus reducing pipeline stalls. The dependencies between the instructions e_1^k to e_6^k are shown in **Fig. 6.8(a)**. In the figure a *solid arrow* implies that the subsequent instruction cannot be started unless the previous instruction has completed, while a *dashed arrow* implies that the subsequent instruction cannot be started unless the previous instruction has started. For example e_6^k uses Z_i, which is updated in e_5^k. Since the update does not require a multiplication (an addition followed by a squaring here), it is completed in one

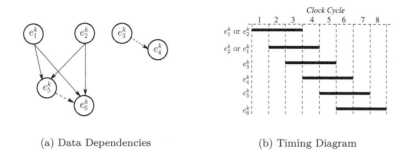

(a) Data Dependencies   (b) Timing Diagram

FIGURE 6.8: Scheduling the Scalar Bit s_k

clock cycle. Thus e_5^k to e_6^k has a dashed arrow, and e_6^k can start one clock cycle after e_5^k. On the other hand, dependencies depicted with the solid arrow involve the multiplier output in the former instruction. This will take L clock cycles, therefore a longer wait.

The dependency diagram shows that in the longest dependency chain, e_5^k and e_6^k has dependency on e_1^k and e_2^k. Thus e_1^k and e_2^k are scheduled before e_3^k and e_4^k. Since the addition in e_6^k has a dependency on e_5^k, operation e_5^k is triggered just after completion of e_1^k and e_2^k; and operation e_6^k is triggered in the next clock cycle. When $L \geq 3$, the interval between starting and completion of e_1^k and e_2^k can be utilized by scheduling e_3^k and e_4^k. Thus, the possible scheduling schemes for the 6 instructions is

$$(\{e_1^k, e_2^k\}, e_3^k, e_4^k, e_5^k, e_6^k) \tag{6.10}$$

Where $\{\ \}$ implies that there is no strict order in the scheduling (either e_1 or e_2 can be scheduled first). An example of a scheduling for $L = 3$ is shown in **Fig. 6.8(b)**. For $L \geq 3^1$, the number of clock cycles required for each bit in the scalar is $2L + 2$. In the next part of this section we show that the clock cycles can be reduced to $2L + 1$ (and in some cases $2L$) if two consecutive bits of the scalar are considered.

6.8.1 Scheduling for Two Consecutive Bits of the Scalar

Consider the scheduling of operations for two bits of the scalar, s_k and s_{k-1} (Algorithm 19). We assume that the computation of bit s_k is completed and the next bit s_{k-1} is to be scheduled. Two cases arise: $s_{k-1} = s_k$ and $s_{k-1} \neq s_k$. We consider each case separately.

When the Consecutive Key Bits are Equal : Fig. 6.9(a) shows the data dependencies when the two bits are equal. The last two instructions to complete for the s_k bit are e_5^k and e_6^k. For the subsequent bit (s_{k-1}), either e_1^{k-1} or e_2^{k-1} has to be scheduled first according to the sequence in (6.10). We see from **Fig. 6.9(a)** that e_1^{k-1} depends on e_6^k, while e_2^{k-1} depends on e_5^k. Further, since e_5^k completes earlier than e_6^k, we schedule e_2^{k-1} before e_1^{k-1}. Thus the scheduling for 2 consecutive equal bits is

$$(\{e_1^k, e_2^k\}, e_3^k, e_4^k, e_5^k, e_6^k, e_2^{k-1}, e_1^{k-1}, e_3^{k-1}, e_4^{k-1}, e_5^{k-1}, e_6^{k-1})$$

An example is shown in **Fig. 6.9(b)**.

---

[1]The special case of $L <= 2$ can trivially be analyzed. The clock cycles required in this case is six.

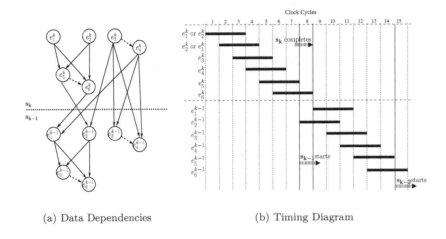

(a) Data Dependencies   (b) Timing Diagram

FIGURE 6.9: Schedule for Two Scalar Bits when $s_{k-1} = s_k$

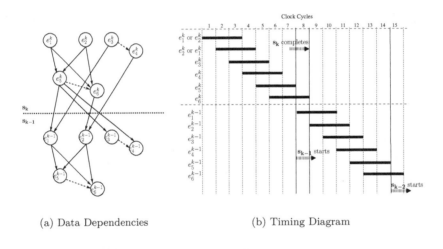

(a) Data Dependencies   (b) Timing Diagram

FIGURE 6.10: Schedule for Two Scalar Bits when $s_{k-1} \neq s_k$

When the Consecutive Key Bits are Not Equal : **Fig. 6.10(a)** shows the data dependency for two consecutive scalar bits that are not equal. Here it can be seen that e_1^{k-1} and e_2^{k-1} depend on e_5^k and e_6^k, respectively. Since, e_5^k completes before e_6^k, we schedule e_1^{k-1} before e_2^{k-1}. The scheduling for two consecutive bits is as follows

$$(\{e_1^k, e_2^k\}, e_3^k, e_4^k, e_5^k, e_6^k, e_1^{k-1}, e_2^{k-1}, e_3^{k-1}, e_4^{k-1}, e_5^{k-1}, e_6^{k-1})$$

An example is shown in **Fig. 6.10(b)**.

Effective Clock Cycle Requirement : Starting from e_1^k (or e_2^k), completion of e_2^k (or e_1^k) takes $L + 1$ clock cycles, for an L stage pipelined *ECM*. After completion of e_1^k and e_2^k, e_5^k starts. This is followed by e_6^k in the next clock cycle. So in all $2L + 2$ clock cycles are required. The last clock cycle however is also used for the next bit of the scalar. So effectively the clock cycles required per bit is $2L + 1$. Compared to the work in [87], our scheduling strategy saves two clock cycles for each bit of the scalar. For an m bit scalar, the saving in clock cycles compared to [87] is $2m$. Certain values of L allow data forwarding to take place. In such cases, the clock cycles per bit reduces to $2L$, thus saving $3m$ clock cycles compared to [87].

6.8.2 Data Forwarding to Reduce Clock Cycles

For a given value of L, Proposition 3 specifies where the pipeline registers have to be placed in the *ECM*. If the value of L is such that a pipeline register is placed at the output of the field multiplier, then data forwarding can be applied to save one clock cycle per scalar bit. For example, consider $L = 4$. This has pipeline registers placed immediately after the multiplier as shown in **Fig. 6.7**. This register can be used to start the instruction e_5^k one clock cycle earlier. **Fig. 6.9** compares the execution of a single bit with and without data forwarding. Though e_2^k (or e_1^k) finishes in the fifth clock cycle, the result of the multiplication is latched into the pipeline register after the fourth clock cycle. With data forwarding from this register, we start e_5^k from the fifth clock cycle, thus reducing clock cycle requirement by one to $2L$.

6.9 Finding the Right Pipeline

The time taken for a scalar multiplication in the *ECM* is the product of the number of clock cycles required and the time period of the clock. For an L stage pipeline, Section 6.7 determines the best time period for the clock. In this section we would first estimate the number of clock cycles required and then analyze the effect of L on the computation time.

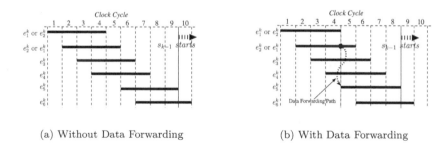

(a) Without Data Forwarding   (b) With Data Forwarding

FIGURE 6.11: Effect of Data Forwarding in the *ECM* for $L = 4$

6.9.1 Number of Clock Cycles

There are two parts in Algorithm 19. First the scalar multiplication in projective coordinates and then the conversion to affine coordinates. The conversion comprises of finding an inverse and 9 multiplications. The clock cycles required is given by $cc_{2scm} = cc_{3scm} + cc_{ita} + cc_{conv}$.

cc_{3scm} is the clock cycles required for the scalar multiplication in projective coordinates. From the analysis in Section 6.8 this can be written as $2mL$ if data forwarding is possible and $m(2L + 1)$ otherwise. For the conversion to affine coordinates, finding the inverse requires cc_{ita} clock cycles (from Equation 6.7), while the 9 multiplications following the inverse

TABLE 6.10: Computation Time Estimates for Various Values of L for an *ECM* over $GF(2^{163}$ and FPGA with 4 input LUTs

L	u_s	DataForwarding Feasible	cc_{3scm}	cc_{ita}	cc_{conv}	cc_{2scm}	ct
1	9	No	978	25	16	1019	$1019t_{cp}^{\#}$
2	4	No	978	44	25	1047	$524t_{cp}^{\#}$
3	3	No	1141	61	34	1236	$412t_{cp}^{\#}$
4	2	Yes	1304	82	43	1429	$357t_{cp}^{\#}$
5	1	No	1793	130	52	1975	$395t_{cp}^{\#}$
6	1	Yes	1956	140	61	2157	$360t_{cp}^{\#}$
7	1	Yes	2282	150	70	2502	$358t_{cp}^{\#}$

requires cc_{conv} clock cycles. The value of cc_{conv} for the *ECM* was found to be $7 + 9L$. Thus,

$$cc_{2scm} = \left[cc_{3scm}\right] + \left[L(l+1) + \sum_{i=2}^{l}\left\lceil\frac{u_i - u_{i-1}}{u_s}\right\rceil\right] + \left[7 + 9L\right] \tag{6.11}$$

6.9.2　Analyzing Computation Time

The procedure involved in analyzing the computation time for an L stage pipeline is as follows.

1. Determine $t_{cp}^{\#}$ (the LUT delay of the critical path of the combinational circuit) using Table 6.8.

2. Compute the maximum operable frequency ($\lceil\frac{t_{cp}^{\#}}{L}\rceil$) and determine the locations of the pipeline registers. Therefore, determine if data forwarding is possible.

3. Determine u_s, the number of cascades in the power block, using Equation 6.8 and the delay of a single 2^n block (Table 6.8).

4. Compute cc_{2scm}, using Equation 6.11.

5. The computation time ct is given by $cc_{2scm} \times \lceil\frac{t_{cp}^{\#}}{L}\rceil$.

For an *ECM* over $GF(2^{163})$, the threshold for the *HBKM* set as 11, an addition chain of $(1, 2, 4, 5, 10, 20, 40, 80, 81)$, and 2^2 exponentiation circuits in the power block, the $t_{cp}^{\#}$ is 23. The estimated computation time for various values of L are given in Table 6.10. The cases $L = 1$ and $L = 2$ are special as for these $cc_{3scm} = 6m$. The table clearly shows that the least computation time is obtained when $L = 4$.

6.10　Detailed Architecture of the *ECM*

Fig. 6.12 shows the detailed architecture for $L = 4$. The input to the architecture is the scalar, reset signal, and the clock. At reset, the curve constants and base point are loaded from ROM. At every clock cycle, the control unit generates signals for the register bank and the arithmetic unit. Registers are selected through multiplexers in the register bank and fed to the arithmetic unit through the buses $A0$, $A1$, $A2$, $A3$, and Qin. Multiplexers

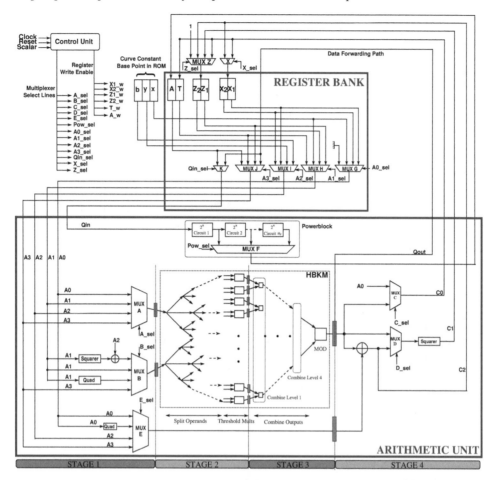

FIGURE 6.12: Detailed Architecture for a 4 Stage Pipelined *ECM*

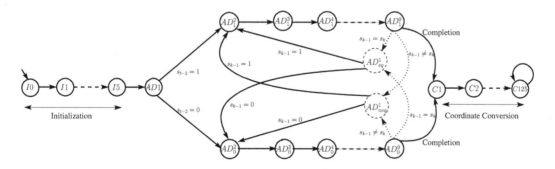

FIGURE 6.13: Finite State Machine for 4-Stage *ECM*

again channel the data into the multiplier. The results are written back into the registers through buses $C0$, $C1$, $C2$, $Qout$. Note the placement of the pipeline registers dividing the circuit in 4 stages and ensuring that each stage has an LUT delay which is less than or equal to $\lceil \frac{23}{4} \rceil = 6$. Note also the pipeline register present immediately after the field multiplier (*HBKM*) used for data forwarding.

TABLE 6.11: Comparison of the Proposed *ECM* with FPGA based Published Results

Work	Platform	Field (m)	Slices	LUTs	Freq (MHz)	Comp. Time (μs)
Orlando [279]	XCV400E	163	-	3002	76.7	210
Bednara [43]	XCV1000	191	-	48300	36	270
Gura [144]	XCV2000E	163	-	19508	66.5	140
Lutz [228]	XCV2000E	163	-	10017	66	233
Saqib [345]	XCV3200	191	18314	-	10	56
Pu [306]	XC2V1000	193	-	3601	115	167
Ansari [33]	XC2V2000	163	-	8300	100	42
Järvinen[1] [163]	Stratix II	163	(11800ALMs)	-	-	48.9
Kim [2] [195]	XC4VLX80	163	24363	-	143	10.1
Chelton [87]	XCV2600E	163	15368	26390	91	33
	XC4V200	163	16209	26364	153.9	19.5
Azarderakhsh[3] [37]	XC4CLX100	163	12834	22815	196	17.2
	XC5VLX110	163	6536	17305	262	12.9
ECCP [314]	XC4V140	233	19674	37073	60	31
ECM [320] (Virtex 4 FPGA)	XC4VLX80	163	8070	14265	147	9.7
	XC4V200	163	8095	14507	132	10.7
	XC4VLX100	233	13620	23147	154	12.5
ECM [320] (Virtex 5 FPGA)	XC5VLX85t	163	3446	10176	167	8.6
	XC5VSX240	163	3513	10195	148	9.5
	XC5VLX85t	233	5644	18097	156	12.3

1. uses 4 field multipliers; 2. uses 3 field multipliers; 3. uses 2 field multipliers

Fig. 6.13 shows the finite state machine for $L = 4$. The states $I0$ to $I5$ are used for initialization (line 2 in Algorithm 19). State $AD1$ represents the first clock cycle for the scalar bit s_{t-2}. States AD_1^2 to AD_1^9 represent the computations when $s_k = 1$, while AD_0^2 to AD_0^9 are for $s_k = 0$. Each state corresponds to a clock cycle in **Fig. 6.11(b)**. Processing for the next scalar bit (s_{k-1}) begins in the same clock cycle as AD_0^9 and AD_1^9 in states AD_{eq}^1 and AD_{neq}^1. The states AD_{eq}^1 or AD_{neq}^1 are entered depending on the equality of s_k and s_{k-1}. If $s_k = s_{k-1}$ then AD_{eq}^1 is entered, else AD_{neq}^1 is entered. After processing of all scalar bits is complete, the conversion to affine coordinates ($cc_{ita} + cc_{conv}$) takes place in states C_1 to C_{125}.

6.11   Implementation Results

In this section, we evaluate the performance of the improved design, compare with the previous version and also with exisiting state of the art implementations on Xilinx Virtex 4 and Virtex 5 platforms. Table 6.11 summarizes the evaluations and comparisions based on place and route results using the Xilinx ISE tool. There have been several implementations of elliptic curve processors on different fields, curves, platforms, and for different applications. Due to the vast variety of implementations available, we restrict comparisons with FPGA implementations for generic elliptic curves over binary finite fields (Table 6.11). In this section, we analyze recent high-speed implementations.

The implementation ECCP [314] is over the field $GF(2^{233})$ and does a scalar multiplication in $31\mu s$. The implementation relied heavily on optimized finite-field primitives and was not pipelined or parallelized. Our implementation on the same field uses enhanced primitives from [314], and therefore has smaller area requirements. Additionally, higher speeds are achieved due to efficient pipelining and scheduling of instructions.

The implementation in [87] uses a 7-stage pipeline, thus achieves high operating clock frequency. However, the unoptimized pipeline and large clock cycle requirement limits performance. In comparison, the *ECM* uses better scheduling there by saving around 1600 clock cycles and a better pipeline, there by obtaining frequencies close to [87], inspite of having only 4 pipeline stages. Further, efficient field primitives and the sub-quadratic Karatsuba multiplier instead of the quadratic Mastrovito multiplier result in 50% reduction in area on Virtex 4.

In [37], two highly optimized digit field multipliers were used. This enabled parallelization of the instructions and higher clock frequency. However, the use of digit field multipliers resulted in large clock cycle requirement for scalar multiplication (estimated at 3380). We use a single fully parallel field multiplier requiring only 1429 clock cycles and an area which is 37% lesser in Virtex 4.

In [195], a computation time of $10.1\mu s$ was achieved while on the same platform our *ECM* achieves a computation time of $9.7\mu s$. Although the speed gained is minimal, it should be noted that [195] uses three digit-level finite field multipliers compared to one in ours, thus has an area requirement which is about three times ours. The compact area is useful especially for cryptanalytic applications where our *ECM* can test thrice as many keys compared to [195].

6.12 Conclusion

This chapter integrates the previously developed finite-field arithmetic blocks to comprise the arithmetic unit (AU) for an elliptic curve processor. The AU is used in a elliptic curve crypto processor to compute the scalar product kP for a NIST specified curve. The initial design is further augmented by implementing the Montgomery's ladder, pipelining the architecture in an optimized manner, and also suitably scheduling the instructions. The final design demonstrates that these principles provide on FPGA platforms one of the best reported timings, and also a compact utilization of the available resources.

Part III

Side Channel Analysis

Chapter 7

Introduction to Side Channel Analysis

"In theory, there is no difference between theory and practice. In practice, there is."

(Lawrence Peter "Yogi" Berra)

7.1 Introduction

As we have seen in the previous chapters, implementation of cryptographic algorithms is complex. These ciphers are complex mathematical constructs, often requiring large-field arithmetic, multiple iterations etc. Hence various techniques are required to make the designs efficient. The ciphers are designed carefully with chosen parameters to thwart the cryptanalysts. Depending on the underlying platform, several hardware and software designs of the same ciphers are developed, to ensure that security comes at a minimal cost to the user. Though conventional attacks are independent of these implementations, most often the standard ciphers, like AES and ECC are designed in a fashion that the attacks are more often not practical. However there is a form of cryptanalysis, known as *side channel analysis* (SCA) which exploits not only the mathematical structures of the ciphers, but also the inherent properties of the implementations. These menacing category of attacks jeopardizes some of the basic assumptions on which the conventional cryptographer designs ciphers, and thus requires special consideration in the context of hardware and embedded security.

Although research in the area of side channel analysis started with the seminal work of [284] in around 1996, several forms of cryptanalysis through other unconventional information channels existed much before. The idea of stealing information through side channels is far older than the personal computer. In World War I, the intelligence corps of the warring nations were able to eavesdrop on one anothers battle orders because field telephones of the day had just one wire and used the earth to carry the return current. Spies connected rods in the ground to amplifiers and picked up the conversations. During the World War II, Bell Labs was aware of attack methods which would use electromagnetic radiations to reveal 75% of the plaintext that was sent in a secured fashion from a distance of 80 feet. Later around 1985, Wim van Eck published the first unclassified technical analysis of the security risks of emanations from computer monitors. Van Eck successfully eavesdropped on a real system, at a range of hundreds of metres, using just $15 worth of equipment plus a television set. This paper showed the feasibility of such attacks to the security community, which had previously believed that such monitoring was a highly sophisticated attack available only to governments. American military scientists began studying these radio waves given off by computer monitors and launched a program, code-named Tempest, to develop shielding techniques. Without these shielding, the image being scanned line by line onto the screen of a standard cathode-ray tube monitor can be reconstructed from a nearby room or even an adjacent building by tuning into the monitors radio transmissions.

Many people assumed that the growing popularity of flat-panel displays would make Tempest problems obsolete, because flat panels use low voltages and do not scan images one line at a time. But in 2003 Markus G. Kuhn, a computer scientist at the University of Cambridge Computer Laboratory, demonstrated that even flat-panel monitors, including those built into laptops, radiate digital signals from their video cables, emissions that can be picked up and decoded from many meters away.

Several side channels and corresponding attacks have been subsequently developed. The challenge in tackling side channel attacks comes from the fact that it violates the classical notions of cryptography. Conventional cryptographic defenses do not work in hindering them. To quote none other than Adi Shamir, it is extremely difficult to envisage new forms of these attacks. According to him, after years of research in provable properties in RSA, like reduction proofs, equivalence to factoring, bit security of RSA, the cipher seemed robust, well studied, and fit for applications like banking etc. where security is needed. However, the work of Boneh, Demillo and Lipton in 1996 showed that a single faulty computation can completely break the scheme by factoring the moduli. Hence, the danger of side channel attacks is from the fact that it can expose the fragility of a mathematically sound cipher and make it unsuitable for applications. Hence, we need a deeper, thorough and theoretical study of the topic. In the following section, we present an overview and define side channel attacks.

7.2   What Are Side Channels?

Side channels are the channels of information which are produced by a device in an unintentional fashion. These channels provide to the cryptanalyst internal state informations which was not available to the classical cryptanalyst. Hence, the proofs or guarantees of security in classical cryptography are no more valid. Examples of such side channels are timing, power, electromagnetic radiations, visual, acoustics, cache, testability features of hardware devices and there may be many more. A very closely related class of attacks is called as fault attacks, where the device under the induction of faults, perform wrong computations. The adversary uses the correct ciphertexts and the faulty ciphertexts and obtains the keys. These class of attacks are extremely dangerous and show that fault tolerance is of utmost importance for cryptographic hardware.

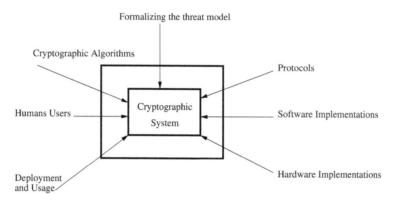

FIGURE 7.1: Side Channel Attacks

7.2.1 Difference of Side Channel Analysis and Conventional Cryptanalysis

Traditionally, the topic of cryptography delves in the subjects of designing secured algorithms for ciphering, signature generation, etc. Security, however, is a much bigger world dealing with several factors: studying the threat models and security goals, designing and analyzing strong cryptographic algorithms, designing robust cryptographic protocols, implementing the algorithms on software or hardware platforms, and finally deploying and using the designs (refer **Fig. 7.1**). The other important aspect is that humans are the users of these products, and often this subject also involves understanding the human behavior for improving the levels of trust. This is really a challenging work.

However, the topic of side channels typically deals with attacks that target the implementation of the ciphering algorithms. They target various properties of the implementation, like power consumption, timing requirement, manifestation of faults, etc. to reveal the underlying operation or information. The side channels could vary depending on several aspects: for example the type of implementation, namely a software vs. hardware implementation, could make different channels more important. It is often difficult to define these channels, but in principle these are covert channels which leak information which the designers of cryptographic algorithms did not consider. Information is leaked because of the implementation being oblivious of these security threats. Often when performance is the key focus designers tend to perform optimizations, which are unaware of these leakage channels. As an example, use of key dependent if-else statements in a program has a chance of potential side channel leakages, as the two branches may be different in terms of their timing requirement, power consumptions etc. thus revealing the key! This shows that optimizations for cryptographic systems have to be carefully done. In other words, a side channel adversary is more powerful than a conventional cryptanalyst, as it has more information sources in the form of observed side channels. Thus designing systems secured against such threats is also more interesting.

7.2.2   Types of Side Channel Attacks

There are several forms of side channels. Some of the popular forms of side channel attacks on hardware and embedded systems are:

1. Timing Attacks

2. Power Attacks

3. Fault Attacks

4. Design for Testability attacks

5. Cache Attacks

These side channel analysis methods can also be combined with each other and also with conventional cryptanalysis techniques to develop even stronger forms of attacks. For example, fault attacks are often combined with algebraic attacks to yield a new class of attacks called *Algebraic Side Channel Attacks*[323].

In the next sections, we provide a brief overview on the above mentioned side channel attacks.

7.3   Kocher's Seminal Works

Paul C. Kocher of Cryptography Research, Inc., wrote in 1996 a fundamental paper to show that careful measurement of the time required to perform private key operations, an attacker can retrieve the key of the RSA algorithm, or any other cryptosystem. The fundamental reason, why such attacks are possible is the difference of time required to process different inputs. Cryptographic codes or designs often ' have several optimizations, conditional statements, distribution of cache hits and misses, different instructions in their assembly codes which make different inputs have varying execution paths, needing different units of time. In the following section, we summarize such a timing based cryptanalysis against a modular exponentiation operation which is central to the RSA cipher.

7.3.1   Timing Attack on Modular Exponentiation

The modular exponentiation, $R \equiv y^x \bmod n$, where n is public and y can be found by an eavesdropper. The attack's objective is to determine the secret x from the timing profile obtained by observing the time required by varying the input y. Note that the value of the secret x must be kept constant throughout the attack. Consider a straightforward implementation of modular exponentiation using a square-and-multiply algorithm.

It is easy to verify that the algorithm performs an exponentiation in time proportional to the length of the exponent x. We assume that x is a w-bit exponent, encoded as $x[0], \cdots, x[w-1]$. The distinct operations performed are multiplication, and squaring. The running variable y is updated in each iteration: each iteration consisting of one squaring

---

Algorithm 7.1: Square and Multiply Algorithm for Modular Exponentiation

---

Input: $y, x, n,$
Output: $s \equiv y^x \bmod n$

1   $s = 1$
2   **for** $(i = n - 1; i \geq 0; i - -)$ **do**
3      $bit = (x >> i)\&1$
4      $s = s^2 \bmod n$
5   **if** *(bit)* **then**
6         $s = s \times y \bmod n$
7   **end**
8   **end**
9   **return** s

---

operation and one conditional multiplication operation. The multiplication is performed in the ith iteration if the corresponding value is one, else it is skipped.

We explain the attack in an iterative way: at any stage of the attack assume that the value of the first $b - 1$-bits of the exponent x are known, and the attacker wants to observe the next bit. That is, the attacker is aware of $x[0], \ldots, x[b - 2]$ and he tries to ascertain $x[b - 1]$.

7.3.1.1   Timing Measurement

The attack assumes accurate timing observation. The following snippet for *timestamp* can be handy to measure the time required by a function P. The time required by the function P is computed by measuring the timestamp before and after calling the function P, and then evaluating the difference between the timestamps. Note if there is no program between two timestamp calls, there is still a small time difference, which is due to overheads. The overhead should be appropriately deducted while computing the running time of the program P.

```
#include <time.h>

unsigned int timestamp(void)
{
    unsigned int bottom;
    unsigned int top;
    asm volatile("xorl %%eax,%%eax\n cpuid \n" ::: "%eax",
     "%ebx", "%ecx", "%edx"); // flush pipeline
    asm volatile("rdtsc\n" : "=a" (bottom), "=d" (top) );
                             // read rdtsc
    asm volatile("xorl %%eax,%%eax\n cpuid \n" ::: "%eax",
     "%ebx", "%ecx", "%edx"); // flush pipeline again
    return bottom;
}
```

7.3.1.2   The Attack Methodology

The attacker measures the time required to perform the loop a large number of times by varying the value of y. Each observed timing can be denoted as $T_j = e + \sum_{i=0}^{w-1} t_i$, where t_i

is the time required to perform the multiplication and squaring for the bit i and e includes measurement error, loop overhead and other sources of inaccuracies.

As stated above we assume that the attacker knows or has correctly evaluated in the previous iterations the first $b-1$-bits, $x[0], \cdots, x[b-2]$ of the secret exponent x. Now the attacker guesses $x[b-1]$. If the guess is correct, subtracting from T yields $T_r = e + \sum_{i=0}^{w-1} t_i - \sum_{i=0}^{b-1} t_i = e + \sum_{i=b}^{w-1} t_i$.

The attacker obtains a distribution by varying the value of y and observing the above timing T_r. Assuming the modular multiplication times are mutually independent and from the measurement error. If the guess is correct, the variance reduces and the observed variance is $Var(e) + (w-b)Var(t)$. For correctly estimated timings (due to correct guesses of the exponent bits) the variance decreases. However if the guess for $x[b-1]$ is wrong, then the variance increases, the resultant variance becomes $Var(e) + [w - (b-1) + 1]Var(t) = Var(e) + [w - b + 2]Var(t)$. This observed increase in variance can be used as an indicator to distinguish a wrong estimate of a bit from a correct one.

7.4   Power Attacks

The seminal paper by Paul Kocher on timing attacks was further extended by another powerful class of attacks, called the power attacks. These attacks work because of the fact that the crypto circuits are eventually implemented using semiconductor logic gates, which are eventually composed of transistors. The current flow through the transistors is dependent on the charge applied (in case of NMOS) or charge removed (in case of PMOS). This charging current which flows to and from the gates eventually consume power which can be observed by the external world with fair accuracy in laboratory environments. These observations leak internal characteristics and states of the crypto-algorithms and thus serve as potential side channel sources.

Like any other side channel analysis method, power attacks are also not theoretical attacks. They exploit the implementation of a given cipher and the power consumption of the design. A set of power consumption measurement is technically known as *trace*. A given trace acquired when the cryptographic hardware operates on inputs is composed of several variations because of the intermediate transitions that the registers in the design go through. The cryptographic operations lead to switchings of the registers which are exhibited in the power trace variations. The power trace is often obtained by placing a small resisitor, say 50 ohms in series with the power or ground inputs. The voltage drop across this resistor is captured by a digital oscilloscope and is recorded as the trace. A typical laboratory set-up is shown in the **Fig. 7.2**.

The device under attack could be a micro-controller, an ASIC or an FPGA design which implements a cryptographic algorithm. In this book, we shall be essentially considering FPGA designs, but the discussions can be extended to other devices as well with minor modifications and slight adjustments. In the **Fig. 7.3** a sample trace for an AES encryption running on an FPGA platform is shown.

Depending on the analysis method and the number of traces captured, there are two broad types of power analysis: Simple Power Analysis (SPA) and Differential Power Analysis (DPA). Broadly, the fact exploited in an SPA is that the power consumption at an instant of time is a function of the operation being carried out by the device. On the other hand, DPA is based on the fact that the power consumption of the same operation at different instants of time depends on the data being processed.

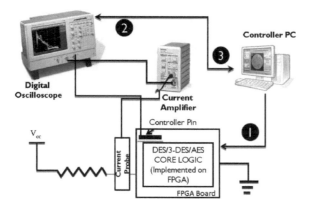

FIGURE 7.2: Side Channel Attack Set Up

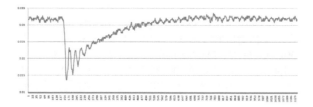

FIGURE 7.3: Power Trace of AES

7.4.1 Simple Power Analysis

Simple power analysis or SPA, as it is abbreviated, is a technique that involves directly interpreting power consumption measurements during *cryptographic operations*. It may be stressed that the SPA works on the hypothesis that the power consumption of the device depends on the operation being performed. The objective of an SPA attack is to obtain the secret key in one or few traces. That makes an SPA quite challenging in practice. **Fig. 7.4** shows that a smart card with a mathematically strong cipher being used in a card accepting device. While the input data and the output data does not reveal the secret key, the figure shows that silent capturing of the power trace by the terminal used to insert the card can reveal the secret key!

However, observation of a power trace can often leak other important information, if not the key. They can be the rounds of a block cipher, the square and multiply operations in case of an asymmetric cipher like RSA.

As a subtle information leakage, it can be a good starting tool for side channel attacks in particular, and cryptanalysis in general, as they can leak the type of cipher under investigation. It may be appreciated that in real life such an information could be very costly. Hence, implementing the ciphers with suitable countermeasures against SPA is important. Fortunately, there are several works describing the design of SPA-resistant cryptosystems.

As an example, consider the modular exponentiation operation as explained previously. We know it is the central operation in an RSA-decryption, which involves the secret key. As a quick reminder, if the secret key is $x = b$, then the decryption algorithm of RSA involves computing: $y^x \bmod n$, where n is the common modulus. An efficient way of performing the operation would be, as discussed, using the square and multiply algorithm. The algorithm

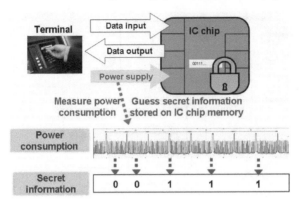

FIGURE 7.4: Simple Power Analysis

shows that at every iteration, *squaring* is performed. However, if the current *bit* in the ith iteration is a one, then a *multiplication* operation is also performed. Hence, it is expected that the power consumption in the ith cycle would be more, if the key bit is one, compared to when it is zero. This helps one to build a distinguisher to determine the key bits from a few power traces. In cases of an unprotected and naïve square and multiply implementation, a single trace is sufficient for most purposes.

7.4.2   An Example SPA of the ECCP Designed

In Chapter 6, we presented the design of an ECCP, which executed the standard Double-and-Add algorithm for performing point multiplication (refer Algorithm 2.3). The state machine for the scalar multiplication in the ECCP has 12 states (**Fig. 6.4**), 4 states ($D1 \cdots D4$) for doubling and 8 states ($A1 \cdots A8$) for addition. Each iteration in the scalar multiplication handles a bit in the key starting from the most significant one to the least significant bit. If the key bit is zero, a doubling is done and no addition is done. If the key bit is one, the doubling is followed by an addition. The dissimilarity in the way a 1 and a 0 in the key is handled makes the ECCP vulnerable to side channel attacks as enumerated below.

- The duration of an iteration depends on the key bit. A key bit of 0 leads to a short cycle compared to a key bit of 1. Thus measuring the duration of an iteration will give an attacker knowledge about the key bit.

- Each state in the FSM has a unique power consumption trace. Monitoring the power consumption trace would reveal if an addition is done thus revealing the key bit.

To demonstrate the attack we used *Xilinx's XPower* [1] tool. Given a *value change dump* (VCD) file generated from a flattened post map or post route netlist, XPower is capable of generating a power trace for a given testbench.

Fig. 7.5 and **Fig. 7.6** are partial power traces generated for the key $(FFFFFFFF)_{16}$ and $(80000000)_{16}$ respectively. The graphs plot the power on the Y axis with the time line on the X axis for a *Xilinx Virtex 4 FPGA*. The difference in the graphs is easily noticeable. The spikes in **Fig. 7.5** occurs in state $A6$. This state is entered only when a point addition is done, which in turn is done only when the key bit is 1. The spikes are not present in

---

[1] http://www.xilinx.com/products/design_tools/logic_design/verification/xpower.htm

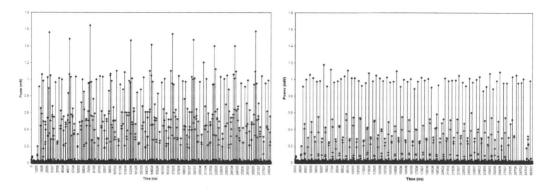

FIGURE 7.5: Power Trace for a Key with all 1   **FIGURE 7.6**: Power Trace for a Key with all 0

Fig. 7.6 as the state $A6$ is never entered. Therefore the spikes in the trace can be used to identify ones in the key.

The duration between two spikes in **Fig. 7.5** is the time taken to do a point doubling and a point addition. This is 12 clock cycles. If there are two spikes with a distance greater than 12 clock cycles, it indicates that one or more zeroes are present in the key. The number of zeroes (n) present can be determined by Equation 7.1. In the equation t is the duration between the two spikes and T is the time period of the clock.

$$n = \frac{t}{4T} - 3 \qquad (7.1)$$

The number of zeroes between the leading one in k and the one due to the first spike can be inferred by the amount of shift in the first spike.

As an example consider the power trace (**Fig. 7.7**) for the ECCP obtained when the key was set to $(B9B9)_{16}$. There are 9 spikes indicating 9 ones in the key (excluding the leading one). Table 7.1 infers the key from the time duration between spikes. The clock has a period $T = 200ns$.

TABLE 7.1: SPA for the key $B9B9_{16}$

i	$t_i - t_{i-1}$	n	Key Inferred
1	-	-	01
2	2400 ns	0	1
3	2400 ns	0	1
4	4000 ns	2	001
5	2400 ns	0	1
6	3200 ns	1	01
7	2400 ns	0	1
8	2400 ns	0	1
9	4000 ns	2	001

The first spike t_1 is obtained at 3506th ns. If there were no zeros before t_1 the spike should have been present at 2706th ns (this is obtained from the first spike of **Fig. 7.5**). The shift is 800 ns equal to four clock cycles. Therefore a 0 is present before the t_1 spike.

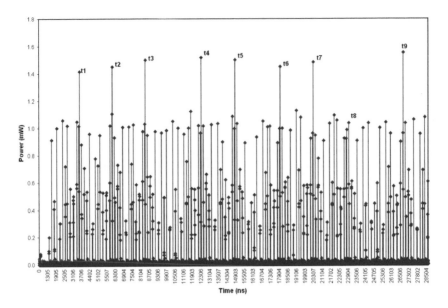

FIGURE 7.7: Power Trace when $k = (B9B9)_{16}$

The key obtained from the attack is $(1011100110111001)_2$, and it matches the actual key.

7.4.3   Differential Power Attacks

Differential Power Attacks or DPA is a power analysis method which exploits the fact that power consumption depends on the data being processed. DPA is essentially a statistical method to performs attacks on ciphers. Though different flavors of DPA exist, a very simple and yet effective method of performing DPA is called as the *Difference of Means* (DOM) method. In this method, we first assume that the power consumption is correlated to a specific *target* bit of an internal register in the hardware. The attacker is typically unaware of this bit. However, he guesses a portion of the key, and based on the guess computes this target bit from the other available data. For example, for a block cipher it could be a specific input bit of an S-box. The attacker guesses, say, a byte of the key and performs a last-round decryption from the ciphertext corresponding to a particular power trace, and determines this target bit. Depending on whether the target bit is one or zero, the power trace is placed in a zero-bit (bin0) or one-bin (bin1). Likewise, all the traces are split in these two bins and finally the average of each bin is computed, and then the difference of the means is computed. The hypothesis is that if the guess of the key portion is correct, then the difference of mean will show high values at those time instants when the target bit is actually computed in the hardware. For a wrong guess, however the difference of mean will be negligible. This helps one to distinguish the correct key from the others.

The dependence can be be explained because of the underlying power models. The leakage of the power profile of the internal state is because the power consumption depends on the Hamming weight or the Hamming distances of the registers. Thus one of the underlying assumptions behind these attacks is that the power consumption of the hardware device is assumed to follow or be influenced by these power models. It may be noted that these power models treat each bit independently, while in real life the influence of each bit may be simultaneous. Though such a multibit power model may be more effective, but notably the Hamming weight or the Hamming distance power models also gives quite effective results in most cases. In this chapter, we study the Hamming weight model more closely. The same discussion can be adapted to Hamming distance model as well.

TABLE 7.2: Dependence of Hamming weight on a target bit

s	HW(s)	Target bit (LSB)
0000	0	0
0001	1	1
0010	1	0
0011	2	1
0100	1	0
0101	2	1
0110	2	0
0111	3	1
1000	1	0
1001	2	1
1010	2	0
1011	3	1
1100	2	0
1101	3	1
1110	3	0
1111	4	1

In order to understand the rationale of the Difference of Means method, we perform a simple experiment. We adhere to the assumption that the power consumption is proportional to the Hamming weight of a state, and study the Hamming weights of any arbitrary 4-bit variable, s. Consider in Table 7.2 the 4-bit value, s and the corresponding Hamming weight are indicated as $HW(s)$. We observe that the distribution is non-uniform (refer to **Fig** 7.8). One can observe the correlation with any target bit, say the LSB of s.

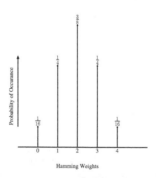

FIGURE 7.8: Distribution of Hamming Weights

If we observe a large number of samples, it is expected that the probability distribution of the s will be uniform. However, the $HW(s)$ will be non-uniform and hence based on our assumption of the power model, the power values will also be skewed. According to the

DOM method, one can split the HWs of the s values into two bins: zerobin and onebin and compute the means of the values in each bin. We observe from the table that the zerobin has values which add to 12 (there are 8 values), whereas the values in the onebin add upto 20 (there are 8 values too). Thus the difference of means of these two values is $\frac{20}{8} - \frac{12}{8} = 1$. It is trivial to observe that if the partitioning was done through a random bit sequence uncorrelated to the Hamming weights, the expected sums in each bin would have been 16, and hence the difference zero. In **Fig 7.9** we show a simulation of 2^{10} runs where the paritioning of the HWs have been done using bits, simulated by the *rand* function in C. One can observe that the DOM is typically close to zero. The same observation holds for any bit length, indicating that a non-zero DOM value indicates that the Hamming weight (i.e. the power consumption) is strongly correlated with the target bit. Let us now analyze

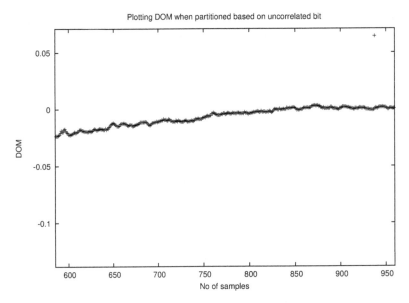

FIGURE 7.9: Distribution of DOM when the Hamming weights are distributed based on an uncorrelated bit

a DPA with the above hindsight on a simple modular exponentiation algorithm. algorithm: $z \equiv y^x \mod 256$. We present the following attack scenario to show the effectiveness of DPA in obtaining the secret key.

In this toy example, the state of the modular exponentiation can be encoded in 8 bits. Consider an attack scenario, where the attacker knows the first four bits of the key, and would like to obtain the next bit: which can be either 0 or 1 with a probability significantly larger than $1/2$. The attacker has access to the hardware, which has the key x embedded inside in some tamper-proof fashion. The attacker thus generates several y's randomly, and observes the corresponding power traces.

Simultaneously, the attacker also feeds in the same input y under which a trace has been obtained. Under our assumption of the attack scenario, the attacker subsequently guesses the next bit and based on the guess computes the value of the temporary variable s using the square and multiply algorithm after the 3rd iteration (note that the square and multiply algorithm starts processing from the MSB of x denoted by 7th iteration and the processing of the LSB denoted by the 0th iteration). The attacker say uses the LSB of the register s after the 3rd iteration to partition the traces either in a zero bin or a one bin. After the attacker has done so for a large number of inputs y, the attacker computes the difference of mean of the two bins. It is expected that for the correct guess of the next bit of x, there will be a significant difference of mean at the 3rd iteration. However, for the wrong guess, since the paritioning of the traces is done based on a random bit which is not correlated to the actual state, s will yield a very small value of the difference of mean. This helps to distinguish between the incorrect key and the correct key.

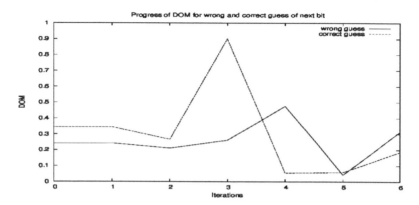

FIGURE 7.10: Plot of DOM for a wrong guess of next bit of x compared to a correct guess with simulated power traces

One can try to experimentally verify the above attack algorithm, either using actual power traces or through simulated power traces obtained from the Hamming weights of the intermediate register s. It may be pointed if the power consumption is based on the Hamming distance power model, then one needs to adapt the attack strategy accordongly. Rather than paritioning the traces on the target bit (LSB of s) value, one needs to partition the traces based on the difference of the LSB of the state s between the 4th iteration and the 3rd iteration. **Fig 7.10** refers to the plot of the DOMs for a run of the attack after observing 2^{10} samples. The correct key in the simulation is $0x8F$, thus the correct next key bit (3rd bit) is 1. It can be observed that using the difference of mean technique the attacker observes the larger DOM (around 0.9) compared to the smaller DOM (around 0.21) for the wrong guess. It should be noted that the plot only shows the absolute value of the DOMs.

We discuss the topic of power analysis in more details in a subsequent chapter, explaining some other improvements of the DOM method using correlations. We also discuss some suitable counter-measures against such power attacks, using a well-known technique called masking.

In the next section, we present an overview of another well known attack technique: called fault attacks. These attacks are extremely powerful attack techniques which extract the keys from faulty computation of an encryption device.

7.5 Fault Attacks

The growing complexity of the cryptographic algorithms and the increasing applications of ciphers in real-time applications has lead to research in the development of high-speed hardware designs or optimized cryptographic libraries for these algorithms. The complex operations performed in these designs and the large state space involved indicates that a complete verification is ruled out. Hence, these designs have a chance of being fault prone. Apart from these unintentional faults, faults can also be injected intentionally. Literature shows several ways of fault injection: accidental variation in operating conditions, like voltage, clock frequency, or focused laser beams in hardware. Software programs can also be subjected to situations, like missing of certain instructions to inflict faults. Apart from the general issue of fault tolerance in any large design, faults bring a completely new aspect when dealing with cryptographic algorithms: *security.*

The first thing that comes to mind is the relation between faults and secrets. In this section, we first attempt to motivate the impact of faults in the leakage of information.

Motivating Example: Consider a pedadogical example comprised of two hardware devices as illustrated in **Fig. 7.11**.

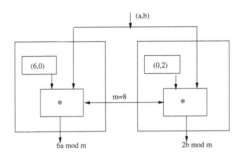

FIGURE 7.11: Effect of Faults on Secrets

The first device has a register storing the values $R1 = (6,0)$, and computes the product $y_{left} = (6,0) \times (a,b)^T = 6a \bmod m$. The value of m is fixed as, say, 8. The second device on the other hand has the register with value $R2 = (0,2)$ and computes $y_{right} = (0,2) \times (a,b)^T = 2b \bmod m$. The users can feed in values of (a,b), st. $(a,b) \in \{2,6\} \times \{2,6\}$. For the rest of the discussion all the computations are mod 8 and are not explicitly stated.

The user can only input the values (a,b) chosen from the 4 values of $\{2,6\} \times \{2,6\}$. On receiving the inputs (a,b) both the hardwares compute the values of y_{left} and y_{right}. However the user is given either y_{left} or y_{right}, chosen on the basis of a random toss of an unbiased coin which is hidden from the user. The challenge of the user is to guess the outcome of the random coin with a probability better than $\frac{1}{2}$. The user is allowed to make multiple queries by providing any of the 4 inputs (a,b). It can be assumed that the random choice is kept constant for all the inputs.

It may be easily observed that $y_{left} = y_{right}$ for all the 4 values of (a,b) which implies that the output y_{left} or y_{right} does not reveal which output is chosen by the random toss. For all the input values of (a,b) the output is 4.

Now consider that one of the hardwares is subjected to a permanent stress, which creates a fault in either the registers $R1$ or $R2$. Hence, either $R1 = r \neq 6$ or $R2 = r \neq 2$. If the fault occurs in $R1$, $y'_{left} = ra$, while $y_{right} = 2b$. Else if the fault occurs in $R2$, $y_{left} = 6a$, while $y'_{right} = rb$. WLOG. assume that the fault is in the first device.

Now the attacker provides two inputs: $(2,2)$ and $(6,6)$ to the hardware devices. The attacker observes both of the outputs. If both the outputs are the same then the attacker concludes that the right output is chosen, while if they are different the left output is chosen with probability 1.

Thus this simple example shows that a fault can leak information, which seemed to be perfectly hidden in the original design. Thus apart from the malfunction of hardware or software designs, algorithms which hide information (like ciphers) should be analyzed wrt. faults. Next, we consider a more non-trivial example of fault-based analysis of the popular RSA cryptosystem.

7.5.1 Fault Analysis of the RSA Cipher

The first fault-based attack was mounted on the well-known public key cryptosystem *RSA*. We know that *RSA* works by considering two keys: a *public key* is known to every one, while a *private key* is *secret*. Encryption of a message is performed using the public key, but decryption requires the knowledge of the private key. All the operations are done mod n, where n is the product of two large distinct prime number p and q. The values of p and q are, however, private and hence not disclosed to all. The encryption key, which is public is a value b, where $1 \leq b \leq \phi(n)$ where $\phi(n)$ is the Euler-Totient function. The decryption key is a private value a, which is selected such that $ab \equiv 1 \, mod \, \phi(n)$. The owner of the private key (p, q, a) publishes the value (b, n), which is the public key.

The encryptor chooses a message x, where $x \in Z_n$. It may be mentioned that $Z_n = \{0, 1, \ldots, n-1\}$. The encryption process is computing the cipher as $y \equiv x^b \, mod \, n$ using the public key b. Since the decryptor knows the value of a, which is the private key, he computes the value of x from y by computing $y^a \equiv (x^b)^a \, mod \, n \equiv x \, mod \, n$. The security of *RSA* is based on the assumption that decryption can be performed only by the knowledge of the private key b. However, to obtain the private information from the public value a requires one to compute the modular inverse of a modulo $\phi(n)$. It is believed that to obtain $\phi(n)$ from n requires the knowledge of the prime factors of n, namely p and q. The security of RSA is thus based on the hardness assumption of factorization of large n.

However, we explain that under situation of faulty computations the value of the secret exponent a can be retrieved by efficient algorithms. In the attack it is assumed that the attacker is in possession of certain number of plaintext and ciphertext pairs. The attacker has the ability to flip one bit of the value a during computation. Say, the i-th bit a_i of a is flipped and modified to $\hat{a}_i$, where $0 \leq i \leq |a|$ and $|a|$ is the bit-length of a. The attacker has access to both fault-free X and faulty plaintexts $\hat{X}$. Therefore, he can compute, $\frac{X}{\hat{X}} = \frac{Y^{\hat{a}}}{Y^a} = \frac{Y^{2^i \hat{a}_i}}{Y^{2^i a_i}} \, mod \, n$. If the ratio is equal to Y^{2^i}, the attacker can be sured that $a_i = 0$. On the other hand if the ratio is $\frac{1}{Y^{2^i}}$, the attacker ascertains that $a_i = 1$. The same technique is repeated for all the values of i, thus a can be retrieved. The attack is also applicable when the fault is induced in Y. It is also possible in cases when the fault flips two or more bits. The details are left to the reader as an exercise.

These attacks show that fault analysis can be a powerful tool for attacking ciphers. Significant research has been performed in the field of fault based cryptanalysis of various ciphers of different types. From the seminal paper of [50] fault attacks have been improved with the ideas of differential analysis to attack block ciphers, like Data Encryption Standard (DES). However, after the acceptance of the 128-bit version of the *Rijndael* block cipher, designed by Vincent Rijmen and Joan Daemen, as the Advanced Encryption Standard (AES) in 2001, the main focus of fault attacks have been AES. We discuss in details some of the state-of-the-art fault analysis methods in Chapter 8.

In the next section, we present an overview on cache-based attacks.

7.6 Cache Attacks

Cache memory attacks are a potent class of side-channel attacks that utilize information leaking from cipher implementations to gain knowledge of the secret key. The information leakage is due to the fact that a cache miss takes considerably more time compared to a cache hit. This difference is manifested through covert channels such as execution time, power consumption, and electro-magnetic radiation.

Depending on the side channel used, cache attacks are categorized into three: trace, access, and timing.

1. **Trace-driven attacks:** In these attacks, the adversary such as in [10, 46, 121, 127, 317, 428] monitors power consumption traces or electro-magnetic radiation to determine if a memory access resulted in a cache hit or miss. These attacks are most applicable on small embedded devices where such side-channels can be easily monitored.

2. **Access-driven attacks:** Examples of these attacks, as in [142, 272, 281, 298, 384]) require the use of a spy process running in the same host as the cryptographic algorithm in order to retrieve memory access patterns made by the cipher. These attacks require a multi-user environment and are a threat to the security of cloud computing [327].

3. **Time-driven attacks:** These attacks, on the other hand, use variations in the encryption time to determine the secret key [44, 58, 318, 312, 384, 386, 387, 388]. They can be applied to a wide range of platforms ranging from small micro-controllers to large server blades. Just as in access attacks, timing attacks are also applicable in virtualized environments as was demonstrated in [406]. Further, timing measurements do not need close proximity to the device. This can result in remote attacks [15, 66, 101]. However, it is considerably more difficult to mount a timing attack compared to trace and access attacks. Unlike these attacks, timing attacks rely on statistical analysis and require significantly more side-channel measurements to distinguish between a cache hit and a miss. The number of measurements depend not only on the system parameters but also on the implementation of the cipher and its algorithm.

In the book, we stress on cache-timing attacks, being one of the most practical forms of cache attacks. In the following section, we provide an overview of the working principle of cache timing attacks, while in Chapter 9 we present an actual attack on a standard block cipher.

7.6.1 Working Principle of Cache-Timing Attacks

Since the initial works of Hu [154], John Kelsey et al. [186], and Dan Page [288], several cache attacks have been introduced on various block ciphers like MISTY1 [387], DES [386], 3-DES [386], AES (like [216, 44, 281, 428]), CLEFIA [317, 318, 319, 428], and CAMELLIA [301]. All these attacks target implementations of block ciphers that use look-up tables to store the non-linear components of the cipher. An obvious method to prevent cache-attacks is to therefore eliminate the use of such look-up tables. The methods available to achieve this are by dedicated instructions for encryption or by replacing the tables with logical equations. However, dedicated instructions, such as Intel's AES-NI [360], cannot be used to implement ciphers other than AES. On the other hand, implementations that use logical equations (with the exception of bitsliced implementations [48]) have a huge overhead on the performance. Bit-sliced implementations are fast but are restricted to non-feedback operating modes. Thus look-up tables are essential for implementations where dedicated instructions are unavailable and high-speed of operations are needed in operating modes requiring feedback.

As an example, consider AES-128 [117] which is a 10-round cipher and takes as input a 16 byte plaintext $P = (p_0, p_1, \cdots, p_{15})$ and a 16 byte secret key $K = (k_0, k_1, \cdots, k_{15})$.

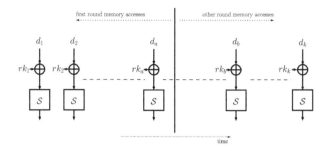

FIGURE 7.12: Memory Accesses in a Block Cipher Implementation

The most widely used software implementation of AES is based on Barreto's code [296]. This performance optimized implementation uses four $1KB$ lookup tables T_0, T_1, T_2, and T_3 for the first 9 rounds of the algorithm, and an additional $1KB$ lookup table T_4 for the final round. The structure of each round is shown in Equation 7.2 and encapsulates the four basic AES operations of *SubByte*, *ShiftRow*, *MixColumn*, and *AddRoundKey*. The input to round i ($1 \leq i \leq 9$) is the state S^i comprising of 16 bytes ($s_0^i, s_1^i, \cdots, s_{15}^i$) and round key K^i split into 16 bytes ($k_0^i, k_1^i, \cdots, k_{15}^i$). The output of the round is the next state S^{i+1}. The first round S^1 comprises of inputs ($P \oplus K$) and round key K^1.

$$
\begin{aligned}
S^{i+1} = \{ &T_0[s_0^i] \oplus T_1[s_5^i] \oplus T_2[s_{10}^i] \oplus T_3[s_{15}^i] \oplus \{k_0^i, k_1^i, k_2^i, k_3^i\}, \\
&T_0[s_4^i] \oplus T_1[s_9^i] \oplus T_2[s_{14}^i] \oplus T_3[s_3^i] \oplus \{k_4^i, k_5^i, k_6^i, k_7^i\}, \\
&T_0[s_8^i] \oplus T_1[s_{13}^i] \oplus T_2[s_2^i] \oplus T_3[s_7^i] \oplus \{k_8^i, k_9^i, k_{10}^i, k_{11}^i\}, \\
&T_0[s_{12}^i] \oplus T_1[s_1^i] \oplus T_2[s_6^i] \oplus T_3[s_{11}^i] \oplus \{k_{12}^i, k_{13}^i, k_{14}^i, k_{15}^i\}\}
\end{aligned}
\tag{7.2}
$$

Consider a 2^n element lookup table used in a block cipher implementation. When stored in the main memory of a processor these 2^n elements are grouped into blocks, which is termed as *memory blocks*. Let 2^v elements of the table map to the same block. When any element in a block gets accessed, the entire block gets loaded into the cache memory and thereafter resides in a cache line unless evicted. Thus, the table can occupy at most 2^{n-v} lines in the cache. These lines require $l = n - v$ bits to be addressed.

From the cache attack perspective, block ciphers can be viewed as k memory accesses made to one or more lookup tables. The index of each access has the form ($d_i \oplus rk_i$), where d_i is the data and rk_i the key material. The block cipher memory accesses can be represented by a sequence as shown in Figure 7.12.

Consider a pair a, b ($1 \leq a \leq b < k$) in the figure, if the access $d_b \oplus rk_b$ collides with $d_a \oplus rk_a$, a cache hit occurs and the equality $\langle d_a \oplus rk_a \rangle = \langle d_b \oplus rk_b \rangle$ can be inferred, where $\langle \cdot \rangle$ is the most significant l bits of the table index. If d_a and d_b can be controlled by the adversary, the XOR of the keys rk_a and rk_b is revealed.

$$
\langle rk_a \oplus rk_b \rangle = \langle d_a \oplus d_b \rangle \ . \tag{7.3}
$$

Depending on controllability of the memory accesses in Figure 7.12, two categories can be defined: the first round memory accesses (these directly depend on the plaintext), and inner round memory accesses (these depend on the plaintext as well as the cipher algorithm). The attacker can easily control all the d_i in the first round. However it becomes increasingly difficult to control d_i as the rounds increase. For example, by manipulating the plaintext inputs and with some amount of additional information, the second round d_i can be controlled. More information is required to control the d_i of the third round and so on. The later rounds of the cipher are several times more difficult to control. The controllability of d_i depends on the cipher structure. For example, CLEFIA has a type-2 generalized Feistel structure, and the inputs are more easily controllable compared to CAMELLIA, which has a classical Feistel structure. More details about the structure can be found in [317] and [301], respectively.

Generally rk_a and rk_b have entropies of n bits each. If the adversary can identify a collision such as in Equation 7.3, then the entropy of the pair of keys reduces from $2n$ to $n + v$. Identifying a collision in the memory access of the cipher can be done by monitoring side-channels such as power consumption, electro-magnetic radiations, or timing of the encryption.

Details of the attacks are presented in a subsequent chapter. In the next section, we provide an overview on an yet another source of leakage in hardware designs: namely the design-for-testability techniques. Scan chains are a very common technique for testing hardware devices. However, attackers have used these techniques originally for testability to control and observe internal states of the cipher, which leads to fairly straightforward attacks against ciphers. In the next section, we present the idea behind the attacks.

7.7   Scan Chain Based Attacks

Cryptographic algorithms are routinely used to perform computationally intense operations over increasingly larger volumes of data, and in order to meet the high throughput requirements of the applications, are often implemented by VLSI designs. The high complexity of such implementations raises concern about their reliability. In order to improve upon the testability of sequential circuits, both at fabrication time and also in the field, Design For Testability (DFT) techniques are provided. However, conventional DFT methodologies for digital circuits have been found to compromise the security of the cryptographic hardware.

Reliability of devices has become a serious concern, with the increase of complexity of ICs and the advent of deep sub-micron process technology. The growth of applications of cryptographic algorithms and their requirement for real time-processing has necessitated the design of crypto-hardware. But along with the design of such devices, testability is a key issue. What makes testability of these circuits more challenging compared to other digital designs, is the fact that popular design for testability (DFT) methodologies, such as scan chain insertion, can be used as a double-edged sword. Scan chain insertion, which is a desirable test technique owing to its high fault coverage and small hardware overhead, open "side channels" for cryptanalysis [422, 174]. Scan chains are used to access intermediate values stored in the flip-flops, thereby ascertaining the secret information, often the key. Conventional scan chains fail to solve the conflicting requirements of effective testing and security [174]. So, one of the solutions that have been suggested is to blow off the scan chains from the crypto ICs, before they are released into the market. But such an approach is unsatisfactory and directly conflicts the paradigm of DFT. In order to solve this problem of efficiently testing cryptographic ICs several research works have been proposed.

7.7.1   Working Principle of Scan-Chain-Attacks on Block Ciphers

In this section, we outline the working principle of scan chain-based-attacks on block ciphers. Similar attacks can be performed on other category of ciphers as well.

Block ciphers, have an iterated structure comprising of rounds (**Fig 7.13**). The rounds are in turn made of substitution and permutation blocks. The substitution layers are complex Boolean mappings, and are realized by an array of smaller mappings, called as S-boxes. The output of the S-boxes are diffused through the permutation layers, to give the output of one round. The plaintext is XORed with the input key, while the output of a round is XORed with a round key before being fed as an input to the next round. The round keys are generated through a key-scheduling algorithm one after the other, starting from the input key. The ciphertext is the output of certain number of rounds, estimated based on classical cryptanalysis to provide sufficient security margin against an adversary. To put some numbers, the DES has a 16 rounds, while the AES has 10, 12, and 14 rounds, depending on whether the key-sizes are 128, 192, and 256 bits.

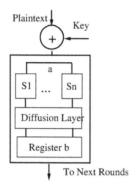

FIGURE 7.13: Generic Structure of a Block Cipher

Side Channel Attacks using Scan Chains: The security of the block cipher is obtained due to the properties of the round function, and the number of rounds in the cipher. However, when the design is prototyped on a hardware platform, and a scan chain is provided to test the design, the attacker uses the scan chain to control the input patterns, and observe the intermediate values in the output patterns. The security of the block cipher is thus threatened, as the output after few rounds is revealed to the adversary. The attacker then analyzes the data and applies conventional cryptanalytic methods on a much lessened cipher.

We next summarize the scan based attack, wrt. **Fig 7.13**. Without loss of generality, let us assume that the S-boxes are bytewise mappings, though the discussion can be easily adapted for other dimensions. The attack observes the propagation of a disturbance in a byte through a round of the cipher. If one byte of the plaintext is affected, say p_0, then one byte of a, a_0 gets changed (see figure). The byte passes through an S-box and produces an output, which is diffused in the output register, b_0.

The diffusion layer of AES-like ciphers are characterized by a property called as, *branch number*, which is the minimum total number of disturbed bytes at the input and output of the layer. For example, the MixColumns step of AES has a branch number of 5, indicating that if b_1 input bytes are disturbed at the input of MixColumns, resulting in b_2 bytes at the output which get affected, then $b_1 + b_2 \geq 5$.

Depending upon the branch number of the diffusion layer, the input disturbance spreads to say t-number of output bits in the register b. The attacker tries to exploit this property to first ascertain the correspondence of the flip-flops of register b, with the output bits in the scan-out pattern. Next the attacker applies a one-round differential attack to determine the secret key.

1. The attacker first resets the chip and loads the plaintext p and the key k, and applies one normal clock cycle. The XOR of p and k is thus transformed by the S-boxes and the diffusion layers, and is loaded into the register b.

2. The chip is now switched to the test mode and the contents of the flip-flops are scanned out. The scanned out pattern is denoted by TP_1.

3. Next, the attacker disturbs one byte of the input pattern and repeats the above two steps. In this case, the output pattern is TP_2.

It may be observed that if the attacker observes the difference between TP_1 and TP_2, the attacker can observe the positions of the contents of the register b. The ones in the difference are all because of the contents of register b. In order to better observe all the bit positions of register b, the attacker repeats the process with further differential pairs. There can be a maximum 256 possible differences in the plaintext byte being changed. However, the ciphers satisfy avalanche criteria, which states that if one input bit is changed, on an average at least half of the output bits get modified. Thus in most cases because of this avalanche criteria of the round, much fewer plaintexts are necessary to obtain the locations of all the registers b.

However, the attacker has only ascertained the location of the values of the register b in the scanned-out patterns. However, it is surely an unintended leakage of information. For example, the difference of the scanned out patterns giving away the Hamming distance after one round of the cipher.

The attacker now studies the properties of the round structures. The S-box is a non-linear layer, with the property that all possible input and output pairs are not possible. As an example, for the present day standard cipher, the Advanced Encryption Standard (AES), given a possible input and output pair, on an average one value of the input to the S-box is possible. That is, if the input to the S-box, denoted by S is x, and the input and output differentials are α, β, then there is one solution on an average to the equation:

$$\beta = S(x) \oplus S(x \oplus \alpha)$$

The adversary can introduce a differential α through the plaintext. However, he uses the scanned out data to infer the value of β. In order to do so, he observes the diffusion of the unknown β through the diffusion layer. In most of the ciphers, like the AES, the diffusion layers are realized through linear matrices.

To be specific in case of AES, a differential $0 < \alpha \leq 255$ in one of the input bytes, is transformed by the S-box to β and then passes to the output after being transformed by the diffusion layer as follows:

$$\begin{pmatrix} \alpha & 0 & 0 & 0 \\ 0 & 0 & 0 & 0 \\ 0 & 0 & 0 & 0 \\ 0 & 0 & 0 & 0 \end{pmatrix} \Rightarrow \begin{pmatrix} \beta & 0 & 0 & 0 \\ 0 & 0 & 0 & 0 \\ 0 & 0 & 0 & 0 \\ 0 & 0 & 0 & 0 \end{pmatrix} \Rightarrow \begin{pmatrix} 2\beta & 0 & 0 & 0 \\ 3\beta & 0 & 0 & 0 \\ \beta & 0 & 0 & 0 \\ \beta & 0 & 0 & 0 \end{pmatrix}$$

Thus the attacker knows that the differential in the scanned-out patterns, TP_1 and TP_2, has the above property. That is there are 4 bytes in the register b, denoted by d_0, d_1, d_2, d_3, such that:

$$d_0 = 2d_2; d_1 = 3d_2; d_2 = d_3 \qquad (7.4)$$

The attacker in the previous attack has ascertained the positions of the 32 bits of the register b in the scanned out pattern. But he does not know the correct pattern. The above property says that the correct pattern will satisfy the above property. If w is the number of ones in the XOR of TP_1 and TP_2, then there are 32_{C_w} possible patterns. Out of that, the correct one will satisfy the above property. The probability of a random string satisfying the above property is 2^{-24}. Thus, if $w = 24$ as an example, then the number of satisfying permutations is $32_{C_4} \times 2^{-24} \approx 1$. Thus, there is a single value which satisfies the above equations. This helps the attacker to get the value of β. The attacker already knows the value of α from the plaintext differential. Thus, the property of the S-box ensures that there is on an average one single value of the input byte of the S-box. Thus, the attacker gets the corresponding byte for a (see figure). The attacker then computes one byte of the key by XORing the plaintext, p_0 with the value of the byte a_0, that is, $k_0 = p_0 \oplus a_0$.

The remaining key bytes may be similarly obtained. In the literature, there are several reported attacks on the standard block ciphers, namely DES and AES [368], but all them follows the above general ideas of attacking through controllability and observability through scan chains.

7.8 Conclusions

In this chapter, we have provided a summary of side channel analysis of implementation of cryptographic algorithms. We have highlighted the differences of such attack methods from conventional cryptanalysis. The attack methodologies have also been explained with focus on timing, power, fault, cache, and scan-based attacks. All these attacks emphasize that one needs closer look at these and their attack techniques to be capable of developing a suitable counter-measures.

Chapter 8

Differential Fault Analysis of Ciphers

"When a secret is revealed, it is the fault of the man who confided it."

(Jean de La Bruyère, Les Caractères, V.)

The growing complexity of the cryptographic algorithms and the increasing applications of ciphers in real-time applications has lead to research in the development of high speed hardware designs or optimized cryptographic libraries for these algorithms. The complex operations performed in these designs and the large state space involved indicates that a complete verification is ruled out. Hence these designs have a chance of being fault prone. Apart from these unintentional faults, faults can also be injected intentionally. Literature shows several ways of fault injection: accidental variation in operating conditions, like voltage, clock frequency, or focussed laser beams in hardware. Software programs can also be subjected to situations, like missing of certain instructions to inflict faults. Apart from the general issue of fault tolerance in any large design, faults bring a complete new aspect when dealing with cryptographic algorithms: *security*.

8.1   Introduction to Differential Fault Analysis

The first fault attack was applied to the *RSA* cryptosytem. Biham and Shamir proposed a new fault based attacking technique which is wildly known as Differential Fault Analysis (DFA)[50]. DFA attack is a very powerful attack model which can threaten a large class of ciphers. However, the actual attack procedure may vary from cipher to cipher, and one has to exploit the fault propagations suitable to extract the key of a given cipher. The foremost DFA proposed was on the DES cipher, which is essentially a Feistel cipher. Later, DFA has been extensively applied on other ciphers, with greater focus on the AES algorithm. Before discussing a fault-based analysis of the AES cipher, we will discuss a general idea on DFA of block ciphers. We will restrict ourselves to the Substitution Permutation Network

(SPN), as AES belongs to this family. However, similar observations and results can be obtained for Feistel structures. Thus fault attacks pose a very powerful threat to hardware implementations of all block ciphers of the modern day.

8.1.1 General Principle of DFA of Block Ciphers

In this section, we study the basic principle of DFA, which shall be subsequently applied for the AES algorithm. As apparent from the name, DFA combines the concepts of differential cryptanalysis with that of fault attacks. DFA is applicable to almost any secret key cryptosystem proposed so far in the open literature. DFA has been used to attack many secret key cryptosystems, including DES, IDEA, and RC5 [50].

There has been considerable body of work about DFA of AES. Some of the DFA proposals are based on theoretical model [54, 300, 132, 285, 256, 264, 390, 341], while others launched successful attacks on ASIC and FPGA devices using previously proposed theoretical models [356, 192, 41, 22, 341]. The key idea of DFA is composed of three steps as

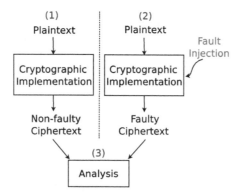

FIGURE 8.1: Three steps of DFA.

shown in **Fig. 8.1**. (1) Run the cryptographic algorithm and obtain non-faulty ciphertexts. (2) Inject faults, i.e., unexpected environmental conditions into cryptographic implementations, rerun the algorithm with the same input, and obtain faulty ciphertexts (3) Analyze relationship between the non-faulty and faulty ciphertexts to significantly reduce the key space.

Practicality of DFA depends on the underlying fault model and the number of faulty ciphertext pairs needed. In the following section we will analyze all the fault models DFA of AES uses and point out their relationships. In this section, we continue the discussion on the working principle of DFA wrt. a generalized block cipher model.

DFA works under the assumption of underlying faults. These faults are often caused by various mechanisms, like: fluctuation of operating voltage, varying the clock frequency, changing the temperature of a device and with the most accurate injection of laser beams. However, in all of the above techniques the faults are created by sudden variation of the operating conditions. It may be noted that apart from the mentioned means of malicious or intentional fault injections, faults can be also unintentional. With the growing complexity of crypto devices, chances of mistakes in the design also increase.

Faults can be categorized depending on whether they are permanent or transient. From the point of view of cryptography, we would like to point out that transient faults are of high concern as they are hard to detect. These faults can be of such a short duration that most simulation based techniques of fault detection may be unable to detect the advent of the faults. However, as we shall soon observe that few faults are enough to leak the entire key of a standard cipher, like AES.

8.1.1.1 Fault Models

The faults can be of varying nature but can be categorized as follows:

1. **Bit model**: This fault model assumes that the fault is localized to 1 bit. The fault control is crucial here, as there is a high probability that a random fluctuation of the operating conditions can lead to more than one bit getting affected. Hence attacks based on such models are often unrealistic and may not be practically viable.

2. **Single byte**: A more practical and most common fault model is the single byte model. This fault model assumes that the faults are spread to bytes and the fault model can be any *random* non-zero value. This non-specificity of the fault value makes these types of DFAs very powerful and practical techniques.

3. **Multiple byte**: In this fault model, it is assumed that the faults propagate to more than 1 byte. More often, these models are more practical, in the sense that the DFAs based on them work even with lesser fault control. In context to DFA of AES, we shall observe a special multiple byte fault model, namely the *Diagonal fault model* which helps to generalize the DFA of AES. The fault values are again arbitrary, and hence makes these attacks very powerful, as they even work when control on the fault induction is less.

8.1.1.2 The Effect of Faults on a Block Cipher

It is expected that the induced fault changes certain bits or bytes during a particular round of the encryption and generates certain differences. Most often the DFAs target the non-linear transformations, namely S-boxes of the block ciphers. As the faults are induced during the encryption process, the fault propagation patterns give some *relations* between the input and output difference of certain S-boxes. In most of the ciphers like AES, the S-boxes are known and therefore, one can easily deduce the *difference distribution table* of the S-box being used. Generally, the S-boxes have inputs which are combined with part of the keys through some mixing operation. Using the difference distribution table and the relations between the input and output difference one reduces the search space of a part of the key. This divide and conquer mechanism helps to recover the entire key quite efficiently for most ciphers. We explain the working in more details for the generalized SPN cipher, as modeled in **Fig. 8.2**.

Fig. 8.2 shows the basic structure of r-round Substitution Permutation Network (SPN) cipher with block-length n-bytes. Each round consists of confusion layer S which is realized by non-linear S-box operation, and a linear transformation called diffusion layer D, followed by an addition with the round key. There is an addition with the whitening key WK at the beginning of the encryption called key-whitening phase. The diffusion layer is generally provided by multiplication with MDS matrix followed by some rotation operations. The diffusion operation plays a major role in DFA. If a byte is modified at the input of the diffusion operation, the induced difference spreads to multiple bytes at the output depending on the *branch number* of the diffusion layer. The disturbed bytes are often referred to as the active bytes in the literature of differential cryptanalysis. Branch number for a diffusion matrix on bytes is used to observe how a non-zero input differential spreads in a cipher through the diffusion layer. Branch number is defined as the sum of the minimum number of active bytes at the input and output of the diffusion layer.

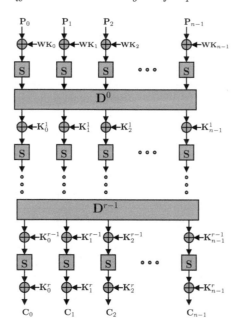

FIGURE 8.2: Basic structure of SPN ciphers

As the diffusion layer is a linear operation wrt. the key mixing operation namely xor, the output difference can be expressed as a linear relation of the input differences. The attacker exploits these properties in the following fashion to obtain the key. Say a single byte fault is induced at the input of $(r-1)^{th}$ (penultimate) round and the corresponding difference at the input of D^{r-1} is $\alpha \neq 0$. If the branch number of the diffusion layer is b, the input byte fault will spread to $b-1$ bytes $(\alpha_{\pi_0}, \ldots, \alpha_{\pi_{b-2}})$ at the output of D_{r-1}, where π denotes the transformation of the diffusion layer. Each of these active bytes then pass through the S-boxes, which non-linearly transform them. The attacker then represents these output bytes in terms of a pair of fault-free and faulty ciphertexts (C, C^*) as follows:

$$\alpha_{\pi_j} = S^{-1}(C_{\pi_j} \oplus K^r_{\pi_j}) \oplus S^{-1}(C^*_{\pi_j} \oplus K^r_{\pi_j}) \tag{8.1}$$

where $j \in \{0, \ldots, b-2\}$ and S^{-1} represent the inverse of the S-box operation. Now the attacker knows the S-box input difference, $C_{\pi_j} \oplus C^*_{\pi_j}$. From the difference distribution table the attacker knows on an average *few* values which satisfy a chosen $(\alpha_{\pi_j}, C_{\pi_j} \oplus C^*_{\pi_j})$ pair.

Further, because of the linear mapping in D^{r-1}, α_{π_j} depends linearly on α. Therefore, the attacker guesses the value of α and gets the values of α_{π_j} i.e., the output differences. Using the input-output difference the attacker retrieves the value $C_{\pi_j} \oplus K_{\pi_j}$ from the difference distribution table of the S-box. As C_{π_j} and $C^*_{\pi_j}$ are known to the attacker, -he can retrieve the value of K_{π_j}. The attacker may need to induce faults multiple times in order to get all the bytes of the round key.

In the next section, we present the fault models used for DFA of AES in the literature and a summary of all the attacks performed [415]. Subsequently, we present the fault attacks on AES.

TABLE 8.1: A Summary of DFA of AES.

Fault Model (A)			No. of Faulty CTs*(B)	Key Space (C)	Experiment (D)
(I) Faults are injected in any location and any round (Section 8.2.1.1)					
Random			2^{128}	2^{128}	N/A
(II) Faults are injected in AddRoundKey in round 0 (Section 8.2.1.2)					
Single bit		[54]	128	1	No
(III)Faults are injected between the output of 7th and the input of 8th round MixColumns (Section 8.2.1.3)					
Single byte		[300]	2	2^{40}	underpowering [356, 192]
Single byte		[264]	2	2^{32}	No
Single byte		[390]	1	2^{8}	No
Multiple byte	DM0	[341]	1	2^{32}	overclocking [341]
Multiple byte	DM1	[341]	1	2^{64}	
Multiple byte	DM2	[341]	1	2^{96}	
Multiple byte	DM3	[341]	2^{128}	2^{128}	
(IV)Faults are injected between the output of 8th and the input of 9th round MixColumns (Section 8.2.1.4)					
Single bit		[132]	≈ 50	1	overclocking [22]
Single byte		[285]	≈ 40	1	underpowering [41]
Single byte		[256]†	6	1	No
Multiple byte	DM0	[256]‡	6	1	No
Multiple byte	DM0	[256]◊	1500	1	No

⋆ CT = ciphertext. † Only 1 byte in a word is faulty. ‡ 2 or 3 bytes in a word are faulty. ◊ All 4 bytes in a word are faulty.

8.2 DFA and Associated Fault Models

DFA exploits a small subspace of all possible faults. The practicality of a fault attack largely relies on the underlying fault model: the nature of the faults and the ability to actually obtain such faults in practice. In the following section, we classify the DFA fault models in four scenarios by the location and round in which faults are injected.

8.2.1 Fault Models for DFA of AES

Table 8.1 is a summary of the published DFA of AES. Faults can be injected either (I) in any location and any round, (II) in AddRoundKey in round 0, (III) between the output of 7th and the input of 8th round MixColumns, or (IV) between the output of 8th and the input of 9th round MixColumns. In each scenario, we analyze the (A) fault models, (B) number of faulty ciphertexts needed, (C) the key space for brute force after obtaining the faulty outputs to recover the secret, and (D) the experimental validation of the attack. The considered transient faults are categorized into single-bit, single-byte, and multiple-byte transient faults. It may be noted that we have purposefully omitted faults of permanent nature: namely stuck-at-1 or stuck-at-0 as they are not relevant from the DFA perspective. Rather, transient faults are more relevant because of their stealthy nature and ability to defeat counter-measures for classical fault tolerance. For detailed discussion in this direction, we would redirect the author to [416].

In the following discussions in this section we elaborate the fault models present in Table 8.1.

8.2.1.1 Faults Are Injected in Any Location and Any Round

In the first fault model in Table 8.1, the attacker injects faults in any random location and any random round. These faults are equivalent to naturally occurring faults. In this case, the attacker will not gain any useful information. Even if he gets all possible 2^{128} faulty ciphertexts, he cannot reduce the key space. Because the key space is 2^{128}, this fault model is impractical for the attacker.

8.2.1.2 Faults Are Injected in AddRoundKey in Round 0

The only fault model an attacker uses in this scenario is single-bit transient fault.

Single-bit transient fault: In [54], the attacker is able to set or reset every bit of the first-round key 1 bit at a time. This attack recovers the entire key using 128 faulty ciphertexts with each faulty ciphertext uniquely revealing 1 key bit. Hence, the key space required to reveal the key is 1. However, as transistor size scales, this attack becomes impractical even with expensive equipments such as lasers to inject the faults, because it requires precise control of the fault location [21].

8.2.1.3 Faults Are Injected between the Output of 7th and the Input of 8th MixColumns

The attacker uses various fault models and analysis in this scenario including single-byte and multiple-byte faults.

Single-byte transient fault: The three different attacks using this fault model are shown in Table 8.1. In the first DFA [300], 2 faulty ciphertexts are needed to obtain the key. This fault model is experimentally verified in [356, 192]. In [356], underpowering is used to inject faults into a smart card with AES ASIC implementation. Although no more than 16% of the injected faults fall into the single byte fault category, only 13 faulty ciphertexts are needed to obtain the key. In [192], the authors underpower an AES FPGA implementation to inject faults with a probability of 40% for single-byte fault injection.

In the second DFA [264], 2 faulty ciphertexts are also needed to reveal the key. Because this attack exploits the faults in a different way, the key space is 2^{32}.

The attack in [390] is similar to [264] but further improved. For the same fault model, the key space is reduced to only 2^8 with a single faulty ciphertext.

Multiple-byte transient fault: [341] proposes a general byte fault model called *diagonal fault model*. The authors divide the AES state matrix into 4 different diagonals and each diagonal has 4 bytes. **A diagonal** is a set of 4 bytes of the AES state matrix, where the ith diagonal is defined as follows:

$$D_i = \{s_{j,(j+i)mod4} \; ; \; 0 \leq j < 4\} \tag{8.2}$$

We obtain the following 4 diagonals.

$$D_0 = (s_{0,0}, s_{1,1}, s_{2,2}, s_{3,3}), \; D_1 = (s_{0,1}, s_{1,2}, s_{2,3}, s_{3,0}),$$

$$D_2 = (s_{0,2}, s_{1,3}, s_{2,0}, s_{3,1}), \; D_3 = (s_{0,3}, s_{1,0}, s_{2,1}, s_{3,2})$$

The diagonal fault model is classified into 4 different cases, diagonal fault models 0, 1, 2, and 3, denoted as DM0, DM1, DM2, and DM3. As shown in **Fig. 8.3**, for DM0, faults can be injected in one of the diagonals; D_0, D_1, D_2, or D_3. For DM1, faults can be injected in at most 2 diagonals. For DM2, faults can be injected in at most 3 diagonals. Finally, for DM3, faults can be injected in at most 4 diagonals. For each of the 4 different diagonals affected, faults propagate to different columns as shown in **Fig. 8.4**. Therefore, if faults are injected into 1, 2, or 3 diagonals, the key space is reduced to 2^{32}, 2^{64}, or 2^{96}, respectively.

The authors also validate the diagonal fault model with a practical fault attack on AES FPGA implementation using overclocking.

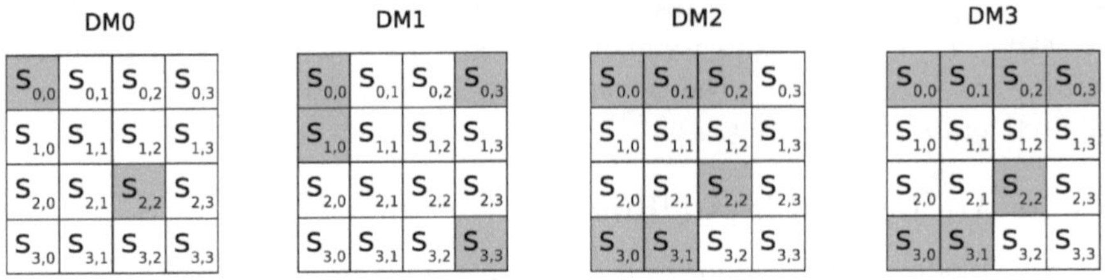

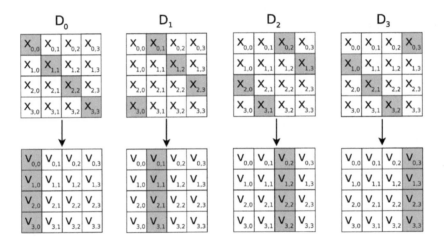

FIGURE 8.3: DFA and diagonal fault models. The first state matrix is an example of DM0. Only diagonal D_0 is affected by a fault. The second state matrix is an example of DM1. Both D_0 and D_3 are corrupted by a fault. The third state matrix is an example of DM2. Three diagonals D_0, D_1, and D_2 are corrupted by a fault. The last state matrix is an example of DM3, all 4 diagonals are corrupted in the fourth state matrix.

FIGURE 8.4: Fault propagation of diagonal faults. The upper row shows the diagonals that faults are injected in. The lower row shows the corresponding columns being affected.

8.2.1.4   Faults Are Injected between the Output of 8th and the Input of 9th MixColumns

Single-bit transient fault: In [132], the attacker needs only 3 faulty ciphertexts to succeed with a probability of 97%. The key space is trivial. [22] validates this single bit attack on a Xilinx 3AN FPGA using overclocking. It is reported that the success rate of injecting this kind of fault is 90%.

Single-byte transient fault: In [285], the authors use a byte level fault model. They are able to obtain the key with 40 faulty ciphertexts, and the key is uniquely revealed. This model is used in a successful attack by underpowering a 65nm ASIC chip [41]. In this attack, 39,881 faulty ciphertexts are collected during the 10 experiments; 30,386 of them were actually the outcome of a single-byte fault. Thus, it has a successful injection rate of 76%.

Multiple-byte transient fault: [256] presents a DFA of AES when the faults are injected in a 32-bit word. The authors propose 2 fault models. In the first model, they assume that at least one of the bytes among the 4 targeted bytes is non-faulty. This means the number of faulty bytes can be 1, 2, or 3 bytes. So this fault model includes the single byte fault model. If only one single byte fault is injected, 6 faulty ciphertexts are required to reveal the secret key. Whereas the second fault model requires around 1500 faulty ciphertexts. These faulty ciphertexts derive the entire key at constant time. Though the second fault model is much more general, the amount of faulty ciphertexts it requires is very large, it is difficult for the attacker to get all the ciphertexts without triggering the CED alarm.

In summary, the attacker can obtain the secret key with 1 or 2 faulty ciphertexts when single or multiple byte transient faults are injected. In the following subsection, we present a detailed analysis on the inter-relationships of the fault models discussed so far.

8.2.2 Relationships between the Discussed Fault Models

As previously mentioned, DFA of AES does not exploit all possible faults. Rather, it exploits a subset of faults, namely single bit, single byte, and multiple byte transient faults injected in selected locations and rounds. Therefore, understanding the relationships among various fault models is the basis for understanding and comparing the various fault attacks on AES. Further the inter-relationships developed also help in analyzing the security of the counter-measured: both conventional as well as for designing new DFA-specific CED. Because DFA of AES targets the last few rounds[1], we synthesize the relationships between different fault models based on the locations and rounds they are injected in.

8.2.2.1 Faults Are Injected in Any Location and Any Round

In this fault model, the attacker cannot derive any useful information from the faults.

8.2.2.2 Faults Are Injected in AddRoundKey in Round 0

As we mentioned previously, this attack uses a very restricted fault model, and it is not practical. Thus, this fault model is also not useful for the attacker.

8.2.2.3 Faults Are Injected between the Output of 7th and the Input of 8th MixColumns

Fig. 8.5(a) summarizes the relationships between the DFA-exploitable fault models by injecting faults in the output of 7th round MixColumns and the input of 8th round MixColumns.

Single-byte faults are, in turn, a subset of the DM0 faults which, in turn, are a subset of the DM1 faults, and so on. The relationship is summarized in (8.3).

$$\text{Single Byte} \subset DM0 \subset DM1 \subset DM2 \subset DM3 \qquad (8.3)$$

A more careful look reveals that 2 byte faults can be either DM0 or DM1 but not DM0. Moreover, 3 byte faults can be either DM0, DM1, or DM2. Four byte faults can be either DM0, DM1, DM2, or DM3. Similarly, the relationship between faulty bytes from 5 to 12 and diagonal fault models are summarized in **Fig. 8.5(a)**.

As shown in **Fig. 8.5(a)**, DM3 includes all possible byte transient faults. The attacks proposed in [341] show that DFA based on DM0, DM1, and DM2 leads to the successful retrieval of the key. Remember that DM3 faults are the universe of all possible transient faults injected in the selected AES round. These faults spread across all 4 diagonals of the AES state and hence, are not vulnerable to DFA as mentioned in Section 8.2.1.3. These

---

[1]In general, the practical faults used in DFA target the 7th, 8th, and 9th rounds.

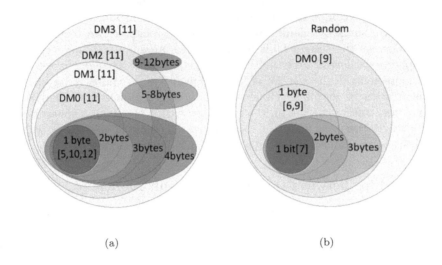

(a)   (b)

FIGURE 8.5: Relationships between DFA fault models when faults are injected between (a) the output of 7th and the input of 8th round MixColumns, (b) output of 8th and the input of 9th round MixColumns.

fault models are multiple-byte transient faults and thus, attacks based on these models are more feasible than those based on single-byte transient faults, which are a subset of the model DM0. The considered fault models are vulnerable to DFA in the following order: (i) the DM0 type faults reduce the key space of AES to 2^{32}, (ii) the DM1 type faults reduce the key space to 2^{64}, and (iii) the DM2 type faults reduce the key space to 2^{96} after a single fault induction. The more encompassing the fault model is, the more realistic the attacks based on it are.

Consider the cardinalities of the identified fault classes, the number of possible DM0, DM1, and DM2 faults are 2^{34}, 3×2^{65}, and 2^{98}, respectively. The number of possible DM3 faults is 2^{128} in the state matrix[2]. If all faults are equiprobable during injection (this is the perspective of conventional fault injection and detection studies), the probability of injecting DM0, DM1, and DM2 faults is negligible. The probability that a randomly injected fault is a DM0, DM1, or DM2 type fault is 2^{-94}, $\frac{1}{3} \times 2^{-63}$, and 2^{-30}, respectively. However, we stress that a DFA attacker does not use uniformly distributed fault injection. Rather, he characterizes the device and uses specific fault injections, which results in high success rates.

8.2.2.4 Faults Are Injected between the Output of 8th and the Input of 9th MixColumns

Fig. 8.5(b) summarizes the relationships between the DFA-exploitable fault models by injecting faults in the output of 8th and the input of 9th round MixColumns. Single-bit transient faults are a subset of single byte faults. Single byte faults are again a subset of

---

[2]The number of faults is calculated based on a simple assumption that the faults are injected at the input to the round. If the faults can be injected anywhere in the AES round, all of these numbers can be proportionally scaled. Further, this is ignoring all permanent and intermittent faults as they are not exploitable from a DFA perspective.

DM0 faults. Two and three byte faults are a subset of DM0 faults. Again, attacks based on multiple byte faults are more feasible than those based on single bit and single byte faults.

In the following section, we detail the above mentioned fault attacks on AES.

8.3 Principle of Differential Fault Attacks on AES

A very central property, which is used in the algorithms to perform a DFA of AES, is the differential features of the AES S-boxes. The following section presents the differential property of the AES S-Box.

8.3.1 Differential Properties of AES S-Box

In this section, we discuss differential properties of S-box, which will be useful for differential fault analysis. In case of the AES, the input to the S-box in each round is the XOR of previous round output and the round key. **Fig. 8.6** shows 2 S-box operation: one with normal input *in* and the other with a difference α to the input. Here *in* is the previous

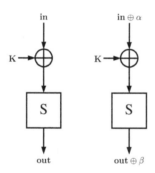

FIGURE 8.6: Difference Across S-box

round output byte and K is the round key byte. The AES S-box is a non-linear operation, therefore input difference α will change to β at the S-box output *out*. Now if we replace the value of $in \oplus K$ by X, we can relate the input output differences by following equation:

$$\beta = S(X \oplus \alpha) \oplus S(X) \tag{8.4}$$

According to the properties of AES, the S-box for a particular value of α and β the above equation can have 0, 2, or 4 solutions of X [275]. For a fixed value of α, in 126 out of 256 choices of β the equation gives 2 solutions of X, and in only one choice of α the equation gives 4 solutions and the rest of the choices of β will not give any solution for X. This implies only 127 out of 256 choices of β produce solutions for X and the average number of solutions of X is 1. It may also be noted that if we know the values of α, β and *in* we can get the values of K from the above equation. This property is being used in most of the advanced DFAs on AES. In the subsequent part of the chapter we explain DFA of AES using these properties.

8.3.2   DFA of AES Using Bit Faults

When AES was introduced at that time side-channel analysis and fault analysis were become 2 very prominent field of research in the research community. The first DFA was already proposed on DES. Therefore, it was a challenge for the researchers in this field to analyze AES in the light of DFA. The initial attempts were further inspired by the practical fault injection techniques, which practically demonstrated that flipping a single bit of an intermediate computation result is possible using relatively less expensive devices like simple camera flash installed on a microscope or laser equipments [367]. However, byte faults are more realistic compared to the bit faults. This constant debate on other fault models and their practicality lead to the emergence of several varieties of fault based attacks on AES.

The DFAs on AES can thus be categorized based on the fault models: bit-level fault model and byte-level fault model. Again byte level fault models are also categorized as: singe-byte and multiple-byte fault models (refer Table 8.1).

We first start with 2 most prominent bit-level DFA of AES. The difference between the 2 attacks is that one targets the last round key and the other focusses on the initial whitening key. In both cases, first the encryption is done in a normal environment on a fixed plaintext, and the fault-free ciphertext is stored. Then again the encryption is done with the same plaintext but in a stressed environment so that a fault is induced as required by the attack algorithm. The induced fault is assumed to be random in nature and the attack algorithm is oblivious of the fault value. Let us first study the DFA which targets the last round of the AES ecryption.

8.3.3   Bit-Level DFA of Last Round of AES

In this attack, originally proposed in [132] it is assumed that the fault is induced at any particular bit of the last round input. However, the exact fault location, i.e., the exact bit where the fault is created is unknown.

Let us consider for the sake of simplicity AES with 128 bits key, though the discussion can be easily extended to the other AES versions. **Fig. 8.7** shows the flow of fault corresponding to the single bit difference at the input of the 10th round. In the figure, K^9 and K^{10} denotes the 9th and 10th round keys respectively. The state matrices S_0, S_1, and S_2 show the corresponding XOR differences of the fault-free and the faulty states. As the fault is induced in a bit, therefore the disturbance is confined within a single byte. So, from the XOR difference of fault-free and faulty ciphertexts one can easily get the location of the faulty byte (note the bit is not evident because of the S-Box).

Consider the fault induced at the $(i,j)^{th}$ byte of the 10th round input state matrix S_0. Let x be the fault-free value at the 10th round input and ε be the corresponding fault value. Note that the attacker is aware of the fault-free (C) and faulty ciphertexts (C^*). As already stated, from the XOR difference of C and C^* the attacker can get the byte position (i,j) where the fault is induced. The (i,j) byte where the bit fault is induced in the byte x can be represented in terms of (C, C^*) as follows:

$$C_{i,l} \oplus C_{i,l}^* = SR(S(x_{i,j})) \oplus SR(S(x_{i,j} \oplus \varepsilon)) \tag{8.5}$$

Note that $l = (j-i) \bmod 4$ provides the corresponding column index where the faulty byte in the jth column and i^{th} row shifts due to the *Shiftrows* operation. In other words, the fault location (i,j) in the difference matrix S_0 changes to (i,l) at the tenth round output.

Having obtained the location of the fault, the attacker is now set to ascertain the value of the fault. Note the similarity of the above equation with that of equation 8.4. The value of $C_{i,l} \oplus C_{i,l}^*$ being known to the attacker, in order to get the value of $x_{i,j}$ he guesses 8 possible values of ε. For each possible value of ε the attacker gets on an average one hypotheses for

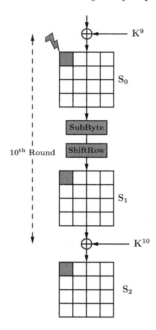

FIGURE 8.7: Basic Structure of Feistel Ciphers

$x_{i,j}$ which will satisfy the above equation (refer Section 8.3.1). Thus for all the 8 possible values of ε, the attacker gets on an average 8 candidates for $x_{i,j}$. In order to identify the unique value for $x_{i,j}$, he obtains another faulty ciphertext by injecting another fault (i.e., the fault location is a different bit) in the same byte. A similar approach leads to another set of 8 values for $x_{i,j}$. Intersection of these 2 sets from the 2 different faulty ciphertexts is expected to determine the exact value of $x_{i,j}$.

This same technique is repeated for the other bytes in order to get all the 16 bytes of x. On an average thus $2 \cdot 16 = 32$ faulty ciphertexts are needed to determine the value of the state matrix x. Thus the attacker obtains the fault-free input of 10th round. Being aware of the fault-free ciphertext C, one can easily retrieve the 10th round key K^{10} from the relation $C = SR(S(x) \oplus K^{10})$. Then as the AES key-schedule is invertible one trivially retrieve the master key.

8.3.4   Bit-Level DFA of First Round of AES

In this section, we describe another bit-level DFA where the fault is induced in the first round of AES encryption. This is a more general attack and applicable to most of the ciphers. The main difference of this attack from the previous ones and the others which follow is the underlying fault model. The fault model is a *bit reset* model, which implies that the attacker has capability to reset a specific bit at a targetted byte location of the AES encryption. The attacker targets the first key whitening operation before the *SubBytes* operation. The plaintext is set to a zero string of length 128 bits, denoted as P_{zero}. The plaintext is fixed throughout the attack, and the objective of the attack is to obtain the whitening key, K.

To start with, an encryption is done using P_{zero} and K under normal environment and the fault-free ciphertexts C_{zero} is obtained and stored. Now a fault is induced according to the fault model discussed. It is assumed that the induced fault resets the lth bit of the (i, j) byte at the input to the first *SubBytes* operation. Let us assume that the fault free input to the *SubBytes* operation is x. Therefore, we can write $x = P_{zero} \oplus K$. The attacker tries to detect the value of l by repeating the following simple steps: He compares the fault-free ciphertext, C_{zero} with that of the faulty one, C^*_{zero}. If they are equal it implies that the lth bit of the $(i,j)^{th}$ byte of x, which was reset due to the fault, was already zero and thus the effect of the reset fault was inconsequential. Thus the corresponding bit of the $(i,j)^{th}$ key byte was zero (as the plaintext is all zero). On the other hand a different value of C_{zero} and C^*_{zero} implies that the induced fault reset the bit $x^l_{i,j}$ with effect. That means the fault-free value of $x^l_{i,j}$ was one and after fault induction it changes to zero. This also means the corresponding bit value of K is one. The fault thus reveals whether a particular bit of the whitening key is 1 or 0. The same technique is repeated for all the 128 bits, and thus 128 faulty ciphertexts are needed to get the master key.

The attack is relatively simple in nature, however is relatively less practical. The main reason is the fault model is very strong as it requires very precise control over the fault location: a specific bit and also an exact location, namely after the key whitening operation and before the first *SubBytes* operation. With reference to a real-life hardware implementation of the block cipher, it is relatively difficult to achieve such a high level of accuracy even with costly equipments. Thus fault attacks on AES with more relaxed fault models and lesser fault induction requirements are desirous and topics of the future sections.

8.4 State-of-the-art DFAs on AES

In this section, we present an overview on some of the more recent fault attacks on AES. These attacks use the more practical fault model, namely the byte faults.

8.4.1 Byte-Level DFA of Penultimate Round of AES

In byte-level DFA, we assume that certain bits of a byte is corrupted by the induced fault and the induced difference is confined within a byte. Due to the fact that the fault is induced in the penultimate round, implies that apart from using the differential properties of S-box (as used in the bit-level DFA on last round of AES), the attacker also uses the differential properties due to the diffusion properties of the MixColumns operation of AES. As already mentioned in the AES diffusion is provided using a 4×4 MDS matrix in the MixColumns. Due to this matrix multiplication, if one byte difference is induced at the input of a round function, the difference is spread to 4 bytes at the round output. **Fig. 8.8** shows the flow of fault.

The induced fault has generated a single byte difference at the input of the 9th round MixColumns. Let f be the byte value of the difference and the corresponding 4-byte output difference is $(2f, f, f, 3f)$, where $2, 1,$ and 3 are the elements of the first row of the MixColumns matrix. The 4-byte difference is again converted to (f_0, f_1, f_2, f_3) by the nonlinear S-box operation in tenth round. The ShiftRows operation will shift the differences to 4 different locations. The attacker has access to the fault-free ciphertext C and faulty ciphertext C^*, which differs only in 4 bytes. Now, we can represent the 4-byte difference $(2f, f, f, 3f)$ in terms of the tenth round key K^{10} and the fault-free and faulty ciphertexts by the following equations:

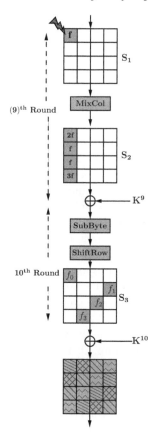

FIGURE 8.8: Differences across the last 2 rounds

$$2\,f = S^{-1}(C_{0,0} \oplus K_{0,0}^{10}) \oplus S^{-1}(C_{0,0}^{*} \oplus K_{0,0}^{10})$$
$$f = S^{-1}(C_{1,3} \oplus K_{1,3}^{10}) \oplus S^{-1}(C_{1,3}^{*} \oplus K_{1,3}^{10})$$
$$f = S^{-1}(C_{2,2} \oplus K_{2,2}^{10}) \oplus S^{-1}(C_{2,2}^{*} \oplus K_{2,2}^{10}) \tag{8.6}$$
$$3\,f = S^{-1}(C_{3,1} \oplus K_{3,1}^{10}) \oplus S^{-1}(C_{3,1}^{*} \oplus K_{3,1}^{10})$$

These four equations can be expressed as the basic equation (8.4). Therefore, it can be represented in the form $A = B \oplus C$ where $A, B,$ and C are bytes in F_{2^8}, having 2^8 possible values each. Now a uniformly random choice of (A, B, C) is expected to satisfy the equation with probability $\frac{1}{2^8}$. Therefore, in this case 2^{16} out of 2^{24} random choices of (A, B, C) will satisfy the equation.

This fact can be generalized. Consider we have M such related equations. These M equations consist of N uniformly random byte variables. The probability that a random choice of N variables satisfy all the M equations simultaneously is $(\frac{1}{2^8})^M$. Therefore, the reduced search space is given by $(\frac{1}{2^8})^M \cdot (2^8)^N = (2^8)^{N-M}$. For our case, we have four equations which consist of five unknown variables: $f,\ K_{0,0}^{10},\ K_{1,3}^{10},\ K_{2,2}^{10},$ and $K_{3,2}^{10}$. Therefore, the four equations will reduce the search space of the variables to $(2^8)^{5-4} = 2^8$. That means out of 2^{32} hypotheses of the 4 key bytes, only 2^8 hypotheses will satisfy the above 4 equations. Therefore, using one fault the attacker can reduce the search space of the 4 key byte to 2^8. Using two such faulty ciphertexts one can uniquely determine the key quartet. This implies for one key quartet one has to induce 2 faults in the required location. For all the 4 key quartets i.e., for the entire AES key an attacker thus needs to induce 8 faults. Therefore using 8 faulty ciphertexts and a fault-free ciphertext, it is expected to uniquely determine the 128-bit key of AES.

8.4.1.1 DFA Using Two Faults

The attack can further be improved. It was shown in [300] that instead of inducing fault in 9th round, if we induce fault in between 7th and 8th round MixColumns, we can determine the 128-bit key using only 2 faulty ciphertexts. **Fig. 8.9** shows the spreading of faults when it is induced in such a fashion. The single byte difference at the input of 8th round MixColumns is spread to 4 bytes. The Shiftrows operation ensures that there is one disturbed byte in each column of the state matrix. Each of the 4-byte difference again spreads to 4 bytes at 9th round MixColumns output. Therefore, the relation between the fault values in the 4 columns of difference-state matrix S_4 is equivalent to 4 faults at 4 different columns of 9th-round input-state matrix as explained in the previous attack. This implies that using 2 such faults we can uniquely determine the entire AES key.

Note that the exact working of the DFA proposed in [300] is slightly different from above, though the underlying principle is the same. The attack maintains a list $\mathcal{D}$ for each column of the difference matrix S_4 assuming a one-byte fault in the input of the penultimate round MixColumns. The size of the table $\mathcal{D}$ is thus 4×255 4-byte values, as the input fault can occur in any byte of a column and can take 255 non-zero values. Assuming that the fault occurs in the difference matrix S_3 in the first column, then equations similar to equation (8.6) can be written, with the left hand side of the equations being a 4-byte tuple $(\Delta_0, \Delta_1, \Delta_2, \Delta_3)$. It is expected that the correct guess of the keys $K_{0,0}^{10}, K_{1,3}^{10}, K_{2,2}^{10}$, and $K_{3,2}^{10}$ should provide a 4-byte tuple which belongs to the list $\mathcal{D}$. There are other wrong keys which also pass this test, and analysis shows that on an average 1036 elements pass this test with a single fault. Repeating the same for all the 4-columns of the difference matrix S_4 reduces the AES key to $1036^4 \approx 2^{40}$ (note that as the fault is assumed to be between 7th and 8th round each column of S_3 has a byte disturbed). However, if 2 faults are induced then with a probability of 0.98 the unique AES key is returned.

This is the best-known DFA of AES to date when the attacker does not have access to the plaintext and the attacker needs to determine the key uniquely. However with access to the plaintexts, the attacker can still improve the attack by performing the DFA using only fault and a further reduced brute force guess. Also it is possible to reduce the time complexity of the attack further from 2^{32} to 2^{30}.

8.4.1.2 DFA Using Only One Fault

The attack proposed in [300] can be further improved when the attacker has access to the plaintexts in addition to the ciphertexts [265]. In that case, the attacker can do brute-force on the possible keys. The objective of this attack or its extensions is to perform the attack using only one fault. While a unique key may not be obtainable with a single fault, the AES key size can reduce to such a small size that a brute force search can be easily performed. It may be noted that reducing the number of fault requirements from 2 to 1 should not be seen in terms of its absolute values. In an actual fault attack, it is very unlikely that the attacker can have absolute control over the fault injection method and hence may need more trials. Rather these attacks are capable of reducing the number of fault requirements by half compared to the attacks proposed in [300].

This attack is comprised of two phases: the first phase reducing the key space of AES to around 2^{36} values, while the second phase reducing it to around 2^8 values.

Consider the **Fig. 8.9**, where from the first column of S_4 we get following 4 differential equations:

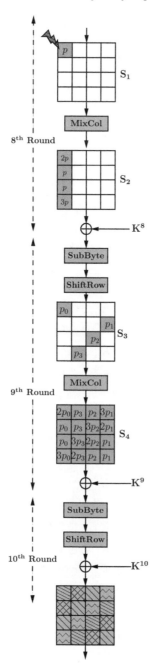

FIGURE 8.9: Differences across the Last Three Rounds

$$2p_0 = S^{-1}(C_{0,0} \oplus K_{0,0}^{10}) \oplus S^{-1}(C_{0,0}^* \oplus K_{0,0}^{10})$$
$$p_0 = S^{-1}(C_{1,3} \oplus K_{1,3}^{10}) \oplus S^{-1}(C_{1,3}^* \oplus K_{1,3}^{10})$$
$$p_0 = S^{-1}(C_{2,2} \oplus K_{2,2}^{10}) \oplus S^{-1}(C_{2,2}^* \oplus K_{2,2}^{10})$$
$$3p_0 = S^{-1}(C_{3,1} \oplus K_{3,1}^{10}) \oplus S^{-1}(C_{3,1}^* \oplus K_{3,1}^{10})$$

$$(8.7)$$

In the above 4 differential equation we only guess the 2^8 values of p_0 and get the corresponding possible 2^8 hypotheses of the key quartet by applying the S-box difference distribution table. Therefore, one column of S_4 will reduce the search space of one quartet of key to 2^8 choices. Similarly, solving the differential equations from all the 4 columns we can reduce the search space of all the 4 key quartets to 2^8 values each. Hence, if we combine all the 4 quartets we get $(2^8)^4 = 2^{32}$ possible hypotheses of the final round key K^{10}. We have assumed here that the initial fault value was in the $(0,0)^{th}$ byte of S_1. If we allow the fault to be in any of the 16 locations, the key space of AES is around 2^{36} values. This space can be brute-force-searched within practical time and hence shows that effectively one fault is sufficient to reduce the key space to practical limits.

The search space of the final round key can be further reduced if we consider the relation between the fault values at the state matrix S_2, which was not utilized in the previous attacks. This step serves as a second phase, which is coupled with the first stage on all the 2^{32} keys (for an assumed location of the faulty byte). We can represent the fault value in the first column of S_2 in terms of the 9th round key K^9 and the 9th round fault-free and faulty output C^9 and C^{*9}, respectively, by the following 4 differential equations:

$$
\begin{aligned}
2\,p_0 = &\; S^{-1}(14(C^9_{0,0} \oplus K^9_{0,0}) \oplus 11(C^9_{1,0} \oplus K^9_{1,0}) \oplus \\
&\; 13(C^9_{2,0} \oplus K^9_{2,0}) \oplus 9(C^9_{3,0} \oplus K^9_{3,0})) \oplus \\
&\; S^{-1}(14(C^{*9}_{0,0} \oplus K^9_{0,0}) \oplus 11(C^{*9}_{1,0} \oplus K^9_{1,0}) \oplus \\
&\; 13(C^{*9}_{2,0} \oplus K^9_{2,0}) \oplus 9(C^{*9}_{3,0} \oplus K^9_{3,0}))
\end{aligned} \tag{8.8a}
$$

$$
\begin{aligned}
p_0 = &\; S^{-1}(9(C^9_{0,3} \oplus K^9_{0,3}) \oplus 14(C^9_{1,3} \oplus K^9_{1,3}) \oplus \\
&\; 11(C^9_{2,3} \oplus K^9_{2,3}) \oplus 13(C^9_{3,3} \oplus K^9_{3,3})) \oplus \\
&\; S^{-1}(9(C^{*9}_{0,3} \oplus K^9_{0,3}) \oplus 14(C^9_{1,3} \oplus K^{*9}_{1,3}) \oplus \\
&\; 11(C^{*9}_{2,3} \oplus K^9_{2,3}) \oplus 13(C^{*9}_{3,3} \oplus K^9_{3,3}))
\end{aligned} \tag{8.8b}
$$

$$
\begin{aligned}
p_0 = &\; S^{-1}(13(C^9_{0,2} \oplus K^9_{0,2}) \oplus 9(C^9_{1,2} \oplus K^9_{1,2}) \oplus \\
&\; 14(C^9_{2,2} \oplus K^9_{2,2}) \oplus 11(C^9_{3,2} \oplus K^9_{3,2})) \oplus \\
&\; S^{-1}(13(C^{*9}_{0,2} \oplus K^9_{0,2}) \oplus 9(C^{*9}_{1,2} \oplus K^9_{1,2}) \oplus \\
&\; 14(C^{*9}_{2,2} \oplus K^9_{2,2}) \oplus 11(C^{*9}_{3,2} \oplus K^9_{3,2}))
\end{aligned} \tag{8.8c}
$$

$$
\begin{aligned}
3\,p_0 = &\; S^{-1}(13(C^9_{0,1} \oplus K^9_{0,1}) \oplus 9(C^9_{1,1} \oplus K^9_{1,1}) \oplus \\
&\; 14(C^9_{2,1} \oplus K^9_{2,1}) \oplus 11(C^9_{3,1} \oplus K^9_{3,1})) \oplus \\
&\; S^{-1}(13(C^{*9}_{0,1} \oplus K^9_{0,1}) \oplus 9(C^{*9}_{1,1} \oplus K^9_{1,1}) \oplus \\
&\; 14(C^{*9}_{2,1} \oplus K^9_{2,1}) \oplus 11(C^{*9}_{3,1} \oplus K^9_{3,1}))
\end{aligned} \tag{8.8d}
$$

In order to utilize the above equations we need the 9th-round key. The 9th-round key can be derived from the final round key by the following conversion matrix:

$$
\begin{pmatrix}
(K^{10}_{0,0} \oplus S[K^{10}_{1,3} \oplus K^{10}_{1,2}] & K^{10}_{0,1} \oplus K^{10}_{0,0} & K^{10}_{0,2} \oplus K^{10}_{0,1} & K^{10}_{0,3} \oplus K^{10}_{0,2} \\
\quad \oplus h_{10}) & & & \\
(K^{10}_{1,0} \oplus S[K^{10}_{2,3} \oplus K^{10}_{2,2}]) & K^{10}_{1,1} \oplus K^{10}_{1,0} & K^{10}_{1,2} \oplus K^{10}_{1,1} & K^{10}_{1,3} \oplus K^{10}_{1,2} \\
(K^{10}_{2,0} \oplus S[K^{10}_{3,3} \oplus K^{10}_{3,2}]) & K^{10}_{2,1} \oplus K^{10}_{2,0} & K^{10}_{2,2} \oplus K^{10}_{2,1} & K^{10}_{2,3} \oplus K^{10}_{2,2} \\
(K^{10}_{3,0} \oplus S[K^{10}_{0,3} \oplus K^{10}_{0,2}]) & K^{10}_{3,1} \oplus K^{10}_{3,0} & K^{10}_{3,2} \oplus K^{10}_{3,1} & K^{10}_{3,3} \oplus K^{10}_{3,2}
\end{pmatrix}.
$$

Thus for each of the possible hypotheses of K^{10} produced by the first stage, and using the ciphertexts (C, C^*), we get the values of (K^9, C^9, C^{*9}). Then the attacker tests the above

4 equations. If it satisfies the candidate key is accepted, else rejected. For completeness, we state the detailed equations as follows:

$$
\begin{aligned}
2p_0 = S^{-1}\big[&14(S^{-1}[K_{0,0}^{10}\oplus C_{0,0}]\oplus K_{0,0}^{10}\oplus S[K_{1,3}^{10}\oplus K_{1,2}^{10}]\oplus h_{10})\oplus\\
&11(S^{-1}[K_{1,3}^{10}\oplus C_{1,3}]\oplus K_{1,0}^{10}\oplus S[K_{2,3}^{10}\oplus K_{2,2}^{10}])\oplus\\
&13(S^{-1}[K_{2,2}^{10}\oplus C_{2,2}]\oplus K_{2,0}^{10}\oplus S[K_{3,3}^{10}\oplus K_{3,2}^{10}])\oplus\\
&9(S^{-1}[K_{3,1}^{10}\oplus C_{3,1}]\oplus K_{3,0}^{10}\oplus S[K_{0,3}^{10}\oplus K_{0,2}^{10}])\big]\oplus\\
S^{-1}\big[&14(S^{-1}[K_{0,0}^{10}\oplus C_{0,0}^*]\oplus K_{0,0}^{10}\oplus S[K_{1,3}^{10}\oplus K_{1,2}^{10}])\oplus\\
&11(S^{-1}[K_{1,3}^{10}\oplus C_{1,3}^*]\oplus K_{1,0}^{10}\oplus S[K_{2,3}^{10}\oplus K_{2,2}^{10}])\oplus\\
&13(S^{-1}[K_{2,2}^{10}\oplus C_{2,2}^*]\oplus K_{2,0}^{10}\oplus S[K_{3,3}^{10}\oplus K_{3,2}^{10}])\oplus\\
&9(S^{-1}[K_{3,1}^{10}\oplus C_{3,1}^*]\oplus K_{3,0}^{10}\oplus S[K_{0,3}^{10}\oplus K_{0,2}^{10}])\big]
\end{aligned}
\tag{8.9}
$$

Similarly, the other 3 faulty bytes can be expressed by the following equations:

$$
\begin{aligned}
p_0 = S^{-1}\big[&14(S^{-1}[K_{0,3}^{10}\oplus C_{0,3}]\oplus K_{0,3}^{10}\oplus K_{0,2}^{10})\oplus\\
&11(S^{-1}[K_{1,3}^{10}\oplus C_{1,3}]\oplus K_{1,3}^{10}\oplus K_{1,2}^{10})\oplus\\
&13(S^{-1}[K_{2,1}^{10}\oplus C_{2,1}]\oplus K_{2,3}^{10}\oplus K_{2,2}^{10})\oplus\\
&9(S^{-1}[K_{3,0}^{10}\oplus C_{3,0}]\oplus K_{3,3}^{10}\oplus K_{3,2}^{10})\big]\oplus\\
S^{-1}\big[&14(S^{-1}[K_{0,3}^{10}\oplus C_{0,3}]\oplus K_{0,3}^{10}\oplus K_{0,2}^{10})\oplus\\
&11(S^{-1}[K_{1,3}^{10}\oplus C_{1,3}]\oplus K_{1,3}^{10}\oplus K_{1,2}^{10})\oplus\\
&13(S^{-1}[K_{2,1}^{10}\oplus C_{2,1}]\oplus K_{2,3}^{10}\oplus K_{2,2}^{10})\oplus\\
&9(S^{-1}[K_{3,0}^{10}\oplus C_{3,0}]\oplus K_{3,3}^{10}\oplus K_{3,2}^{10})\big]\oplus
\end{aligned}
\tag{8.10}
$$

$$
\begin{aligned}
p_0 = S^{-1}\big[&14(S^{-1}[K_{0,2}^{10}\oplus C_{0,2}]\oplus K_{0,2}^{10}\oplus K_{0,1}^{10})\oplus\\
&11(S^{-1}[K_{1,1}^{10}\oplus C_{1,1}]\oplus K_{1,2}^{10}\oplus K_{1,1}^{10})\oplus\\
&13(S^{-1}[K_{2,0}^{10}\oplus C_{2,0}]\oplus K_{2,2}^{10}\oplus K_{2,1}^{10})\oplus\\
&9(S^{-1}[K_{3,3}^{10}\oplus C_{3,3}]\oplus K_{3,2}^{10}\oplus K_{3,1}^{10})\big]\oplus\\
S^{-1}\big[&14(S^{-1}[K_{0,2}^{10}\oplus C_{0,2}^*]\oplus K_{0,2}^{10}\oplus K_{0,1}^{10})\oplus\\
&11(S^{-1}[K_{1,1}^{10}\oplus C_{1,1}^*]\oplus K_{1,2}^{10}\oplus K_{1,1}^{10})\oplus\\
&13(S^{-1}[K_{2,0}^{10}\oplus C_{2,0}^*]\oplus K_{2,2}^{10}\oplus K_{2,1}^{10})\oplus\\
&9(S^{-1}[K_{3,3}^{10}\oplus C_{3,3}^*]\oplus K_{3,2}^{10}\oplus K_{3,1}^{10})\big]
\end{aligned}
\tag{8.11}
$$

$$
\begin{aligned}
3p_0 = S^{-1}\big[&14(S^{-1}[K_{0,1}^{10}\oplus C_{0,1}]\oplus K_{0,1}^{10}\oplus K_{0,0}^{10})\oplus\\
&11(S^{-1}[K_{1,0}^{10}\oplus C_{1,0}]\oplus K_{1,1}^{10}\oplus K_{1,0}^{10})\oplus\\
&13(S^{-1}[K_{2,3}^{10}\oplus C_{2,3}]\oplus K_{2,1}^{10}\oplus K_{2,0}^{10})\oplus\\
&9(S^{-1}[K_{3,2}^{10}\oplus C_{3,2}]\oplus K_{3,1}^{10}\oplus K_{3,0}^{10})\big]\oplus\\
S^{-1}\big[&14(S^{-1}[K_{0,1}^{10}\oplus C_{0,1}^*]\oplus K_{0,1}^{10}\oplus K_{0,0}^{10})\oplus\\
&11(S^{-1}[K_{1,0}^{10}\oplus C_{1,0}^*]\oplus K_{1,1}^{10}\oplus K_{1,0}^{10})\oplus\\
&13(S^{-1}[K_{2,3}^{10}\oplus C_{2,3}^*]\oplus K_{2,1}^{10}\oplus K_{2,0}^{10})\oplus\\
&9(S^{-1}[K_{3,2}^{10}\oplus C_{3,2}^*]\oplus K_{3,1}^{10}\oplus K_{3,0}^{10})\big]
\end{aligned}
\tag{8.12}
$$

We thus have 4 differential equations and the combined search space of (K^9, C^9, C^{*9})

and p_0 is $2^{32} \cdot 2^8 = 2^{40}$. Therefore, the above 4 equations will reduce this search space of K_{10} to $\frac{2^{40}}{(2^8)^4} = 2^8$. Hence using only one faulty ciphertext one can reduce the search space of AES-128 key to 256 choices. However, the time complexity of the attack is 2^{32} as we have to test all the hypothesis of K^{10} by the above equations: (8.9), (8.10), (8.11), and (8.12). In the next subsection, we present an improvement to reduce the time complexity of the attack to 2^{30} from 2^{32}.

8.4.1.3   DFA with Reduced Time Complexity

The above second phase of the analysis is based on 4 equations: (8.9), (8.10), (8.11), and (8.12). All the 2^{32} possible key hypotheses are tested by these 4 equations. The key hypotheses which are satisfied by all 4 equation are considered and rest are discarded.

However, if we consider the above 4 equations in pairs we observe that each possible pair does not contain all the 16 bytes of the AES. For example, the pair of equations (8.10) and (8.11) contains 14 key bytes excluding $K_{0,0}^{10}$ and $k_{0,1}^{10}$. This fact can be utilized to reduce the time complexity of the attack. We use this observation to split the lists of key which are exported in the first phase of the attack and subsequently filtered in the second phase.

In the first phase of the attack, we have 4 quartets $\{K_{0,0}^{10}, K_{1,3}^{10}, K_{2,2}^{10}, K_{3,1}^{10}\}$, $\{K_{0,1}^{10}, K_{1,0}^{10}, K_{2,3}^{10}, K_{3,2}^{10}\}$, $\{K_{0,2}^{10}, K_{1,1}^{10}, K_{2,0}^{10}, K_{3,3}^{10}\}$, and $\{K_{0,3}^{10}, K_{1,2}^{10}, K_{2,1}^{10}, K_{3,0}^{10}\}$ Let us assume one value of the first quartet is (a_1, b_1, c_1, d_1). As per the property of the S-Box there will be another value of $K_{0,0}^{10}$ which satisfies the system of equation (8.7) with rest of the key byte values remaining same. Let us assume the second value of $K_{0,0}^{10}$ is a_2, then the 4-tuple (a_2, b_1, c_1, d_1) also satisfies the system of equation (8.7).

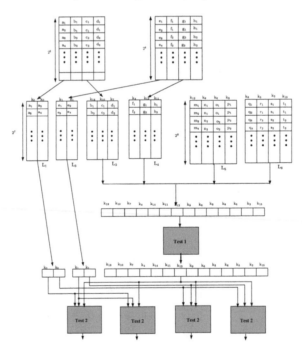

FIGURE 8.10: Model for data-flow parallelization in the second phase

Using this idea, we can divide the list for the quartet $\{K_{0,0}^{10}, K_{1,3}^{10}, K_{2,2}^{10}, K_{3,1}^{10}\}$ into 2 sublists, L_1, L_2. As depicted in **Fig. 8.10** The list L_1 contains the pair values for the key byte $K_{0,0}^{10}$ (note that the key byte $K_{0,0}^{10}$ has always an even number of possible choices). The list L_2 contains the distinct values for the remaining part of the quartet, $\{K_{1,3}^{10}, K_{3,1}^{10}\}$. Thus, the expected size of the lists L_1 and L_2 is 2^7 each, compared to the previous list size of 2^8 when $\{K_{0,0}^{10}, K_{1,3}^{10}, K_{3,1}^{10}\}$ were stored together.

Similarly, we store the possible values of quartet $\{K_{0,1}^{10}, K_{1,0}^{10}, K_{2,3}^{10}, K_{3,2}^{10}\}$ in 2 lists, L_3 and L_4. Here L_3 stores the pair values for the key byte $K_{0,1}^{10}$, while the list L_4 contains the distinct values for the key bytes $\{K_{1,0}^{10}, K_{2,3}^{10}, K_{3,2}^{10}\}$. Here also the expected size of the lists are 2^7. The other 2 quartets $\{K_{0,2}^{10}, K_{1,1}^{10}, K_{2,0}^{10}, K_{3,3}^{10}\}$ and $\{K_{0,3}^{10}, K_{1,2}^{10}, K_{2,1}^{10}, K_{3,0}^{10}\}$ are stored in list L_6 and L_5. Both the lists have expected size of 2^8.

Next we select the key bytes from the 6 lists, $L_1, L_2, L_3, L_4, L_5, L_6$ to solve the equations of the second phase of the attack such that the time complexity is reduced.

Because of the observations regarding the pair of equations (8.9) and (8.12); and (8.10) and (8.11), the second phase can be divided into 2 parts. In part one we test the keys generated from the first phase of the attack by the pair of equations (8.10) and (8.11). In **Fig. 8.10** this is denoted as *Test1*. As the 2 equations for *Test1* do not require key bytes $K_{0,0}^{10}$ and $K_{0,1}^{10}$ we only consider all possible keys generated from lists L_2, L_4, L_5, L_6. There are 2^{30} such possible keys. In the second part, we combine each of the 14 byte keys satisfying *Test1* with one of the 4 possible values arising out of the 4 combination of the pair of values for $K_{0,0}^{10}$ in L_1 and $K_{0,1}^{10}$ in L_3. These keys are further tested in parallel by the equations (8.9) and (8.12). In **Fig. 8.10**, we refer to this test as *Test2*.

The size of the lists L_2 and L_4 is 2^7; and the size of lists L_5 and L_6 is 2^8. Therefore the number of possible keys generated from these 4 lists is $2^7 \times 2^7 \times 2^8 \times 2^8 = 2^{30}$. These 2^{30} keys are fed as input to *Test1* which is expected to reduce the key hypotheses by 2^8. Therefore, each instance of *Test2* will receive input of $(\frac{2^{30}}{2^8}) = 2^{22}$ expected key hypotheses. The chance of each key satisfying *Test2* is 2^{-16} which implies each instance of *Test2* will result in 2^6 key hypotheses.

The above attack procedure is summarized in Algorithm 8.1.

Algorithm 8.1: Parallelized Fault Attack on AES

Input: 128 bit faulty and fault-free ciphertexts C and C'
Output: 2^8 possible key hypotheses

1 Step 1: Produce 4 lists storing $\{K_{0,0}^{10}, K_{1,3}^{10}, K_{2,2}^{10}, K_{3,1}^{10}\}$, $\{K_{0,1}^{10}, K_{1,0}^{10}, K_{2,3}^{10}, K_{3,2}^{10}\}$, $\{K_{0,2}^{10}, K_{1,1}^{10}, K_{2,0}^{10}, K_{3,3}^{10}\}$, and $\{K_{0,3}^{10}, K_{1,2}^{10}, K_{2,1}^{10}, K_{3,0}^{10}\}$

2 Step 2: Store the key bytes in 6 lists L_1 to L_6 (as mentioned previously).

3 Step 3: Each of the possible 14 byte keys generated by combining list L_2, L_4, L_5, and L_6, is tested by the equations (8.10) and (8.11) (*Test1*).

4 Step 4: Each of the 14 byte keys satisfying *Test1* is combined with 4 possible $K_{0,0}^{10}, K_{0,1}^{10}$ pair values taken from 4 columns of the lists L_1 and L_3.

5 Step 5: Run in parallel the 4 instances of *Test2* (check equations (8.9) and (8.12)) each with one of the four 16 byte keys of Step 4 as a input.

It may be easily observed that the time required is because of step 3, which is equal to 2^{30}, making the overall attack 4 times faster on an average, and still reducing the overall keyspace of AES to around 2^8 values. The summary of the entire attack is presented in Algorithm 8.2.

The above fault models are based on single byte fault models, which assume that the fault is localized in a single byte. However due to impreciseness in the fault induction, the fault can spread to more than one bytes. Such a *multiple-byte* fault requires a revisit at

---

Algorithm 8.2: DFA on AES-128 State

    Input: C, C^*
    Output: List L_k of tenth round key K^{10}

1   Solve the four sets of equations of S_4 (**Fig. 8.9**) independently.;

2   Get 2^{32} hypotheses of K^{10}.;

3   **for** *Each candidates of K^{10}* **do**
4   Get K^9 from K^{10} using AES-128 Key Scheduling.;
5   Get unique choices of 14 bytes of K^{10} except $K^{10}_{0,0}, K^{10}_{0,1}$.;
6   Test the 2nd and 3rd equations of S_2;
7   **if** *Satisfied* **then**
8   **for** *Each candidates of* $(K^{10}_{0,0}, K^{10}_{0,1})$ **do**
9   Test the 1st and 4th equations of S_2;
10   **if** *Satisfied* **then**
11   Save K^{10} to L_k.;
12   **end**
13   **end**
14   **end**
15   **end**

16   **return** L_k

---

the DFA methods. In [341], a technique for performing DFA when such faults occur where presented, which generalize further the DFA proposed in [28] and later extended in [197]. The underlying fault models assumed in this attack were already introduced in section 4.1.3 and were called as *diagonal fault models*. In the next section, we outline the idea of these attacks.

8.5 Multiple-Byte DFA of AES-128

In this section, we present the DFAs under the multiple byte fault models. The DFAs are efficient to obtain the AES key using 2 to 4 faults, when the faults corrupt upto 3 diagonals of the 4 diagonals of the AES state matrix at the input of the 8th round MixColumns. In the next subsection, we first observe the DFAs when the fault is confined to one diagonal of the state matrix, i.e., the fault is according to the fault model $DM0$.

8.5.1 DFA According to Fault Model $DM0$

We first show that faults which are confined to one diagonal are equivalent and can be used to retrieve the key using the same method.

8.5.1.1 Equivalence of Faults in the Same Diagonal

Let us first observe the propagation of a fault injected in diagonal D_0 through the round transformations from the input of the 8th round to the output of the 9th round.

Fig. 8.11 shows some cases of fault induction in diagonal D_0. The faults vary in the number of bytes that are faulty in D_0 at the input of the 8 round. We emphasize the fact that irrespective of the number or positions of bytes that are faulty in D_0, due to the subsequent ShiftRows operation the fault is confined to the first column C_0 of the state matrix at the end of the 8th round. So the fault propagation in the 9th round for all these cases is similar and leads to the same byte inter-relations at the end of the 9th round.

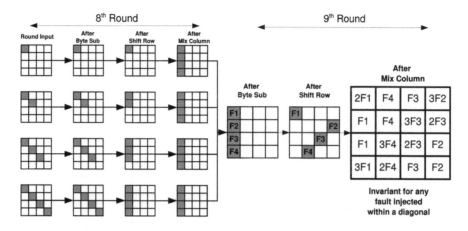

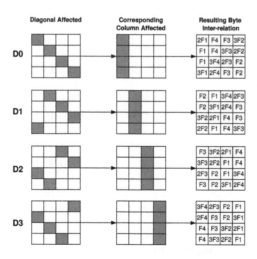

FIGURE 8.11: Equivalence of Different kinds of Faults induced in Diagonal D_0 at the Input of 8th Round of AES

In general any fault at the input of the 8th round in the ith diagonal, $0 \leq i \leq 3$, leads to the ith column being affected at the end of the round. There are 4 diagonals and faults in each diagonal maps to 4 different byte inter-relations at the end of the 9th round. These relations are depicted in **Fig. 8.12**. These relations will remain unchanged for any combination of faults injected within a particular diagonal. Each of the 4 sets of relations in **Fig. 8.12** will be used to form key dependent equations. Each of the equation sets will comprise of 4 equations of similar nature as shown in equation 8.6.

FIGURE 8.12: Byte Inter-relations at the end of 9th Round corresponding to different Diagonals being Faulty

As before these equations reduce the AES key to an average size of 2^{32}. If the attacker is unaware of the exact diagonal, he can repeat for all the above 4 sets of equations, and the key size will still be $2^{32} \times 4 = 2^{34}$, which can be brute forced feasibly with present-day computation power.

Next we consider briefly the cases when the faults spread to more than one diagonal.

8.5.2   DFA According to Fault Model $DM1$

In **Fig. 8.13**, we observe the propagation of faults when the diagonals, D_0 and D_1 are affected at the input of the 9th-round MixColumns.

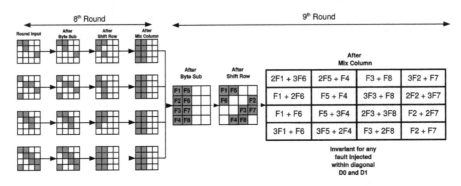

After Mix Column			
2F1 + 3F6	2F5 + F4	F3 + F8	3F2 + F7
F1 + 2F6	F5 + F4	3F3 + F8	2F2 + 3F7
F1 + F6	F5 + 3F4	2F3 + 3F8	F2 + 2F7
3F1 + F6	3F5 + 2F4	F3 + 2F8	F2 + F7

Invariant for any fault injected within diagonal D0 and D1

FIGURE 8.13: Fault Propagation if Diagonals D_0 and D_1 are Affected

We observe that the nature of the faults in the state matrix at the input of the 9th round MixColumns and hence at the output remains invariant for all possible faults in these two diagonals. This property is exploited to develop equations which are used to retrieve the correct key.

We denote the fault values in the first column of the output of the 9th round MixColumns by a_0, a_1, a_2, a_3, where each a_i is a byte $0 \le i \le 3$. Then using the inter-relationships among the faulty bytes one can easily show that:

$$a_1 + a_3 = a_0$$
$$2a_1 + 3a_3 = 7a_2$$

We can express a_0, a_1, a_2, a_3 in terms of the fault-free ciphertext (CT), faulty ciphertext (CT^*) and 4 bytes of the 10th round key ($\mathbf{K_{10}}$). The equations reduce the key space of 4 bytes of the key to 2^{16}. Similarly, performing the analysis for other columns, helps to reduce the AES key to a size of $(2^{16})^4 = 2^{64}$. Using two such faulty inductions it is expected that the unique key is returned.

Depending on the combination of 2 diagonals affected out of the 4 diagonals, there are 6 such sets of equations. Hence even in such case, the attacker reduces the AES key space to 6 possible keys, which he can easily brute force.

In the next section, we present an attack strategy if the fault gets spread to at most 3 diagonals. This fault model, $DM2$ thus covers the first 2 models of fault.

8.5.3   DFA According to Fault Model $DM2$

In **Fig. 8.14**, we observe the propagation of faults when the diagonals, D_0, D_1, and D_2 are affected.

From **Fig. 8.14**, we note that for all possible faults corrupting the diagonals D_0, D_1, and D_2, the nature of the faults at the input of the 9th-round MixColumns is an invariant. The fault nature at the output of the 9th-round MixColumns is as seen in the figure, also an invariant. We denote the fault values in the first column of the output of the 9th-round MixColumns by a_0, a_1, a_2, a_3, where each a_i is a byte $0 \le i \le 3$.

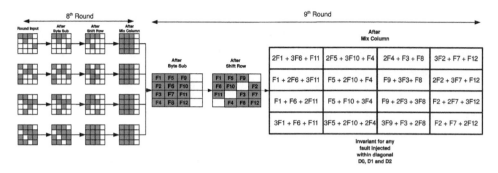

FIGURE 8.14: Fault Propagation if diagonals D_0, D_1 and D_2 are affected

The following equation can be obtained by observing the inter-relationships (refer to **Fig. 8.13**):

$$11a_0 + 13a_1 \;=\; 9a_2 + 14a_3$$

As before in the case of faults modeled by $DM1$, we can express a_0, a_1, a_2, a_3 in terms of the fault-free ciphertext (CT), faulty ciphertext (CT'), and the 10th round key $(\mathbf{K_{10}})$. One equation reduces 4 bytes of the key to 2^{24} values. We can have similar equations for each of the remaining 3 columns of the state matrix after the 9th round MixColumns, and thus the AES key space reduces to an expected value of $(2^{24})^4 = 2^{96}$. However, using 4 faults and taking the intersection of the key space, it is expected that the key space reduces to a unique value.

It may be noted that when the faults occur according to the model $DM3$, that is all the 4 diagonals are affected, the DFA fails.

8.6   Extension of the DFA to Other Variants of AES

In the previous sections, we described DFAs using different fault models on AES with 128-bit key. However, AES has two more variants: AES-192 and AES-256 with key length 192 and 256 bits. These two variants of AES follows different key scheduling. If we observe the key scheduling algorithm, we see that for AES-192 and AES-256 obtaining last round is not sufficient to retrieve the master key. It requires retrieving the last two round keys, rather any two consecutive round keys. For the sake of simplicity we target to recover the last two round keys. Furthermore, in case of AES-192, the last round key and the last two columns of penultimate round key is sufficient. This is because the first two columns of the penultimate round key can be directly derived from the final round key.

The first complete DFA on AES-192 and AES-256 was proposed in [219]. The proposed attacks were based on two different fault models which requires 6 and 3000 pairs of fault-free and faulty ciphertexts. A new attack was proposed in [376] which first time exploited the relations between the round keys of the key scheduling algorithm. The attack on AES-192 required three pairs of correct and faulty ciphertexts and the attack on AES-256 required two pairs of correct and faulty ciphertexts and two pairs of correct and faulty plaintexts. The attack was further improved in [196] where the DFA on AES-192 required two pairs of fault-free and faulty ciphertexts, and on AES-256 required three pairs of fault-free and faulty ciphertexts. Recently, a DFA on AES-256 was proposed in [27], which required two pairs of fault-free and faulty ciphertexts and a brute-force search of 16 bits with time complexity of 2^{32}.

8.6.1 DFA on AES-192 States

A DFA on AES-192 has been proposed by Kim [196], which exploits all the available information. According to our analysis a single byte fault should reveal 120-bit of the secret key. AES-192 has a 192-bit key, and therefore one would expect the most efficient attack would need two single byte faults. Kim's attack required two faults and uniquely determines the key.

8.6.2 DFA on AES-256 States

In this section, we propose a two-phase DFA on AES-256 states. The analysis says that using a single byte fault induction one can reveal maximum of 120 bits of the secret key. AES-256 has a 256-bit key. Therefore, two fault induction should be able to reveal $(120 \cdot 2) = 240$ bits of the key.

According to the AES-256 key schedule, retrieving one round key is not enough to get the master key. Algorithm 6 shows that the penultimate round key is not directly related to the final round key. Therefore, the attack on AES-128 cannot be directly applicable to AES-256.

We propose an attack which requires two faulty ciphertexts C_1^* and C_2^* and a fault free ciphertext C. The first faulty ciphertext C_1^* is generated by inducing a single byte fault between the MixColumns operations in the eleventh and twelfth round, whereas C_2^* is generated by inducing a singe byte fault in between the MixColumns operations in the tenth and eleventh round. **Fig. 8.15(a)** shows the flow of faults corresponding to C_1^*, whereas **Fig. 8.15(b)** shows the flow of faults corresponding to C_2^*.

The proposed attack works in two phases. In the first phase of the attack, we reduce the possible choices of final round key to 2^{16} hypotheses and in the second phase of the attack we deduce 2^{16} hypotheses for the penultimate round key leaving 2^{16} hypotheses for the master key.

8.6.2.1 First Phase of the Attack on AES-256 States

In order to get the final round key we directly apply the first phase of the DFA on AES-128, described in Section 8.4.1.2, to the faulty ciphertext C_1^* (**Fig. 8.15(a)**). Therefore, using the relation between the faulty bytes in state matrix S_4 we reduce the possible values of the final round key K^{14} to 2^{32} hypotheses. Next we consider the second faulty ciphertext C_2^* (**Fig. 8.15(b)**), where in state matrix S_3 we have a relationship between the faulty bytes that is similar to the state matrix S_4 of C_1 (**Fig. 8.15(a)**). We define X as the output of the 13th round SubBytes operation in the computation that produced the fault-free ciphertext. We also define ρ and ε as the differences at the output of 13th round SubBytes operation corresponding to two faulty ciphertexts C_1^* and C_2^*, respectively. These two differences can be expressed as:

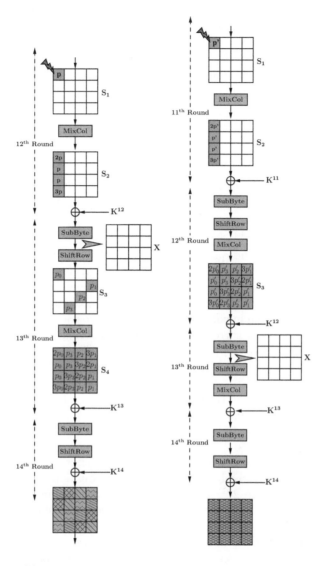

(a) Flow of Faults in the Last Three Rounds of AES-256

(b) Flow of Faults in the Last Four Rounds of AES-256

FIGURE 8.15: Flow of Faults

$$\rho = SR^{-1}\Big(MC^{-1}\big(SR^{-1}(SB^{-1}(C \oplus K^{14})) \oplus$$
$$SR^{-1}(SB^{-1}(C_1^* \oplus K^{14})))\big)\Big)$$

$$\varepsilon = SR^{-1}\Big(MC^{-1}\big(SR^{-1}(SB^{-1}(C \oplus K^{14})) \oplus$$
$$SR^{-1}(SB^{-1}(C_2^* \oplus K^{14})))\big)\Big)$$

Therefore, the fault values in the first column of S_3 (**Fig. 8.15(b)**) can be represented in terms of X and ε by four equations similar to equation (8.4). In that case $\varepsilon_{0,0}$, $\varepsilon_{1,0}$, $\varepsilon_{2,0}$, and $\varepsilon_{3,0}$ are the values corresponding β and $2p_0'$, p_0', p_0', and $3p_0'$ are the values corresponding to α in the four equations, respectively.

Similarly, from the first column of state matrix S_2 of **Fig. 8.15(a)**, we get four more differential equations which correspond to the first column of X and ρ. Therefore, corresponding to first column of X, we get two sets of differential equations. Again each byte of ε and ρ corresponds to one quartet of K^{14}.

For example $\rho_{0,0}$ can be expressed as:

$$
\begin{aligned}
\rho_{0,0} = \big(&14(SB^{-1}(C_{0,0} \oplus K_{0,0}^{14}) \oplus SB^{-1}(C_{1(0,0)}^* \oplus K_{0,0}^{14})) \oplus \\
&11(SB^{-1}(C_{1,3} \oplus K_{1,3}^{14}) \oplus SB^{-1}(C_{1(1,3)}^* \oplus K_{1,3}^{14})) \oplus \\
&13(SB^{-1}(C_{2,2} \oplus K_{2,2}^{14}) \oplus SB^{-1}(C_{1(2,2)}^* \oplus K_{2,2}^{14})) \oplus \\
&9(SB^{-1}(C_{3,1} \oplus K_{3,1}^{14}) \oplus SB^{-1}(C_{1(3,1)}^* \oplus K_{3,1}^{14}))\big)
\end{aligned}
\tag{8.13}
$$

We already know that each of the quartets are independently calculated and produces 2^8 hypotheses. Therefore, the four pairs $(\varepsilon_{0,0}, \rho_{0,0})$, $(\varepsilon_{1,0}, \rho_{1,0})$, $(\varepsilon_{2,0}, \rho_{2,0})$, and $(\varepsilon_{3,0}, \rho_{3,0})$ correspond to four quartets of K^{14} and each having 2^8 values.

In order to solve two sets of differential equations of first column of X, with minimum time complexity, we consider them in pairs. First, we choose two equations, for example from the second set we choose equations corresponding to $X_{0,0}$ and $X_{1,0}$. We guess the values of p corresponding to each choice of $(\rho_{0,0}, \rho_{1,0})$ and derive the possible values of $X_{0,0}, X_{1,0}, \varepsilon_{0,0}$, and $\varepsilon_{1,0}$. We test these values by the corresponding equations in the first set. If they satisfy the relationships they are accepted, otherwise they are rejected. It may be observed that the mapping between a byte of ρ and the corresponding byte of ε is one-to-one, as both the bytes are derived from same key quartet.

Therefore, in the two equations of the second set we guess $2^8 \cdot 2^8 \cdot 2^8 = 2^{24}$ hypotheses for $(\rho_{0,0}, \rho_{1,0}, p)$ which is reduced to 2^{16} hypotheses by corresponding two equations of the first set. Each of these 2^{16} hypotheses are combined with 2^8 hypotheses for $\rho_{2,0}$ in the third equation of the second set and tested by the corresponding equation in the first set. Again, the possible hypotheses reduce to 2^{16}. Then these values are combined with 2^8 hypotheses for $\rho_{3,0}$ in the fourth equation of the second set and verified using the corresponding equation in the first set, which will again reduce the number of possible hypotheses to 2^{16}. Therefore, finally we will have 2^{16} hypotheses for K^{14} each corresponding to one value for $(X_{0,0}, X_{1,0}, X_{2,0}, X_{3,0})$. Throughout the process the time consuming part of the calculation is where 2^{24} hypotheses are made and the rest is negligible. We, therefore, consider the time complexity of this process to be 2^{24}.

It can also be explained in straightforward way. There are eight equations, in which p, p_0', $(X_{0,0}, X_{1,0}, X_{2,0}, X_{3,0})$ and K^{14} are unknown. The total search space of these variables would be 2^{80}. Therefore, the reduced search space produced by these eight equations is $\frac{2^{80}}{(2^8)^8} = 2^{16}$.

In the second phase of the attack we deduce the values of penultimate round key K^{13} corresponding to 2^{16} choices of K^{14}.

8.6.2.2 Second Phase of the Attack on AES-256 States

In order to get the penultimate round key, we consider the last three columns of S_3 in **Fig. 8.15(b)**. For, one choice of K^{14}, the differential equations from the last three columns of S_4 will reduce the number of hypotheses for $(X_{0,1}, X_{1,1}, X_{2,1}, X_{3,1})$, $(X_{0,2}, X_{1,2}, X_{2,2}, X_{3,2})$, and $(X_{0,3}, X_{1,3}, X_{2,3}, X_{3,3})$ to 2^8 for each set. Then we get the last three columns of K^{12} from K^{14} as $K_{i,j}^{12} = K_{i,j}^{14} \oplus K_{i,j-1}^{14}$, where $0 \leq i \leq 3$ and $1 \leq j \leq 3$.

Now from the first column of S_2 we get following four equations:

$$
\begin{aligned}
2\,p' = SB^{-1}\big(&14(SB^{-1}(X_{0,0}) \oplus K_{0,0}^{12}) \oplus 11(SB^{-1}(X_{1,0}) \oplus K_{1,0}^{12}) \oplus \\
&13(SB^{-1}(X_{2,0}) \oplus K_{2,0}^{12}) \oplus 9(SB^{-1}(X_{3,0}) \oplus K_{3,0}^{12})\big) \oplus \\
SB^{-1}\big(&14(SB^{-1}(X_{0,0} \oplus \varepsilon_{0,0}) \oplus K_{0,0}^{12}) \oplus 11(SB^{-1}(X_{1,0} \oplus \varepsilon_{1,3}) \oplus K_{1,0}^{12}) \oplus \\
&13(SB^{-1}(X_{2,0} \oplus \varepsilon_{2,2}) \oplus K_{2,0}^{12}) \oplus 9(SB^{-1}(X_{3,0} \oplus \varepsilon_{3,1}) \oplus K_{3,0}^{12})\big)
\end{aligned}
\tag{8.14}
$$

$$
\begin{aligned}
p' = SB^{-1}\big(&9(SB^{-1}(X_{0,3}) \oplus K_{0,3}^{12}) \oplus 14(SB^{-1}(X_{1,3}) \oplus K_{1,3}^{12}) \oplus \\
&11(SB^{-1}(X_{2,3}) \oplus K_{2,3}^{12}) \oplus 13(SB^{-1}(X_{3,3}) \oplus K_{3,3}^{12})\big) \oplus \\
SB^{-1}\big(&9(SB^{-1}(X_{0,3} \oplus \varepsilon_{0,3}) \oplus K_{0,3}^{12}) \oplus 14(SB^{-1}(X_{1,3} \oplus \varepsilon_{1,2}) \oplus K_{1,3}^{12}) \oplus \\
&11(SB^{-1}(X_{2,3} \oplus \varepsilon_{2,1}) \oplus K_{2,3}^{12}) \oplus 13(SB^{-1}(X_{3,3} \oplus \varepsilon_{3,0}) \oplus K_{3,3}^{12})\big)
\end{aligned}
\tag{8.15}
$$

$$
\begin{aligned}
p' = SB^{-1}\big(&13(SB^{-1}(X_{0,2}) \oplus K_{0,2}^{12}) \oplus 9(SB^{-1}(X_{1,2}) \oplus K_{1,2}^{12}) \oplus \\
&14(SB^{-1}(X_{2,2}) \oplus K_{2,2}^{12}) \oplus 11(SB^{-1}(X_{3,2}) \oplus K_{3,2}^{12})\big) \oplus \\
SB^{-1}\big(&13(SB^{-1}(X_{0,2} \oplus \varepsilon_{0,2}) \oplus K_{0,2}^{12}) \oplus 9(SB^{-1}(X_{1,2} \oplus \varepsilon_{1,1}) \oplus K_{1,2}^{12}) \oplus \\
&14(SB^{-1}(X_{2,2} \oplus \varepsilon_{2,0}) \oplus K_{2,2}^{12}) \oplus 11(SB^{-1}(X_{3,2} \oplus \varepsilon_{3,3}) \oplus K_{3,2}^{12})\big)
\end{aligned}
\tag{8.16}
$$

$$
\begin{aligned}
3\,p' = SB^{-1}\big(&11(SB^{-1}(X_{0,1}) \oplus K_{0,1}^{12}) \oplus 13(SB^{-1}(X_{1,1}) \oplus K_{1,1}^{12}) \oplus \\
&9(SB^{-1}(X_{2,1}) \oplus K_{2,1}^{12}) \oplus 14(SB^{-1}(X_{3,1}) \oplus K_{3,1}^{12})\big) \oplus \\
SB^{-1}\big(&11(SB^{-1}(X_{0,1} \oplus \varepsilon_{0,1}) \oplus K_{0,1}^{12}) \oplus 13(SB^{-1}(X_{1,1} \oplus \varepsilon_{1,0}) \oplus K_{1,1}^{12}) \oplus \\
&9(SB^{-1}(X_{2,1} \oplus \varepsilon_{2,3}) \oplus K_{2,1}^{12}) \oplus 14(SB^{-1}(X_{3,1} \oplus \varepsilon_{3,2}) \oplus K_{3,1}^{12})\big)
\end{aligned}
\tag{8.17}
$$

Each of the above equations requires one column of X and one column of K^{12}. Therefore, the last three equations can be solved as we already know the values of the last three columns of X and K^{12}. In order to reduce the time complexity, we conduct a pairwise analysis. We first choose equations (8.15) and (8.16). We have 2^8 hypotheses for both $(X_{0,3}, X_{1,3}, X_{2,3}, X_{3,3})$ and $(X_{0,2}, X_{1,2}, X_{2,2}, X_{3,2})$. Each of these hypotheses can be evaluated using these two equations that will reduce the value to 2^8 choices. Those which satisfy these equations are combined with the 2^8 choices for $(X_{0,1}, X_{1,1}, X_{2,1}, X_{3,1})$ and further tested by using (8.17) which will again reduce the combined hypotheses of the last three column to 2^8 possibilities. The values of $(X_{0,0}, X_{1,0}, X_{2,0}, X_{3,0})$ are already reduced to one possibility for a particular value of K^{14} in the first phase of the attack. Therefore, this results on 2^8 hypotheses for X. For each of these hypotheses we get the first column of K^{12} and test using (8.14). This will further reduce the number of hypotheses for X to 1. The time complexity here is around 2^{16} as we consider two columns of X.

Therefore, one hypothesis for K^{14} will produce one value for X which in turn produces one value for K^{13} by the following: $K^{13} = MC(SR(X)) \oplus C^{13}$, where C^{13} is the output from the 13th round, which is known to the attacker from the ciphertext C and K^{14} previously ascertained. Hence one hypothesis for K^{14} will produce one hypothesis for K^{13}. Therefore, the 2^{16} hypotheses of K^{14} will produce 2^{16} hypotheses for K^{13}. In which case the total time complexity will be $2^{16} \cdot 2^{16} = 2^{32}$. So, finally we have 2^{16} hypotheses for (K^{13}, K^{14}) which corresponds to 2^{16} hypotheses for the 256-bit master key. Two faulty ciphertexts thus reveal 240-bit of the AES-256 key. The summary of the attack is presented in Algorithm 8.3.

Algorithm 8.3: DFA on AES-256 State

Input: C, C_1^*, C_2^*
Output: List of 256-bit key L_k

1 /* $X_{i,j} = \langle X_{0,j}, X_{1,j}, X_{2,j}, X_{3,j} \rangle$*/;
2 /* $K_{i,j}^{12} = \langle K_{0,j}^{12}, K_{1,j}^{12}, K_{2,j}^{12}, K_{3,j}^{12} \rangle$*/;

3 Solve four sets of equations of S_4 (**Fig. 8.15(a)**) independently.;
4 Get 2^{32} hypotheses for K^{14}.;
5 Solve the two set of equations of $X_{i,0}$.;
6 Get 2^{16} hypotheses for K^{14}.;

7 **for** *each candidate of K^{14}* **do**
8   Guess the possible candidates of $X_{i,1}$, $X_{i,2}$, and $X_{i,3}$;
9   Get the values of $K_{i,1}^{12}$, $K_{i,2}^{12}$, and $K_{i,3}^{12}$ from K^{14};
10   **for** *Each candidate of $X_{i,3}, X_{i,2}, X_{i,1}$* **do**
11   Test second, third and fourth equations of S_2(**Fig. 8.15(b)**);

12   **if** *Satisfied* **then**
13   Get $K_{i,0}^{12}$ from K^{14} and X;
14   Test First equation of S_2 (**Fig. 8.15(b)**) ;

15   **if** *Satisfied* **then**
16   Get K^{13} from X;
17   Get 256-bit key from AES-256 Key Scheduling algorithm;
18   save the 256-bit key to L_k;
19   **end**
20   **end**
21   **end**
22 **end**
23 **return** L_k

8.7   DFA of AES Targeting the Key Schedule

In the previous sections we described how an induced difference at the state of a particular round of AES can be exploited to reveal the secret key. In order to protect AES from such attacks, a designer has to use some countermeasures which will not allow the attacker to induce faults in AES round operations. Even if fault is induced, the attacker will not be able to get the faulty ciphertexts to apply a DFA. Subsequently, the attackers have developed new attacking technique known as DFA on AES key schedule which work even if the rounds of the AES are protected against faults. In this kind of DFAs, faults are induced at the round keys. Therefore, even if the rounds are protected against DFA, the attack will work as the protection will not be able to distinguish between a fault-free round key and a faulty round key.

However, the DFA on AES key schedule are more challenging than DFA on AES state. A difference induced in a round key will spread to more number of bytes in the subsequent round keys during the key schedule operation, which in turn creates more number of unknown variables in the differential equations. Therefore, the differential equations are more complex than the differential equations in a DFA on AES state.

The first complete DFA on AES key schedule was proposed in [88]. The attack was targeted on AES-128 and required less than thirty pairs of fault-free and faulty ciphertexts. This attack was improved in [297] which was based on multi-byte fault model where the faults are injected during the execution of AES key scheduling. The attack retrieved the 128-bit AES key using around 12 pairs of fault-free and faulty ciphertexts. The required number of fault induction in the initial attacks show the complexity of DFA on AES key schedule. An improved attack in [377] showed that a DFA on AES key schedule is possible using two pairs of fault-free and faulty ciphertexts and a brute-force search of 48-bit. Subsequently, there are two more attacks proposed in [198] and [194] using two pairs of fault-free and faulty ciphertexts each. Furher optimized attacks on the AES key schedule was proposed in [26] which required only one pair of fault-free and faulty ciphertexts.

8.7.1 Attack on AES-128 Key Schedule

In this section, we propose a two phase attack which will reduce the AES-128 key space to 2^8 hypotheses using only one faulty ciphertext. The required faulty ciphertext is generated by inducing a single-byte fault in the first column of the eighth round key while it is being generated. Therefore, the induced byte fault is then propagated to subsequent round keys. **Fig. 8.16** shows the flow of this fault as per the AES-128 key schedule. These faulty round keys subsequently corrupt the AES state matrix during the encryption process. The flow of faults in the AES states is shown in **Fig. 8.17**.

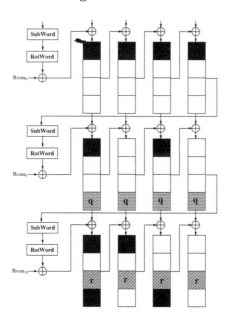

FIGURE 8.16: Flow of faults in AES-128 key schedule

In the first phase of the attack, we reduce the search space of the final round key to 2^{40} hypotheses. In the second phase, we further reduce this search space to 2^8 hypotheses.

8.7.1.1 First Phase of the Attack on AES-128 Key Schedule

The faulty eighth-round key corrupts the AES state matrix during the AddRoundKey operation. **Fig. 8.17** shows that the faults in K^8 corrupts the first row of the state matrix at the input of ninth round. Subsequently, the faults are propagated to all 16 bytes

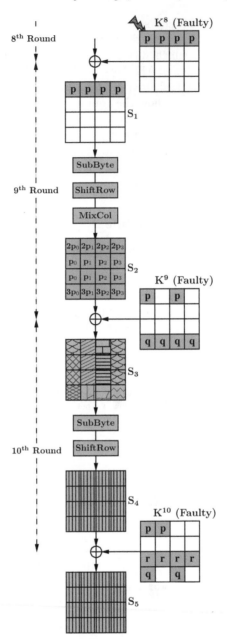

FIGURE 8.17: Flow of faults in the last three rounds of AES-128

in the `MixColumns` operation. The faulty bytes in state matrix S_2 can be represented by the fault-free and faulty ciphertexts C and C^*. The first column S_2 will produce a set of four differential equations similar to equations (8.6) which corresponds to the key quartet $(K_{0,0}^{10}, K_{1,3}^{10}, K_{2,2}^{10}, K_{3,1}^{10})$. Similarly, from other three columns we get three more sets of equations corresponding to key quartets $(K_{0,1}^{10}, K_{1,0}^{10}, K_{2,3}^{10}, K_{3,2}^{10})$, $(K_{0,2}^{10}, K_{1,1}^{10}, K_{2,0}^{10}, K_{3,3}^{10})$, $(K_{0,3}^{10}, K_{1,2}^{10}, K_{2,1}^{10}, K_{3,0}^{10})$. We refer to these four key quartets as K_{q0}, K_{q1}, K_{q2}, and K_{q3} respectively.

It may be observed that unlike the proposed DFA on AES-128, here the number of unknown variable are more. We have p, q, and r as extra unknown variables. Therefore, existing solving techniques will not be applicable to these equations. It may be noted that these three unknown variables are derived from key schedule operation and related by following equations:

$$
\begin{aligned}
q &= S[K_{0,3}^8] \oplus S[K_{0,3}^8 \oplus p] \\
&= S[K_{0,3}^9 \oplus K_{0,2}^9] \oplus S[K_{0,3}^9 \oplus K_{0,2}^9 \oplus p] \qquad (8.18) \\
&= S[K_{0,3}^{10} \oplus K_{0,1}^{10}] \oplus S[K_{0,3}^{10} \oplus K_{0,1}^{10} \oplus p] \\
r &= S[K_{3,3}^9] \oplus S[K_{3,3}^9 \oplus q] \\
&= S[K_{3,3}^{10} \oplus K_{3,2}^{10}] \oplus S[K_{3,3}^{10} \oplus K_{3,2}^{10} \oplus q] \qquad (8.19)
\end{aligned}
$$

In the first three sets of equations there are 8 unknown variables (p, q, r, p_i) and the corresponding quartet of key bytes K_{qi}; where i corresponds to the i-th quartet. We observe that the fourth set of equations does not contain p. In order to get the quartets K_{q0}, K_{q1}, K_{q2} from the first three sets of equations, we need to test all possible 2^{32} values for (p, q, r, p_i). For, each of these hypotheses we get one hypothesis for K_{q0}, K_{q1}, and K_{q2} each. Therefore, for all possible 2^{32} choices we get 2^{32} hypotheses of each of the quartets. In the last set of equations, we have only q, r, and p_3. Therefore, in the last set of equations we get 2^{24} possible hypotheses for K_{q3}. Hence, all the possible choices of K^{10} are given by $(2^{32})^3 \cdot 2^{24} = 2^{120}$ which is not practical.

In order to solve the individual set of equations in practical time we apply a divide-and-conquer technique. We observe that the key bytes $K_{0,3}^{10}, K_{0,1}^{10}, K_{3,2}^{10}, K_{3,3}^{10}$, and (p, q) are also contained in (8.18) and (8.19). Therefore, we can combine these equations with the last three sets of equation corresponding to K_{q1}, K_{q2}, and K_{q3}. This will reduce the possible choices for the corresponding 12 key bytes.

In the first step we test the possible values of (p, q) For, each of these values we guess the 2^8 values of p_1 in the second set of equations. For each (p, q, p_1) we get the values of 3 key bytes $K_{0,1}^{10}, K_{1,0}^{10}$, and $K_{3,2}^{10}$ from the corresponding equations. Therefore, for one value of (p, q) we get 2^8 hypotheses for $(K_{0,1}^{10}, K_{1,0}^{10}, K_{3,2}^{10})$. Similarly, we guess p_3 in fourth set of equations and get 2^8 hypotheses for $(K_{0,3}^{10}, K_{1,2}^{10}, K_{3,0}^{10})$. Therefore, for one hypothesis for (p, q) we get a total of $2^8 \cdot 2^8 = 2^{16}$ hypotheses for 6 key bytes $(K_{0,1}^{10}, K_{1,0}^{10}, K_{3,2}^{10}, K_{0,3}^{10}, K_{1,2}^{10}, K_{3,0}^{10})$. These values are tested by using (8.18), which will reduce the possible values of these 6 key bytes to $\frac{2^{16}}{2^8} = 2^8$ hypotheses.

In the second step, for each hypothesis for the six key bytes, we guess the values of p_2 and get the 3 key bytes $(K_{0,2}^{10}, K_{1,1}^{10}, K_{3,3}^{10})$ from the third set of equations. Therefore, we have a total of $2^8 \cdot 2^8 = 2^{16}$ hypotheses for nine key bytes $(K_{0,1}^{10}, K_{1,0}^{10}, K_{3,2}^{10}, K_{0,3}^{10}, K_{1,2}^{10}, K_{3,0}^{10}, K_{0,2}^{10}, K_{1,1}^{10}, K_{3,3}^{10})$. We use these and get the corresponding values of r from (8.19). Therefore, now using the values of r we can deduce the other 3 key bytes $(K_{2,3}^{10}, K_{2,0}^{10}, K_{2,1}^{10})$ from the corresponding equations in the last three sets of equations. So, in the second step we deduce 2^{16} hypotheses for 12 key bytes from the last 3 sets of equations.

In the third step, we test the 2^8 values for p_0 and get the corresponding choices of the 4 key bytes $\{K_{0,0}^{10}, K_{1,3}^{10}, K_{2,2}^{10}, K_{3,1}^{10}\}$ from the first set of equations. Therefore, in the third step we deduce a total of $2^{16} \cdot 2^8 = 2^{24}$ hypotheses for the 16 key bytes of K^{10} corresponding to one hypothesis for (p, q). Therefore, for all possible 2^{16} hypotheses for (p, q), we will get $2^{24} \cdot 2^{16} = 2^{40}$ hypotheses for K^{40}.

However, the complexity of this attack is still quite high. In our experiments, we found out that for a desktop with an *Intel Core^{TM}2 Duo* processor clocked at 3 GHz speed takes around two and half days to perform brute-force search of 2^{40} possible keys.

8.7.1.2   Second Phase of the Attack on AES-128 Key Schedule

In this phase of the attack we deduce differential equations from the differences in the state matrix S_1 (**Fig. 8.17**). In the first row of the state matrix we have 4-byte differences (p, p, p, p). The faulty byte p at the first column of the state matrix can be represented by:

$$
\begin{aligned}
p = S^{-1}\big[&14(S^{-1}[K_{0,0}^{10} \oplus C_{0,0}] \oplus K_{0,0}^9) \oplus 11(S^{-1}[K_{1,3}^{10} \oplus C_{1,3}] \oplus K_{1,0}^9)\oplus \\
&13(S^{-1}[K_{2,2}^{10} \oplus C_{2,2}] \oplus K_{2,0}^9) \oplus 9(S^{-1}[K_{3,1}^{10} \oplus C_{3,1}] \oplus K_{3,0}^9)\big] \oplus \\
S^{-1}\big[&14(S^{-1}[K_{0,0}^{10} \oplus C_{0,0}^* \oplus p] \oplus (K_{0,0}^9 \oplus p)) \oplus 11(S^{-1}[K_{1,3}^{10} \oplus C_{1,3}^*] \oplus K_{1,0}^9)\oplus \\
&13(S^{-1}[K_{2,2}^{10} \oplus C_{2,2}^* \oplus r] \oplus K_{2,0}^9) \oplus 9(S^{-1}[K_{3,1}^{10} \oplus C_{3,1}^*] \oplus (K_{3,0}^9 \oplus q))\big]
\end{aligned} \tag{8.20}
$$

Similarly, the other three faulty bytes can be expressed by the following:

$$
\begin{aligned}
p = S^{-1}\big[&14(S^{-1}[K_{0,1}^{10} \oplus C_{0,1}] \oplus K_{0,1}^9) \oplus 11(S^{-1}[K_{1,0}^{10} \oplus C_{1,0}] \oplus K_{1,1}^9)\oplus \\
&13(S^{-1}[K_{2,3}^{10} \oplus C_{2,3}] \oplus K_{2,1}^9) \oplus 9(S^{-1}[K_{3,2}^{10} \oplus C_{3,2}] \oplus K_{3,1}^9)\big] \oplus \\
S^{-1}\big[&14(S^{-1}[K_{0,1}^{10} \oplus C_{0,1}^* \oplus p] \oplus (K_{0,1}^9)) \oplus 11(S^{-1}[K_{1,0}^{10} \oplus C_{1,0}^*] \oplus K_{1,1}^9)\oplus \\
&13(S^{-1}[K_{2,3}^{10} \oplus C_{2,3}^* \oplus r] \oplus K_{2,1}^9) \oplus 9(S^{-1}[K_{3,2}^{10} \oplus C_{3,2}^* \oplus q] \oplus (K_{3,1}^9 \oplus q))\big]
\end{aligned} \tag{8.21}
$$

$$
\begin{aligned}
p = S^{-1}\big[&14(S^{-1}[K_{0,2}^{10} \oplus C_{0,2}] \oplus K_{0,2}^9) \oplus 11(S^{-1}[K_{1,1}^{10} \oplus C_{1,1}] \oplus K_{1,2}^9)\oplus \\
&13(S^{-1}[K_{2,0}^{10} \oplus C_{2,0}] \oplus K_{2,2}^9) \oplus 9(S^{-1}[K_{3,3}^{10} \oplus C_{3,3}] \oplus K_{3,2}^9)\big] \oplus \\
S^{-1}\big[&14(S^{-1}[K_{0,2}^{10} \oplus C_{0,2}^*] \oplus (K_{0,2}^9) \oplus p) \oplus 11(S^{-1}[K_{1,1}^{10} \oplus C_{1,1}^*] \oplus K_{1,2}^9)\oplus \\
&13(S^{-1}[K_{2,0}^{10} \oplus C_{2,0}^* \oplus r] \oplus K_{2,2}^9) \oplus 9(S^{-1}[K_{3,3}^{10} \oplus C_{3,3}^*] \oplus (K_{3,2}^9 \oplus q))\big]
\end{aligned} \tag{8.22}
$$

$$
\begin{aligned}
p = S^{-1}\big[&14(S^{-1}[K_{0,3}^{10} \oplus C_{0,3}] \oplus K_{0,3}^9) \oplus 11(S^{-1}[K_{1,3}^{10} \oplus C_{1,3}] \oplus K_{1,3}^9)\oplus \\
&13(S^{-1}[K_{2,1}^{10} \oplus C_{2,1}] \oplus K_{2,3}^9) \oplus 9(S^{-1}[K_{3,0}^{10} \oplus C_{3,0}] \oplus K_{3,3}^9)\big] \oplus \\
S^{-1}\big[&14(S^{-1}[K_{0,3}^{10} \oplus C_{0,3}] \oplus (K_{0,3}^9)) \oplus 11(S^{-1}[K_{1,3}^{10} \oplus C_{1,3}] \oplus K_{1,3}^9)\oplus \\
&13(S^{-1}[K_{2,1}^{10} \oplus C_{2,1} \oplus r] \oplus K_{2,3}^9) \oplus 9(S^{-1}[K_{3,0}^{10} \oplus C_{3,0} \oplus q] \oplus (K_{3,3}^9 \oplus q))\big] \oplus
\end{aligned} \tag{8.23}
$$

In the first phase of the attack we have already reduced p, q, r, and K^{10} to 2^{40} choices. Using these values we can get the 9th round fault-free and faulty outputs. As per the attack on the AES-128 key scheduling algorithm (**Fig. 8.16**), we can directly deduce the 9th round key from the 10th round key. Therefore, for each value of K^{10} we get the corresponding values of K^9 and can test it using the four equations. There are four equations, and the total search space is 2^{40}. Therefore, the four equations reduce the search space to $\frac{2^{40}}{(2^8)^4} = 2^8$. Hence, in the second phase of the attack we have only 2^8 hypotheses for K^{10}. These can then be used to drive 2^8 hypotheses for the master key.

Though the final search space is 2^8, the time complexity of the attack is still 2^{40} since the second phase of the attack still needs to test each of the 2^{40} keys generated from the first phase of the attack.

8.7.1.3   Time Complexity Reduction

In the first phase of the attack, we have four sets of equations corresponding to four key quartets K_{q0}, K_{q1}, K_{q2}, and K_{q3}. These four sets of equations produce 2^{40} values of 16-byte key K^{10}. Each of these keys are tested by four equations in the second phase of the attack. However, none of these equations require all 16 bytes of the key. For example, the first equation required $K_{0,0}^{10}, K_{1,3}^{10}, K_{2,2}^{10}, K_{3,1}^{10}$ and nine more key bytes corresponding to four ninth round key bytes $K_{0,0}^9, K_{1,0}^9, K_{2,0}^9, K_{3,0}^9$. Therefore, in the first equation we need 13 bytes of K^{13}. Similarly, in the rest of the three equations, each requires ten bytes of K^{10}. In the first phase of the attack we use (8.18) and (8.19) since their dependencies are between the key bytes $K^{10}_{0,3}$, $K^{10}_{0,1}$, and $K^{10}_{3,3}$, $K^{10}_{3,2}$.

Therefore, in order to reduce the time complexity of the attack in the second phase we only test one equation at a time. We start with the third equation, as it only requires eleven bytes of K^{10} (ten key bytes plus one for $K^{10}_{0,3}$ since it depends on $K^{10}_{0,1}$ in (8.18)). Those which satisfy this equation are accepted and combined with the other five key bytes, and are subsequently tested using rest of the three equations. Those which do not satisfy these equations are simply discarded.

It is clear from the analysis in Section 8.4.1.3 that the number of unique choices of the eleven key bytes required by the third equation is $\frac{2^{40}}{2^5} = 2^{35}$. Therefore, we need only to test 2^{35} hypotheses out of the 2^{40} possibilities for the 16-byte key. Those which satisfy the test are combined with 2^5 possible hypotheses for the remaining five key bytes and subsequently tested using rest of the three equations. The first test will reduce the possible hypotheses for 11 key bytes to $\frac{2^{35}}{2^8} = 2^{27}$. Therefore, the rest of the three equations are tested using the $2^{27} \cdot 2^5 = 2^{32}$ hypotheses for the 16-byte key, which will reduce the number of hypotheses to $\frac{2^{32}}{(2^8)^3} = 2^8$.

So, finally we get 2^8 hypotheses for K^{10}, and we test a maximum of 2^{35} hypotheses for the key. Therefore, the time complexity of the attack is reduced to 2^{35} from 2^{40}. As a single fault in the AES key schedule is also able to reduce the number of key hypotheses of AES-128 to 2^8 we claim that faults in the AES-128 datapath and key schedule are both equal in terms of leakage of the key (reduction of key space), though the time complexity of the attack is higher for the key schedule. The proposed attack summary is presented in Algorithm 8.4.

Algorithm 8.4: DFA on AES-128 Key Scheduling

Input: C, C^*
Output: List L_k of tenth round key K^{10}

1 **for** *Each candidate of* { p, q } **do**
2   **for** *Each candidate of* (p_1, p_3) **do**
3   Get $(K^{10}_{0,1}, K^{10}_{1,0}, K^{10}_{3,2})$ and $(K^{10}_{0,3}, K^{10}_{1,2}, K^{10}_{3,0})$ from equations of 2nd and 4th column of S_2 (**Fig. 8.17**).;
4   Test equation (8.18);
5   **if** *Satisfied* **then**
6   **for** *Each candidate of* (p_2, p_0) **do**
7   Get $(K^{10}_{0,2}, K^{10}_{1,1}, K^{10}_{3,3})$ from equations of 3rd column of S_2.;
8   Get r from equation (8.19).;
9   Get $(K^{10}_{2,3}, K^{10}_{2,0}, K^{10}_{2,1})$ from equations of last three columns of S_2 .;
10   Get $(K^{10}_{0,0}, K^{10}_{1,3}, K^{10}_{2,2}, K^{10}_{3,1})$ from equations of 1st column of S_2. ;
11   Get K^9 from K^{10} using AES-128 Key Scheduling.;
12   Test third equation of S_1.;
13   **if** *Satisfied* **then**
14   **for** *Each values of* $\{K^{10}_{0,0}, K^{10}_{1,0}, K^{10}_{3,0}, K^{10}_{1,3}, K^{10}_{2,3}\}$ **do**
15   Get K^9 from K^{10} using AES-128 Key Scheduling.;
16   Test rest of the three equations of S_1.;
17   **if** *Satisfied* **then**
18   Save K^{10} to L_k.;
19   **end**
20   **end**
21   **end**
22   **end**
23   **end**
24   **end**
25 **end**

26 **return** L_k

8.7.2 Proposed Attack on AES-192 Key Schedule

In this section, we propose an attack on AES-192 using only two faulty ciphertexts. The most recent attack to date requires around 4 to 6 faulty ciphertexts [194]. Due to the different key scheduling algorithm the attack described above for the AES-128 can not be directly applied to AES-192, since the knowledge of last round key is not sufficient to get the master key. From Algorithm 6 we know that the first two columns of the eleventh round key K^{11} can easily be retrieved from the first three columns of the 12th round key K^{12} by following simple XOR operations since: $K^{11}_{i,j} = K^{12}_{i,j} \oplus K^{12}_{i,j-1}$ where $0 \le i \le 4$ and $0 \le j \le 1$. The last two columns of K^{11} cannot be directly recovered from K^{12}. Therefore, unlike the attack on AES-128, an extra eight byte need to be derived to get the master key.

We propose a two phase attack which requires two faulty ciphertexts C^*_1 and C^*_2. These two faulty ciphertexts are generated by inducing a single-byte fault at two different locations of the first column of the tenth round key. **Fig. 8.18** and **Fig. 8.19** show how these faults propagate in the key schedule.

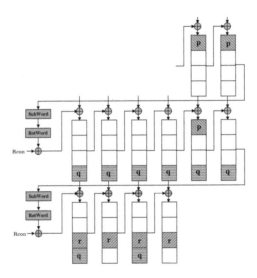

FIGURE 8.18: Flow of Faults in AES-192 Key Schedule when Fault is Induced at $K^{10}_{0,0}$.

The propagation of these fault in the AES-192 state matrix in the last three rounds is shown in **Fig. 8.20(a)** and **Fig. 8.20(b)**. At the input to the eleventh round, state matrix S_1, there is a difference in only four bytes. However, unlike the AES-128, the fault is not propagated to all the bytes at the out put of penultimate round. In **Fig. 8.20(a)** the fault is propagated to only 14 bytes, whereas in **Fig. 8.20(b)** the fault affects 13 bytes in the penultimate round output.

In order to get the last two round keys of AES-192 we again follow a two phase attack strategy. In the first phase of the attack we reduce the final round key to 2^8 choices and in the second phase we first uniquely determine the final round key and then reduce the penultimate round key to 2^{10} possible choices.

8.7.2.1 First Phase of the Attack on AES-192 Key Schedule

In the first phase of the attack we consider the relationship between the fault values at state matrix S_3 (**Fig. 8.20(a)** and **Fig. 8.20(b)**). In **Fig. 8.20(a)**, which corresponds to first faulty ciphertext C^*_1, the first column of state matrix S_2 consists of 2 faulty bytes p_0 and q_0. These 2 faulty bytes will produce a relation $\langle (2p_0 \oplus q_0), (p_0 \oplus q_0), (p_0 \oplus 3q_0), (3p_0 \oplus 2q_0) \rangle$

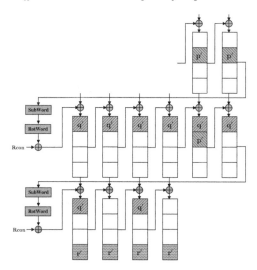

FIGURE 8.19: Flow of Faults in AES-192 Key Schedule when Fault is Induced at $K_{1,0}^{10}$.

at the output of MixColumns (in S_3). Therefore, this relation will produce four equations similar to equations (8.6). In the same way, from the rest of the three columns of S_3 we get $\langle 2p_1, p_1, p_1, 3p_1 \rangle$, $\langle 0, 0, 0, 0 \rangle$, and $\langle q_1, q_1, 3q_1, 2q_1 \rangle$. Using second and fourth relations we get two more sets of equations. However, from the third relation which does not have any difference, we get a set of two equations corresponding to fault value p and q in K^{11}. It may be observed that the third byte of this relation is zero. Therefore, from this value we can get $r = C_{2,0} \oplus C_{1(2,0)}^*$.

Similarly, from the four columns of S_3 of **Fig. 8.20(b)**, we get relations $\langle 3p_0', 2p_0', p_0', p_0' \rangle$, $\langle 0, 0, 0, 0 \rangle$, $\langle 2q_0, q_0, q_0, 3q_0 \rangle$, and $\langle (2q_1 \oplus 3p_1), (q_1 \oplus 2p_1), (q_1 \oplus p_1), (3q_1 \oplus p_1) \rangle$. These four relations will produce four more sets of equations. Each of these sets of equations corresponds to one key quartet of twelfth round key K^{12}. Like the previous attack we also name these quartets K_{q0}, K_{q1}, K_{q2}, and K_{q3} respectively.

Therefore, each faulty ciphertext produces four sets of equations. These sets of equations are not mutually independent, and are related by two variables. For the faulty ciphertext C_1^*, the variables are (q, r) whereas for faulty ciphertext C_2^*, the variables are (q', r'). As with the propagation of faults in the AES-192 key schedule, the variables r and r' can be deduced from q and q' respectively (**Fig. 8.18** and **Fig. 8.19**). They are related by following equation:

$$r = S(K_{3,3}^{11}) \oplus S(K_{3,3}^{11} \oplus q) \tag{8.24a}$$

$$r' = S(K_{0,3}^{11}) \oplus S(K_{0,3}^{11} \oplus q') \tag{8.24b}$$

Similarly, q and q' are related to p and p' by following equations:

$$q = S(K_{1,3}^{11} \oplus K_{1,2}^{11}) \oplus S(K_{1,3}^{11} \oplus K_{1,2}^{11} \oplus p) \tag{8.25a}$$

$$q' = S(K_{0,3}^{11} \oplus K_{0,2}^{11}) \oplus S(K_{0,3}^{11} \oplus K_{0,2}^{11} \oplus p') \tag{8.25b}$$

Then r and r' can directly be calculated from the ciphertexts C_1^* and C_2^* as $r = C_{2,0} \oplus C_{1(2,0)}^*$ and $r' = C_{2,0} \oplus C_{2(2,0)}^*$. Now to solve the eight sets of equations we guess the values of (q, q'). We start with two sets of equations corresponding to quartet K_{q0}. In the second set of equations, for one hypothesis for (q, q') we get 2^8 hypotheses for the quartet K_{q0}

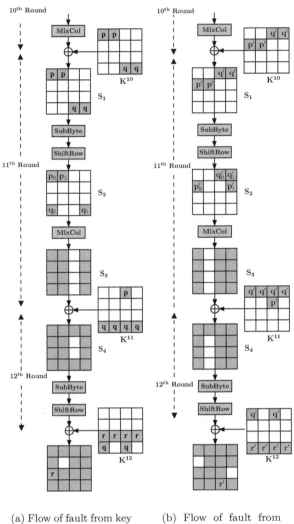

(a) Flow of fault from key byte $K_{0,0}^{10}$

(b) Flow of fault from key byte K_{10}^{10}

FIGURE 8.20: Flow of faults in the last three rounds of AES-192

corresponding to 2^8 hypotheses for p_1'. Therefore, for all possible values of (q, q') we get 2^{24} hypotheses for K_{q0}. Each of these hypotheses are tested using the first set of equations.

There are eight equations in the two sets corresponding to quartet K_{q0}, that contain nine unknown variables; namely q, q', p_0, p_3, p_1' and the quartet K_{q0}. Therefore, the reduced search space is given by $(2^8)^{9-8} = 2^8$. This implies that out of 2^{24} choices of q, q', K_{q0}, only 2^8 choices satisfy both the sets of equations.

Next we derive the second quartet K_{q1} from its corresponding two sets of equations. We can directly deduce the values of $K_{0,1}^{12}$ corresponding to the values of q' in second set of equations. These values can be used in the first set of equations to get the corresponding values of $2p_1$ and p_1. Using these values we can derive the three key bytes $K_{1,0}^{12}, K_{2,3}^{12}, K_{3,2}^{12}$ from the remaining three equations of the first set.

This gives an expected 2^8 hypotheses for (q, q') from the previous step. Each of these hypotheses will give one expected hypothesis for $K_{0,1}^{12}$, which in turn give one expected hypothesis for the three key bytes $K_{1,0}^{12}, K_{2,3}^{12}, K_{3,2}^{12}$. Therefore, the 2^8 hypotheses for (q, q', K_{q0}) will produce 2^8 hypotheses for the quartet K_{q1}, giving 2^8 hypotheses for (q, q', K_{q0}, K_{q1}).

For the third quartet, K_{q2}, we can apply the same approach and one hypotheses for $K_{3,3}^{12}$ corresponding to one hypotheses for q from its first set of equations. This value will in turn allow a hypothesis for $K_{0,2}^{12}$ and $K_{2,0}^{12}$ from the first and third equations of the second set. However, p' is unknown. Therefore, we have to consider all possible 2^8 hypotheses for p' which in turn produces 2^8 hypotheses for $K_{1,1}^{12}$. This implies, for one hypothesis for q we get 2^8 hypotheses for the third quartet K_{q2}. From the previous steps we have 2^8 hypotheses for q. Therefore, in this step, we get 2^{16} hypotheses for $(q, q', K_{q0}, K_{q1}, K_{q2})$.

In the next step we consider fourth quartet K_{q3}. The two sets of equations are similar to the two sets of equations corresponding to quartet K_{q0}. Therefore, for one hypothesis for q we get 2^8 hypotheses for the quartet K_{q3} from the first set of equations. Each of these are tested using the second set of equations. We have nine variables in the two sets of differential equations in which we choose the values of q and q' from the 5-tuple $(q, q', K_{q0}, K_{q1}, K_{q2})$. Therefore, the total number for resulting hypotheses is $(2^8)^7 \cdot 2^{16} = (2^8)^9$. We have eight equations in two sets, which will reduce the hypotheses to $(2^8)^{9-8} = 2^8$ for the 6-tuple $(q, q', K_{q0}, K_{q1}, K_{q2}), K_{q2})$. Therefore, in the first phase of the attack, we have 2^8 choices of the final round key K^{12}.

8.7.2.2 Second Phase of the Attack on AES-192 Key Schedule

In the second phase of the attack, we define differential equations based on the relationship between the faulty bytes in state matrix S_1. The fault values (p, q) and (p', q') in S_1 of (**Fig. 8.20(a)** and **Fig. 8.20(b)**) will give eight differential equations. Each of these equations corresponds to one column of K^{11}. Using AES-192 key scheduling algorithm we can directly define the first two columns K^{11} from K^{12} as $K_{i,j}^{11} = K_{i,j}^{12} \oplus K_{i,j-1}^{12}$ for $0 \leq i \leq 3$ and $0 \leq j \leq 1$.

The values of p can be deduced from K^{12} using equation $p = S^{-1}(K_{0,2}^{12} \oplus C_{0,2}) \oplus S^{-1}(K_{0,2}^{12} \oplus C_{1(0,2)}^*)$. Therefore, $p, K_{q0}, K_{q1}, K_{i,0}^{11}$, and $K_{i,1}^{11}$ can be directly derived from K^{12} where $0 \leq i \leq 3$. There is an expected 2^8 hypotheses for K^{12} from the first phase of the attack. We consider the two equations corresponding to two values of p in S_1. In these two equations the search space is 2^8, which can be reduced to $\frac{2^8}{2^{16}} = \frac{1}{2^8}$. One would expect that only one value will satisfy both the equations leaving one hypotheses for K^{12}.

An attacker can then deduce the fourth column $K_{i,3}^{11}$. The 2 bytes $K_{0,3}^{11}$ and $K_{3,3}^{11}$ of the fourth column can directly be calculated using equations (8.24a) and (8.24b). For one hypothesis for (q, r, q', r'), we get four hypotheses for $(K_{0,3}^{11}, K_{3,3}^{11})$. The other two key bytes, $K_{1,3}^{11}$ and $K_{2,3}^{11}$, can be derived from three more differential equations from S_1. The faulty byte q in the fourth column of S_1 (**Fig. 8.20(a)**), p' in the first column and q' in the fourth column of S_1 (**Fig. 8.20(b)**), will produce equations which correspond to $K_{i,3}^{11}$. In these equations only $K_{1,3}^{11}$ and $K_{2,3}^{11}$ are unknown, and the possible values for key bytes $K_{0,3}^{11}, K_{3,3}^{11}$ had already been reduced to an expected four hypotheses. One would expect that these will allow one hypothesis for $K_{i,3}^{11}$ to be determined (two hypotheses will remain with probability $\frac{2^{18}}{(2^8)^3} = \frac{1}{2^6}$).

For the third column of K^{11}, we can get the values of two key bytes $K_{0,2}^{11}$ and $K_{1,2}^{11}$ from (8.25a) and (8.25b). However, for one value for $K_{0,3}^{11}, K_{1,3}^{11}, q, q'$ we get two hypotheses for $K_{0,2}^{11}$ from (8.25a) and two hypotheses for $K_{1,2}^{11}$ from (8.25b) giving a total of four hypotheses. For key bytes $K_{2,2}^{11}$ and $K_{3,2}^{11}$ we can only determine one equation, i.e., from q' at the third column of S_1 (**Fig. 8.20(b)**). This gives an expected four hypotheses for $(K_{2,2}^{11}, K_{3,2}^{11})$ and 2^{16} hypotheses for $(K_{2,2}^{11}, K_{2,3}^{11})$. Therefore, the resulting number of expected hypotheses is $\frac{2^{16} \cdot 4}{2^8} = 2^{10}$. So, finally we get an expected 2^{10} hypotheses for $K_{i,2}^{12}$, implying the expected hypotheses for K^{11} is reduced to 2^{10}.

Therefore, the two phase attack on AES-192 using two faulty ciphertexts can reduce a 192-bit key to 2^{10} hypotheses. The above attack is one of the most efficient attack on the AES-192 key schedule to date and is summarized in Algorithm 8.5.

Algorithm 8.5: DFA on AES-192 Key Scheduling

Input: C, C_1^*, C_2^*
Output: List L_k of (K^{11}, K^{12})

1 Get r and r' from C, C_1^*, C_2^*.;
2 Derive equations from S_3 of **Fig. 8.20(a)** and **Fig. 8.20(b)**.;
3 **for** *Each candidate of (q, q', p')* **do**
4   Get $K_{q0}, K_{q1}, K_{q2}, K_{q3}$ by solving corresponding two sets of equations of S_3.;
5   Get K^{12} from K_{q0}, K_{q1}, K_{q2}, and K_{q3}.;
6   **for** *Each candidate of K^{12}* **do**
7   Get $K_{i,0}^{11}$ and $K_{i,1}^{11}$ (two columns of K^{11}).;
8   Test two equations of p of S_1.;
9   **if** *Satisfied* **then**
10   Save (p, p', q, q', K^{12}).;
11   **end**
12   **end**
13 **end**
14 Get $K_{0,3}^{11}$ and $K_{3,3}^{11}$ from equations (8.24a) and (8.24b).;
15 **for** *Each candidate of $(K_{0,3}^{11}, K_{3,3}^{11})$* **do**
16   Get $K_{1,3}^{11}$, and $K_{2,3}^{11}$ from equations of q, p' and q' of S_1.;
17   Get $K_{0,2}^{11}$ and $K_{1,2}^{11}$ from equations (8.25a) and (8.25b).;
18   **for** *Each candidate of $(K_{0,2}^{11}, K_{1,2}^{11})$* **do**
19   Get $K_{2,2}^{11}$ and $K_{3,2}^{11}$ from equations of q' of S_1.;
20   Save (K^{11}, K^{12}) to L_k.;
21   **end**
22 **end**
23 **return** L_k

8.7.3   Proposed Attack on AES-256 Key Schedule

In this section, we present a two-phase attack on AES-256 to uniquely determine the secret key. The attack requires three faulty ciphertexts, that we will refer to as C_1, C_2, and C_3. The first two faulty ciphertexts C_1 and C_2 are generated by inducing a single byte fault in the first column of twelfth round key (**Fig. 8.21**). The third faulty ciphertext C_3 is generated by inducing fault in the first column of the eleventh round key (**Fig. 8.22**). **Fig. 8.23(a)** and **Fig. 8.23(b)** show how the fault propagates in the AES state matrix.

In the first phase of the attack we uniquely determine the 14-th round key K^{14} using C_1 and C_2. In the second phase of the attack we uniquely determine the penultimate round key K^{13} using C_3.

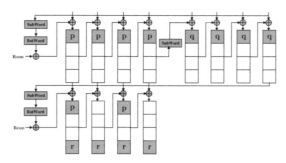

FIGURE 8.21: Flow of Faults in AES-256 Key Schedule when the Fault is Induced at $K_{0,0}^{12}$

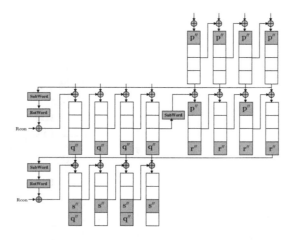

FIGURE 8.22: Flow of Faults in AES-256 Key Schedule when the Fault is Induced at $K_{0,0}^{11}$

8.7.3.1 First Phase of the Attack of AES-256 Key Schedule

In the first phase of the attack, we deduce the differential equations from the relationship between the faulty bytes in state matrix S_3 (**Fig. 8.23(a)**). From the first column of S_3 we get relation $\langle 2p_0, p_0, p_0, 3p_0 \rangle$, which corresponds to C_1. Similarly, from C_2 we get $\langle 2p_0', p_0', p_0', 3p_0' \rangle$. These two relations will give two sets of equations. Therefore, together we get eight sets of equations, each set corresponds to the one quartet of key bytes. As with the previously described attacks, we refer to these quartets as K_{q0}, K_{q1}, K_{q2}, and K_{q3}. There are two sets of equations each corresponding to a quartet. In order to use these sets of equations, we need to guess the values of p, q, r, p_i and p', q', r', p_i', where i corresponds to the i-th quartet. In which case the total possible hypotheses is $(2^8)^8 = 2^{64}$, which would make an exhaustive search impossible. We apply a divide-and-conquer strategy to these equations.

The second and third equation of each set of equations contain only two unknown variables except the key bytes. Therefore, we can directly solve these equations by guessing the values of p_i and p_i'. For example we guess p_0 in the first set of equations of K_{q0} and derive 2^8 hypotheses for $(K_{1,3}^{14}, K_{2,2}^{14})$. Each of these hypotheses are tested using corresponding equations in the second set of equations of K_{q0}. Those which satisfy these equations are accepted and rest are discarded. There are four equations and four unknowns $(K_{1,3}^{14}, K_{2,2}^{14}, p_0, p_0')$, so one would expect one hypothesis to remain.

Similarly, we can uniquely determine the values of $(K_{1,0}^{14}, K_{2,3}^{14})$, $(K_{1,1}^{14}, K_{2,0}^{14})$, and

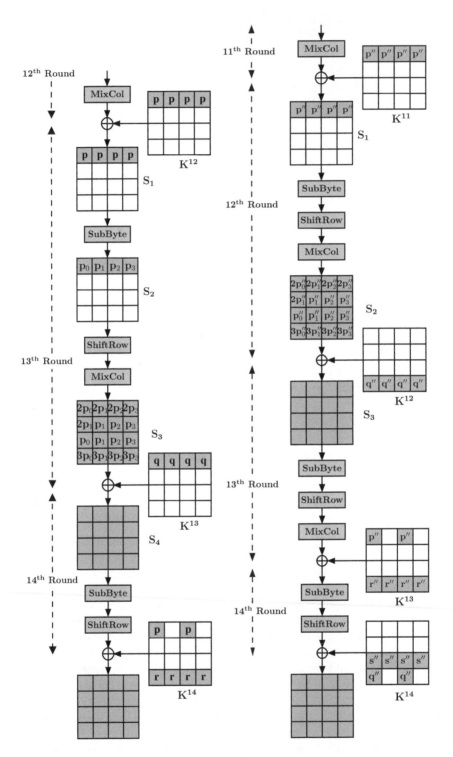

(a) Flow of faults from key byte $K_{0,0}^{12}$ (b) Flow of faults from key byte $K_{0,0}^{11}$

FIGURE 8.23: Flow of faults in the AES-256 rounds

$(K_{1,2}^{14}, K_{2,1}^{14})$, and the corresponding values of $p_1, p_2, p_3, p_1', p_2'$, and p_3' from the second and third equations of two sets of equations of K_{q1}, K_{q2}, K_{q3}. Next, we guess the values of r and r'. For each hypothesis, we get one hypothesis for $K_{3,1}^{14}$ using fourth equation of two sets of equations of K_{q0}. Similarly, we get the values $K_{3,2}^{14}, K_{3,3}^{14}$, and $K_{3,0}^{14}$ corresponding to other three key quartets. There are eight equations and six unknown variables (namely r, r', and four key bytes) so an attacker should be able to determine these bytes.

An attacker would then only need to solve the first equation of each of the eight sets of equations. In these equations we have eight unknown variable (q, p, q', p'), and the four key bytes. As per **Fig. 8.21**, q and q' can be derived from p and p' using the following:

$$q = S(K_{0,3}^{13} \oplus K_{0,2}^{13}) \oplus S(K_{0,3}^{13} \oplus K_{0,2}^{13} \oplus p) \qquad (8.26)$$

$$q' = S(K_{0,3}^{13} \oplus K_{0,2}^{13}) \oplus S(K_{0,3}^{13} \oplus K_{0,2}^{13} \oplus p') \qquad (8.27)$$

Similarly, r, r' can be deduced from q, q' using the following:

$$r = S(K_{3,3}^{14} \oplus K_{3,2}^{14}) \oplus S(K_{3,3}^{14} \oplus K_{3,2}^{14} \oplus q) \qquad (8.28)$$

$$r' = S(K_{3,3}^{14} \oplus K_{3,2}^{14}) \oplus S(K_{3,3}^{14} \oplus K_{3,2}^{14} \oplus q') \qquad (8.29)$$

The values of $r, r', K_{3,3}^{14}$, and $K_{3,2}^{14}$ are already known from the previous steps. Therefore, we get the values of q, and q' from (8.28) and (8.29). Therefore, an attacker would only need to guess the values of p and p' to get the values of $K_{0,0}^{14}, K_{0,1}^{14}, K_{0,2}^{14}$, and $K_{0,3}^{14}$ from the corresponding sets of equations. There are eight equations and six unknown variables, which implies that an attacker would be able to determine p, p' and $K_{0,0}^{14} K_{0,1}^{14}, K_{0,2}^{14}, K_{0,3}^{14}$.

Therefore, finally we have one choice of p, p', q, q', r, r', and K^{14} using two faulty ciphertexts C_1^* and C_2^*.

8.7.3.2 Second Phase of th Attack of AES-256 Key Schedule

In the second phase of the attack, we use a third faulty ciphertext produced by a one byte fault in the first column of the 11th round key, as shown in **Fig. 8.22**. The propagation of the fault in the last three rounds is shown in **Fig. 8.23(b)**. In order to reduce the number of hypotheses for K^{13} we use the relationship between the faulty byte in the 13th round. As we have the 14th round key, we can decrypt one round and get the output of the 13th round for a fault-free and faulty outputs. We define the output of the 13th round of C, C_1^*, and C_2^* as C^{13}, C_1^{13*}, and C_2^{13*} respectively. In case of the third faulty ciphertext C_3^* we cannot compute the output of the 13th round as the values of q'' and s'' in the final round key are not known.

Therefore, we follow the technique proposed in Section 8.6.2.1. Let X be the fault-free output of the 13th round SubBytes operation and ϵ be the corresponding fault value. Therefore, ϵ can be written as

$$\epsilon = SR^{-1}\Big(MC^{-1}\Big(SR^{-1}(SB^{-1}(C \oplus K^{14})) \oplus$$

$$SR^{-1}(SB^{-1}(C_3^* \oplus K^{14*})) \oplus (K^{13} \oplus K^{13*})\Big)\Big)$$

where K^{14*} and K^{13*} are the 14th and 13th round faulty keys used to generate faulty ciphertext C_3. K^{14} is already known to us. Therefore, in order to get K^{14*} and $(K^{13} \oplus K^{13*})$ we need to know the values of p'', q'', r'', and s''. However, as per **Fig. 8.22**, r'' can be directly deduced from K^{14} and q'' by the following equation:

$$r'' = S(K_{3,3}^{12}) \oplus S(K_{3,3}^{12} \oplus q'')$$
$$= S(K_{3,3}^{14} \oplus K_{3,2}^{14}) \oplus S(K_{3,3}^{14} \oplus K_{3,2}^{14} \oplus q'') \qquad (8.30)$$

Therefore, now we need to guess p'', q'', and s'' to get the possible hypotheses for ϵ.

The possible fault values in the first column of S_2 (**Fig. 8.23(b)**) can be represented in terms of first column of X and ϵ which will produce four differential equations. Similarly, from the rest of the three columns of S_2 we get three more sets of equations. The values for $X_{0,0}, X_{0,1}, X_{0,2}, X_{0,3}$ can also be represented by the faulty ciphertexts C_1^* and C_2^*. In **Fig. 8.23(a)**, the first row of S_1 can be expressed in terms of $(X_{0,0}, X_{0,1}, X_{0,2}, X_{0,3})$, (p_0, p_1, p_2, p_3), which will produce a set of four differential equations. Similar, equations can also be generated from C_2^*.

In these eight equations, only $X_{0,0}, X_{0,1}, X_{0,2}, X_{0,3}$ are unknown; the rest of the variables have been determined in the first phase of the attack. Therefore, using these equations we can uniquely determine the values of $X_{0,0}, X_{0,1}, X_{0,2}, X_{0,3}$. It may be noted that these 4 bytes of X correspond to the first equations of the four sets of equations generated from S_2 (**Fig. 8.23(b)**). We use the four bytes of X; and get the corresponding values of $2\,p_0''$, $2\,p_1''$, $2\,p_2''$, $2\,p_3''$. If we multiply these values with the inverse of 2 we get the corresponding values of p_0'', p_1'', p_2'', and p_3''.

We have 2^{24} choices of ϵ corresponding to the all possible values of p'', q'', and s''. For, each possible value of ϵ we will get one hypothesis for the quartet of X from each of the four sets of equations. Therefore, from all the four sets of equations we get one hypothesis for X corresponding to one hypothesis for ϵ. Therefore, we expect to have 2^{24} hypotheses for X corresponding to 2^{24} hypotheses for ϵ.

In the next step, we deduce four differential equations corresponding to four faulty bytes p'', p'', p'', p'', in S_1 (**Fig. 8.23(b)**) as described in Section 8.6.2.2. Each of these four equations requires one column of the twelfth round key K^{12}. The last three columns of K^{12} can be computed from K^{14} as $K_{i,j}^{12} = K_{i,j}^{14} \oplus K_{i,j-1}^{14}$ where $0 \le i \le 4$ and $1 \le j \le 3$. Therefore, we can test each value of X using the last three of the four equations which corresponds to last three columns of K^{12}. The value of p'' is already known while considering ε.

There are 2^{24} values of X in the three equations that will be expected to be reduced to one hypothesis, since $\frac{2^{24}}{(2^8)^3} = 1$. In some cases there could be more than one remaining hypothesis for X satisfying the last three equations. In which case the false hypotheses can be eliminated since $K^{13} = (MC(SR(X)) \oplus C^{13})$. Using the value of K^{13} and K^{14} we verify these hypotheses using the key schedule.

The described attack would determine K^{13} and K^{14} allowing the 256-bit master key of AES-256 using three faulty ciphertexts. The summary of the attack is given in Algorithm 8.6.

8.8 DFA countermeasures

In this section, we present an overview on some popular countermeasure techniques against Differential Fault Attacks. The faults which are more useful for DFA are transient in nature, as they die away and does not exist after a time instance. Thus there detection is more tricky, as opposed to permanent faults. As observed in the previous sections, the attacks exploit some properties in the fault propagations. Hence, the countermeasures are built to prevent this access of the faulty ciphertext to the adversary by two methods: *detection*, and *infection*.

Algorithm 8.6: DFA on AES-256 Key Scheduling

Input: C, C_1^*, C_2^*, C_3^*
Output: List L_k of (K^{13}, K^{14})

1 Derive equations from S_3 (**Fig. 8.23(a)**) corresponding to C_1^*, and (**Fig. 8.23(b)**) corresponding to C_2^*.;

2 Solve 2nd and 3rd equations corresponding to each quartet of key.;

3 Determine 2nd and 3rd bytes of each quartets and p_i, p_i' $(0 \leq i \leq 3)$.;

4 **for** *Each candidate of* (r, r') **do**

5   Solve equations of (r, r') of S_3.;

6   **if** *Solution found* **then**

7   Save (r, r') and 4th bytes of each quartets.

8   **end**

9 **end**

10 Get q and q' from equations (8.28) and (8.29).;

11 **for** *Each candidate of* (p, p') **do**

12   Solve equations of (p, p') of S_3.;

13   **if** *Solution found* **then**

14   Save (p, p') and 1st bytes of each quartets.

15   **end**

16 **end**

17 Get K^{14} from K_{q0}, K_{q1}, K_{q2}, and K_{q3},;

18 Derive two sets of equations of X from (p, p') of S_1.;

19 Determine $X_{0,0}, X_{0,1}, X_{0,2}, X_{0,3}$ by solving these equations.;

20 Derive equations of X from S_2(**Fig. 8.23(b)**);

21 **for** *Each candidate of* (p'', q'', s'') **do**

22   Determine ϵ;

23   Determine P_i'' from $X_{0,i}$ $(0 \leq i \leq 3)$;

24   Determine X from equations of S_2(**Fig. 8.23(b)**);

25   Get $K_{i,j}^{12}$ from K^{14} $(1 \leq j \leq 3)$;

26   Test last three equations of P'' of S_1(**Fig. 8.23(b)**);

27   **if** *Satisfied* **then**

28   Get $K_{i,0}^{12}$ from X and K^{14};

29   Test first equation of P'' of S_1(**Fig. 8.23(b)**);

30   **if** *Satisfied* **then**

31   Get K^{13} from X.;

32   Save (K^{13}, K^{14}).;

33   **end**

34   **end**

35 **end**

36 **return** L_k

The detection mechanisms rely on specialized circuits, which are called as *concurrent error detection* (CED) [364], which identifies a faulty computation through several redundancy techniques. For example, the detection countermeasure is usually implemented by duplicating the computation and finally comparing the results of two computations. When a fault is thus detected, the adversary prevents the faulty ciphertext from being exposed to the adversary. But in this countermeasure, the comparison step itself is prone to fault attacks. The infection countermeasure on the other hand, aims to destroy the fault invariant by diffusing the effect of a fault in such a way that it renders the faulty ciphertext unexploitable. Infection countermeasures are preferred to detection as they avoid the use of attack vulnerable operations such as comparison.

We first provide an overview on the four types of redundancy which are used to buid CED based countermeasures agonst DFA.

8.8.1 Hardware Redundancy

Hardware redundancy duplicates the function and detects faults by comparing the outputs of two copies.

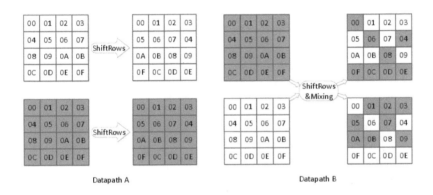

Datapath A   Datapath B

FIGURE 8.24: Datapath mixing

In [170], the authors propose a novel hardware-redundancy technique for AES to detect faults. Because an attacker can potentially inject the same faults to both of the AES circuits, the straightforward hardware redundancy can be bypassed by the attacker. Furthermore, in case of implementations where the Key-Schedule is done prior to the encryption and is stored in a memory may not be protected by such countermeasures. This is because the faults can target the memory storing the key, and thus the hardware redundancy checks will miss the fault induction as repeating the encryption will yield the same result each time!

As shown in **Fig. 8.24**, the idea is to mix byte states between the operations in two pieces of hardware, in different ways and at different locations. Because the entire hardware is duplicated, hardware redundancy has low performance overhead, and the hardware overhead is approximately 200%.

To reduce the hardware overhead, [270] proposes a partial hardware-redundancy technique as shown in **Fig. 8.25**. This technique focuses on parallel AES architecture and S-box protection. The idea is to add an additional S-box to every set of four S-boxes, and perform two tests of every S-box per encryption cycle (10 rounds). Although the hardware overhead is reduced to 26%, this process has a fault coverage of 25% at a certain clock cycle, because it can only check one S-box among every four in one clock cycle.

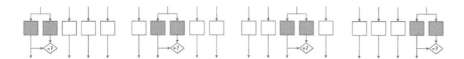

FIGURE 8.25: Partial hardware redundancy.

8.8.2 Time Redundancy

Time redundancy computes the same input twice using the same function and compares the results.

In [236], the authors propose time redundancy with a Double-Data-Rate (DDR) mechanism. The pipelined AES data path logic is partitioned into two classes, where non-adjacent stages in the pipeline are driven by two opposite clock signals. The DDR architecture allows us to halve the number of clock cycles per round, though maybe with a light impact on clock frequency as compared to a design without protection. This takes advantage of the free cycles for recomputing the round on the same hardware. Two successive round operation outputs obtained from two copies of the same input data are checked for possible mismatches. It shows an almost maximal fault coverage on the datapath at the cost of 36% hardware overhead. Under some conditions, this technique allows the encryption to be computed twice without affecting the global throughput. However, this technique becomes difficult to implement as technology scales.

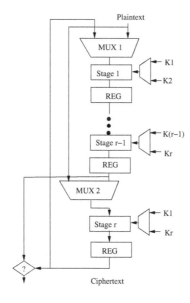

FIGURE 8.26: Slid CED Architecture for Time Redundancy

A technique that is suited for any pipeline-based block cipher design is proposed in [311] (**Fig. 8.26**). The key idea is to use different pipeline stages to check against each other by *sliding* the computations from one stage to another. The attack is based on the popular *slide attack* [51]. Let us assume the pipeline has r stages, denoted as R_i, $1 \leq i \leq r$. In the normal computation, the plaintext will be computed by the first stage and then the second stage and so on. The rth stage will produce the ciphertext. Consider two successive encryptions with the same key, K, with the round keys denoted as $K_1, K_2, \ldots, K_r$. The first encryption is on a plaintext P, and the ciphertext is hence $C = Enc(P, K)$. The intermediate state after the first round of the first encryption is $P' = R_1(P, K_1)$. When the first round is operating, at the same time the plaintext is encrypted redundantly by the last stage of the pipeline, which is otherwise idle at this instance. The result P' (if there is no fault) is fed back by the multiplexer (MUX-1 in **Fig. 8.26**) to the first stage of the pipeline and is encrypted with the round key K_2. Thus at the same time instance two different redundant encryptions are getting operated. This continues and when the ciphertext C is produced by the rth stage, the $(r-1)^{th}$ stage produces $C' = R_{r-1}(R_{r-2}(\ldots(R_1(P', K_2), \ldots, K_{r-1})K_r))$. It is trivial to check if there is no fault, then $C = C'$, which is checked by the comparator. Compared to the original design, this CED provides a throughput of 50-90.0% percent, depending on the frequency of the redundant check from every one to ten rounds (in case of AES-128). Hardware overhead is only 2.3% percent.

8.8.3 Information Redundancy

In order to reduce the overheads of the above redundancy techniques, information redundancy methods are developed. Information redundancy techniques rely on error detecting codes (EDC). A few check bits are generated from the input message which propagate along with the input message and are finally validated when the output message is generated. Parity code and robust code are proposed for CED in various research [45, 258, 187, 260, 259, 188, 190].

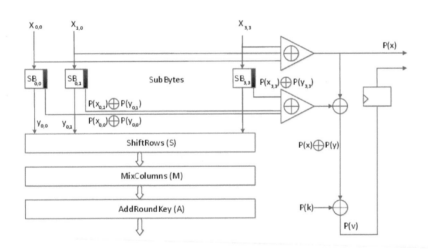

FIGURE 8.27: Parity-1 CED.

8.8.3.1 Parity-1

A technique in which a parity bit is used for the entire 128-bit state matrix is developed in [412]. The parity bit is checked once for the entire round as shown in **Fig. 8.27**. This approach targets low-cost CED. Parity-1 is based on a general CED design for Substitution Permutation Networks (SPN) [179], in which the input parity of SPN is modified according to its processing steps into the output parity and compared with the output parity of every round. The authors adapt this general approach to develop a low-cost CED. First, they determine the parity of the 128-bit input using a tree of XOR gates. Then for the nonlinear S-box, inversion in $GF(2^8)$ and a linear affine transformation. They add one additional binary output to each of the 16 S-boxes. This additional S-box output computes the parity of every 8-bit input and the parity of the corresponding 8-bit output.

Each of the modified S-boxes is 8-bit by 9-bit. The additional single-bit outputs of the 16 S-boxes are used to modify the input parity for SubBytes. Because ShiftRows implements a permutation, it does not change the parity of the entire state matrix from its input to output. MixColumns does not change the parity of the state matrix from inputs to outputs either. Moreover, MixColumns does not change the parity of each column. Finally, the bitwise XOR of the 128-bit round key needs a parity modification by a single precomputed parity bit of the round key. Because the output of a round is the input to the next round, the output parity of a round can be computed with the same hardware for computing the input parity of the previous round.

Although this technique has only 22.3% hardware overhead, it has 48%-53% fault coverage for multiple bit random fault model.

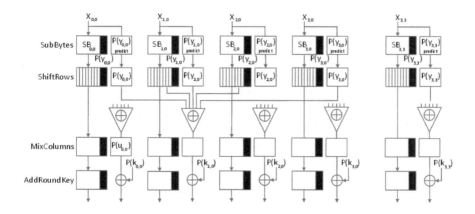

FIGURE 8.28: Parity-16 CED.

8.8.3.2 Parity-16

Parity-16 is first proposed in [45]. In this technique, each predicted parity bit is generated from an input byte. Then, the predicted parity bits and actual parity bits of output are compared to detect the faults.

In [45], the authors propose the use of a parity bit that is associated with each byte of the state matrix of a 128-bit iterated hardware implementation with LUT-based S-boxes as shown in **Fig. 8.28**. Predicted parity bits on S-box outputs are stored as additional bits in the ROMs (nine bits instead of eight in the original S-boxes). In order to detect errors in the memory, the authors propose increasing each S-box to 9-bit by 9-bit in such a way that all the ROM words addressed with a wrong input address (i.e. S-boxes input with a wrong associated parity), deliberately store values with a wrong output parity so that the CED will detect the fault. As before, the parity bit associated with each byte is not affected by ShiftRows. In Parity-1, the global parity bit on the 128 bits remains unchanged after MixColumns. Conversely, at the byte level, the parity after MixColumns is affected. Therefore, parity-16 requires the implementation of prediction functions in MixColumns. Finally, the parity bits after AddRoundKey are computed as before, by adding the current parity bits to those of the corresponding round key. This technique incurs 88.9% hardware overhead because of the LUT size is doubled. The throughput is 67.86% of the original.

8.8.3.3   Parity-32

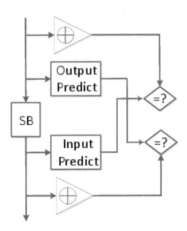

FIGURE 8.29: Parity-32 CED.

As shown in **Fig. 8.29**, a technique that strengthen fault detection on S-boxes is proposed in [269]. With respect to parity-16, this technique still uses one parity bit for each byte in all the operations except SubBytes. It adds one extra parity bit for each of the inputs and outputs of the S-box in SubBytes; one parity bit for the input byte and one for the output byte. The actual output parity is compared with the predicted output parity, and the actual input parity bit is compared with the predicted input parity. It has 37.35% hardware overhead and 99.20% fault coverage.

8.8.3.4   Robust Code

Robust codes are first proposed in [177]. The idea is to use non-linear EDC instead of linear codes, like parity. Robust codes can be used to extend the error coverage of any linear prediction technique for AES. The advantage of non-linear EDC is that it has uniform fault coverage, unlike the linear codes like parity. Thus, if all the data vectors and error patterns are equiprobable, then the probability of injecting an undetectable fault is the same for all of them.

The architecture of AES with robust protection is presented in **Fig. 8.30**. In this architecture, two extra units are needed. One is the prediction unit at the round input, and it includes a linear predictor, a linear compressor, and a cubic function. The other one is the comparison unit at the output of the round, and it includes a compressor, a linear compressor, and a cubic function This architecture protects the encryption and decryption as well as Key-Scheduler or Key Expansion module.

A linear predictor and linear compressor is designed to generate a 32-bit output, and we call them the linear portion. The output of the linear portion is linearly related to the output of the round of AES as shown in **Fig. 8.30**. They offer a relatively compact design compared to the original round of AES. They simplify the round function by XORing the bytes in the same column. The effect of MixColumns is removed by the linear portion. As a result, the linear portion is greatly simplified as it no longer needs to perform multiplication associated with the MixColumns or InvMixColumns. For the cubic function, the input is cubed in $GF(2^r)$ to produce the r-bit output, and thus it is non-linear with respect to the output of the round.

In the comparison unit, the compressor and the linear compressor are designed to generate a 32-bit output from the 128-bit round output. The bytes in the same column of the output is XORed. Again, the 32-bit output is cubed in the cubic function to generate r-bit output. This output is then compared with the output from the prediction unit.

This technique provides $1 - 2^{-56}$ fault coverage, and it has a 77% hardware overhead.

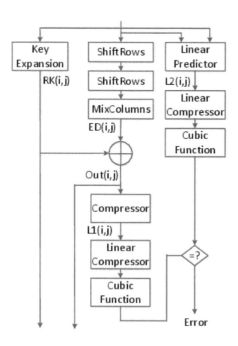

FIGURE 8.30: Robust Code

Although these countermeasures can thwart DFA, the designer needs to be cautious when implementing information redundancy-based techniques. Because they increase the correlation of the circuit power consumption with the processed data, the side channel leakage is also increased [235].

8.8.4 Hybrid Redundancy

In [181, 182, 180], the authors consider CED at the operation, round, and algorithm levels for AES. In these schemes, an operation, a round, or the encryption and decryption are followed by their inverses. To detect faults, the results are compared with the original input.

The underlying assumption is that a complete encryption device operating in ECB mode consists of encryption and decryption modules. Thus, a low-cost and low-latency systematic CED is proposed for encryption and decryption datapaths. They describe algorithm-level, round-level, and operation-levels CEDs that exploit the inverse relationship properties of AES. Because AES uses the same set of round keys for both encryption and decryption, they can be generated a priori, stored in the key RAM, and retrieved in any order depending upon

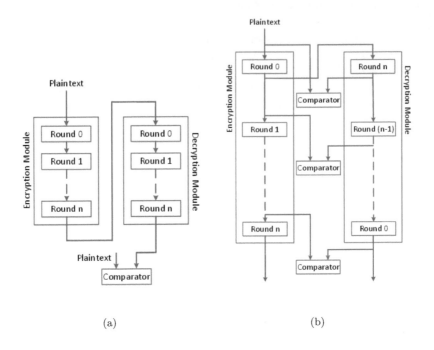

(a)   (b)

FIGURE 8.31: Hybrid redundancy (a) Algorithm level (b) Round level

whether encryption or decryption is in progress. They then extend the proposed techniques
to full duplex mode by trading off throughput and CED capability.

As shown in **Fig. 8.31(a)**, the algorithm-level CED approach exploits the inverse relationship between the entire encryption and decryption. Plaintext is first processed by
the encryption module. After the ciphertext is available, the decryption module is enabled
to decrypt the ciphertext. While the decryption module is decrypting ciphertext, the encryption module can process the next block of data or be idle. A copy of plaintext is also
temporarily stored in a register. The output of decryption is compared with this copy of
the input plaintext. If there is a mismatch, an error signal will be raised, and the faulty
ciphertext will be suppressed.

For AES, the inverse relationship between encryption and decryption exists at the round
level as well. Any input data passed successively through one encryption round are recovered
by the corresponding decryption round.

For almost all the symmetric block cipher algorithms, the first round of encryption
corresponds to the last round of decryption; the second round of encryption corresponds
to the next-to-the-last round of decryption, and so on. Based on this observation, CED
computations can also be performed at the round level. At the beginning of each encryption
round, the input data is stored in a register before being fed to the round module. After
one round of encryption is finished, output is fed to the corresponding round of decryption.
Then, the output of the decryption round is compared with the input data saved previously.
If they are not the same, encryption is halted and an error signal is raised. Encryption with
round-level CED is shown in **Fig. 8.31(b)**.

Depending on the block ciphers and their hardware implementation, each round may
consume multiple clock cycles. Each round can be partitioned into operations and sub-
pipelined to improve performance. Each operation can consume one or more clock cycles,
such that the operations of encryption and corresponding operations of decryption satisfy

the inverse relationship. As shown in **Fig. 8.32(a)**, applying input data to the encryption operation and the output data of the encryption operation to the corresponding inverse operation in decryption yields the original input data. The boundary on the left shows the rth encryption round while the boundary on the right shows the $(n - r + 1)^{th}$ decryption round, where r is the total number of rounds in encryption/decryption. **Fig. 8.32(a)** also shows that the first operation of the encryption round corresponds to the mth operation of the decryption round, which is the last operation of the decryption round. Output from operation one of encryption is fed into the corresponding inverse operation m of decryption.

Although these techniques has close to 100% fault coverage, their throughput is 73.45% of the original AES in half-duplex mode. It can suffer from more than 100% throughput overhead if the design is in full-duplex mode. The hardware overhead is minimal if both encryption and decryption are on the chip. However, if only encryption or decryption is used in the chip, it will incur close to 100% hardware overhead.

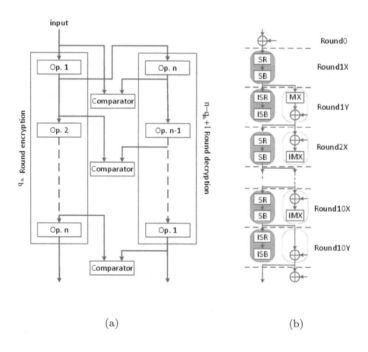

(a)   (b)

FIGURE 8.32: Hybrid redundancy. (a) Operation level. (b) Optimized version.

To reduce the hardware overhead of the previous technique, [349] proposes a novel hardware optimization, and thus, reduced the hardware utilization significantly. **Fig. 8.32(b)** shows the architecture. It divides a round function block into two sub-blocks and uses them alternatively for encryption (or decryption) and error detection. Therefore, no extra calculation block is needed, even though only a pipeline register, a selector and a comparator are added. The number of operating cycles is doubled, but the operating frequency is boosted because the round function block in the critical path is halved. Therefore, the technique provides 85.6% throughput compared to 73.45% in the previous one. The hardware overhead also decrease from 97.6% to 88.9%.

8.8.5 Other Techniques

In [258, 187, 260], parity is obtained for S-box implementation in finite field arithmetic with polynomial basis. In [259, 188, 190], parity is obtained for S-box implementation in finite field arithmetic with normal basis. In [189], an AES parity detection method with mixed basis is proposed. All these parity schemes share the same limitation. If an even number of faults occur in the same byte, none of these schemes can detect them.

While traditional CED techniques have their strengths and limitations, techniques based on algorithmic invariances can offer new tradeoff choices. An invariance-based CED is proposed in [143]. It utilizes a round-level invariance of the AES and checks for the invariance property. Because the invariance does not constrain the input pattern of the round, it is very flexible and the fault coverage is very high. Because the invariance property is a permutation property, the hardware overhead only includes the comparator and muxes that are used to select the regular or the permuted datapath. A new CED technique based on normal basis has been proposed in [414], which shows improved fault coverage and suitability for 8-bit architectures.

8.9 Invariance based DFA Countermeasures

The detection countermeasures (discussed before) are usually implemented by performing redundant computations and finally comparing the results of two computations. But in this countermeasure, the comparison step itself is prone to fault attacks. The infection countermeasure on the other hand, aims to destroy the fault invariant by diffusing the effect of a fault in such a way that it renders the faulty ciphertext unexploitable. Infection countermeasures are preferred in this sense as they avoid the use of attack vulnerable operations such as comparison. But they have an adverse effect on performance.

In FDTC 2012, Lomné *et. al* [225] showed that infection countermeasures which use deterministic diffusion to infect the intermediate output are not secure and emphasized on the need of randomness in these countermeasures. In LatinCrypt 2012, Gierlichs *et. al* [131] proposed an infection countermeasure for AES which infects the faulty computation with random values. Despite the use of randomness in the infection mechanism, the countermeasure for AES128 [131] was attacked by Battistello and Giraud in FDTC 2013 [42]. They observed that if a fault is injected in any byte of the last three rows of the 10th round input, then the erroneous byte remains unaffected by the infection method and can be exploited to retrieve the corresponding key byte. This attack assumes a *constant byte fault model* to retrieve 12 bytes of AES128 key using 36 faults on average and recovers the remaining 4 key bytes corresponding to the top row using a brute-force search.

8.9.1 An Infective Countermeasure Scheme

In the rest of the discussion, we use the following notations:
RoundFunction - The round function of AES128 block cipher which operates on a 16 byte state matrix and 16 byte round key. In a *RoundFunction*, the SubBytes, ShiftRows and MixColumns transformations are applied successively on the state matrix, followed by the KeyXor operation. AES128 has 10 rounds in addition to the initial Key Whitening step, which we refer to as the 0th round.
S - The SubBytes operation in the *RoundFunction*.
SR - The ShiftRows operation in the *RoundFunction*.

MC - The MixColumns operation in the *RoundFunction*.
I^i - The 16 byte input to the ith round of AES128, where $i \in \{0, \ldots, 10\}$.
K - The 16 byte secret key used in AES128.
k^j - The 16 byte matrix that represents $(j-1)^{th}$ round key, $j \in \{1, \ldots, 11\}$, derived from the main secret key K.
β - The 16 byte secret input to the dummy round.
k^0 - The 16 byte secret key used in the computation of dummy round.
The 16 bytes $(m_0 \ldots m_{15})$ of a matrix are arranged in 4×4 arrays and follow a column major order. We denote multiplication symbol by $\cdot$, a bitwise logical AND operation by $\wedge$, a bitwise logical OR operation by $\vee$, a bitwise logical NOT operation by $\neg$ and a bitwise logical XOR operation by $\oplus$.

We first explain the countermeasure for AES128 proposed in [131], followed by a brief description of the attack [42] mounted on it.

8.9.2 Infection Countermeasure

Algorithm 8.7: Infection Countermeasure [131]

Input: P, k^j for $j \in \{1, \ldots, n\}$, (β, k^0), $(n = 11)$ for AES128
Output: $C = \text{BlockCipher}(P, K)$

1. State $R_0 \leftarrow P$, Redundant state $R_1 \leftarrow P$, Dummy state $R_2 \leftarrow \beta$

2. $C_0 \leftarrow 0$, $C_1 \leftarrow 0$, $C_2 \leftarrow \beta$, $i \leftarrow 1$

3. while $i \leq 2n$ do

4. $\lambda \leftarrow RandomBit()$ // $\lambda = 0$ implies a dummy round

5. $\kappa \leftarrow (i \wedge \lambda) \oplus 2(\neg\lambda)$

6. $\zeta \leftarrow \lambda \cdot \lceil i/2 \rceil$ // ζ is actual round counter, 0 for dummy

7. $R_\kappa \leftarrow RoundFunction(R_\kappa, k^\zeta)$

8. $C_\kappa \leftarrow R_\kappa \oplus C_2 \oplus \beta$ // infect C_κ to propagate a fault

9. $\epsilon \leftarrow \lambda(\neg(i \wedge 1)) \cdot SNLF(C_0 \oplus C_1)$ // check if i is even

10. $R_2 \leftarrow R_2 \oplus \epsilon$

11. $R_0 \leftarrow R_0 \oplus \epsilon$

12. $i \leftarrow i + \lambda$

13. end

14. $R_0 \leftarrow R_0 \oplus RoundFunction(R_2, k^0) \oplus \beta$

15. return(R_0)

Algorithm 8.7 depicts the infection countermeasure proposed in [131] for AES128. At the beginning of this algorithm, plaintext P is copied to both R_0 and R_1 and a secret value β is copied to R_2. In this algorithm, every round of AES is executed twice. The redundant round which operates on R_1, occurs before the cipher round which operates on R_0. There are dummy rounds which occur randomly across the execution of this algorithm, in addition to one compulsory dummy round in step 14. The input to the dummy round is a secret value β and a secret key k^0, which is chosen such that $RoundFunction(\beta, k^0) = \beta$. To prevent the information leakage through side channels *e.g. power analysis,* dummy SubByte, ShiftRow and MixColumn operations are added to the 0th round and a dummy MixColumn operation is added to the 10th round of AES128. The intermediate computation of cipher, redundant and dummy round is stored in C_0, C_1 and C_2 respectively. A random bit λ decides the course of the algorithm as follows:

1. $\lambda = 0$, dummy round is executed.

2. $\lambda = 1$ and parity of i is even, cipher round is executed.

3. $\lambda = 1$ and parity of i is odd, redundant round is executed.

After the computation of every cipher round, the difference between C_0 and C_1 is transformed by Some Non Linear Function($SNLF$) which operates on each byte of the difference $(C_0 \oplus C_1)$. $SNLF$ maps all but zero byte to non-zero bytes and $SNLF(0) = 0$. Authors in [131] have suggested to use inversion in $GF(2^8)$ as $SNLF$. In case of fault injection in either cipher or redundant round, the difference $(C_0 \oplus C_1)$ is non-zero and the infection spreads in subsequent computations through R_0 and R_2 according to steps 9-11. Also, if the output of dummy round, C_2, is not β, the infection spreads in the subsequent computations through the steps 8-11. Finally in the step 14, the output of last cipher round is xored with the output of dummy round and β, and the resulting value is returned.

8.9.3   Attacks on the Infection Countermeasure

In the absence of any side channel and with the countermeasure [131] in place, it seems difficult to identify whether a fault is injected in the target round by analysing the faulty ciphertext. For example, in the implementation of AES128 without countermeasure, if a fault is injected in the input of 9th round, then the expected number of faulty ciphertext bytes which differ from the correct ciphertext is 4. In this countermeasure, the presence of compulsory dummy round ensures that the expected number of different bytes is 16 when the 9th round computation is faulty. Moreover, the occurence of random dummy rounds makes it difficult to inject the same fault in both the branches of the computation.

Despite the strength of the countermeasure [131], authors in [42] showed how to attack it using a *constant byte fault model.* They observed that only one dummy round occurs after the 10th cipher round of AES128, which limits the infection to only 4 bytes if the 10th round's computation is faulty. The attack details are as follows:

Suppose a fault f disturbs I_1^{10}, i.e. the first byte of second row in 10th cipher round input I^{10}. The difference between the faulty and redundant intermediate state after the step 7 of Algorithm 8.7 is:

$$
R_0 \oplus R_1 = \begin{pmatrix} 0 & 0 & 0 & 0 \\ 0 & 0 & 0 & \varepsilon \\ 0 & 0 & 0 & 0 \\ 0 & 0 & 0 & 0 \end{pmatrix}
$$

where $\varepsilon = S[I_1^{10} \oplus f] \oplus S[I_1^{10}]$.

R_2 and R_0 are infected in steps 10 and 11. After the infection steps, we obtain:

$$R_0 \oplus R_1 = \begin{pmatrix} 0 & 0 & 0 & 0 \\ 0 & 0 & 0 & \varepsilon \oplus SNLF[\varepsilon] \\ 0 & 0 & 0 & 0 \\ 0 & 0 & 0 & 0 \end{pmatrix}$$

Finally, in the step 14, dummy round operates on infected R_2 which further infects R_0. But, the ShiftRow operation of dummy round shifts the infection to column 3 and leaves the faulty byte of R_0 in column 4 unmasked. The output of compulsory dummy round differs from β in column 3 and therefore, the final difference between the correct ciphertext C and faulty ciphertext C^* is:

$$\therefore C \oplus C^* = \begin{pmatrix} 0 & 0 & \beta'_8 \oplus \beta_8 & 0 \\ 0 & 0 & \beta'_9 \oplus \beta_9 & \varepsilon \oplus SNLF[\varepsilon] \\ 0 & 0 & \beta'_{10} \oplus \beta_{10} & 0 \\ 0 & 0 & \beta'_{11} \oplus \beta_{11} & 0 \end{pmatrix} \tag{8.31}$$

where β'_8, β'_9, β'_{10}, β'_{11} are the infected bytes of the compulsory dummy round output. Since the byte C^*_{13} is unaffected by the infected output of dummy round, it is exploited to retrieve the byte k^{11}_{13} of the 10th round key using two more pairs of faulty and correct ciphertexts. Similarly, the remaining 11 key bytes corresponding to last three rows of k^{11} can be retrieved. For details on attack procedure, the reader is referred to [42].

If a fault is injected in any byte of the last three rows of I^{10}, the resulting erroneous byte is left unmasked and hence is exploited in the attack. However, if a fault is injected in any byte of the top row, the erroneous byte is masked by the infected output of compulsory dummy round. *This attack does not target the remaining 4 key bytes that correspond to the top row and they are computed using a brute force search.*

Observation 1: Ideally, the countermeasure should infect the entire result if a fault is injected in any of the rounds. But Algorithm 8.7 fails to protect the last round and it is exploited in the attack. Moreover, in this algorithm, the last cipher round is always the penultimate round. Thus, using a side channel, one can always observe a posteriori whether a fault was injected in the last but one round.

The countermeasure can be further subjected to DFA assuming random byte fault models, with some more observations. Next we present additional flaws in the countermeasure [131] which were considered while developing the countermeasure presented in section4.

8.9.3.1 Further Loop Holes in the Countermeasure: Attacking the Infection Technique

It might seem that if the output of compulsory dummy round infects the erroneous byte of 10th round's output, then the attack [42] can be thwarted. However, in this section, we demonstrate that the infection caused by compulsory dummy round is ineffective and can be removed.

8.9.4 Infection Caused by Compulsory Dummy Round

In Algorithm 8.7, since the input as well as the output of dummy round is β, *i.e.* $RoundFunction(\beta, k^0) = \beta$, we can write:

$$MC(SR(S(\beta))) \oplus k^0 = \beta$$

Using this relation, the xor of $RoundFunction(R_2, k^0)$ and β in step 14 of Algorithm 8.7 can now be expressed as:

$$RoundFunction(R_2, k^0) \oplus \beta = MC(SR(S(R_2))) \oplus k^0 \oplus MC(SR(S(\beta))) \oplus k^0$$
$$= MC(SR(S(R_2))) \oplus MC(SR(S(\beta)))$$

Since SubByte operation is the only non-linear operation in the above equation,

$$\therefore RoundFunction(R_2, k^0) \oplus \beta = MC(SR(S(R_2) \oplus S(\beta))) \tag{8.32}$$

If $R_2 = \beta$ then the execution of compulsory dummy round in step 14 has no effect on the final output R_0, but if $R_2 \neq \beta$ then the output of compulsory dummy round infects the final output R_0. However, this infection can be removed using the above derived equation and the desired faulty ciphertext can be recovered.

On the basis of Equation 8.32, the xor of correct ciphertext C and faulty ciphertext C^* in Equation 8.31 can now be expressed as:

$$C \oplus C^* = \begin{pmatrix} 0 & 0 & 3 \cdot x & 0 \\ 0 & 0 & 2 \cdot x & \varepsilon \oplus SNLF[\varepsilon] \\ 0 & 0 & 1 \cdot x & 0 \\ 0 & 0 & 1 \cdot x & 0 \end{pmatrix}$$

where $x = S[\beta_{13} \oplus SNLF[\varepsilon]] \oplus S[\beta_{13}]$ (for details refer [146]). Ideally, every byte of C^* should be infected with an independent random value but here the compulsory dummy round in Algorithm 8.7 infects only column 3 of C^* and that too, with interrelated values and leaves the rest of the bytes unmasked.

In the following discussion, we show the significance of this result, by attacking the top row of I^{10}. Subsequently, we show that the infection can be removed even if the fault is injected in the input of the 9th cipher round. We prove this by mounting the classical Piret & Quisquater's attack [126] on the countermeasure [131].

8.9.4.1 Attacking the Top Row

We now demonstrate the attack on the top row of I^{10} to retrieve the remaining 4 bytes of k^{10}.

Suppose a fault f disturbs I_0^{10} i.e. the first byte of 10th cipher round input I^{10}. The difference between the faulty and redundant intermediate state after the step 7 of Algorithm 8.7 is:

$$R_0 \oplus R_1 = \begin{pmatrix} \varepsilon & 0 & 0 & 0 \\ 0 & 0 & 0 & 0 \\ 0 & 0 & 0 & 0 \\ 0 & 0 & 0 & 0 \end{pmatrix}$$

where $\varepsilon = S[I_0^{10} \oplus f] \oplus S[I_0^{10}]$.

R_2 and R_0 are infected in steps 10 and 11. After the infection steps, we obtain:

$$R_0 \oplus R_1 = \begin{pmatrix} \varepsilon \oplus SNLF[\varepsilon] & 0 & 0 & 0 \\ 0 & 0 & 0 & 0 \\ 0 & 0 & 0 & 0 \\ 0 & 0 & 0 & 0 \end{pmatrix}$$

Finally, in the step 14, dummy round operates on infected R_2 which further infects R_0. In this case, the ShiftRow operation of dummy round does not shift the infection and the erroneous byte of R_0 in column 1 is masked. The final difference between the correct ciphertext C and faulty ciphertext C^* is:

$$\therefore C \oplus C^* = \begin{pmatrix} \varepsilon \oplus SNLF[\varepsilon] \oplus \beta_0' \oplus \beta_0 & 0 & 0 & 0 \\ \beta_1' \oplus \beta_1 & 0 & 0 & 0 \\ \beta_2' \oplus \beta_2 & 0 & 0 & 0 \\ \beta_3' \oplus \beta_3 & 0 & 0 & 0 \end{pmatrix} \quad (8.33)$$

where β_0', β_1', β_2', β_3' are the infected bytes of the compulsory dummy round output. and $\varepsilon = S[I_0^{10} \oplus f] \oplus S[I_0^{10}]$. Here, we cannot use the attack technique described in [42] directly, because the erroneous byte of 10th cipher round has also been infected with the output of compulsory dummy round in step 14. *This is different from the case when fault is injected in any of the last three rows of 10th cipher round input.* In order to carry out the attack [42], we need to remove the infection caused by the dummy round. Now, we can use Equation 8.32 to write the above matrix as:

$$C \oplus C^* = \begin{pmatrix} \varepsilon \oplus SNLF[\varepsilon] \oplus 2 \cdot y & 0 & 0 & 0 \\ 1 \cdot y & 0 & 0 & 0 \\ 1 \cdot y & 0 & 0 & 0 \\ 3 \cdot y & 0 & 0 & 0 \end{pmatrix} \quad (8.34)$$

where $y = S[\beta_0 \oplus SNLF[\varepsilon]] \oplus S[\beta_0]$ (for details refer [146]). We can use the value of $1 \cdot y$ from $C \oplus C^*$ to remove the infection from C^* and therefore unmask the erroneous byte. As a consequence, we can perform the attack suggested in [42] to get the key byte k_0^{11}. *By attacking the top row, now the attacker has the flexibility to mount the attack on any of the 12 bytes of 10th cipher round instead of always targeting the last three rows.*

Observation 2: It is quite evident from this attack that the infection mechanism used in the countermeasure [131] is not effective. The purpose of this infection countermeasure is defeated as we can easily remove the infection and recover the desired faulty ciphertext. This is a major flaw in this countermeasure as it makes even the 9th round susceptible to the fault attack which we will illustrate in the following discussion.

8.9.5 Piret & Quisquater's Attack on the Countermeasure

The presence of compulsory dummy round in the countermeasure [131] ensures that a fault in the 9th cipher round input of AES128 infects all 16 bytes in the output. Even though the countermeasure infects all the bytes of the resulting ciphertext, we show that we can again remove the infection caused by compulsory dummy round using Equation 8.32 and obtain the desired faulty ciphertext. To mount this attack, we consider the following two facts:

1. The authors of [131] have mentioned that an attacker can affect the *RandomBit* function in the Algorithm 8.7, so that the random dummy round never occurs. To counteract this effect, they added a compulsory dummy round at the end of the algorithm which ensures that the faulty ciphertext is infected in such a way that no information is available to the attacker.

2. Also, because of performance issues, Algorithm 8.7 should terminate within a reasonable amount of time and hence, the number of random dummy rounds should be limited to a certain value.

First, we show that if random dummy rounds never occur in the while loop, then despite the presence of compulsory dummy round in step 14, we can mount the Piret & Quisquater's

attack [126] on this countermeasure and *recover the entire key using only 8 faulty ciphertexts*. Subsequently, we show that even if the random dummy rounds occur, we can still
mount this attack [126].

Attack in the Absence of Random Dummy Rounds. Consider the scenario where
the attacker influences the *RandomBit* function so that no dummy round occurs except
the compulsory dummy round in step 14. We observe that if a fault is injected in the 9th
cipher round, then the rest of the computation is infected thrice. Once, after the 9th cipher
round in step 11, then after the 10th cipher round in step 11 and finally after the execution
of compulsory dummy round in step 14. To be able to mount Piret & Quisquater's attack
[126], we first analyze the faulty ciphertext and identify whether a fault was injected in the
input of 9th cipher round. After identifying such faulty ciphertexts, we remove the infection
caused by the output of compulsory dummy round and 10th cipher round. Once the infection is removed, we can proceed with the attack described in [126].
The attack procedure can be summarized as follows:

1. Suppose a random fault f is injected in the first byte of the 9th cipher round input.
   Before the execution of step 14, the output of faulty computation differs from the
   output of correct computation in 4 positions *viz.* 0, 13, 10 and 7 which comprises a
   diagonal. But the execution of compulsory dummy round in step 14 infects all the 16
   bytes of the faulty computation. Therefore, the resulting faulty ciphertext T^* differs
   from the correct ciphertext T in 16 bytes. We use Equation 8.32 to represent this
   difference as:

$$T \oplus T^* = \begin{pmatrix} m_0 \oplus 2F_1 \oplus 1F_2 & 1F_3 & 3F_4 \oplus 1F_5 \oplus 1F_6 & 3F_7 \\ 1F_1 \oplus 3F_2 & 1F_3 & 2F_4 \oplus 3F_5 \oplus 1F_6 & m_1 \oplus 2F_7 \\ 1F_1 \oplus 2F_2 & 3F_3 & m_2 \oplus 1F_4 \oplus 2F_5 \oplus 3F_6 & 1F_7 \\ 3F_1 \oplus 1F_2 & m_3 \oplus 2F_3 & 1F_4 \oplus 1F_5 \oplus 2F_6 & 1F_7 \end{pmatrix}$$
(8.35)

   where F_i, $i \in \{1,\ldots,7\}$, represents the infection caused by the compulsory dummy
   round in step 14 and m_j, $j \in \{0,1,2,3\}$, represents the difference between the correct
   and faulty computation before the execution of step 14 in Algorithm 8.7 (for details
   refer [146]). Now, we can deduce the values of F_1 and F_2 from column 1, F_3 from
   column 2, F_4, F_5 and F_6 from column 3 and F_7 from column 4 and thus remove the
   infection caused by the compulsory dummy round from T^*.

2. After removing the infection caused by compulsory dummy round, we get:

$$T \oplus T^* = \begin{pmatrix} m_0 & 0 & 0 & 0 \\ 0 & 0 & 0 & m_1 \\ 0 & 0 & m_2 & 0 \\ 0 & m_3 & 0 & 0 \end{pmatrix}$$

   We can now remove the infection caused by the 10th cipher round. Each m_j can be
   written as $z_j \oplus SNLF[z_j]$, $j \in \{0,1,2,3\}$, where $SNLF[z_j]$ represents the infection
   caused in step 11 of Algorithm 8.7, after the execution of 10th cipher round and
   z_j represents the difference between the outputs of correct and faulty computations
   before step 11 (for details refer [146]). If $SNLF$ is implemented as inversion in $GF(2^8)$,
   we get two solutions of z_j for every m_j. Since the 4 equations represented by m_j are
   independent, we obtain 2^4 solutions for $T \oplus T^*$. Here, T is known, therefore we have
   2^4 solutions for T^* as well.

3. After removing the infection caused by 10th cipher round, the attacker makes hypotheses on 4 bytes of the 10th round key k^{11} and uses the faulty and correct output

of 9th cipher round to verify the following relations:

$$2 \cdot f' \oplus SNLF[2 \cdot f'] = S^{-1}[T_0 \oplus k_0^{11}] \oplus S^{-1}[T_0^* \oplus k_0^{11}]$$
$$1 \cdot f' \oplus SNLF[1 \cdot f'] = S^{-1}[T_{13} \oplus k_{13}^{11}] \oplus S^{-1}[T_{13}^* \oplus k_{13}^{11}]$$
$$1 \cdot f' \oplus SNLF[1 \cdot f'] = S^{-1}[T_{10} \oplus k_{10}^{11}] \oplus S^{-1}[T_{10}^* \oplus k_{10}^{11}]$$
$$3 \cdot f' \oplus SNLF[3 \cdot f'] = S^{-1}[T_7 \oplus k_7^{11}] \oplus S^{-1}[T_7^* \oplus k_7^{11}]$$

where $SNLF[b \cdot f']$, $b \in \{1,2,3\}$ is the infection caused in step 11, after the execution of 9th cipher round. The above set of equations is solved for all 2^4 possible values of T^* (for the complexity analysis of the attack, refer [146]).

Identifying Desired Faulty Ciphertexts. As done in [126], we call a ciphertext resulting from a fault injected in the input of 9th round as desired faulty ciphertext, otherwise we call it undesired. It is not difficult to identify whether the given faulty ciphertext is desired or not. With the countermeasure [131] in place, if a fault affects a byte of column i in the 9th round input, where $i \in \{0,1,2,3\}$, we observed that the following relations hold in the xor of faulty and correct ciphertext:

$$(T \oplus T^*)_{(4 \cdot (i+1))\%16} = (T \oplus T^*)_{(4 \cdot (i+1))\%16+1}$$
$$(T \oplus T^*)_{(4 \cdot (i+1))\%16+2} = 3 \cdot (T \oplus T^*)_{(4 \cdot (i+1))\%16}$$
$$(T \oplus T^*)_{(4 \cdot (i+3))\%16+2} = (T \oplus T^*)_{(4 \cdot (i+3))\%16+3} \quad (8.36)$$
$$(T \oplus T^*)_{(4 \cdot (i+3))\%16} = 3 \cdot (T \oplus T^*)_{(4 \cdot (i+3))\%16+2}$$

where $(T \oplus T^*)_j$ represents the jth byte in matrix $T \oplus T^*$. One can see from Equation 8.35, that the above relation arises because the compulsory dummy round uses the same value to mask more than one byte of the faulty computation.

Attack Considering Random Dummy Rounds. In the attack explained above, we assumed that the attacker influences the *RandomBit* function in the countermeasure [131] so that the dummy rounds do not occur in the while loop. Now, we consider the case where the number of random dummy rounds occuring in every execution of Algorithm 8.7 is exactly d^3. Since $\lambda = 0$ corresponds to a dummy round and $\lambda = 1$ corresponds to an AES round, we can view the computation of Algorithm 8.7 as if decided by a binary string of length $(22+d)$, where $(22+d)^{th}$ *RoundFunction* is always the 10th cipher round. We choose to inject the fault in $(22 + d - 2)^{th}$ round as it can be a 9th cipher or a 10th redundant or a dummy round. This increases the probability of injecting the fault in 9th cipher round.

Assuming that every string of length $(22 + d)$, consisting of exactly 22 1's and d 0's, is equally likely, then the probability that $(22 + d - 2)^{th}$ *RoundFunction* is a 9th cipher round is the same as that of a binary string of length $(22 + d)$ that ends in '111'. Since the while loop in Algorithm 8.7 always terminates with the execution of 10th cipher round, the binary string always ends with a 1. Therefore this probability is: $\frac{(19+d)!/((19)!\cdot(d)!)}{(21+d)!/((21)!\cdot(d)!)}$ [146]. If $d = 20$ then the probability that 40th *RoundFunction* is a 9th cipher round is nearly 0.26.

Simulation Results. We carried out Piret & Quisquater's attack [126] on Algorithm 8.7 using a random byte fault model with no control over fault localization. We implemented the Algorithm 8.7 in C and used the GNU Scientific Library(GSL) for *RandomBit* function. The simulation details are as follows:

---

[3]If the value of d varies across different executions, one can still compute a mean value of d by observing the number of *RoundFunctions* through a side channel.

1. The value of d is kept constant and 1000 tests are performed.

2. Each test executes Algorithm 8.7 until 8 desired faulty ciphertexts are obtained. However, as the target $(22 + d - 2)^{th}$ $RoundFunction$ can also be a dummy or 10th redundant round, the undesired faulty ciphertexts obtained in such cases are discarded. Equation 8.36 can be used to distinguish between desired and undesired faulty ciphertexts.

3. An average of the faulty encryptions over 1000 tests is taken, where number of faulty encryptions in a test = (8 desired faulty ciphertext + undesired faulty ciphertexts).

4. Subsequently, the value of d is incremented by 5 and the above procedure is repeated.

The probability that the targeted $RoundFunction$ is a 9th cipher round decreases with higher values of d but it still remains non-negligible. In other words, higher the value of d, more is the number of faulty encryptions required in a test as evident from **Fig. 8.33**:

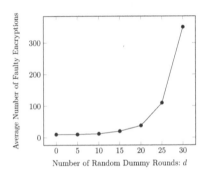

FIGURE 8.33: Piret & Quisquater's Attack on Algorithm 8.7

Observation 3: The feasibility of Piret and Quisquater's attack shows that the infection method employed in the countermeasure [131] fails to protect against classical fault attacks.

8.10 Improved Countermeasure

In this section, we propose an improved countermeasure based upon the principles used in the Algorithm 8.7. The *observations* enumerated in this chapter were used as a guideline for developing this countermeasure. As evident from the attacks explained earlier, the infection countermeasure for protecting AES against the differential fault attacks should have the following properties:

1. If a fault is injected in any of the cipher, redundant or dummy round, all bytes in the resulting ciphertext should be infected.

2. As shown, merely infecting all bytes in the output is not sufficient. Therefore, the infection technique should result in such a faulty ciphertext that any attempts to make hypothesis on the secret key used in AES are completely nullified.

3. The countermeasure itself should not leak any information related to the $RoundFunction$ computations which can be exploited through a side channel.

Given below is an algorithm, which is designed to possess all the aforementioned properties. It uses cipher, redundant and dummy rounds along the lines of Algorithm 8.7 but exhibits a rather robust behaviour against fault attacks.

Following additional notations are used in this algorithm:

1. **rstr**: A 't' bit random binary string, consisting of $(2n)$ 1's corresponding to AES rounds and $(t - 2n)$ 0's corresponding to dummy rounds.

2. **BLFN**: A Boolean function that maps a 128 bit value to a 1 bit value. Specifically, $BLFN(0) = 0$ and for nonzero input $BLFN$ evaluates to 1.

3. γ: A one bit comparison variable to detect fault injection in AES round.

4. δ: A one bit comparison variable to identify a fault injection in dummy round.

Algorithm 8.8: Improved Countermeasure

---

1 Inputs : P, k^j for $j \in \{1, \ldots, n\}$, (β, k^0), $(n = 11)$ for AES128
2 Output : $C = \text{BlockCipher}(P, K)$

    1. State $R_0 \leftarrow P$, Redundant state $R_1 \leftarrow P$, Dummy state $R_2 \leftarrow \beta$

    2. $i \leftarrow 1$, $q \leftarrow 1$

    3. $rstr \leftarrow \{0, 1\}^t$ // $\#1(rstr) = 2n, \#0(rstr) = t - 2n$

    4. while $q \leq t$ do

    5. $\lambda \leftarrow rstr[q]$ // $\lambda = 0$ implies a dummy round

    6. $\kappa \leftarrow (i \wedge \lambda) \oplus 2(\neg\lambda)$

    7. $\zeta \leftarrow \lambda \cdot \lceil i/2 \rceil$ // ζ is actual round counter, 0 for dummy

    8. $R_\kappa \leftarrow RoundFunction(R_\kappa, k^\zeta)$

    9. $\gamma \leftarrow \lambda(\neg(i \wedge 1)) \cdot BLFN(R_0 \oplus R_1)$ // check if i is even

    10. $\delta \leftarrow (\neg\lambda) \cdot BLFN(R_2 \oplus \beta)$

    11. $R_0 \leftarrow (\neg(\gamma \vee \delta) \cdot R_0) \oplus ((\gamma \vee \delta) \cdot R_2)$

    12. $i \leftarrow i + \lambda$

    13. $q \leftarrow q + 1$

    14. end

    15. return(R_0)

Apart from these elements, Algorithm 8.8 exhibits the following features which makes it stronger than Algorithm 8.7:

1. In Algorithm 8.8, matrix R_2 represents the state of the dummy round and is initialized to a random value β. This state matrix R_2 bears no relation with any of the intermediate states or the round keys of AES. When a fault is induced in any of the rounds, Algorithm 8.8 outputs a matrix R_2. For fault analysis to succeed, the faulty

output should contain some information about the key used in the cipher. However, the new countermeasure outputs matrix R_2 which is completely random and does not have any information about the key used in the AES, which makes the differential fault analysis impossible. Since in the case of fault injection Algorithm 8.8 outputs dummy state R_2, the pair (β, k^0) should be refreshed in every execution[4].

2. In Algorithm 8.8, more than one dummy round can occur after the execution of last cipher round and consequently the 10th cipher round is not always the penultimate round.

3. Since the number of dummy rounds in Algorithm 8.8 is kept constant, the leakage of timing information through a side channel is also prevented.

For a clear illustration, Table 8.2 shows the functioning of Algorithm 8.8.

TABLE 8.2: Computation of Algorithm 8.8

Step	Redundant Round	Cipher Round	Dummy Round
5.	$\lambda = 1, i$ is odd	$\lambda = 1, i$ is even	$\lambda = 0$
6.	$\kappa \leftarrow 1$	$\kappa \leftarrow 0$	$\kappa \leftarrow 2$
7.	$\zeta \leftarrow \lceil i/2 \rceil$	$\zeta \leftarrow \lceil i/2 \rceil$	$\zeta \leftarrow 0$
8.	$R_1 \leftarrow RoundFunction(R_1, k^\zeta)$	$R_0 \leftarrow RoundFunction(R_0, k^\zeta)$	$R_2 \leftarrow RoundFunction(R_2, k^0)$
9.	$\gamma \leftarrow 0$	$\gamma \leftarrow BLFN(R_0 \oplus R_1)$	$\gamma \leftarrow 0$
10.	$\delta \leftarrow 0$	$\delta \leftarrow 0$	$\delta \leftarrow BLFN(R_2 \oplus \beta)$
11.	$R_0 \leftarrow R_0$	$R_0 \leftarrow (\neg(\gamma) \cdot R_0) \oplus ((\gamma) \cdot R_2)$	$R_0 \leftarrow (\neg(\delta) \cdot R_0) \oplus ((\delta) \cdot R_2)$
12.	$i \leftarrow i + 1$	$i \leftarrow i + 1$	$i \leftarrow i + 0$
13.	$q \leftarrow q + 1$	$q \leftarrow q + 1$	$q \leftarrow q + 1$

If any of the cipher or redundant round is disturbed, then during the computation of cipher round, $(R_0 \oplus R_1)$ is non-zero and $BLFN(R_0 \oplus R_1)$ updates the value of γ to 1. As a result, R_0 is replaced by R_2 in step 11. Similarly, if the computation of dummy round is faulty, $(R_2 \oplus \beta)$ is non-zero and δ evaluates to 1. In this case too, R_0 is replaced by R_2. Also, if the state of comparison variables γ and δ is 1 at the same time, then in step 11, R_0 is substituted by R_2 as this condition indicates fault in comparison variables themselves. In case of undisturbed execution, Algorithm 8.8 generates a correct ciphertext.

8.11   Conclusions

The chapter presents an overview on fault analysis and fault models. After introducing Differential Fault Analysis the chapter starts with a detailed analysis, comparisions and inter-relationships between various fault models which are assumed for DFA on AES. Subsequently we discuss the fault attacks on AES: starting from early efforts to recent attacks on the cipher. The chapter deals with the attacks in two different directions: single and multiple byte fault model based attacks, and attacks which target the data path and the key-schedule. Finally, the chapter concludes with some suitable countermeasures based on detection and infection and tries to provide a comparative study of the schemes.

---

[4]One should note that even a new pair of (β, k^0) cannot protect Algorithm 8.7 against the attacks described in this chapter.

Chapter 9

Cache Attacks on Ciphers

"History is malleable. A new cache of diaries can shed new light, and archeological evidence can challenge our popular assumptions."

(Ken Burns)

American Director

The memory organization in a processor can significantly affect its performance. Of all the memory that is present, the cache is arguably the most important when performance is considered. Cache memories used in processors are equipped with several additional features to meet the high throughput requirements of the processor. The pitfall with cache memories is that they result in side-channel leakage leading to attacks on ciphers. The side-channel leakage is exploited in several flavors of attacks, which are described in this chapter.

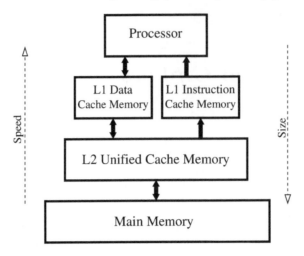

FIGURE 9.1: Memory Hierarchy Structure

9.1   Memory Hierarchy and Cache Memory

Modern superscalar CPU architectures are plagued with the *von Neumann bottleneck* due to the high-speed with which CPUs process instructions and the comparative low speed of memory access. The possibility of using high-speed memory technologies that match CPU processing speeds is restricted by cost factors. To mitigate this speed difference superscalar CPU architectures are built with memory as a hierarchy of levels, with small and fast memories close to the processor and large, slower, less expensive memories below it. A memory stores a subset of the data that is present in the memory below it, while the lowest memory level (generally main-memory, which uses low-cost capacitive DRAMs), contains all the data. The aim is to provide the user with large cheap memories, while providing access at processor speeds.

Memories close to the processor are called *cache memories* and are built with SRAM technology, which offer high access speeds, but are large and expensive. Depending on the data it contains, cache memories are categorized as either *data*, *instruction*, or *unified* (that store both data and instructions). Cache memories are also categorized based on their closeness to the processor as L1, L2, and L3, with L1 being the closest to the processor and L3 the furthest. Most modern desktop and server processors have dedicated L1 data and L1 instruction caches; and a larger unified L2 cache memory. Some servers also contain an L3 cache before the main-memory (**Fig. 9.1**). The L1 caches data present in L2, while L2 caches data present in L3 or the main-memory.

Cache memories work by exploiting the *principle of locality*, which states that programs access a small portion of their address space in any given time instant. The entire memory space of the processor is divided into *blocks*, typically of 64 or 128 contiguous bytes. A memory access results in a *cache hit* if the data is available in the cache memory. For example, an *L1-data cache hit* is obtained if the data accessed is available in the L1-data cache memory. In this case the data is available to the processor quickly and there are no delays. A *cache miss* occurs if the data accessed is not available in the cache memory. In this case the block containing the data is loaded into the cache from a memory lower in the hierarchy. This is a slow process and during which the processor may stall. There are three

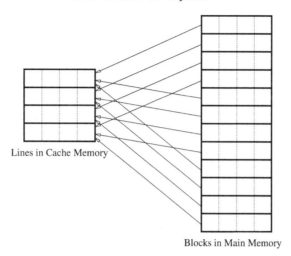

Lines in Cache Memory

Blocks in Main Memory

FIGURE 9.2: Direct Mapped Cache Memory with $2^b = 4$

types of cache misses: compulsory misses, capacity misses, and conflict misses. *Compulsory misses* are cache misses caused by the first access to a block that has never been used in the cache. *Capacity misses* occur when blocks are evicted and then later reloaded into the cache. This occurs when the cache cannot contain all the blocks needed during execution of a program. *Conflict misses* occur when one block replaces another in the cache.

9.1.1 Organization of Cache Memory

The cache memory is organized into lines with each line capable of holding a block of memory. Suppose each block has a capacity to store 2^δ words, and there are 2^b lines in the cache, then at-most $2^{b+\delta}$ words can be stored in the cache. An address translation mechanism is required to determine which cache line a block should gets stored into. In the most simple approach, every 2^b-th block gets mapped into the same cache line. This mapping is called *direct-mapping* and is depicted in **Fig. 9.2**. The address translation mechanism computes two components: the word address A_{word} and the line address A_{line}. If A is the address of the data that is to be accessed then

$$A_{word} = A \bmod 2^\delta$$
$$A_{line} = \lfloor A/2^\delta \rfloor \bmod 2^b \ .$$

Note that the size of the address A_{word} is δ bits while the size of the line address is b bits. Problems arise due to the many-to-one mapping from blocks to lines (as seen in **Fig. 9.2**). The cache controller needs to know which block is present in a cache line before it can decide if a hit or a miss has occurred. This is done by using an identifier called the *tag*. The identifier denoted A_{tag} for the address A is given by

$$A_{tag} = \lfloor \lfloor A/2^\delta \rfloor /2^b \rfloor \ .$$

Thus every line in the cache has an associated tag as shown in **Fig. 9.3**. For every memory access, the tag for the address (A_{tag}) is compared with the tag stored in the cache. A match results in a cache hit, otherwise a cache miss occurs.

Time-driven cache attacks on block ciphers monitor these hits and misses that occur

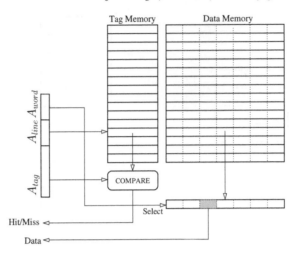

FIGURE 9.3: Organization of Direct Mapped Cache Memory

due to look-up tables used in the implementation. A look-up table is defined as a global array in a program. For example, the C construct for a look-up table is as follows.

```
const unsigned char T0[256] = { 0x63, 0x7C, 0x77, 0x7B, ... };
```

Assuming that the base address for T0 is 0x804af60, Table 9.1 shows how the table gets mapped for a $4KB$ direct-mapped cache with a cache line size of 64 bytes. Every block in the table maps to a distinct cache line provided that the table has lesser blocks than the lines in the cache.

The drawback of the direct mapped scheme is poor cache utilization and *cache thrashing*. Consider a program which continuously reads data from addresses A and then A'. The addresses are such that they map into the same line in the cache (i.e. $A_{line} = A'_{line}$). Thus every memory access would result in a cache miss, considerably slowing down the program even though the other lines in the cache are unused. This is called cache thrashing.

An improved address translation scheme divides the cache into 2^s sets. Each set groups $w = 2^b/2^s$ cache lines. A block now maps to a set instead of a line, and can be present in any of the w cache lines in the set. A cache which uses such an address translation scheme is called a $w-way\ set\ associative\ cache$. The address translation for such a scheme is defined as follows.

$$A_{word} = A \bmod 2^\delta$$
$$A_{set} = \lfloor A/2^\delta \rfloor \bmod 2^s$$
$$A_{tag} = \lfloor \lfloor A/2^\delta \rfloor / 2^s \rfloor$$

TABLE 9.1: Mapping of Table T0 to a Direct-Mapped Cache of size $4KB$ ($2^\delta = 64$ and $2^b = 64$)

Elements	Address	line	Tag
T0[0] to T0[63]	0x804af40 to 0x804af7f	61	0x804a
T0[64] to T0[127]	0x804af80 to 0x804afbf	62	0x804a
T0[128] to T0[191]	0x804afc0 to 0x804b0ff	63	0x804a
T0[192] to T0[255]	0x804b000 to 0x804b03f	0	0x804b

If $w = 2$, the thrashing in the previous example is eliminated as the data corresponding to the addresses A and A' can simultaneously reside in the cache. However, the problem arises again if a program is executed that makes continuous accesses to three or more data from different addresses that share the same cache set.

9.1.2 Improving Cache Performance for Superscalar Processors

As seen in the previous section, a poorly designed cache can slow down a program instead of accelerating it. Therefore, it is important to understand the effect of the cache memory in a program's execution. The average memory access time is often used as a metric for the purpose. For a system with a single level of cache memory, the metric is defined as follows.

$$Average memory access time = Hit time + MissRate \times MissPenalty \ ,$$

where *Hit time* is the time to hit in the cache, while *Miss Penalty* is the time required to replace the block from memory (i.e. the miss time). *Miss Rate* is the fraction of the memory accesses that miss the cache.

9.2 Timing Attacks Due to CPU Architecture

This category of timing attacks, often called *micro-architecture attacks* [16, 76], uses the fact that the behavior of the program is altered due to certain components in the CPU architecture. For public-key cipher implementations, branch prediction hardware [11, 13, 12] and instruction cache memories [8, 9] have been identified as sources of leakage. Data cache memories are a source of leakage for any cipher implementation that use look-up tables, which are accessed at key dependent locations. They have been used against stream ciphers [427], public-key ciphers [298], and block ciphers. In this chapter, we focus on block ciphers, though many of the discussions can be also generalized for other ciphers. But it should also be noted that different algorithms have their own features, which can be exploited in combination with other micro-architectural features.

9.2.1 Attacks on Block Ciphers using Data Cache Memories

A round of a typical symmetric key block cipher comprises of three functions: key mixing, substitution (S-box), and diffusion (**Fig. 9.4**). Due to the ease of implementation and high degree of flexibility in terms of content, the S-box is generally implemented as look-up tables, which are accessed one or more times a round. We provide an overview on the table based software implementation of such ciphers, which are central to the cache attacks.

9.2.1.1 Table-based Implementation of the AES

In 2001, the National Institute of Standards and Technology (NIST) recommended the use of Rijndael as the Advanced Encryption Standard (AES) [117]. AES is a symmetric key block cipher and can use key sizes of either 128, 192, or 256 bits to encrypt and decrypt 128-bit blocks. We summarize the AES-128 standard, which uses a key size of 128 bits. The input to AES-128 is arranged in a 4×4 matrix of bytes called *state*. The state undergoes a series of transformations in 10 rounds during the encryption process.

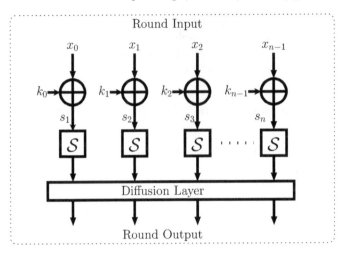

FIGURE 9.4: A Round of a Typical Iterated Block Cipher

Algorithm 9.1: AES-128

Input: 128-bit plaintext input block $\mathbf{x}$ and 128-bit round keys $\mathbf{k}^{(0)}$, $\mathbf{k}^{(2)}$, $\cdots$, $\mathbf{k}^{(10)}$
        generated from a secret key using the AES-128 key generation algorithm
Output: 128-bit ciphertext

1 **begin**
2      $r \leftarrow 1$;
3      $\mathbf{s}^{(0)} \leftarrow \mathsf{AddRoundKeys}(\mathbf{x}, \mathbf{k}^{(0)})$;
4   **while** $r <= 9$ **do**
5          $\mathbf{s}^{(\mathbf{r})} \leftarrow \mathsf{SubBytes}(\mathbf{s}^{(\mathbf{r-1})})$;
6          $\mathbf{s}^{(\mathbf{r})} \leftarrow \mathsf{ShiftRows}(\mathbf{s}^{(\mathbf{r})})$;
7          $\mathbf{s}^{(\mathbf{r})} \leftarrow \mathsf{MixColumns}(\mathbf{s}^{(\mathbf{r})})$;
8          $\mathbf{s}^{(\mathbf{r})} \leftarrow \mathsf{AddRoundKeys}(\mathbf{s}^{(\mathbf{r})}, \mathbf{k}^{(\mathbf{r})})$;
9   **end**
10      $\mathbf{s}^{(10)} \leftarrow \mathsf{SubBytes}(\mathbf{s}^{(9)})$;
11      $\mathbf{s}^{(10)} \leftarrow \mathsf{ShiftRows}(\mathbf{s}^{(10)})$;
12      $\mathbf{y} \leftarrow \mathsf{AddRoundKeys}(\mathbf{s}^{(10)}, \mathbf{k}^{(10)})$;
13   **return y** ;
14 **end**

Algorithm 9.1 presents the AES-128 algorithm. The first operation on the input is the *AddRoundKeys*, which serves to provide the initial randomness by mixing the input key. The state is then subjected to 9 rounds to further increase the diffusion and confusion in the cipher [370]. Each round comprises of 4 operations on the state: *SubBytes*, *ShiftRows*, *MixColumns*, and *AddRoundKeys*. The state is then subjected to a final round, which has all operations except the *MixColumns* operation. The four AES operations are defined as follows:

- *AddRoundKeys* : Each element in the state is subjected to a bitwise XOR with a 128-bit round key. The round key is generated from the secret key by a key expansion algorithm [117].

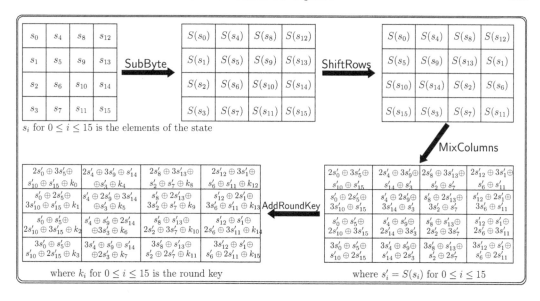

FIGURE 9.5: Transformations of the state in a Round of AES ($1 \leq r \leq 9$)

- *SubBytes :* Each element in the state is replaced by an affine transformation of its inverse in the field $GF(2^8)$. For a byte s_i in the state, this operation is denoted by $S(s_i)$.

- *ShiftRows :* Provides a cyclic shift of the i-th row in the state by i bytes towards the left (where $0 \leq i \leq 3$). That is each byte in the i-th row is cyclically shifted to the left by i bytes.

- *MixColumns :* Provides a column-wise linear transformation of the state matrix. Each column of the state matrix is considered as a polynomial of degree 3 with coefficients in $GF(2^8)$ and multiplied by the polynomial $\{03\}\alpha^3 + \{01\}\alpha^2 + \{01\}\alpha + \{02\}$ mod $(\alpha^4 + 1)$. The combination of *ShiftRows* and *MixColumns* provide the necessary diffusion for the cipher.

Starting from the 4×4 byte state, **Fig. 9.5** shows the transformation it undergoes in a round (for $1 \leq r \leq 9$).

9.2.1.2 Software Implementations of AES

Of all operations, the SubBytes is the most difficult to implement. On 8-bit micro-controllers, a 256-byte look-up table is ideal to perform this operation. The table provides the necessary flexibility in terms of content, small footprint, and speed. For 32-bit platforms, more efficient implementations can be built using larger tables. We give a brief description of this method, which are known as T-table implementations. T-table implementations were first proposed in [104] and have been adopted by several crypto-libraries such as OpenSSL[1].

---

[1] http://www.openssl.org

Consider 4 look-up tables defined as follows:

$$T_0[z] = \begin{bmatrix} 02 \bullet S(z) \\ S(z) \\ S(z) \\ 03 \bullet S(z) \end{bmatrix}; T_1[z] = \begin{bmatrix} 03 \bullet S(z) \\ 02 \bullet S(z) \\ S(z) \\ S(z) \end{bmatrix}; T_2[z] = \begin{bmatrix} S(z) \\ 03 \bullet S(z) \\ 02 \bullet S(z) \\ S(z) \end{bmatrix}; T_3[z] = \begin{bmatrix} S(z) \\ S(z) \\ 03 \bullet S(z) \\ 02 \bullet S(z) \end{bmatrix}$$
(9.1)

Each table is of 1024 bytes mapping a byte z of the state to a 32 bit value. Using these tables, the first nine AES rounds can be expressed as follows

$$\begin{aligned} \mathbf{s}^{(r+1)} =& T_0[s_0^{(r)}] \oplus T_1[s_5^{(r)}] \oplus T_2[s_{10}^{(r)}] \oplus T_3[s_{15}^{(r)}] \oplus [k_0^{(r)}\ k_1^{(r)}\ k_2^{(r)}\ k_3^{(r)}]^T\ \| \\ & T_0[s_4^{(r)}] \oplus T_1[s_9^{(r)}] \oplus T_2[s_{14}^{(r)}] \oplus T_3[s_3^{(r)}] \oplus [k_4^{(r)}\ k_5^{(r)}\ k_6^{(r)}\ k_7^{(r)}]^T\ \| \\ & T_0[s_8^{(r)}] \oplus T_1[s_{13}^{(r)}] \oplus T_2[s_2^{(r)}] \oplus T_3[s_7^{(r)}] \oplus [k_8^{(r)}\ k_9^{(r)}\ k_{10}^{(r)}\ k_{11}^{(r)}]^T\ \| \\ & T_0[s_{12}^{(r)}] \oplus T_1[s_1^{(r)}] \oplus T_2[s_6^{(r)}] \oplus T_3[s_{11}^{(r)}] \oplus [k_{12}^{(r)}\ k_{13}^{(r)}\ k_{14}^{(r)}\ k_{15}^{(r)}]^T \end{aligned}$$
(9.2)

A byte of the state in the current round ($\mathbf{s}^{(r)}$) is denoted $s_i^{(r)}$ and the next round state is denoted $\mathbf{s}^{(r+1)}$, where $0 \leq r \leq 9$ and $0 \leq i \leq 15$. The final round cannot use these tables due to the absence of the *MixColumns* operation.

Cache attacks are applicable on ciphers which are implemented with such look-up tables and executed on platforms with cache memories. These attacks were first hypothesized by Kocher and then Kelsey et al. in [202, 185], theoretically formulated by Page [288], and practically demonstrated by Tsunoo et al. [387]. Depending on the attack model and adversarial capabilities, cache attacks are categorized into three: trace-driven, time-driven, and access-driven. In this section we explain each category and provide a selected survey of cache attacks under each category.

9.3   Trace-Driven Cache Attacks

These attacks are based on the assumption that the adversary is able to monitor the cache activity of an executing cipher. The resulting *trace* records if the cache produced a hit or a miss for every memory access. For example consider the first three memory accesses of the first round of a cipher's implementation, which uses a single look-up table to implement S-box operations. These accesses are to indices $x_0 \oplus k_0$, $x_1 \oplus k_1$, and $x_2 \oplus k_2$ in the look-up table S (as shown in **Fig. 9.4**). Assuming that no part of the table is cached at the start of encryption (a *clean cache*), the following cache traces are possible[2]: (MMM), (MMH), (MHM), and (MHH), where M and H denotes a cache miss and hit respectively. Such traces can be captured by monitoring the power or electro-magnetic radiation of the cryptographic device.

Suppose there are 2^δ elements of the look-up table that share a memory block (the size of the memory block is equal to the cache line size) and the look-up table occupies l memory blocks. Thus the table has $l \cdot 2^\delta$ elements, and to address each element of the table requires $n = \delta + \log_2 l$ bits. $\log_2 l$ bits is the line address while δ bits is the word address (Section 9.1.1). Thus n is the entropy of a memory access to the table. By observing cache traces, this entropy can be reduced.

Consider for a given input, suppose the trace MHx (where x can be either M or H)

---

[2]Note that the first operation would always result in a compulsory M due to the clean cache assumption.

is observed from the power or electro-magnetic traces of the cryptographic device, the adversary can then infer that the first and second access were to the same memory block of the table (a *collision*) therefore will have the same line address (Section 9.1.1). The following relation can then be built: $\langle x_0 \oplus k_0 \rangle = \langle x_1 \oplus k_1 \rangle$, where $\langle \cdot \rangle$ indicates the address of the memory block (the top $\log_2 l$ bits of the table index). Thus the XOR of the secret keys k_0 and k_1 can be inferred.

$$\langle k_0 \oplus k_1 \rangle = \langle x_0 \oplus x_1 \rangle \tag{9.3}$$

Since k_0 and k_1 together have an initial entropy of $2n$, the entropy reduces to $n + \delta$ after the cache traces are obtained. Equation 9.3 is the basic relation which can be deduced from the cache traces. Trace-driven attacks use this relation along with cipher properties to get more information about the secret key. There have several trace-driven attacks that have been published. For example [288, 46, 216, 121, 58, 10, 127]. In this section we survey the various reported trace-driven attacks.

9.3.1 A Theoretical Cache Trace Attack on DES

In 2002, Page formulated the first ever cache attack on a block cipher [288]. He showed how the secret key of DES [118] can be recovered from its cache traces. DES has a Fesitel structure with eight S-box accesses per round. An implementation of DES was considered, which used a table to implement each S-box (the implementation thus used eight look-up tables). Cache traces of the first two rounds of the cipher were considered and an assumption made that the cache is initially clean at the start of encryption. The first round would therefore have a trace comprising of 8 cache misses: (MMMMMMMM). On the other hand, the trace for the second round would comprise of misses and hits. For example (MMMH-MMHM). The cache hits infer collisions with the respective first round memory accesses. Thus, in the example, collisions are present in the fourth and seventh tables.

The attack works as follows. Consider one of the eight look-up tables. The table is accessed once in each round. For the first two rounds, the index to the table (i_1 for the first round and i_2 for the second round) is first expressed in terms of the input and the key. For example $i_1 = F_1(x[\cdots], k[\cdots])$ and $i_2 = F_2(x[\cdots], k[\cdots])$, where F_1 and F_2 are some non-linear functions on few bits of the input and few bits of the key denoted $x[\cdots]$ and $k[\cdots]$ respectively. Next, inputs are selected such that a cache hit in the concerned table is obtained in the second round. From this cache hit, a collision is inferred resulting in the equality $\langle i_1 \rangle = \langle i_2 \rangle$. The entire key space for $k[\cdots]$ can then be searched to filter out keys that satisfy this equality. By taking several different inputs that result in the desired collision, the key space can be reduced further until a unique key is found.

To demonstrate the attack, Page simulated a direct mapped cache of size $1KB$ having a cache line size of 4 bytes. Each table in the DES implementation is of 16 bytes, therefore the table can hold at-most $\frac{16}{4} = 4$ cache lines (or $l = 4$). The presence of a collision gives $\log_2 l = \log_2 4 = 2$ bits of information about the memory block in the table accessed. To uniquely identify the entire 56 bit key of DES when the first look-up table is considered, 2^{10} inputs need to be chosen that satisfy the required conditions and a key space of 2^{32} needs to be searched.

9.3.2 Trace-Driven Attacks on AES

Since the standardization of Rijndael as the AES, there have been several efforts to attack the cipher using cache attacks. Two of the initial cache trace attacks were from Lauradoux in [216] and Fournier and Tunstall in [121]. Both works target a 256 byte single table AES implementation. If cache traces of the first round are considered then relationships between the key bytes can be constructed of the form $\langle k_i^{(0)} \oplus k_j^{(0)} \rangle$, where $0 \le i, j \le 15$ and $k_i^{(0)}$ and $k_j^{(0)}$ are the AES whitening keys as described in Algorithm 9.1. If $\log_2 l$ bits of information are revealed about the memory accesses, then the first round attack can reduce the key space from 2^{128} to $2^{128-15 \cdot \log_2 l}$ keys. Assuming 16 elements of the table fit in a single cache line (thus the number of blocks occupied by the table is $l = 256/16 = 16$), the key space for AES-128 is reduced to 2^{68} keys. Fournier and Tunstall also showed that if the second round cache traces were also considered then relationships between the two rounds can be used to reduce the key space further. For example, if the first look-up in two rounds collide, then the following relationship can be built (refer Algorithm 9.1 and **Fig. 9.5**):

$$
\begin{aligned}
\langle s_0^{(0)} \rangle &= \langle s_0^{(1)} \rangle \\
\langle s_0^{(0)} \rangle &= \langle 2 \cdot S(s_0^{(0)}) \oplus 3 \cdot S(s_5^{(0)}) \oplus S(s_{10}^{(0)}) \oplus S(s_{15}^{(0)}) \oplus k_0^{(1)} \rangle \\
\langle x_0 \oplus k_0^{(0)} \rangle &= \langle 2 \cdot S(x_0 \oplus k_0^{(0)}) \oplus 3 \cdot S(x_5 \oplus k_5^{(0)}) \\
&\quad \oplus S(x_{10} \oplus k_{10}^{(0)}) \oplus S(x_{15} \oplus k_{15}^{(0)}) \oplus k_0^{(1)} \rangle
\end{aligned}
\tag{9.4}
$$

Further, the key expansion algorithm of AES can be used to represent $k_0^{(1)}$ as $k_0^{(0)} \oplus S(k_{13}^{(0)}) \oplus 1$. Thus there are 5 key bytes involved in the relation: $k_0^{(0)}$, $k_5^{(0)}$, $k_{10}^{(0)}$, $k_{13}^{(0)}$, and $k_{15}^{(0)}$. The values of these bytes are unknown, however $\log_2 l$ bits of their XOR relationship can be determined from the first round attack (i.e., the first round attack gives $\langle k_0^{(0)} \oplus k_5^{(0)} \rangle$, $\langle k_0^{(0)} \oplus k_{10}^{(0)} \rangle$, $\langle k_0^{(0)} \oplus k_{13}^{(0)} \rangle$, $\langle k_0^{(0)} \oplus k_{15}^{(0)} \rangle$). Consequently the key space for the tuple of 5 key bytes reduces from 2^{40} to 2^{24} (assuming $\log_2 l = 4$). A search in the key space of 2^{24} which satisfy Equation 9.4 is required to completely recover the key bytes.

The attack in [121] used adaptively chosen plaintexts. First x_1 is varied until a cache hit is obtained in the second table access, then x_2 is varied until the third access results in a cache hit, and so on until 15 cache hits are obtained in the first round. The first round cache trace would then look as follows: (MHHHHHHHHHHHHHHHH). In [127], Gallais, Kizhvatov, and Tunstall observed that while varying x_i (for $1 \le i \le 14$), to obtain a collision in the i-th memory access, the information in the cache trace to the right of i is ignored (*i.e.* all traces for j ($i < j \le 15$) are ignored). They then provided an improved attack that utilizes information in these parts of the trace as well. This reduced the expected number of traces required in the first round of attack from 125 (in [121]) to around 15. They also applied these enhancements to improve the second round attack on AES.

9.3.3 Trace-Driven Attacks on the Last Round of AES

The last round of AES does not have the *MixColumns* operation therefore popular implementations like OpenSSL[3] use a different look-up table exclusively for the last round. This results in known ciphertext attacks, which are more powerful than the first and second round attacks in terms of the number of cache traces required. A byte of ciphertext c_i can be expressed as $y_i = S(s_i^{(9)}) \oplus k_i^{(10)}$, where $0 \le i \le 15$ and the elements of the state at the input of the last round is denoted $s_i^{(9)}$ (Algorithm 9.1). Note that here we have neglected the *ShiftRows* operation of the last round as it does not affect the attack's efficiency. The inverse S-box operation (S^{-1}) can be used to express the index of the look-up table of the last round in terms of the ciphertext and key as follows:

$$
s_i^{(9)} = S^{-1}(y_i \oplus k_i^{(10)})
\tag{9.5}
$$

---

[3] http://www.openssl.org

In [10], Aciiçmez and Koç showed that if collisions in the last round exists, say between the i_1 and i_2 accesses ($0 \leq i_1, i_2 \leq 15$), then the following relation can be constructed.

$$\langle s_{i_1}^{(9)} \rangle = \langle s_{i_2}^{(9)} \rangle$$
$$\langle S^{-1}(y_{i_1} \oplus k_{i_1}^{(10)}) \rangle = \langle S^{-1}(y_{i_2} \oplus k_{i_2}^{(10)}) \rangle \tag{9.6}$$

Due to the non-linearity of the S-box, only the correct values of $k_{i_1}^{(10)}$ and $k_{i_2}^{(10)}$ obey the relation for every ciphertext sample.

9.3.4 Trace-Driven Attack Based on Induced Cache Miss

In the previous trace-driven attacks discussed, a cache which is not cleaned at the start of encryption either rendered the attack ineffective or adversely affected its efficiency. In [46], Bertoni et al. presented an attack which works well even with an unclean cache. However, a more powerful adversary is required, who is capable of invalidating a single cache line. The attack is based on the observation that if two encryptions on the same input are performed one after the other, the second encryption would have significant number of cache hits. This is because the first encryption loads the S-box table into the cache, while the second encryption directly reads data off the cache. The attack steps are as follows:

1. For an input **x** perform an encryption.

2. Invalidate a cache line occupied by the table.

3. Encrypt **x** again and this time obtain the cache trace by monitoring its power consumption.

In the second encryption, if a cache miss is observed in the i-th memory access of the first round, it can be inferred with significant probability that the invalidated cache line was accessed during the i-th memory access, where $0 \leq i \leq 15$. This reveals the most significant bits of the index of the table access (*i.e.* $\langle s_i \rangle$), and consequently bits of the key since $\langle k_i^{(0)} \rangle = \langle s_i^{(0)} \oplus x_i \rangle$. Bertoni et al. demonstrated this attack on the AES block cipher with the S-box implemented using a table of 256 bytes. The attack was demonstrated using the Simplescalar[4] simulator and software power models to determine the cache trace.

9.4 Access-Driven Cache Attacks

Cache memories are a shared resource in a system. If a process running in a system fetches a block of data into the cache, the data will remain in the cache memory unless evicted. The eviction can be done by any process in the system and can result in a covert timing channel. The channel was first discovered by Wray in [411] and Hu in [154]. Attacks on cryptographic algorithms using the shared feature in cache memories were suggested independently by Percival in [298] and Osvik, Shamir, and Tromer in 2005 [280]. These attacks are known as *access-driven* attacks and use time as a side-channel instead of power or electro-magnetic traces. We briefly describe selected works in this category of cache attacks.

---

[4]http://www.simplescalar.com

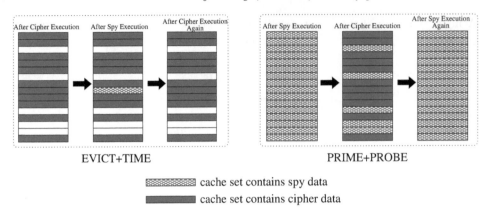

cache set contains spy data

cache set contains cipher data

FIGURE 9.6: Cache Sets Corresponding to Table $\mathcal{T}_j$ for Evict+Time and Prime+Probe Access Driven Attacks

9.4.1   Access-Driven Attacks on Block Ciphers

Consider the T-table implementation for AES (Section 9.2.1.2). For the first round, the table $\mathcal{T}_j$ is accessed at index $s_{i+j}^{(0)} = (x_{i+j} \oplus k_{i+j}^{(0)})$ for $0 \leq j \leq 3$ and $i \in \{0, 4, 8, 12\}$, where x_{i+j} is an input byte and $k_{i+j}^{(0)}$ the corresponding whitening key byte. Suppose the key byte $k_{i+j}^{(0)}$ is guessed (the guess represented by $\tilde{k}_{i+j}^{(0)}$), then a corresponding index to table $\mathcal{T}_j$ can be computed as $\tilde{s}_{i+j}^{(0)} = x_{i+j} \oplus \tilde{k}_{i+j}^{(0)}$. If the guessed key is correct (*i.e.* $k_{i+j}^{(0)} = \tilde{k}_{i+j}^{(0)}$) then the computed index is also correct (*i.e.* $s_{i+j}^{(0)} = \tilde{s}_{i+j}^{(0)}$) and viceversa.

In [280, 384, 281], Osvik, Tromer, and Shamir showed two methods that an adversary monitoring the covert timing channels in cache memories can use to identify when the equality $\langle s_{i+j}^{(0)} \rangle = \langle \tilde{s}_{i+j}^{(0)} \rangle$ holds. The methods *evict+time* and *prime+probe* require that the adversary knows (or learns) the memory location of the table $\mathcal{T}_j$. We summarize the methods below:

Evict + Time : For every possible value of the table index ($\langle \tilde{s}_{i+j}^{(0)} \rangle$) perform the following

1. Trigger an encryption (Algorithm 9.1) for a random input **x**.

2. For a guess of $\tilde{s}_{i+j}^{(0)}$, determine the memory address of $\mathcal{T}_j[\tilde{s}_{i+j}^{(0)}]$ and compute the cache set it gets mapped into. Denote this cache set as M.

3. Perform operations so that all data present in cache set M is evicted.

4. Trigger a second encryption with **x** again and time it.

Fig. 9.6 shows the various stages of the cache sets used by the table $\mathcal{T}_j$. There are two possible outcomes after the second encryption:

- If $\langle s_{i+j}^{(0)} \rangle = \langle \tilde{s}_{i+j}^{(0)} \rangle$ implying $(\langle k_{i+j}^{(0)} \rangle = \langle \tilde{k}_{i+j}^{(0)} \rangle)$, then the cache set M is always accessed by both encryptions (in steps 1 and 4). Particularly, the second encryption would *always* (with probability = 1) result in a cache miss for the access $\mathcal{T}_j[s_{i+j}^{(0)}]$.

- If $\langle s_{i+j}^{(0)} \rangle \neq \langle \tilde{s}_{i+j}^{(0)} \rangle$ implying $(\langle k_{i+j}^{(0)} \rangle \neq \langle \tilde{k}_{i+j}^{(0)} \rangle)$, then for a value of **x**, the cache set M is not accessed at $\mathcal{T}_j[\tilde{s}_{i+j}^{(0)}]$. However, the set *may* be accessed by the other memory accesses to $\mathcal{T}_j$. Thus for the second encryption (in step 4), the probability of a cache miss is ≤ 1 for the access $\mathcal{T}_j[s_{i+j}^{(0)}]$.

If several values of $\mathbf{x}$ are considered, the ever-present cache miss at $\mathcal{T}_j[s_{i+j}^{(0)}]$ when $\langle s_{i+j}^{(0)} \rangle = \langle \tilde{s}_{i+j}^{(0)} \rangle$, would cause a slight increase in the expected encryption time compared to when $\langle s_{i+j}^{(0)} \rangle \neq \langle s_{i+j}^{(0)} \rangle$ where the cache miss at $\mathcal{T}_j[s_{i+j}^{(0)}]$ is not always present. This difference in time can be detected by an adversary to determine the correct value of $\langle s_{i+j}^{(0)} \rangle$ thereby obtaining $\langle k_{i+j}^{(0)} \rangle$.

In [56], Bogdanov, Eisenbarth, and Paar use the Evict+Time strategy to mount a differential cache-collision attack on AES. The main idea of the attack is to choose pairs of plaintexts such that they cause *wide-collisions*; five AES S-box operations (one in the 2nd round and four in the 3rd) possess either pairwisely equal or pairwisely distinct values. The evict+time technique is used to identify plaintexts pairs with wide collisions. An existence of a wide collision would cause on average the second encryption to be faster by a margin of 5 compared to when there is no wide collision. The wide collisions are then used to construct a set of four non-linear equations, which when solved result in parts of the key.

Prime + Probe: In the evict+time method, the time for the memory access to $\mathcal{T}_j[s_{i+j}^{(0)}]$ (where $0 \leq j \leq 3$ and $i \in \{0, 4, 8, 12\}$) gets reflected in the total execution time of the cipher, thus leading to the attack. However, this technique delivers a low success due to the presence of additional memory accesses and other code that executes during the encryption. Further, there is considerable noise from sources such as instruction scheduling, conditional branches, and cache contention thus resulting in a low signal to noise ratio (SNR). In the prime+probe method, smaller codes are timed thus leading to a larger attack success. The steps involved in the prime+probe is as follows:

1. Define an array A as large as the cache memory and read a value of A for every memory block (thus filling the entire cache with A).

2. Trigger an encryption with a random input $\mathbf{x}$.

3. For a guess of $\langle \tilde{s}_{i+j}^{(0)} \rangle$, determine the cache set that $\mathcal{T}_j[\langle \tilde{s}_{i+j}^{(0)} \rangle]$ gets mapped into. Denote this cache set as M.

4. Access A at indices which get mapped to the cache set M and time the accesses. **Fig. 9.6** shows the various stages of the cache sets used by the table $\mathcal{T}_j$.

If $\langle \tilde{s}_{i+j}^{(0)} \rangle$ is correct (*i.e.* $\langle \tilde{s}_{i+j}^{(0)} \rangle = \langle s_{i+j}^{(0)} \rangle$), then $A's$ data present in the cache set M would be evicted with probability $= 1$ during the encryption in step 2. However, this probability can be less than one if $\langle \tilde{s}_i^{(0)} \rangle$ is incorrect. Further, an eviction of $A's$ data at M would result in a cache miss in the fourth step; identified by a longer memory access time. However, if $A's$ data at M is not evicted, then the last step would have a cache hit therefore a shorter access time. The correct $\langle \tilde{s}_{i+j}^{(0)} \rangle$ (thus $\langle \tilde{k}_i^{(0)} \rangle$) can therefore be identified by repeating the four steps with several inputs.

9.4.2 Second Round Access-Driven Attack on AES

For a table with $l \cdot 2^\delta$ elements each element has an entropy $n = \delta + \log_2 l$, where 2^δ is the number of elements in the table sharing a memory block and l is the number of memory blocks occupied by the table. The first round attack can reveal at most $\log_2 l$ bits of each key byte. In order to reveal the entire key byte, the second round of AES needs to be targeted [280, 384, 281]. Consider the first table access in the second round. From Algorithm 9.1, **Fig. 9.5**, and the key scheduling algorithm of AES, this is

$$s_0^{(1)} = 2 \cdot S[x_0 \oplus k_0^{(0)}] \oplus 3 \cdot S[x_5 \oplus k_5^{(0)}] \oplus S[x_{10} \oplus k_{10}^{(0)}] \oplus S[x_{15} \oplus k_{15}^{(0)}] \oplus k_0^{(0)} \oplus S(k_{13}^{(0)}) \oplus 1 \ . \quad (9.7)$$

The value of $\langle s_0^{(1)} \rangle$ is affected by keys $k_0^{(0)}$, $k_5^{(0)}$, $k_{10}^{(0)}$, $k_{13}^{(0)}$, and $k_{15}^{(0)}$ each occupying one byte. The first round attack reveals $\log_2 l$ bits of each of these key bytes leaving δ bits unknown, Thus there is a space of $5 \cdot 2^\delta$ keys that need to be searched. The evict+time or prime+probe methods can be used along with Equation 9.7 to identify the correct key from this key space.

9.4.3   A Last Round Access Driven Attack on AES

As described in Section 9.3.3, the last round of some implementations of AES use a different table (called $\mathcal{T}_4$). This table is exclusively used in the last round and can lead to known ciphertext attacks. A byte of the ciphertext can be expressed as $y_i = k_i^{(10)} \oplus S(s_i^{(9)})$ where $0 \leq i \leq 15$ (here we have ignored the last round *ShiftRows* operation as it does not affect the attack complexity). Thus $k_i^{(10)} = y_i \oplus S(s_i^{(9)})$. Evict+time or prime+probe methods can be used to determine $\langle S(s_i^{(9)}) \rangle$ and therefore $\langle k_i^{(10)} \rangle$ can be determined.

Neve and Seifert in [272] developed two ways to determine all bits of $k_i^{(10)}$. The first method called the *non-elimination method*, is based on the fact that for a given value of y_i, the input to the *SubBytes* in the last round (*i.e.* $s_i^{(9)}$) is fixed. This implies that the cache set accessed for a given y_i is always the same. Now consider that $y_i = t_1$ corresponds to $s_i^{(9)} = o_1$, where $0 \leq t_1, o_1 \leq 255$. Similarly $y_i = t_2$ corresponds to $s_i^{(9)} = o_2$, where $0 \leq t_2, o_2 \leq 255$. Thus,

$$\begin{aligned} t_1 &= k_i^{(10)} \oplus S(o_1) \\ t_2 &= k_i^{(10)} \oplus S(o_2) \end{aligned} \qquad (9.8)$$

The access attack reveals $\langle o_1 \rangle$ and $\langle o_2 \rangle$. This leaves 2^δ possible key options for $k_i^{(10)}$. This key space can then be reduced by using the relation $t_1 \oplus t_2 = S(o_1) \oplus S(o_2)$ obtained from Equation 9.8. Further reduction of key space is possible by considering different pairs of values for y_i. The authors in [272] estimate that 186 pairs are required to uniquely identify the correct key.

The second method is based on eliminating incorrect values of $s_i^{(9)}$. It uses the fact that the table $\mathcal{T}_4$ is accessed only 16 times and not all memory blocks of the table are likely to be accessed during the encryption. The memory blocks not accessed can be detected by the evict+time or the prime+probe methods. It is certain that $S(s_i^{(9)})$ is not one of the values in the unaccessed blocks. Thus if n blocks of $\mathcal{T}_4$ are not accessed during the encryption, then $n \cdot 2^\delta$ values of $s_i^{(9)}$ can be eliminated. By using different inputs to the cipher, more values of $s_i^{(9)}$ can be eliminated until a unique value is obtained. This corresponds to a unique value of $k_i^{(10)}$.

9.4.4   Asynchronous Access-Driven Attacks

The access-driven attacks discussed so far were synchronous, where in, it is assumed that the adversary can trigger an encryption. A less restrictive form of the attack is the asynchronous mode, where a non-privileged adversary running concurrently in an independent user space, need only monitor the cache activity to determine cache sets accessed by the executing cipher. No triggering of encryptions is required. Instead, the only requirements is that the adversary executes in the same processor and in parallel with the cipher. Asynchronous access driven attacks were pioneered by Percival in [298], who demonstrated an attack on RSA. Osvik et al. and Neve then explored the feasibility of asynchronous attacks on AES [280, 384, 281, 272], though the practicality of the work remains unclear. Aciiçmez et al.[14] were the first to present a practical asynchronous access-driven using instruction caches on OpenSSL's DSA, while [142] demonstrated the first practical asynchronous attack on AES.

In an asynchronous attack, the adversary runs a spy process which periodically reads or writes data into cache lines and monitors the time it took. An eviction of the spy's data by another process (such as an executing cipher) from the cache will result in a longer memory access time due to the cache miss that occurs. Thus giving a clue about the memory access patterns of the cipher process. Such leakages are also possible when the spy and cipher are executing in different security zones. Such attacks are important in cloud computing virtualized environments [327], where several users share the same hardware, albeit in different security zones.

A system vulnerable to such asynchronous attacks utilizes at least one of the following features in the computer system: symmetrical multithreading [281, 298] or pre-emptive operating system (OS) scheduler [272, 142].

Symmetrical multithreading allows multiple processes to execute simultaneously on a single processor. The hardware resources including the cache memories are shared between the processes. The cache memory acts as a covert channel transmitting information about the memory access patterns of the cipher.

Pre-emptive OS Scheduling divides CPU time into equally spaced intervals called *slices*. At the beginning of a slice, a process gets allocated the CPU and executes until it voluntarily relinquishes the CPU or the time slice completes. A new process may then get allocated to the CPU by a process known as *context-switching*. In [272], Neve and Seifert suggests that spy processes can exploit such schedulers to obtain covert information about a cipher's execution, though no explicit details about the construction was given. In [385], Tsafrir, Etsion, and Feitelson present a practical malicious code that can exploit context-switching in OS schedulers. The intuition is that it starts executing at the beginning of a slice, but yields the processor before the slice completes. Another process is then scheduled for the remaining time interval in the slice. The authors show several applications of the malicious code such as denial of services, bypassing profiling and administrative polices, etc. Gullasch, Bangerter, and Krenn use such a malicious code to develop a fine-grained access-driven cache timing attack in [142].

9.4.5 Fine-Grained Access-Driven Attacks on AES

The previous access-driven cache-timing attacks on AES [280, 384, 281, 272] used the fact that the spy determines all the cache sets accessed by AES only after the encryption is complete. Due to the large granularity of measurements in the attacks, it was not possible for the spy to determine intermediate accesses done by AES. In [142], Gullasch, Bangerter, and Krenn show a way of exploiting the OS scheduler to obtain information about every single cache access performed by AES.

In order to practically mount the attack, the Completely Fair Scheduler (CFS), which is typically used in the Linux kernels, is exploited. About 100 spy threads are launched in the system. When a spy thread gets scheduled into the processor, it first makes the cache measurements, and then waits until most of the time slice is complete before blocking itself.

The cipher then executes in the small time interval that remains in the time slice. Typically the cipher is made to execute for only 200 clock cycles before getting blocked again. This interval is just sufficient for the cipher to make one memory access. The next spy thread then gets scheduled into the processor and the single access made by the cipher is determined by measuring the memory access time to access its data. In this way, the cipher is executed very slowly, and each memory access it makes can be tracked by the spy.

9.5   Time-Driven Cache Attacks

Time-driven attacks differ from access-driven attacks as they do not require the use of cache memory as a resource shared between multiple processes. Instead the adversary uses execution time of the cipher as the side-channel[5]. Execution time is influenced by several factors such as instruction processing, memory accesses, interrupts, and page faults. Of all these factors, it is only the variations in the execution time caused due to memory accesses that is of interest from the side-channel attack perspective. Since the variations due to memory access is relatively small compared to the variations due to other sources, the signal-to-noise ratio is low. Consequently, large number of time measurements need to be made before the secret key of the cipher can be retrieved. An advantage however is the fact that time measurements do not need to be done in the system hosting the encryption. They can even be done over the network leading to *remote timing attacks*. We provide a brief description of the state-of-the-art remote timing attacks before discussing the various time-driven attacks on block ciphers.

9.5.1   Remote Timing Attacks

A typical remote timing attack uses a sever-client architecture. The server executes the cipher, while the adversary runs in the client or is an eves-dropper. The server and client can reside in the same host or in different hosts connected by a network as shown in **Fig. 9.7**. Communication between the server and client is by network sockets. In the attack, the client triggers encryptions on the server and measures the time required for the operation to complete. This time, known as *round-trip time*, is denoted by T in **Fig. 9.7**. The round-trip time comprises of 3 components [101]:

$$T = A \cdot ExecutionTime + ProbagationTime + Jitter \ . \tag{9.9}$$

The *ExecutionTime* is the time required to perform an encryption. That is, from the time the crypto-program receives its input to the time it produces an output. It is variations in this component that is useful for the attack. The scaling factor A accommodates clock skew between the server and client. The *ProbagationTime* is the average latency of the communication, while the *Jitter* absorbs all the randomness introduced by the network, load on the machines, and any other source. The value of *Jitter* would vary depending on the distance between the server and client. For public-key ciphers the variation in *ExecutionTime* is strong enough to overcome the jitter in LANs. In [66] and [65], two attacks over LANs were demonstrated. The former was on RSA while the latter on ECDSA. For block

---

[5]The evict+time attack discussed in Section 9.4.1 falls into both time-driven as well as access-driven categories. Like time-driven attacks, the encryption time of the cipher is used as the side-channel and like access-driven attacks, the cache sets accessed by the cipher is obtained by a spy which shares the cache memory of the cipher process.

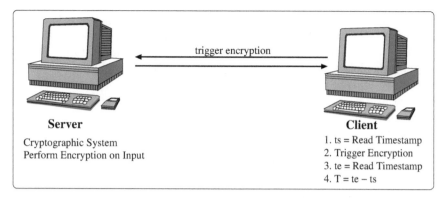

FIGURE 9.7: Remote Timing Attacks

ciphers, the variations in *ExecutionTime* is comparatively small, making attacks over the LAN more difficult. The remote timing attacks demonstrated on block ciphers were with the server and client running on the same host and communicating via TCP/IP sockets ([15] and [406]). These attacks are applicable in the current cloud computing infrastructures, where several users (including malicious users) share the same hardware but in different virtualized environments. The attack in [406] is demonstrated in one such environment. Further, time-driven attacks could possibly threaten future networks, where increased network speeds would reduce the amount of jitter in the measurements making variations in the *ExecutionTime* more easily observable. Most time-driven attacks use these variations to distinguish between a hit and a miss. This is discussed in the next part of the section.

9.5.2 Distinguishing between a Hit and Miss with Time

Distinguishing between a cache hit and miss can be easily done when power traces of the processor is captured. For a pair of memory accesses to a look-up table in a cipher's implementation, Page showed that the entropy of the key can be reduced from $2n$ bits to $n+\delta$ bits (see Section 9.3). At about the same time, Tsunoo et al. showed how similar information

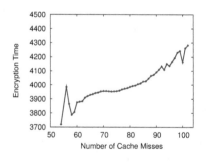

(a) Encryption Time vs Cache Misses

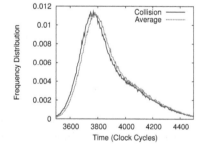

(b) Frequency Distribution of Encryption Time

FIGURE 9.8: Distributions of Encryption Time of OpenSSL AES Block Cipher on Intel Core 2 Duo (E7500)

about the keys can be obtained by using timing instead of power traces [387]. The model by Tsunoo et al. uses the fact that the execution time is linearly proportional to the number of cache misses due to the look-up table used in the cipher's implementation. This is seen in **Fig. 9.8(a)**, which plots the execution time versus number of cache misses due to the look-up tables for the OpenSSL implementation of AES executing on an Intel Core 2 Duo machine. Thus, on average, a longer execution time would imply the presence of higher number of cache misses during the encryption. **Fig. 9.8(b)** shows two timing distributions for an implementation of AES. The only difference between the two distributions is that on average, one of the distributions has one lesser cache miss compared to the other. This distribution, called *collision* in **Fig. 9.8(b)**, can be clearly distinguished by the shorter encryption time.

This principle to distinguish a hit from a miss was used in the first practical cache attack [387]. The cipher targeted was MISTY1 [248] implemented on an Intel Pentium III system running at 600MHz. The attack required around 2^{17} chosen plaintexts and successfully retrieved the key in over 90% of the attacks. The attack was improved in [388] to reduce the number of measurements required to around 2^{14}. In [386], encryption time was used to distinguish between a cache hit and a cache miss in DES. The attack required around 2^{23} known plaintexts to retrieve the DES key. Later Aciiçmez, Schindler, and Koç used the same principle to mount a first round time-driven cache attack on AES [15].

9.5.3 Second Round Time-Driven Attack on AES

The first round attack on AES is able to determine relations of the form $\langle k_i^{(0)} \oplus k_j^{(0)} \rangle$, where $k_i^{(0)}$ and $k_j^{(0)}$ ($0 \leq i < j \leq 15$) are a pair of whitening key bytes (see Section 9.2.1.1). On a typical system with a 64-byte cache line, the first round attack can reduce the entropy of an AES-128 key from 128 bits to 80 bits for the standard T-table implementation (Section 9.2.1.2). In order to reduce the entropy further, Aciiçmez, Schindler, and Koç suggest targeting the second round [15]. Here we provide the basic second round attack technique.

Let $\tilde{\mathbf{k}}^{(0)}$ be a guess of the whitening key. If there is a collision between the states $s_0^{(0)}$ and $s_0^{(1)}$ (*i.e.* the first access in the first and second rounds respectively), then from Equation 9.4 the following relation is obtained.

$$\langle x_0 \rangle = \langle 2 \cdot S(x_0 \oplus \tilde{k}_0^{(0)}) \oplus 3 \cdot S(x_5 \oplus \tilde{k}_5^{(0)}) \oplus S(x_{10} \oplus \tilde{k}_{10}^{(0)}) \oplus S(x_{15} \oplus \tilde{k}_{15}^{(0)}) \oplus S(\tilde{k}_{13}^{(0)}) \oplus 1 \rangle \quad (9.10)$$

There are 5 unknown key bytes involved: $\tilde{k}_0^{(0)}$, $\tilde{k}_5^{(0)}$, $\tilde{k}_{10}^{(0)}$, $\tilde{k}_{13}^{(0)}$, and $\tilde{k}_{15}^{(0)}$. For each guess of the 5 bytes, a set is created (thus there are 2^{40} sets). A random plaintext is chosen and the encryption time is found. The encryption time is added into all sets which satisfy Equation 9.10 for the corresponding plaintext and key guess. Several such plaintexts and corresponding encryption time are taken, after which the average time in each of the 2^{40} key sets is found. The set in which the average time is the least corresponds to the correct key.

The reason for the attack to work is as follows. Since the plaintexts are chosen at random, there will be several plaintexts which do not cause a collision between the states $s_0^{(0)}$ and $s_0^{(1)}$ during the execution of the cipher and several other plaintexts which do cause the collision. Further, each of these plaintexts will satisfy Equation 9.10 for several wrong keys. Said another way, for a set corresponding to a wrong key, the encryption time that gets added may or may not have the required collision (*i.e.* between $s_0^{(1)}$ and $s_0^{(1)}$). However, for the set corresponding to the correct key, the encryption time that gets added will always have the collision between $s_0^{(0)}$ and $s_0^{(1)}$. Thus, on average, the encryption time added to the correct set will have a cache miss less compared to the encryption time added to a wrong set. The smaller number of cache misses in the correct set will result in a smaller average execution time. This is used to distinguish the correct key.

9.5.4 Theoretical Analysis of Time-Driven Attacks

Mathematically analyzing side-channel attacks is important to quickly evaluate the security of a crypto-system. For DPA, there have been several works that develop such mathematical frameworks. For example, Mangard in [241] develops a framework to evaluate the success of a DPA attack in terms of the number of power traces captured.

For cache attacks, the success depends on the implementation of the crypto-system under attack and the cache architecture. A brief theoretical analysis of time-driven attacks was made in [15] and [386], while Tiri et al. delivered a comprehensive treatment in [380]. The latter work adopts the statistical framework developed by Mangard [241] for time-driven cache attacks on block ciphers and shows the relationship between the attack's success (in terms of number of timing measurements), the cache line size, and the number and size of the look-up tables used in the cipher's implementation.

The model by Tiri et al. uses the fact that the encryption time is directly proportional to the number of cache misses that occur due to the look-up tables present in the cipher's implementation (as was seen in **Fig. 9.8(a)**). If the cipher makes n accesses to a table $\mathcal{T}$ occupying l memory blocks, the probability of obtaining m cache misses is given by

$$\Pr[m] = \frac{1}{l^n}\binom{l}{m}\sum_{j=1}^{m}(-1)^{m-j}\binom{m}{j}j^k \ . \tag{9.11}$$

Further, the number of cache misses forms a Gaussian distribution with mean (μ) and variance (σ^2) defined to be

$$\mu = \sum_{m=1}^{l} m \cdot \Pr[m]$$
$$\sigma^2 = \sum_{m=1}^{l} m^2 \cdot \Pr[m] - \mu^2 \ . \tag{9.12}$$

In a similar way another Gaussian distribution is obtained, which represents the number of cache misses during an encryption given that one collision is always present (*ever-present*) for a specific memory access. The distinguishability between the two distributions is used in time-driven attacks (for example, **Fig. 9.8(b)**, where the distribution called collision has the ever-present collision, while the average case distribution does not). Tiri et al. used estimation techniques from [241] to compute the number of measurements required to distinguish the two distributions with a certain level of confidence.

9.5.5 Profiled Time-Driven Attack on AES

In 2005, Bernstein developed a first round time-driven attack on AES [44] capable of retrieving the whitening keys $k_i^{(0)}$, where $0 \le i \le 15$ (Algorithm 9.1). Unlike the previous attacks discussed so far, Bernstein's attack has two phases: a profiling phase followed by an attack phase. During the *profiling phase*, the adversary learns the characteristics of the system by building a timing profile called *template* using a known AES key. With this template, any other secret key used in the AES implementation on that system (or an exactly similar system) can be attacked. During the *attack phase*, another timing profile is

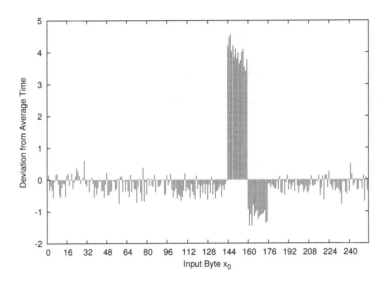

FIGURE 9.9: Timing Profile for $\mathcal{D}_0$ vs x_0 for AES on an Intel Core 2 Duo (E7500)

built for the secret key. A statistical comparison of this timing profile with the template reveals the secret key. Below we provide details of the attack.

Building a Timing Profile: The AES input has sixteen bytes as seen in Section 9.2.1.1. For each byte an array of size 256 is defined, which stores the average execution time. We denote these arrays by $\mathcal{A}_i$ for $0 \leq i \leq 15$ and the 256 elements as $\mathcal{A}_i[j]$ for $0 \leq j \leq 255$. The adversary finds the encryption time for a randomly chosen input (say $\mathbf{x} = (x_0||\cdots||x_i||\cdots x_{15})$, $0 \leq i \leq 15$) and updates the average timing of $\mathcal{A}_i[x_i]$ for all 16 arrays. This is repeated for around 2^{24} inputs. The average time (t_{avg}) for all encryptions is computed and deviation vectors found as follows $\mathcal{D}_i[j] = \mathcal{A}_i[j] - t_{avg}$ for $0 \leq i \leq 15$ and $0 \leq j \leq 255$. Each deviation vector forms a *timing profile* for an input byte. **Fig. 9.9** shows the timing profile for the first input byte of AES. It plots the value of x_0 on the x-axis and $\mathcal{D}_0[x_0]$ on the y-axis. To attack a key byte, two such timing profiles are required. One for a known key and the other for an unknown key.

Extracting Keys from the Timing Profiles: Each vertical line in the timing profile provides an average deviation $\mathcal{D}_i[j]$ where $0 \leq i \leq 15$ and $0 \leq j \leq 255$. This deviation is an invariant with respect to the index of the look-up table accessed in the i-th memory access of the first round of AES. As seen in Algorithm 9.1, the i-th memory access to the look-up table in the first round has the form $s_i^{(0)} = x_i \oplus k_i^{(0)}$. Thus the time deviation is an invariant with respect to $s_i^{(0)}$ (*i.e.* $\mathcal{D}_i[s_i^{(0)}]$ is an invariant).

Now consider two timing profiles for the i-th byte ($0 \leq i \leq 15$) : one from a known key (denoted $\hat{k}_i^{(0)}$) and another from an unknown key (denoted $\tilde{k}_i^{(0)}$). Further, $\mathcal{D}_i[s_i^{(0)}]$ is an invariant and there are two ways to obtain this invariant. Using $\hat{k}_i^{(0)}$ the invariant can be obtained from $\hat{x}_i \oplus \hat{k}_i^{(0)}$ for some $\hat{x}_i$ ($0 \leq \hat{x}_i \leq 255$) and using $\tilde{k}_i^{(0)}$ the invariant can be obtained from $\tilde{x}_i \oplus \tilde{k}_i^{(0)}$ for some $\tilde{x}_i$ ($0 \leq \tilde{x}_i \leq 255$). Thus with reference to the deviation of time, $\mathcal{D}_i[\tilde{x}_i \oplus \tilde{k}_i^{(0)}] = \mathcal{D}_i[\hat{x}_i \oplus \hat{k}_i^{(0)}]$. With respect to the timing profiles, the invariant has shifted from $\hat{x}_i$ in the known timing profile to $\tilde{x}_i$ in the unknown timing profile. If this shift can be determined then the unknown key can be computed as $\tilde{k}_i^{(0)} = \tilde{x}_i \oplus \hat{x}_i \oplus \hat{k}_i^{(0)}$.

To determine the shift, the unknown key byte is guessed (say *kguess*) and for every possible value of x ($0 \leq x \leq 255$), a correlation coefficient is computed as follows:

$$CC_{kguess} = \sum_{x=0}^{255} \mathcal{D}_i[x \oplus \hat{k}_i^{(0)}] \times \mathcal{D}_i[x \oplus kguess] \qquad (9.13)$$

There are thus 256 values of CC_{kguess}, which are arranged in a decreasing order. The key guess corresponding to the maximum value of CC_{kguess} is most likely the unknown secret byte of the key ($\tilde{k}_i^{(0)}$).

Analysis of Bernstein's Attack : The reason for the attack to work is the fact that for a given platform and an i ($0 \leq i \leq 15$), execution time varies depending on the value of $x_i \oplus k_i^{(0)}$. This variation in execution time is attributed to several causes such as number of cache misses that occur during the encryption, interrupts, context switches, etc. However, in the attack, we are only interested in the variation obtained after taking the average of several encryptions. This measurement is not influenced by events that are non-periodic with respect to time, provided an appropriate threshold is used to filter out excessively large encryption times. The factors which causes variation in the average encryption time is as follows.

- *Conflict Misses.* These cache misses occur due to memory accesses which evict the recently accessed data. Conflict misses can be non-periodic. But as pointed out by Neve, Seifert, and Wang [273, 271], conflict misses can also be periodic in nature. Periodic conflict misses, cause cache misses in the same cache set at regular intervals of time. This periodic form of conflict misses affect the average encryption time, because they evict the same data from the cache in every encryption.

- *Micro-architectural Effects.* There can be small variations in the time depending on the micro-architecture of the system, and the data being accessed. Bernstein gives an example of recently occurring stores to memory affecting the load time in certain locations. Another example is loads from memory, which causes conflicts in cache banks. Further micro-architectural components in cache memory, like the hardware prefetchers have been found to also affect information leakage.

Loaded Cache Variant: In [72], Canteaut, Lauradoux, and Seznec claim that the AES execution will behave differently depending on the initial state of the cache. If the cache is clean of any AES data before the start of encryption then the timing side-channels mostly detect cache misses. These variation in execution time are significant because data read from the RAM takes considerably more time than data read from the cache. In Bernstein's attack, the cache is flushed of all AES data at the start of encryption. This is forced by making system calls and by array manipulations. Both these operations can have a major influence in the state of the cache.

If the encryption starts with a loaded cache, the variations in execution time does not depend on the cache misses anymore. The variations in time are due conflict misses or the micro-architecture of the processor. The variations due to the micro-architecture are more subtle, therefore Canteaut, Lauradoux, and Seznec provide a stronger variant of Bernstein's attack for such models. The variant attack uses the correlation between the execution time and the value of subsets of the bits of $s_i^{(0)}$ (for $0 \leq i \leq 15$) instead.

Second Round Attack Variant: In theory, all bits of the whitening key can be obtained from Bernstein's first round attack. This is unlike other first round cache attacks where the amount of information obtained about the whitening key is limited to a few most significant bits of each byte. In practice however, the result is not different from any other first round cache attack. The recovered bits are limited just as in any other cache attack. In [271], Neve, Seifert, and Wang provide a second round profiled cache-timing attack to reveal the remaining key bits. The attack works by building templates based on $s_i^{(1)}$ instead of $s_i^{(0)}$ for $0 \leq i \leq 15$. Results show that all bits of the key are recovered with the same number of timing measurements as the first round attack.

9.6   Countermeasures for Timing Attacks

Timing attacks on software implementations of ciphers uses the fact that the time required to perform an operation varies depending on the cipher's input and key. Just like any other SCA, a timing attack has two phases: an online phase followed by an offline phase. The *online phase* monitors the time of the device, while the *offline phase* predicts the secret key from the timing. There have been several timing attacks published since Kocher's work in 1996 [202]. These attacks target various ciphers, platforms, and implementations. However there are certain minimum criteria required for any attack to succeed. The following enumerates these criteria.

1. There should be variations in the way a crypto-system processes its inputs. These variations must be manifested through the time required to execute an operation.

2. The variations must depend on the secret key of the crypto-system.

3. The adversary must be able to monitor the timing with an instrument powerful enough to measure the variations in the signal carrying the timing information.

4. The number of measurements that needs to be monitored depends on how much information can be garnered from a measurement, the noise, and the offline capabilities of the adversary to extract the signal.

5. The attacker should know the design of the crypto-system. Note that in certain cases the information needed can be learnt from the side-channel itself.

6. The attacker should have a synchronization signal to know when the crypto-system starts and/or completes its processing.

If any of these criterion are not met, then timing attacks are prevented. It is therefore not surprising that countermeasures try to make difficult to fulfill one or more of these criteria. Completely preventing a criterion can be done, for example by eliminating the cache memory from processor designs. However, this leads to significant performance degradation, which far super seeds the security gains obtained. Thus the aim of practical countermeasures is to obtain the right balance between security and performance.

This section summarizes countermeasures for cache attacks from [288, 289, 280, 216, 298, 384, 121, 44, 72, 64, 98, 53, 402, 165, 245]. The techniques to counter timing attacks form a subset of these. Depending on where they are applied, countermeasures can be categorized as application layer or hardware layer countermeasures. The remaining of the section discusses each category.

9.6.1 Application-Layer Countermeasures

Application level countermeasures are easy to apply and can provide sufficient levels of security against certain trace-driven, time-driven, and access-driven attacks. However they suffer from significant shortcomings. First, most of the application layer countermeasures are heavy and inefficient. Further, all applications sharing the same host require to apply these countermeasures to protect against a common vulnerability. This adversely affects performance and energy requirements of the system. Nevertheless these countermeasures provide a quick fix to prevent cache attacks. We therefore survey some of these countermeasures here.

Implementations without Look-up Tables: For cache attacks, which rely on look-up tables used in the cipher's implementation, an obvious countermeasure would be to not use look-up tables. One method is to design new ciphers which have no S-boxes, for example [200]. For the general class of ciphers that do use S-boxes, implementations without look-up tables would have a drastic affect on performance. An alternate non-look-up table based implementation is the use of bitslicing [48, 322], which allows multiple encryptions to be done concurrently in a single processor. Bitslicing yields high speeds of encryption, however is restricted to certain non-feedback modes of operation, and therefore cannot be universally applied.

In [313], we suggested a hybrid countermeasure for AES, which can protect against cache attacks as well as provide the necessary performance. Our method is based on the fact that attacks can exploit only the first, second, third, and the last round of AES. The countermeasure therefore chose to implement these rounds without a look-up table, while implementing the remaining intermediate rounds with look-up tables. The implementations without look-up tables in the first, second, three and last rounds shield the implementation against cache attacks, while the look-up tables used in the intermediate rounds provide the necessary performance.

Cache Warming: Loading the contents of the look-up tables prior to encryption. As a result the accesses to the look-up table during the cipher execution would be cache hits. In addition to the warming, the elements of the table should not be evicted during the encryption [44]. This is not easy to satisfy.

Small Tables: Consider an implementation of a cipher with a look-up table of size $l \cdot 2^\delta$, where l is the number of memory blocks occupied by the table and 2^δ the number of elements in the table that share the same memory block. The number of bits required to access an element in the table is $\delta + \log_2 l$. Most cache attacks are not able to distinguish between elements that lie in the same block. Assuming that the table is aligned to a memory block, these cache attacks can only retrieve $\log_2 l$ bits leaving the remaining δ bits uncertain. The uncertainty can be increased by having small tables (thereby reducing l) or packing more elements into a memory block.

In the extreme, if the entire look-up table can be made to fit in a single cache line, then the adversary cannot ascertain any bit. In such cases $\log_2 l = 0$, that is the adversary retrieves 0 bits. The problem however is that S-boxes used in most ciphers are considerably larger than the memory block. Therefore compressing them into a single block is not easy. In [317] and [319], we provided techniques that can be used to compress S-boxes of standard ciphers like CLEFIA into a single memory block. One technique we proposed is suited for S-boxes based on the multiplicative inverse in a finite field. We implemented these S-boxes using composite field isomorphisms [286]. This allowed the use of smaller tables which stored sub-field operations.

Data-Oblivious Memory Access Pattern: This allows the pattern of memory accesses to be performed in an order that is oblivious to the data passing through the algorithm. To a certain extent, modern microprocessors provide such data oblivious memory accesses by reordering instructions. For example, four memory accesses to different locations say, A, B, C, and D, would get executed in any of the 4! ways (say $BCDA$ or $DCAB$). This reordering would increase the difficulty of trace-driven and certain time-driven and access-driven attacks. However, the reordering is restricted to memory accesses which do not have data dependencies. For block ciphers, such independent memory accesses are present within a round but not across rounds, therefore only partially fulfills data-oblivious requirements.

A naïve method to attain complete data-oblivious memory accesses is to read elements from every memory block of the table, in a fixed order, and use just the one needed. Another option is to add noise to the memory access pattern by adding spurious accesses, for example by performing a dummy encryption in parallel to the real one. A third option is to mask the sensitive table accesses with random masks that are stripped away at the end of the encryption. Alternatively, the table can be permuted regularly to thwart attacks using statistical analysis.

Generic program transformations are also present for hiding memory accesses [135]. However, there are huge overheads in performance and memory requirements. More practical proposals have been developed using shuffling [431] and permutations [432].

Constant and Random Time Implementations: A combination of the countermeasures discussed so far can be used to deliver constant time implementations [44, 72]. To obtain such implementations requires cache warming to ensure that all memory accesses result in cache hits. A timing probe which measures the current execution time for the cipher, and a compensation loop which is designed to increase the encryption time until the worst case execution time is obtained. Additionally to prevent evictions of the table occurring during an interrupt, an interrupt detector is required to re-warm the cache.

As opposed to constant time implementations, adding a random delay to each execution time can be used to increase the attack difficulty. The countermeasure was first proposed for DPA in [94]. Tunstall and Benoit in [389] and later Coron and Kizhvatov in [99, 100] provide improvements by modifying the distribution of the delay.

9.6.2   Countermeasures Applied in the Hardware

Subtle changes in the hardware can make attacks much more difficult with little overhead in the performance. In this section we survey some of the hardware modifications that have been suggested to counter cache attacks.

Non-Cached Memory Accesses: Certain memory pages can be flagged as non-cacheable. This would prevent memory accesses loading data into the cache. Consequently, every memory access would read data from the RAM, and every access would thereby be a cache miss preventing all cache attacks.

Specialized Cache Designs: have been proposed for thwarting cache attacks. They work on the fact that information leakage is due to sharing of cache resources, thus leading to *cache interference*. These solutions provide means of preventing access-driven attacks. Their effectiveness in blocking time-driven attacks has not yet been analyzed. In [298], Percival suggests eliminating cache interference by modifying the cache eviction algorithms. The modified eviction algorithms would minimize the extent to which one thread can evict data from another thread.

In [290], Page proposed to partition cache memory, which is a direct-mapped *partitioned cache* that can dynamically be partitioned into protected regions by the use of specialized cache management instructions. By modifying the instruction set architecture and tagging memory accesses with partition identifiers, each memory access is hashed into a dedicated partition. Such cache management instructions are only available to the operating system. While this technique prevents cache interference from multiple processes, the cache memory is under-utilized due to rigid partitions. For example, a process may use very few cache lines of its partition, but the unused cache lines are not available to another process.

In [402], Wang and Lee provide an improvement on the work by Page using a construct called *partition-locked cache* (PLCache), which the cache lines of interest are locked in cache, thereby creating a private partition. These locked cache lines cannot be evicted by other cache accesses not belonging to the private partition. In the hardware, each cache line requires additional tags comprising of a flag to indicate if the the line is locked and an identifier to indicate the owner of the cache line. The under-utilization of Page's partitioned cache still persists because the locked lines cannot be used by other processes, even after the owner no longer requires them.

Wang and Lee also propose a *random-permutation cache* (RPCache) in [402], where as the name suggests, randomizes the cache interference, so that the difficulty of the attack increases. The design is based on the fact that information is leaked only when cache interference is present between two different processes. RPCache aims at randomizing such interferences so that no useful information is gleaned. The architecture requires an additional hardware called the *permutation table*, which maps the set bits in the effective address to obtain new set bits. These are then used to index the cache set array. Changing the contents of the permutation table will invalidate the respective lines in the cache. This causes additional cache misses and a randomization in the cache interference. In [403], Wang and Lee use an underlying direct-mapped cache and dynamically reprogrammable cache mapping algorithms to achieve randomization. From the security perspective, this technique is shown to be as effective in preventing attacks as RPCache, but with less overheads on the performance. In [204], Kong et al. show that partition locked and random permutation caches, although effective in reducing performance overhead, are still vulnerable to advanced cache attack techniques. They then go on to propose modifications to Wang and Lee's proposals to improve the security [206, 205].

In [113], Domnitser et al. provide a low-cost solution to prevent access-driven attacks based on the fact that the cipher evicts one or more lines of the spy data from the cache. The solution, which requires small modifications of the replacement policies in cache memories, restricts an application from holding more than a pre-determined number of lines in each set of a set-associative cache. With such a cache memory, the spy can never hold all cache lines in the set, therefore the probability that the cipher evicts spy data is reduced. By controlling the number of lines that the spy can hold, tradeoff between performance and security can be achieved.

Specialized Instructions: A few recent microprocessors support specialized instructions for ciphers. For example Intel supports the AES-NI for their new processors [360], which allows AES encryption or decryption using a combination of six instructions. These instructions have dedicated hardware support [247] and therefore do require to use look-up tables. Dedicated hardware has the added advantage of boosting performance. With Intel's AES-NI, speed of encryptions can be increased more than an order of magnitude. The drawback however is that such dedicated hardware are only applicable for AES based crypto-systems. There are several other ciphers that are used in many applications, which cannot gain from these instructions. These ciphers are still vulnerable to attacks. An alternate direction is to develop improved instruction sets, which would be friendly for the general cipher algorithm. For example, bit-permutation instructions were suggested in [429, 218] as a means to speed up a typical block cipher. For public-key ciphers, several instruction enhancements have been suggested such as [137, 138, 395].

In [193], we suggested a new instruction to be added to the microprocessor ISA called PERMS. This instruction allows any arbitrary permutation of the bits in an n bit word, and can be used to accelerate diffusion layer implementations in block ciphers, thereby providing high-speed encryptions.

Prefetching: Prefetching data into cache memory is present in modern microprocessors to reduce the memory latencies by anticipating accesses. In [216], prefetching algorithms is suggested as a means to counter cache attacks, since it would confuse the adversary while distinguishing between a cache hit and a miss.

While prefetching was in fact demonstrated to make access-driven attacks slightly more difficult [110]. It has the opposite effect in profiled time-driven cache attacks.

Controlling Time: Current timing attacks require distinguishing between events by their execution time. This requires highly accurate timing measurements to be made. A popular method for making these measurements is by the RDTSC (*read time stamp counter*) instruction, which is present in most modern day processors. This instruction allows the processor's time stamp counter (TSC) to be read. A typical measurement would look as follows:

```
t1 = RDTSC();
function();      /* the operation that needs to be timed */
t2 = RDTSC();
t = t2 - t1;
return t;
```

Since the TSC is incremented in every clock cycle, RDTSC can provide nanoscale accuracy. Denying the user access to RDTSC instructions can prevent cache-timing attacks (both time-driven and access-driven). However, the main drawback is that several benign applications (such as Linux kernels, multimedia games, and certain cryptographic algorithms [245]) rely on RDTSC. These applications will cease to function if the instruction is disabled. A less stringent way is to therefore *fuzzy* the timestamp returned by the RDTSC instruction. This is possible because unlike timing attacks, benign applications do not require highly accurate timing measurements. Time fuzzing can be either done by reducing the accuracy of the measurement (such as by masking least significant bits of the timestamp [280]) or by reducing the precision of the measurement (such as by injecting noise into the timestamp [165]).

If $t1$ is the current value of the TSC, then masking returns $\lfloor \frac{t1}{E} \rfloor$, where E is a time duration called *epoch*. Consequently, t has the form $\lfloor \frac{t2}{E} \rfloor - \lfloor \frac{t1}{E} \rfloor$. The size of the epoch is crucial. It should be large enough to protect against timing attacks, yet small enough to not affect benign applications. In [394], Vattikonda et al. propose a way to bypass masking schemes. The technique uses the fact that timing attacks do not need absolute timing measurements, rather it is only required to distinguish between two or more events. In the proposal, the adversary first loops continuously to synchronize with the start of the epoch. This is denoted by $t1e = \lfloor \frac{t1}{E} \rfloor$. Then the operation to be timed is called, and an RDTSC instruction is invoked in a tight loop till the end of the epoch (detected by the change in the RDTSC value). A counter c counts the number of RDTSC invocations made. The value of c in the end of the loop can be used to distinguish between events executed by the operation, as a smaller value of $t2e = \lfloor \frac{t2}{E} \rfloor$ will lead to a larger value of c.

```
c = 0;
/* Synchronize to the start of epoch */
```

```
t1e = RDTSC();
while(t1e != RDTSC());
function()     /* the operation that needs to be timed */
/* Continuously scan TSC until end of epoch */
t2e = RDTSC();
while(t2e != RDTSC()) c = c + 1;
return c and (t2e - t1e)
```

In the noise injection technique, a random offset between $[0, E)$ is added to the timestamp value returned by RDTSC. There are however two possible problems. The first is likely to occur when multiple RDTSC instructions are invoked. The first invocation of RDTSC returns a value of the form $t1 + r1$, while the second invocation return has the form $t2 + r2$, where $t1$ and $t2$ are the timestamp values and $r1$ and $r2$ are the random numbers $(0 \leq r_1, r_2 < E)$. If the two invocations are done in quick succession then $t1 = t2$, while it is possible that $r1 > r2$. This gives the impression of time moving backwards. The second drawback of the noise injection scheme is that the randomness is limited by the size of E. If sufficient number time measurements are made and average taken, the effect of the injected noise can be eliminated.

In [245], Martin, Demme, and Sethumadhavan propose a scheme called *Timewarp*. The scheme prevents the attack in [394] by restricting the TSC reading to end of an epoch. Additionally the RDTSC instruction is delayed by a random time (less than an epoch) before the result is returned. Noise is further added to the TSC value to increase the difficulty of the attack.

Even without using the RDTSC instructions, it is possible to make highly accurate timing measurements. For example on multi-processor systems, a counter can be run in a tight loop in a different thread, which can be used to make sufficiently precise timing measurements. These are called *virtual time-stamp counters* (VTSC). To prevent use of such counters, [245] proposes to add hardware in the processor, which detects these loops and injects random delays into them.

9.7 Conclusions

The chapter presents an overview on memory hierarchy and the impact of cache memory for improving the performance of processors. Subsequently, we deal with the impact of cache in leading to timing attacks against table based software implementations of ciphers like AES. The chapter presents a detailed overview on the three types of cache attacks: namely trace-driven, access-driven, and time-driven. Finally we present some discussions on possible mitigations that can be adopted at either the application or hardware level againt these attacks.

Chapter 10

Power Analysis of Cipher Implementations

"Every contact leaves a trace."

(Edmond Locard)

Pioneer in forensic science who became known as the Sherlock Holmes of
France, 1877-1966

Power analysis of ciphers is a methodology to determine the key of cryptosystems by
analyzing the power consumption of a device. The attacks exploit the dependence of power

consumption of cryptographic implementations on the underlying operations and internal data. In this chapter, we make a detailed study of power-based attacks: to understand the causes and threats arising out of them.

10.1 Power Attack Setup and Power Traces

The cryptographic device performs various operations as defined by the ciphering algorithm. The key, which is the target of an attack, is used several times in combination with the input, often the plaintext to result in the ciphertext. Power attacks, in addition to controlling the input plaintext, and obtaining the output ciphertext also relies on the power traces. These power traces contain leaked information of intermediate values, often stored in hardware registers.

(a) Laboratory Setup for Power Analysis

(b) Components of a Power Attack Setup

FIGURE 10.1: Power Attack Set Up

A successful power attack on a cryptographic device requires proper understanding of the power characteristic of the device. However, the central requirement of a power attack is the capability to obtain an accurate power trace. Hence developing a proper setup which will enable us to collect power traces accurately is of primary importance. **Fig. 10.1(a)** shows a laboratory environment with the schematic of the setup shown in 10.1(b).

The encryption algorithm is implemented in various kinds of platforms, ranging from microcontrollers to FPGAs and ASICs. For our discussion in this chapter, we shall consider implementations on FPGAs experimented on SASEBO-GII platforms (**Fig. 10.2(a)**).

As depicted in **Fig. 10.1**, the power analysis experimental bed comprises of three distinct components.

1. **Design Under Test:** The design under test for our experimentation is a standard SASEBO BOARD which is used for evaluation. We provide a short description of the SASEBO evaluation board here. More details of the same can be found in [346]. There are two FPGAs in this board. One is known as control FPGA (Spartan 3A XC3S400A) and another is known as cryptographic FPGA (Virtex 5 xc5vlx50). Control FPGA

contains the codes for communication with CPU [346]. It acts as a controller which provides input and required control signals to cryptographic FPGA. Cryptographic FPGA contains the implementation of the cryptographic algorithm to be attacked. Communication with CPU is done through a USB cable. Plain text is given to this board through CPU and cipher text is sent to CPU for verification. Signals from this board is given to oscilloscope to plot power traces.

The detailed diagram of SASEBO is shown in **Fig. 10.2**.

 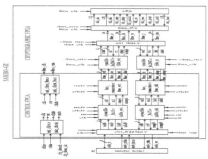

(a) The SASEBO-GII Board   (b) Diagram of SASEBO-GII [346]

FIGURE 10.2: Power Attack Platform using SASEBO-GII

2. **Oscilloscope:** The oscilloscope is used for acquiring power traces. Upon receiving trigger signal, power traces is obtained and is sent to CPU. Triggering is very important for obtaining power traces. Triggering indicates start of the encryption and help us to identify the desired power traces. The oscilloscope should have a high sampling rate. We use a Tektronix MSO4034B Mixed Signal Oscilloscope with specifications 2.50 Gs/s, 350 MHz and 4 channels. We do not use any dedicated probes.

3. **CPU:** The heart of this setup is the CPU. The whole setup along with the operation of the other components are controlled by CPU. Interface between CPU and SASEBO board and CPU and oscilloscope is developed using *C#* codes. Plain text is sent to FPGA and cipher text is received for the verification. Power trace is received from the oscilloscope and is used to attack the scheme.

10.1.1   Power Traces of an AES hardware

As an example, we consider in this chapter the rolled AES architecture (**Fig. 10.3**) described in Chapter 4. For simplicity we consider the 128 bit version of AES, though the discussion can easily be extended to the other versions. The AES-128 design implemented on Xilinx Virtex 5 FPGA(xc5vlx50) has a signal called *trigger* signal which aligns the acquired power traces so that each trace profile correspond to same sequence of operations in an encryption run. This signal is tapped from the controller pin on the FPGA board and is fed to the second channel of the oscilloscope. The plaintext input to the design are generated from the PC and cipher text is fed back to the PC for the correctness verification. The power trace from the SASEBO GII is accquired by the oscilloscope and the power trace values are stored in the PC. An example power trace for a full 10 round encryption is shown in **Fig. 10.4**.

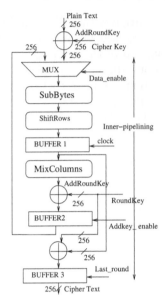

FIGURE 10.3: The Rolled Encryption Unit subjected to Power Analysis

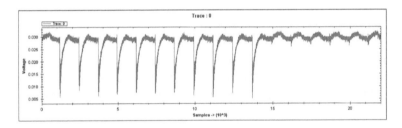

FIGURE 10.4: Power Trace of an AES-128 encryption

A closer inspection shows the 10 rounds of encryption. Each of the 10 rounds correspond to the power consumption in a clock cycle of time period of 500 ns (i.e., 2 MHz clock in the cryptographic FPGA of the SASEBO board). In **Fig. 10.5** we show the zoomed out trace of the last round of the encryption. The last round power trace is used in the subsequent attack, as one can develop a ciphertext only attack using power analysis. Also in AES-128 recovering the last round key helps to recover the initial key of the cipher.

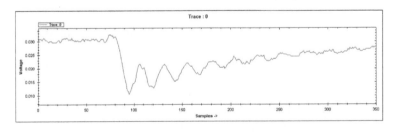

FIGURE 10.5: Power Trace of the last round of AES

10.1.2 Quality of Power Measurements

The quality of a measurement setup can be described by the amount of noise present in the measured power traces which are usually voltage or current signals. The two most important kinds of noise in power traces are electronic noise and algorithmic noise. The electronic noise refers to the fluctuations in power traces when the same operation is repeated several times on the device. The factors attributing to this comprise of noise of the power supply, noise of clock generator and conduction and radiation emissions from the components connected to the device under attack. The algorithmic or switching noise occurs because of contributions of logic cells to the power traces which are not under attack. The power measurement captured from the setup is actually the total power consumption of the FPGA device. But often the power dissipation from a small circuit of the entire hardware is targetted in an attack to reveal the key. The power from all other parts of the device is a noise to the attacker which forms the switching noise.

The power consumption of CMOS based cryptographic devices is an analog high-frequency (HF) signal which means the frequency components or bandwidth of the power consumption signals are in GHz range. The measurement of such signals is a highly challenging task as they are affected in propagation from the logic cells on the device to the oscilloscope by factors like thermal noise, crosstalk, filtering etc. The quality of the experimental setup is determined by how it copes with these high-frequency effects. **Fig. 10.6** shows the blurring of the power signals of the last two rounds of AES-128, when the encryption with the same plaintext and key input provides different power traces. Such noisy power traces would imply that more power traces are required to obtain the actual key. To have the most accurate power traces, a high bandwidth (GHz range) path is required from the logic cells on the FPGA device to the oscilloscope. But depending on the quality of the setup, the parasitics in the mentioned path limit the bandwidth and hence cause deviations in measurements. These parasitics in the form of on-chip bypass capacitances are mostly located in the power supply grid of the FPGA which provide stable voltage supply to the device. Also the bonding wires on the I/O pads create parasitic inductance. These parasitic components filter out the high bandwidth components and blurs the individual consumption peaks due to individual logic cells leading to switching noise.

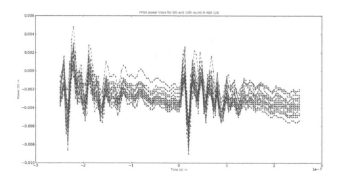

FIGURE 10.6: Electronic Noise for 9th and 10th round of AES-128

A proper experimental setup should aim for faster power trace acquisition over huge number of plaintexts as required in the attacks. In order to obtain several power traces without intervention the captured power traces will be sent online from the mixed signal oscilloscope (MSO) to the PC as soon as they are captured. This will facilitate on-the fly processing of power traces. Also the MSO has 4 analog channels and 16 digital channels which facilitates on-chip debugging of the cryptographic design on FPGA platform. The TPP series passive probes of the MSO have an analog bandwidth of 1 GHz and less than 4 pF of capacitive loading. As the parasitic elements as mentioned above are less, it enables a proper path for power trace signals with high bandwidth to propagate from the SASEBO-GII FPGA board to the MSO and leads to increased accuracy in the power trace measurements.

10.2   Power Models

Power analysis depends largely on power simulation, which predicts the power variation of a device wrt. the change of internal values. The internal value is often computed from the ciphertext and an assumed portion of the key, and the *power model* maps the internal value to a power level. Again like our modeling of critical path and path delay in Chapter 3, actual values of the power are not important, but rather their relative ordering is crucial. Various forms of power models and variations have been suggested, but CMOS circuits which is the most common forms of technologies used in the present hardware design industry use the Hamming weight and Hamming distance power models to predict the variation of power. We present an overview on these models underneath.

10.2.1   Hamming Weight Power Model

In this model, we assume that the power consumption of a CMOS circuit is proportional to the value at the tth time instance, say v_t. The model is oblivious of the state at the $(t-1)^{th}$ time instance, v_{t-1}. Thus, given the state v_t, the estimated power is denoted as $HW(v_t)$, where HW is the Hamming Weight function. It may be argued that this if an inaccurate model, given the fact that the dynamic power of a CMOS circuit rather depends on the transition $v_{t-1} \rightarrow v_t$ than on the present state. However the Hamming Weight model provides an idea of power consumption in several occasions. Consider situations where the circuit is pre-charged to a logic 1 or 0 (ie. $v_{t-1}=0$ or 1), the power is in that case either directly or inversely proportional to the value v_t. In situations where the initial value v_t is also uniformly distributed, the dependence still holds directly or inversely owing to the fact that the transition power due to a $0 \rightarrow 1$ toggle or $1 \rightarrow 0$ switch are not same. This is because of different charge and discharge paths of a CMOS gate **Fig. 10.7**. Thus assuming that the actual power is better captured by $P = HW(v_{t-1} \oplus v_t)$, there may exist a correlation between P and $HW(v_t)$ due to this asymmetric power consumption of CMOS gates.

10.2.2   Hamming Distance Power Model

This is a more accurate model of the power consumption of a CMOS gate. Here the power consumption of a CMOS circuit is assumed to be proportional to the Hamming Distance of the input and the output vector. In short, the power consumption is modeled as $P = HD(v_{t-1}, v_t) = HW(v_{t-1} \oplus v_t)$, where HD denotes the Hamming Distance between two vectors. This is a more accurate model as it captures the no of toggles in a net of the circuit. However in order to use the model the attacker needs more knowledge than that for using the Hamming Weight model. The attacker here needs to know the state of the circuit in successive clock cycles. This model is useful for modeling the power consumption of registers

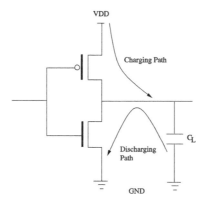

FIGURE 10.7: Different Power Consumption for $0 \to 1$ and $1 \to 0$ transition for CMOS switch

and buses. On the contrary, they are incapable for estimating the power consumption due to combination circuits as these transitions are unknown due to the presence of unknown transitions because of glitches.

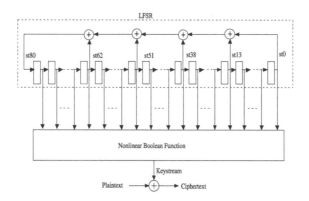

FIGURE 10.8: Non-linear filter generator based stream cipher

In order to illustrate the above models consider as an example, a Linear Feedback Shift Register (LFSR), which forms the basic building blocks of keystream generators of Stream Ciphers and are well suited for hardware implementations. The stream cipher using the LFSR and a nonlinear function is shown in **Fig. 10.8**. The stream cipher was implemented on Xilinx FPGA platform XC3S400-5PQ208 device and the respective power traces were taken as voltage drop across 1-ohm resistance put across V_{ccint} and *GND*. The power traces for 80 consecutive clock cycles after deasserting reset is shown in **Fig. 10.9**.

The power traces were taken at a resolution of 20ns/pt. Using the above discussed power models, namely Hamming Weight and Hamming Distance for each clock cycle after the start of the execution are shown in **Fig. 10.10(a)** and **Fig. 10.10(b)**. The similarity of the Hamming distance and the Hamming weight plots (**Fig. 10.10(a)** and **Fig. 10.10(b)**) with **Fig. 10.9** can be observed visually.

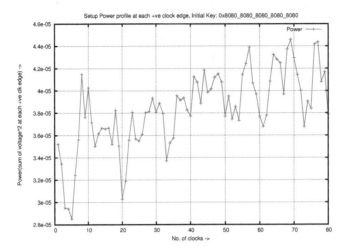

FIGURE 10.9: Power profile of the implemented stream cipher as obtained from the setup

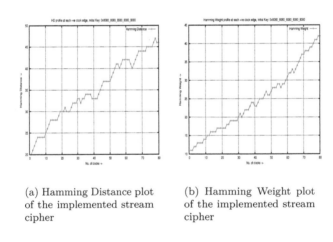

(a) Hamming Distance plot of the implemented stream cipher

(b) Hamming Weight plot of the implemented stream cipher

FIGURE 10.10: Power Models

10.2.3   Why Do Gates Leak?

In this section using the Hamming Distance power model, we discuss why a CMOS gate can be subjected to power analysis. Consider a gate, denoted as $y = f(x)$, where x comprises of the inputs. As an example, let us consider 4 different energy consumptions due to transitions of the gate, namely $P_{0 \to 0}$, $P_{0 \to 1}$, $P_{1 \to 0}$, and $P_{1 \to 1}$. Consider the transitions of an AND gate, denoted as $y = AND(a, b) = a \wedge b$, where a and b are bits, in Table 10.1. The energy levels, as stated before, are annotated in the fourth column. This column can be used to estimate the average energy when the output bit is 0 or 1, namely $E(q = 0)$ and $E(q = 1)$ respectively. We show that the power consumption of the device is correlated by the *value* of the output bit. It may be emphasized that this observation is central to the working of a DPA attack.

TABLE 10.1: Transitions of an AND gate

a	b	q	Energy
$0 \to 0$	$0 \to 0$	$0 \to 0$	$E_{0 \to 0}$
$0 \to 0$	$0 \to 1$	$0 \to 0$	$E_{0 \to 0}$
$0 \to 0$	$1 \to 0$	$0 \to 0$	$E_{0 \to 0}$
$0 \to 0$	$1 \to 1$	$0 \to 0$	$E_{0 \to 0}$
$0 \to 0$	$0 \to 0$	$0 \to 0$	$E_{0 \to 0}$
$0 \to 0$	$0 \to 1$	$0 \to 1$	$E_{0 \to 1}$
$0 \to 0$	$1 \to 0$	$0 \to 0$	$E_{0 \to 0}$
$0 \to 0$	$1 \to 1$	$0 \to 1$	$E_{0 \to 1}$
$0 \to 0$	$0 \to 0$	$0 \to 0$	$E_{0 \to 0}$
$0 \to 0$	$0 \to 1$	$0 \to 0$	$E_{0 \to 0}$
$0 \to 0$	$1 \to 0$	$1 \to 0$	$E_{1 \to 0}$
$0 \to 0$	$1 \to 1$	$1 \to 0$	$E_{1 \to 0}$
$0 \to 0$	$0 \to 0$	$0 \to 1$	$E_{0 \to 0}$
$0 \to 0$	$0 \to 1$	$0 \to 0$	$E_{0 \to 1}$
$0 \to 0$	$1 \to 0$	$1 \to 0$	$E_{1 \to 0}$
$0 \to 0$	$1 \to 1$	$1 \to 1$	$E_{1 \to 1}$

The average energies when $q = 0$ or $q = 1$ are:

$$E(q = 0) \quad = \quad (3E_{1 \to 0} + 9E_{0 \to 0})/12$$
$$E(q = 1) \quad = \quad (3E_{0 \to 1} + E_{1 \to 1})/4$$

Observe that if the four transition energy levels are different, then in general $|E(q = 0) - E(q = 1)| \neq 0$. This simple computation shows that if a large number of power traces are accumulated and divided into two bins: one for $q = 0$ and the other for $q = 1$, the means for the 0-bin and 1-bin computed, and then the difference-of-mean (DOM) computed, it is expected to find a non-zero difference. This forms the basis of Differential Power Analysis (DPA), where the variation of power of a circuit wrt. data is exploited. This is more powerful than the Simple Power Analysis (SPA) as detailed in Chapter 7. In the following section, we provide a discussion on the Difference-of-Mean (DoM) technique to perform a DPA on a block cipher like AES.

10.3 Differential Power Analysis Using Difference of Mean

The basic principle of the DoM method is based on the fact that the power consumption of a device is correlated with a target bit or a set of bits. In the simplest form, we obtain a large number of power consumption curves and the corresponding ciphertexts. The attacker then applies a divide and conquer strategy: he assumes a portion of the key which is required to perform the deciphering for a portion of the cipher for one round. Based on the guessed key he computes a target bit, typically the computation of which requires evaluation of an S-Box. Depending on whether the target bit is 0 or 1, the traces are divided into a 0-bin and 1-bin. Then the mean of all the traces in the 0-bin and 1-bin are computed and finally we compute Difference-of-Mean (DoM) of the mean curves. It is expected that for the correct key guess, there will be a time instance for which there is a non-negligible value, manifesting as a spike in the difference curve. The correlation of the power consumption of the device on the target bit is thus exploited to distinguish the correct key from the wrong ones. We state the above attack more elaborately in the form of an algorithm.

10.3.1   Computing DoM for Simulated Power Traces on AES

In this section, let us consider a sample run of the AES algorithm. We provide several runs of the AES algorithm with NSample randomly chosen plaintexts. Consider an iterated AES hardware where a register is updated by the output of the AES round every encryption. The power trace is stored in the array sample[NSample][NPoint], where NPoint is corresponding to the power consumption after each round of the encryption. For each of the power traces we also store the corresponding ciphertexts in the array Ciphertext[NSample]. For simulation we compute the power by either the Hamming Weight or Hamming Distance model. For our simulation on the AES algorithm, we keep NSample as 8000 and NPoint as 12. One can check that the power consumption is corresponding to the state of the register before the encryption, then updated by the initial key addition, followed by the state after each of the 9 rounds of AES, and finally the ciphertext after the 10th round.

The attack algorithm first *targets* one of the key bytes, key, for which one the 16 S-Boxes of the last round is targetted. We denote the corresponding ciphertext byte in the array Ciphertext[NSample] by the variable cipher. For each of the NSample runs, the analysis partitions the traces, sample[NSample][NPoint] into a zero-bin and one-bin, depending on a target bit at the input of a target S-Box. For computing or estimating the target bit at the input of the target S-Box, the attack guesses the target key byte, and then computes the Inverse-SBox on the XOR of the byte cipher and the guessed key byte, denoted as key. One may observe that the ciphertexts for which the target byte in the ciphertext, cipher is same, always goes to the same bin. Thus the traces can be stored in a smaller array, sample[NCipher][NPoint], where NCipher is the number of cipher bytes (which is ofcourse 256).

10.3.2   Simulation of the Power Traces and Computing the DoM

For each run of the encryption algorithm, acting on each plaintext, a corresponding power trace is supposed to be stored. One may obtain the power trace from an actual experiment on a device, like microcontrollers, FPGAs or ASICs. For an example, we simulate the power trace by observing the Hamming Weights (HWs) of the encryptions for all the NPoint instances. Instead of storing each trace separately we combine by adding those for which traces for which the ciphertext has the same value for the target ciphertext byte, cipher.

The following algorithm provides an overview on the Difference-of-Mean algorithm technique. It essentially splits the traces into the two bins based on a target bit, say the LSB. The algorithm then computes the average of all the 0-bin and the 1-bin traces, and then computes the difference of the means, denoted as DoM. It is expected that the correct key will have a significant Difference of Mean, compared to the wrong keys which have almost a negligible DoM. We then store the highest value of the DoM as the biasKey[NKey] for each of the key guesses. The key which has the highest bias value is returned as the correct key.

Fig. 10.11(a) we observe the progress of the bias values with increase in the number of iterations. In the experiment we target the 0th byte of the tenth round key. Likewise, one can target any key byte and obtain the entire AES key using a divide and conquer strategy. In the initial experiment, we assume that the power consumption of the AES architecture is proportional to the Hamming Weights of the registers after each round. **Fig. 10.11(a)** shows the maximum DoM, referred here as bias of all the 256 keys against the number of iterations on which the attack is run. It can be observed in the figure that the correct key byte separates out quite fast from the wrong ones. To make the attack more realistic and

---

Algorithm 10.1: Power Analysis by Computing Difference-of-Mean

---

Input: sample[NSample][NPoint],Ciphertext[NSample]
Output: biasKey[NKey],biasIndex[NKey]

```
1  for (cipher = 0; cipher < NCipher; cipher++) do
2      partialCipher = inverseSBox[cipher ⊕ key]
3      if (partialCipher & 1) then
4          for (j = 0; j < NPoint; j++) do
5              sumBin1[j] += sample[cipher][j]
6              countBin1 += freqSample[cipher]
7          end
8      end
9      else
10         for (j = 0; j < NPoint; j++) do
11             sumBin0[j] += sample[cipher][j]
12             countBin0 += freqSample[cipher]
13         end
14     end
15 end
16 bias = 0
17 for (j = 0; j < NPoint; j++) do
18     meanDiff[j] = sumBin0[j]/countBin0 - sumBin1[j]/countBin1
19     if (bias < abs(meanDiff[j])) then
20         bias = abs(meanDiff[j])
21         index = j
22     end
23     biasKey[key] = bias
24     biasIndex[key] = index
25 end
```

---

also to observe the effect of noise, we super-impose the power traces as discussed above with a Gaussian noise. As shown in **Fig. 10.11(b)** one can observe that the separation of the correct key from the other ones happens slowly, but nevertheless is clearly visible.

10.3.3 DOM and the Hamming Distance vs. Hamming Weight Model

This experiments show that DoM can be used as a distinguisher for the keys of a cipher. The inherent reason being that the power profile of the device is dependent on data. The DoM technique is based on correct classification of the power traces into two bins depending on the function of the taget bit. Assuming the power model is Hamming Weight, we perform the classification based on the 0 or 1 value of a target bit. The attack outlined previously was an example of such a hypothesis. The attack can be easily adapted for a Hamming Distance power model, where the classification of the power traces is based on the change or transitions of the target bit across two successive clock cycles. The rest of the attack remains the same.

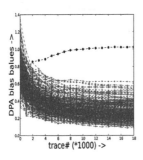 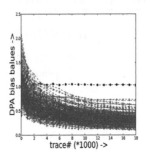

(a) Progress of Bias of keys for Power profiles with no noise

(b) Progress of Bias of keys for Power profiles with no noise

FIGURE 10.11: Progress of Bias of keys for simulated Power Profiles of AES-128

10.4   PKDPA: An Improvement of the DoM technique

The basic DoM (Difference of Mean) method, as described may be improved in several ways. Researchers have proposed different schemes to measure the efficiency of DPA, one of the popular objectives being to reduce the number of traces/measurements required to mount a successful attack[47, 59]. A DPA enhancement is proposed in [47] which exploits the bias of a linear combination of output bits of the Substitution-Box (S-Box) of the block ciphers. To enhance DPA some authors [251] have introduced the multi-bit DPA attacks which use multiple bits instead of a single bit to devise a distinguisher. In [425], the authors present a DPA enhancement whereby they find the keys registering maximum DPA bias for all target bits and then perform a majority voting to arrive at the correct key. Although effective in reducing the number of traces required to perform the attack, the majority voting will not return the correct key till it does not produce the highest DPA bias for *any* of the target bits.

In this section, we present an attack method which is based on an effective choice of *window* to observe the *probable* keys [342]. The central idea behind the proposed attack is to obtain a set of keys, which have a high probability of being the correct key, the DoM being the indicator for the probability. The attack, called as the Probabilistic Key DPA (PKDPA) looks for a set of keys with high DoM values. The cardinality of the set is defined as the *window-size*. So PKDPA analyzes a window of keys instead of a single key. The specifications of PKDPA for finding the correct key corresponding to a single S-Box are given below:

In the following subsection, we present an experiment on the PKDPA to show the efficiency of the method.

10.4.1   Application of PKDPA to AES

The attack has been mounted on a standard iterative implementation of AES. We first show that for a trace count of 2500, classical DoM based DPA does not return any conclusive result. It is evident from the differential plots given in **Fig. 10.12** that the correct key, which is 12, cannot be distinctively identified except for the case of the 2nd target bit

---

Algorithm 10.2: Probabilistic Key DPA (PKDPA)

Input: Plaintext/Ciphertext,power traces,target S-Box,window-size,key guesses
Output: Correct Key

1   Choose target S-Box, specify window-size and obtain power traces
2   **for** *All target bits (ie. each output bit of the S-Box) and all possible key guesses* **do**
3   Perform DoM test.
4   **end**
5   Extract probable keys (the keys whose DoM value lies inside the chosen window-size) based on the corresponding DoM values.
6   **for** *Each probable key* **do**
7   Find frequency of occurrence
8   **end**
9   **if** *Frequency of occurrence of a key* $\geq \left\lceil \frac{1}{2}(\# \text{ of output bits of the S-Box}) \right\rceil$ **then**
10   return correct key
11   **end**
12   **else**
13   Obtain more power traces and goto step 4
14   **end**

(**Fig. 10.12(a)**). In fact a precise look at the results show that for the 3rd and 6th target bits, DPA returns key 244 as the correct key. This could even trick an attacker into believing that 244 might be the correct key. Thus we see that for 2500 traces DPA leads to indecisive results. We deploy a probable key analysis using the same number of traces.

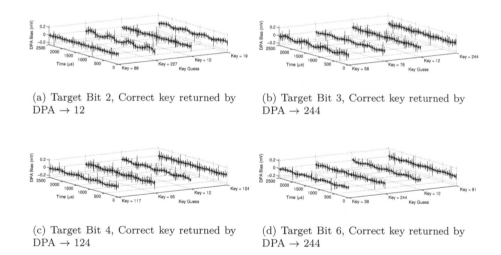

(a) Target Bit 2, Correct key returned by DPA → 12

(b) Target Bit 3, Correct key returned by DPA → 244

(c) Target Bit 4, Correct key returned by DPA → 124

(d) Target Bit 6, Correct key returned by DPA → 244

FIGURE 10.12: AES Differential plots for some target bits of S-Box-15 with 2500 traces.

In order to depict the attack, we define **probable key matrix** as a $w \times t$ matrix, where w is the windo size chosen for the attack, and t is the number of target bits. The ith column of the matrix is populated with the top w keys which are returned by a DoM based DPA targeting the ith bit chosen from the t target bits. The elements in the ith column are also arranged in descending order of their DoM, and thus the first row of the matrix actually represents the keys which have registered highest DPA bias. In other words, these keys are the ones that a classical DPA attack would have returned as correct keys. The window-size (w) for the experiment is 10 and hence we have total of 10 probable keys in each column which are arranged in decreasing order of their DPA bias.

As the number of output bits of an AES S-Box is 8 so we get a (10×8) probable key matrix. **Table 10.2** shows the probable key matrix for 2,500 traces. From the frequency analysis (**Table 10.3**), we infer that key 12 is the most frequent key with frequency of occurrence being 4. So by probable key analysis, key 12 is concluded to be the correct key.

TABLE 10.2: AES Probable Key Matrix for S-Box 15 with 2500 Traces

Bit1	Bit2	Bit3	Bit4	Bit5	Bit6	Bit7	Bit8
11	**12**	244	124	86	244	242	147
23	86	76	95	64	38	143	107
61	227	58	244	69	67	128	42
133	19	217	**12**	210	17	44	88
197	161	164	142	127	124	174	137
35	38	69	139	60	103	41	**12**
22	191	52	117	218	91	36	122
220	164	123	74	193	196	68	125
238	105	**12**	73	18	82	133	159
178	26	193	147	89	78	202	96

TABLE 10.3: Frequency Matrix for unmasked AES S-Box 15 with 2500 Traces

Key	Freq.	Key	Freq.	Key	Freq.	Key	Freq.	Key	Freq.	Key	Freq.	Key	Freq.
12	4	96	1	41	1	73	1	105	1	142	1	210	1
244	3	11	1	42	1	74	1	107	1	143	1	217	1
38	2	17	1	44	1	76	1	117	1	159	1	218	1
69	2	18	1	52	1	78	1	122	1	161	1	220	1
86	2	19	1	58	1	82	1	123	1	174	1	227	1
124	2	22	1	60	1	88	1	125	1	178	1	238	1
133	2	23	1	61	1	89	1	127	1	191	1	242	1
147	2	26	1	64	1	91	1	128	1	196	1	Remaining
164	2	35	1	67	1	95	1	137	1	197	1	keys do
193	2	36	1	68	1	103	1	139	1	202	1	not occur

The choice of the window size is critical for the success of the attack. In the following we discuss the relation between the choice of the window size and success of the attack through a theoretical framework.

10.4.2 Choosing the Window-Size

Let us consider a ($m \times n$) S-Box. If we set the window-size to w, then we will have an ($w \times n$) probable key matrix. We now define a random variable M_i such that

$$M_i = \left\{ \begin{array}{ll} 1 & \text{if any key occurs in the } i^{th} \text{ column of the probable key matrix} \\ 0 & \text{otherwise} \end{array} \right\}$$

The probability of occurrence of any randomly chosen key in a column of the probable key matrix is

$$Pr[M_i = 1] = \frac{w}{2^m}, \quad \text{where } 2^m \text{ is \# of keys guessed}$$

Under the assumption that $(M_1, M_2, \cdots, M_n)$ are independent random variables, we can write

$$M = \sum_{i=1}^{n} M_i$$

For, a random key $Pr[M < \frac{n}{2}]$ should be very high. Now, it can be noted that according to PKDPA if a key other than the correct key occurs more than or equal to $\lceil \frac{n}{2} \rceil$ times than it leads to an error. So, $Pr[M \geq \frac{n}{2}]$ gives the error probability of PKDPA. From the point of view of probable key analysis, we want to keep $Pr[M \geq \frac{n}{2}]$ for a randomly chosen key as low as possible. We then argue that with the error probability significantly low for a wrong key, if some key occurs more than or equal to $\lceil \frac{n}{2} \rceil$ times, then it must be the correct key with a very high probability. This is because $Pr[M \geq \frac{n}{2}]$ is high for a correct key as it will be correlated to all the target bits and hence tend to appear in all columns. Hence we can use this to devise a good distinguisher between the correct key and wrong keys. In the following paragraphs we try to draw a relation between the parameter window-size and error probability. We proceed by applying the theorem for multiplicative form of *Chernoff bound* [145], which is stated as follows:

Theorem 18 *[145] Let random variables $(X_1, X_2, \cdots, X_n)$ be independent random variables taking on values 0 or 1. Further, assume that $Pr(X_i = 1) = p_i$. Then, if we let $X = \sum_{i=1}^{n} X_i$ and μ be the expectation of X, for any $\delta > 0$, we have*

$$Pr[X \geq (1 + \delta)\mu] \leq \left(\frac{e^\delta}{(1 + \delta)^{(1+\delta)}} \right)^{\mu} \tag{10.1}$$

We are interested to find the Chernoff bound for the error probability $Pr[M \geq \frac{n}{2}]$ of a random (or wrong) key. For the random variable M defined earlier, the expectation $\mu = E(M)$ and $\delta > 0$ are as below.

$$E(M) = \left(\frac{w}{2^m} \right) n \tag{10.2}$$

$$\delta = \left\{ \frac{2^{(m-1)}}{w} \right\} - 1 \tag{10.3}$$

By Theorem 18, the error probability of a random key occurrence in the probable key matrix is bounded by

$$Pr\left[M \geq \frac{n}{2}\right] \leq \left[\frac{e^{\left\{ \frac{2^{(m-1)}}{w} - 1 \right\}}}{\left\{ \frac{2^{(m-1)}}{w} \right\}^{\left(\frac{2^{(m-1)}}{w} \right)}} \right]^{\left(\frac{w}{2^m} \right)n} \tag{10.4}$$

The R.H.S of Equation 10.4, thus gives an upper bound of the error probability of a randomly chosen (wrong) key to pass the test. From the condition that $\delta > 0$, we can easily derive the upper bound for the window-size.

$$\left\{ \frac{2^{(m-1)}}{w} \right\} - 1 > 0$$

$$\Rightarrow \quad w < 2^{(m-1)}$$

TABLE 10.4: Error Probabilities(ϵ) for different window-sizes (AES)

w	1	5	10	15	20	25	30	35
ϵ	1.9714e-007	1.0873e-004	0.0015	0.0064	0.0174	0.0364	0.0645	0.1022
$1-\epsilon$	0.99999980286	0.99989127	0.9985	0.9936	0.9826	0.9636	0.9355	0.8978

We now give some theoretical results about the variation of error probability with the window-size. For AES we choose $m = n = 8$ and plot the upper bound of the error probability given in Equation 10.4 for all possible values of the window-size ($w < 2^{(m-1)}$) for the AES algorithm in **Fig. 10.13**. We also plot the value of confidence defined as (1 - error probability).

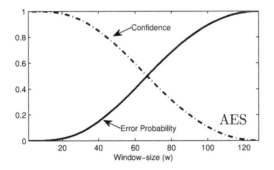

FIGURE 10.13: Error probability and Confidence vs. Window-size for the AES circuit

From **Fig. 10.13** one can infer that as we go on increasing the window-size the error probability of PKDPA also increases and attains very high value if w is close to $2^{(m-1)}$. In general we can say that the probability of error is directly proportional to the chosen window-size.

$$Pr\left[M \geq \frac{n}{2}\right]_{w_1} > Pr\left[M \geq \frac{n}{2}\right]_{w_2}, \quad \text{if} \quad w_1 > w_2$$

Table **10.4** shows the error probabilities for AES w.r.t some discrete window-sizes. In the next paragraph we study the effect of window-size on the number of traces required to mount the attack.

The estimates of error probability and confidence have been plotted in **Fig. 10.14** w.r.t the window-size. In addition to that we plot the number of traces that are required to attack AES S-Box - 15 against window-size (w). One can infer from the figure that ideal size of the window varies between 9 and 18. In this range least number of traces are required to mount PKDPA. If we increase w beyond 18 the trace count also increases rapidly. We also see that beyond a certain value of the window-size i.e., 34 there is a drastic increase in the number of required traces. Actually from our practical results we have found that for $w > 34$, the probability $Pr\left[M \geq \frac{n}{2}\right]$ for wrong keys becomes significantly high. It can be seen that the theoretical value of the error probability (ϵ) for $w = 35$ given in **Table 10.4** is also high. From our experimental results we have found that for all practical purposes $w = 10$ (AES) yields good results.

The plots in **Fig. 10.13** imply that the probability of error with window-size $w = 1$ is

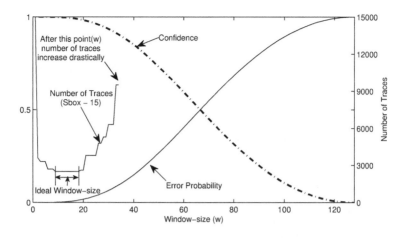

FIGURE 10.14: Error probability, Confidence and # of Traces (S-Box - 15) vs. Window-size for AES

the least and steadily increases with $w > 1$. It is interesting to note that $w = 1$ actually represents classical DPA where we look only for the key with the highest DPA bias. From **Table 10.4** we can see that the probability of error (ϵ) is significantly low for $w = 1$. However, if we choose $w = 10$ (AES) then ϵ still remains very low. Conversely, we can say that the level of confidence $(1 - \epsilon)$ in classical DPA is very high while for PKDPA it is still considerably high. In practice, we see that by slightly lowering the level of confidence we are able to considerably reduce the number of traces required for a successful attack. However, one should be careful in choosing the window size as choosing a very high window-size could lead to drastic increase in required number of traces.

There are several other improvements and variants of the Differential Power Attacks. The most commonly known method is called the Correlation Power Attack (CPA), where correlation coefficient is used as a statistical distinguisher to identify the wrong keys from the correct one. In the next section, we provide a detailed discussion of the method.

10.5 Correlation Power Attack

Like in the DoM based DPA attack, the Correlation Power Attack (CPA) also relies on targeting an intermediate computation, typically the input or output of an S-Box. These intermediate values are as seen previously computed from a known value, typically the ciphertext and a portion of the key, which is guessed. The power model is subsequently used to develop a *hypothetical* power trace of the device for a given input to the cipher. This hypothetical power values are then stored in a matrix for several inputs and can be indexed by the known value of the ciphertext or the guessed key byte. This matrix is denoted as **H**, the hypothetical power matrix. Along with this, the attacker also observes the actual power traces, and stores them in a matrix for several inputs. The actual power values can be indexed by the known value of the ciphertext and the time instance when the power value was observed. This matrix is denoted as **T**, the real power matrix. It may be observed that one of the columns of the matrix **H** corresponds to the actual key, denoted as k_c. In order to distinguish the key from the others, the attacker looks for *similarity* between the columns of the matrix $\mathbf{H}$ and those of the matrix $\mathbf{T}$. The similarity is typically computed using the Pearson's Correlation coefficient as defined in details below.

10.5.1 Computing Correlation Coefficient for Simulated Power Traces for AES

Like previously, we consider an iterative AES circuit and simulate its power profile using either a Hamming Weight or Hamming Distance model. As for DoM computations we used a Hamming Weight model, for variation here we use the Hamming Distance model.

The real power matrix is stored in an array trace[NSample][NPoint], where NPoint and NSample denotes the timing for which the power trace is observed and the number of power traces acquired respectively. As discussed for the computation of DoM the value of NPoint is 12 for AES, denoting those time instances when the AES round causes change in the value of the output register, thus leading to a power consumption due to the transitions. For the hypothetical power consumption, the attacker obtains The hypothetical power matrix is obtained by starting from the Ciphertext. The attacker targets a specific key byte key, and finds out the corresponding byte in the ciphertext, denoted as Cipher. **Fig. 10.15** shows the last round toggling in the registers storing the state of AES during the computations. One may note from **Fig. 10.15** that due to the ShiftRow operation the Hamming Distance computations should be properly expressed for the iterated AES architecture. For example, note the toggling in the register R1, can be found by $HD(S_1, S(S_{13}) \oplus k_1)$, where HD denotes the Hamming Distance of the two bytes. While the second term in the HD function is directly available to the attacker from the ciphertext byte denoted by Cipher=C_1, for the first term the attacker needs to guess a key byte. The attacker thus guesses the key byte, k_5 and performs XOR with the corresponding ciphertext byte, denoted as SCipher=C_5 and performs Inverse SubByte to obtain the state S_1. The attacker thus develops the hypothetical power values by obtaining the Hamming Distance between Cipher and Inverse SubByte of (SCipher $\oplus$ key).

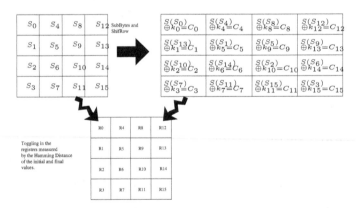

FIGURE 10.15: Computing Hamming Distance in the Registers due to Last Round Transformation of AES

In the following, we detail the computation of the Hypothetical power trace. The attacker targets a specific register (see **Fig. 10.15**) and observes the corresponding ciphertext byte, Cipher. As described before to compute the hypothetical power value, the attacker needs to apply Inverse Shift Row to obtain the corresponding byte position which affects this register position.

TABLE 10.5: Target Ciphertext Byte wrt. Register Position to Negotiate Inverse Shift Row

Register Position	0	1	2	3	4	5	6	7	8	9	10	11	12	13	14	15
Target CipherText Byte	0	5	10	15	4	9	14	3	8	13	2	7	12	1	6	11

Algorithm 10.3: Correlation Power Analysis

Input: trace[NSample][NPoint],hPower[NSample][NKey],
Ciphertext[NSample],meanH[i],meanTrace[j],i, j
Output: result[NKey][NPoint]

```
1  for (k = 0; k < NCipher; k++) do
2    {
3      temph = hConsumedPower[i][k] - meanH[i]
4      tempt = trace[j][k] - meanTrace[j]
5      sumHT += temph*tempt
6      sumSqH += temph*temph
7      sumSqT += tempt*tempt
8    }
9      result[i][j] = sumHT/sqrt(sumSqH*sumSqT)
10 end
```

Table 10.5 shows the mapping between the target register position and the ciphertext byte which is to be traced back to the last round to find the previous value of the register. We call this ciphertext byte as **SCipher**. The attacker in order to trace back this byte guesses the key byte, denoted as **key** and obtains InvSubByte[SCipher $\oplus$ key]. The Hamming Distance between this traced back byte and the present ciphertext byte, **Cipher** provides an estimate of the hypothetical power.

10.5.2   Computation of the Correlation Matrix

The actual power value for all the **NSample** encryptions are observed and stored in the array **trace[NSample][NPoint]**. The attacker first scans each column of this array and computes the average of each of them, and stores in **meanTrace[NPoint]**. Likewise, the hypothetical power is stored in an array **hPower[NSample][NKey]** and the attacker computes the mean of each column and stores in **meanH[NKey]** by scanning each column of the hypothetical matrix. The attacker then computes the correlation value to find the similarity of the ith column of the matrix **hPower** and the jth column of **trace**. The correlation is computed as follows and stored in the array **result[NKey][NPoint]**:

$$result[i][j] = \frac{\sum_{k=0}^{NSample}(hPower[i][k]-meanH[i])(trace[j][k]-meanTrace[j])}{\sum_{k=0}^{NSample}(hPower[i][k]-meanH[i])^2 \sum_{k=0}^{NSample}(hPower[i][k]-meanH[i])^2}$$

Algorithm 10.3 summarizes the steps to compute the correlation matrix and perform the correlation power attack. It may be noted that i denotes the candidate key, and j represents a time instant in the power trace when the correlation is computed. It is expected that after sufficient number of traces the correct key will have a significant peak in its correlation plot wrt. the time interval of encryption.

10.5.3   Experimental Results on Simulated Traces

In this section, we present the result of CPA on simulated traces which are obtained by the Hamming Distance between the successive rounds of encryption. We present results for this *ideal* power trace. However in reality, as discussed the power profiles also have a Gaussian noise along with. To simulate it we add a noise component to the power profile and redo the experiments. As can be observed from the **Fig. 10.16**, the correct key in both the cases is distinguishable from the other keys. Also it may be noted that in case of the ideal trace (i.e. power trace with no noise) the distinction occurs with even lesser number of traces, and is also more compared to that with noise.

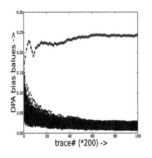
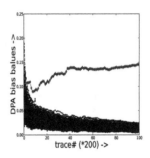

(a) Progress of Bias of keys for CPA attack with Ideal Power profiles

(b) Progress of Bias of keys for CPA attack with Power profiles Injected with Noise

FIGURE 10.16: Progress of Bias of keys for CPA on simulated Power Profiles of AES-128

The efficiency of a CPA analysis is often measured by several metrics as published in the literature. In the following section, we provide an overview on some of the most important metrics, namely Guessing Entropy and Mean Time to Disclosure.

10.6   Metrics to Evaluate a Side Channel Analysis

In order to evaluate the several attack methods and also to compare the severalcryptographic designs wrt. these attacks several formal metrics have been developed. It is important to have an understanding of these security metrics which are based on formalizing these side channel analysis techniques. In this section, we provide an overview on some of the fundamental metrics and then try to use them to evaluate the previously discussed attacks.

10.6.1   Success Rate of a Side Channel Adversary

The description of the side channel analysis presented before shows that the side channel adversaries works on a divide and conquer strategy, where the key space is divided into several equivalent classes. The attack is normally unable to distinguish keys which belong to the same class or partition, but is capable to distinguish between teo keys which falls in different partitions. Thus one can formalize the adversary as an algorithm which targets

---

Algorithm 10.4: Formal Definition of Success Rate of a Side Channel Attack

---

Input: K, L, E_K
Output: 0 (failure), 1 (success)

1 $k \in_R K$
2 $s = \gamma(k)$
3 $\mathbf{g} = [g_1, \ldots, g_o] \leftarrow A_{E_k, L}$
4 **if** $s \in g$ **then**
5   **return** 0
6 **end**
7 **else**
8   **return** 1
9 **end**

---

a given implementation of a cryptographic algorithm, formally denoted as E_K, where K denotes the key space. The adversary also assumes a leakage model for the key denoted as L. The leakage model provides some information of the key or some other desirable information. Also the adversary is bounded in terms of computational resources and thus the adversary $A_{E_K, L}$ is an algorithm with time complexity τ, memory complexity m, making q queries to the target implementation of the cryptographic algorithm. Note that the leakage function is not capable of distinguishing certain keys, hence inducing a partition S on the entire key space K. The mapping from K to S can be captured by a function γ such that $s = \gamma(k)$, where $s \in S$ and $k \in K$, and $|S| << |K|$. The objective of the adversary is to determine the corresponding equivalence class to which a chosen key k belongs denoted as $s = \gamma(k)$ with a non-negligible probability.

As an analogy consider the Hamming Weight or Hamming Distance leakage model, which divides the entire key space into equivalence classes or partitions, which the attacker tries to distinguish with sufficient observations. The output of the adversary is based on the ciphertext (black-box information) and the leakage (side channel information) outputs a *guess vector*, which are the key classes sorted in terms of descending order of being a likely candidate. We thus define an order-o (o $\leq$ |S|) adversary when the adversary produces the guessing vector as $\mathbf{g} = [g_1, \ldots, g_o]$, where g_1 is the most likely candidate, and so on. Now having defined the adversary let us try to understand formally the side channel experiment to define the metrics.

More precisely, the side channel attack is defined as an experiment $\mathsf{Exp}_{A_{E_K, L}}$ where $A_{E_K, L}$ is an adversary with time complexity τ, memory complexity m and making q queries to the target implementation of the cryptographic algorithm. In the experiment for any k chosen randomly from K, when the adversary, $A_{E_k, L}$ outputs the guessing vector g, the attack is considered as a success if the corresponding key class denoted as $s = \gamma(k)$ is such that $s \in g$. More formally the experiment for a side channel attack of order-o is as follows. The experiment returns a 0 or 1 indicating a success or failure of the attack.

The oth order success rate of the side channel attack $A_{E_K, L}$ against the key classes or partitions S is defined as:

$$\mathbf{Succ}^{\mathsf{o}}_{\mathbf{A}_{\mathbf{E_K}, \mathbf{L}}}(\tau, m, k) = \mathsf{Pr}[\mathsf{Exp}_{A_{E_K, L}} = 1]$$

10.6.2   Guessing Entropy of an Adversary

The above metric for an oth order attack implies the success rate for an attack where the remaining workload is o-key classes. Thus the attacker has a maximum of o-key classes to

---

Algorithm 10.5: Formal Definition of Guessing Entropy

Input: K, L, E_K
Output: Key class i

1 $k \in_R K$
2 $s = \gamma(k)$
3 $\mathbf{g} = [g_1, \ldots, g_o] \leftarrow A_{E_k, L}$
4 **return** i such that $g_i = s$

---

which the required k may belong. While the above definition for a given order is fixed wrt. the remaining work load, the following definition of **guessing entropy** provides a more flexible definition for the remaining work load. It measures the average number of key candidates to test after the attack. We formally state the definition.

The **Guessing Entropy** of the adversary $A_{E_k, L}$ against a key class variable S is defined as:

$$\mathbf{GE_{A_{E_K}, L}}(\tau, m, k) \;=\; \mathsf{E}[\mathrm{Exp}_{A_{E_K}, L}]$$

In order to evaluate the Guessing Entropy (GE) we observe the ranks of the various guessed key values in the guessing vector. For the experiments on CPA with the simulated power traces (both without and with noise), **Fig. 10.17** we plot the ranking of the correct key wrt. the wrong keys. The plots show that the correct key rank reduces fast to zero, thus showing that the guessing entropy reduces to 0 at that point, and the key is identified after a certain number of traces. The figures show that with noise the Guessing Entropy reaches zero slower and after more number of traces, as when the power traces are without any noise value.

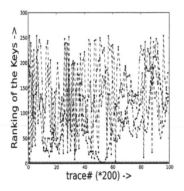
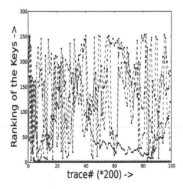

(a) Guessing Entropy of Keys (No Noise)

(b) Guessing Entropy of Keys (with Noise)

FIGURE 10.17: Guessing Entropy Plots for CPA on Simulated Power Traces

The above experiments on CPA were based on simulated power traces, and thus do not exactly capture the real-life scenario. For completeness we also present in the following section we present an overview on using real-life power traces for performing the correlation power analysis.

10.7 CPA on Real Power Traces of AES-128

In this section, we present some snap-shots of a power attack on a real-life implementation of AES-128. The vulnerability of the design against power attacks often vary with the architecture of the design. The power attacks target the dependence of the power values on some target state. However, depending on the architecture, the actual power value also contains accompanying noise, in the form of electric and algorithmic noise. The architecture often has an impact on the extent of algorithmic noise, which affects the performance of a CPA. The architecture thus has a role on the *Signal-to-Noise* (SNR) ratio which has an impact on the Success-rate or Guessing Entropy of an attack. We first define the SNR of a power trace, which is an important metric to evaluate the extent of signal in a power trace of a given architecture.

10.7.1 SNR of a Power Trace

In order to define SNR we follow the formalism of DPA or CPA as by Standaert et al in []. Let the AES block cipher be represented by E with r rounds, and let S be a random variable representing a key dependent intermediate variable of E. S is called the target and satisfies $S = F_k^*(X)$, where X is a random variable representing a part of known plaintext or ciphertext and $F_k^* : X \to S$ is a function dependent on a part of the secret key $k^* \in K$ (referred to as subkey). The function F is determined by both the algorithm of the cipher and the leakage model of the hardware device. We denote by L_t, the random variable that represents the side channel leakage of an implementation of E at time instant t, $0 \le t < rT$ where T is the number of samples collected per round. We further denote by $L_t(s)$ the random variable $(L_t|S = s)$. In DPA, the attacker collects traces $\{l_1, \ldots, l_q\}$ that has resulted from the encryption (or decryption) of a sequence of q plaintexts (or ciphertexts) $\{p_1, \ldots, p_q\}$ (or $\{c_1, \ldots, c_q\}$) using the fixed but unknown key with subkey $k^* \in K$ in a physical implementation of E. It should be noted that each l_i is a vector of size rT i.e. l_i contains the leakages of rT points: 0 to $rT - 1$ in time during the ith encryption (or decryption). Then a distinguisher D is used which by taking the leakage vector $\{l_1, \ldots, l_q\}$ and the corresponding input vector $\{x_1, \ldots, x_q\}$ as inputs, outputs a distinguishing vector $D = \{d_k\}_{k \in K}$. For a successful attack, $k^* = \mathrm{argmax}_{k \in K} d_k$ holds with a non-negligible probability.

In DPA, it is often assumed that the power consumptions of a CMOS device at a sample point is linearly dependent on the intermediate value manipulated at that point. Suppose the target S is manipulated at a time instant t^*, referred to as *instance of interest*. According to conventional leakage model:

$$
\begin{aligned}
L_t^* &= aS + N \\
&= aF_{k^*}(X) + N
\end{aligned}
$$

where a is some real constant, $N \sim N(0, \sigma)$ accounts for a Gaussian distribution for noise. Here, aS is the deterministic part of the leakage. Since X is known, the attacker can compute the target intermediate value under each key hypothesis $\{F_k(x_i)\}_{i=1}^q$ for $k \in K$. In univariate DPA, the attacker is provided with the leakage of point of interest t^* , $L_{t*} = aF_{k*}(X) + N$ and computes the distinguishing vector $D = \{d_k\}_{k \in K}$ such that $d_k = D(aF_{k*}(X) + N, F_k(X))$ where D is a univariate distinguisher. It should be noted that a univariate distinguisher takes the leakage of a single sample point as input and generates output based on it. In Correlation Power Analysis (CPA), Pearson's correlation coefficient (Corr) is used as the distinguisher i.e., the attacker computes

$d_k = Corr(aF_{k*}(X) + N, F_k(X))$ for $k \in K$ and returns the key k as the correct key such that d_k is maximum.

In most of the practical scenarios, the point of interest t^* is not known before hand. Thus, in practice, DPA attacks are multivariate in nature, i.e., they takes the leakages of multiple sample points as the input. Most common form of multivariate DPA attacks apply an univariate distinguisher on each of the sample points and then, simply chooses the best result among those. However, in a different strategy, the attacker sometimes uses multivariate distinguisher which jointly evaluates the power consumptions at multiple sample points. Such multivariate distinguishers are common in profiling attacks like Template attack [86], Stochastic attack [350, 183]. However, non-profiling attacks are vulnerable to a decrease in the success rate resulting from the integration of the output of a sample point which has more signal component corresponding to the noise (often measured using the metric SNR) to that of sample points with low signal-to-noise ratio. Thus, the definition of SNR and the ability to measure can be quite handy to evaluate DPA: for developing improvements of the classical DPA and also for assessing the vulnerability of a given architecture against these attacks.

Consider an AES implementation running on a hardware platform. We compute the target variable S by taking the 128-bit Hamming Distance between the ciphertext and the input to the previous round. We investigate the behaviour of the leakages of an AES implementation over a range of sample points due to the computation of the intermediate variable. For example, we examine the signal-to-noise ratio for 20,000 power traces around 300 sample points around the register update for the last round.

Recalling, that the power leakage is $L_t = aS + N$, where aS is the deterministic data dependent part of the power targetted by CPA. The overall power consumption of the device can be depicted using the (conceptual) frequency distribution in **Fig. 10.18**. It can be seen that the overall power consumption is centered around distinct voltage levels, which indicate the various Hamming Distance classes, denoted by S. However, because of the expected Gaussian noise N, the voltage levels are spread across each of these voltage levels.

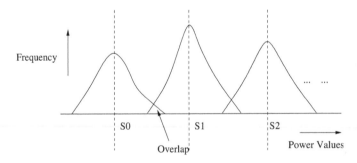

FIGURE 10.18: Conceptual Frequency Plot of a power profile

The variation of the data-dependent leakage is computed as $Var(E[L_t|S])$, which indicates the variations in leakage due to the target S at sample point t. It is intuitive to see this statistic captures the deterministic component of the power leakage and is useful to the attacker (more the variation, more the detectability!). It thus may be stated that the variations in this parameter indicate the *leakage* of the target variable S. Thus, $Var(E[L_t|S])$ captures the *signal* content of a power trace. The noise component of the power consumption can be computed as $(L_t - E[L_t|S])$. It may be observed that in **Fig. 10.18** each of the normal distributions, which are due to the noise, starts overlapping if this variance increases. Thus the variance of the noise distribution computed as $Var(L_t - E[L_t|S])$ captures the *noise* of the power traces at the instance t. Thus we have the following definition of the signal-to-noise ratio (SNR) of a power trace.

The ratio SNR, thus quantifies the amount of information at a sample point and is computed as:

$$SNR_t \quad = \quad \frac{Var(E[L_t|S])}{Var(L_t - E[L_t|S])}$$

The SNR is a very useful metric for assessing the threat of a power attack on a given implementation. The power consumption of the device can be denoted as $L_t = P_{det} + N$, where P_{det} is the deterministic component of power and N is the noise. Thus the correlation between the total leakage L_t and the hypothetical power value for the ith key H_i as $Corr(H_i, L_t)$ and expanded as:

$$
\begin{aligned}
Corr(H_i, L_t) \quad &= \quad Corr(H_i, P_{det} + N) \\
&= \quad \frac{Cov(H_i, (P_{det} + N))}{\sqrt{Var(H_i)(Var(P_{det}) + Var(N))}} \\
&= \quad \frac{E(H_i \cdot (P_{det} + N)) - E(H_i)E(P_{det} + N)}{\sqrt{Var(H_i)Var(P_{det})}\sqrt{1 + \frac{Var(N)}{Var(P_{det})}}} \\
&= \quad \frac{Corr(H_i, P_{det})}{\sqrt{1 + \frac{1}{SNR}}}
\end{aligned}
$$

In the above equations, Cov and E denotes the Covariance and Expectation of random variables. Also note that we have used the fact that P_{det} and N are statistically independent. The above result can be used to evaluate an architecture using simulated traces. The simulations, as described previously, are based on a power model and derived with the knowledge of the key. In such cases there is no noise, and the CPA computes the Correlation $Corr(H_i, P_{det})$. However the real correlation can be computed using the knowledge of the SNR using the above equation.

Having defined the SNR of the power traces, we investigate the performance of the CPAs on few architecture topologies. We start from the iterative version. The following results are however based on actual power traces.

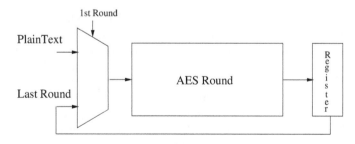

FIGURE 10.19: An Iterative AES: Target for the Power Attack

10.7.2 DPA of an Iterative Architecture

The architecture of an iterative AES architecture is shown in **Fig. 10.19**. The attack technique is the same as mentioned in the previous sections. The power traces are collected and correlated with the hypothetical power values, which again depend on the key. In this architecture, as all the S-Boxes are in parallel, when we target a specific S-Box, the 15 others are also operational.

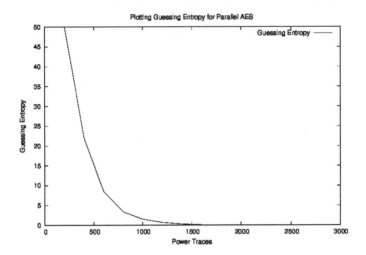

FIGURE 10.20: Plot of Guessing Entropy for CPA on Parallel Architecture for AES

They add to the algorithmic noise for the attack. To emphasize this point, we call this architecture a *parallel architecture* as opposed to the serialized architecture (in the next section). We acquire 70,000 power traces divided into sets with 3000 traces each. We perform the CPA attack on them, compute the average guessing entropy for them. The corresponding plot is illustrated in **Fig. 10.20**.

10.7.3   DPA on a Serialized Architecture of AES

The architecture depicted in **Fig. 10.21** shows a serialized implementation of the AES algorithm. As can be seen, a multiplexer is used to select the 8 bits of the 128-byte state and is accordingly transformed by the S-Box.

From the perspective of the attack, it may be observed that while a particular S-Box operation takes place, there are no other S-Box computation in parallel, unlike the iterative architecture previously discussed. We have in total 40,000 traces and they are divided into 40 sets of 1,000 traces. The experimental setup has a vertical scale of 5 mV and a resolution of 2.5 GS/s.

The guessing entropy is calculated by taking the average of the 40 results. The plot shown in **Fig. 10.22** shows the progress of the guessing entropy for the serialized architecture for the zeroth S-Box. The plot shows that within few traces one can leak the key bytes for a serialized architecture, owing to the reduced algorithmic noise.

10.7.4   Shuffling Architecture

A very popular technique to increase the resistance against CPA is called as *shuffling*. In this architecture the sequence of S-Box operations are randomly chosen and performed in an arbitrary order. The technique is a better countermeasure than the insertion of dummy operations as it does not have a negative effect on the overall throughput.

Thus shuffling can be quite easy to implement by making the select lines of the mul-

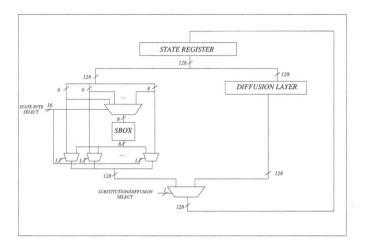

FIGURE 10.21: A Serialized Architecture for AES

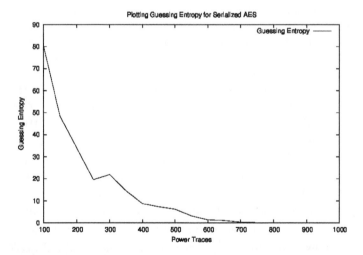

FIGURE 10.22: Plot of Guessing Entropy for CPA on Serialized Architecture for AES

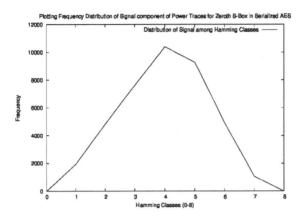

FIGURE 10.23: Frequency Plot of Signal Component of Power Traces for the zeroth S-Box of Serialized Architecture for AES

tiplexer in **Fig. 10.21** arbitrary. However shuffling schemes have their limitations, as the randomness provided is quite limited. In particular, if one observes the total power consumed over the 16 clock cycles for the S-Box operations one can still perform a CPA attack. However compared with the serialized implementation the SNR is low, and thus making it harder to perform a CPA. We compare the above architectures by measuring their relative SNRs, as discussed below.

For computing the SNR for the serialized architecture, we observe the power trace during say the zeroth S-Box computation. Then with the knowledge of the corresponding key byte (note that we are computing the SNR for performing an evaluation and hence we are aware of the key), we compute the Hamming Distance corresponding to the zeroth S-Box. Note that since we are targeting a particular S-Box, the Hamming classes can be 9: from 0 to 8. Then we divide the power traces into the the possible into these 9 classes, and compute the average of each class, p_i. We also note the frequencies of each class, ie. the number of traces falling into each of the Hamming classes, f_i. The averaging is expected to remove the effect of noise, and hence is expected to give a measure of the *signal*. We compute the variance by using the standard formula: $Var(E[L_t|S]) = \frac{\Sigma_{i=0}^{8} f_i p_i^2}{\Sigma_{i=0}^{8} f_i} - (\frac{\Sigma_{i=0}^{8} p_i f_i}{\Sigma_{i=0}^{8} f_i})^2$. Now the average is deducted from the power traces, thus removing the signal and providing the noise distribution. We perform similar computations as for the signal to find the variance of the noise. The ratio is finally computed to provide the SNR.

For the shuffled scheme, we compute the SNR for the total power for all the 16 S-Box computations. This increases the SNR, as can be checked that if a specific S-Box is targetted the SNR is theoretically expected to be $\frac{1}{256}^{th}$ compared to the serialized implementation. For our computations of the SNR we sum the power values in the traces for the sample points corresponding to each of the sixteen cycles, and then they are divided into the Hamming classes.

It may be noted that since we are considering the total power for all the S-Boxes, the Hamming classes vary from 0 to 128. The same technique as above is applied for computing the variance of the signal, and the noise to compute the SNR. **Fig. 10.24** shows the SNR

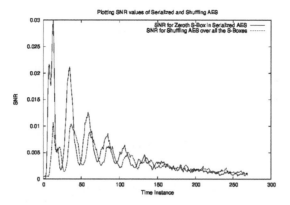

FIGURE 10.24: Comparison of SNR values of Serialized Architecture for AES vs the Shuffled Architecture

values of both the architectures to indicate that the average SNR for the shuffled architecture is almost one-third of the serialized architecture.

We also show the guessing entropy of a CPA attack mounted on the shuffled architecture in **Fig. 10.25**. This may be compared with that in the serialized architecture where the guessing entropy reduced to 0 value quite fast indicating indicating increased vulnerability against CPA.

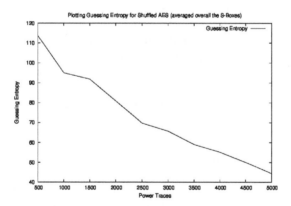

FIGURE 10.25: Plot of Guessing Entropy for CPA on Shuffled Architecture for AES (averaged over all the S-Boxes)

10.8 Popular Countermeasures against Power Analysis: Masking

Several schemes have been proposed to counter against the threats from power attacks. The objective of these countermeasures is to make the power consumption of the device independent of the data processed. Noise generators, insertion of random delays are some of the popular techniques. The other line of countermeasures is by building circuits assuming logic styles with data independent power consumption. However, these methods are often costly and not in accordance with the normal CAD methodology.

The most popular approach is to randomize the intermediate results which are computed using conventional gates. The assumption is based on the fact that the power consumption of the devices are uncorrelated with the actual data as they are *masked* with a random value. The popularity of masking over other techniques are because it can be applied at algorithmic level or at the gate level and does not rely on specially designed gates. Further, the process of converting an unmasked digital circuit can be converted into a masked version in an automated fashion.

In masking every intemediate value which is related to the key is concealed by a random value m which is called as the *mask*. Thus, we transform the intermediate value v as $v_m = v * m$, where m is randomly chosen and varies from encyption to encryption. The attacker does not know the value m. The operation $*$ could be either exclusive or, modulo addition, or modulo multiplication. *Boolean masking* is a special term given to the phenomenon of applying $\oplus$ as the above operation to conceal the intermediate value. If the operation is addition or multiplication, the masking is often referred to as *arithmetic masking*.

Masking can be broadly classified into two types depending on whether it is applied at the algorithmic level or at the gate level.

10.8.1 Masking at the Algorithmic Level

In these class of masking, the intermediate computations of an algorithm are masked. Depending on the nature of the masking scheme, namely Boolean or arithmetic, the non-linear functions of the given cipher are redesigned. Several such masking schemes have been proposed depending on the type of the algorithm for both symmetric and asymmetric algorithms. In the following we provide a description of these schemes. It may be pointed out that the AES S-Box is the only non-linear layer in the cipher. The other layers being linear can be quite conveniently masked in an additive fashion using the exclusive or operator. Hence, we focus on the S-Box.

10.8.1.1 Masking the AES S-Box

As discussed before in Chapter 4, a compact realization of the AES S-Box can be achieved by using the composite fields. The transformation from $GF(2^8)$ to $GF(2^4)^2$ is again linear, and thus can be masked using *XORs* quite conveniently. We consider the masking of the Galois field inverse in composite fields.

Recall the circuit description in chapter 4. Let the irreducible polynomial of an element in $GF(2^4)^2$ be $r(Y) = Y^2 + Y + \mu$ (note we assume $\tau = 1$). Let an element in the composite field be $\gamma = (\gamma_1 Y + \gamma_0)$ and let the inverse be $\delta = (\gamma_1 Y + \gamma_0)^{-1} = (\delta_1 Y + \delta_0) \bmod (Y^2 + \tau Y + \mu)$.

Thus, the inverse of the element is expressed by the following equations:

$$\delta_1 = \gamma_1(\gamma_1^2 \mu + \gamma_1 \gamma_0 + \gamma_0^2)^{-1} \tag{10.5}$$
$$\delta_0 = (\gamma_0 + \gamma_1)(\gamma_1^2 \mu + \gamma_1 \gamma_0 + \gamma_0^2)^{-1} \tag{10.6}$$

Equivalently, we can write:

$$\delta_1 = \gamma_1 d' \tag{10.7}$$

$$\delta_0 = (\gamma_1 + \gamma_0)d' \tag{10.8}$$

$$d = \gamma_1^2 \mu + \gamma_1 \gamma_0 + \gamma_0^2 \tag{10.9}$$

$$d' = d^{-1} \tag{10.10}$$

Next we consider the masking of these operations. The masked values corresponding to the input is thus, $(\gamma_1 + m_h)Y + (\gamma_0 + m_l)$, of which the inverse is to be computed such that the output of the equations of Equation are also masked by random values, respectively m'_h, m'_l, m_d, m'_d.

Let us consider the masking of Equation 10.7. Thus we have:

$$\delta_1 + m'_h = \gamma_1 d' + m'_h \tag{10.11}$$

$$\tag{10.12}$$

Hence we need to compute $\gamma_1 d' + m'_h$. However, because of the additive masking, we have both γ_1 and d' masked. Thus, we can compute the *masked value* $(\gamma_1 + m_h)(d' + m'_d)$, and then add some *correction terms* to obtain $\gamma_1 d' + m'_h$.

To elaborate, the correction terms will be:

$$(\gamma_1 d' + m'_h) + (\gamma_1 + m_h)(d' + m'_d) = (\gamma_1 + m_h)m'_d + m_h d' + m'_h \tag{10.13}$$

However we may note that in that case the operation uses terms like d' we should mask. Thus one has to take care when adding correction terms that no intermediate values are correlated with values, which an attacker can predict.

We thus mask d' in the correction term as follows: $(\gamma_1 + m_h)m'_d + m_h(d' + m'_d) + m_h m'_d + m'_h$.

Thus, the entire computation can be written as:

$$\begin{aligned}
\delta_1 + m'_h &= (\gamma_1 + m_h)(d' + m'_d) + \\
&\quad (\gamma_1 + m_h)m'_d + m_h(d' + m'_d) + m_h m'_d + m'_h \\
&= f_{\gamma_1}((\gamma_1 + m_h), (d' + m'_d), m_h, m'_h, m'_d)
\end{aligned}$$

We thus have:

$$f_{\gamma_1} = (\gamma_1 + m_h)m'_d + m_h(d' + m'_d) + m_h m'_d + m'_h$$

Likewise, one can derive the remaining 2 equations (Equation 10.8, and 10.9) in the masked form. For Equation 10.8, we have:

$$\begin{aligned}
\delta_0 + m'_l &= (\gamma_1 + \gamma_0)d' + m'_l \\
&= (\gamma_1 d' + m'_h) + (\gamma_0 + m_l)(d' + m'_d) + (d' + m'_d)m_l \\
&\quad + (\gamma_0 + m_l)m'_d + m'_h + m'_l + m_l m'_d \\
&= (\delta_1 + m'_h) + (\gamma_0 + m_l)(d' + m'_d) + (d' + m'_d)m_l \\
&\quad + (\gamma_0 + m_l)m'_d + m'_h + m'_l + m_l m'_d \\
&= f_{\gamma_0}((\delta_1 + m'_h), (\gamma_0 + m_l), (d' + m'_d), m_l, m'_h, m'_l, m'_d)
\end{aligned}$$

Thus continuing for Equation 10.9 we have:

$$
\begin{aligned}
d + m_d &= \gamma_1^2 p_0 + \gamma_1 \gamma_0 + \gamma_0^2 + m_d \\
&= (\gamma_1 + m_h)^2 p_0 + (\gamma_1 + m_h)(\gamma_0 + m_l) + (\gamma_0 + m_l)^2 + (\gamma_1 + m_h)m_l + (\gamma_0 + m_l)m_h \\
&\quad + m_h^2 p_0 + m_l^2 + m_h m_l + m_d \\
&= f_d((\gamma_1 + m_h), (\gamma_0 + m_l), p_0, m_h, m_l, m_d)
\end{aligned}
$$

The masking of Equation 10.10 involves performing the following operations on $d + m_d$ and obtained the masked inverse, $d' + m_d'$. Thus one needs to develop a circuit for $f_{d'}$ for which:

$$
\begin{aligned}
d' + m_d' &= f_{d'}(d + m_d, m_d, m_d') \\
&= d^{-1} + m_d'
\end{aligned}
$$

Masking Equation 10.10 involves masking an inverse operation in $GF(2^4)$. Hence the same masking operations as above can be applied while reducing the inverse to that in $GF(2^2)$. Thus, we can express an element in $GF(2^4)$ $\delta = \Gamma_1 Z + \Gamma_0$, where Γ_1 and $\Gamma_0 \in GF(2^2)$. Interestingly, in $GF(2^2)$ the inverse is a linear operation making masking easy! Thus we have, $(\Gamma + m)^{-1} = \Gamma^{-1} + m^{-1}$. This reduces the gate count considerably.

10.8.1.2 Security of the Masking Scheme

The security of masking is discussed in the following. As pointed out in [52] we provide a formal definition for secured masking. Consider an encryption algorithm $enc(x, k)$, where x and k are respectively the plaintext and the input key. The input plaintext gets modified and generates the ciphertext $enc(x, k)$ through several intermediate states denoted as $I_1(x, k), \dots, I_t(x, k)$. Varying the plaintext the adversary may obtain several values of the intermediate states and can observe the joint distributions for the intermediate states for different values of the key k. Generally, the joint distributions of these intermediate points vary depending on the plaintext and the key; this helps the attackers to build distinguishers which are exploited to recover the key. A dth order adversary obtains the value of at most d-indermediate points for each value of $(x, enc(x, k))$ (note that k is fixed for the attacker).

The masking operation tries to make these distributions indistinguishable by randomizing the computations. The randomization is often done through the choice of a random number $r \in R = \{0, 1\}^s$. Thus the intermediate computations are transformed to $I_1(x, k, r), \dots, I_t(x, k, r)$. Informally, the masking fails to provide security when the joint distribution, denoted as $D_{x,k}(r)$, depends on (x, k).

Definition 10.8.1 *An algorithm that evaluates an encryption function enc is order d perfectly masked if for all d-tuples $I_1, \dots, I_d$ of intermediate results we have that:*

$$
D_{x,k}(R) = D_{x',k'}(R) \text{ for all pairs } (x, k), (x', k')
$$

For $d = 1$ we say that an algorithm is perfectly masked.

Thus for the above masking scheme we need to argue that all the data dependent intermediate operations fulfill definition 10.8.1.2. The intermediate values in the above masking are masked data $(a + m_a)$, masked multiplication $(a + m_a)(b + m_b)$, multiplication of masked values with masks $(a + m_a)m_b$, masked squarings $(a + m_a)^2$, and $(a + m_a)^2 p$. The proof presented in [282] is divided into two parts: first it shows that all the above intermediate computations leads to outputs whose distributions are independent of the inputs, and secondly the summation of the intermediate states are done securely.

We state the results without proofs.

Lemma 1 *Let $m \in GF(2^n)$ be uniformly distributed in $GF(2^n)$ and is independently chosen of $a \in GF(2^n)$, then for all values of $a \in GF(2^n)$ $(a + m)$ is also uniformly distributed. Thus the distribution of $a + m$ is independent of a.*

Lemma 2 *Let $a, b \in GF(2^n)$ be arbitrary. Let $m_a, m_b \in GF(2^n)$ be independently and uniformly distributed in $GF(2^n)$. Then the probability distributions of $(a + m_a)(b + m_b)$ is:*

$$Pr((a + m_a)(b + m_b)) = \begin{cases} \frac{2^{n+1} - 1}{2^{2n}} & \text{if } i = 0, \text{ ie. if } m_a = a \text{ or } m_b = 0 \\ \frac{2^n - 1}{2^{2n}} & \text{if } i \neq 0 \end{cases} \quad (10.14)$$

Thus, the distribution of $(a + m_a)(b + m_b)$ is independent of a and b. We call this distribution as the random product distribution. *As a special case, when $b = 0$, we have $(a + m_a)m_b$ which is independent of a.*

Lemma 3 *Let $a \in GF(2^n)$ be arbitrary and $p \in GF(2^n)$ a constant. Let $m_a \in GF(2^n)$ be independently and unformily distributed in $GF(2^n)$. Then the distribution of $(a + m_a)^2$ and $(a + m_a)^2 p$ is independent of a. More generally any bijective mapping on an uniformly distributed finite set will retain the uniform distribution in the output.*

The above results show that the masking scheme performs operations which are secure, in the sense that they produce distributions which are independent of the input if the masks are chosen independently and unformly. However when we combine the above masked values more intermediate computations are performed. We need to ensure that the composition is also secure. The following result gives a guarantee for the same.

Lemma 4 *Let $a_i \in GF(2^n)$ be arbitrary and $M \in GF(2^n)$ be independent of all a_i, and uniformly distributed in $GF(2^n)$. Then the distribution of $\Sigma_i a_i + M$ is (pairwise) independent of a.*

One should note that the independence is for all values of i. Thus for the independence every summation of variables must start with the addition of an independent mask M. This result shows that the order in which the terms are added is important.

10.8.1.3 Circuit Complexity and Reuse of Masks

The above masking of the non-linear transformation of the AES S-Box can be explained through the top-level diagram in **Fig. 10.26**.

The circuit can be however be made more efficient and more compact through the reuse of the mask values. The reuse of the mask values can however make the circuit vulnerable to higher order differential power attacks, but it remains secure against first order attacks, if properly implemented. The application of the mask values must ensure conformity with lemma 4. Thus a direct implementation of the following formulae after sharing of the masks are not secured. They become secured only when an independent value is added to the first intermediate value that is computed.

The objective of reusing the masks is to look for opportunities of making mask values identical which leads to the reduction in the multiplications required, though this may come at the cost of some increased additions. The ordering of the operations is also crucial to

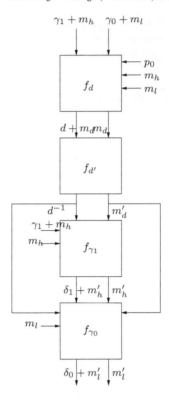

FIGURE 10.26: Masked AES S-Box using Field Isomorphism

ensure the prevention of any accidental unmasking of data. Following are some suggested reuse of masks to simplify the circuitry.

In order to reduce the complexity of f_{γ_1} the following reuse of masks is performed. Using $m_d' = m_l$ and $m_h' = m_h$, we have the following:

$$
\begin{aligned}
f_{\gamma_1} &= (\gamma_1 + m_h)(d' + m_l) + \\
&\quad (\gamma_1 + m_h)m_l + m_h(d' + m_l) + m_h m_l + m_h
\end{aligned}
$$

For the sake of reducing the gate count of the circuit for f_{γ_0} we can choose $m_l' = m_l$ and $m_d' = m_h = m_h'$. Thus we have:

$$
\begin{aligned}
f_{\gamma_0} &= (\delta_1 + m_h) + (\gamma_0 + m_l)(d' + m_h) + (d' + m_h)m_l \\
&\quad + (\gamma_0 + m_l)m_h + m_h + m_l + m_l m_h
\end{aligned}
$$

Likewise for reducing the gate count of f_d we choose $m_h = m_d$. Thus,

$$
\begin{aligned}
f_d &= (\gamma_1 + m_h)^2 p_0 + (\gamma_1 + m_h)(\gamma_0 + m_l) + (\gamma_0 + m_l)^2 + (\gamma_1 + m_h)m_l + (\gamma_0 + m_l)m_h \\
&\quad + m_h^2 p_0 + m_l^2 + m_h m_l + m_h
\end{aligned}
$$

In the following we detail the time steps in which the above intermediate computations are performed for the overall security. We divide the intermediate computations into *masked S-Box computations* and *correction terms*, to stress that while the former are computations which are any way performed in the unmasked S-Box circuit, the later are extra correction steps and adds to the overhead of the computation.

TABLE 10.6: Sequence of Masking Operations

Clk	Masked S-Box computations	Correction Terms
1	$(\gamma_1 + m_h)^2 p_0$	$(\gamma_1 + m_h)m_l$
2	$(\gamma_1 + m_h)(\gamma_0 + m_l)$	$(\gamma_0 + m_l)m_h$
3	$(\gamma_0 + m_l)^2$	$m_h^2 p_0$
4	$(\gamma_1 + m_h)(d' + m_l)$	m_l^2
5	$(\gamma_0 + m_l)(d' + m_h)$	$m_h m_l$
6	-	m_h
7	-	$(d' + m_l)m_h$
8	-	$(d' + m_h)m_l$

10.8.2 Masking at the Gate Level

One of the most popular countermeasures to prevent DPA attacks at gate level is masking. Although there are various techniques to perform masking, the method of masking has finally evolved to the technique proposed in [382]. The principle of this masking technique is explained briefly, in reference to a 2 input and gate. The same explanation may be extended to other gates, like or, XOR etc. The gate has two inputs a and b and the output is $q = a$ and b. The corresponding mask values for a, b and q are respectively m_a, m_b and m_q. Thus the masked values are: $a_m = a \oplus m_a, b_m = b \oplus m_b, q_m = q \oplus m_q$. Hence the masked and gate may be expressed as: $q_m = f(a_m, b_m, m_a, m_b, m_q)$. The design proposed in [382] proposes a hardware implementation for the function f for the masked and gate, which may be easily generalised to a masked multiplier. This is because the 2-input and gate is a special of case of an n-bit multiplier, as for the and gate we have $n = 1$. The masked multiplier (or masked and gate by assuming $n = 1$) is depicted in *Fig. 10.27*. The correctness of the circuit may be established by the following argument:

$$
\begin{aligned}
q_m &= q \oplus m_q \\
&= (ab) \oplus m_q \\
&= (a_m \oplus m_a)(b_m \oplus m_b) \oplus m_q \\
&= (a_m b_m \oplus b_m m_a \oplus a_m m_b \oplus m_a m_b \oplus m_q)
\end{aligned}
$$

However, it should be noted that the order of the computations performed is of extreme importance. The correct order of performing the computations are as follows:

$$
q_m = a_m b_m + (m_a b_m + (a_m m_b + (m_a m_b + m_q)))
$$

The ordering follows to ensure that the unmasked values are not exposed during the computations. Further it should be emphasized that one cannot reuse the mask values. For example one may attempt to make one of the input masks, m_a same as the output mask, m_q. While this may seem to be seemingly harmless can defeat the purpose of the masking. We discuss this aspect in details below.

In the above product let us denote the intermediate terms as $P_1 = a_m b_m$, $P_2 = m_a b_m$, $P_3 = a_m m_b$, $P_4 = m_a m_b$. First let us observe that adding any of two of these products gives a data dependent distribution. For example, consider $P_1 + P_2 = ab_m$. This distribution depends on a, since $a = 0$ gives the constant zero distribution, while $a \neq 0$ gives a uniform distribution. Likewise, $P_1 + P_3 = ba_m$, $P_2 + P_4 = bm_b$, which are all dependent on b for their distributions.

Consider, $P_1 + P_4 = a_m b_m + m_a m_b = (a + m_a)(b + m_b) + m_a m_b = ab_m + m_a b$. This distribution depends on both a and b. Fixing $a = b = 0$, we have the zero distribution, else we have a uniform distribution. This makes the distribution data dependent, and thus does not work. Likewise, $P_2 + P_3$ does not work as the resulting value is $am_b + m_a b$, which again depends on a and b. Hence this also does not work.

Hence, the only way of adding the terms seem to be my adding the output mask. When we are attempting to reuse the masks by setting $m_q = m_a$, we have $P_1 + m_a = ab_m + m_a(b_m + 1)$. Resulting distribution depends on a, as when $a = 0$, we have the *random product* distribution, else when $a \neq 0$, we have the uniform distribution. Similarly, $P_3 + m_a = am_b + m_a(m_b + 1)$ also is data dependent.

So, we start with $P_2 + m_a$ or $P_4 + m_a$. For the first choice, we observe $P_2 + m_a = m_a b_m + m_a = m_a(b_m + 1)$, which is a *random product* distribution. Next, we add P_4, and obtain $(P_2 + m_a) + P_4 = m_a(b + 1)$ which depends on b. Trying $(P_2 + m_a) + P_3 = am_b + m_a(b + 1)$, which is again data dependent. This can be easily observed as setting $a = 0$ and $b = 1$ we have the zero distribution, else we have a uniform distribution.

However, trying $(P_2 + m_a) + P_1 = m_a(b_m + 1) + a_m b_m = ab_m + m_a$, which is a uniform distribution and is data independent. As we still need to combine P_3 and P_4, we attempt them as either of the following:

$$
\begin{aligned}
((P_2 + m_a) + P_1) + P_3 &= ab_m + m_a + a_m m_b \\
&= ab + m_a(m_b + 1) \\
((P_2 + m_a) + P_1) + P_4 &= ab_m + m_a + m_a m_b \\
&= ab_m + m_a(m_b + 1)
\end{aligned}
$$

The former distribtion depends on $q = ab$, as when $q = 0$ we get the *random product* distribution, else when $q \neq 0$ we get different distribution depending on the value of q. The later is also data dependent as when $a = 0$ we get the *random product* distribution, else we get the uniform distribution.

This shows that though in the above masking of the AND gate, every term is not data dependent, there is no way to add them without revealing a distribution which is not data dependent. This shows the importance of lemma 4, which tells us to add a uniform and independently chosen mask (in this case mask m_q) to make the addition of the intermediate terms always data independent.

10.8.3 The Masked AND Gate and Vulnerabilities due to Glitches

The circuit for computing the above masked AND gate is shown in **Fig. 10.27**. The same circuit can be applied for masking a $GF(2^n)$ multiplier as well. We observe that the masked multiplier (or, AND gate) requires four normal multipliers (or, AND gates) and four normal n-bit (or 1-bit) XOR gates. Also it may be observed that the multipliers (or, AND gates) operate pairwise on (a_m, b_m), (b_m, m_a), $(a_m m_b)$ and (m_a, m_b). Each of the element of the pairs has no correlation to each other (if the mask value is properly generated) and are independent of the unmasked values a, b and q. As discussed in section 10.2.3, one can obtain a transition table and obtain the expected energy for generating $q = 0$ and $q = 1$. The gate now has 5 inputs and thus there can be $4^5 = 1024$ transitions like *table 10.1*). If we perform a similar calculation as before for unmasked gates, we find that the energy required to process $q = 0$ and $q = 1$ are identical. Thus if we compute the mean difference of the power consumptions for all the possible 1024 transitions for the two cases: $q = 0$ and $q = 1$, we should obtain theoretically zero. Likewise the energy levels are also not dependent on the inputs a and b and thus supports the theory of masking and show that the masked gate should not leak against a first order DPA. However in this analysis we assume that the CMOS gates switch once per clock cycle, which is true in the absence of glitches.

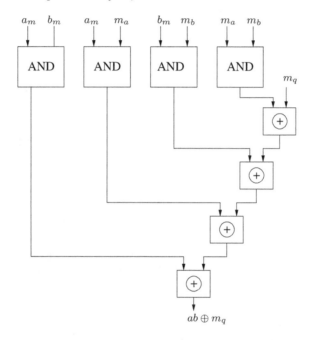

FIGURE 10.27: Architecture of a masked multiplier

But glitches are a very common phenomenon in digital circuits, as a result of which the CMOS gates switch more than once in a clock signal before stabilizing to their steady states. One of the prime reasons of glitches in digital circuits is different arrival times of the input signals, which may occur in practice due to skewed circuits, routing delays etc. As can be seen in the circuit shown in **Fig. 10.27** the circuit is unbalanced which leads to glitches in the circuit.

The work proposed in [242] investigates various such scenarios which causes glitches and multiple toggles of the masked AND gate. The assumption is that each of the 5 input signals toggle once per clock cycle and that one of the inputs arrive at different time instance than the others. Moreover we assume that the delay between the arrival time of two distant signals is more than the propagation time of the gate. As a special case, consider situations when only one of the five inputs arrives at a different moment of time than the remaining four inputs.

There exist 10 such scenarios as each one of the 5 input signals can arrive either before or after the four other ones. In every scenario there exist $4^5 = 1024$ possible combinations of transitions that can occur at the inputs. However, in each of the ten scenarios where the inputs arrive at two different moments of time, the output of the masked and gate performs two transitions instead of one. One transition is performed when the single input performs a transition and another one is performed when the other four input signals perform a transition. Thus the Transition Table for such a gate in this scenario would consist of 2048 rows and we observe that the expected mean for the cases when $q = q_m \oplus m_q = 0$ is different from that when $q = 1$. Similar results were found in other scenarios as well.

In [243], the exact reason behind the attacks on masked AND gates were searched for. For each of the 1024 transitions resulting in the circuit due to the toggles in the input lines the transitions were monitored for each of the internal lines. The number of transitions in the lines are denoted by $T(a_m), T(b_m), T(m_a), T(m_b), T(m_q), \ldots, T(i_1), \ldots, T(i_7)$. It can be observed that the masking causes the correlation of the number of transitions $T(a_m), T(b_m), T(m_a), T(m_b), T(m_q), T(i_1), T(i_2), T(i_3), T(i_4)$ with the unmasked signals, a, b, and c zero. The inputs are masked and hence it can be explained why the number of transitions $T(a_m), T(b_m), T(m_a), T(m_b), T(m_q)$ are uncorrelated with the value of q.

The 4 multipliers never operate on inputs like a_m and the corresponding mask m_a, rather they operate on independent inputs like a_m along with b_m and m_b. These makes the number of transitions at the output of the multipliers are also uncorrelated with the unmasked values. Hence, it was exactly pin-pointed that it was the XOR gates which was responsible for the correlation between power and the value of q.

This was counterintuitive as normally the output of the XOR gate switches whenever any of the input changes. Since the inputs to 4 XOR gates (**Fig. 10.27**) i_1, i_2, i_3 and i_4 are uncorrelated to the unmasked values (as it was stated previously that the multipliers process values which are not correlated to the unmasked values), it was expected that the outputs of the XOR gates should be also uncorrelated to the unmasked values. However XOR gates *absorbs* certain transitions when both the values change simultaneously or within a small interval of time. It was shown that due to the difference of arrival time between the inputs to the XOR gates, the number of absorbed transitions of the XOR gates were correlated to unmasked values a, b, and q. The absorbed transitions again depend on the arrival times of the input signals i_1 to i_4, which depends on the unmasked values. Thus the joint distribution of the arrival times of $i_1, \ldots, i_4$ was established as the source of side channel leakage of the masked gates.

The above discussion shows that the absorption property of the XORs are responsible for the power attacks. On a closer look it may be observed that out of the 4 XOR gates of the masked AND gate, the one combining the mask m_q and the output line of a multiplier i_4 operates on data none of which depends on the unmasked inputs a or b. Hence the actual responsible XOR gates are the other three XOR gates. If the architecture can ensure that these XOR gates do not absorve any transition then the overall circuit can be secured. One possible solution is to properly time the circuit with suitable enabling signals. We may also want to properly balance the circuit, with the care that arbitrary balancing might lead to the exposure of unmasked values. However adding such measures also increases the circuit complexity.

10.9   Conclusions

In this chapter, we provided an overview on power attacks on implementations of cryptographic algorithms. The chapter provided an insight into the measurement setup, the underlying power models explaining why the gates are vulnerable to power analysis. Subsequently, Differential Power Analysis is explained using the Difference of Mean method, along with some improvements over the basic technique. We discussed techniques for performing power attacks using correlation analysis, thus defining the method of Correlation Power Analysis. Metrics for evaluating a Differential Power Analysis is subsequently discussed. The chapter presented power analysis results for both simulated power traces, along with actual attacks on real traces captured from FPGAs for various types of AES architectures. The chapter concluded with popular countermeasures, with an emphasis on masking techniques and their limitations against first order power attacks.

Chapter 11

Testability of Cryptographic Hardware

"Sed quis custodiet ipsos custodes? (Who watches the watchmen?)"

(Satires of Juvenal)

1st or 2nd Century Roman Satirist.

11.1 Introduction

With the increase in the applications and complexity of cryptodevices, reliability of such devices has raised concern. Scan chains are the most popular testing technique due to their high fault coverage and least hardware overhead. However, scan chains open side channels for cryptanalysis as discussed in Chapter 7. Scan chains are used to access intermediate values stored in the flip-flops, thereby, ascertaining the secret information, often known as key. These attack techniques exploit the fact that most of modern day ICs are designed for testability. If scan chains are used for testing then they serve as a double-edged sword. In this test scheme all flip-flops (FFs) are connected in a chain and the states of the FFs can be scanned out through the chain. Scan testing equips a user with two very powerful features namely controllability and observability. Controllability refers to the fact that the user can set the FFs to a desired state, while observability refers to the power to observe the content of the FFs. Both these desirable features of a scan-chain testing methodology can be fatal from cryptographic point of view. In cryptographic algorithms, knowledge of intermediate

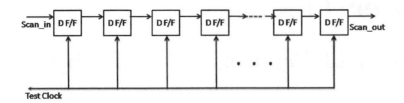

FIGURE 11.1: Design of a Scan Chain

values of the cipher can seriously reduce the complexity of breaking it. As seen in Section 7.7 of Chapter 7, the availability of scan chains to an attacker can be used efficiently to determine the key of a block cipher.

Such kinds of attacks can have profound practical importance as the security of the system can be compromised using unsophisticated methods. For example, keys can be extracted from popular pay TV set-top boxes via scan-chains at a cost of few dollars. Naturally, the attack can be prevented by eliminating the test capabilities from the design. However, this increases the risk of shipping chips with defects, which may hamper the normal functionality of the designs. Hence, research is needed to study the scan-chain based attacks against designs of standard ciphers with the objective of developing suitable DFT techniques for cryptographic hardware.

In order to solve this challenging problem of efficiently testing cryptographic chips, several interesting solutions have been proposed. An important constraint on these designs is their hardware cost, test time, and the amount of testability achieved. In this chapter, we extend the attack on block ciphers as introduced in Chapter 7 to stream ciphers. Subsequently we provide an overview on some possible strategies to be incorporated in the design of test methodologies to make the design testable, yet secure.

11.2   Scan Chain Based Attacks on Cryptographic Implementations

Scan chains are a technique used in DFT. The objective is to make testing easier by providing a simple way to set and observe every flip-flop in an IC. A special signal called scan enable is added to a design. When this signal is asserted, every flip-flop in the design is connected as a chain of registers. One input pin provides the data to this chain, and one output pin is connected to the output of the chain. On each clock event, an input pattern can be scanned-in to the registers. Then after a normal run of the device, the updated contents of the registers are scanned out of the scan chain. A standard scan chain is shown in **Fig. 11.1**. The test data is given through the scan_in line and the output pattern is scanned out through the scan_out line as shown in the figure.

Scan chains provides an access to internal states of a cipher, which can be used to attack both stream and block ciphers. As we have seen in Chapter 7, block ciphers can be quite easily attacked using the scan chains. The attacks essentially have two important steps: obtaining the correspondence of the scan chains and the internal flip flops, and secondly of utilizing them to obtain internal states which are required to retrieve the secret key. For block ciphers, the second step is quite easy as the output after one round is exposed to the attacker. However, the attack is slightly more complicated for stream ciphers. In the present section, we provide an overview on the attacks on stream ciphers. These attacks show that the scan chains provide controllability and observability to attack any cryptographic algorithm.

11.2.1 Scan Chain Based Attack on Stream Ciphers

In this section, we consider a popular structure of a stream cipher family. **Fig. 11.2** depicts a stream cipher with s independent Linear Feedback Shift Registers (LFSRs), which are combined by a Boolean function F to produce the pseudo-random key stream. The key-stream is XORed with the Data-bits to produce the cipher stream. To be more specific consider the hardware shown in **Fig. 11.2**, where each LFSR is expanded to show that that they comprise of a Shift Register (SR) and a Configurable Register (CR). The CR is loaded with the co-efficients of the primitive polynomial from the memory. To configure the LFSRs, a part of the input key, called the seed, is used to retrieve the primitive polynomials from the memory. The encryption hardware thus has a w bits seed, out of which w_1 bits are used for memory addressing, while the rest, w_2 bits are used to load the SRs of the LFSRs. The size of the LFSRs are all n bits. The attacker is aware of w, but he does not know the value of w_1, and the bit positions of the seed which are used to access the memory. Similarly he does not know w_2 and their positions, which initialize the SRs. We assume that the attacker also does not know the primitive polynomials, the structure of the scan-chain and the initial seed which has been used.

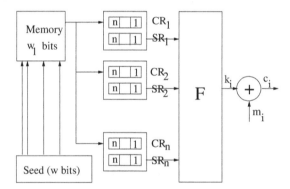

FIGURE 11.2: Generic Structure of a Stream Cipher

The stream cipher can be attacked through the use of scan-chains, enabling the adversary to obtain the value of the message data from the ciphertext. The attack has three broad stages: First, the attacker scans out the entire contents of the internal CR and SR flip-flops at the beginning, but he does not know their positions in the scan-chains.

In the first stage of the attack, the adversary ascertains the structure of the seed. For this the attacker inputs an all zero-input seed and applies one clock cycle. Thus the memory gets accessed at a location, $addr(0)$, the content of which is denoted by $(addr(0))$, and the corresponding polynomial gets loaded into the CR registers. Now the attacker sets the device back to test mode and scans out the data. It may be noted that all the SRs get the value directly from the seed and are thus all zero. Hence the number of ones in the scanned out data patterns is $s.wt(addr(0))$, as there are s-LFSRs. Now the attacker sets one of the input seed bits to one and the above steps are repeated. Depending on whether this bit goes to the memory or goes to the SRs, the number of ones is either $s.wt(addr(1))$ or $s.wt(addr(0)) + 1$. Since both of these cannot be same (as $s > 1$), and the attacker knows the value of $s.wt(addr(0))$, he comprehends whether the set bit is a part of the w_1 bits or not. Continuing this for all the w bits of the seed, the attacker knows the bits in the seed which are used to initialize the SRs. The attacker also knows the positions of the CR registers in the scanned out pattern.

In the second step, the attacker identifies the ordering of the CR and SR registers. The attacker first feeds an all one input, through the scan input pin in test mode. Thus with out loss of generality, if we assume that the LFSRs have even number of bits, the feedback bit is zero. If now the device is scanned out, one can identify the location of the $SR[n]$ bits (see figure) in the scanned out pattern. Similarly toggling between normal and test mode, one can identify all the groups of the SR bits. At this point however he does not know the relation-ship of the SR bits in the scanned out pattern with the corresponding LFSRs.

For this the attacker applies a simple trick and sets the CR bits to $10\ldots01$ through the scan chains (note he already has ascertained the positions of the CR bits in the scanned out pattern). The adversary also sets one of the $SR[1]$ bits to one. After n clock cycles, all the SR bits of a particular register becomes one, and their positions are revealed in the scan chain.

Now, the attacker uses the scanned out data at the beginning and uses his knowledge of SR and CR registers in the scanned out data, to determine the contents of the SR and CR registers at the beginning. This information helps him to obtain the key-stream, which helps to obtain the message bits from the ciphertext bits.

The above generic technique for attacking stream ciphers using scan chains is illustrated next, with an example attack on the Trivium stream cipher.

11.3   Scan Attack on Trivium

Before stating the attack, we briefly describe the Trivium Stream cipher. Trivium is a hardware based stream cipher enlisted in phase 3 of the **eStream**[383] project. It may be noted that although the attack is targeted for the implementation of Trivium in [375], the attack may be adapted to other implementations as well. However, as any side channel analysis the attack is dependent on the implementation.

11.3.1   Brief Description of Trivium

Trivium operates in two phases: key initialization and key-stream generation.

11.3.1.1   Key and IV Setup

First, the key and the Initialization Vector (IV) are used to initialize the internal states of the cipher which are then updated using Equation (11.2) but without generating the key-stream.

$$
\begin{aligned}
(s_1, s_2, s_3, \ldots, s_{93}) &\leftarrow (K_1, K_2, K_3, \ldots, K_{80}, 0, 0, \ldots, 0) \\
(s_{94}, s_{95}, s_{96}, \ldots, s_{177}) &\leftarrow (IV_1, IV_2, IV_3, \ldots, IV_{80}, 0, 0, \ldots, 0) \\
(s_{178}, s_{179}, s_{180}, \ldots, s_{288}) &\leftarrow (0, 0, \ldots, 1, 1, 1)
\end{aligned}
\tag{11.1}
$$

$$\text{for } i \quad = \quad 1 \text{ to } 4 \times 288 \text{ do}$$

$$t_1 \quad \leftarrow \quad s_{66} \oplus s_{91}.s_{92} \oplus s_{93} \oplus s_{171}$$

$$t_2 \quad \leftarrow \quad s_{162} \oplus s_{175}.s_{176} \oplus s_{177} \oplus s_{264}$$

$$t_3 \quad \leftarrow \quad s_{243} \oplus s_{286}.s_{287} \oplus s_{288} \oplus s_{69}$$

$$(s_1, s_2, s_3, ..., s_{93}) \quad \leftarrow \quad (t_3, s_1, s_2, ..., s_{92})$$

$$(s_{94}, s_{95}, s_{96}, ..., s_{177}) \quad \leftarrow \quad (t_1, s_{94}, s_{95}, ..., s_{176})$$

$$(s_{178}, s_{179}, s_{180}, ..., s_{288}) \quad \leftarrow \quad (t_2, s_{178}, s_{179}, ..., s_{287})$$

$$\text{end for} \tag{11.2}$$

11.3.2 KeyStream Generation

The state update function is given by Equation (11.3). The variable z_i denotes the key-stream bit while N denotes the number of bits to be generated and $N \leq 2^{64}$.

$$\text{for } i \quad = \quad 1 \text{ to } N \text{ do}$$

$$t_1 \quad \leftarrow \quad s_{66} \oplus s_{93}$$

$$t_2 \quad \leftarrow \quad s_{162} \oplus s_{177}$$

$$t_3 \quad \leftarrow \quad s_{243} \oplus s_{288}$$

$$z_i \quad \leftarrow \quad t_1 \oplus t_2 \oplus t_3$$

$$t_1 \quad \leftarrow \quad t_1 \oplus s_{91}.s_{92} \oplus s_{171}$$

$$t_2 \quad \leftarrow \quad t_2 \oplus s_{175}.s_{176} \oplus s_{264}$$

$$t_3 \quad \leftarrow \quad t_3 \oplus s_{286}.s_{287} \oplus s_{69}$$

$$(s_1, s_2, s_3, s_4, ..., s_{93}) \quad \leftarrow \quad (t_3, s_1, s_2, s_3, s_4, ..., s_{92})$$

$$(s_{94}, s_{95}, s_{96}, s_{97}, ..., s_{177}) \quad \leftarrow \quad (t_1, s_{94}, s_{95}, s_{96}, s_{97}, ..., s_{176})$$

$$(s_{178}, s_{179}, s_{180}, s_{181}, ..., s_{288}) \quad \leftarrow \quad (t_2, s_{178}, s_{179}, s_{180}, s_{181}, ..., s_{287})$$

$$\text{end for} \tag{11.3}$$

11.3.3 The Attack

11.3.3.1 Objective of the Attacker

The aim is to obtain the message stream from the stream of ciphertexts. The adversary observes the cryptogram $c_1, c_2, c_3, \cdots, c_l$ and then gets the possession of the device. The intention is to obtain the plaintexts $m_1, m_2, m_3, \cdots, m_l$ using scan-chain based side channel analysis.

11.3.3.2 Attack on Trivium

Here we show the attack on the implementation of Trivium in [375]. Trivium has a total of 288 internal state registers. The control circuitry in [375] requires an 11-bit counter which adds 11 more registers while 3 registers are required for the temporary variables. So the scan chain for trivium has a total of 302 registers.

As already mentioned in section 7.8, a scan attack consists of two phases, ascertaining which bit corresponds to which register and deciphering the cryptogram. Scan based attacks try to exploit the information gained about the internal state of the cipher. All hardware that has been designed keeping DFT in mind have a scan-in and scan-out line. This allows the user to scan in a desired pattern in test mode, run the circuit in normal mode and then scan out the pattern to verify the functioning of the device. In case of crypto devices this feature equips an attacker with a tool by virtue of which he can gain knowledge about the internal intermediate state of the crypto algorithm. He exploits this knowledge to break the cryptosystem. Literature shows that these attacks are quite easy to implement and do not require any sophisticated set-up.

11.3.3.3   Ascertaining Bit Correspondence

As far as Trivium is concerned the first phase of the attack can be broken down in 3 parts i.e., ascertaining the location of the internal state bits, the counter bits and the temporary registers. Once the attacker gets hold of the crypto-chip, he tries to scan out the data to get the state of the registers. What the attacker does not know is the correspondence between the actual bits and the pattern he has scanned out. However, by some clever use of key and IV setup and by using certain properties of the state update function he can easily find the exact positions of the bits in the scanned out pattern. The following procedure details the steps the attacker takes:

1. **Ascertaining location of counter bits**

   The attacker can ascertain the positions of the counter bits by exploiting the Key-IV input pattern. As per the design in [375] the user is needed to give a padded input pattern as, $(Key_{80}, 0^{13}, IV_{80}, 0^{112}, 1^3)$ through the Key_IV padding line. Here Key_{80} represents the 80 bits of the key while 0^{13} denotes a sequence of 13 0's. Since this pattern is given from outside, so the attacker inputs a pattern of all zeros i.e., 0^{288}. He then runs the system in normal mode for $(2^{10} - 1)$ cycles. Since the internal state of the cipher is set to all zeros, so according to Equation (11.3), running the cipher will have no change on the 288-bit internal state register and the temporary registers which always remain to an all zero state. The only thing that changes is the 11-bit counter. Since the system runs for $(2^{10} - 1)$ cycles, so 10 bits of the counter will be set to 1. The attacker then scans out the pattern and the bits which are 1, are concluded to be the 10 counter bits. The 11th counter bit can be determined by scanning in the scanned out pattern again and running the system for 1 cycle. This sets the 11th counter bit to 1. The attacker now scans out the pattern to get the bit position. The attacker requires a total of 288 clock cycles to scan-in the pattern and the same number of clock cycles to scan-out the pattern.

   It might be noted that to mount the scan attack the attacker need not know which bit of the counter corresponds to which bit-position but only the positions of all the counter-bits as a whole. The number of clock-cycles required is $(288 + 2^{10} - 1 + 288 + 288 + 1 + 288) = 2176$.

2. **Ascertaining the internal state bits**

   This part of the attack is straight-forward. The attacker here again tries to exploit the key-IV input pattern. He first resets the circuit and then gives a pattern in which only $key_1 = 1$ and remaining bits are 0 during Key-IV setup Equation (11.1) .i.e.,

   $$(s_1, s_2, s_3, s_4, \cdots, s_{288}) \quad \leftarrow \quad (1, 0^{79}, 0^{13}, 0^{80}, 0^{112}, 0^3).$$

   He then runs the system for 1 clock-cycle to load the first key bit, after which he scans out the entire pattern in test-mode. The output pattern will have 1's in two positions. Out of these one will correspond to the counter LSB which the attacker already knows while the other corresponds to s_1. So the bit position of s_1 in the output pattern is ascertained. He proceeds likewise setting to 1 only the bit he wants to find in the input pattern and then running the corresponding number of clock-cycles in normal mode. Typically, to find the ith bit position he has to run the system for i clock periods. He thus finds the bit positions for all the 288 state bits in the output pattern. The number of clock-cycles required is $\sum_{i=1}^{288} i + 288^2 = 124560$.

3. Ascertaining the temporary register bits

The attacker has already determined the positions of $(288 + 11) = 299$ internal registers. He then finds the temporary registers t_1, t_2, t_3. The following equations can be derived from Equation (11.2),

$$
\begin{aligned}
t_1 &\leftarrow s_{66} \oplus s_{91}.s_{92} \oplus s_{93} \oplus s_{171} \\
t_2 &\leftarrow s_{162} \oplus s_{175}.s_{176} \oplus s_{177} \oplus s_{264} \\
t_3 &\leftarrow s_{243} \oplus s_{286}.s_{287} \oplus s_{288} \oplus s_{69}
\end{aligned}
$$

The attacker sets the input pattern in such a way that when he runs the cipher in normal mode after key-IV load, only one of the temporary registers changes their value to 1 while the others are 0. For example, the attacker can set $s_{66} = 1$ i.e.,

$$
(s_1, s_2, s_3, s_4, \ldots, s_{288}) \leftarrow (0^{65}, 1, 0^{12}, 0^{13}, 0^{80}, 0^{112}, 0^3).
$$

He then loads the Key-IV pattern in normal mode and runs for 1 more clock cycle which will set $t_1 = 1$. He scans out the pattern and as he already knows all other bit positions he can get the position of t_1. This requires 2×288 clocks, 288 for scanning in and 288 for scanning out. He repeats the process to get t_2. Once he obtains t_1 and t_2, the position of t_3 becomes evident. Thus, he requires a total of 4×288 clocks.

This concludes the first phase of the attack with the attacker now having the knowledge of all the bits positions in the internal state of the cipher. He then advances to the next phase where he attempts to decipher the cryptogram from the knowledge of the internal state.

11.3.4 Deciphering the Cryptogram

In a stream cipher, we XOR the plain text bit to the key stream bit to get the ciphertext bit. So, if we have key steam bit K_i and cipher text C_i, plaintext bit P_i can be obtained as

$$
P_i = K_i \oplus C_i
$$

So our basic motive is to get all the key stream bits. The attacker had scanned out the internal state of Trivium after getting hold of the device. Now, he has ascertained the position of s-bits in the scan-chain. This information will be used to decipher the cryptogram and to obtain the plaintext. We proceed by knowing the previous state from the current state. Table 1 gives a clear picture about the relation of present and previous states of Trivium. As is clear from the encryption algorithm, current state is a right shift of previous state with first bit being a non-linear function of some other bits. So, our task remains to calculate 'a'.'b' and 'c'. Observe the following equations:

$$t_1 = s_{66} \oplus s_{93} \tag{11.4}$$

$$t_1 = t_1 \oplus s_{91} \cdot s_{92} \oplus s_{171} \tag{11.5}$$

$$(s_{94}, s_{95}, \cdots, s_{177}) \leftarrow (t_1, s_{94}, \cdots, s_{176}) \tag{11.6}$$

Equations (11.4) and (11.5) can be combined to get,

$$t_1 = s_{66} \oplus s_{93} \oplus s_{91} \cdot s_{92} \oplus s_{171} \tag{11.7}$$

This should be noted that if we give a clock at this configuration of Trivium, register s_{94} gets loaded with t_1 and other bits are shifted to their right. So, we can say that what is s_{67} now, must have been s_{66} in the previous state and what is s_{93} now, must have been s_{92} in the previous state and so on. Hence, from Equations (11.6) and (11.7) and by referring to table. 11.1 we have the following equation:

$$s_{94} = a \oplus s_{67} \oplus s_{92} \cdot s_{93} \oplus s_{172}$$
$$\Rightarrow a = s_{94} \oplus s_{67} \oplus s_{92} \cdot s_{93} \oplus s_{172}$$

Similarly, 'b' and 'c' can be deduced by the following set of equations:

$$s_{178} = b \oplus s_{163} \oplus s_{176} \cdot s_{177} \oplus s_{265}$$
$$\Rightarrow b = s_{178} \oplus s_{163} \oplus s_{176} \cdot s_{177} \oplus s_{265}$$

And,

$$s_1 = c \oplus s_{244} \oplus s_{287} \cdot s_{288} \oplus s_{70}$$
$$\Rightarrow c = s_1 \oplus s_{244} \oplus s_{287} \cdot s_{288} \oplus s_{70}$$

Hence, we can compute all the previous states given a single current state of the internal registers. Once obtained a state, one can easily get the key stream bit by following Equation (11.3). The key stream bit when XORed with the ciphertext bit of the state produces corresponding plaintext bit.

Present State	Previous State
$(s_1, s_2, \cdots, s_{93})$	$(s_2, s_3, \cdots, s_{93}, a)$
$(s_{94}, s_{95}, \cdots, s_{177})$	$(s_{95}, s_{96}, \cdots, s_{177}, b)$
$(s_{178}, s_{179}, \cdots, s_{288})$	$(s_{179}, s_{180}, \cdots, s_{288}, c)$

TABLE 11.1: Internal states of Trivium

As a summary, the scan attacks are a very powerful attack model. Thus several ciphers have been attacked in literature, following similar controllability and observability through scan chains. These works show that both block and stream ciphers, and even public key algorithm hardwares cannot be *tested safe* through scan chains. This raises the important question, of how to test cryptographic devices through specially designed scan chains so that while the normal user gets controllability and observability needed for testability, while the attacker does not get the same. Further constrain of a low hardware overhead makes the task even more challenging. Allowing untested components in a cryptographic circuit is also dangerous, as it may be the avenues for further attacks. Thus testing features are a necessity, without opening side channels to the adversary.

11.4 Testability of Cryptographic Designs

The previous attacks, clearly show the vulnerability of ciphers implemented with scan chains. The security of cryptographic algorithms lies in a secret information, commonly known as the key. During the side channel attacks, scan-chains are used to access intermediate values stored in the flip-flops, thereby ascertaining the key. Conventional scan-chains fail to solve the conflicting requirements of effective testing and security [174]. On one hand, for high fault coverage we need larger controllability and observability in the design. On the other hand, high controllability and observability leads to succesful attacks, thus rendering poor security. In order to solve this challenging problem of efficiently testing cryptographic chips some research work has been proposed.

In [149] a scan chain design based on scrambling was proposed. The design uses a scrambling technique to provide both security and testability for crypto chips. This technique dynamically reorders the flip-flops in a scan chain to protect the secrets. However, statistical analysis of the information scanned out from chips can still determine the scan chain structure and the secret information[55, 421]. Furthermore, the area overhead incurred by dynamic reordering of scan chains is high. The wiring complexity increases very fast with the number of flip-flops in the design, making the proposal inefficient for real life crypto devices. The scrambler uses a control circuit which determines the reordering of the scan flip flops in discrete time steps, thus requiring flip flops for their implementation. The control circuit uses a separate test key in order to program the interconnections. Thus, if one uses scan chains to test the scrambler circuit the attack proposed in [422] can be used to decode the test key and hence break the scheme of reordering.

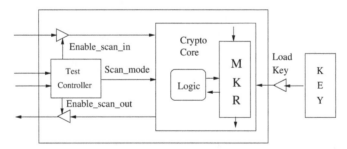

FIGURE 11.3: Secure Scan Architecture with Mirror Key Register [55]

An interesting alternative and one of the best method was proposed in [55, 421] where a secure scan chain architecture with mirror key register was used to provide both testability and security. **Fig 11.3** shows the diagram of the secure scan architecture. The design uses the idea of a special register called as the mirror key register (MKR), which is loaded with the key, stored in a separate register, during encryption. However, during encryption, the design is in a secure mode and the scan chains are disabled. When the design is in the test mode, the design is in the insecure mode and the scan chains are enabled. During this time the MKR is detached from the key register. The transition from the insecure mode to the secure mode happens, by setting the Load_key signal high and the Enable_scan_in and Enable_scan_out signals low. However, the transition from the secure mode to the insecure mode happens only through a power_off state and reversing the above control signals. It is expected that the power off removes the content of the MKR, and thus does not reveal the key to a scan-chain based attacker.

But this method has the following shortcomings:

- Security is derived from fact that switching off power destroys the data in registers. So, if the secret is permanently stored on-chip (example credit cards, cell-phone simcards, access cards) even after turning the power off the information exists inside the chip. This can be extracted from a device having such a scan chain in the insecure mode.

- At-speed testing or on-line testing is not possible with this scheme.

- The cryptographic device can be a part of a critical system that remains ON continuously (like satellite monitoring system). In such devices power-off is not possible. Hence testing in such a scenario requires alternative solutions.

- One of the most secured mode of operation of a block cipher like AES is Cipher Block Chaining (CBC) where the ciphertext at any instant of time depends on the previous block of ciphertext [368]. If testing is required at an intermediate stage then the device needs to be switched off. Thus for resuming data encryption all the previous blocks have to be encrypted again. This entire process has also to be synchronized with the receiver which is decrypting the data. Therefore such modes of block ciphers cannot be tested efficiently using this scheme.

In [161] a secured chain architecture was proposed based on lock and key technique. The architecture also uses a test key like [149] to secure the vital information of the chip. The design has a Test Security Controller (TSC) which compares the key. When the key is succesfully entered a finite state machine (FSM) switches the chip to a secured mode allowing normal scan based testing. Otherwise the device goes to an insecure mode and remains stuck until an additional Test Control pin is reset. The design suffers from the problem of large overhead due to the design of the TSC. The TSC itself uses a large number of flip-flops (for LFSRs and FSMs) which requires BIST for testing leading to an inefficient design. Further the design uses an additional key (known as test key) for security. If the cipher uses an n bit key for its operation (like 128 bits for AES-Rijndael) a brute force attack would require 2^n operations to break the system. Any successful attack should break the key with a complexity less than that of a brute force effort. If the design uses additional key bits for security of TSC (say t bits) then with a total of $n + t$ bits of key the design provides security equivalent to that of $min(n, t)$ bits. Hence, using additional key bits for scan chains is not a viable solution.

In [263] a scan tree based architecture with aliasing free compactor was proposed for testing of cryptographic devices. However, the design has the weakness of a large area overhead due to the design of compactors and its testing circuit. Normal CAD flow also does not support the design of scan tree structures.

One of the recent techniques in implementing secure scan-chains is the Flipped-scan [357] technique. In this scheme inverters are introduced at random points in the scan-chain. Security lies in the fact that an attacker cannot guess the positions of the inverters with a probability significantly greater that $\frac{1}{2}$. However, this scheme is vulnerable to an attack which we call the reset attack. In standard VLSI design, each FF is accompanied by either a synchronous or asynchronous RESET which initializes the FF to zero. An attacker can assert the reset signal and obtain the scan-out pattern by operating the crypto chip in test mode. The scan-out pattern would look like series of 0's interleaved with series of 1's. The places where polarity is reversed are the locations where an inverter has been inserted. The attack is detailed below.

11.4.0.1   Reset Attack on Flipped-Scan Mechanism

In standard VLSI design, each FF is accompanied by either a synchronous or asynchronous RESET which initializes the FF to zero. An attacker can assert the reset signal

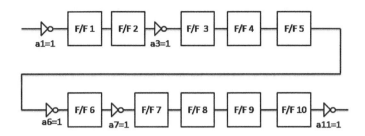

FIGURE 11.4: Example Demonstrating Attack on Flipped-Scan

and obtain the scan-out pattern by operating the crypto chip in test mode. The scan-out pattern would look like series of 0's interleaved with series of 1's. The places where polarity is reversed are the locations where an inverter has been inserted. The following example illustrates the attack.

Example 22 *Suppose there is a scan-chain of* 10 *D-FFs; and inverters are placed at position numbers* 1, 3, 6, 7 *and* 11, *out of* 11 *possible positions as shown in* **Fig. 11.4.** *We apply a reset signal and scan out the pattern. We will get a pattern equal to* $X_1, X_2, \cdots, X_{10}$, *where* $X_i = a_{i+1} \oplus a_{i+2} \cdots \oplus a_{11}$, *where* a_i *is* 1 *if there is an inverter in the* i_{th} *link and* $a_i = 0$ *otherwise.*

We will get this pattern in the order $X_{10}, X_9, \cdots, X_1$. *In this example,*

$$
\begin{aligned}
X_{10} &= a_{11} \\
X_9 &= a_{10} \oplus a_{11} \\
X_8 &= a_9 \oplus a_{10} \oplus a_{11} \\
&\vdots \\
X_1 &= a_2 \oplus a_3 \cdots a_{11}
\end{aligned}
$$

From the above set of equations it follows that we will get a sequence $X = \{0, 0, 1, 1, 1, 0, 1, 1, 1, 1\}$. *As previously stated inverters have been inserted at those positions where polarity is reversed in the pattern. Here, the positions where inverters were placed are* 3,6,7 *and* 11. *Presence of inverter at the* 11th *position was detected using the fact that first bit obtained while scanning out is* 1. *It can be easily deduced whether there is an inverter in the first position or not by feeding in a bit and observing if the output toggles or not. Thus, inverters are placed at positions* 1,3,6,7 *and* 11. *By the above procedure, one can always ascertain the location of inverters. Therefore, the design in [357] is no longer secure.*

In [261] a prevention scheme is proposed as an improvement over the Flipped scan-chain. The proposal is based on insertion of XOR gates at random points in the scan chain. We call the scheme *Xor-Chain*. One of the inputs to the XOR gate is the present input of the flip-flop from the one preceding it in the chain while the other input in the current output of the flip-flop. Actually it is a data-dependent inverter which conditionally invert the present input based on the past input. Clearly, this configuration passes the reset attack on the flipped scan architecture, as in case of reset, scan-chain output will be all zeros, i.e., the XOR gates become transparent.

Fig. 11.5 shows a XOR-chain architecture having six D-FFs. In this structure XOR gates are inserted before 2nd, 4th and 5th FFs. In order to test a circuit, we first reset the chip and then feed in a pattern to the chain architecture. The proposed XOR-chain

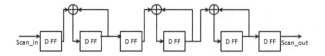

FIGURE 11.5: XOR-Chain Architecture[261]

architecture can be used for testability as we can have a unique output pattern for a given input pattern. The following theorem, summarizes the fact that the XOR-chain maintains a one-to-one correspondence between the test input and output patterns, and thus can be used to test the device.

Theorem 19 *[261] Let $X = \{X_1, X_2, \cdots, X_n\}$ be the vector space of inputs to the XOR-chain and $Y = \{Y_1, Y_2, \cdots, Y_n\}$ be the vector space of outputs from the XOR-chain. Then there is a one-to-one correspondence between X and Y, if the XOR chain is reset before feeding in the pattern X.*

The proof has essentially two parts. First we try to prove the one-to-one correspondence between the input and what gets into the FFs.

Let the existence of an XOR gate be denoted by a variable $a_i \in (0,1)$ such that if $a_i = 1$ then there is an XOR gate before the ith FF. Otherwise, if $a_i = 0$ there is no XOR gate. At any instant of time t the state of the internal FFs of the XOR-chain can be expressed as follows:

$$S_1^t = X_{n-t} \oplus S_1^{t-1}.a_1$$
$$S_2^t = S_1^{t-1} \oplus S_2^{t-1}.a_2$$
$$S_3^t = S_2^{t-1} \oplus S_3^{t-1}.a_3$$
$$...$$
$$S_n^t = S_{n-1}^{t-1} \oplus S_n^{t-1}.a_n$$

where,

$$n \implies \text{the total number of FFs,}$$
$$S_i^t \implies \text{the state(value) of the } i^{th} \text{ FF in the } t^{th} \text{ clock cycle,}$$
$$X_{n-t} \implies \text{the input to the XOR-chain at the } t^{th} \text{ clock cycle.}$$

Solving the above system of equations by multiplying these equations with appropriate values of a_i and subsequent XORing, we get the following expression:

$$a_1.S_2^t \oplus a_1.a_2.S_3^t \oplus \ldots (a_1.a_2...a_{n-1}).S_n^t = S_1^t \oplus X_{n-t} \oplus (a_1.a_2...a_n).S_n^{t-1}$$

For testing, before scanning in a pattern, the circuit is always reset. Hence, all FFs are initially holding 0. In the above equation S_n^{t-1} is the state of the nth FF at the $(t-1)^{th}$ clock cycle. However, that should be 0 because of the initial reset. So the term $(a_1.a_2...a_n).S_n^{t-1}$ is always 0 independent of the values of $a_1, a_2, ...a_n$. Thus the resultant equation can be rewritten as:

$$X_{n-t} = a_1.S_2^t \oplus a_1.a_2.S_3^t \oplus \ldots (a_1.a_2...a_{n-1}).S_n^t \oplus S_1^t$$

It can be inferred from above that given the states of all the FFs at an instant (i.e., $S_1^t, ..., S_n^t$) and the configuration of the XOR-chain(i.e., $a_1, ..., a_n$) one can find out what the input to the chain was. Thus we can conclude that given a fixed X and $(a_1, a_2, .., a_n)$, the states of internal FFs have a one-to-one mapping with vector space X.

In order to mount a scan attack on a crypto hardware in general and stream cipher in particular, an attacker must first ascertain the structure of the scan-chain. So the main aim of any prevention mechanism is to thwart such an attempt. Similar, to the philosophy of flipped scan chain, security of our scheme relies on the fact that if the positions of the XOR gates are unknown to the attacker, then it is computationally infeasible for him to break the structure of the scan-chain. As a rule of thumb in designing we insert $m = \lfloor n/2 \rfloor$ XOR gates in a scan-chain with n FFs. We show in the following that even if the attacker has the knowledge of the number of XOR gates (m) among the number of FFs, the probability of successfully determining the structure is about $1/2^n$. The following theorem states the fact that it is infeasible for the attacker to determine the scan structure.

Theorem 20 *[261] For a XOR scan-chain with n FFs and $m = \lfloor n/2 \rfloor$ XOR gates. The probability to guess the correct structure by an attacker with knowledge of n is nearly $1/2^n$.*

Let the number of FFs be n and the number of XOR gates be m. Hence, the number of structures possible is ^nC_m, where ^nC_m means the number the ways of choosing m unordered elements from n elements. Lets us assume that attacker uses the knowledge that the number of XOR gates is half the number of FFs, so that we have $m = \lfloor n/2 \rfloor$. Therefore, the probability to guess the correct structure is now $1/^nC_{\lfloor n/2 \rfloor}$

In order to compute the bound, we use the fact the maximum value of ^nC_r is when $r = \lfloor n/2 \rfloor$. We combine this with the fact that the maximum binomial coefficient (given by the above value) must be greater that the average of all binomial coefficients, i.e., when r runs from 0 to n.

But, $^nC_{\lfloor n/2 \rfloor} > 2^n/(n+1) \Rightarrow {}^nC_{\lfloor n/2 \rfloor} > 2^{n-log_2(n+1)}$. And for large values of n, $n - log_2(n+1) \approx n$. Hence, the probability of guessing the correct scan structure is nearly $1/2^n$.

The XOR-chain model requires insertion of *XOR* gates at random points of a scan chain. In terms of gate count the XOR-chain is far more costly than its nearest counterpart *flipped-scan*. Table 11.2 compares the hardware overhead of the proposed prevention scheme with [357].

Prevention Mechanism	No. of insertions	Total Transistor Count
Flipped Scan	$\lfloor (n+1)/2 \rfloor$	$(n+1)$
Xored Scan	$\lfloor n/2 \rfloor$	$5n$

TABLE 11.2: Hardware Overhead Comparison

Subsequently, several developments and interesting solutions on scan chains for secured testing have evolved [125, 124, 361, 362]. But in spite of the defences, this topic remains an important field of activity with the emergence of new attacks [166].

11.5   Conclusions

The chapter described the potential security threats due to conventional scan chains for providing DFT (Design for Testability) to cryptographic hardware. We presented a case-study of an attack on a generic stream cipher hardware module, and then later show an actual attack on a standard stream cipher called Trivium. Finally, we discussed some potential countermeasures to allow testability, but reducing the attack opportunities to an adversary.

Part IV

Hardware Intellectual Property Protection

Chapter 12

Hardware Intellectual Property Protection through Obfuscation

"The intellectual property situation is bad and getting worse. To be a programmer, it requires that you understand as much law as you do technology."

Eric Allman

12.1   Introduction

Reuse-based System-on-Chip design using hardware intellectual property (IP) cores has become a pervasive practice in the industry. These IP cores usually come in the following three forms: synthesizable Register Transfer Level (RTL) descriptions in Hardware Description Languages (HDLs) ("Soft IP"); gate-level designs directly implementable in hardware ("Firm IP"); and GDS-II design database ("Hard IP"). The approach of designing complex systems by integrating tested, verified and reusable modules reduces the SoC design time and cost dramatically [73].

Unfortunately, recent trends in IP-piracy and reverse-engineering efforts to produce counterfeit ICs have raised serious concerns in the IC design community [73, 277, 172, 85, 215]. IP piracy can take diverse forms, as illustrated by the following scenarios:

- A chip design house buys the IP core from the IP vendor, and makes an illegal copy or "clone" of the IP. The IC design house then uses the IP without paying the required royalty, or sells it to another IC design house (after minor modifications) claiming the IP to be its own design [172].

- An untrusted fabrication house makes an illegal copy of the GDS-II database supplied by a chip design house, and then manufactures and sells counterfeit copies of the IC under a different brand name [77].

- A company performs post-silicon reverse-engineering on an IC to manufacture its illegal clone [336].

These scenarios demonstrate that all parties involved in the IC design flow are vulnerable to different forms of IP infringement, which can result in loss of revenue and market share. *Obfuscation* is a technique that transforms an application or a design into one that is functionally equivalent to the original but is significantly more difficult to reverse engineer. Software obfuscation to prevent reverse-engineering has been studied widely in recent years [97, 430, 155, 153, 95, 96]; however, the techniques of software obfuscation are not directly applicable to HDL because the obfuscated HDL can result in potentially unacceptable design overhead when synthesized.

Although design modifications to prevent the illegal manufacturing of ICs by fabrication houses have been proposed [336] before, such techniques are not useful in preventing the theft of soft IPs. Furthermore, they do not provide protection against possible IP piracy from the SoC design house. In this chapter, we present two low-overhead techniques each of which can serve as the basis for a secure SoC design methodology through design obfuscation and authentication performed on the RTL design description. We follow a key-based obfuscation approach, where normal functionality is enabled only upon application of a specific input initialization key sequence. The majority of commercial hardware IPs come in the RTL ("soft") format, which offers better portability by allowing design houses to map the circuit to a preferred platform in a particular manufacturing process [231].

In this chapter, we have demonstrated design obfuscation for both gate-level [77] and RTL IPs. The main idea behind the IP protection technique for gate-level designs are: (a) finding the optimal modification locations in a gate-level netlist by structural analysis, and (b) designing a gate-level modification circuit to optimally modify the netlist. While direct structural analysis and the structural modification proposed in [77] is suitable for gate-level IPs, the proposed obfuscation approach for gate-level IPs cannot be used for RTL IPs for the following reasons: (a) RTL IPs do not directly provide high-level structural information; and (b) any obfuscation performed on an RTL IP should maintain its portability. Since a majority of the hardware IPs are actually delivered in RTL format, there is a need to develop low-overhead protection measures for them against piracy. In this chapter, we propose a anti-piracy approach for RTL IPs based on effective key-based hardware obfuscation. The basic idea is to judiciously obfuscate the control and data flow of an RTL IP in a way that prevents its normal mode operation without application of an enabling key at its primary input.

We provide two RTL IP obfuscation solutions, which differ in level of protection and computation complexity: 1) the first technique, referred to as the "STG modification approach", converts a RTL description to gate level; obfuscates the gate level netlist; and then de-compiles back to RTL; 2) the second technique, referred to as the "CDFG modification approach", avoids the forward compilation step and applies obfuscation in the register transfer level by modifying its control and data flow constructs, which is facilitated through generation of a CDFG of the RTL design. The first approach can provide higher level of obfuscation but is computationally more expensive than the second one.

We derive appropriate metrics to quantify the obfuscation level for both the approaches. We compare the two approaches both qualitatively and quantitatively. We show that an important advantage of the proposed obfuscation approach is that the level of protection can be improved with minimal additional hardware overhead by increasing the length of the initialization key sequence. We show that this is unlike conventional encryption algorithms e.g. the *Advanced Encryption Standard* (AES) whose hardware implementations usually incur much larger overhead for increasing key length.

Finally, along with obfuscation, we show that the proposed approaches can be extended to embed a hard-to-remove "digital watermark" in the IP that can help to authenticate the IP in case it is illegally stolen. The authentication capability provides enhanced security while incurring little additional hardware overhead.

The rest of the chapter is organized as follows. In Section 12.2, we present related work and the motivation behind this work. In Section 12.3, we describe the functional obfuscation technique for IP based on modifications of the *State Transition Graph* (STG) of the circuit, for gate–level designs. In Section 12.4 we describe the extension of the idea to generate RTL designs. In Section 12.5, we describe IP protection based on the *Control and Data Flow Graph* (CDFG) extracted from the RTL. In Section 12.5.2, we compare the relatives merits and demerits of the two proposed techniques. In Section 12.6, we present theoretical analysis of the proposed obfuscation schemes to derive metrics for the level of obfuscation. In Section 12.7, we present automated design flows, and simulation results for several open-source IP cores. In Section 12.8, we describe a technique to decrease the overhead by utilizing the normally unused states of the circuit.

12.2　Related Work

Hardware IP protection has been investigated earlier in diverse contexts. Previous work on this topic can be broadly classified into two main categories: (1) *Obfuscation* based protection, and (2) *Authentication* based protection.

Hardware Obfuscation: In obfuscation based IP protection, the IP vendor usually affects the human readability of the HDL code [379], or relies on cryptographic techniques to encrypt the source code [70]. In [379], the code is re-formatted by changing the internal net names and removing the comments, so that the circuit description is no longer intelligible to the human reader. RTL obfuscation for VHDL descriptions has been explored in [68], where the authors use rudimentary transformations of the code such as variable name changes, inlining of code, loop unrolling, statement order changing, etc. to make the code difficult to understand. However, usually the IP interface and port names cannot be modified or obfuscated to comply with the specifications. As the above two techniques do not modify the functionality of the IP core, they cannot prevent an IP from being stolen by an adversary and used as a "black-box" circuit module. In [70], the HDL source code is encrypted and the IP vendor provides the key to de-crypt the source code only to its customers using a particular secure design platform. A similar approach has been proposed in [407], where an infrastructure for IP evaluation and delivery for FPGA applications has been proposed based on Java applets. However, the above techniques force the use of a particular design platform, a situation that might be unacceptable to many SoC designers who seek the flexibility of multiple tools from diverse vendors in the design flow. Also, none of the above techniques prevent possible reverse-engineering effort at later stages of the design and manufacturing flow (to produce IC clones or insert hardware Trojan), and thus does not benefit the other associated parties (e.g. the SoC designers and the system designers). One important point to note is that a given hardware obfuscation technique should not affect any change in the standard interface of a hardware IP module. In other words, obfuscation of a hardware IP module should have minimum impact on the workflow of an IC designer.

Hardware Watermarking: To protect the rights of the IP vendor through authentication, the approaches proposed are directed towards embedding a well-hidden *Digital Watermark* in the design [73, 277, 172, 85, 215] to authenticate the design at a later stage. Since this digital watermark (or signature) is extremely difficult to discover and remove from the IP, it is easy to prove an illegal use of such a component in litigation. The signature is typically in the form of an input-output response pair hosted in the memory or combinational parts of the circuit [73, 277], but secure hashing to insert multiple small watermarks in the design has also been proposed [215]. Another noted approach is *constraint-based watermarking* [172], where the watermarks are design features which result from constraints applied to optimization and constraint-satisfaction problems during design. The authentication-based IP protection schemes are efficient and sophisticated techniques to prove the ownership of an IP which has a digital signature embedded in it. However, their main shortcoming is they are *passive*, in the sense that they cannot prevent the stolen IP from being used in the first place. They can only help to prove the ownership in case of litigation.

Software Obfuscation: It has been shown that it is possible to recover software source-code by decompilation of binary or byte-code. One of the most popular approaches of preventing such reverse-engineering is to obfuscate the control-flow of a program to produce "spaghetti code" that is difficult to de-compile from the binary form to a higher level program [430, 155, 153, 223]. Another technique is the so-called "code morphing" [95], where a section of the compiled code is substituted with an entirely new block that expects the same machine state when it begins execution of the previous section, and leaves with the same machine state after execution as the original. Other software obfuscation approaches include self-modifying code [168] (code that generates other code at run-time), self-decryption of partially encrypted code at run-time [352, 35], and code redundancy and voting to produce "tamper-tolerant software" (conceptually similar to hardware redundancy for fault tolerance) [162]. A general shortcoming of these approaches is that they do not scale well in terms of memory footprint and performance as the size of the program (or the part of the program to be protected) increases [84]. Hence, RTL obfuscation approaches motivated along similar lines are also likely to result in inefficient circuit implementations of the obfuscated RTL with unacceptable design overhead. Also, the value of such techniques is the matter of debate because it has been theoretically proven that software obfuscation in terms of obfuscating the "black-box functionality" does not exist [40]. In contrast, we modify both the structure and the functionality of the circuit description under question; hence the above result of impossibility of obfuscation is not applicable in our case.

12.3 Functional Obfuscation through State Transition Graph Modification

We start with the description of the scheme for gate–level designs. Later, we extend it for RTL designs.

12.3.1 Goals of the Obfuscation Technique

In order to achieve comprehensive protection of hardware IPs, the proposed approach focuses on obfuscating the functionality and structure of an IP core by modifying the gate-level netlist, such that it both obfuscates the design and embeds authentication features in it. The IC is protected from unauthorized manufacturing by the fact that the system designer depends on input from the chip designer to use the IC. Consequently, the manufacturing house cannot simply manufacture and sell un-authorized copies of an IC without the knowledge of the design house. In addition, by adopting a *Physically Unclonable Function* (PUF) based activation scheme, the security can be increased further since it ensures that the activation pattern is specific to each IC instance. The embedded authentication feature helps in proving illegal usage of an IP during litigation. Finally, the obfuscation remains transparent to the end user who has the assurance of using a product that has gone through an anti-piracy secure design flow.

12.3.2 Hardware IP Piracy: Adversary's Perspective

An adversary trying to determine the functionality of an obfuscated gate-level IP core can take resort to either (1) simulationÂŰ-based reverseÂŰ engineering to determine functionality of the design, or (2) structural analysis of the netlist to identify and isolate the original design from the obfuscated design. The proposed obfuscation approach targets to achieve simulation mismatch for the maximum possible input vectors, as well as structural mismatch for maximum possible circuit nodes. To achieve structural mismatch between the reference and the obfuscated design, we modify the state transition function as well as internal logic structure.

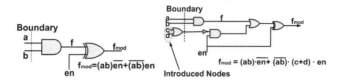

(a) Simple scheme using XOR gate   (b) Scheme using expansion of logic cone

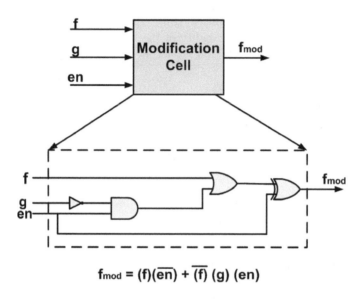

$$f_{mod} = (f)(\overline{en}) + \overline{(f)} \, (g) \, (en)$$

(c) Modification cell

FIGURE 12.1: Schemes for Boolean function modification and modification cell.

12.3.2.1   Modification Scheme Employing Input Logic-cone Expansion

Consider the simple example shown in Fig. 12.1(a). It shows a modified 2-ÂŰinput AND gate. If $en = 0$, it works as an ordinary AND gate; however, if $en = 1$, the original functionality of the AND gate is obfuscated because the output is inverted. Simulation of the simple circuit of Fig. 12.1(a) against an ordinary 2ÂŰ-input AND gate will report 4 possible input vectors with $en = 1$ as failing patterns. To increase the number of failing patterns for this circuit we must increase its input logic cone size, while ensuring that it continues to function properly when $en = 0$. Fig. 12.1(b) shows an alternative scheme, where the input logic cone has been expanded to include the node c and d. A complete enumeration of the truth-table of the modified circuit will show failures for 13 input patterns.

The modification scheme of Fig. 12.1(b) can be generalized to a form shown in Fig. 12.1(c). Here, f is the Boolean function corresponding to an internal node and g is any arbitrary Boolean logic function. It is worthwhile to note that the simple modification scheme of Fig. 12.1(a) is a special case with $g = 1$. As shown, the modified logic function is of the form:

$$f_{mod} = f{\cdot}\overline{en} + \overline{f}{\cdot}g{\cdot}en \tag{12.1}$$

Let us call the function g as the *Modification Kernel Function* (MKF). It is clear that for

$en = 1$, if $g = 1$ for a given set of primary inputs and state element output state, $f_{mod} = \overline{f}$ and the test pattern is a failing test pattern. To increase the amount of dissimilarity between the original and modified designs, we should try to make g evaluate to logic-1 as often as possible. At first glance, the trivial choice seems to be $g = 1$. However, in that case the input logic cone is not expanded and thus the number of failing vectors reported by a formal verification approach is limited. For any given set of inputs, this is achieved by a logic function which is the logical-OR of the input variables.

12.3.3 Obfuscation Metric

We now derive a metric that quantifies the level of obfuscation, i.e. the mismatch between the original and the obfuscated design. Let, f be a function of the set P_1 of primary inputs and state-element outputs and g be a function of a set P_2 of primary inputs and state element (SE) outputs. Let $P_1 \bigcap P_2 = P$, $|P_1| = p_1$, $|P_2| = p_2$, $|P| = p$, $P_1 \bigcup P_2 = \Gamma$ and $|\Gamma| = \gamma = p_1 + p_2 - p$. Further, let g be a Boolean OR function with p_2 inputs. Then, for $(2^{p_2} - 1)$ of its input combinations, g is at logic-1. Consider $en = 1$. Then, for all these $(2^{p_2} - 1)$ input combinations of P_2, $f_{mod} = \overline{f}$, causing a failing vector. Corresponding to each of these $(2^{p_2} - 1)$ combinations of P_2, there are $(p_1 - p)$ other independent primary inputs to f. Hence, the total number of failing vectors when $g = 1$ is:

$$N_{g1} = 2^{(p_1-p)} \cdot (2^{p_2} - 1) \tag{12.2}$$

For the other "all zero" input combination of P_2, $f = 0$. Let the number of possible cases where $f = 1$ at $g = 0$ be N_{g0}. Then, the total number of failing input patterns:

$$N_{failing} = N_{g1} + N_{g0} = 2^{(p_1-p)} \cdot (2^{p_2} - 1) + N_{g0} \tag{12.3}$$

In the special case when $P_1 \bigcap P_2 = P = \phi$, N_{g0} is given simply by the number of possible logic-1 entries in the truth-table of f.

The total input space of the modified function has a size 2^γ. We define the *obfuscation metric (M)* as:

$$M = \frac{N_{failing}}{2^{\gamma+1}} = \frac{2^{(p_1-p)} \cdot (2^{p_2} - 1) + N_{g0}}{2^{p_1+p_2-p+1}} \tag{12.4}$$

The "+1" factor in the denominator is due to the en signal. Note that $0 < M \leq \frac{1}{2}$. As an example, for $f = ab + cd$, with $g = a + b$, $M = \frac{13}{32}$. As a special case, consider $p = p_1 = p_2$, i.e. the signal g is derived from the same set of primary inputs of f. Then,

$$M = \frac{1}{2}\left(1 + \frac{N_{g0} - 1}{2^{p_1}}\right) = \frac{1}{2}\left(1 + \frac{N_{g0} - 1}{2^{p_2}}\right) \tag{12.5}$$

In this case, N_{g0} is either 0 or 1; hence $M = \frac{1}{2}$ if $N_{g0} = 1$ and $M = \frac{1}{2}\left(1 - 2^{-p_1}\right)$ if $N_{g0} = 0$. Note that M attains the maximum (ideal) value of 0.5 in this case when $N_{g0} = 1$. The theoretical maximum, however, is not a very desirable option because it keeps the input space limited to 2^{p_1} possible vectors. Again, if $p = 0$, i.e., g is generated by a completely different set of primary inputs which were not included in f, then:

$$M = \frac{1}{2}\left(1 + \frac{N_{g0}2^{-p_1} - 1}{2^{p_2}}\right) \tag{12.6}$$

Larger values of N_{g0} and smaller values of p_2 for a given p_1 help to increase M. Note that unlike the first case, N_{g0} is guaranteed to be non-zero. This property effectively increases the value of M in case (b) than that in case (a) for most functions. However, in the second case, $M < \frac{1}{2}$, i.e. M cannot attain the theoretical maximum value.

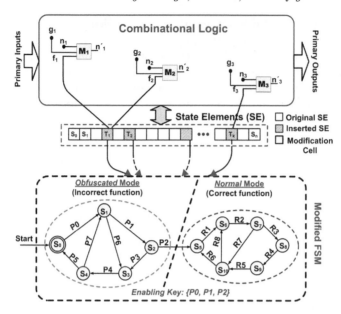

FIGURE 12.2: The proposed functional and structural obfuscation scheme by modification of the state transition function and internal node structure.

Selection of the Modification Kernel Function (g): Although the above analysis points to the selection of primary inputs or state element outputs to design the MKF (g) satisfying the condition $p = 0$, in practice, this could incur a lot of hardware overhead to generate the OR-functions corresponding to each modified node. An alternative approach is to select an internal logic node of the netlist to provide the Boolean function g. It should have the following characteristics:

1. The modifying node should have a very large fan-in cone, which in turn would substantially expand the logic cone of the modified node.

2. It should not be in the fan-out cone of the modified node.

3. It should not have any node in its fan-in cone which is in the fan-out cone of the modified node.

Conditions (2) and (3) are essential to prevent any *combinational loop* in the modified netlist. Such a choice of g does not, however, guarantee it to be an ORÂŰ-function and is thus sub-ÂŰoptimal.

12.3.4   System-level Obfuscation

In this section, we present the secure SoC design methodology for hardware protection based on the analysis presented in the previous section.

12.3.4.1   State Transition Function Modification

The first step of the obfuscation procedure is the modification of the state transition function of a sequential circuit by inserting a small Finite State Machine (FSM). The inserted FSM has all or a subset of the primary inputs of the circuit as its inputs (including the clock and reset signals) and has multiple outputs. At the start of operations, the FSM is

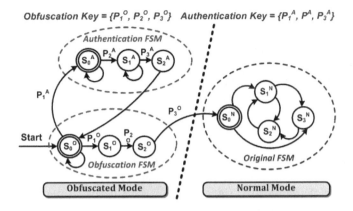

FIGURE 12.3: Modification of the initialization state space to embed authentication signature.

reset to its initial state, forcing the circuit to be in the *obfuscated* mode. Depending on the applied input sequence, the FSM then goes through a state transition sequence and only on receiving N specific input patterns in sequence, goes to a state which lets the circuit operate in its *normal* mode. The initial state and the states reached by the FSM before a successful initialization constitute the "pre-initialization state space" of the FSM, while those reached after the circuit has entered its normal mode of operation constitute the "post-initialization state space". Fig. 12.2 shows the state diagram of such a FSM, with $P0{\rightarrow}P1{\rightarrow}P2$ being the correct initialization sequence. The input sequence $P0$ through $P2$ is decided by the IP designer.

The FSM controls the mode of circuit operation. It also modifies selected nodes in the design using its outputs and the *modification cell* (e.g. M_1 through M_3). This scheme is shown in Fig. 12.2 for a gate–level design that incorporates modifications of three nodes n_1 through n_3. The MKF can either be a high fan-in internal node (avoiding combinational loops) in the unmodified design, or the OR-function of several selected primary inputs. The other input (corresponding to the *en* port of the modification cell) is a Boolean function of the inserted FSM state bits with the constraint that it is at logic-0 in the *normal* mode. This modification ensures that when the FSM output is at logic-0, the logic values at the modified nodes are the same as the original ones. On the other hand, in the *obfuscated* mode, for any FSM output that is at logic-1, the logic values at the modified nodes are inverted if $g = 1$ and logic-0 if $g = 0$. Provided the modified nodes are selected judiciously, modifications at even a small number of nodes can greatly affect the behavior of the modified system. This happens even if the *en* signal is not always at logic-0. In our implementation, we chose to have the number of outputs of the inserted FSM as a user-specified parameter. These outputs are generated as random Boolean functions of the state element bits at design time with the added constraint that in the *normal* mode, they are at logic-0. The randomness of the Boolean functions adds to the security of the scheme. Such a node modification scheme can provide higher resistance to structural reverse-engineering efforts than the scheme in [78].

12.3.5 Embedding Authentication Features

The proposed obfuscation scheme allows us to easily embed authentication signature into a gate-level design with negligible design overhead. Such an embedded signature acts as a *digital watermark* and hence helps to prevent attack from trusted parties in the design flow with knowledge of initialization sequence. Corresponding to each state in the *pre-initialization state space*, we arrange to have a particular pattern to appear at a sub-set of the primary outputs when a pre-defined input sequence is applied. Even if a hacker arranges to by-pass the initialization stage by structural modifications, the inserted FSM can be controlled to have the desired bit-patterns corresponding to the states in the *pre-initialization state space*, thus revealing the watermark. For post-silicon authentication, scan flip-flops can be used to bring the design to the obfuscated mode. Because of the prevalent widespread use of full-scan designs, the inserted FSM flip-flops can always be controlled to have the desired bit-patterns corresponding to the states in the *authentication FSM*, thus revealing the watermark. Fig. 12.3 illustrates the modification of the state transition function for embedding authentication signature in the *obfuscated mode* of operation.

To mask or disable the embedded signature, a hacker needs to perform the following steps, assuming a purely random approach:

1. Choose the correct inserted FSM state elements (n_p) from all the total state elements (n_t). This has $\binom{n_t}{n_p}$ possible choices.

2. Apply the correct input vector at the n_i input ports where the vectors are to be applied to get the signature at the selected n_o output ports. This is one out of 2^{n_i} choices.

3. Choose the n_o primary outputs at which the signature appears from the total set of primary outputs (n_{po}). This has $\binom{n_{po}}{n_o}$ possibilities.

4. For each of these recognized n_o outputs, identify it to be one among the possible $2^{2^{(n_i+n_p)}}$ Boolean functions (in the *obfuscated* mode) of the n_i primary inputs and n_p state elements, and change it without changing the normal functionality of the IP.

Hence, in order to mask one signature, the attacker has to make exactly one correct choice from among $N = \binom{n_t}{n_p} \cdot 2^{n_i} \cdot \binom{n_{po}}{n_o} \cdot 2^{2^{(n_i+n_p)}}$ possible choices, resulting in a masking success probability of $P_{masking} \cong \frac{1}{N}$. To appreciate the scale of the challenge, consider a case with $n_t = 30$, $n_p = 3$, $n_i = 4$, $n_o = 4$ and $n_{po} = 16$. Then, $P_{masking} \sim 10^{-47}$. In actual IPs, the masking probability would be substantially lower because of higher values of n_p and n_t.

12.3.6   Choice of Optimal Set of Nodes for Modification

To obfuscate a design, we need to choose an optimal set of nodes to be modified, so that maximum obfuscation is achieved under the given constraints. We estimate the level of obfuscation by the amount of verification mismatch reported by a Formal Verification based equivalence checker tool. Formal equivalence checker tools essentially try to match the input logic cones at the state-elements and the primary outputs of the reference and the implementation [400]. Hence, nodes with larger fanout logic cone would be preferred for modification since that will in turn affect the input logic of comparatively larger number of nodes. Also, large input logic cone of a node is generally indicative of its higher *logic depth*; hence any change at such a node is likely to alter a large number of primary outputs. Thus, in determining the suitability metric for a node as a candidate for modification, we need to consider both these factors. We propose the following metric to be used as the *suitability metric* for a node:

$$M_{node} = \left(\frac{w_1 \cdot FO}{FO_{max}} + \frac{w_2 \cdot FI}{FI_{max}} \right) \times \frac{FO \cdot FI}{FI_{max} \cdot FO_{max}} \qquad (12.7)$$

where FI and FO are the number of nodes in the fan-in and the fan-out cone of the node, respectively. FI_{max} and FO_{max} are the maximum number of fan-in and fan-out nodes in the circuit netlist and are used to normalize the metric. w_1 and w_2 are weights assigned to the two factors, with $0 \leq w_1, w_2 \leq 1$ and $w_1 + w_2 = 1$. We chose $w_1 = w_2 = 0.5$, which gives the best results in terms of obfuscation, as shown in the next section. Note that $0 < M_{node} \leq 1$. Because of the widely differing values of FO_{max} and FI_{max} in some circuits, it is important to consider both the sum and the product terms involving $\frac{FO}{FO_{max}}$ and $\frac{FI}{FI_{max}}$. Considering only the sum or the product term results in an inferior metric that fails to capture the actual suitability of a node, as observed in our simulations.

12.3.7 The *HARPOON* Design Methodology

The overall hardware obfuscation design flow is shown in Fig. 12.4. First, from the synthesized gate-level HDL netlist of an IP core, the fan-in and fan-out cones of the nodes are obtained. Then, an iterative ranking algorithm is applied to find the most suitable N_{max} modifiable nodes, where N_{max} is the maximum number of nodes that can be modified within the allowable overhead constraints. The ranking is a multi-pass algorithm, with the metric for each node being dynamically modified based on the selection of the node in the last iteration. The algorithm takes into account the overlap of the fan-out cones of the nodes which have been already selected and eliminates them from the fan-out cones of the remaining nodes. On the completion of each iteration, the top ranking node among the remaining nodes is selected, so that selection of N_{max} nodes would take N_{max} iterations. In this way, as the iterations progress, the nodes with more non-overlapping fan-out cones are assigned higher weight. We observed the superiority of this iterative approach over a single-pass ranking approach for all the benchmark circuits we considered.

A *"don't touch"* list of nodes can be optionally input to the to direct it not to modify certain nodes, e.g. nodes which fall in the critical path. In large benchmarks, we observed that there were sufficient nodes with high fanouts, such that skipping a few *"don't touch"* nodes still maintains the effectiveness of node modification algorithm in achieving functional and structural obfuscation. For each node to be modified, proper MKF (g) is selected either on the basis of its fan-in cone size, or by OR-ing several primary inputs which were originally not present in its input logic cone. The FSM is then integrated with the gate-level netlist and the selected nodes are modified. The modified design is re-synthesized and flattened to generate a new gate-level netlist. The integrated FSM and the modification cells are no longer visually identifiable in the resultant netlist. This re-synthesis is performed under timing constraint, so that it maintains circuit performance.

The IP vendor applies the hardware obfuscation scheme to create a modified IP and supplies it to the design house, along with the activating sequences. The design house receives one or multiple IPs from the IP vendors and integrates them on chip. To activate the different IPs, the designer needs to include a low-overhead *controller* in the SoC. This controller module can perform the initialization of the different IP blocks in two different ways. In the first approach, it serially steers the different initialization sequences to the different IP blocks from the primary inputs. This controller module will include an integrated FSM which determines the steering of the correct input sequences to a specific IP block. Multiplexors are used to steer initialization sequences to the IP blocks, or the primary inputs and internal signals during normal operation. The chip designer must modify the test-benches accordingly to perform block-level or chip-level logic simulations.

In the second approach, the initialization sequences is stored permanently on-chip in a ROM. In the beginning of operations, the controller module simply reads the different input sequences in parallel and sends them to the different IP blocks for initialization. The advantage of this approach is that the number of initialization cycles can be limited.

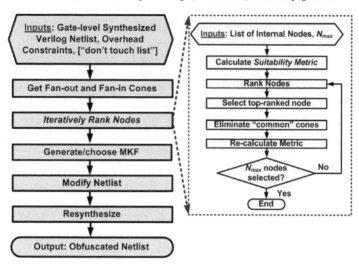

FIGURE 12.4: Hardware obfuscation design flow along with steps of the iterative node ranking algorithm.

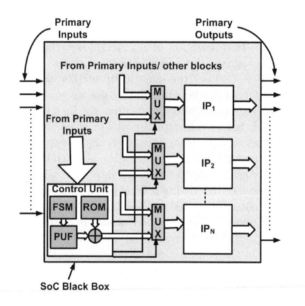

FIGURE 12.5: SoC design modification to support hardware obfuscation. An on-chip controller combines the input patterns with the output of a PUF block to produce the activation patterns.

However, additional overhead is incurred for storing the input sequences in an on-chip ROM. To increase the security of the scheme, the chip designer can arrange an instance-specific initialization sequence to be stored in an one-time programmable ROM. In that case, following the approach in [30], we can have the activating patterns to be simple logic function (e.g. and XOR) of the patterns read from the ROM and the output of a *Physically Unclonable Function* (PUF) block. The patterns are written to the ROM post-manufacturing after receiving instructions from the chip designer, as suggested in [30]. Because the output of a PUF circuit is not predictable before manufacturing, it is not

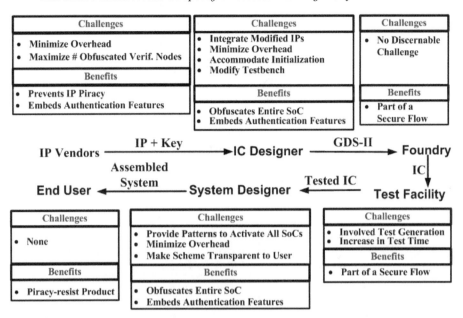

FIGURE 12.6: Challenges and benefits of the *HARPOON* design methodology at different stages of a hardware IP life cycle.

possible to have the same bits written into the programmable ROMs for each IC instance. Fig. 12.5 shows this scheme.

The manufacturing house manufactures the SoC from the design provided by the design house and passes it on to the test facility. If a PUF block has been used in the IC, the test engineer reports the output on the application of certain vectors back to the chip designer. The chip designer then calculates the specific bits required to be written in the one-time programmable ROM. The test engineer does so and blows off an one-time programmable fuse, so that the output of the PUF block is no longer visible at the output. The test engineer then performs post-manufacturing testing, using the set of test vectors provided by the design house. Ideally, all communication between parties associated with the design flow should be carried out in an encrypted form, using symmetric or asymmetric cryptographic algorithms such as Diffie-Hellman [336]. The tested ICs are passed to the system designer along with initialization sequence (again in an encrypted form) from the design house.

The system designer integrates the different ICs in the board-level design and arranges to apply the initialization patterns during "booting" or similar other initialization phase. Thus, the initialization patterns for the different SoCs need to be stored in Read Only Memory (ROM). In most ASICs composed of multiple IPs, several initialization cycles are typically needed at start-up to get into the "steady-stream" state, which requires accomplishing certain tasks such as initialization of specific registers [254]. The system designer can easily utilize this inherent latency to hide the additional cycles due to initialization sequences from the end user.

Finally, this secure system is used in the product for which it is meant. It provides the end-user with the assurance that the components have gone through a secure and piracy-proof design flow. Fig. 12.6 shows the challenges and benefits of the design flow from the perspectives of different parties associated with the flow. It is worth noting that the proposed design methodology remains valid for a SoC design house that uses custom logic blocks instead of reusable IPs. In this case, the designer can synthesize the constituent logic blocks using the proposed obfuscation methodology for protecting the SoC.

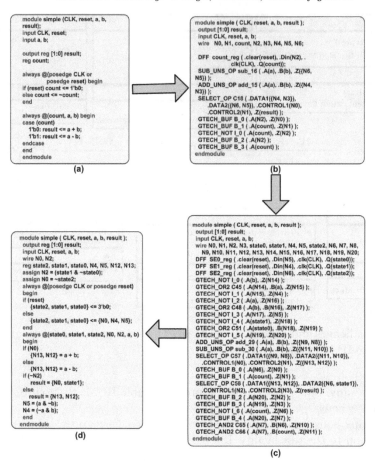

FIGURE 12.7: Example of a Verilog RTL description and its obfuscated version [82]: a) original RTL; b) technology independent, unoptimized gate-level netlist obtained through RTL compilation; c) obfuscated gate-level netlist; d) decompiled obfuscated RTL.

12.4   Extension of STG Modification for RTL Designs

As noted previously in Section 12.1, most hardware IPs are distributed in a technology-independent, RTL form. In this section, we extend the technique described in the previous sections to generate obfuscated RTL IP designs. This technique has three main steps:

- Logic synthesis of the RTL to an unmapped, unoptimized gate-level netlist, composed of generic Boolean gates.

- Functional obfuscation of the netlist by structural modifications following the principle outlined in the previous section, and,

- Subsequent decompilation of the obfuscated netlist back to an obfuscated version of the original RTL.

The modified, re-synthesized (to allow better intermingling of the inserted circuit modification), gate-level design is then decompiled to regenerate the RTL of the code, without

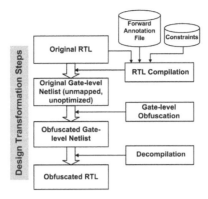

FIGURE 12.8: Design transformation steps in course of the proposed RTL obfuscation process.

maintaining high level HDL constructs. Instead, the modified netlist is traversed recursively to reconstruct the Boolean equations for the primary output nodes and the state element inputs, expressed in terms of the primary inputs, the state-element outputs and a few selected high fanout internal nodes. The redundant internal nodes are then removed. This "partial flattening" effect hides all information about the modifications performed in the netlist. Optionally, the obfuscation tool maintains a list of expected instances of library datapath elements, and whenever these are encountered in the netlist, their outputs are related through proper RTL constructs to their inputs. This ensures regeneration of the same datapath cells on resynthesis of the RTL.

As an example, consider the simple Verilog module *"simple"* which performs addition or subtraction of two bits depending on the value of a free running 1-bit counter, as shown in Fig. 12.7(a). Fig. 12.7(b)-(d) shows the transformation of the design through the proposed obfuscation process. The decompiled RTL in Fig. 12.7(d) shows that the modification cell and the extra state transition logic are effectively hidden and isolation of the correct initialization sequence can be difficult even for such a small design. Major semantic effect of obfuscation is the change and replacement of high level RTL constructs (such as if...else, for, while, case, assign etc.) in the original RTL, and replacement of internal nodes and registers. Furthermore, internal register, net and instance names are changed to arbitrary identifiers to make the code less comprehensible.

After the gate-level modification, the modified netlist is decompiled to produce a description of the circuit, which although being technically a RTL and functionally equivalent to the modified gate-level netlist, is extremely difficult to comprehend to a human reader. In addition, the modifications made to the original circuit remain well-hidden. A forward annotation file indicates relevant high-level HDL constructs and macros to be preserved through this transformation. These are maintained during the RTL compilation and decompilation steps. From the unmapped gate-level netlist, we look for specific generic gates, that can be decompiled to an equivalent RTL construct, e.g. multiplexor can be mapped to an equivalent if...then...else construct or a case construct. The datapath modules or macros are transformed into appropriate operands. For example, an equation $n1 = s1{\cdot}d1 + s2{\cdot}d2 + s3{\cdot}d3$ can be mapped to a case construct. Fig. 12.8 shows the design transformation steps during the obfuscation process. We present an analysis of the security of this scheme in Section 12.6.

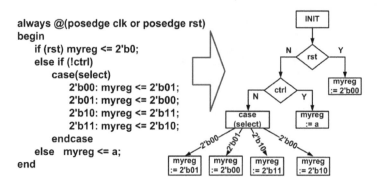

FIGURE 12.9: Transformation of a block of RTL code into CDFG [83].

12.5   Obfuscation through Control and Dataflow Graph (CDFG) Modification

In this section, we describe the extension and modification of the functional obfuscation technique, which operates directly on the RTL description of circuits (rather the CDFG derived from the HDL description code blocks), and generates RTL descriptions as output. It avoids the intermediate gate-level transformation described in the last section.

12.5.1   CDFG Obfuscation Methodology

Similar to the STG modification based scheme, the main idea of this approach is to efficiently integrate a *mode control FSM* into the design through judicious modification of control and data flow structures derived from the RTL, such that the design works in two different modes *obfsucated* and *normal*. The operations of the *mode control FSM* is the same as that depicted in Fig. 12.2, with the circuit starting in the *obfuscated mode* and then moving to the *normal mode* only after the successful application of a pre-defined input sequence. The *mode control FSM* is integrated inside the CDFG derived from the RTL in a way that makes it extremely hard to isolate from the original IP. The FSM is realized in the RTL by expanding a judiciously selected set of registers, which we refer to as *host registers* and modifying their assignment conditions and values. Once the FSM has been integrated, both control and data flow statements are conditioned based on the mode control signals derived from this FSM. The proposed obfuscation scheme comprises of four major steps described below.

Parsing the RTL and Building CDFG: In this step, the given RTL is parsed and each concurrent block of RTL code is transformed into a CDFG data structure. Fig. 12.9 shows the transformation of an "always @()" block of a Verilog code to its corresponding CDFG. Next, small CDFGs are merged (whenever possible) to build larger combined CDFGs. For example, all CDFGs corresponding to non-blocking assignments to clocked registers can be combined together without any change of the functionality. This procedure creates larger CDFGs with substantially more number of nodes than the constituent CDFGs, which helps to obfuscate the *hosted* mode-control FSM better.

"Hosting" the Mode Control FSM: Instead of having a stand-alone mode control FSM as in [77], the state elements of the mode-control FSM can be hosted in existing registers in the design to increase the level of obfuscation. This way, the FSM becomes an integral part of the design, instead of controlling the circuit as a structurally isolated

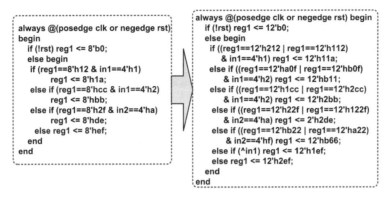

FIGURE 12.10: Example of hosting the registers of the mode-control FSM [83].

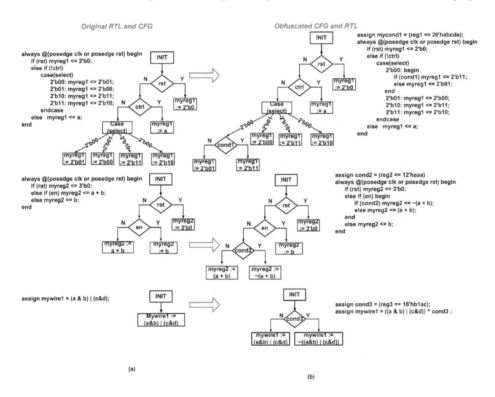

FIGURE 12.11: Examples of control-flow obfuscation: (a) original RTL, CDFG; (b) obfuscated RTL, CDFG [83].

element. An example is shown in Fig. 12.10, where the 8-bit register *reg1*, referred as the "host register", has been expanded to 12-bits to host the mode-control FSM in its left 4-bits. When these 4-bits are set at values $4'h1$ or $4'h2$, the circuit is in its *normal* mode, while the circuit is in its *obfuscated mode* when they are at $4'ha$ or $4'hb$. Note that extra RTL statements have been added to make the circuit functionally equivalent in the *normal* mode. The obfuscation level is improved by distributing the mode-control FSM state elements in a non-contiguous manner inside one or more registers, if possible.

Modifying CDFG Branches: After the FSM has been hosted in a set of selected *host registers*, several CDFG nodes are modified using the control signals generated from this

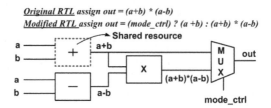

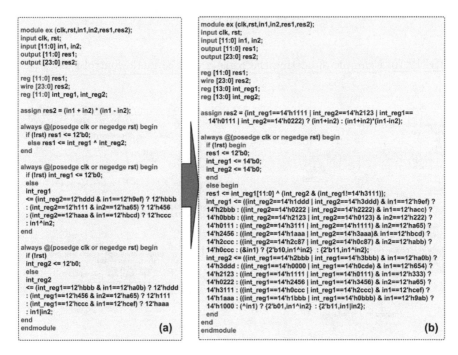

FIGURE 12.12: Example of datapath obfuscation allowing resource sharing [83].

FIGURE 12.13: Example of RTL obfuscation by CDFG modification: (a) original RTL; (b) obfuscated RTL [83].

FSM. The nodes with large fanout cones are preferentially selected for modification, since this ensures maximum change in functional behavior at minimal design overhead. Three example modifications of the CDFGs and the corresponding RTL statements are shown in Fig. 12.11. The registers *reg1*, *reg2* and *reg3* are the *host registers*. Three "case()", "if()" and "assign" statements in Fig. 12.11(a) are modified by the mode-control signals *cond1*, *cond2* and *cond3*, respectively. These signals evaluate to logic-1 only in the *obfuscation mode* because the conditions $reg1 = 20'habcde$, $reg2 = 12'haaa$ and $reg3 = 16'hb1ac$ correspond to states which are only reachable in the *obfuscation mode*. Fig. 12.11(b) shows the modified CDFGs and the corresponding CDFG statements.

Besides changing the control-flow of the circuit, functionality is also modified by introducing additional datapath components. However, such changes are done in a manner that ensures sharing of the additional resources during synthesis. This is important since datapath components usually incur large hardware overhead. An example is shown in Fig. 12.12, where the signal *out* originally computes $(a+b) \times (a-b)$. However, after modification of the RTL, it computes $(a+b)$ in the *obfuscated mode*, allowing the adder to be shared in the two modes and the outputs of the multiplier and the adder to be multiplexed.

TABLE 12.1: Comparison of Decompilation-based and CDFG-based Obfuscation Approaches

Approach	Advantages	Disadvantages
STG Modfication	(a) Higher level of obfuscation	(a) Loses major RTL constructs
		(b) Greater hardware and computational overheads
CDFG Modification	(a) Works directly on RTL descriptions	(a) Hiding modifications is more challenging
	(b) Preserves RTL constructs	

Generating Obfuscated RTL: After the modifications have been preformed on the CDFG, the obfuscated RTL is generated from the modified CDFGs, by traversing each of them in a *depth-first* manner. Fig. 12.13(a) shows an example RTL code and Fig. 12.13(b) shows its corresponding obfuscated versions. A 4-bit FSM has been *hosted* in registers int_reg1 and int_reg2. The conditions $int\_reg1[13:12]=2'b00$, $int\_reg1[13:12]=2'b01$, $int\_reg2[13:12]=2'b00$ and $int\_reg1[13:12]=2'b10$ occur only in the obfuscated mode. The initialization sequence is $in1=12'h654 \rightarrow in2=12'h222 \rightarrow in1=12'h333 \rightarrow in2=12'hacc \rightarrow in1=12'h9ab$. Note the presence of *dummy state transitions* and out-of-order state transition RTL statements. The outputs *res1* and *res2* have been modified by two different *modification signals*. Instead of allowing the inputs to appear directly in the sensitivity list of the "if()" statements, it is possible to derive internal signals (similar to the ones shown in Fig. 12.11(b)) with complex Boolean expressions which are used to perform the modifications. The output *res1* has been modified following the datapath modification approach using resource sharing.

12.5.1.1 Embedding Authentication Features

Authentication features might be embedded in the RTL by the same principle as described in Section 12.3.5. RTL statements describing the state transitions of the *authentication FSM* can be integrated with the existing RTL in the same way the statements corresponding to the *obfuscation FSM* is hidden. In case the *unused states* are difficult to derive from the original RTL, it can be synthesized to a gate-level netlist and the same technique based on *sequential justification* as described in Section 12.3.5 might be applied.

12.5.2 Comparison between the Two Approaches

Table 12.1 compares the relative advantages and disadvantages of the two proposed techniques. Although the decompilation based approach potentially can hide the modifications better than the direct RTL modification based approach (as shown by our theoretical analysis of their obfuscation levels in Section 12.6 and by our simulation results), it also loses major RTL constructs and creates a description of the circuit which might result in an unoptimized implementation on re-synthesis. Hence, we provide the IP designer with a choice where either of the techniques might be chosen based on the designer's priority. For example, if the IP is going to released to a untrustworthy SoC design houses with a prior record of practising IP piracy, the STG modification system might be used. On the other hand if the IP is to released to a comparatively more trustable SoC design house where the design specifications are very aggressive, the CDFG modification based approach might be used.

12.5.3   Obfuscation-based Secure SoC Design Flow

The proposed obfuscation based techniques can be utilized to develop a piracy-proof SoC design and manufacturing flow, as described in [77]. The SoC designer receives different obfuscated IPs from the same or different vendors, and then integrates them on the SoC. A special integrated controller module receives patterns from the primary inputs and controls the systematic initialization of the IP modules in the SoC. The system designer integrates several such SoCs on a board, and uses initialization sequences from a secure, tamper-proof microcontroller [106] enhanced with a secure EEPROM [105] to enable all the SoCs. This prevents unauthorized reading/observations of the initialization sequence keys during the initialization phase. Typically, the latency incurred in the initialization can be easily masked in the latency inherent in a "bootup" or a similar process. Thus, the end user remains oblivious to the embedded security measures in the SoCs. By supporting obfuscated IP cores in the design flow, all the parties (the IP vendor, the SoC designer and the system designer) are benefited by being protected from piracy.

12.6   Measure of Obfuscation Level

In general, it is a difficult problem to detect through analysis the complete functionality of a given circuit, irrespective of the form (RTL/gate–level) it has been described in. A related problem of detecting whether a given circuit has a *hardware Trojan* inserted in it has been shown capable of evading most traditional testing and verification techniques, since such analysis is equivalent to the *Halting problem*, according to *Rice's theorem* [157, 324]. Next, we present a quantitative analysis on the level of difficulty for breaking the proposed obfuscation-based protection.

We try to analyze the security of the proposed schemes against three different attacks: (a) attacks based on manual effort of visually trying to identify the modifications in the RTL; (b) attacks through simulation-based functional analysis, and (c) attacks through structural analysis and reverse-engineering. In all the cases, we assume a challenging situation for the IP owner where the adversary has access to an unobfuscated version of the original RTL.

12.6.1   Manual Attacks by Visual Inspection

To estimate the obfuscation level against a manual mode of attack, we propose a new metric called *semantic obfuscation metric* (M_{sem}), which depicts how many of the original high-level RTL constructs have been replaced by new ones. We define M_{sem} by:

$$M_{sem} = \frac{abs(N_{c,orig} + N_{w,orig} + N_{e,obfus} - N_{raw,obfus})}{max(\{N_{c,orig} + N_{w,orig} + N_{e,obfus}\}, N_{raw,obfus})} \qquad (12.8)$$

where $N_{c,orig}$ is the total number of high-level RTL constructs in the original RTL; $N_{e,obfus}$ is the number of extra state elements included in the obfuscated design; $N_{w,orig}$ is the total number of internal `wire` declarations in the original RTL and $N_{raw,obfus}$ is the number of `reg`, `assign` and `wire` declarations in the obfuscated RTL. Note that $0{\leq}M_{sem}{\leq}1$, with a higher value implying better obfuscation. M_{sem} represents a measure of semantic difference between the obfuscated and the unobfuscated versions of the RTL, by taking into consideration the constructs introduced in the obfuscated code and the constructs removed from the original code. This is the weakest attack, with the adversary having very little chance of figuring out the obfuscation scheme for large RTLs which have undergone a complete change of the "look-and-feel".

12.6.2 Simulation-based Attacks

For a logic simulation based approach where random input vectors are sequentially applied to take the circuit to the *normal mode*, the probability of discovering the initialization key sequence is $\frac{1}{2^{M \cdot N}}$ for a circuit with M primary input ports and a length-N initialization key sequence. For example, in a circuit with $M = 64$ primary inputs and a length $N = 4$ initialization key sequence, this probability is $\sim 10^{-77}$. In practice, most IPs will have larger number of primary inputs and the length N can be made larger, resulting in smaller detection probability. Thus, we can claim that it is extremely challenging to break the scheme using simulation based reverse-engineering.

12.6.3 Structural Analysis-based Attack

For the structural analysis based attack, the two proposed obfuscation schemes present different challenges to an adversary. For the STG modification scheme, the adversary has to analyze the circuit in terms of the Boolean logic structure of the internal nodes, while in the CDFG modification based scheme, the adversary has to analyze the high-level RTL structure of the code. This is the strongest attack, and to be acceptable, the proposed obfuscation approaches must provide adequate protection against this attack. We describe the complexity of the two analyses that follow.

12.6.3.1 Structural Analysis against STG Modification

Analysis based on structure of the internal nodes is most conveniently done by the construction and manipulation of Reduced Ordered Binary Decision Diagrams (ROBDD) [67] corresponding to the internal circuit nodes. To detect the node modification scheme, the adversary's algorithm must be able to solve several sub-problems in succession. We estimate the computational complexity of each of these sub-problems below to derive an estimate of the computational complexity of the entire problem.

Let the total number of primary outputs of the circuit be P, the total number of state elements in the original circuit be S and the total number of state elements inserted in the modified circuit be T. Then, it is sufficient to analyze the structures of these $(P + S + T)$ nodes between the original and the modified designs, out of which $(P + S)$ are also present in the original design. Suppose, the adversary finds F nodes out of these $(P + S + T)$ nodes to have contrasting logic structures by a ROBDD-based analysis. This dissimilarity is due to two reasons: (a) direct effect of the node modification scheme on some of these nodes, and (b) indirect effect of these modified nodes on other nodes. Either way, from eqn. (12.1), the affected nodes would have their values inverted only if simultaneously $en = 1$ and $g = 1$. To isolate the inserted FSM, the adversary must detect this node modification scheme for each dissimilar node.

Finding the Correct ROBDD Representation of the Modified Nodes: To detect the effect of a particular *en* signal originating from the inserted state machine on a modified node, the adversary's algorithm should be able to represent the ROBDD of the modified node with the *en* signal as the root node, as shown in Fig. 12.14. Improving the variable ordering to minimize the size of a BDD is an *NP-complete* problem [57]. Hence, it follows that the computational complexity to find a particular representation of the ROBDD of the modified function which has *en* as the root node is also *NP-complete* with respect to the number of variables in the Boolean logic expression for the node. Hence, deciphering

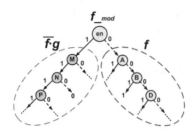

FIGURE 12.14: Binary Decision Diagram (BDD) of a modified node.

the modification scheme for a modified node with fanin cone size f_i has a computational complexity $O(2^{f_i})$.

Graph Isomorphism Comparison: After the ROBDD of the modified node has been expressed in the form shown in Fig. 12.14, each sub-graph below the node *en* should be compared with the ROBDD graph for f for isomorphism. Proving graph isomorphism is a problem with computational complexity between P and NP, with the best-known heuristic having complexity $2^{O(\sqrt{n \log n})}$ for a graph with n vertices [169]. Hence, establishing the equivalence for f through graph isomorphism has a computational complexity $2^{O(\sqrt{f_i \log f_i})}$ for a node with fanin cone size f_i. Let $\overline{f_i}$ be the average fanin cone size of the failing verification nodes. Hence, overall this sub-problem has a computational complexity $O(2^{\overline{f_i}} \cdot 2^{O(\sqrt{\overline{f_i} \log \overline{f_i}})})$, which must be solved for each of the F dissimilar nodes.

Compare Point Matching: So far we have assumed that the adversary would be able to associate the dissimilar nodes in the obfuscated design with the corresponding nodes in the original design and would then try to decipher the obfuscation scheme. This is expected to be relatively easy for the primary output ports of the IP because the IP vendor must maintain a standard interface even for the obfuscated version of the IP, and hence the adversary can take advantage of this name matching. However, the names of the state elements can be changed arbitrarily by the IP vendor and hence, finding the corresponding state elements to compare is a *functional compare point matching* problem [32], which is extremely computationally challenging because of the requirement to search through $(S_N)!$ combinations, where S_N is the number of dissimilar state elements. Hence, we propose the following metric to quantify the level of protection of the proposed STG modification based obfuscation scheme in providing protection against structural analysis:

$$M_{str} = F \cdot 2^{\overline{f_i}} \cdot 2^{\sqrt{\overline{f_i} \log \overline{f_i}}} + (S_N)! \qquad (12.9)$$

Observations from the Metric: From the above metric, the following can be observed which act as a guide to the IP designer to design a well-obfuscated hardware IP following the STG modification-based scheme:

1. Those nodes which have larger fanin cones should be preferably modified because this would increase $\overline{f_i}$ in eqn.(12.9), thus increasing M_{str}.

2. An inserted FSM with larger number of flip-flops increases its obfuscation level because S_N increases. Also, as shown previously in this section, there is an exponential dependence of the probability of breaking the scheme by simulation based reverse-engineering on the length of the initialization key sequence. Hence, it is evident that FSM design and insertion to attain high levels of obfuscation incur greater design overhead. Thus the IP designer must trade-off between design overhead and the level of security achievable through obfuscation.

3. Modification of a larger number of nodes increases F, which in turn increases the level of obfuscation.

12.6.3.2   Structural Analysis against CDFG Modification-based Approach

The structural analysis of the CDFG modification based obfuscation scheme is estimated by the degree of difficulty faced by an adversary in discovering the *hosted* mode-control FSM and the modification signals. Consider a case where n mode-control FSM state-transition statements have been hosted in a RTL with N blocking/non-blocking assignment statements. However, the adversary does not know a-priori how many registers host the mode-control FSM. Then, the adversary must correctly figure out the hosted FSM state transition statements from one out of $\sum_{k=1}^{n} \binom{N}{k}$ possibilities. Again, each of these choices for a given value of k has $k!$ - associated ways to arrange the state transitions (so that the *initialization key sequence* is applied in the correct order). Hence, the adversary must correctly identify one out of $\sum_{k=1}^{n} \left(\binom{N}{k} \cdot k! \right)$ possibilities. The other feature that needs to be deciphered to break the scheme are the mode control signals. Let M be the total number of blocking, non-blocking and dataflow assignments in the RTL, and let m be the size of the modification signal pool. Then, the adversary must correctly choose m signals out of M, which is one out of $\binom{M}{m}$ choices. Combining these two security features, we propose the following metric to estimate the complexity of the structural analysis problem for the CDFG modification based design:

$$M_{str} = \sum_{k=1}^{n} \left(\binom{N}{k} \cdot k! \right) \cdot \binom{M}{m} \tag{12.10}$$

A higher value of M_{str} indicates a greater obfuscation efficiency. As an example, consider a RTL with values $N = 30$, $M = 100$, in which a FSM with parameter $n = 3$ is hosted, and let $m = 20$. Then, $M_{obf} \approx 1.35 \times 10^{25}$. In other words, the probability of the hacker reverse-engineering the complete scheme is about 1 in 10^{25}. In practice, the values of n and M would be much higher in most cases, making M_{str} larger and thus tougher for the hacker to reverse-engineer the obfuscation scheme.

12.6.4   Quantitative Comparison

The value of M_{str} is expected to be better in the STG modification based approach, because of the exponential dependance of this metric on the average fanin cone size of the modified nodes (eqn. 12.9), compared to the combinatorial dependence on the number of RTL statements for the CDFG modification based approach (eqn. 12.10). The value of M_{sem} is again expected to be superior in the STG modification based approach because the changes in the appearance of the RTL is more drastic in this case, whereas the CDFG modification based approach makes comparatively lesser changes to the high-level RTL constructs, as it is based on intelligent utilization of mostly existing RTL constructs. However, the run-time of the obfuscation algorithm is expected to be higher in the STG modification based approach, because it performs recursive backtracking to construct the logic equations of the internal nodes. All these predicted trends were supported by our simulation results presented in Section 12.7.

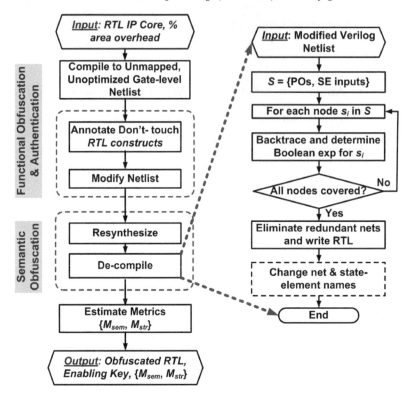

FIGURE 12.15: Flow diagram for the proposed STG modification-based RTL obfuscation methodology [82].

12.7   Results

In this section we first describe the automated design flows for the two proposed obfuscation techniques, followed by the simulation results of application of the techniques to open-source IPs and benchmark circuits.

12.7.1   Design Flow Automation

Fig. 12.15 shows the entire STG modification based RTL obfuscation design flow. The design flow starts with the *compilation* of RTL description of the IP core to a unmapped, unoptimized gate-level Verilog netlist. The maximum allowable area overhead is entered as a design constraint, from which the maximum number of modifiable nodes (N_{max}) is estimated. Additionally, the tool has a list of user-mentioned constructs and macros in a forward annotation file. These elements are preserved during the RTL compilation and decompilation processes by treating them as *don't touch* modules. The N_{max} nodes to be modified are chosen based on the algorithm described in [77], which ensures maximum perturbation of the design. The modified netlist is re-synthesized and the resultant netlist is then decompiled to a RTL code. The names of the internal nodes and instances are changed by a simple string substitution scheme.

Fig. 12.16 shows the steps of the proposed CDFG modification based design obfuscation methodology. The input to the flow is the original RTL, the desired obfuscation level

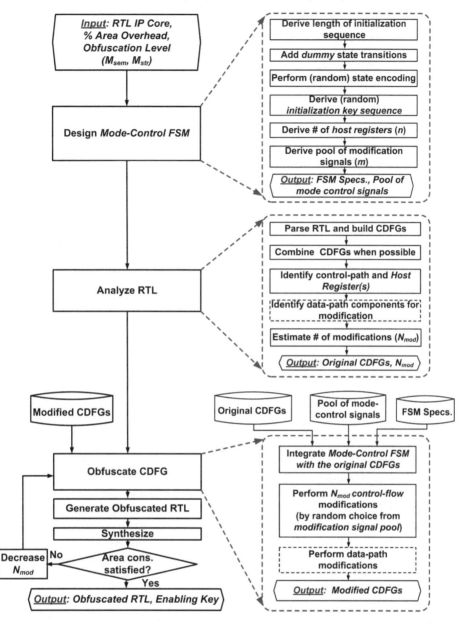

FIGURE 12.16: Flow diagram for the proposed CDFG modification-based RTL obfuscation methodology [83].

represented by the obfuscation metrics (M_{sem} and M_{str}), and the maximum allowable area overhead. It starts with the design of the mode-control FSM based on the target M_{sem} and M_{str}. The outputs of this step are the specifications of the FSM which include its state transition graph, the state encoding, the pool of modification signals, and the *initialization key sequence*. Random state encoding and a random *initialization key sequence* are generated to increase the security. Note that in the STG modification-based approach, we do not start with explicit target values of the metrics, because these two parameters cannot be predicted a-priori in this technique. However, the target area overhead is an indirect

TABLE 12.2: Functional and Semantic Obfuscation Efficiency and Overheads for IP Cores for 10% area overhead target (CDFG Modification based Results at iso-delay)

			STG Modification based Approach							
IP	Sub–	Nodes	Obfuscation Efficiency				Design Overhead			
Cores	Modules	Modified (%)	Failing Verif. Nodes (%)	M_{sem}	$\log_{10} M_{str}$	Area (%)	Delay (%)	Power (%)	Run time (s)	
	key_sel	0.93	100.00	0.98	51.56	6.65	1.39	4.85	32	
DES	crp	0.83	100.00	0.91	55.87	5.54	0.66	5.43	37	
	Key Expand	0.95	90.30	0.92	43.17	5.29	0.00	4.56	28	
AES	Sbox	0.95	100.00	0.96	45.78	4.95	2.42	5.31	29	
	Inverse Sbox	0.97	85.25	0.94	46.22	5.51	2.60	5.62	35	
	DCT	0.90	88.95	0.96	60.19	4.64	1.00	5.06	27	
FDCT	ZIGZAG	0.95	100.00	0.92	52.12	5.74	0.88	5.67	30	

			CDFG Modification based Approach							
IP	Sub–	# of	Obfuscation Efficiency				Design Overhead			
Cores	Modules	Modifications	Failing Verif. Nodes (%)	M_{sem}	$\log_{10} M_{str}$	Area (%)	Delay (%)	Power (%)	Run time (s)	
	post_norm	20	98.16	0.69	36.81	8.22	0.00	9.14	27	
	pre_norm	20	94.16	0.70	32.91	9.39	0.00	9.79	25	
FPU	pre_norm_fmul	20	90.00	0.77	23.13	8.30	0.00	9.69	20	
	except	10	100.00	0.73	23.16	7.56	0.00	8.73	14	
	control_wopc	20	92.79	0.75	42.12	8.74	0.00	8.97	29	
TCPU	mem	10	97.62	0.71	19.69	8.29	0.00	9.76	15	
	alu	10	97.62	0.81	15.01	9.59	0.00	9.88	15	

estimate of these parameters, and the decompilation process automatically ensures a high value of M_{sem}, while an optimal node modification algorithm ensures a high value of M_{str}.

12.7.2 Implementation Results

12.7.2.1 Implementation Setup

The above design flows were developed using C and the TCL scripting language and were directly integrated in the *Synopsys Design Compiler* environment. Synthesis was performed using *Synopsys Design Compiler*, using a LEDA 250 nm library. All formal equivalence checking was performed using *Synopsys Formality*. All work was performed on a Linux workstation with 2 GB of main memory and a dual-core 1.5 GHz processor.

A FSM with a length-4 initialization key sequence was designed for mode-control in both the schemes. In the STG modification based scheme, we chose high fan-in internal nodes as MKFs, as described in [77]. The STG modification scheme was applied on three open-source Verilog IP cores, viz. "Data Encryption Standard" (DES), "Advanced Encryption Standard" (AES) and "Discrete Cosine Transform" (FDCT) collected from [278]. The CDFG modification based obfuscation technique was applied for two Verilog IP cores – a single precision IEEE-754 compliant floating-point unit ("FPU"), and a 12-bit RISC CPU ("TCPU"), both obtained from [278]. For the STG modification based approach, each gate-level modified design was verified using *Formality* with the corresponding de-compiled RTL to verify the correctness of the procedure.

12.7.2.2 Obfuscation Efficiency and Overheads

Table 12.2 shows the structural and semantic obfuscation metrics and design overheads for 10% target area overhead constraint for each module. Note that the value of the M_{str} metric is in a logarithmic scale. The effectiveness of the schemes was very high; most of the modified designs considered reported close to 100% equivalence checking failure (for the primary outputs and outputs of state elements) when compared with their unmodified counterparts, thus having a very high value of the computational complexity metric M_{str}. However, the value of M_{str} is orders of magnitude higher for the STG modification based

TABLE 12.3: Overall Design Overheads for Obfuscated IP Cores (STG Modification based Results at Iso-delay)

STG Modification based Approach			
IP Core	**Area (%)**	**Delay (%)**	**Power (%)**
DES	6.09	1.10	5.05
AES	5.25	2.00	5.45
FDCT	5.22	0.95	5.55
Average	5.52	1.35	5.35
CDFG Modification based Approach			
FPU	8.48	9.36	0.00
TCPU	8.54	9.73	0.00
Average	8.51	9.55	0.00

approach, as predicted in Section 12.6. The value of M_{sem} was very close to the ideal value of 1.0 for the STG modification based approach; however, it is closer to 0.75 on average for the CDFG modification based approach. Again, this is an expected trend as predicted in Section 12.6.

For all the individual circuit modules, the observed area overhead was less than 10%, the power and delay overheads were within acceptable limits (target delay overhead was set at 0% for the CDFG modification based scheme). The maximum run-times of the obfuscation programs for the individual modules was 29 seconds for the CDFG modification based approach, and 37 seconds for the STG modification based approach. Table 12.3 shows the overall design overheads after re-synthesis of the multi-module IP cores from the obfuscated RTL, which are again all within acceptable limits.

12.7.3 Effect of Key Length

The security offered by the two proposed approaches increases with the increase in the key length. We investigate the following aspects of the proposed techniques (a) design and performance overheads to support multiple-length keys, and (b) effect of increasing key lengths on design and performance overheads. We compare the proposed techniques with hardware implementations of the AES encryption/decryption algorithm.

12.7.3.1 Support for Multiple-length Keys

Most commercially available IP cores for AES can be operated in three different modes with three different input key lengths – 128 bit, 192 bit and 256 bit [18, 19]. This flexibility allows the SoC designers to trade-off between the available security (which increases with increase of key length) and performance (which decreases with increase of key length). Usually, a "*key_length*" input control signal determines the input key length. The same feature can be implemented in our proposed techniques, where the length of the initialization key sequence can be varied. Fig. 12.17 shows such a system which supports initialization key sequences of length 3, 4 or 5. However, in case of commercially available AES cores,

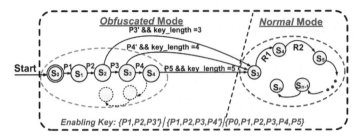

FIGURE 12.17: Scheme with *initialization key sequences* of varying length (3, 4 or 5).

TABLE 12.4: Area Overhead for Multi-length Key Support

Scheme	Area Overhead (%)
STG Modification	2.26 (av.)
CDFG Modification	3.16 (av.)
Ref. [19] (AES 48-cycle core)	17.88
Ref. [19] (AES 96-cycle core)	24.59

TABLE 12.5: Comparison of Throughput with Increasing Key Length

Scheme	Decrease in Throughput (%)	
	1.5X key length	2X key length
STG Modification	2.70 (av.)	3.96 (av.)
CDFG Modification	3.07 (av.)	4.72 (av.)
Ref. [19] (AES 48-cycle core)	14.10	24.83
Ref. [19] (AES 96-cycle core)	14.04	24.56

this flexibility comes at a price – the multi-key IP core versions usually have greater area than the baseline designs supporting only a single key length [19].

Table 12.4 shows the area overhead effect of supporting multiple keys lengths on the proposed schemes for the IP modules presented in Table 12.3, compared to two versions of a commercially available AES core [19]. The key lengths for our proposed schemes were 4 (baseline), 6 (1.5X) and 8 (2X), while those for the AES implementations were 128 (baseline), 192 (1.5X) and 256 (2X). From this table, it is clearly evident that the proposed approaches are more scalable than the AES hardware implementations with respect to the increase in key length.

12.7.3.2   Effect of Increasing Key Length

For symmetric key cryptographic algorithms such as AES, in general the security increases with the length of the key, as the complexity of breaking the encryption is an exponential function of the key length. However, an increasing key length usually results in lower throughput. Similar trends are expected for the two proposed obfuscation schemes

TABLE 12.6: Area and Power Overhead for ISCAS-89 Benchmarks Utilizing Unused States (at Iso-delay)

Circuit	# of Gates	% Ar. Ov.1	% Ar. Ov.2	%Pow. Ov.1	%Pow. Ov.2
s1196	370	18.44	24.84	2.45	6.00
s1238	373	16.31	27.15	4.63	10.71
s1423	505	6.11	6.08	2.015	3.07
s1488	431	12.81	16.93	7.24	12.76
s5378	1102	14.45	18.69	8.76	25.78
s9234	5807	6.53	9.04	9.28	13.15
s13207	2488	7.93	8.17	7.54	16.28
s15850	2983	7.67	8.99	5.63	6.15
s35932	7966	1.34	1.955	6.93	9.49
s38417	8822	0.09	0.56	1.81	5.27
s38584	9019	0.85	3.03	5.10	10.77

with respect to the length of the initialization key sequence. We investigated the scalability of the two proposed techniques with respect to the increase in the length of the initialization key sequence for the proposed approaches vis-a-vis that for commercially available hardware implementations of AES with respect to the key length. Again, for the proposed obfuscation schemes we considered a key length of 4 to the baseline case, while a 128-bit key for AES was considered baseline. Table 12.5 shows the decrease in throughput with the increase of key length. Once again, the simulation results showed that the proposed schemes had superior scalability of throughput than the hardware implementations of AES when the key length is increased.

12.8   Discussions

In this section, we describe a technique to decrease the hardware overhead by while utilizing the normally "unused states" (states which never arise during normal operations).

12.8.1   Using Unreachable States during Initialization

Referring to Fig. 12.3, the states in the *initialization FSM* and the *obfuscation FSM* are encoded by using states which are unreachable during normal operations. By doing this, one can ensure that the circuit would not operate in the correct mode prior to its initialization. This can help to eliminate the need to introduce a separate FSM to control the mode of operation, potentially decreasing the hardware overhead. We present simulation results for a method of obfuscation based on finding unused states for a suite of gate-level sequential circuits, and two open-source RTL IP cores.

Table 12.6 shows the area and power overhead (at iso-delay) in ISCAS-89 circuits following the decompilation based methodology where normally unused states of the circuit are

TABLE 12.7: Area and Power Overhead for IP Cores Utilizing Unused States (at Iso-delay)

IP	Module	% Ar. Ov.1	% Ar. Ov.2	%Pow. Ov.1	%Pow. Ov.2
AES	sbox	5.95	7.46	15.19	17.67
	inv_sbox	6.99	8.25	8.98	15.27
	key_expand	3.93	5.47	13.80	15.93
	Overall	4.57	6.07	13.03	16.14
DES	key_sel	4.81	8.91	2.66	5.35
	crp	4.75	6.77	1.75	4.79
	Overall	4.77	7.69	2.03	4.97

used to encode the states in the obfuscated mode. The unused states were found using *sequential justification* by *Synopsys Tetramax*. The results were taken without integrating any mode-control FSM, considering 5–6 randomly chosen state-elements in the original circuit, having an initialization state space with 4 states, and (for result set "1") an authentication state space consisting of 4 states. State encoding with 6 state elements were required in cases where sufficient unused states are not available from 5 state elements. Table 12.7 shows the corresponding figures for two open-source IP cores.

12.9   Conclusions

The design and manufacturing of complex modern SoCs is made feasible by the existence of pre-verified, high-performance hardware intellectual property cores. However, this makes the hardware IP cores susceptible to piracy. We have presented a paradigm of hardware IP protection based on *Design Obfuscation*, whereby the design is made less understandable and more difficult to reverse-engineer. The proposed obfuscation approaches provide active defense against IP infringement at different stages of SoC design and fabrication flow, thus protecting the interests of multiple associated parties. The obfuscation steps can be easily automated and integrated in the IP design flow and it does not affect the test/verification of a SoC design for legal users. We have shown that they incur low design and computational overhead and cause minimal impact on end-user experience. The proposed approaches are easily scalable to large IPs (e.g. processor) and in terms of level of security. Further improvement in hardware overhead can be obtained by utilizing a normally unused states of the circuit.

In the next chapter, we introduce another major threat in the domain of hardware security, which is drawing a lot of research attention globally: *hardware Trojans*, The issue of Hardware Trojans also arises from the horizontal model of semiconductor design and manufacturing. We give examples of hardware Trojans, their modes of operation, the threats posed by them, and then move to design and testing techniques to mitigate the threats.

Part V

Hardware Trojans

Chapter 13

Overview of Hardware Trojans

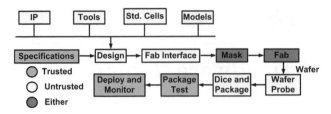

FIGURE 13.1: Vulnerable steps of a modern IC life cycle [107].

- *"The cyber threat is serious, with potential consequences similar in some ways to the nuclear threat of the Cold War. The cyber threat is also insidious, enabling adversaries to access vast new channels of intelligence about critical U.S. enablers (operational and technical; military and industrial) that can threaten our national and economic security."*

- *"Current DoD actions, though numerous, are fragmented. Thus, DoD is not prepared to defend against this threat. DoD red teams, using cyber attack tools which can be downloaded from the Internet, are very successful at defeating our systems."*

United States Department of Defense
"TASK FORCE REPORT: Resilient Military Systems and the Advanced Cyber Threat"

13.1 Introduction

The horizontal business model becoming prominent in recent years in semiconductor design and manufacturing, has relinquished the control that IC design houses had over the design and manufacture of ICs, thus making them vulnerable to different security attacks. Fig. 13.1 illustrates the level of trust at different steps of a typical IC life-cycle [107]. Each party associated with the design and manufacture of an IC can be a potential adversary who inserts malicious modifications, referred as *hardware Trojans* [17]. Concern about this vulnerability of ICs and the resultant compromise of security has been expressed globally [109, 36], especially since several unexplained military mishaps are attributed to the presence of malicious hardware Trojans [17, 199].

Ideally, any undesired modification made to an IC should be detectable by pre-silicon verification/simulation and post-silicon testing. However, pre-silicon verification or simulation requires a golden model of the entire IC. This might not be always available, especially for IP based designs where IPs can come from third-party vendors. Besides, a large multi-module design is usually not amenable to exhaustive verification. Post-silicon, the design can be verified either through destructive de-packaging and reverse-engineering of the IC [107], or by comparing its functionality or circuit characteristics with a golden version of the. However, existing state-of-the-art approaches do not allow destructive verification of ICs

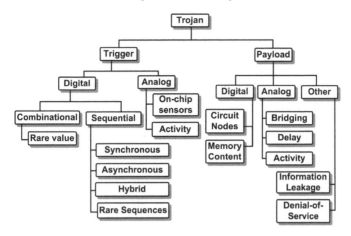

FIGURE 13.2: Trojan taxonomy based on trigger and payload mechanisms.

to be scalable. Moreover, as pointed out in [107], it is possible for the adversary to insert Trojans in only some ICs on a wafer, not the entire population, which limits the usefulness of a destructive approach.

Traditional post-manufacturing logic testing is not suitable for detecting hardware Trojans. This is due to the stealthy nature of hardware Trojans and inordinately vast spectrum of possible Trojan instances an adversary can employ. Typically, the adversary would design a Trojan that triggers a malfunction only under rare circuit conditions in order to evade detection. Due to the finite size of the testset, the rare condition for activation of the Trojan might not be realized during the testing period, especially if the Trojan acts as a sequential state machine or "time-bomb" [408]. Special algorithms must be developed to increase the accuracy of logic testing techniques, and would be decsribed in the next chapter. On the other hand, the techniques for detecting Trojans by comparison of the "side-channel parameters" such as power trace [23] or delay [167], are limited by the large process-variation effect in nanoscale IC technologies, reduced detection sensitivity for ultra-small Trojans and measurement noise [23].

In the next section, we give classification and examples of different hardware Trojans.

13.2 Trojan Taxonomy and Examples

Different methods of classifying hardware Trojans based on various characteristics have been proposed. In [38], the authors propose a simple classification of Trojans – *combinational* (whose activation depends on the occurrence of a particular condition at certain internal nodes of the circuit) and *sequential* (whose activation depends on the occurrence of a specific sequence of rare logic values at internal nodes). In [401], the authors classify Trojans based on three attributes: *physical, activation* and *action*. Some classifications (e.g. [408, 167]) are based on the activation mechanisms (referred as *Trojan triggers*) and the part of the circuit or the functionality affected by the activation of the Trojan (referred as *Trojan payload*). In this chapter, we follow and expand the Trojan taxonomy proposed in [408], where the Trojans are classified based on their trigger and payload mechanisms, as shown in Fig. 13.2.

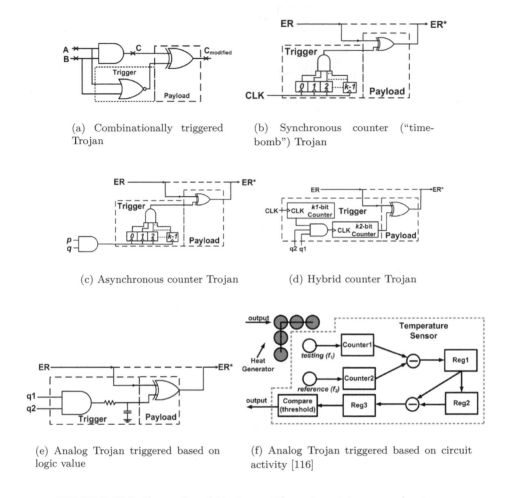

(a) Combinationally triggered Trojan

(b) Synchronous counter ("time-bomb") Trojan

(c) Asynchronous counter Trojan

(d) Hybrid counter Trojan

(e) Analog Trojan triggered based on logic value

(f) Analog Trojan triggered based on circuit activity [116]

FIGURE 13.3: Examples of Trojans with various trigger mechanisms.

The trigger mechanisms can be of two types: *digital* and *analog*. *Digitally triggered* Trojans can again be classified into *combinational* and *sequential* types.

Fig. 13.3(a) shows an example of a *combinationally triggered* Trojan where the occurrence of the condition $A = 0$, $B = 0$ at the trigger nodes A and B causes a payload node C to have an incorrect value at $C_{modified}$. Typically, an adversary would choose an extremely rare activation condition so that it is very unlikely for the Trojan to trigger during conventional manufacturing test.

Sequentially triggered Trojans (the so-called âŞtime bombsâŤ), on the other hand, are activated by the occurrence of a sequence, or a period of continuous operation. The simplest sequential Trojans are synchronous stand-alone counters, which trigger a malfunction on reaching a particular count. Fig. 13.3(b) shows a synchronous k-bit counter which activates when the count reaches $2^k - 1$, by modifying the node ER to an incorrect value at node $ER^\star$. An asynchronous version is shown in Fig. 13.3(c), where the count is increased not by the clock, but by a rising transition at the output of an AND gate with inputs p and q. The trigger mechanism can also be *hybrid*, where the counts of both a synchronous and an asynchronous counter simultaneously determine the Trojan trigger condition, as shown in Fig. 13.3(d). Note that more complex state machines of different types and sizes can

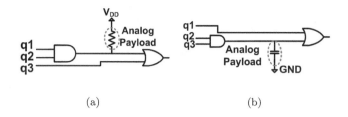

(a)   (b)

FIGURE 13.4: Examples of analog payload Trojans.

be used to generate the trigger condition based on a sequence of rare events. In general, it is more challenging to detect sequential Trojans using conventional test generation and application, because it requires satisfying a sequence of rare conditions at internal circuit nodes to activate them. The number of such sequential trigger conditions for arbitrary Trojan instances can be unmanageably large for a deterministic logic testing approach.

The trigger-mechanism can also be *analog* in nature, where on-chip sensors are used to trigger a malfunction. Fig. 13.3(e) shows an example of an analog trigger mechanism where the inserted capacitance is charged through the resistor if the condition $q_1 = 1$, $q_2 = 1$ is satisfied, and discharged otherwise, causing the logic threshold to be crossed after a large number of cycles. A different analog Trojan trigger mechanism (see Fig. 13.3(f)) was proposed in [116], where higher circuit activity and the resultant rise of temperature was used to trigger the malfunction, through a pair of ring oscillators and a counter.

Trojans can also be classified based on their *payload* mechanisms into two main classes – *digital* and *analog*. Digital Trojans can either affect the logic values at chosen internal payload nodes, or can modify the contents of memory locations. Analog payload Trojans, on the other hand, affect circuit parameters such as performance, power and noise margin. Fig. 13.4(a) shows an example where a bridging fault is introduced using an inserted resistor, while Fig. 13.4(b) shows an example where the delay of the path is affected by increasing the capacitive load.

Another form of analog payload would be generation of excess activity in a circuit (similar to that shown in Fig. 13.3(f)), to accelerate the aging process of an IC and shorten its life-span, without affecting its functionality.

Apart from triggering logic errors in the IC, the Trojan can also be designed to assist in software-based attacks like privilege escalation, login backdoor and password theft [199]. A type of hardware trojan attracting considerable research attention in recent years is the "information leakage" Trojan, which leaks secret information via an interface "backdoor". It could also involve side-channel attack where the information is leaked through the power trace [222, 221]. We would investigate a Trojan that helps the leakage of secret information, later in this chapter. Another type of Trojan payload proposed is that implementing a "Denial of Service" (DoS) attack, which causes a system functionality to be unavailable.

In the rest of the section, we describe two novel Trojan designs, capable of causing potent "information leakage attacks".

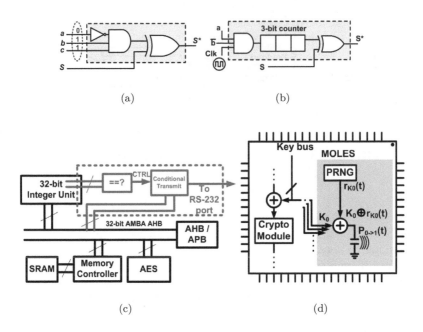

(a)   (b)

(c)   (d)

FIGURE 13.5: Examples of (a) combinational and (b) sequential hardware Trojans that cause malfunction conditionally; Examples of Trojans leaking information (c) through logic values and (d) through side-channel parameter [221].

13.3   Multi-level Attacks

In this section, we describe a novel hardware Trojan that involves the nexus of multiple malicious parties at different stages of the design, manufacturing, and/or deployment stages. Although some specific instances of multi-level attack (MLA) have been explored in diverse contexts, e.g. [7], where with the help of *focused ion beams* an inserted dormant Trojan is connected to the functional unit in the fab, in this chapter we examine it in its general form as an issue arising out of modern design and manufacturing practices. We present the general model of multi-level attacks, gives an example of such an attack, analyse its effectiveness theoretically as well as through experimental validation. We elucidate the concept of multi-level attacks with an example of an attack on a hardware implementation of the *Advanced Encryption Standard* (AES) algorithm, which leads to leakage of the secret key. We show that multi-level attacks pose stronger threat in terms of evading existing defence mechanisms than the attacks involving a single party with access to a single level of IC life-cycle.

Fig. 13.6 shows possible nexus that might exist between different parties associated with the design, manufacturing and deployment in the life-cycle of IP-based cryptographic hardware. Fig. 1(a) and 1(b) consider the hardware life-cycle for Application Specific Integrated Circuit (ASIC) and field programmable gate array (FPGA) realization, respectively. Nexus between two or more stages can be leveraged to mount extremely strong attacks, leading to IP piracy, post-deployment malfunction or information leakage. Due to the distributed nature of these attacks, they can easily evade security verification at individual stages.

Consider an iterative implementation of the Advanced Encryption Standard (AES) algorithm as shown in Fig. 13.7(a). As described in earlier chapters, a typical AES encryp-

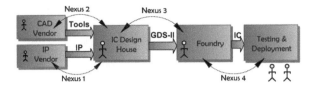

(a) Multi-level threat for an IP-based cryptographic IC design and manufacturing flow

(b) Multi-level threat for an IP-based FPGA design flow

FIGURE 13.6: Example of multi-level attacks for both ASIC and FPGA realizations of cryptographic hardware.

tion consists of ten rounds of a series of operations - *AddRoundKey*, *SubBytes*, *ShiftRows* and *MixColumns*, with the tenth round replacing the *MixColumns* step with an extra *AddRoundKey* step. This particular implementation of AES takes 10 clock cycles to complete the encryption of a single 128-bit block of plain-text.

Let us assume that the malicious adversary is the designer of the AES hardware herself, who wants to know the secret encryption key after the hardware has been deployed. For this, the malicious designer develops a nexus with the person in charge of deploying the encryption hardware in-field. Typically, such encryption hardware is designed in the form of hardware intellectual property cores (IP cores) in hardware description language (HDL), which can be directly synthesized and either used as a building block in a cryptographic IC or mapped on a FPGA. The person in charge of deployment would allow an AES IP core infected with a Trojan to be included. The encryption key is usually hard-coded in a tamper-resistant non-volatile memory module on the circuit board, hence the deployer cannot directly access the key. Since multiple parties are involved here in trying to discover some secret information, this is an example of a *multi-level attack*.

The knowledge of how the hardware Trojan might be triggered is a secret shared only between the two co-operating malicious parties. The structure of the inserted Trojan circuit is shown in Fig. 13.7(a) and the associated timing diagram of the Trojan signals is shown in Fig. 13.7(b). The hardware Trojan is triggered (activated) by the application of three consecutive patterns (denoted by $P1$, $P2$, $P3$ in Fig. 13.7(b)) at chosen bit positions of the input plain-text, which are easily controllable by the in-field adversary. The probability of triggering such a Trojan accidentally by non-motivated application of plain-text is extremely small. To see this, consider that the Trojan is triggered by the occurrence of consecutively three different bit patterns each of length thirty at thirty different bit positions of the plain-text. Then, the probability of successfully applying one of the patterns is $\frac{1}{2^{30}}$. Since the choices of the patterns are independent of each other, the probability of successfully

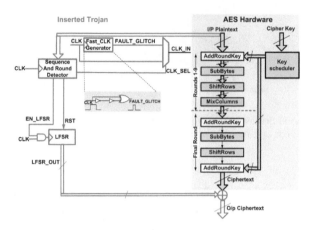

(a) AES hardware with Trojan

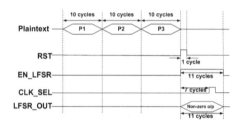

(b) Timing diagram of the Trojan signals

FIGURE 13.7: Example of a designer-embedded Trojan in the hardware implementation of the AES cryptographic hardware.

applying all the three patterns in correct sequence and triggering the Trojan is given by:

$$P_{trigger} = \left(\frac{1}{2^{30}}\right)^3 = \frac{1}{2^{90}} \approx 10^{-27} \tag{13.1}$$

which is minuscule. Hence, we can safely assume that only the deployer can trigger the Trojan by a "chosen plain-text" attack, by controlling the plain-text input to the encrypter.

The Trojan activates after detecting this sequence of patterns through a sequence detector. The Trojan also includes a delay-based glitch generator circuitry which generates glitches ($FAULT\_GLITCH$) by XOR-ing the system clock with a delayed version of itself, as shown in Fig. 13.7(a). On activating, the Trojan waits for seven clock cycles before enabling a multiplexor through the CLK_SEL signal that lets a narrow glitch ($FAULT\_GLITCH$) being applied at the clock input instead of the system-clock. This causes a *setup time violation* in the input flip-flops when the seventh round cipher-text is fed-back to the input of the encryption hardware to start the eighth round encryption [355]. Thus, the inserted Trojan hardware injects a *fault* in the AES circuit at the beginning of the eighth round during encryption. It has been shown [262] that by analyzing two faulty cipher-texts corresponding to two known plain-texts, the 128-bit AES key can be deduced exactly without any brute-force search. If only one plain-text cipher-text pair is known, the key can be deduced exactly by a brute-force search of the order of 2^{32}.

The adversaries want that *only they and no other party* would be able to deduce the secret key from the faulty cipher-text. To achieve this, she can mask the cipher-text by adding a *Linear Feedback Shift Register* (LFSR) to the design. The LFSR remains active for the time taken to encrypt a single plain-text by the AES hardware. The state transitions of the LFSR is controlled by the *EN_LFSR* signal which is synchronized with the event of multiple successful pattern matches. This concept takes its motivation from the type of information leakage Trojan described in [221]. The infeasibility of recovering the key with a modified faulty cipher-text is shown next in Section 13.3.1.

13.3.1 Difficulty of Recovering Encryption Key from Modified Faulty Cipher-text

Let us assume that the output cipher byte c_i is being masked by XOR-ing with eight selected output bits of the *LFSR*. Therefore c_i must be part of one of the four ninth-round system of equation proposed in the paper [262]. Let us assume the corresponding quartet of key bytes are $\{k_p, k_q, k_r, k_s\}$ and the corresponding system of equations is:

$$2\delta = S^{-1}(x_1 \oplus k_p) \oplus S^{-1}(x_1' \oplus k_p)$$
$$\delta = S^{-1}(x_2 \oplus k_q) \oplus S^{-1}(x_2' \oplus k_q)$$
$$\delta = S^{-1}(x_3 \oplus k_r) \oplus S^{-1}(x_3' \oplus k_r)$$
$$3\delta = S^{-1}(x_4 \oplus k_s) \oplus S^{-1}(x_4' \oplus k_s)$$

where x_1, x_2, x_3, x_4 are the actual cipher-text, and x_1', x_2', x_3', x_4' are the corresponding faulty cipher-text values. Here $\delta \in \{0, \ldots, 255\}$ and S^{-1} represents the *InverseSubByte* operation of AES. We now prove by contradiction that the masked output cipher-text will not reveal the secret key.

Let us assume that the masked cipher reveals the actual key and x_1 in above equation represents c_i and the corresponding faulty cipher byte and the masked faulty cipher bytes are x_1' and $x_1' \oplus \alpha$, where α is a non-zero masked value generated by the LFSR. Therefore, the above equation should give same quartet of key bytes $\{k_p, k_q, k_r, k_s\}$ with the masked value. In that case only the first equation changes and the rest of the equations remain unchanged. Hence, from the first equation we can write,

$$S^{-1}(x_1 \oplus k_p) \oplus S^{-1}(x_1' \oplus \alpha \oplus k_p)$$
$$= S^{-1}(x_1 \oplus k_p) \oplus S^{-1}(x_1' \oplus k_p)$$

which implies

$$S^{-1}(x_1' \oplus \alpha \oplus k_p) = S^{-1}(x_1' \oplus k_p)$$

which implies $x_1' = x_1' \oplus \alpha$ and $\alpha = 0$, since the S^{-1} mapping is bijective. This conclusion contradicts our assumption.

13.3.2 Effectiveness of Multi-level Attacks

We now try to quantitatively estimate the effectiveness of an attack based on the nexus between multiple parties at different levels. Consider the example given in the previous section. In this case, note that it is not fruitful to consider whether the nexus between the designer and the deployer makes it easier for either party to launch an attack. It would be generally infeasible (even for the deployer) to launch a fault-attack on the AES encrypter by suddenly increasing the clock frequency to the encrypter. The effectiveness of the attack can be realized by estimating the difficulty in discovering the inserted hardware Trojan, and

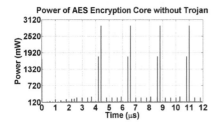
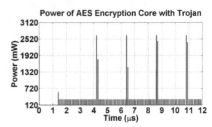

(a) Power trace of circuit without Tro-   (b) Power trace of circuit with Trojan.
jan

FIGURE 13.8: Power traces of circuits with and without Trojan.

TABLE 13.1: Simulated Increase in Average Power

Design	Average Power (mW)	% Increase (w.r.t. golden)
AES without Trojan (golden)	120.60	0.00
AES with Trojan (LFSR inactive)	120.68	0.07
AES with Trojan (LFSR active)	120.86	0.22

then using it to retrieve the encryption key, for somebody who is not part of the nexus. To discover the scheme, a third-party (who is not part of the nexus) must perform two tasks successfully:

- Activate the inserted Trojan by applying the three correct patterns ($P1$, $P2$ and $P3$), and,

- Identify the bit positions of the output cipher-text whose values have been inverted by the Trojan LFSR.

In general, if each of the Trojan activation sequence vectors is M-bit long and the length of the initialization sequence is N, the complexity of activating the Trojan by a brute-force method is $O(2^{M \cdot N})$. To perform the second task successfully by brute force (since a third-party has no way of knowing this information), P bit positions out of 128 bits AES cipher-text must be chosen, and corresponding to each of the assumed choices, an average of 2^{32} operations must be performed to calculate the key. Only one of these operations of overall complexity $O\left(\binom{128}{P} \cdot 2^{32}\right)$ will yield the correct key. Hence, for a third-party to actually launch a successful fault-attack on the above hardware will require brute-force operations of complexity $O\left(2^{M \cdot N}\binom{128}{P} \cdot 2^{32}\right)$. For example, with $M = 10$, $N = 3$, $P = 15$ (i.e. 15 bits of the output cipher-text were flipped), the above complexity is $\approx 2^{126}$, which is comparable to the complexity of finding an 128-bit AES encryption key by a brute-force search.

13.3.3   Results: Multi-level Attacks

The iterative AES encryption core infected with a length-3, 10-bit pattern detector and a 32-bit LFSR-based hardware Trojan as described in Section 13.3 was implemented in Verilog and simulated using *ModelSim*. The design was synthesized using *Xilinx ISE* to map it to a *Xilinx Spartan-3E* FPGA board. *Xilinx XPower* was used to simulate the

TABLE 13.2: Hardware Overhead

Design	Slices	Slice Flip-flops	4-input LUTs
AES without Trojan (golden)	3229	2437	5835
AES with Trojan	3260	2487	5898
Overhead (%)	0.96	2.05	1.08

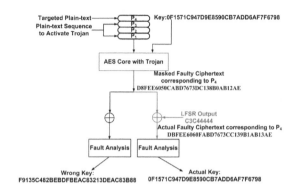

FIGURE 13.9: Experimental setup to simulate multi-level attack.

transient power trace of the circuit. Fig. 13.8 shows the simulated power traces of the circuit with and without Trojan. Table 13.1 shows the percentage increase in the average power consumption of the infected design as compared to the golden design, and Table 13.2 shows the hardware overhead. As is evident from these two tables, the Trojan is small relative to the original circuit and has negligible effect on the average power consumption, and is thus extremely difficult to detect using side-channel techniques which are commonly affected by experimental noise and process variation effects.

To show the effectiveness of the above multi-level attack scenario, a fault attack was launched using a glitch as shown in Fig. 13.9. When the effect of the masking by the output of the LFSR was not considered, the fault analysis technique described in [262] yielded an incorrect key, which was different in all the sixteen bytes compared to the original key. When the effect of the masking was taken into consideration, the correct key was recovered through the fault analysis attack, as expected.

13.3.4 Extension of the Multi-level Attack Model

The attack model exemplified in the last two sections is not limited to cryptographic applications. ASIC or FPGA hardware used in any application where national, business or personal security is at stake can be attacked using such techniques. Also, more nexus scenarios can be envisaged between different parties. A general observation is that if a party at a higher level of design abstraction is part of the nexus, more parties would be probably required to conduct the operation successfully. For example, from the cases considered in the previous section, a nexus where the back-end designer and the fab engineer are involved requires two persons, whereas a nexus where a logic designer is involved would require three parties.

13.3.5 Prevention Techniques against Multi-level Attacks

The state-of-the-art of techniques to detect hardware Trojans would find it difficult to detect the Trojans arising out of multi-level nexus. This is because parties that are part of the nexus would ensure that either (a) the Trojans are designed such that they

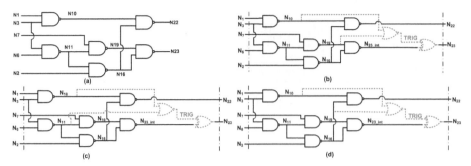

FIGURE 13.10: The *c17 ISCAS–85* circuit and three different inserted combinational Trojans. Trojan–1 and Trojan–3 are triggered and cause malfunction for 2 out of 32 possible input vectors. Trojan–2 is triggered relatively more often and cause malfunction for 4 out of the 32 possible input vectors.

can evade the detection techniques using simulation, verification or post-silicon testing, or (b) the malicious parties would neutralize such steps. Consider the scenario where every personnel associated with the design and manufacturing flow is potentially untrusted. Then, one of the possible prevention techniques is to verify the design against every preceding level of design abstraction, by first reverse-engineering the design back to higher levels of design abstraction. For example, the GDS-II of the design should be independently reverse-engineered and compared with the design at gate-level, RTL and behavioral level. Such a technique can however, be extremely expensive, and may not guarantee security against all forms and complexities of multi-level attacks.

13.4   Effect of Hardware Trojan on Circuit Reliability

In this section, we study the effect of undetected hardware Trojans on circuit reliability. This is to give the reader an quantitative estimate of the adverse effect that an undetected hardware Trojan might have, on the reliability and expected lifetime of a circuit. In spite of great strides that have been made in the understanding of the behavior of hardware Trojans and their detection techniques, the great variety exhibited by hardware Trojans, makes them almost impossible for the current state-of-the-art techniques to *guarantee* the detection of surreptitiously inserted hardware Trojans. Hence, it is useful to have an idea of how much adverse effect (in terms of affecting the operational lifetime) an *undetected MHL* has on the host circuit. We show in Section 13.4.1 that the trends suggested by our relatively simple reliability model for the failure mode of a hardware Trojan infected circuit closely fits our simulation results. Later in the chapter, we would show that relatively simple ring–oscillator based hardware Trojans (inserted in a FPGA by direct modification of the FPGA configuration bitstream), with relatively small hardware footprint, can be extremely effective in raising the operating temperature of a FPGA, thus decreasing the operational lifetime of the FPGA by orders of magnitude. As would be evident from the analyses that follow, our reliability metrics present a *lower bound* on the reliability of an infected circuit, because they are derived assuming no special design or testing technique.

In this section, we will treat circuit reliability and associated metrics from a relatively abstract mathematical viewpoint, without concentrating on the actual cause of circuit failure. Our definitions and notation would follow those given in [207], and would use relatively simple analytical models of circuit failure.

Suppose a circuit starts operating at time $t = 0$ and remains operational until it is hit by a failure for the first time at time $t = T$. Then T is the *lifetime* of the component, and let T be a random variable distributed according to the *probability density function* (pdf) $f(t)$. If $F(t)$ is the cumulative distribution function (cdf) for T, then $f(t)$ and $F(t)$ are related by:

$$f(t) = \frac{\mathrm{d}\,F(t)}{\mathrm{d}\,t}, \quad F(t) = \text{Prob.}\{T \leq t\} = \int_0^t f(\tau)\,\mathrm{d}\tau \tag{13.2}$$

Being a density function, $f(t)$ satisfies:

$$f(t) \geq 0 \quad \text{for } t \geq 0 \quad \text{and} \quad \int_0^\infty f(t)\,\mathrm{d}t = 1 \tag{13.3}$$

The cdf, $F(t)$, of a given circuit is the probability that the circuit will fail at or before time t. Its counterpart, *reliability* ($R(t)$) is the probability that the circuit will survive at least until time t, and is given by:

$$R(t) = \text{Prob.}\{T > t\} = 1 - F(t) \tag{13.4}$$

Perhaps the most important quantitative metric used to estimate reliability is the *failure rate* or *hazard rate*, denoted by $\lambda(t)$, and defined as:

$$\lambda(t) = \frac{f(t)}{1 - F(t)} = \frac{f(t)}{R(t)} \tag{13.5}$$

$\lambda(t)$ denotes the conditional instantaneous probability of a circuit failing, given it is yet to fail at time t. Since $\frac{\mathrm{d}\,R(t)}{\mathrm{d}\,t} = -f(t)$, we have $\lambda(t) = -\frac{1}{R(t)}\frac{\mathrm{d}\,R(t)}{\mathrm{d}\,t}$. For circuits which have a failure rate that is constant over time (which is the most commonly considered model for ICs), i.e. $\lambda(t) = \lambda$, we have:

$$\frac{\mathrm{d}\,R(t)}{\mathrm{d}\,t} = -\lambda R(t) \tag{13.6}$$

Solving eqn. (13.6) with the initial condition $R(t) = 0$ leads to:

$$R(t) = e^{-\lambda t} \quad \text{for } t \geq 0 \tag{13.7}$$

Eqn. (13.7) leads to the following expressions:

$$f(t) = \lambda e^{-\lambda t} \quad \text{and} \quad F(t) = 1 - e^{-\lambda t} \quad \text{for } t \geq 0 \tag{13.8}$$

Besides λ, another important parameter that characterizes circuit reliability is the *mean time to failure* (MTTF), which is the expected lifetime of the circuit, and is given (assuming a constant failure rate) by:

$$\text{MTTF} = \text{E}[T] = \int_0^\infty t f(t)\,\mathrm{d}t = \int_0^\infty \lambda t e^{-\lambda t}\,\mathrm{d}t = \frac{1}{\lambda} \tag{13.9}$$

A major part of our analysis for different types of hardware Trojans would be devoted to modelling how the presence of a undetected hardware Trojan modifies the values of the failure rate and MTTF of a circuit. Depending on the nature of the inserted hardware Trojan, the circuit may or may not recover its original functionality. However, in the analyses that follow, we would assume the interval between the start of functioning of a circuit and its first functional failure due to the activation of a hardware Trojan as defining the lifetime of the circuit.

TABLE 13.3: Combinational Trojans: Trigger Condition and Trojan Activation Probability

Trojan	Trigger Condition	Troj. Activation Probability
Trojan–1	$N10 = 0, N19 = 0$	2/32
Trojan–2	$N10 = 0, N11 = 0$	4/32
Trojan–3	$N10 = 0, N16 = 0$	2/32

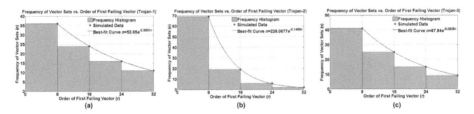

FIGURE 13.11: Failure trends of the $c17$ circuit with three types of inserted combinational Trojans (shown in Figs. 13.10(b)–(d)).

TABLE 13.4:   Combinational Trojans and Associated Mean Time to Failure

Trojan	b_{est}	$\mathbf{MTTF_{trojan,est}} = \frac{1}{b}$	$\mathbf{MTTF_{trojan,est}}$(95% Conf. Int.)	$\mathbf{MTTF_{trojan,av}}$
Trojan–1	0.0501	19.96	[19.09,20.94]	19.15
Trojan–2	0.1489	6.72	[5.79,6.93]	6.81
Trojan–3	0.0628	15.92	[15.47,16.41]	16.35

13.4.1   Hardware Trojan and Reliability: Analysis and Results

In this section, we give examples of different common and widely studied hardware Trojans, and analyse their effect on circuit reliability.

13.4.1.1   Combinational Trojans

As a running example, we would use the $c17$ circuit from the *ISCAS–85* combinational circuit suite. The $c17$ circuit was chosen because of its inherent simplicity (the entire circuit consists of six two-input NAND gates), and this choice does not take into consideration the fact that the Trojan concerned is easily detectable. However, as would be evident from the analysis, the technique of estimating the reliability and the quantitative metrics derived are applicable for circuits of arbitrary complexity. Fig. 13.10(a) shows the $c17$ circuit. It has five primary inputs ($N1$, $N2$, $N3$, $N6$ and $N7$); two primary outputs ($N22$ and $N23$), and four internal nodes ($N10$, $N11$, $N16$ and $N19$).

Figs. 13.10(b)–(d) show the $c17$ circuit with three different inserted simple combinational Trojans. Each of these three Trojans consists of one NOR gate and one XOR gate, and each of them are triggered and cause circuit malfunction by the simultaneous occurrence of logic–0 at two selected internal nodes of the circuit. Table 13.3 shows the trigger conditions and the activation probabilities of the three inserted Trojans obtained by exhaustive simulation of the possible input values.

Assuming that the only effect of combinational Trojans is functional failure of the circuit, and does not include *aging*, the presence of a combinational Trojan modulates the reliability of the infected circuit to:

$$R(t) = e^{-\lambda_{eff}t} \tag{13.10}$$

where the *effective failure rate* λ_{eff} is the sum of the failure rate of the original (Trojan-free) circuit (λ_{org}) and λ_{tro} is the contribution of the included Trojan in increasing the failure rate. Thus,

$$\lambda_{eff} = \lambda_{org} + \lambda_{tro} \tag{13.11}$$

If $MTTF_{org}$ is the original $MTTF$ and $MTTF_{eff}$ is the effective $MTTF$ due to the presence of the Trojan, the change in $MTTF$ value is given by:

$$\Delta MTTF = MTTF_{eff} - MTTF_{org} = \frac{MTTF_{org}}{1 + \frac{\lambda_{org}}{\lambda_{tro}}} \tag{13.12}$$

To observe the actual failure trend of the $c17$ circuit, we simulated the three circuits shown in Figs. 13.10(b)-(d) with 100 sets of random vectors, each set consisting of 32 vectors. However, each set of 32 vectors did not consist of all possible vectors 00000 to 11111, and hence, the set of test vectors were truly random. Figs. 13.11(a)-(c) show frequency histogram of the number of failures (n) that occur in the intervals 0-8, 9-16, etc., in a set of 32 vectors, considering the average over 100 vector sets. The upper range of the intervals are denoted by r. Thus, the time is discretized in terms of the number of vectors applied. This curve is representative of the failure probability density function of the Trojan-infected circuit. The best–fitted curves of the form $n = ae^{-br}$ were obtained using *MATLAB*.

The parameter b, which is interpreted as representative of the $MTTF$ of the circuit, can also be estimated by averaging the time to failure for the different vector sets, following the *Method of Moments* [207]. Table 13.4 shows the estimated and average value (as obtained by averaging the first instance of failure of the vector sets) of the $MTTF$ (considering only the presence of Trojan), along with the 95% confidence interval for the estimated value. Note that the MTTF is in terms of the number of input vectors applied before the first circuit failure. From the plots and the table, it is evident that the data and the data trends fitted very well to the theoretically predicted trend.

13.4.2 Synchronous Counter-based Sequential Trojan

A synchronous counter-based Trojan acts as a "silicon time-bomb" and causes malfunction after an inserted free-running counter driven by the system clock reaches a terminal count value. The synchronous counter-based Trojan modulates the circuit failure probability density function differently compared to the conditional triggered Trojans, because the Trojan is guaranteed to be activated after the count has reached its terminal value. Let T_{tro} be the time required for the counter to reach its terminal count. Then, for $0 \le t < T_{tro}$, the circuit failure probability function ($F(t)$) is identical to that of the original Trojan, whereas for $t \ge T_{tro}$, $F(t) = 1$. This implies the following form of the failure probability density function:

$$f(t) = \lambda e^{-\lambda t} \left[u(t) - u(t - T_{tro}) \right] + e^{-\lambda T_{tro}} \delta(t - T_{tro}) \tag{13.13}$$

where $u(t)$ is the *unit step function* defined by:

$$u(t) = \begin{cases} 1 & \text{for } t \ge 0 \\ 0 & \text{otherwise} \end{cases} \tag{13.14}$$

and $\delta(t)$ is the *unit impulse function* defined by:

$$\delta(t) = \begin{cases} 1 & \text{for } t = 0 \\ 0 & \text{otherwise} \end{cases} \tag{13.15}$$

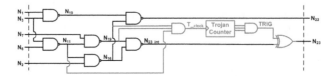

FIGURE 13.12: *c17* with an asynchronous binary counter-type Trojan. The reset signal for the Trojan counter has not been shown for simplicity.

TABLE 13.5: Asynchronous Sequential Trojan: Trigger Condition and Trigger Probability[†]

Trojan	States	Troj. Cnt. Inc. Cond.	Trigg. Cond.	Troj. Act. Prob. (est.)
Trojan-4	$2^3 = 8$	↑ for $T_{clock} = N11\&N16\&N19$	$T_{count} = 3'b111$	0.0406
Trojan-5	$2^4 = 16$	↑ for $T_{clock} = N11\&N16\&N19$	$T_{count} = 4'b1111$	0.0191

[†]The Trojan activation probability was estimated by simulations with a set of 3200 random vectors.

Clearly, $f(t) \geq 0$ for non-negative value of t as defined above, and it can be easily verified that the above definition of $f(t)$ satisfies $\int_0^\infty f(t)\,dt = 1$ as follows:

$$\int_0^\infty f(t)\,dt = \int_0^{T_{tro}} \lambda e^{-\lambda t}\,dt + e^{-\lambda T_{tro}} \int_0^\infty \delta(t - T_{tro})\,dt = 1 \qquad (13.16)$$

using the *sampling property* of $\delta(t)$, i.e. $\int_{-\infty}^\infty f(t)\delta(t - t_0)\,dt = f(t_0)$. The *failure probability* $F(t)$ is the given by:

$$F(t) = \int_0^t f(\tau)\,d\tau = \begin{cases} 1 - e^{-\lambda t} & \text{for } t < T_{tro} \\ 1 & \text{for } t \geq T_{tro} \end{cases} \qquad (13.17)$$

To determine the $MTTF$, we consider two different cases: (a) $\frac{1}{\lambda} \geq T_{tro}$ and (b) $\frac{1}{\lambda} < T_{tro}$. When $\frac{1}{\lambda} \geq T_{tro}$, the circuit is expected to fail due the activation of the Trojan before it fails due to other reasons. However, there is still a finite probability of the circuit failing in the time interval $0 \leq t < T_{tro}$. Hence, if $\frac{1}{\lambda} \geq T_{tro}$,

$$MTTF_{eff} = T_{tro} - T_{tro}\int_0^{T_{tro}} f(t)\,dt = T_{tro}\left[1 - (1 - e^{-\lambda T_{tro}})\right] = e^{-\lambda T_{tro}}T_{tro} \qquad (13.18)$$

and the corresponding $\Delta MTTF$ is:

$$\Delta MTTF = -\left(\frac{1}{\lambda} - e^{-\lambda T_{tro}}T_{tro}\right) = -T_{tro}\left(\frac{1}{k} - e^{-k}\right) \qquad (13.19)$$

where $k = \lambda T_{tro}$ is a dimensionless parameter and $0 < k < 1$.

When $\frac{1}{\lambda} < T_{tro}$, the circuit is expected to fail due to other reasons before it fails due to the activation of the Trojan. Hence, if $\frac{1}{\lambda} < T_{tro}$,

$$MTTF_{eff} = MTTF_{org} = \frac{1}{\lambda} \qquad (13.20)$$

and the corresponding change in $MTTF$ is:

$$\Delta MTTF = 0 \qquad (13.21)$$

TABLE 13.6: Asynchronous Sequential Trojans and Associated Mean Time to Failure [†]

Trojan	b_{est}	$\text{MTTF}_{\text{trojan,est}} = \frac{1}{b}$	$\text{MTTF}_{\text{trojan,est}}$ 95% Conf. Int.	$\text{MTTF}_{\text{trojan,av}}$
Trojan–4	0.0595	16.81	[14.91,19.28]	19.10
Trojan–5	0.0351	28.52	[26.32,31.12]	30.22

†The MTTF is in terms of the number of clock cycles passed before the first circuit failure.

13.4.3 Asynchronous Counter-based Sequential Trojan

The asynchronous counter-based sequential Trojan is triggered by successive occurrence of rare events at chosen internal circuit nodes (instead of the system clock). Eqns. (13.11) and (13.12) are still valid. In addition, if the number of state transitions required before the Trojan causes a circuit malfunction is larger, the value of $MTTF$ can be also be expected to be greater.

Fig. 13.12 shows the $c17$ circuit with an inserted sequential Trojan. The Trojan is an asynchronous binary counter which increases its count whenever a positive edge occurs on the net T_{trojan}, which in turn is derived by AND–ing nodes $N11$, $N16$ and $N19$. The Trojan flips the logic–value at the primary output node $N23$ whenever the count reaches $(2^n - 1)$. Two different such Trojans were considered: Table 13.5 shows the Trojan clocking and activation conditions, along with the activation probability estimated through simulations using 3200 test vectors. Fig. 13.13 shows the simulated failure trends of the $c17$ circuit infected with two types of Trojans: 3–bit asynchronous counter (Trojan-4) and 4-bit asynchronous counter (Trojan-5). Table 13.6 shows the $MTTF$ extracted from the best–fitted curve and by averaging the simulation data. Again, the $MTTF$ derived from the best–fit curve and from the simulation data agree very well, and as expected, the circuit with the more difficult to activate Trojan (Trojan-5) has a smaller $MTTF$.

Thus, in all the types of Trojan considered by us, we found close match to the theoretically predicted results. Next, we consider an interesting example of a hardware Trojan, whereby ring oscillators are instantiated in a FPGA, to cause rise of operating temperature. Such rise of operating temperature causes decrease in IC reliability, which would be estimated quantitatively in Section 13.5.8.

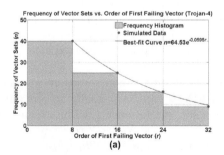 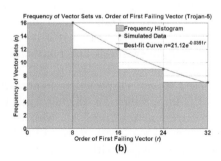

FIGURE 13.13: Failure trends of the $c17$ circuit with two types of inserted sequential Trojans (described in Sec. 13.4.3).

13.5 Hardware Trojan Insertion by Direct Modification of FPGA Configuration Bitstream

As mentioned previously, hardware Trojans can be inserted at various stages of the design and manufacturing flow: specifications, design, fabrication, testing and assembly and packaging [178]. Electronic Design Automation (EDA) CAD tools being indispensable in modern IC design, they are a potential source of Trojan insertion. For example, a logic synthesis CAD tool might make surreptitious modification to the design to insert hardware Trojans, and not reveal the modifications to the user [178]. Although CAD tools have been described as a possible source of hardware Trojans [378], interestingly, it has not been explored by researchers. A possible reason for this might be that most industry-standard CAD tools are closed source, and it is not possible to modify their source code to bestow Trojan insertion capabilities on them. However, as discussed in [334], add-on scripts can be another possible source of Trojan insertion.

Field programmable gate arrays (FPGAs) in recent years have become an alternative to application specific ICs (ASICs) in many applications, graduating from chiefly a proto-typing platform a couple of decades ago. They provide the unique flexibility of using the same design platform for implementing multiple applications, while offering continuously improving power and throughput. An added advantage of FPGA based design is that the required CAD tools are provided by the FPGA vendors, with the free versions of the software offering basic functionality being sufficient for most designs. FPGAs are configured ("programmed") by loading a binary file, termed as a "configuration bitstream", on the FPGA's "configuration memory" from a PC or over the network. The syntax and semantics of this binary file is usually proprietary, with only some basic information available about the bitstream organization in the public domain, e.g. in [159]. However, interestingly, utilizing this relatively scarce information, useful software tools have been designed in the academic community, mainly to have greater control over the configuration process [257].

In this chapter, we demonstrate a software-based Trojan insertion technique for FPGAs which are configured using unencrypted configuration bitstreams. Till date, most of the proposed hardware Trojans for FPGAs have been inserted in the high-level design description (typically in Verilog/VHDL hardware description language). In contrast, the goal of the proposed attack is to directly modify the configuration bitstream file (a binary file with a **.bit** extension in the *Xilinx* FPGA design platform) to insert Trojans into it. The attack works as an add-on program that modifies the original configuration bitstream file to insert hardware Trojans. The strength of the attack lies in the fact that since at present there is no verification mechanism for the correctness of FPGA configuration bitstreams (other than an in-built CRC generating and matching mechanism, which can be disabled, as described later), such a modification would be extremely difficult to detect pre-deployment. A major strength of the proposed attack is that it leaves no trace of Trojan insertion in the log files generated during logic synthesis and place-and-route, as the Trojan is inserted after these steps have been completed.

The proposed attack is especially potent, given the dynamic re-configuration capability of modern FPGAs in which an already configured FPGA can be partially re-configured online to add extra functionality [230]. Also, although support for encrypted bitstreams are also available in many modern high-end FPGA families (e.g. the *Xilinx Virtex* family), but there are also many families with numerous deployed FPGAs (e.g. the *Xilinx Spartan* family) which do not support bitstream encryption. Moreover, bitstream encryption (typically performed by a *Triple-DES* engine inside the FPGA) has also been recently reported to be broken by side-channel attacks [255].

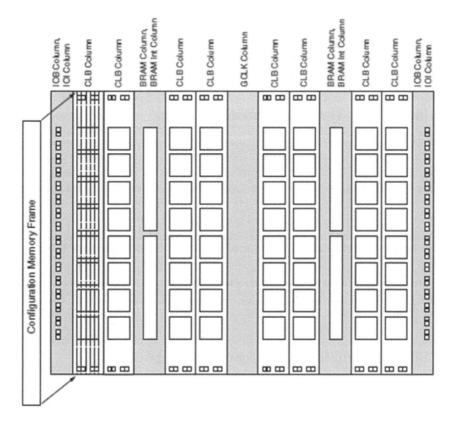

FIGURE 13.14: Xilinx Virtex-II configuration bitstream file organization [159, 257].

TABLE 13.7: Virtex-II (XC2V40) Column Types and Frame Count [159]

Column Type	Columns	Frames per Column
Input/Output Block (IOB)	2	4
Input/Output Interface (IOI)	2	22
Configurable Logic Block (CLB)	8	22
Block RAM (BRAM)	2	62
BRAM Interconnect (BRAM_INT)	2	22
Global Clock (GCLK)	1	4

We next present an in–depth description of the organisation of a typical Xilinx configuration bitstream file in depth, including its correlation with the FPGA architecture.

13.5.1   Xilinx Configuration Bitstream Structure

In this section, we describe the structure of a *Xilinx* configuration bitstream file in the light of the FPGA architecture (which is essential in understanding the proposed attack). Most of the description about the configuration bitstream is taken from [159, 257].

13.5.2   Xilinx Virtex-II FPGA Builiding Blocks

In Virtex-II FPGAs, *Configurable Logic Block*s (CLBs) are the basic building blocks of user logic. They typically occupy the majority of the FPGA floor-plan and are organized in rows and columns. A CLB consists of four *slices*, and each slice contains two flip-flops (FFs) used for clocked logic; two four-input lookup tables (LUTs) used for logic functions, and multiplexers. Each CLB contains a single switch-matrix which connects the external routing to the internal logic. The *input/output blocks* (IOBs) contain the input/output logic for each pin on the device. The IOB signals can optionally be latched or registered. *Block BRAM* (BRAM) provide memory buffers for user designs. The *BRAM Interconnect* (BRAM_INT) provides the routing interface to the BRAMs and the configuration for the dedicated multipliers providing high-speed 18x18 multiplication. Separate "columns" in the bitstream are dedicated to represent the above resources (CLB, IOB, BRAM, etc.), as shown in Table 13.7 [159].

13.5.3   Xilinx Configuration Bitstream File Organisation

The Xilinx Virtex-II configuration bitstream in stored in a *configuration memory*, which is arranged in *frames* that are 1-bit wide and stretches from the top edge of the device to the bottom, as shown in Fig. 13.14. These frames are the smallest addressable segments of the configuration memory space; therefore, all operations must act on whole configuration frames. Configuration memory frames do not directly map to any single piece of hardware; rather, they configure a narrow vertical slice of many physical resources [159]. The size of the frame depends on the family (e.g. Virtex-II) and the particular FPGA device (e.g. XC2V40) for which the configuration file is being generated. The number of configuration bits can be related to the frame count by:

$$\text{No. of Configuration Bits} = \text{Frame Count} \times \text{Frame Size} \qquad (13.22)$$

Other than the configuration bits in the frames, the .bit file also contains other auxiliary parts, for example, a "header" of ASCII encoded name of the top-level module of the design, the device family, timestamp; cyclic redundancy check (CRC) words, and a long trailing series of zeros at the end of the files to signify "no operation" (NOOP). The default size of the configuration bitstream can be deduced as:

$$\text{Bitstream size} = \text{No. of Configuration Bits} + \text{Overhead} \qquad (13.23)$$

The order in which the different sections are present in the bitstream configuration file is: header words, frame words, CRC words, and trailing (NOOP) words.

13.5.3.1   Configuration Memory Addressing

Each configuration frame has a unique 32-bit address that is composed of a block address (BA), a major address (MJA), a minor address (MNA), and a byte number. The major address identifies a specific column within a block, and the minor address identifies a specific frame within a column [159].

13.5.4 Configuration Process

Configuration takes place by writing the configuration bitstream file to one of the configuration ports on the FPGA. The bitstream consists of a 32-bit *synchronization word* and a sequence of *packets* that contain header and data information for writing to the various configuration registers (15 in number). The purpose of the synchronization word is to align the device configuration logic with the beginning of the first packet in the bit stream. Each packet targets a specific configuration register to set configuration options, program configuration memory, or toggle internal signals. Bit stream data packets consist of a 32-bit header and a body of variable length. There are two packet types: Type-1, used for smaller body (up to $2^{11} - âĂŞ1$ words), and Type-2, used for larger packets (up to $2^{27} - âĂŞ1$ words).

13.5.5 Cyclic Redundancy Check (CRC)

The configuration bitstream contain a 16-bit CRC word at the end of both Type-1 and Type-2 frames, after the special "configuration directive" bit pattern 0X30012001. The reference document [159] mentions that for Type-1 frames, the constant CRC 0x00009A32 is used, while that for Type-2 frames is either calculated using the polynomial $x^{16}+x^{15}+x^2+1$, or a default value 0x0000DEFC ("DEFC" was probably chosen to remind us of the fact that it is the "default CRC"). During programming the FPGA with the configuration bitstream, the device performs a CRC check on-the-fly, and allows successful configuration only if the CRC check passes.

13.5.6 Disabling CRC Check

We found that calculation of the CRC with the polynomial mentioned in [159] does not tally with the observed CRC, which is not surprising, given that the user guide is listed as "obsolete/under obsolescene" on the official Xilinx website. This was a major stumbling block in the attack, as without the correct CRC value, the FPGA will not accept a modified configuration bitstream. Fortunately, we found a workaround by noting that Xilinx allows disabling of CRC check by setting the "**-g CRC:Disable**" option in the *BitGen* tool of ISE, either from the command prompt or through GUI. While performing the modifications at the bitstream level, this is equivalent to setting the 29th bit of the 32-bit "Configuration Options Register" (COR) to 1. The value of the COR is found after the special bit pattern 0x30000001. When CRC checking is disabled, the CRC matching mechanism uses the default CRC value 0x0000DEFC. Hence, the CRC matching mechanism can be made to accept an arbitrarily modified bitstream file by making the modifications; searching the bitstream for the string 0x30000001 (for COR) and 0x30012001 (for the CRC); making the 29th bit of COR to be 1, and then overwriting the four bytes following 0x30012001 by 0x0000DEFC.

13.5.7 Bitstream Modification Technique

As a consequence of the above observation, a modification of the configuration bitstream to add a hardware Trojan can occur in two different cases:

1. There is no overlap between the inserted Trojan circuitry and the original circuitry with regards to the resources on the FPGA occupied by them. In this case, the part of the bitstream that configures the Trojan circuitry on the FPGA is simply "dropped into" the existing bitstream file at a position where no resources have been utilized originally (i.e. the values at those positions is a continuous string of zeros) to configure unutilized resources of the FPGA for the extra circuit. In this case, the functionalities

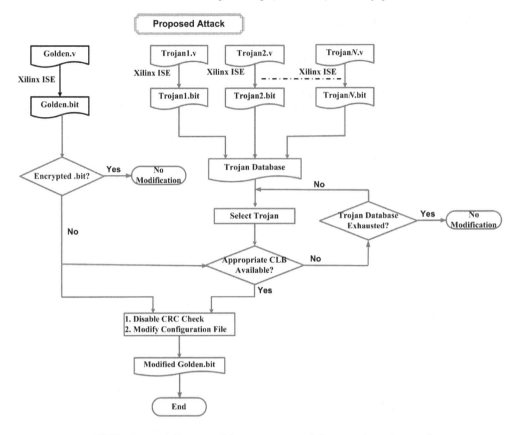

FIGURE 13.15: Proposed bitstream modification-based attack.

of the original circuit and the Trojan are independent of each other as there is no connection between the ports of the original design and the hardware Trojan. We call these Type-I Trojans in this chapter.

2. The configuration bitstream corresponding to the Trojan to be inserted overlaps (partially or fully) with the bitstream corresponding to the original design in the .bit file. In this case, the original circuit and the Trojan circuits are connected with each other in some way. We term such Trojans as Type-II Trojans.

In the first case, the Trojan insertion operation by bitstream modification is relatively easier to perform. In contrast, Trojan insertion in the second case requires detailed knowledge of the correlation between the routing of the interconnects in the FPGA fabric with the bitstream. Even in a relatively low-end (by modern standards) FPGA model such as Virtex-II (device XC2V40), this is an extremely complicated exercise in the absence of supporting documentation to provide at least some basic information. Even this has been attempted previously [274]. However, the approach taken by the authors in [274] does not work directly on the .bit file, but first derives the design description in another proprietary plaintext format called the *Xilinx Design Language* ("**.xdl**" being the file extension); modifies the .xdl file, and then transforms it back to the .bit format. However, the .xdl format again has no official public documentation, and future support for this format by the FPGA CAD tools is not guaranteed by Xilinx. Hence, in this work we adopt the more generic approach of directly modifying the .bit file, and we consider only Type-I Trojans.

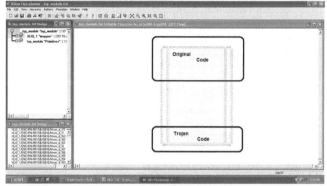

(a) Resources Occupied in Upper and Lower Halves

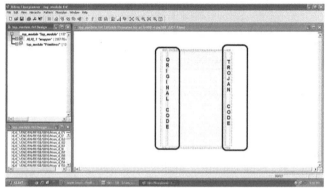

(b) Resources Occupied in Left and Right Halves

FIGURE 13.16: Examples of two possible cases of Type-I Trojan insertion.

Fig. 13.15 shows the steps of the proposed attack. "Golden.bit" represents the .bit file corresponding to the original design. The modification program takes this as one of the inputs, and searches a database of .bit files corresponding to different Type-I Trojans sequentially. The Type-I Trojans are designed such that they are physically restricted within only one of the four halves (*upper, lower, right* and *left*) of the FPGA, both in terms of on-chip resource usage as well as the I/O pin usage. The modification program first checks the bit in the 1-th index of the "Status Register" (STAT) at address 0x00111. If this bit is 1, the following configuration bitstream is triple-DES encrypted, otherwise if it is 0, the configuration bitstream is unencrypted [159]. If the program finds that the "Golden.bit" file is encrypted, it exits without performing any modification. Otherwise, the Trojan insertion algorithm identifies the blocks in the bitstream based on which "column" they represent; finds the resources on the FPGA which are unutilized by the original design; finds whether it is possible to integrate the selected Trojan bitstream with the original bitstream; finally, if integration is possible, integrates the two bitstreams and disables the CRC. If it fails in finding a proper Trojan .bit file, it exits without performing the modification. Note that the proposed attack depends on the availability of resources in proper locations of the FPGA to be successful. Fig. 13.16 shows two possible cases of successful Trojan insertion where there is no connection or overlap between the original circuit and the Trojan circuit.

To correctly parse the bitstream, it is essential to know the different types of columns in the bitstream (IOB, BRAM, CLB, etc.); the number of each type of column for a given device; the number of frames per column; and the number of 4-byte words in a frame. After

FIGURE 13.17: Demonstration of successful configuration of the RO-based Trojan insertion.

knowing these information [159], the sizes of the blocks is calculated as follows (assuming we are considering the "CLB" type columns, and from Table 13.7):

- No. of Frames in a CLB column = 22

- No. of 4-byte words in each frame (for Virtex-II device XC2V40) = 26

- No. of Columns on the FPGA = 8

∴ Total configuration bytes for CLB = 22*104*8 = 18,304

Similar calculations are to be carried out for all column types.

13.5.8   Demonstration of the Bitstream Modification-based Attack

The modification scheme described in the previous section was implemented by writing a C program. To demonstrate the proposed Trojan insertion attack, we modified the configuration bitstream corresponding to an 128-bit *Advanced Encryption Standard* (AES) cipher circuit, to insert a ring-oscillator based Trojan. A ring-oscillator based Trojan is a "free-running Trojan", which performs redundant circuit switching to dissipate power, thus increasing the circuit operating temperature without affecting the functionality of the original circuit directly. Such a Trojan has been reported previously in the literature [91], although the Trojan was inserted at the HDL level. Operating temperature is a major factor that affects the lifetime of a circuit, with higher operating temperature adversely affecting the expected lifetime as measured by the *Mean Time to Failure* (MTTF), through effects such as *Negative Bias Temperature Instability* (NBTI) of the PMOS devices [20, 207]. The effect of elevated operating temperature is quantified by a factor that signifies the acceleration of the ageing process [207]. Under elevated operating temperature, the acceleration factor is given by:

$$AF = e^{\frac{E_a}{k_B T_{org}} - \frac{E_a}{k_B T_{MHL}}} \tag{13.24}$$

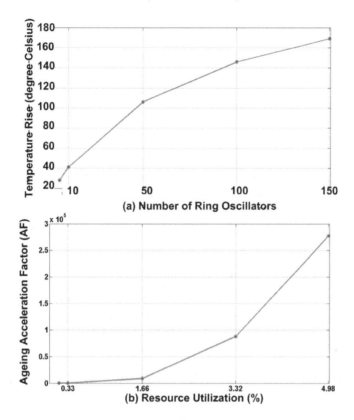

FIGURE 13.18: Effects of inserting 3–stage ring–oscillator based MHL in Virtex-II FPGA: (a) rise of temperature as a function of the number of inserted 3-stage ring oscillators; (b) theoretical aging acceleration factor as a function of percentage FPGA resource utilization by ring-oscillator Trojans.

and the modified $MTTF$ is given by:

$$MTTF_{eff} = \frac{MTTF_{org}}{AF} \tag{13.25}$$

where E_a is the *activation energy* (in electron-volts), k_B is the *Boltzmann constant* ($\approx$ 0.8625×10^{-4} electron–volt per degree kelvin), $MTTF_{eff}$ is the effective mean time to failure, $MTTF_{org}$ is the original mean time to failure T_{org} is the operating temperature of the original (MHL-free) circuit and T_{MHL} is the operating temperature of the MHL-infected circuit (both in degree kelvin). We inserted a varying number of three-stage ring oscillators, and observed the rise in temperature (measured by a digital thermometer in contact with the IC package), as shown in Fig. 13.18(a). We found that with 150 inserted ring oscillators occupying less than 20% of the total FPGA resources, the temperature increases by over 160° Celsius. Fig. 13.18(b) shows the theoretical ageing acceleration factor with representative values of $T_{org} = 300K$ and $E_a = 0.9eV$. We did not observe any functional failure of the cipher circuit in spite of operating it at such elevated temperatures for 20 consecutive days (~480 hours). This is not surprising, given the expected time-to-failure of such FPGAs are $\sim 10^8$ hours at room temperature. We arranged to have two LEDs on the FPGA board would be lighted ON when the AES and the ring oscillators would each be correctly mapped on the FPGA. We were able to demonstrate the correct working of the modification program by successfully programming the FPGA with modified configuration bitstream, the elevated operating temperature, and the two LEDs lighting up, as shown in Fig. 13.17.

Next we discuss some possible hardware techniques to prevent or detect the proposed attack.

13.5.9   Prevention/Detection Techniques against the Proposed Attack

13.5.9.1   Grounding Unused Pins in a FPGA

This method would prevent against Trojans that surreptitiously leak the secret key through covert channels using the unutilized I/O pins in the FPGA, as the Trojan would not find any port to the outside world through which the key is to be leaked. However, this method cannot protect against those key-leaking Trojans which aid in leaking the key through side-channel information, as well as Trojans which leak the key through the already used FPGA pins, or network ports.

13.5.9.2   Online Temperature Monitoring

We can have on-board temperature sensors to perform real-time temperature monitoring, so that if an inserted Trojan increases the circuit operating temperature by redundant switching, the effect would be detected and defensive action (e.g. shutting down the FPGA) can be undertaken proactively.

13.5.9.3   Filling-up Unused Resources of the FPGA

The proposed attack works by analysing the bitstream file and finding unused resources in the FPGA. However, if the designer intentionally fills up all unused portions of the FPGA with dummy logic, the adversary would find it difficult to find place to insert the Trojan. Of course, the difficulty with this approach is that it might adversely affect the overall power consumption and performance.

13.5.10   Logic Distribution to Balance Power Consumption from the I/O Power Pins

If the adversary follows a scheme of locating the important portions of the circuit mapped on the FPGA by finding the I/O power pins on the FPGA that consume the maximum power, the scheme can be foiled by following a custom placement of the logic blocks of the circuit which distributes them across the FPGA. This will make the logic blocks across the FPGA to harness power from the nearest I/O power pin, and thus somewhat equalize the power consumption for the different power pins.

13.5.10.1   Dedicated Hardware Logic to Check CRC Status

This is applicable only if the adversary has followed a method of disabling the CRC in the bitstream, like we have done in our proposed attack. There can be a custom logic block on the PCB between the configuration memory and the FPGA to check the configuration register values whether CRC checking has been disabled, and if that is the case, to disallow loading the bitstream on the FPGA.

13.5.10.2   Scrambling and De-scrambling the Bitstream File

We can scramble the configuration bitstream by software means, and have dedicated hardware logic to de-scramble it before it is actually loaded in FPGA. This is to make it difficult for an adversary to insert hardware Trojans by direct modification of the bitstream. Even if we assume that read-back is possible in-field from the configuration memory, the adversary would not be able to calculate the exact bitstream to be put into the configuration memory, so that the hardware de-scrambler de-scrambled it as intended. Here, the challenge is to keep the scrambling algorithm secret. This is a low-cost alternative to FPGAs supporting encrypted bitstreams.

13.6 Conclusion

The issue of hardware Trojans and effective countermeasures against them have drawn considerable interest in recent times. In this chapter, we have presented a comprehensive study of different Trojan types, and demonstrated a few potent attacks. Considering the varied nature and size of hardware Trojans, it is likely that a combination of techniques, both during design and testing, would be required to provide an acceptable level of security. Design-time approaches would span various levels of design descriptions. On the other hand, post-silicon validation would require a combination of logic and side-channel test approaches to cover Trojans of different types and sizes under large parameter variations. In the next chapters, we explore different approaches to detect and/or provide protection against hardware Trojans.

Chapter 14

Logic Testing based Hardware Trojan Detection

> "The addition of any function not visualized in the original design will inevitably degenerate structure. Repairs also, will tend to cause deviation from structural regularity since, except under conditions of the strictest control, any repair or patch will be made in the simplest and quickest way. No search will be made for a fix that maintains structural integrity."
>
> L. A. Belady and M. M. Lehman
> "Programming System Dynamics or the Metadynamics of Systems in Maintenance and Growth",
> Research Report RC3546, IBM, 1971.

14.1 Introduction

In this chapter, we propose a novel testing methodology, referred to as *MERO* (**M**ultiple **E**xcitation of **R**are **O**ccurence) protection against hardware Trojans. MERO comprises of a statistical test generation approach for Trojan detection and a coverage determination approach for quantifying the level of trust. The main objective of the proposed methodology is to derive a set of test patterns that is *compact* (minimizing test time and cost), while maximizing the Trojan detection coverage. The basic concept is to detect rare or low probability conditions at the internal nodes, and then derive an optimal set of vectors than can trigger each of the selected low probability nodes *individually to their rare logic values multiple times* (e.g. at least N times, where N is a given parameter). As analyzed in Section 14.2.1, this increases the probability of detection of an arbitrary Trojan instance. By increasing the toggling of nodes that are random-pattern resistant, it improves the probability of activating an unknown Trojan compared to purely random patterns. The proposed methodology is conceptually similar to the *N-detect test* [31, 302] used in stuck-at ATPG (automatic test pattern generation), where a test set is generated to detect each single stuck-at fault in a circuit by at least N different patterns to improve test quality and defect coverage [302]. In this chapter, we focus on digital Trojans [408], which can be inserted into a design either in a design house (e.g. by untrusted CAD tool or IP) or in a foundry. We do not consider the Trojans where the triggering mechanism and/or effect are analog in nature (e.g. thermal fluctuations).

Since the proposed detection is based on functional validation using logic values, it is robust with respect to parameter variations and can reliably detect very small Trojans, e.g. the ones with few logic gates. Thus, the technique can be used as *complementary to the side-channel Trojan detection approaches* [23, 309, 38, 167], which are more effective in detecting large Trojans (e.g. ones with area $> 0.1\%$ of the total circuit area). In side-channel approaches existence of a Trojan is determined by noting its effect in a one or more physical side-channel parameters, such as current or delay. Besides, the MERO approach can be used to increase the detection sensitivity of many side-channel techniques such as the ones that monitor the power/current signature, by increasing the activity in a Trojan circuit [38]. Using an integrated Trojan coverage simulation and test generation flow, we validate the approach for a set of ISCAS combinational and sequential benchmark circuits. Simulation results show that the proposed test generation approach can be extremely effective for detecting arbitrary Trojan instances of small size, both combinational and sequential.

The rest of the chapter is organized as follows. Section 14.2 describes the mathematical justification of the MERO methodology, the steps of the MERO test generation algorithm and the Trojan detection coverage estimation. Section 14.3 describes the simulation setup and presents results for a set of ISCAS benchmark circuits with detailed analysis. Section 14.4 concludes the chapter.

14.2   Statistical Approach for Trojan Detection

As described in Section 14.1, the main concept of our test generation approach is based on generating test vectors that can excite candidate trigger nodes individually to their rare logic values multiple (at least N) times. In effect, the probability of activation of a Trojan by the simultaneous occurrence of the rare conditions at its trigger nodes increases. As an example, consider the Trojan shown in Fig. 13.5(a). Assume that the conditions $a = 0$, $b = 1$ and $c = 1$ are very rare. Hence, if we can generate a set of test vectors that induce these rare conditions at these nodes individually N times where N is sufficiently large, then a Trojan with triggering condition composed jointly of these nodes is highly likely to be activated by the application of this test set. The concept can be extended to sequential Trojans, as shown in Fig. 13.5(b), where the inserted 3-bit counter is clocked on the simultaneous occurrence of the condition $ab' = 1$. If the test vectors can sensitize these nodes such that the condition

$ab' = 1$ is satisfied at least 8 times (the maximum number of states of a 3-bit counter), then the Trojan would be activated. Next, we present a mathematical analysis to justify the concept.

14.2.1 Mathematical Analysis

Without loss of generality, assume that a Trojan is triggered by the rare logic values at two nodes A and B, with corresponding probability of occurrence p_1 and p_2. Assume T to be the total number of vectors applied to the circuit under test, such that both A and B have been individually excited to their rare values *at least* N times. Then, the expected number of occurrences of the rare logic values at nodes A and B are given by $E_A = T \cdot p_1 \geq N$ and $E_B = T \cdot p_2 \geq N$, which lead to:

$$T \geq \frac{N}{p_1} \quad \text{and} \quad T \geq \frac{N}{p_2} \tag{14.1}$$

Now, let p_j be the probability of simultaneous occurrence of the rare logic values at nodes A and B, an event that acts as the trigger condition for the Trojan. Then, the expected number of occurrences of this event when T vectors are applied is:

$$E_{AB} = p_j \cdot T \tag{14.2}$$

In the context of this problem, we can assume $p_j > 0$, because an adversary is unlikely to insert a Trojan which would never be triggered. Then, to ensure that the Trojan is triggered at least once when T test vectors are applied, the following condition must be satisfied:

$$p_j \cdot T \geq 1 \tag{14.3}$$

From inequality (14.1), let us assume $T = c \cdot \frac{N}{p_1}$. where $c \geq 1$ is a constant depending on the actual test set applied. Inequality (14.3) can then be generalized as:

$$S = c \cdot \frac{p_j}{p_1} \cdot N \tag{14.4}$$

where S denotes the number of times the trigger condition is satisfied during the test procedure. From this equation, the following observations can be made about the interdependence of S and N:

1. For given parameters c, p_1 and p_j, S is proportional to N, i.e. the expected number of times the Trojan trigger condition is satisfied increases with the number of times the trigger nodes have been individually excited to their rare values. This observation forms the main motivation behind the MERO test generation approach for Trojan detection.

2. If there are q trigger nodes and if they are assumed to be mutually independent, then $p_j = p_1 \cdot p_2 \cdot p_3 \cdots p_q$, which leads to:

$$S = c \cdot N \cdot \prod_{i=2}^{q} p_i \tag{14.5}$$

As $p_i < 1 \quad \forall i = 1, 2, \cdots q$, hence, with the increase in q, S decreases for a given c and N. In other words, with the increase in the number of trigger nodes, it becomes more difficult to satisfy the trigger condition of the inserted Trojan for a given N. Even if the nodes are not mutually independent, a similar dependence of S on q is expected.

Algorithm 14.1: Procedure MERO

Generate reduced test pattern set for Trojan detection

Inputs: Circuit netlist, list of rare nodes (L) with associated rare values, list of random patterns (V), number of times a rare condition should be satisfied (N)

Outputs: Reduced pattern set (R_V)

```
 1: Read circuit and generate hypergraph
 2: for all nodes in L do
 3:     set number of times node satisfies rare value (A_R) to 0
 4: end for
 5: set R_V = Φ
 6: for all random pattern in V do
 7:     Propagate values
 8:     Count the # of nodes (C_R) in L with their rare value satisfied
 9: end for
10: Sort vectors in V in decreasing order of C_R
11: for all vector v_i in decreasing order of C_R do
12:     for all bit in v_i do
13:         Perturb the bit and re-compute # of satisfied rare values (C'_R)
14:         if (C'_R > C_R) then
15:             Accept the perturbation and form v'_i from v_i
16:         end if
17:     end for
18:     Update A_R for all nodes in L due to vector v_i
19:     if v'_i increases A_R for at least one rare node then
20:         Add the modified vector v'_i to R_V
21:     end if
22:     if (A_R ≥ N) for all nodes in L then
23:         break
24:     end if
25: end for
```

---

3. The trigger nodes can be chosen such that $p_i \leq \theta \quad \forall i = 1, 2, \cdots q$, so that θ is defined as a *trigger threshold* probability. Then as θ increases, the corresponding selected rare node probabilities are also likely to increase. This will result in an increase in S for a given T and N, i.e. the probability of Trojan activation would increase if the individual nodes are more likely to get triggered to their rare values.

All of the above predicted trends were observed in our simulations, as shown in Section 14.3.

14.2.2   Test Generation

Algorithm 14.1 shows the major steps in the proposed reduced test set generation process for Trojan detection. We start with the golden circuit netlist (without any Trojan), a random pattern set (V), list of rare nodes (L) and number of times to activate each node to its rare value (N). First, the circuit netlist is read and mapped to a *hypergraph*. For each node in L, we initialize the number of times a node encounters a rare value (A_R) to 0. Next, for each random pattern v_i in V, we count the number of nodes (C_R) in L whose rare value is satisfied. We sort the random patterns in decreasing order of C_R. In the next step, we consider each vector in the sorted list and modify it by perturbing one bit at a time. If a modified test pattern increases the number of nodes satisfying their rare values, we accept the pattern in the reduced pattern list. In this step we consider only those rare nodes with $A_R < N$. The process repeats until each node in L satisfies its rare value at least N times. The output of the test generation process is a minimal test set that improves the coverage for both combinational and sequential Trojans compared to random patterns.

14.2.3 Coverage Estimation

Once the reduced test vector set has been obtained, computation of Trigger and Trojan coverage can be performed for a given *trigger threshold* (θ) (as defined in Section 14.2.1) and a given number of trigger nodes (q) using a random sampling approach. From the Trojan population, we randomly select a number of q-trigger Trojans, where each trigger node has signal probability less than equal θ. We assume that the Trojans comprised of trigger nodes with higher signal probability than θ will be detected by conventional test. From the set of sampled Trojans, Trojans with false trigger conditions which cannot be justified with any input pattern are eliminated. Then, the circuit is simulated for each vector in the given vector set and checked whether the trigger condition is satisfied. For an activated Trojan, if its effect can be observed at the primary output or scan flip-flop input, the Trojan is considered "covered", i.e. detected. The percentages of Trojans activated and detected constitute the *trigger coverage* and *Trojan coverage*, respectively.

14.2.4 Choice of Trojan Sample Size

In any random sampling process an important decision is to select the sample size in a manner that represents the population reasonably well. In the context of Trojan detection, it means further increase in sampled Trojans, renders negligible change in the estimated converge. Fig. 14.1 shows a plot of percentage deviation of Trigger and Trojan coverage ($q = 4$) from the asymptotic value for two benchmark circuits with varying Trojan sample size. From the plots, we observe that the coverage saturates with nearly 100,000 samples, as the percentage deviation tends to zero. To compromise between accuracy of estimated coverage and simulation time, we have selected a sample size of 100,000 in our simulations.

14.2.5 Choice of N

Fig. 14.2 shows the trigger and Trojan coverage for two ISCAS-85 benchmark circuits with increasing values of N, along with the lengths of the corresponding test-set. From these plots it is clear that similar to *N-detect* tests for stuck-at fault where defect coverage typically improves with increasing N, the trigger and Trojan coverage obtained with the MERO approach also improves steadily with N, but then both saturate around $N = 200$ and remain nearly constant for larger values of N. As expected, the test size also increases with increasing N. We chose a value of $N = 1000$ for most of our experiments to reach a balance between coverage and test vector set size.

14.2.6 Improving Trojan Detection Coverage

As noted in previous sections, Trojan detection using logic testing involves simultaneous triggering of the Trojan and the propagation of its effect to output nodes. Although the proposed test generation algorithm increases the probability of Trojan activation, it does not explicitly target increasing the probability of a malicious effect at payload being observable. MERO test patterns, however, achieve significant improvement in Trojan coverage compared to random patterns, as shown in Section 14.3. This is because the Trojan coverage has strong correlation with trigger coverage. To increase the Trojan coverage further, one can use the following low-overhead approaches:

1. *Improvement of test quality*: We can consider number of nodes observed along with number of nodes triggered for each vector during test generation. This means, at step 13-14 of Algorithm 14.1, a perturbation is accepted if the sum of triggered and

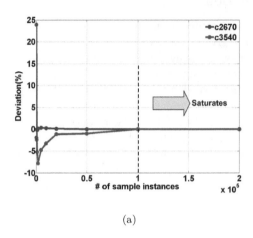

(a)

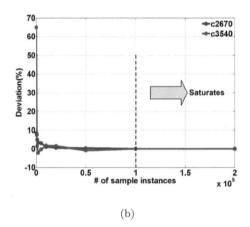

(b)

FIGURE 14.1: Impact of sample size on trigger and Trojan coverage for benchmarks c2670 and c3540, $N = 1000$ and $q = 4$: (a) deviation of trigger coverage, and (b) deviation of Trojan coverage.

observed nodes improves over previous value. This comes at extra computational cost to determine the number of observable nodes for each vector. We note that for a small ISCAS benchmark c432 (an interrupt controller), we can improve the Trojan coverage by 6.5% with negligible reduction in trigger coverage using this approach.

2. *Observable test point insertion*: We note that insertion of very few observable test points can achieve significant improvement in Trojan coverage at the cost of small design overhead. Existing algorithm for selecting observable test points for stuck-at fault test [130] can be used here. Our simulation with c432 resulted in about 4% improvement in Trojan coverage with 5 judiciously inserted observable points.

3. *Increasing N and/or increasing the controllability of the internal nodes*: Internal node controllability can be increased by judiciously inserting few controllable test points or increasing N. It is well-known in the context of stuck-at ATPG, that scan insertion improves both controllability and observability of internal nodes. Hence, the proposed

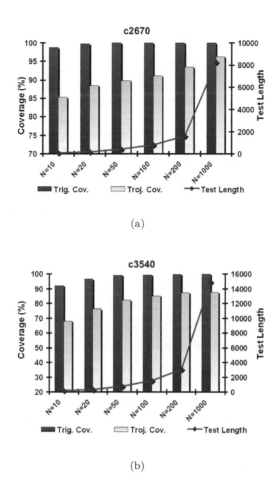

FIGURE 14.2: Impact of N (number of times a rare point satisfies its rare value) on the trigger/Trojan coverage and test length for benchmarks (a) c2670 and (b) c3540.

approach can take advantage of low-overhead design modifications to increase the effectiveness of Trojan detection.

14.3 Results

14.3.1 Simulation Setup

The test generation and the Trojan coverage determination methodology was implemented in three separate C programs. All the three programs can read a Verilog netlist and create a *hypergraph* from the netlist description. The first program, named as *RO-Finder* (**R**are **O**ccurence **Finder**), is capable of functionally simulating a netlist for a given set of input patterns, computing the signal probability at each node and identifying nodes with low signal probability as rare nodes. The second program, MERO implements Algorithm

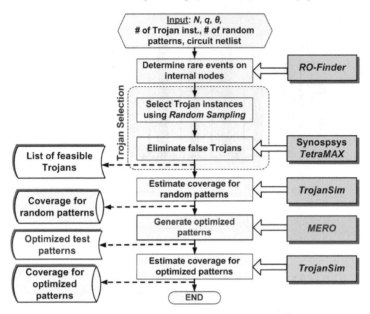

FIGURE 14.3: Integrated framework for rare occurrence determination, test generation using MERO approach, and Trojan simulation.

TABLE 14.1: Comparison of Trigger and Trojan Coverage Among ATPG Patterns [246], Random (100K, input weights: 0.5), and MERO Patterns for $q = 2$ and $q = 4$, $N = 1000$, $\theta = 0.2$

Circuit	Nodes (Rare/ Total)	ATPG Patterns				Random (100K Patterns)				MERO Patterns			
		q = 2		q = 4		q = 2		q = 4		q = 2		q = 4	
		Trigger Cov. (%)	Trojan Cov. (%)	Trigger Cov. (%)	Trojan Cov. (%)	Trigger Cov. (%)	Trojan Cov. (%)	Trigger Cov. (%)	Trojan Cov. (%)	Trigger Cov. (%)	Trojan Cov. (%)	Trigger Cov. (%)	Trojan Cov. (%)
c2670	297/1010	93.97	58.38	30.7	10.48	98.66	53.81	92.56	30.32	100.00	96.33	99.90	90.17
c3540	580/1184	77.87	52.09	16.07	8.78	99.61	86.5	90.46	69.48	99.81	86.14	87.34	64.88
c5315	817/2485	92.06	63.42	19.82	8.75	99.97	93.58	98.08	79.24	99.99	93.83	99.06	78.83
c6288	199/2448	55.16	50.32	3.28	2.92	100.00	98.95	99.91	97.81	100.00	98.94	92.50	89.88
c7552	1101/3720	82.92	66.59	20.14	11.72	98.25	94.69	91.83	83.45	99.38	96.01	95.01	84.47
s13207‡	865/2504	82.41	73.84	27.78	27.78	100	95.37	88.89	83.33	100.00	94.68	94.44	88.89
s15850‡	959/3004	25.06	20.46	3.80	2.53	94.20	88.75	48.10	37.98	95.91	92.41	79.75	68.35
s35932‡	970/6500	87.06	79.99	35.9	33.97	100.00	93.56	100.00	96.80	100.00	93.56	100.00	96.80
Avg.	**724/2857**	**74.56**	**58.14**	**19.69**	**13.37**	**98.84**	**88.15**	**88.73**	**72.30**	**99.39**	**93.99**	**93.50**	**82.78**

‡These sequential benchmarks were run with 10,000 random Trojan instances to reduce run time of *Tetramax*

14.1 described in Section 14.2.2 to generate the reduced pattern set for Trojan detection. The third program, *TrojanSim* (**Trojan Sim**ulator), is capable of determining both Trigger and Trojan coverage for a given test set using random sample of Trojan instances. A q-trigger random Trojan instance is created by randomly selecting the trigger nodes from the list of rare nodes. We consider one randomly selected payload node for each Trojan. Fig. 14.3 shows the flowchart for the MERO methodology. Synopsys *TetraMAX* was used to justify the trigger condition for each Trojan and eliminate the false Trojans. All simulations and test generation were carried out on a Hewlett-Packard Linux workstation with a 2 GHz dual-core processor and 2GB main memory.

14.3.2   Comparison with Random and ATPG Patterns

Table 14.1 lists the trigger and Trojan coverage results for a set of combinational (ISCAS-85) and sequential (ISCAS-89) benchmarks using stuck-at ATPG patterns (generated using

TABLE 14.2: Reduction in Test Length by MERO Approach Compared to 100K Random Patterns and Associated Runtime, $q = 2$, N=1000, θ=0.2

Ckt.	MERO Test Length	% Reduction	Run-time (s)
c2670	8254	**91.75**	30051.53
c3540	14947	**85.05**	9403.11
c5315	10276	**89.72**	80241.52
c6288	5014	**94.99**	15716.42
c7552	12603	**87.40**	160783.37
s13207[†]	26926	**73.07**	23432.04
s15850[†]	32775	**67.23**	39689.63
s35932[†]	5480	**94.52**	29810.49
Avg.	**14534**	**85.47**	**48641.01**

[†]These sequential benchmarks were run with 10,000 random Trojan instances to reduce run time of *Tetramax*

the algorithm in [246]), weighted random patterns and MERO test patterns. It also lists the number of total nodes in the circuit and the number of rare nodes identified by *RO-Finder* tool based on signal probability. The signal probabilities were estimated through simulations with a set of 100,000 random vectors. For the sequential circuits, we assume full-scan implementation. We consider 100,000 random instances of Trojans following the sampling policy described in Section 14.2.4, with one randomly selected payload node for each Trojan. Coverage results are provided in each case for two different trigger point count, $q = 2$ and $q = 4$, at $N = 1000$ and $\theta = 0.2$.

Table 14.2 compares reduction in the length of the testset generated by the MERO test generation method with 100,000 random patterns, along with the corresponding run-times for the test generation algorithm. This run-time includes the execution time for *Tetramax* to validate 100,000 random Trojan instances, as well as time to determine the coverage by logic simulation. We can make the following important observations from these two tables:

1. The stuck-at ATPG patterns provide poor trigger and Trojan coverage compared to MERO patterns. The increase in coverage between the ATPG and MERO patterns is more significant in the case of higher number of trigger points.

2. From Table 14.2, it is evident that the reduced pattern with N=1000 and $\theta = 0.2$ provides comparable trigger coverage with significant reduction in test length. The average improvement in test length for the circuits considered is about 85%.

3. Trojan coverage is consistently smaller compared to trigger coverage. This is because in order to detect a Trojan by applying an input pattern, besides satisfying the trigger condition, one needs to propagate the logic error at the payload node to one or more primary outputs. In many cases although the trigger condition is satisfied, the malicious effect does not propagate to outputs. Hence, the Trojan remains triggered but undetected.

14.3.3 Effect of Number of Trigger Points (q)

The impact of q on coverage is evident from the Fig. 14.4, which shows the decreasing trigger and Trojan coverage with the increasing number of trigger points for two combinational benchmark circuits. This trend is expected from the analysis of Section 14.2.1. Our use of *TetraMAX* for justification and elimination of the false triggers helped to improve the Trojan coverage.

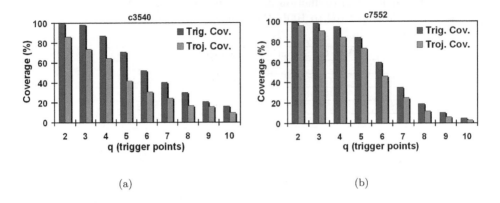

FIGURE 14.4: Trigger and Trojan coverage with varying number of trigger points (q) for benchmarks (a) c3540 and (b) c7552, at $N = 1000$, $\theta = 0.2$.

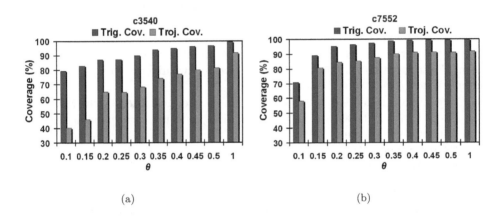

FIGURE 14.5: Trigger and Trojan coverage with *trigger threshold* (θ) for benchmarks (a) c3540 and (b) c7552, for $N = 1000$, $q = 4$.

14.3.4   Effect of Trigger Threshold (θ)

Fig. 14.5 plots the trigger and Trojan coverage with increasing θ for two ISCAS-85 benchmarks, at $N = 1000$ and $q = 4$. As we can observe, the coverage values improve steadily with increasing θ while saturating at a value above 0.20 in both the cases. The improvement in coverage with θ is again consistent with the conclusions from the analysis of Section 14.2.1.

14.3.5   Sequential Trojan Detection

To investigate the effectiveness of the MERO test generation methodology in detecting sequential Trojans, we designed and inserted sequential Trojans modeled following Fig. 13.5(b), with 0, 2, 4, 8, 16 and 32 states, respectively (the case with zero states refers to a combinational Trojan following the model of Fig. 13.5(a)). A cycle-accurate simulation was performed by our simulator *TrojanSim*, and the Trojan was considered detectable only when the output of the golden circuit and the infected circuit did not match. Table 14.3

TABLE 14.3: Comparison of Sequential Trojan Coverage between Random (100K) and MERO Patterns, $N = 1000$, $\theta = 0.2$, $q = 2$

Ckt.	Trigger Cov. for 100K Random Vectors (%)						Trigger Cov. for MERO Vectors (%)					
	Trojan State Count						Trojan State Count					
	0	2	4	8	16	32	0	2	4	8	16	32
s13207	100.00	100.00	99.77	99.31	99.07	98.38	100.00	100.00	99.54	99.54	98.84	97.92
s15850	94.20	91.99	86.79	76.64	61.13	48.59	95.91	95.31	94.03	91.90	87.72	79.80
s35932	100.00	100.00	100.00	100.00	100.00	100.00	100.00	100.00	100.00	100.00	100.00	100.00
Avg.	**98.07**	**97.33**	**95.52**	**91.98**	**86.73**	**82.32**	**98.64**	**98.44**	**97.86**	**97.15**	**95.52**	**92.57**

Ckt.	Trojan Cov. for 100K Random Vectors (%)						Trojan Cov. for MERO Vectors (%)					
	Trojan State Count						Trojan State Count					
	0	2	4	8	16	32	0	2	4	8	16	32
s13207	95.37	95.37	95.14	94.91	94.68	93.98	94.68	94.68	94.21	94.21	93.52	92.82
s15850	88.75	86.53	81.67	72.89	58.4	46.97	92.41	91.99	90.62	88.75	84.23	76.73
s35932	93.56	93.56	93.56	93.56	93.56	93.56	93.56	93.56	93.56	93.56	93.56	93.56
Avg.	**92.56**	**91.82**	**90.12**	**87.12**	**82.21**	**78.17**	**93.55**	**93.41**	**92.80**	**92.17**	**90.44**	**87.70**

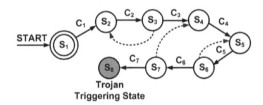

FIGURE 14.6: FSM model with no loop in state transition graph.

presents the trigger and Trojan coverage respectively obtained by 100,000 randomly generated test vectors and the MERO approach for three large ISCAS-89 benchmark circuits. The superiority of the MERO approach over the random test vector generation approach in detecting sequential Trojans is evident from this table.

Although these results have been presented for a specific type of sequential Trojans (counters which increase their count conditionally), they are representative of other sequential Trojans whose state transition graph (STG) has no "loop". The STG for such a FSM has been shown in Fig. 14.6. This is a 8-state FSM which changes its state only when a particular internal node condition C_i is satisfied at state S_i, and the Trojan is triggered when the FSM reaches state S_8. The example Trojan shown in Fig. 13.5(b) is a special case of this model, where the conditions C_1 through C_8 are identical. If each of the conditions C_i is as rare as the condition $a = 1, b = 0$ required by the Trojan shown in Fig. 13.5(b), then there is no difference between these two Trojans as far as their rareness of getting triggered is concerned. Hence, we can expect similar coverage and test length results for other sequential Trojans of this type. However, the coverage may change if the FSM structure is changed (as shown with dotted line). In this case, the coverage can be controlled by changing N.

### 14.3.6	Application to Side-channel Analysis

As observed from the results presented in this section, the MERO approach can achieve high trigger coverage for both combinational and sequential Trojans. This essentially means that the MERO patterns will induce activity in the Trojan triggering circuitry with high probability. A minimal set of patterns that is highly likely to cause activity in a Trojan is attractive in power or current signature-based side-channel approach to detect hardware Trojan. The detection sensitivity in these approaches depends on the induced activity in the Trojan circuit by applied test vector. It is particularly important to enhance sensitivity for the Trojans where the leakage contribution to power by the Trojan circuit can be easily masked by process or measurement noise. Hence, MERO approach can be extended to generate test vectors for side-channel analysis, which requires amplifying the Trojan impact on side-channel parameter such as power or current.

## 14.4	Conclusions

Conventional logic test generation techniques cannot be readily extended to detect hardware Trojans because of the inordinately large number of possible Trojan instances. In this chapter, we have presented a statistical Trojan detection approach using logic testing where the concept of multiple excitation of rare logic values at internal nodes is used to generate test patterns. Simulation results show that the proposed test generation approach achieves about 85% reduction in test length over random patterns for comparable or better Trojan detection coverage. The proposed detection approach can be extremely effective for small combinational and sequential Trojans with small number of trigger nodes, for which side-channel analysis approaches cannot work reliably. Hence, the proposed detection approach can be used as complementary to side-channel analysis based detection schemes. Future work can be directed towards improving the test quality which will help in minimizing the test length and increasing Trojan coverage further.

Chapter 15

Side-channel Analysis Techniques for Hardware Trojans Detection

- *"Cyber is a complicated domain. There is no sliver bullet that will eliminate the threats inherent to leveraging cyber as a force multiplier, and it is impossible to completely defend against the most sophisticated cyber attacks."*

James R. Gosler and Lewis von Thaer
"TASK FORCE REPORT: Resilient Military Systems and the Advanced Cyber Threat"

15.1   Introduction

In Chapter-14, we saw an example of the application of logic testing in detecting hardware Trojans. However, it was mentioned and shown that such a technique, while effective for simple and ultra-small Trojan circuits (consisting of a few gates) with simple trigger conditions, generally finds its difficult to effectively detect larger Trojans with complex trigger conditions. In addition, logic testing based techniques are simply unable to detect Trojans which do not affect the logic functionality of the original circuit.

An alternative to logic technique is to apply techniques which rely on detecting the variations in the measurement of observable physical "side-channel" parameters like power signature [23, 38, 308, 309] or delay [167, 310] of an IC in order to identify a structural change in the design. Such approaches have the advantage that they do not require triggering a malicious change and observing its impact at the primary output. The major disadvantage is in terms of the extensive process variations which can cause extreme variations in the measured side-channel parameter e.g. 20X power and 30% delay variations in 180 nm technology [60]. Existing side-channel approaches suffer from one or more of the following shortcomings: 1) they do not scale well with increasing process variations; 2) they consider only die-to-die process variations and do not consider local within-die variations; and 3) they require design modifications which can potentially be compromised by an adversary. The detection sensitivity degrades with increasing parameter variations or decreasing Trojan size. Besides, effect of process variations is augmented by measurement noise (electrical and environmental) which makes isolation of a Trojan effect further difficult.

In this chapter, we propose two novel techniques for side-channel parameter analysis based Trojan detection that are effective under large process-induced noise and parameter variations. The first technique is a multiple-parameter based side-channel analysis based approach for effective detection of complex Trojans under large process-induced parameter variations. The concept takes its inspiration from multiple-parameter testing [191], which considers the correlation of the intrinsic leakage (I_{DDQ}) to the maximum operating frequency (F_{max}) of the circuit in order to increase the sensitivity of I_{DDQ} testing to distinguish fast, intrinsically leaky ICs from defective ones. The basic idea is to exploit the intrinsic dependencies of variations in the supply current and operating frequency on process variations to identify the ICs affected with malicious hardware in a non-invasive manner. Instead of using only the power signature (which is highly vulnerable to parameter variations [23, 60]), the proposed side-channel approach achieves high signal-to-noise ratio (SNR) using the intrinsic dependencies between active-mode supply current (I_{DDT}) and maximum operating frequency (F_{max}) of a circuit to identify the ICs affected with malicious hardware in a non-invasive manner. We provide a theoretical analysis regarding the effect of various components of process variations on the relationship between the parameters. The proposed approach requires no modification to the design flow and incurs no hardware overhead.

In this chapter, we propose a Trojan detection technique using region-based side-channel analysis where the effect of Trojan compared to the effect of process noise is magnified by using a suitable vector generation algorithm. The vector generation approach can selectively activate one region at a time while minimizing activity in other regions of the circuit under test (CUT). Assuming that the effect of the Trojan on the side-channel parameter will manifest itself only on the measured value for a single region, we can use the measurements from other regions as the golden comparison point to identify the presence of a Trojan within that region. By decreasing the golden current for comparison, the sensitivity of Trojan detection can be increased using partitions which have mutually exclusive activity for the chosen vector set. The test vectors can also be designed [81] to increase the activity in parts of the Trojan circuit, even if the Trojan's malicious output does not get generated or propagated to the primary outputs during the testing process. Besides, we propose a novel side-channel analysis approach which we refer as *self-referencing*. The concept is to decompose a large design into a group of functional blocks, and then consider one functional block at a time to determine the existence of Trojan using only transient supply current (I_{DDT}) measurement. Next, we will use a *Region Slope Matrix* to compare the current values of different regions and reduce the effect of process variations. Any effect due to the presence of a Trojan is reflected in the matrix values and helps identify the infected chips from the golden chips, even under process variations. The method can also be used to localize the Trojan and identify the region in which it is present.

15.2   Motivation for the Proposed Approaches

Most side-channel analysis based techniques concentrate on minimization of the "background signal level" or equivalently maximization of the Trojan signal level [39], characterization and elimination of the experimental noise [23], or characterization of the measurement port transfer function [308] to accurately extract the side-channel information. Moreover, none of the proposed techniques considers simultaneous elimination of the effects of "inter-die" or global process variation (the variation between different ICs), as well as "intra-die" or local process variation (the variation in the same IC) on the measured parameter. The main motivation behind the proposed approaches is the development of a side-channel analysis based Trojan detection technique which systematically eliminates both global and local process variation effects. To achieve this, we measure multiple side-channel parameters from the population of untrusted ICs and compare their values with the golden trend line, obtained by measurement followed by destructive testing of a few ICs or from extensive simulations and parametric testing. Since the different side-channel parameters are similarly affected by process variation effects, they can be used to identify whether the deviation from golden nominal values are caused due to process effect or due to presence of Trojan circuit which affects the parameters in a completely different manner. We argue theoretically that it is impossible for the attacker to mimic the trend due to process variations when inserting the Trojan in order to make it undetectable by this approach. Using techniques to increase the sensitivity of Trojan detection for ultra-small Trojans which produce imperceptible change

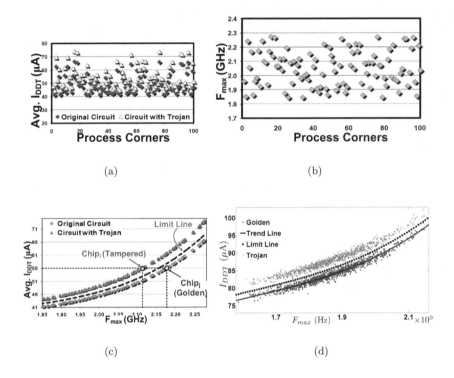

FIGURE 15.1: (a) Average I_{DDT} values at 100 random process corners (with maximum variation of $\pm 20\%$ in inter-die V_{th}) for c880 circuit. The impact of Trojan (8-bit comparator) in I_{DDT} is masked by process noise. (b) Corresponding F_{max} values. (c) The F_{max} vs. I_{DDT} plot shows the relationship between these parameters under inter-die process variations. Trojan-inserted chips stand out from the golden trend line. (d) The approach remains effective under both inter-die and random intra-die process variations. A limit line is used to account for the spread in I_{DDT} values from the golden trend line.

in the side-channel parameters amidst process noise, we demonstrate that the use of this novel multiple-parameter approach allows higher detection sensitivity compared to existing side-channel Trojan detection approaches.

15.3   Multiple-parameter Analysis based Trojan Detection

In order to use side-channel analysis for Trojan detection, we need to distinguish between the Trojan contribution and process noise by comparing the side-channel information for the golden and the untrusted ICs. However, the effect of process variations on F_{max} and I_{DDT} can mask the effect due to a Trojan circuit. Average I_{DDT} and F_{max} results for an 8-bit ALU circuit (c880 from ISCAS-85 benchmark suite) are plotted in Fig. 15.1(a) and Fig. 15.1(b) for 100 chips which lie at different process corners, assuming only die-to-die or *inter-die* variations in transistor threshold voltage (V_{th}), where all transistors in a die experience similar variations. The effect of a combinational Trojan (8-bit comparator circuit) is only observed in the current; it does not affect the F_{max} because it is not inserted on the critical path of the circuit. The spread in I_{DDT} due to variation easily masks the effect of the Trojan, making it infeasible to isolate from process noise, as shown in Fig. 15.1(a). The problem becomes more severe with decreasing Trojan size or increasing variations in transistor parameters. To overcome this issue, the intrinsic relationship between I_{DDT} and F_{max} can be utilized to differentiate between the original and tampered versions. The plot for I_{DDT} vs. F_{max} for the ISCAS–85 circuit c880 is shown in Fig. 15.1(c). It can be observed that two chips (e.g. $Chip_i$ and $Chip_j$) can have the same I_{DDT} value, one due to presence of Trojan and the other due to process variation. By considering only one side-channel parameter, it is not possible to distinguish between these chips. However, the correlation between I_{DDT} and F_{max} can be used to distinguish malicious changes in a circuit under process noise. The presence of a Trojan will cause the chip to deviate from the trend line. As seen in Fig. 15.1(c), the presence of a Trojan causes a variation in I_{DDT} when compared to a golden chip, while it does not have similar effect on F_{max} as induced by process variation - i.e. the expected correlation between I_{DDT} and F_{max} is violated by the presence of the Trojan.

Note that in the proposed multiple-parameter approach, F_{max} is used for calibrating the process corner of the chips. In practice, the delay of any path in the circuit can be used for this purpose. Hence, it becomes difficult for an attacker to know in advance which path delay will be used for calibrating process noise. Since a typical design will have exponentially large number of paths, it is infeasible for an attacker to manipulate all circuit paths in order to hide the Trojan effect. Furthermore, even if the path is guessed by the attacker, a Trojan is likely to increase both delay and activity of the path on which it is inserted. Hence, a chip containing the Trojan will deviate from the expected I_{DDT} vs. F_{max} trend line, where both current and frequency increase or decrease simultaneously. Finally, in order to alter the F_{max} in a way that the Trojan evades multiple-parameter detection approach (i.e., it falls within the limit line in Fig. 15.1(c)), the adversary needs to know the exact magnitude of process variation for each path of each chip, which is difficult to estimate at fabrication time [60].

Fig. 15.1(d) shows the effect of random intra-die process variation effects on the I_{DDT} and F_{max} values for 1000 instances of the c880 circuit with and without Trojan. We performed Monte Carlo simulations in HSPICE using inter-die ($\sigma = 10\%$) and intra-die ($\sigma = 6\%$) variations in V_{th}. In this case, the transistors on the same die can have random variations on top of a common inter-die shift from the nominal process corner. The trend line is obtained by using polynomial curve fitting of order three in MATLAB, which matches the trend obtained by considering only inter-die process variation effects. We observe that there is a spread in the values from the trend line due to random intra-die variations, but the spread is much reduced in comparison to the spread in each side-channel parameter alone, because we consider the multiple-parameter relationship. By computing the spread in I_{DDT} values for a given F_{max}, corresponding to a particular inter-die process corner, we can estimate the *sensitivity* of the approach in terms of Trojan detection. Any Trojan which consumes current less than the amount of spread will remain undetected. The limit line is obtained by scaling the trend line by the spread factor, which is computed using the mean and standard deviation of the actual spread in I_{DDT} values for a given F_{max} for the sample of ICs and allows us to identify all the Trojan instances without any error, even for a small Trojan. Next, we provide a theoretical basis for the existence of a trend line between I_{DDT} and F_{max} under process variations.

15.3.1 Theoretical Analysis

The basic idea of the multiple-parameter approach is to exploit the correlated changes in I_{DDT} and F_{max} with process variations. For a short channel transistor, the ON current [344]

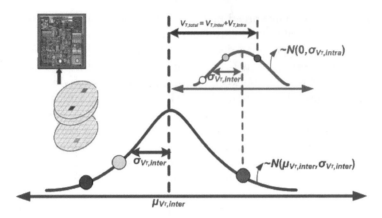

FIGURE 15.2: Effect of process variations on device threshold voltage in an IC.

of a switching gate can be expressed as:

$$I_g = k_g(V_{DD} - V_{th})^\alpha \tag{15.1}$$

where V_{DD} is the supply voltage, α is the *velocity saturation index* with $1 \leq \alpha \leq 2$, V_{th} is the transistor *threshold voltage*, and k_g is a gate-dependant constant. Consider the i-th IC from a lot of manufactured ICs.The effect of process variations can cause the threshold voltage to vary from die-to-die (Inter-die variations) or within-die (Intra-die variations). As shown in Fig. 15.2, if these variations are modelled using Gaussian distributions around the nominal threshold voltage of the process, the V_{th} of a transistor on a die can be expressed as the sum of the *nominal* threshold voltage (V_T), the *inter-die* component of variation (ΔV_{Ti}) for the i-th IC, and Δv_{Tg}, the *random* component of variation. The ΔV_{Ti} value is common for every device in the i-th IC, while the Δv_{Tg} value varies from gate to gate. Eqn. (15.1) can be re-written as:

$$I_g = k_g(V_{DD} - V_T - \Delta V_{Ti})^\alpha \left[1 - \frac{\Delta v_{Tg}}{V_{DD} - V_T - \Delta V_{Ti}}\right]^\alpha \tag{15.2}$$

Expanding binomially, assuming $\frac{\Delta v_{Tg}}{V_{DD} - V_T - \Delta V_{Ti}} \ll 1$ and discarding higher-order terms, the above equation can be approximated as:

$$I_g \approx (V_{DD} - V_T - \Delta V_{Ti})^\alpha [k_g - c_i \cdot k_g \cdot \Delta v_{Tg}] \tag{15.3}$$

where $c_i = \frac{\alpha}{V_{DD} - V_T - \Delta V_{Ti}}$ is a constant that depends on the IC being considered. Summing over all the switching gates in the IC, the total transient current of the i-th IC is given by:

$$I_{ddt,i} = \sum_{g \in IC_i} I_g \approx (V_{DD} - V_T - \Delta V_{Ti})^\alpha \left[k_{av}n_{tot,i} - c_i \sum_{g \in IC_i} k_g \Delta v_{Tg}\right] \tag{15.4}$$

where $k_{av} \cdot n_{tot,i} = \sum_{g \in IC_i} k_g$ and $n_{tot,i}$ is the total number of switching gates in the IC. The term $\sum_{g \in IC_i} k_g \Delta v_{Tg}$ represents the sum of several random variables, each distributed with mean $\mu = 0$ and variance (say) σ^2. Hence, by the *Central Limit Theorem* [291], their sum follows a Normal distribution with mean $\mu = 0$ and a reduced variance $\frac{\sigma^2}{n_{\text{tot,i}}}$, and is approximately zero. Hence, the above equation can be approximated by:

$$I_{\text{ddt,i}} \approx k_{av} \cdot n_{\text{tot,i}} \cdot (V_{DD} - V_T - \Delta V_{Ti})^\alpha \tag{15.5}$$

On the other hand, the gate delay can be expressed as:

$$t_{dg} = \beta_g (V_{DD} - V_{th})^{-\alpha} \tag{15.6}$$

where β_g is another gate-dependant constant. Applying the same approximations, the delay of the gate is given by:

$$t_{dg} \approx (V_{DD} - V_T - \Delta V_{Ti})^{-\alpha} [\beta_g + \beta_g c_i \Delta v_{Tg}] \tag{15.7}$$

Summing the delays for the gates on the critical path of the i-th IC:

$$T_{\text{crit,i}} = \sum_{g \in P_{\text{crit,i}}} t_{dg} \approx \beta_{av} \cdot n_{\text{crit,i}} \cdot (V_{DD} - V_T - \Delta V_{Ti})^{-\alpha} \tag{15.8}$$

where $n_{\text{crit,i}}$ is the number of gates on the critical path $P_{\text{crit,i}}$ of the i-th IC. Hence, the maximum operating frequency of the i-th IC is given by:

$$f_{\text{max,i}} = \frac{1}{T_{\text{crit,i}}} \approx \frac{1}{\beta_{av} n_{\text{crit,i}}} \cdot (V_{DD} - V_T - \Delta V_{Ti})^\alpha \tag{15.9}$$

Combining equations (15.5) and (15.9), the relationship between $I_{\text{ddt,i}}$ and $f_{\text{max,i}}$ is given by:

$$\frac{I_{\text{ddt,i}}}{f_{\text{max,i}}} \approx k_{av} \cdot \beta_{av} \cdot n_{\text{tot,i}} \cdot n_{\text{crit,i}} \tag{15.10}$$

This shows that the relationship between the transient switching current and the maximum operating frequency of an IC at different process corners is linear, based on first-order approximation. In the presence of a Trojan circuit in the i-th IC with $n_{\text{trojan,i}}$ switching gates, the value of the transient current changes to:

$$I_{\text{ddt,i,trojan}} \approx k_{av} \cdot (n_{\text{tot,i}} + n_{\text{trojan,i}}) \cdot (V_{DD} - V_T - \Delta V_{Ti})^\alpha, \tag{15.11}$$

while the expression for the maximum operating frequency remains unchanged, if the Trojan is not inserted on the critical path. Hence, for the i-th IC, in the presence of Trojan, the relationship between $I_{\text{ddt,i}}$ and $f_{\text{max,i}}$ changes to:

$$\frac{I_{\text{ddt,i,trojan}}}{f_{\text{max,i}}} \approx k_{av} \cdot \beta_{av} \cdot (n_{\text{tot,i}} + n_{\text{trojan,i}}) \cdot n_{\text{crit,i}} \tag{15.12}$$

Comparing equations (15.10) and (15.12), we observe that the primary effect of the inserted Trojan is the change in the slope of the linear relationship between the transient current and the maximum operating frequency in a tampered IC. From these two equations, we can observe that there is a strong correlation between dynamic current and circuit delay (which, for the critical path of the circuit, translates to maximum operating frequency or F_{max}) through the common parameter V_{th}. Due to process variation, if the current changes by V_{th} shift, frequency ($f = \frac{1}{t_d}$) also shifts in the same direction.

The I_{DDT} vs. F_{max} relationship for a Trojan-free design can be determined either at design time by simulation or by monitoring a number of golden ICs. Once the relationship is determined, we need to define the *limit line* that distinguishes variation-induced shift from Trojan-induced one. Judicious selection of the limit line should minimize the probability of false negatives as well as take into consideration other design marginalities (such as cross talk and power supply noise). Note that although F_{max} is a unique parameter and does not depend on the applied input vector, the average I_{DDT} is a function of the applied input vector, and hence, should be measured for a set of input vectors for each golden IC. A set of patterns that maximizes the activity in the Trojan circuit, while reducing the background current, is likely to provide the best signal-to-noise ratio.

15.3.2   Improving Detection Sensitivity

The minimum size of Trojan which can be detected by any side-channel approach, in particular for the multiple-parameter approach based on the choice of current and frequency measurements for a given amount of process noise is quantified by the detection sensitivity. In a single V_{th} (or F_{max}) point, the sensitivity can be expressed as:

$$Sensitivity = \frac{I_{tampered} - I_{original}}{I_{original}} \times 100\% \qquad (15.13)$$

from equations (15.5) and (15.11). The detection sensitivity of the proposed approach reduces with decreasing Trojan size and increasing circuit size. In order to extend the approach for detecting small sequential/combinational Trojans in large circuits (with $> 10^5$ transistors), we need to improve the SNR using appropriate side-channel isolation techniques. Clearly, the sensitivity can be improved by increasing the current contribution of the Trojan circuit relative to that of the original circuit. Next, we describe a test generation technique used to reduce $I_{original}$ and increase its difference from $I_{tampered}$.

15.3.2.1   Test Vector Selection

A complex circuit under test (CUT) is typically comprised of several functional modules, which are interconnected according to their input/output dependencies. Our test generation approach tries to maximize the contribution of Trojan circuit in supply current while minimizing the effect of background current. The technique also needs to ensure that the test set increases the activity in an arbitrary Trojan circuit. Fig. 15.3 illustrates the overall methodology for the proposed multiple-parameter based Trojan detection technique, along with the steps of the test vector generation algorithm [114], described later in this chapter.

The first step of the approach is to divide the circuit into several functional modules $\{M_I\}$. Sometimes, the circuit under test is designed with clearly-defined functional blocks which can be selectively activated by using control signals. An example of such a circuit which is amenable to simple functional decomposition is a pipelined processor, where the different pipeline stages correspond to the different regions. Any large functional block is furthered partitioned by *hypergraph partitioning*, which is used to identify partitions which have minimum cut-sets between them. This allows us to isolate the activity in one partition from causing activity in other regions. The region-based partitioning described in [38] can also be used for creating partitions in circuits which do not have well-defined functional blocks or for creating sub-blocks within a functional block. The decomposition should follow a set of properties to maximize the effectiveness of the approach:

1. The blocks should be reasonably large to cancel out the effect of random parameter variations, but small enough to minimize the background current.

2. The blocks should be functionally as independent of each other as possible so that the test generation process can increase the activity of one block (or few blocks) while minimizing the activity of all others.

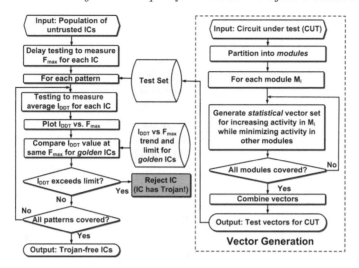

FIGURE 15.3: Major steps in the multiple-parameter Trojan detection approach.

Next, we consider each module separately to generate test vectors for activating it. The test vector generation algorithm needs to take into account two factors:

1. Only one region must be activated at a time. If the inputs to different modules are mutually exclusive and the regions have minimal interconnection, it is easy to maximally activate one region while minimizing activity in other regions. If complex interconnections exist between the modules, the inputs need to be ranked in terms of their sensitivity towards activating different modules and the test generation needs to be aware of these sensitivity values.

2. When a particular region is being activated, the test vectors should try to activate possible Trojan trigger conditions and should be aimed at creating activity within most of the innumerable possible Trojans. This motivates us to consider a modified version of the statistical test generation approach (*MERO*) proposed in [81] for maximizing Trojan trigger coverage. Note that, unlike functional testing approaches, the Trojan payload need not be affected during test time, and the observability of Trojan effect on the side-channel parameter is enough to signify the presence of the Trojan.

For each module M_i, we use connectivity analysis in order to assign weights to the primary inputs in terms of their tendency to maximize activity in the region under consideration while minimizing activity in other regions. This step can also identify control signals which can direct the activity exclusively to particular regions. Next, we generate weighted random input vectors for activating the region under consideration and perform functional simulation using a graph-based approach, which lets us estimate the activity within each region for each pair of input vectors. We sort the vectors based on a metric C_{ij} which is higher for a vector pair which can maximally activate module M_i while minimizing activity in each of the other modules. Then, we prune the vector set to choose a reduced but highly efficient vector set generated by the *MERO* algorithm, which is motivated by the N-detect test generation technique [31]. In this approach, we identify internal nodes with rare values within each module, which can be candidate trigger signals for a Trojan. Then we identify the subset of vectors which can take the rare nodes within the module to their rare values at least N times, thus increasing the possibility of triggering the Trojans within the region. Once this process is completed for all the regions, we combine the vectors and generate a test suite which can be applied to each chip for measuring supply current corresponding to each of its regions.

For a functional test of a multi-core processor, we can use specially designed small test programs which are likely to trigger and observe rare events in the system such as events on the memory control line or most significant bits of the datapath, multiple times. In general a design is composed of several functional blocks and activity in several functional blocks can be turned off using input conditions. For example in a processor, activity in the floating point unit (FPU), branch logic or memory peripheral logic can be turned off by selecting an integer ALU operation. Many functional blocks are pipelined. In these cases, we will focus on one stage at a time and provide initialization to the pipeline such that the activities of all stages other than the one under test are minimized by ensuring that the corresponding stage inputs do not change.

For each IC from a population of untrusted ICs, the dynamic current (I_{DDT}) values are collected for a pre-defined set of test vectors, which are generated with the vector generation algorithm. The operating frequencies (F_{max}) for these ICs are determined using structural or functional delay testing approach. Next, average I_{DDT} vs. F_{max} measurements for the untrusted ICs are compared against that of a golden IC for each test pattern. A mismatch between the two allows us to identify a Trojan by effectively removing the contribution of process noise.

15.3.2.2 Power Gating and Operand Isolation

Complex designs are typically modular and comprise of several independent functional modules. To prevent unwanted switching of logic elements, low-power designs conventionally use power gating techniques such as *clock gating, supply gating* or *operand isolation*. We propose to employ the already-existing power gating controls to improve Trojan detection sensitivity by reducing $I_{original}$, without introducing any modifications to the design. Similar to power gating, one can also use Operand Isolation techniques to suppress activity in one part of the circuit, when activating other blocks. These approaches are supplementary to the test vector generation technique described earlier and are applicable to circuits in which the region-based test generation is not very effective. We applied these techniques to the Advanced Encryption Standard (AES) circuit, as described in Fig. 15.4. The module inside the CUT for which Trojan detection is being carried out is kept active, and most

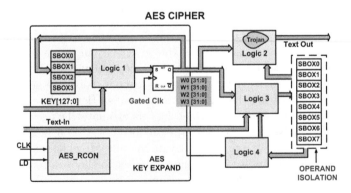

FIGURE 15.4: Schematic showing the functional modules of the AES cipher test circuit. The AES "Key Expand" module is clock-gated and operand isolation is applied to the "SBOX" modules to reduce the background current, thereby improving detection sensitivity. The Trojan instance is assumed to be in the logic block 2.

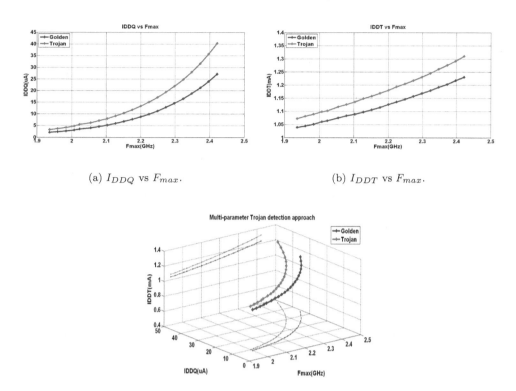

(a) I_{DDQ} vs F_{max}.

(b) I_{DDT} vs F_{max}.

(c) 3-D plot of I_{DDQ}, I_{DDT} and F_{max}.

FIGURE 15.5: The correlation among I_{DDT}, I_{DDQ} and F_{max} can be used to improve Trojan detection confidence.

other modules can be power gated. It should be noted that depending on the functionality of the CUT, it might not be always possible to switch-off certain units whose outputs feed other dependent modules. Thus, when testing for Trojan in module 4, we cannot shut off the modules 1 and 3 that affect the controllability (and hence the activity) of the internal nodes in 4. One major concern against using power gating is that if we introduce power gating during test-time as a method to increase our Trojan detection sensitivity, the attacker can use these control signals to disable the Trojan during test time. Note that the adversary should not be able to exploit the sensitivity improvement techniques to reduce the Trojan contribution during testing. However, in this case, it is difficult for the adversary to distinguish between the normal functional mode and Trojan detection mode, since the decision about which blocks are turned-off or biased is taken dynamically. Hence, the attacker cannot use the power gating techniques to reduce the current contribution of the inserted Trojan.

15.3.2.3 Use of Other Side-channel Parameters

It should be noted that various measurable parameters can be used for multiple-parameter side-channel-based Trojan detection where at least one parameter is affected by the Trojan and other parameters are used to calibrate the process noise. Besides I_{DDT} and F_{max}, other circuit parameters such as quiescent or leakage current (I_{DDQ}) can also be used to increase the confidence level. Apart from contributing to the dynamic current

(I_{DDT}), a Trojan will also contribute to the leakage current (I_{DDQ}). Moreover, similar to I_{DDT}, the value of I_{DDQ} increases monotonically with the F_{max} for a given design from one process corner to another. Thus any decision derived from studying the I_{DDT} vs. F_{max} relation can be reinforced by observing the I_{DDQ} vs. F_{max} relation for the same set of ICs. For example, if one of the ICs is observed to have considerably larger I_{DDT} and I_{DDQ} values but smaller F_{max} compared to the other, then it is highly likely to be structurally different and to be affected with a Trojan intrusion. Similar to I_{DDT}, the value for I_{DDQ} is input-dependent, thus, carefully chosen input vectors can reduce the leakage current (by 30–40%). Thus a low-leakage vector can improve the I_{DDQ} sensitivity of a Trojan. Fig. 15.5(a) shows the I_{DDQ} vs. F_{max} plot for the 8-bit ALU benchmark with and without Trojan instances. To understand the joint effect of the three variables, we simulated the c880 ISCAS-85 circuit with and without an 8-bit comparator Trojan. Fig. 15.5(c) shows a 3-D plot of I_{DDT}, I_{DDQ} and F_{max}, with projections on the I_{DDQ}–F_{max} and I_{DDT}–F_{max} planes for the corresponding 2-D plots. We can observe that a Trojan instance clearly isolates a chip in the multiple-parameter space from process induced variations.

15.3.2.4 Test Conditions

During side-channel testing, the choice of testing conditions can have a significant impact on sensitivity of Trojan detection. For instance, the placement of the current sensor to measure I_{DDT} for the chip is an important parameter. It should be noted that in case of a non-invasive approach for Trojan detection, the current sensors are not inserted within the chip. Also, if they are inserted within the chip, they can be tampered with, by the attacker. However, it is advisable to measure the current as close to the pins as possible. If we measure the current drawn from the power supply, the averaging effect of the bypass capacitors on the board-level can cause a negative impact on Trojan detection sensitivity. Also, if the current sensing can be done at individual VDD pins at the chip-level, instead of at the common supply node at the board-level, we can divide the background current to a considerably smaller value. It can also help in isolating the Trojan effect if the functional regions being activated draw supply current dominantly from different VDD pins. In this context, a region-based Trojan detection approach described in [308], explains how one can use the I_{DDT} values for different regions to calibrate the process noise assuming that the Trojan affects only one or few of the regions' currents. Moreover, the I_{DDT} values obtained for different test vector sets which selectively activate one region compared to another can be used as reference parameters, as described in [114], in order to detect a Trojan which is localized in one region of the IC.

The value of the supply voltage and the operating frequency during testing can also be used to get better Trojan detection sensitivity by our approach. As the supply voltage is reduced below nominal, the gates start switching slowly. Also, the dynamic and leakage current get reduced. As we measure average current over a clock period as the current corresponding to a pair of test vectors, the value contains components from both switching current and the leakage current. Based on the equations derived in Section 15.3.1, and the trend lines in Fig. 15.5(a), a trend line exists between F_{max} and I_{DDT} and the relation between F_{max} and I_{DDQ} is non-linear. We can see that if the measured average current is dominated by the leakage component, the relationship has a non-linear trend. If the trend remains close to linear, it is easier to get a limit line and determine a threshold for characterizing process variations. We can reduce the leakage component by measuring the average leakage current for the same vector and subtracting it from the measured switching current to extract the actual I_{DDT}. On the other hand, we can get similar sensitivity by measuring the current for shorter period of time (i.e. at high operating frequency) which leaves very little margin beyond the critical path delay, or by testing at a lower supply voltage, when the gate delays increase and eat up the slack for the particular operating frequency. If other low-power design techniques are built into the design, like applying body-bias to reduce leakage or clock/supply gating or adaptive voltage scaling for different functional regions, these can be used to our advantage in order to increase Trojan detection sensitivity.

15.4   Results

In this section, we describe the simulation and measurement setup for validating the proposed approach and provide corresponding results.

15.4.1   Simulation Verification

15.4.1.1   Test Setup

We used two test cases to validate the proposed Trojan detection approach: 1) an AES cipher circuit with an equivalent area of slightly over 25,000 two-input NAND gates (i.e $> 10^5$ transistors) and about 30% of the total area contributed by memory elements and 2) a 32-bit pipelined Integer Execution Unit (IEU) with about 20,000 two-input gates. Both designs were synthesized using Synopsys Design Compiler and mapped to a LEDA library. Circuit simulations were carried out for the 70 nm *Predictive Technology Model* (PTM) using the Synopsys *Nanosim* power simulator [305]. To consider the effect of process variations in order to determine the trend line and estimate the Trojan detection sensitivity, we used $\pm 20\%$ variation over the nominal V_{th} in our simulations. Finally, we used Monte Carlo simulations in HSPICE with random variations in inter-die and intra-die threshold voltage of the transistors to understand the effectiveness of our approach in detecting different Trojans.

We introduced four types of Trojan circuits in the two test circuits, with each Trojan type having an area an order of magnitude smaller than the previous type.

1. Trojan I: It consists of a 24-bit counter with a "gated" clock and occupies $\sim 1.1\%$ of the AES circuit area. The gating signal for the clock is an internal signal with very low signal probability (obtained by simulating each test circuit with random input patterns). When the clock is not gated, the counter counts through the states and when it reaches the maximum count, an AND gate connected to all the outputs triggers the Trojan output and an XOR gate modifies the payload node. The low signal probability of the internal gating signal makes it highly unlikely that the counter will reach the maximum count within the testing period.

2. Trojan II: It consists of a 10-bit counter which occupies $\sim 0.4\%$ of the AES circuit area. Instead of a clock signal, the counter has an internal signal as its state transition enable. The counter moves from one state to the next only when it encounters a positive edge on this internal signal. An internal signal with very low activity is chosen from both the test circuits.

3. Trojan III: The third Trojan is a variant of Trojan II with less number of flip-flops. It contains a 3-bit counter and occupies only $\sim 0.11\%$ of the AES circuit area.

4. Trojan IV: This is a purely combinational Trojan which occupies a meagre 0.04% of

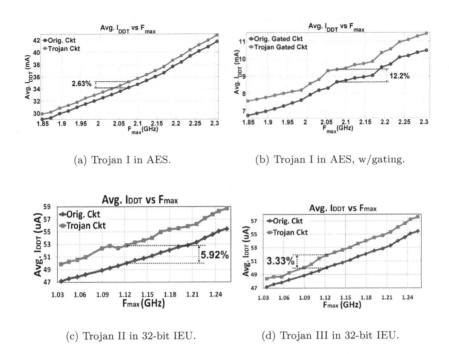

(a) Trojan I in AES.   (b) Trojan I in AES, w/gating.

(c) Trojan II in 32-bit IEU.   (d) Trojan III in 32-bit IEU.

FIGURE 15.6: I_{DDT} vs. F_{max} relationship for both golden and tampered AES and IEU circuits showing the sensitivity of our approach for detecting different Trojan circuits.

TABLE 15.1: Trojan Detection Sensitivity for Different Trojan Sizes in AES

Trojan Type	Trojan Size	Sensitivity	
		w/o gating	w/ gating
I (seq, 24-FF)	1.10%	2.63%	12.20%
II (seq, 10-FF)	0.40%	1.70%	8.60%
III (seq, 3-FF)	0.11%	0.81%	3.53%
IV (comb, 8-bit)	0.04%	0.23%	1.12%

the AES circuit area. It compares an 8-bit input to a pre-defined constant and triggers a malfunction only when the input matches with it. The Trojan trigger condition is derived from eight rare nodes of the circuit, such that the probability of occurrence of all eight rare values at the Trojan input is extremely low.

15.4.1.2   Results

Fig. 15.6(a) shows a plot of I_{DDT} vs. F_{max} for the AES circuit, with and without an inserted Trojan of type I. From this plot, it is observed that the current differential due to the Trojan circuit is only 2.63% at different process corners. For smaller Trojan circuits (Trojan II-IV), this difference can be less prominent and is, therefore, likely to be masked by process noise or design marginalities. Thus the clock gating and operand isolation as discussed in Section 15.3.2.2 were implemented to improve the Trojan detection sensitivity in the AES test circuit. As a result of selective gating, it was possible to reduce the average activity per node significantly (from 0.16 to 0.05). Fig. 15.6(b) shows the average I_{DDT}

TABLE 15.2: Trojan Detection Sensitivity for Different Trojan Sizes in IEU

Trojan Type	Trojan Size	Sensitivity	
		high act. vectors	low act. vectors
I (seq, 24-FF)	1.40%	2.14%	3.83%
II (seq, 10-FF)	0.50%	1.00%	1.80%
III (seq, 3-FF)	0.14%	0.72%	1.29%
IV (comb, 8-bit)	0.05%	0.45%	0.84%

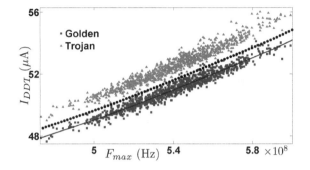

FIGURE 15.7: Effect of random process variations is observed by performing Monte Carlo simulations with inter-die $\sigma = 10\%$ and random intra-die $\sigma = 6\%$ for the 32-bit IEU circuit with Trojan IV inserted. Using a 2% sensitivity limit line to accommodate for the random process variation effects, we can obtain 99.8% detection accuracy and limit the false alarms to 0.9%.

vs. F_{max} plots for Trojan I, with power gating applied, which increases the sensitivity from 2.63% (Fig. 15.6(a)) to 12.2%. The sensitivity for different Trojan sizes is shown in Table 15.1. From the above results we conclude that selective gating or operand isolation can be extremely effective in improving the resolution of side channel analysis using current signature. Fig. 15.6(c) and 15.6(d) show I_{DDT} vs. F_{max} trends for the 32-bit IEU circuit, which shows sensitivity reduction with decrease in Trojan size. These sensitivity values can be improved by choosing proper low-activity vectors which reduce the background current. the improvement in sensitivity for different Trojan circuits due to low activity vectors is shown in Table 15.2.

Fig. 15.7 shows the results of performing Monte Carlo simulations for 1000 instances of the 32-bit IEU circuit with and without Trojan IV inserted. Here we consider both die-to-die and within-die variations as well as uncorrelated variations between NMOS and PMOS threshold voltages. Using a 2% sensitivity limit line, we obtain 99.3% Trojan detection accuracy, with 0.3% false alarms. Hence, the multiple-parameter approach is shown to work even under random process variation effects on top of inter-die variations. However, these results were obtained at nominal supply voltage of 1V and relatively low operating frequency of 200 MHz (clock period = 5 ns). As described in Section 15.3.2.4, we can use supply voltage scaling and frequency scaling during testing to make the measured supply current get dominated by the switching current (I_{DDT}) only by reducing the slack when no switching activity takes place in the circuit. This can give better Trojan detection sensitivity as shown in Fig. 15.8. By decreasing the clock period to 3 ns, we limit the idle time within the measurement period. Also, by reducing the supply voltage to 0.8V, the switching speed of the gates gets reduced and the slack decreases further.

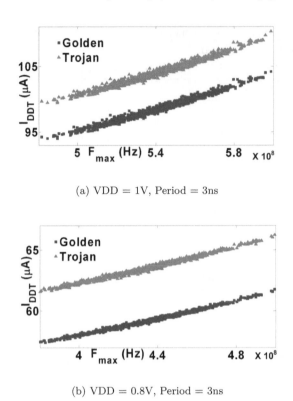

(a) VDD = 1V, Period = 3ns

(b) VDD = 0.8V, Period = 3ns

FIGURE 15.8: Choosing a faster clock period (3ns) and lowering the supply voltage from 1V to 0.8V gives better Trojan detection accuracy.

15.4.2 Hardware Validation

15.4.2.1 Test Setup

Hardware validation of the proposed multi-parameter approach was performed using an FPGA-platform where FPGA chips were used to emulate the ASIC scenario. We wanted to observe the effectiveness of the proposed approach to isolate the Trojan effect in presence of process variations, when a golden design and its variant with Trojan are mapped to the FPGA devices. Such an FPGA-based test setup provides a convenient platform for hardware validation using different Trojan types, sizes and even different designs. The selected FPGA device was Xilinx Virtex-II XC2V500 fabricated in 120nm CMOS technology. We designed a custom test board with socketed FPGAs for measuring current from eight individual supply pins as well as the total current, using 0.5 Ω precision current sense resistors. The test circuit was the 32-bit IEU with a 5-stage pipelined multiplier which has a logic utilization of 90% of the FPGA slices. The Trojan circuit was a sequential circuit (input-triggered counter) with different number of flip-flops. I_{DDT} was monitored for two types of input vectors: those which performed low-activity logic operations and those which performed high-activity multiplication operations. The Trojan size was varied from 256 (1.76% of design size) to 4 (0.03%) flip-flops.

In order to measure I_{DDT}, we measured the voltage drop across the sense resistor, using high-side current sensing strategy. To increase accuracy of measurements amidst measurement noise, the sense resistors were connected between the core V_{DD} pins and the bank of

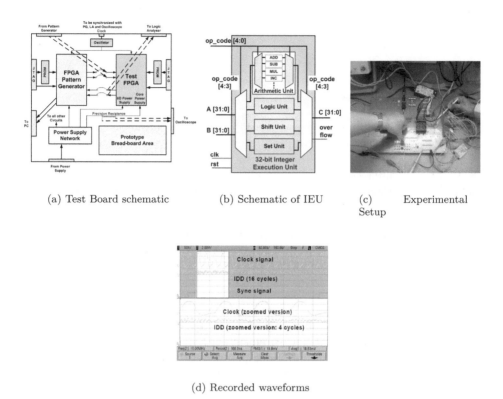

(a) Test Board schematic (b) Schematic of IEU (c) Experimental Setup

(d) Recorded waveforms

FIGURE 15.9: (a) Test PCB schematic. (b) Test circuit schematic. (c) Experimental setup. (d) Snapshot of measured I_{DDT} waveform from oscilloscope.

bypass capacitors. A differential probe was used to measure the voltage waveforms, which were recorded using an Agilent mixed-signal oscilloscope (100 MHz, 2 Gsa/sec). The waveforms were synchronized with a 10 MHz clock input and are recorded over 16 cycles corresponding to a pattern of 16 input vectors. A "SYNC" signal is used to correspond to the first input vector in the set, so that the current can be measured for the same vectors in all cases. Frequency (an estimate of F_{max}) was measured using a 15-inverter chain ring oscillator circuit, mapped to different parts of the FPGA, with an on-chip counter as described

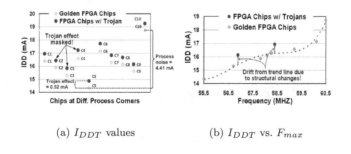

(a) I_{DDT} values (b) I_{DDT} vs. F_{max}

FIGURE 15.10: Measurement results for 10 FPGA chips showing I_{DDT} vs. F_{max} trend for the IEU test circuit with and without a 16-bit sequential Trojan (0.14% of original design).

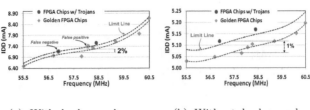

(a) With background current.

(b) Without background current.

FIGURE 15.11: Measured I_{DDT} vs. F_{max} results for 8 golden and 2 Trojan chips for the IEU circuit with and without a 4-bit sequential Trojan (0.03% of original design).

in [295]. We performed experiments with 10 FPGA chips from the same lot, which were placed in the same test board using a BGA socket, with the same design mapped into each chip. The test setup is shown in Fig. 15.9.

15.4.2.2 Results

The experimental results for multiple-parameter testing approach are shown in Fig. 15.10. The results show that while measurements of I_{DDT} only (Fig. 15.10(a)) may not be able to capture the effect of a Trojan under parameter variations, multiple-parameter based side-channel analysis can be effective to isolate it. For a set of golden chips, I_{DDT} vs. F_{max} follows an expected trend under process noise and deviation from this trend indicates the presence of structural changes in the design. Fig. 15.10(b) shows this scenario for 10 FPGA chips, 8 golden and 2 with Trojans (16-bit sequential Trojan). The ones with Trojans stand out from the rest in the I_{DDT} vs. F_{max} space. Note that some design marginalities, such as small capacitive coupling, which cause localized variation, can make the I_{DDT} vs. F_{max} plot for golden chips to deviate from the linear trend. Also, better trend can be obtained by performing measurements over larger population of chips, than was available.

Fig. 15.11(a) shows the measured I_{DDT} vs. F_{max} trend for a 4-bit sequential Trojan, which occupied 0.03% of logic resources in the FPGA. By drawing a limit line with a sensitivity of 2%, we get errors in Trojan detection. Lowering the sensitivity to 1% will decrease the number of false negatives (Trojan chips classified as golden), but increase the number of false positives (golden chips classified as Trojan). To improve the sensitivity of Trojan detection, we subtracted the background current (current measured with no input activity)

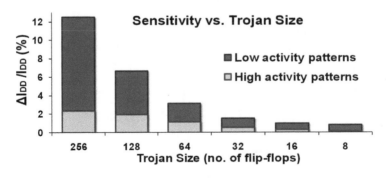

FIGURE 15.12: Sensitivity of Trojan detection decreases with Trojan size but improves by proper test vector selection.

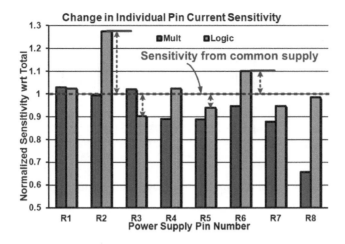

FIGURE 15.13: Sensitivity of Trojan detection can be improved by measuring current from multiple supply pins.

for each chip and the corresponding I_{DDT} vs. F_{max} trend is shown in Fig. 15.11(b). Even with a sensitivity of 1%, we can now clearly identify the Trojan chips without any errors. Fig. 15.12 shows the variation in Trojan detection sensitivity with Trojans of various sizes and with sets of input test vectors with differing activity levels. It is clear from this graph, that the sensitivity of Trojan detection decreases with decrease in Trojan size, and for very small Trojans, we need to use sensitivity improvement techniques to avoid classification errors. The sensitivity towards Trojan detection by measuring from individual pins compared to the sensitivity when measuring the total current is plotted in Fig. 15.13. It can be observed that when activating the multiplier which is spread out over a large part of the FPGA, we do not get much improvement in sensitivity. However, the supply current corresponding to the logic operations shows clear improvement in sensitivity of ~1.25X over the overall current sensitivity, for the pin R2 which is closest to the placement of the logic block of the IEU on the FPGA. The sensitivity can potentially be improved further by integrating current sensors into the packaging closer to the pins and by using current integration circuitry to perform the averaging.

15.5 Integration with Logic-testing Approach

As shown in Section 15.4, sensitivity of Trojan detection with the proposed side channel approach reduces with Trojan size. Hence, while such an approach can be extremely effective for complex, sequential Trojans, it may not detect ultra-small Trojans reliably. On the other hand, logic testing based approaches can detect such Trojans with high confidence. However, it is extremely challenging to detect structurally and functionally complex Trojans using logic testing. This is because a finite set of generated test vectors are usually unable to trigger the Trojans and/or manifest their malicious effect. As shown in [81], the logic testing approach generally achieves poor Trojan detection coverage for Trojans with more than 8 inputs. However, for side-channel analysis based approaches, it is not essential to activate the *entire* Trojan circuit - even activating a small part of the Trojan circuit might

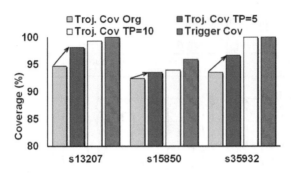

FIGURE 15.14: Improvement of Trojan coverage by logic testing approach with insertion of observable test points (5 and 10).

be sufficient to detect the Trojan if the effect on the side-channel parameter being measured is substantial, relative to the background value. Hence, the proposed methodology can also be integrated with logic-testing based Trojan detection approaches (such as *MERO* [81]) to provide comprehensive coverage for Trojans of different types and sizes.

The overall coverage can be estimated by a statistical sampling approach, in which a random sample of Trojan instances of a specific size (e.g. 100K) is chosen from the Trojan population and the percentage of Trojans in the sample detected by a given test-set is determined using functional simulation. Trojan detection coverage for a particular test set is defined as:

$$Coverage = \frac{\# \ of \ Trojans \ detected}{\# \ of \ sampled \ Trojans} \times 100\% \qquad (15.14)$$

One can also use coverage enhancement techniques like test-point insertion to enhance logic-testing based Trojan detection. Similar to current sensor integration for improving sensitivity of side-channel technique, we can insert low-overhead test-points to increase the observability of poorly observable internal circuit nodes and making them primary outputs. to reduce pin overhead, we can use multiplexing of the test points on existing pins. Similarly, controllable test point insertion can be used to improve trigger coverage. In order to observe the effect of observable test points, we performed simulations with 5 and 10 inserted test points (TP). To select the test points, the nodes were ranked in descending order based on the following metric:

$$M = \frac{f_{in} + f_{out}}{abs(f_{in} - f_{out}) + 1} \qquad (15.15)$$

where f_{in} and f_{out} represent the sizes of the fanin and fanout cones of a node, respectively. The metric indicates that nodes closer to the primary inputs/outputs have less chance of getting selected. Fig. 15.14 shows the effect of test point insertion on the Trojan coverage as compared to a baseline case with no inserted test point, for three sequential (ISCAS'89) benchmark circuits with $N = 1000$, $q = 2$ and $\theta = 0.2$. As observed from this plot, test point insertion helps to improve the Trojan coverage considerably for some circuits and helps to reduce the gap between trigger coverage and Trojan coverage.

We computed the Trojan detection coverage for different ISCAS-85 benchmark circuits for a population of 100,000 10-input combinational Trojans, using the *MERO* logic testing algorithm as well as the combined side-channel and *MERO* approach, as shown in Table 15.3. We used the sensitivity value derived in Section 15.3.2 to determine if a Trojan is detected using side-channel approach. It can be readily observed that although the logic testing approach in isolation achieves relatively poor coverage for large Trojans (size >= 8

TABLE 15.3: Trojan Coverage for ISCAS-85 Benchmark Circuits

Benchmark	Troj. Cov. (*MERO*) (%)	Troj. Cov. (total) (%)
c880	48.37	100.00
c1355	20.00	100.00
c1908	70.37	100.00
c2670	31.44	100.00
c3540	12.50	100.00
c5315	4.82	100.00
c6288	36.92	100.00
c7552	4.52	99.84
Average	28.62	99.98

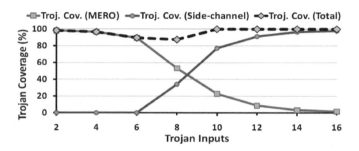

FIGURE 15.15: Complementary nature of *MERO* and Side-channel analysis for maximum Trojan detection coverage in 32-bit IEU.

inputs), the total coverage is almost 100% for most circuits when the two approaches are combined.

We also analysed the *complementary* nature of coverage by the logic testing and side-channel approaches of Trojan detection. Fig. 15.15 shows the Trojan coverage for logic testing approach (*MERO*) and side-channel approach without any sensitivity improvement techniques applied, as well as the total coverage for the combined approach, for a 32-bit Integer Execution Unit (IEU) for Trojans of different sizes. It can be observed that for larger Trojans with 8 or more inputs, the detection coverage of the *MERO* approach is much inferior to that for the side-channel based multi-parameter testing. On the other hand, smaller Trojans are easier to trigger and detect using logic testing, but their contribution to side-channel parameter may be difficult to distinguish. From this analysis, we note that Trojans of different types and sizes can be detected with high confidence by the combined approach.

15.5.1 Motivation of Self-Referencing Approach

We now demonstrate a scalable side-channel approach to hardware Trojan detection based on a concept called "self-referencing". The basic idea is to use supply current signature of one region of a chip as reference to that of another to eliminate the process noise. Such calibration or referencing is possible due to the spatial correlation of process variation effects across regions in a chip. We show that such an approach can be extremely effective in nullifying all forms of process noise, namely inter-die, intra-die random and intra-die systematic variations [60]. Since process noise is eliminated by comparing current signature

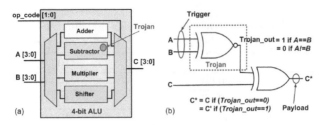

FIGURE 15.16: (a) An simple test circuit: a 4-bit Arithmetic Logic Unit (ALU). (b) A combinational Trojan inserted into the subtractor.

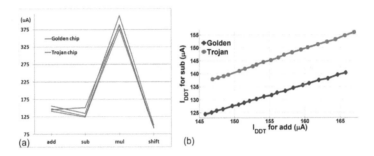

FIGURE 15.17: (a) Comparison of supply current between golden and tampered chip for four regions of a 4-bit ALU. (b) Correlation of region currents at different process points for golden and tampered ICs.

of regions in an IC, the method is scalable with increasing process noise. To increase the Trojan detection sensitivity, we propose a region-based vector generation approach, which tries to maximize the Trojan effect while minimizing the background current. Current values of n regions are then compared with all other using a slope heuristic and the resultant region slope matrix is used to compare a chip with another. We validate the proposed approach using both simulation and measurements for several large open source designs.

The idea of self-referencing can be illustrated using an example 4-bit ALU, as shown in Fig. 15.16(a). The ALU contains four distinct functional units (FUs) – adder, subtractor, multiplier and shifter, which are activated based on the input "opcode" value. There are two 4-bit operands and a 4-bit output. In such a circuit, a single region or FU can be selectively activated by proper choice of opcode, we can easily generate test vectors which target separate activation of the four regions. We consider three different process corners (nominal $\pm 25\%$) for the entire design (modeled as a change in the transistor threshold voltage V_T) and simulate the design in HSPICE for four different vector pairs which activate each of the four regions separately. We also measure the background current. The Trojan circuit, as shown in Fig. 15.16(b) was designed to invert an output bit of the subtractor if two input bits were equal. We simulated the circuit with the Trojan in the subtractor module (occupying 2.7% area of the ALU) at the nominal process corner for the same set of vectors.

Fig. 15.17(a) shows the plot of the average I_{DDT} values for the four different vectors activating the four different regions without the background current. We can observe the tampered circuit consumes more current for the vector which activates the subtractor region. We plot the current for one region (adder) with respect that for another (subtractor) for a set of golden and tampered chips at 20 different process points in Fig. 15.17(b). We expect a correlation between the region currents across process corners. However, since there is a Trojan in the subtractor, it shows uncorrelated behavior in supply current. Hence, the current for the adder can be used to calibrate the process noise and check for the presence of Trojan in other modules. In real life, since we do not know the region which contains the Trojan, we need to compare each region with all others. This also allows us to cancel out the effect of random and systematic intra-die process variations, as explained next.

15.5.2 Analysis of Process Variations on Self-Referencing

Consider an IC that has been partitioned into N different regions, such that each region can be preferentially activated while the activity of the other partitions are minimized. Consider that the region R_i has been preferentially activated, and consider a gate $g \in R_i$ whose output goes from logic-0 to logic-1. Then, the current drawn by g is approximately given by $I_g = k(V_{DD} - V_{Tg})^2$, where k is a constant depending on the process and the nature of the gate, V_{DD} is the supply voltage and V_{Tg} is the threshold voltage of the i-th gate. Now, V_{Tg} can be expressed as $V_{Tg} = V_T + \Delta V_{Ti} + \Delta v_{Tg1} + \Delta v_{Tg2}$, Here, ΔV_{Ti} represents the effect of the "systematic intra-die" component of variation, and has the same value for all gates in the region R_i; Δv_{Tg1} represents the effect of the "inter-die" component of process variation, and has the same value for all gates in the IC, and Δv_{Tg2} is the effect of the "random intra-die" component of process variation, and has random values for different gates of the IC. Hence,

$$
\begin{aligned}
I_g &= k\left[V_{DD} - (V_T + \Delta V_{Ti} + \Delta v_{Tg1} + \Delta v_{Tg2})\right]^2 \\
&= k\left[(V_{DD} - V_T - \Delta v_{Tg1})^2 + (\Delta V_{Ti} + \Delta v_{Tg2})^2 - 2(V_{DD} - V_T - \Delta v_{Tg1})(\Delta V_{Ti} + \Delta v_{Tg2})\right]
\end{aligned}
$$
(15.16)

Ignoring all second order terms involving both random and systematic shifts of the threshold voltage, the above equation can be approximated by:

$$
I_g \approx \underbrace{k\left[(V_{DD} - V_T)^2 - 2(V_{DD} - V_T)(\Delta v_{Tg1} + \Delta V_{Ti})\right]}_{\text{constant for each gate } g \in R_i} - \underbrace{2(V_{DD} - V_T)\Delta v_{Tg2}}_{\text{random for each gate } g \in R_i}
$$
(15.17)

Summing the currents for all the switching gates of the region R_i, the total switching current for region R_i is:

$$
I_i = \sum_{g \in R_i} I_g = kn_i\left[(V_{DD} - V_T)^2 - 2(V_{DD} - V_T)(\Delta v_{Tg1} + \Delta V_{Ti})\right] - 2(V_{DD} - V_T)\sum_{g \in R_i} \Delta v_{Tg2}
$$
(15.18)

where n_i is the number of switching gates in region R_i. Now, the term $\sum_{g \in R_i} \Delta v_{Tg2}$ represents the sum of n_i (normally distributed) random variables, each with mean $\mu = 0$ and standard deviation σ_T (let). Hence, by the *Central Limit Theorem* [291], the term $\sum_{g \in R_i} \Delta v_{Tg2}$ is approximately normally distributed with mean $\mu = 0$ and a reduced standard deviation $\frac{\sigma_T}{\sqrt{n_i}}$. Hence, for reasonably large value of n_i, this term is approximately equal to zero, and the expression for I_i can be approximated by:

$$
I_i \approx \sum_{g \in R_i} I_g = kn_i\left[(V_{DD} - V_T)^2 - 2(V_{DD} - V_T)(\Delta v_{Tg1} + \Delta V_{Ti})\right]
$$
(15.19)

Similarly, for a region R_j. the switching current is given by:

$$
I_j \approx \sum_{g \in R_j} I_g = kn_j\left[(V_{DD} - V_T)^2 - 2(V_{DD} - V_T)(\Delta v_{Tg1} + \Delta V_{Tj})\right]
$$
(15.20)

Hence, the difference between the currents of regions R_i and R_j can be expressed as:

$$I_i - I_j|_{observed} = k\left[(V_{DD} - V_T)^2 - 2(V_{DD} - V_T)\Delta v_{Tg1}\right](n_i - n_j)$$
$$- 2k(V_{DD} - V_T)(n_i\Delta V_{Ti} - n_j\Delta V_{Tj}) = c_1(n_i - n_j) + \underbrace{c_2(n_i\Delta V_{Ti} - n_j\Delta V_{Tj})}_{\text{due to } systematic\ intra\text{-}die \text{ variation}}$$

$$(15.21)$$

where c_1, c_2 are constants. If the contribution due to the intra-die systematic component is negligible, the above expression can be re-written as:

$$I_i - I_j|_{observed} \approx c_1(n_i - n_j) \qquad \text{and} \qquad I_i|_{observed} \approx c_1 n_i \qquad (15.22)$$

Hence, the mutual region slope metric for regions R_i and R_j is

$$S_{ij,observed} = \frac{I_i - I_j}{I_i} = \frac{n_i - n_j}{n_i} \qquad (15.23)$$

In the *nominal* case, in the absence of any process variation effects, $\Delta V_{Ti} = \Delta V_{Tj} = \Delta v_{Tg1} = \Delta v_{Tg2} = 0$; hence , $I_i - I_j|_{golden} = c_3(n_i - n_j)$, $I_i = c_3 n_i$ and

$$\boxed{S_{ij,golden} = \frac{n_i - n_j}{n_i} = S_{ij,observed}} \qquad (15.24)$$

Similarly, it can be shown that $S_{ji,golden} = S_{ji,observed}$. This shows that under negligible *systematic intra-die* variations, the ratio of the difference in the switching currents of two regions and the current of each region should remain approximately unchanged. This equality fails to be satisfied in case one of the regions is modified by the insertion of a Trojan, because then the switching current of the gates constituting the Trojan circuit disturbs the balance. This observation is the main motivation behind using the region slope values for reducing the process noise. For a circuit with N regions, if we compute the region slope values for all pairs of regions, we obtain an $N \times N$ region slope matrix, with zeros on the diagonal. It is observed that systematic variations still cause some variations in the Region Slope values, but the effect of process variation has been reduced greatly compared to the variations in individual current values, thus giving us improved sensitivity for Trojan detection.

Next, we describe the major steps which constitute our self-referencing approach for Trojan detection.

15.5.3   Self-Referencing Methodology

For a large design, the golden supply current for a high activity vector can be large compared to the additional current consumed by a small Trojan circuit, and the variation in the current value due to process variation can be very large. This can mask the effect of the Trojan on the measured current, leading to difficulty in detecting a Trojan-infected chip. Most side-channel analysis based approaches perform calibration of the process noise by using golden chips at different process corners. This helps us obtain a limiting threshold value beyond which any chip is classified as Trojan. Since the variation in the measured value can cause a golden chip to be misclassified as a Trojan (we refer to this case as a *false positive – FP*), the limit line has to be close to the nominal golden value. On the other hand, if the Trojan effect does not change the value beyond the limit, the Trojan-containing chip can be misclassified as a golden one (we refer to this case as a *false negative – FN*). To limit the probability of false positives and false negatives, the limiting values need to be chosen carefully.

The Trojan detection sensitivity of this approach reduces with decreasing Trojan or increasing circuit size. In order to detect small sequential/combinational Trojans in large circuits ($> 10^5$ transistors), we need to improve the SNR (Signal-to-Noise Ratio) using appropriate side-channel isolation techniques. At a single V_T point the sensitivity, for an approach where transient current values are compared for different chips, can be expressed as:

$$Sensitivity = \frac{I_{tampered,nominal} - I_{golden,nominal}}{I_{golden,process\ variation} - I_{golden,nominal}} \quad (15.25)$$

Clearly, the sensitivity can be improved by increasing the current contribution of the Trojan circuit relative to that of the original circuit. We can divide the original circuit into several small regions and measure the supply current (I_{DDT}) for each region. The relationship between region currents also helps to cancel the process variation effects. In Fig. 15.17(a), if we consider the "slope" or relative difference between the current values of 'add' and 'sub' regions, we can see that there is a larger shift in this value due to Trojan than in the original current value due to process variations. We refer to this approach as the *self-referencing* approach, since we can use the relative difference in the region current values to detect a Trojan by reducing the effect of process variations.

The major steps of the self-referencing approach are as follows. First, we need to perform a *functional decomposition* to divide a large design into several small blocks or regions, so that we can activate them one region at a time. Next, we need a vector generation algorithm which can generate vectors that maximize the activity within one region while producing minimum activity in other regions. Also, the chosen set of test vectors should be capable of triggering most of the feasible Trojans in a given region. Then, we need to perform self-referencing among the measured supply current values. For this we use a region slope matrix as described earlier. Finally, we reach the decision making process which is to compare the matrix values for the test chip to threshold values derived from golden chips at different process corners, in order to detect the presence or absence of a Trojan. Next we describe each of the steps in detail.

15.5.3.1 Functional Decomposition

The first step of the proposed self-referencing approach is decomposition of a large design into functional blocks or regions. Sometimes, the circuit under test is designed with clearly-defined functional blocks which can be selectively activated by using control signals, like the 4-bit ALU circuit which we considered for our example in Section 15.5.1. Another type of circuit which is amenable to simple functional decomposition is a pipelined processor, where the different pipeline stages correspond to the different regions. However, there can be circuits which are available as a flattened gate-level netlist. For this we could use a hyper-graph based approach to identify partitions which have minimum cut-sets between them. This allows us to isolate the activity in one partition from causing activity in other regions. As for the *multi-parameter* approach, the region-based partitioning described in [38] can also be used for creating partitions in circuits which do not have well-defined functional blocks or for creating sub-blocks within a functional block. The decomposition should follow a set of properties to maximize the effectiveness of the approach:

1. The blocks should be reasonably large to cancel out the effect of random parameter variations, but small enough to minimize the background current. It should also be kept in mind that if the regions are too small, the number of regions can become unreasonably large for the test vector generation algorithm to handle.

2. The blocks should be functionally as independent of each other as possible so that

the test generation process can increase the activity of one block (or few blocks) while minimizing the activity of all others.

3. The decomposition process can be performed hierarchically. For instance, a system-on-a-chip (SoC) can be divided into the constituent blocks which make up the system. But, for a large SoC, one of the blocks could itself be a processor. Hence, we need to further divide this structural block into functional sub-blocks.

15.5.3.2 Statistical Test Vector Generation

In order to increase the Trojan detection sensitivity, proper test vector generation and application are necessary to reduce the background activity and amplify the activity inside the Trojan circuit. If we partition the circuit into several functional and structurally separate blocks, we can activate them one at a time and observe the switching current for that block with respect to the current values for other blocks. The test vector generation algorithm needs to take into account two factors:

1. Only one region must be activated at a time. If the inputs to different modules are mutually exclusive and the regions have minimal interconnection, it is easy to maximally activate one region while minimizing activity in other regions. If complex interconnections exist between the modules, the inputs need to be ranked in terms of their sensitivity towards activating different modules and the test generation needs to be aware of these sensitivity values.

2. When a particular region is being activated, the test vectors should try to activate possible Trojan trigger conditions and should be aimed at creating activity within most of the innumerable possible Trojans. This motivates us to consider a statistical test generation approach like the one described in [81] for maximizing Trojan trigger coverage. Note that, unlike functional testing approaches, the Trojan payload need not be affected during test time, and the observability of Trojan effect on the side-channel parameter is ensured by the region-based self-referencing approach described earlier.

Fig. 15.18 shows a flow chart of the test vector generation algorithm on the right. For each region, we assign weights to the primary inputs in terms of their tendency to maximize activity in the region under consideration while minimizing activity in other regions. This step can also identify control signals which can direct the activity exclusively to particular regions. Next, we generate weighted random input vectors for activating the region under consideration and perform functional simulation using a graph-based approach, which lets us estimate the activity within each region for each pair of input vectors. We sort the vectors based on a metric C_{ij} which is higher for a vector pair which can maximally activate region R_i while minimizing activity in each of the other regions. Then, we prune the vector set to choose a reduced but highly efficient vector set generated by a statistical approach such as *MERO* [81]. In this approach (motivated by the *N-detect* test generation technique), within a region, we identify internal nodes with rare values, which can be candidate trigger signals for a Trojan. Then we identify the subset of vectors which can take the rare nodes within the region to their rare values at least N times, thus increasing the possibility of triggering the Trojans within the region. Once this process is completed for all the regions, we combine the vectors and generate a test suite which can be applied to each chip for measuring supply current corresponding to each of its regions.

For functional test of a multi-core processor, we can use specially designed small test programs which are likely to trigger and observe rare events in the system such as events on the memory control line or most significant bits of the datapath multiple times. In general

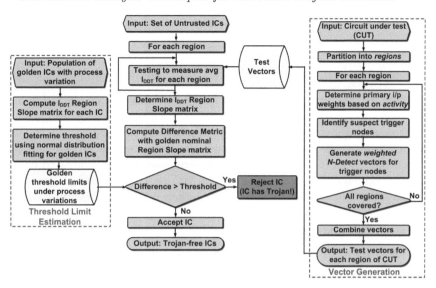

FIGURE 15.18: The major steps of the proposed self-referencing methodology. The steps for test vector generation for increasing sensitivity and threshold limit estimation for calibrating process noise are also shown.

a design is composed of several functional blocks and activity in several functional blocks can be turned off using input conditions. For example in a processor, activity in the floating point unit (FPU), branch logic or memory peripheral logic can be turned off by selecting an integer ALU operation. Many functional blocks are pipelined. In these cases, we will focus on one stage at a time and provide initialization to the pipeline such that the activities of all stages other than the one under test are minimized by ensuring that the corresponding stage inputs do not change. Next we describe how the self-referencing approach can be applied to compare the current values for different regions and identify the Trojan-infected region.

15.5.3.3   Side-channel Analysis Using Self-Referencing

In this step, we measure the current from different blocks which are selectively activated, while the rest of the circuit is kept inactive by appropriate test vector application. Then the average supply current consumed by the different blocks is compared for different chip instances to see whether the relations between the individual block currents are maintained. Any discrepancy in the "slope" of the current values between different blocks indicates the presence of Trojan. This approach can be hierarchically repeated for further increasing sensitivity by decomposing the suspect block into sub-blocks and checking the self-referencing relationships between the current consumed by each sub-block.

The flowchart for this step is shown in Fig. 15.18. Note that the best Trojan detection capability of region-based comparison will be realized if the circuit is partitioned into regions of similar size. The region slope matrix is computed by taking the relative difference between the current values for each region. We estimate the effect of process variations on the "slopes" to determine a threshold for separating the golden chips from the Trojan-infested ones. This can be done by extensive simulations or measurements from several known-golden chips. as previously discussed, for a design with n regions, the region slope matrix is an $n \times n$ matrix, with entries that can be mathematically expressed as:

$$S_{ij} = \frac{I_i - I_j}{I_i} \; \forall i, j \in [1, n] \tag{15.26}$$

For each region, we get $2n - 1$ slope values, of which one of them is '0', since the diagonal elements S_{ii} will be zero.

The intra-die systematic variation is eliminated primarily because we use the current from an adjacent block, which is expected to suffer similar variations, to calibrate process noise of the block under test. The intra-die random variations can be eliminated by considering switching of large number of gates. In our simulations we find that even switching of 50 logic gates in a block can effectively cancel out random deviations in supply current.

15.5.3.4   Decision Making Process

In this step, we make a decision about the existence of Trojan in a chip. The variation in slope values for different regions for a chip from the golden nominal values are combined by taking the L^2 norm (sum of squares of difference of corresponding values) between the two region slope matrices. This difference metric for any chip k is defined as

$$D(k) = \sum_{i=1}^{N} \sum_{j=1}^{N} (S_{ij}|_{Chip\; k} - S_{ij}|_{golden, nominal})^2. \tag{15.27}$$

The limiting "threshold" value for golden chips can be computed by taking the difference $D(golden, process\; variations)$ as defined by

$$Threshold = \sum_{i=1}^{N} \sum_{j=1}^{N} (S_{ij}|_{golden, process\; variation} - S_{ij}|_{golden, nominal})^2. \tag{15.28}$$

Any variation beyond the threshold is attributed to the presence of a Trojan. The steps for computing the golden threshold limits are illustrated on the left side of Fig. 15.18. Since unlike conventional testing, a go/no-go decision is difficult to achieve, we come up with a measure of confidence about the trustworthiness of each region in a chip using an appropriate metric. We compare the average supply current consumed by the different blocks for different chip instances to see whether the expected correlation between the individual block currents is maintained. The Trojan detection sensitivity of the self-referencing approach can be defined as

$$Sensitivity = \frac{D(tampered, nominal)}{Threshold} \tag{15.29}$$

Since, the slope values are less affected by process variations compared to the current values alone, we expect to get better sensitivity compared to eqn. (15.25). Note that since we perform region-based comparison, we can localize a Trojan and repeat the analysis within a block to further isolate the Trojan. This approach can be hierarchically repeated to increase the detection sensitivity by decomposing a suspect block further into sub-blocks and applying the self-referencing approach for those smaller blocks. We can also see that the region-based self-referencing approach is scalable with respect to design size and Trojan size. For the same Trojan size, if the design size is increased two-fold, we can achieve same sensitivity by dividing the circuit into twice as many regions. Similarly we can divide the circuit into smaller regions to increase sensitivity towards detection of smaller Trojan circuits.

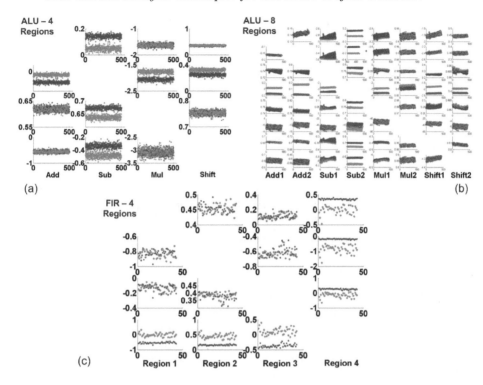

FIGURE 15.19: Self-referencing methodology for detecting Trojan in the 32-bit ALU and FIR circuits. Blue and red lines (or points) denote golden and Trojan chips, respectively.

15.5.4 Self-referencing Simulation Results

We used two test cases to validate the proposed Trojan detection approach: 1) a 32-bit integer Arithmetic Logic Unit (ALU), and 2) a Finite Impulse Response (FIR) digital filter. The size of the ALU circuit can be scaled by changing the word size parameter. We considered 4 structurally different blocks - adder (*add*), subtracter (*sub*), multiplier (*mul*) and shifter (*shift*) which can be selectively activated by the *opcode* input bits. However, the FIR filter had a flattened netlist and was manually partitioned into four regions with the minimum interconnections, and the test vector generation tool (written in MATLAB) was used to generate test vectors to selectively activate each block. We inserted a small (<0.01% of total area) Trojan in the subtracter of the ALU and the 4th region of the FIR filter. Both designs were synthesized using *Synopsys Design Compiler* and mapped to a *LEDA* standard cell library. Circuit simulations were carried out for the 70nm *Predictive Technology Model* (PTM) [292] using *Synopsys HSPICE*. To estimate the effect of process variations, we used Monte Carlo simulations for a maximum of ±20% variation in the nominal V_T value, inter-die variations with $\sigma = 10\%$ and random intra-die variations with $\sigma = 6\%$. We simulated the circuits and separately measured the supply current for different regions for 500 golden chips and 500 infected chips.

The simulated region slope matrix values are plotted in Fig. 15.19(a). The Trojan-infected chip instances can be easily distinguished from the golden ones, even in the presence of process noise. The row and column corresponding to the subtracter (2nd region) show visibly different values for the golden (blue) and Trojan (red) values. Next, we performed simulations with multiple vector pairs activating the same module to show that the Trojan in the subtracter is only selectively activated on the application of one of the two vector

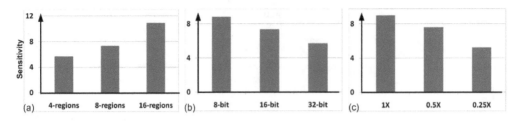

FIGURE 15.20: Sensitivity analysis with (a) different number of regions, (b) different circuit sizes, and (c) different Trojan sizes.

TABLE 15.4: Probability of Detection and Probability of False Alarm (False Positives)

Circuit Name	TN(%)	FP(%)	FN(%)	TP(%)
32-bit ALU	99.10	0.90	5.90	94.10
FIR	97.72	2.28	6.60	93.40

pairs activating the subtracter module. The region slope matrix for this case is shown in Fig. 15.19(b). This matrix contains 8 regions, since each of the four structurally separate regions of the ALU are further divided into two sub-blocks corresponding to the two different vector pairs which share the same opcode values. It can be readily observed that increasing the number of regions increases the sensitivity of Trojan detection.

Fig. 15.19(c) shows the simulation results for the FIR design. The test vectors are chosen by the MATLAB tool and used to dominantly activate different regions of the design. The region slope matrix is computed for 50 golden chips and 50 Trojan-infected chips and we can successfully detect the Trojan-infected region (region 4). Fig. 15.20 shows the variation in sensitivity of the self-referencing approach by varying different parameters of the ALU. For a 16-bit ALU, we see that increasing the number of regions helps increase the sensitivity in Fig. 15.20(a). In Fig. 15.20(b), we plot the sensitivity of the approach for increasing circuit sizes. Finally in Fig. 15.20(c), we show that increasing the number of regions also helps to keep the sensitivity nearly constant as we scale down the Trojan size. The percentage of true positives, true negatives, false positives and false negatives as obtained from the Monte Carlo simulations are presented in Table 15.4. We used a process point with 20% V_T variation to compute the threshold. For smaller circuits and larger Trojans the sensitivity is higher and hence, the accuracy of classification is also better.

15.5.5 Experimental Results

We used a custom test board with socketed *Xilinx Virtex-II XC2V500* FPGAs to measure current from eight individual supply pins as well as the total current, using 0.5Ω precision current sense resistors to sense the I_{DDT} and an *Agilent* mixed-signal oscilloscope (100MHz, 2 Gsa/sec) to record the data. The test circuit was a 32-bit DLX processor with a 5-stage pipeline which contains the previously-described 32-bit ALU as part of its execution unit, occupying over 80% of the FPGA slices. The Trojan circuit was a 16-bit serial-in parallel-out shift register (sequential Trojan) occupying 0.08% of total area. We performed experiments with 10 FPGA chips from the same lot. We insert a Trojan in two of the ten chips inside the subtracter sub-region of the ALU. The region slope matrix is constructed using the measured current values for the five pipeline stages of the DLX processor in the 10 FPGA chips. We use the 8 golden chips to determine the threshold limit and use our self-referencing approach to test 4 test chips (2 golden and 2 Trojan). As can be clearly seen from Fig. 15.21, the Trojan containing chips are easily identified as well as the region

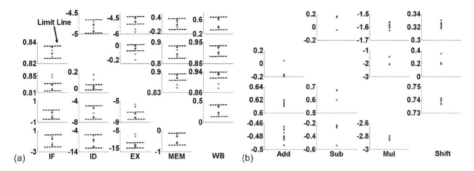

FIGURE 15.21: Experimental results for 8 golden and 2 tampered FPGA chips. Region slope matrix for (a) 32-bit DLX processor; (b) 32-bit ALU. The limit lines are obtained by analyzing the 8 golden chips. The red points denote the values for the Trojan-containing test chips while the blue points denote the values for the golden chips.

which contains the Trojan in both cases. Next, we repeat the procedure using test vectors which only activate the four sub-regions inside the 32-bit ALU and identify that the Trojan is located within the subtracter.

15.5.6 Conclusions

In this chapter, we have described techniques for hardware Trojan detection that depend on the effect of an inserted Trojan on the current consumption of the circuit. The main challenge is to have high Trojan detection sensitivity in the presence of process variation noise. In addition, we have shown how to increase the sensitivity of the techniques further by combining them with logic testing techniques. We have demonstrated the effectiveness of the two proposed experimental techniques, and have given theoretical justifications for them.

Chapter 16

Design Techniques for Hardware Trojan Threat Mitigation

"Byrne's Law: In any electrical circuit, appliances and wiring will burn out to protect fuses."

Robert Byrne

16.1 Introduction

In the two previous chapters, we have examined testing techniques for Trojan detection. Logic-testing based Trojan detection techniques are effective for small Trojans that do affect the circuit logic functionality, and side-channel analysis based testing techniques are effective for complex Trojans that affect the side-channel parameters (current signature, delay, etc.) substantially. However, there can be a third line-of-thought while somebody is trying to protect against hardware Trojans: what if the original circuit, by its very design, provides protection against Trojan insertion, or at least, resists attempts of Trojan insertion?

In this chapter, we explore three conceptually different design techniques directed towards Trojan detection following the above–mentioned line–of–thought. The first technique relies on obfuscation of circuit functionality through structural modifications that help in reducing the potency of an inserted hardware Trojan. The technique is developed based on the argument that any successful attempt to insert a hardware Trojan would require a through understanding of the circuit functionality on part of an adversary. However, as a result of the adopted functional obfuscation technique through structural modifications, an adversary might find it difficult to correctly comprehend the circuit functionality. This in turn might result in an inserted Trojan to either not trigger, or become more vulnerable to logic testing based Trojan detection techniques, like that proposed in Chapter 14. A conceptually similar protection scheme has been earlier suggested in [399] for software, whereby by decreasing the comprehensibility of a program, malicious software modification is prevented.

The second technique relies on structural and functional isolation of modules on a FPGA to prevent the possibility of them interacting in a malicious manner.

The third and final technique provides a FPGA-based design infrastructure to insert extra logic that performs run-time execution monitoring to detect and prevent any imminent circuit logic malfunction.

16.2 Obfuscation-based Trojan Detection/Protection

16.2.1 Methodology of Circuit Obfuscation-based Trojan Detection/Protection

The obfuscation in our scheme is achieved by two important modifications of the *state transition graph* (STG) of the circuit:

- The size of the reachable state-space is "blown up" by a large (exponential) factor using extra state elements.

- Certain states, which were *unreachable* in the original design are used and made reachable only in the *obfuscated mode* of operation.

These two modifications make it difficult for an adversary to design a functionally potent and well-hidden Trojan, as shown through the analysis presented in Sections (16.2.2)–(16.2.4). As would be evident from the following, this modification of the STG is different in methodology and goals from the ones proposed in [29, 77, 30, 336], in which no state-space explosion is attempted.

Fig. 16.1(a) shows the proposed obfuscation scheme based on the change in the STG of the circuit. On power-up, the circuit is initialized to a state (S_0^O) in the *obfuscated mode*. On the application of an input sequence $K_1{\rightarrow}K_2{\rightarrow}K_3$ in order, i.e. the *initialization key sequence*, the circuit reaches the state S_0^N, which is the *reset state* in the *original state space*, allowing *normal mode* of operation. The states S_0^O, S_1^O and S_2^O constitute the *initialization state space*. The application of even a single incorrect input vector during the initialization process takes the circuit to states in the *isolation state space*, a set of states from which it is not possible to come back to the *initialization state space* or enter the *original state space*. The *initialization state space* and the *isolation state space* together constitute the *obfuscation state space*. All state encodings in the *obfuscation state space* are done using *unreachable* state bit combinations for selected state elements of the circuit. This ensures that the circuit cannot perform its normal functionality until the correct initialization key sequence has been applied. The initialization latency (typically < 10 clock cycles) can be

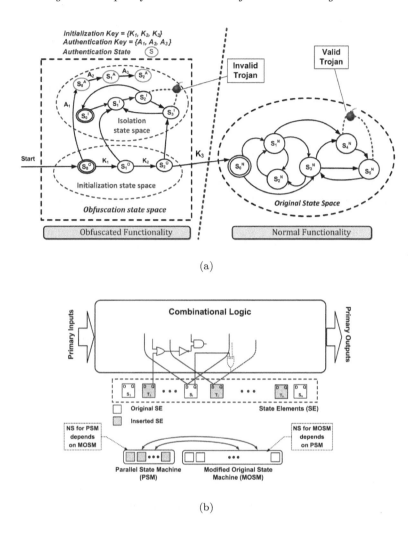

FIGURE 16.1: The obfuscation scheme for protection against hardware Trojans: (a) modified state transition graph and (b) modified circuit structure.

easily hidden from the end-user by utilizing the inherent latency of most ASICs during a "boot-up" or similar procedure on power-ON [77]. We consider the post-manufacturing testing phase to be "trusted" such that there is no possibility of the secret initializaton key to be leaked to the adversary in the fab. This is a commonly accepted convention which was first explicitly stated in [107]. To protect against the possibility of an user releasing the initialization key sequence of the design in the public domain, *user-specific initialization key sequence* or in the extreme case *instance-specific* initialization key sequence might be employed.

To "blow up" the size of the *obfuscation state space*, a number of extra state elements are added depending on the allowable hardware overhead. The size of the *obfuscation state space* has an exponential dependence on the number of extra state elements. An inserted *parallel finite state machine* (PSM) defines the state transitions of the extra state elements. However, to hide possible structural signature formed by the inserted PSM, the circuit description of the PSM is *folded* into the *modified state machine in the original circuit*

(MOSM) (as shown in Fig. 16.1(b)) to generate an integrated state machine. A logic re-synthesis step is performed, including logic optimization under design constraints in terms of delay, area or power. In effect, the circuit structures such as the input logic cones of the original state elements change significantly compared to the unobfuscated circuit, making reverse-engineering of the obfuscated design practically infeasible for a adversary. This effect is illustrated in Section 16.2.5 through an example benchmark circuit.

To increase the level of structural difference between the obfuscated and the original circuits, the designer can choose to insert *modification cells* as proposed in [77] at selected internal nodes. Furthermore, the level of obfuscation can be increased by using more states in the obfuscated state space. This can be achieved by: 1) adding more state elements to the design and/or 2) using more unreachable states from the original design. However, this can increase the design overhead substantially. In Section 16.4.1 we describe a technique to reduce the design overhead in such cases.

Selected states in the *isolation state space* can also serve the purpose of authenticating the ownership of the design, as described in [77]. Authentication for sequential circuits is usually performed by embedding a *digital watermark* in the STG of the design [276, 381], and our idea of hiding such information in the unused states of the circuit is similar to [426]. A *digital watermark* is a unique characteristic of the design which is usually not part of the original specification and is known only to the designer. Fig. 16.1 shows such a scheme where the states S_0^A, S_1^A and S_2^A in the *isolation state space* and the corresponding output values of the circuit are used for the purposes of authenticating the design. The design goes through the state transition sequence $S_0^O \rightarrow S_0^A \rightarrow S_1^A \rightarrow S_2^A$ on the application of the sequence $A_1 \rightarrow A_2 \rightarrow A_3$. Because these states are unreachable in the normal mode of operation, they and the corresponding circuit output values constitute a property that was not part of the original design. As shown in [77], the probability of determining such an embedded watermark and masking it is extremely small, thus establishing it as a robust watermarking scheme.

16.2.2   Effect of Obfuscation on Trojan Insertion

As mentioned before, to design a functionally catastrophic but hard-to-detect Trojan, the adversary would try to select a "rare" event at selected internal "trigger nodes" to activate the Trojan. To select a sufficiently rare trigger condition for the Trojan to be inserted, the adversary would try to estimate the signal probability [268] at the circuit nodes by simulations. To do so with a certain degree of confidence, a minimum number of simulations with random starting states and random input vectors must be performed [413]. However, the adversary has no way to know whether the starting state of the simulations is in the *normal state space* or the *obfuscation state space*. If the initial state of the simulations lie in the *obfuscation state space*, there is a high probability that the simulations would remain confined in the *obfuscation state space*. This is because the random test generation algorithm of the adversary most likely would be unable to apply the correct input vector at the correct state to cause the state transition to the *normal state space*. Essentially, the STG of the obfuscated circuit has two *near-closed* (NC) set of states [93], which would make accurate estimation of the signal probabilities through a series of random simulations extremely challenging. An algorithm was proposed in [93] to detect the *NC sets* of a sequential circuit; however, the algorithm requires: (a) knowledge of the state transition matrix of the entire sequential circuit, which is not available to the adversary, and (b) a list of all the *reachable states* of the circuit, which is extremely computationally challenging to enumerate for a reasonably large sequential circuit. Hence, we can assume that the adversary would be compelled to resort to a random simulation based method to estimate the signal probabilities at internal circuit nodes.

16.2.3   Effect of Obfuscation on Trojan Potency

To decrease the *potency* of the inserted Trojan, the designer of the obfuscated circuit must ensure that if the adversary starts simulating the circuit in the *obfuscation state space*, the probability of the circuit being driven to the *normal state space* is minimal. Consider a sequential circuit originally with N state elements and M *used states*, to which n state-elements are added to modify the STG to the form shown in Fig. 16.1(a). Let the number of states in the *obfuscation state space* be $S_i = f_1 \cdot 2^n \cdot (2^N - M) = f_1 \cdot 2^n \cdot B$, where $B = (2^N - M)$, and $f_1 < 1$ represents a *utilization factor* reflecting the overhead constraint.

Let I denote the set of states in the *obfuscation state space*, U denote the set of states in the *normal state space*, and T denote the set of states actually attained during the simulations by the adversary. Let, p be the number of primary inputs (other than the clock and reset) where the initialization *key* sequence is applied, and let the length of the initialization key sequence be k. Then, it takes k correct input vectors in sequence to reach the *normal state space* from state S_0^O, $k - 1$ correct input vectors from state S_1^O, and so on. Then, the probability that the simulation started in the *initialization state space* and was able to reach the *normal state space* by the application of random input vectors:

$$P\left(T \subseteq \left\{I \bigcup U\right\}\right) = \frac{k}{S_i + M} \cdot \left(\frac{1}{2^p} + \frac{1}{2^{2p}} + \cdots \frac{1}{2^{pk}}\right) \tag{16.1}$$

$$\approx \frac{k \cdot 2^{-p}}{\left(f_1 \cdot 2^n \cdot B + M\right)\left(1 - 2^{-p}\right)} \tag{16.2}$$

assuming $2^{-pk} \ll 1$. Similarly, the probability that the simulations started in the *initialization state space* or the *isolation state space* and remained confined there:

$$P\left(T \subseteq \left\{I \bigcup U'\right\}\right) = \left[1 - \frac{k \cdot 2^{-p}}{\left(f_1 \cdot 2^n \cdot B + M\right)\left(1 - 2^{-p}\right)}\right] \cdot \frac{f_1 \cdot 2^n \cdot B}{f_1 \cdot 2^n \cdot B + M} \tag{16.3}$$

where U' denotes the complement set of U. Again, the probability that the simulations started in the *normal state space*, and remained confined there is:

$$P\left(T \subseteq U\right) = \frac{M}{f_1 \cdot 2^n \cdot B + M} \tag{16.4}$$

To maximize the probability of keeping the simulations confined in the *obfuscation state space*, the designer should ensure:

$$P\left(T \subseteq \left\{I \bigcup U'\right\}\right) \gg P\left(T \subseteq U\right) + P\left(T \subseteq \left\{I \bigcup U\right\}\right) \tag{16.5}$$

Approximating $M \gg \frac{k \cdot 2^{-p}}{1 - 2^{-p}}$, and simplifying, this leads to:

$$f_1 \cdot 2^n \cdot B \gg M \tag{16.6}$$

This equation essentially implies the size of the *obfuscation state space* should be much larger compared to the size of the *normal state space*, a result that is intuitively expected. From this analysis, the two main observations are:

- The size of the *obfuscation state space* has an exponential dependence of the number of extra state elements added.

- In a circuit where the size of the used state space is small compared to the size of the unused state space, higher levels of obfuscation can be achieved at lower hardware overhead.

As an example, consider the ISCAS-89 benchmark circuit $s1423$ with 74 state elements (i.e. $N = 74$), and $> 2^{72}$ unused states (i.e., $2^N - M > 2^{72}$) [424]. Then, $M < 1.42 \times 10^{22}$, and considering 10 extra state elements added (i.e. $n = 10$), $f_1 > 0.0029$ for eqn. (16.6) to hold. Thus, expanding the state space in the modified circuit by about 3% of the available unused state space is sufficient in this case.

16.2.4   Effect of Obfuscation on Trojan Detectability

Consider a Trojan designed and inserted by the adversary with q trigger nodes, with *estimated* rare signal probabilities $p_1, p_2, \ldots p_q$, obtained by simulating the obfuscated circuit. Then, assuming random input vectors, the adversary expects the Trojan to be activated once (on average) by the application of

$$N = \frac{1}{\prod\limits_{i=1}^{q} p_i} \tag{16.7}$$

test vectors. However, let the *actual* rare logic value probabilities of these internal nodes be $p_i + \Delta p_i$, for the i-th trigger node. Then, the Trojan would be *actually* activated once (on average) by:

$$N' = \frac{1}{\prod\limits_{i=1}^{q} (p_i + \Delta p_i)} = \frac{N}{\prod\limits_{i=1}^{q} (1 + \frac{\Delta p_i}{p_i})} \tag{16.8}$$

test vectors. The difference between the estimated and the actual number of test vectors before the Trojan is activated is $\Delta N = N - N'$, which leads to a percentage normalized difference:

$$\frac{\Delta N}{N}(\%) = \left(1 - \frac{1}{\prod\limits_{i=1}^{q} (1 + \frac{\Delta p_i}{p_i})} \right) \times 100\% \tag{16.9}$$

To appreciate the effect that Δp and q has on this change on the average number of vectors that can activate the Trojan, assume $\frac{\Delta p_i}{p_i} = f$ $\forall i = 1, 2 \ldots q$; then eqn. (16.9) can be simplified to:

$$\frac{\Delta N}{N}(\%) = \left(1 - \frac{1}{(1 + f)^q} \right) \times 100\% \tag{16.10}$$

Fig. 16.2 shows this fractional change plotted vs. the number of trigger nodes (q) for different values of the fractional mis-estimation of the signal probability (f). From this plot and eqns. (16.9) and (16.10), it is evident that:

- The probability of the Trojan getting detected by logic testing increases as the number of Trojan trigger nodes (q) increases. However, it is unlikely that the adversary will have more than 10 trigger nodes, because otherwise as shown by our simulations, it becomes extremely difficult to trigger the Trojans at all.

- For values $2 \leq q \leq 10$, the number of random input patterns required to activate the trojan decreases sharply with q. The improvement is more pronounced at higher values of f. This observation validates the rationale behind an obfuscation-based design approach that resists the adversary from correctly estimating the signal probabilities at the internal circuit nodes.

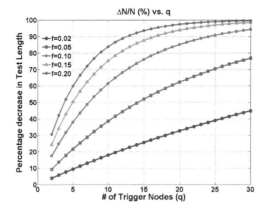

FIGURE 16.2: Fractional change in average number of test vectors required to trigger a Trojan, for different values of average fractional mis-estimation of signal probability f and Trojan trigger nodes (q).

16.2.5 Effect of Obfuscation on Circuit Structure

The re-synthesis of the circuit after its integration with the RTL description corresponding to the *obfuscation state space* flattens the circuit into a single netlist, resulting in drastic changes to the input logic cones of the primary outputs and the state elements. This makes it infeasible to manually or automatically analyze and identify the modifications made to a practical circuit with reasonably large number of gates, even if the adversary is in possession of an unmodified version of the original circuit netlist. To appreciate this effect, consider the

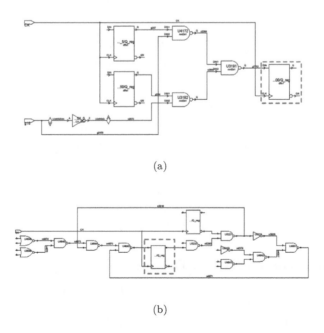

(a)

(b)

FIGURE 16.3: Comparison of input logic cones of a selected flip-flop in $s15850$: (a) original design and (b) obfuscated design.

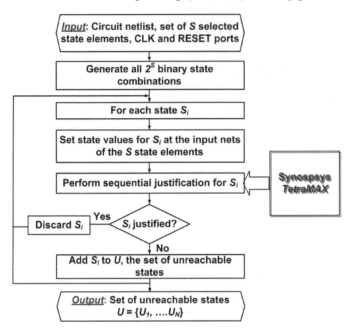

FIGURE 16.4: Steps to find unreachable states for a given set of S state elements in a circuit.

input logic cones (up to 4 levels) of a selected flip-flop in the gate -level netlist of the $s15850$ ISCAS-89 benchmark, and its obfuscated version, shown in Fig. 16.3. Similarly significant structural difference was observed for all the benchmark circuits considered by us. If the adversary is not in possession of an unmodified *reference* gate-level design, this task is even more difficult, as the adversary would have no idea about the netlist structure of the original design. The theoretical complexity of reverse-engineering similar key–based obfuscation schemes for circuits has been analysed in [229, 208], where such systems were shown to be "provably secure" because of the high computational complexity.

16.2.6 Determination of Unreachable States

The construction of the *obfuscation state space* requires the determination of *unreachable states* in a given circuit. Fig. 16.4 shows the steps of determining the set of unreachable states for a selected set of S state elements in a given circuit. First, all the possible 2^S state bit combinations are generated for the S state elements. Then, each state of these 2^S states are subjected to *full sequential justification* at the inputs of the selected S state elements, using *Synopsys Tetramax*. The justified states are discarded, while the states which fail justification are collected to form the set U of structurally unreachable states.

16.2.7 Test Generation for Trojan Detection

Since deterministic test pattern generation for the Trojan population is practically infeasible due to the inordinately large number of possible Trojans, we apply a statistical approach to sample and simulate a representative set of Trojan instances (10–20 K) from the total population of Trojans. First, the signal probabilities at the internal nodes of the circuit are estimated by the application of a large set of random vectors to the circuit. From the signal probability (S_p) of the internal nodes, which indicate the rareness of a logic-0 or

---

Algorithm 16.1: Procedure *OBFUSCATE*

Generate the obfuscated netlist from a given circuit netlist

Inputs: Circuit netlist, maximum area overhead (*max_area_overhead*), total number of states in the *obfuscation state space*, length of *initialization key sequence* (k)

Outputs: Obfuscated circuit netlist, *initialization key sequence*

1: Set no. of extra state elements to be added: $n \leftarrow 8$
2: Set no. of original state elements to be used for state encoding: $S \leftarrow 5$
3: **repeat**
4:    **repeat**
5:      Select S state elements randomly from circuit netlist
6:      Determine unreachable states for S state elements using sequential justification
7:    **until** sufficient unreachable states found
8:    Generate state encodings for the extra state elements
9:    Generate random state transitions for the extra state elements
10:    Generate random *initialization key sequence* of length k
11:    Generate RTL for *obfuscation state space*
12:    Integrate generated RTL with existing netlist
13:    Re-synthesize modified circuit
14:    Calculate *area_overhead*
15:    $n \Leftarrow n - 1, S \Leftarrow S - 1$
16: **until** *area_overhead* $\leq$ *max_area_overhead*

---

logic-1 event in those nodes, we select a set of candidate trigger nodes with S_p less than a specified trigger threshold (θ). Next, starting from a large set of *weighted random vectors*, a smaller testset is generated to excite each of these candidate trigger nodes to its rare value at least N times, where N is a given parameter. This is done because excitation of each rare node individually to its corresponding rare value multiple times is likely to increase the probability of the Trojans triggered by them to get activated, as shown by the analysis in [81]. We have observed through extensive simulations on both combinational (ISCAS-85) and sequential (ISCAS-89) benchmark circuits, that such a statistical test generation methodology can achieve higher Trojan detection coverage than weighted random vector set, with 85% reduction in test length on average [81]. Note that for sequential circuits, we assume a *full-scan* implementation. Sequential justification is applied to eliminate *false Trojans*, i.e. Trojans which cannot be triggered during the operation of the circuit.

16.2.8   Determination of Effectiveness

To determine the decrease in *potency* of the Trojans by the proposed scheme, we reduce a given vector set to eliminate those vectors with state values in the *obfuscation state space*. We then re-simulate the circuit with the reduced test set to determine the Trojan coverage. The decrease in the Trojan coverage obtained from the reduced test set indicates the Trojans which are activated or effective only in the *obfuscation state space* and, hence, become benign.

To determine the increase in *detectability* of the Trojans, we compare the S_p values at the Trojan trigger nodes between two cases: 1) a large set of random vectors, and 2) a modified set of random vectors which ensure operation of the obfuscated design in only *normal mode*. The increase in Trojan detectability is estimated by the percentage of circuit nodes for which the S_p values differ by a pre-defined threshold. The difference in estimated S_p prevents an adversary from exploiting the true rare events at the internal circuit nodes in order to design a hard-to-detect Trojan. On the other hand, true non-rare nodes may appear as rare in the obfuscated design, which potentially serve as *decoy* to the adversary. The above two effects are summed up by the increase in Trojan detection coverage due to the obfuscation. The coverage increase is estimated by comparing the respective coverage values obtained for the obfuscated and the original design for the same number of test patterns.

16.3   Integrated Framework for Obfuscation

Algorithm-16.1 shows the steps of the procedure *OBFUSCATE*, which performs the obfuscation of a given gate-level circuit. The input arguments are the gate-level synthesized Verilog netlist of the given circuit, the maximum allowable area overhead, the total number of states in the *obfuscation state space*, and the length of the input key sequence (k). Initially, the number (n) of extra state elements to be added and the number (S) of existing state elements to be used for state-encoding in the initialization state space are both set to five. These S state-elements are randomly chosen for state-encoding in the *initialization state space*, and their unreachable states are determined by the method described in Section 16.2.6. If the number of unreachable states found is not sufficient for the required number of states in the *obfuscation state space*, another random selection of S state elements is made and the process is continued until sufficient unreachable states are found. Once this is done, state encoding for the extra state elements and random state transitions for the 2^n states of the n extra state elements is generated. Next, an initialization key sequence of length k is selected randomly. The RTL of state transitions of the two separate set of flip-flops for the *initialization state space* is generated. As mentioned in Section 16.2.1, the RTL is constructed in a way that ensures that the chosen original state elements and the extra state elements act together as parts of the same FSM during the initialization phase.

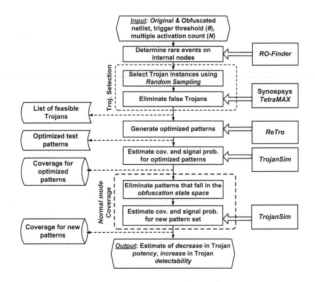

FIGURE 16.5: Framework to estimate the effectiveness of the obfuscation scheme.

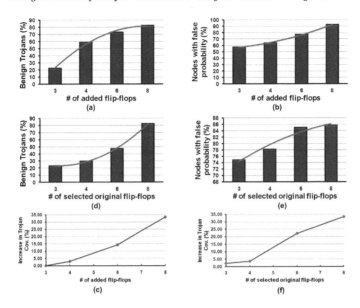

FIGURE 16.6: Variation of protection against Trojans in *s1196* as a function of (a), (b) and (c): the number of added flip-flops in state encoding (S); (d), (e) and (f): the number of original state elements used in state encoding (n). For (a), (b) and (c), four original state elements were selected for state encoding, while for (d), (e) and (f), four extra state elements were added.

The RTL is then integrated with the original gate-level netlist, with appropriate control signals to enable the operation in the two different modes. The modified circuit is then re-synthesized under input design constraints using *Synopsys Design Compiler* to generate the obfuscated version of the circuit. If the area of the re-synthesized circuit is larger than the user-specified area overhead constraint, S and n are each decreased by one and the process is repeated until the area constraint is satisfied for the obfuscated design.

We assumed the Trojan model shown in Fig. 13.5(a). We wrote three C programs to estimate the effectiveness of the proposed obfuscation scheme for protection against Trojans. The computation of signal probabilities at the internal nodes is done by the program *RO-Finder* (**R**are **O**ccurrence **Finder**). The testset for Trojan detection achieving multiple excitation of rare trigger conditions is performed by the program *ReTro* (**Re**duced pattern generator for **Tro**jans). The generation of the reduced pattern set by the elimination of the patterns with states in the *obfuscation state space* is performed by a TCL program. The decrease in the Trojan *potency* and the increase in the Trojan *detectability* are then estimated by a cycle-accurate simulation of the circuit by the simulator *TrojanSim* (**Trojan Sim**ulator). *TetraMax* is used for sequential justification of the Trojan triggering conditions. Fig. 16.5 shows the steps to estimate the effectiveness of the obfuscation scheme [79]. The entire flow was integrated with the *Synopsys* design environment using TCL scripts. A *LEDA* 250nm standard cell library was used for logic synthesis. All simulations, test generation and logic synthesis were carried out on a Hewlett-Packard Linux workstation with a 2GHz dual-core processor and 2GB RAM.

TABLE 16.1: Effect of Obfuscation on Security Against Trojans (100,000 random patterns, 20,000 Trojan instances, $q = 2$, $k = 4$, $\theta = 0.2$)

Benchmark Circuit	Trojan Instances	Obfus. Flops $(n + S)$	Obfuscation Effects		
			Benign Trojans (%)	False Prob. Nodes (%)	Func. Troj. Cov. Incr. (%)
s1488	192	8	38.46	63.69	0.00
s5378	2641	9	40.13	85.05	1.02
s9234	747	9	29.41	65.62	1.09
s13207	1190	10	36.45	83.59	0.56
s15850	1452	10	40.35	68.95	2.65
s38584	342	12	33.88	81.83	0.45

TABLE 16.2: Effect of Obfuscation on Security Against Trojans (100,000 random patterns, 20,000 Trojan instances, $q = 4$. $k = 4$, $\theta = 0.2$)

Benchmark Circuit	Trojan Instances	Obfuscation Effects		
		Benign Trojans (%)	False Prob. Nodes (%)	Func. Troj. Cov. Incr. (%)
s1488	98	60.53	71.02	12.12
s5378	331	70.28	85.05	15.00
s9234	20	62.50	65.62	25.00
s13207	36	80.77	83.59	20.00
s15850	124	77.78	79.58	18.75
s38584	11	71.43	77.21	50.00

16.4   Results

To verify the trends predicted in Section 16.2.3, we investigated the effects of adding extra state elements (n) and unreachable states determined from variable number of existing state elements (S) on the level of protection against Trojans. Fig. 16.6 shows the variation in the percentage of Trojans rendered benign, percentage of internal nodes with false signal probability, and the percentage increase in detectability of Trojans for the *s1196* benchmark circuit. These plots clearly show the increasing level of protection against Trojans with the increasing size of the *obfuscation state space*, which matches the theoretical predictions in Section 16.2.3.

Table 16.1 and Table 16.2 show the effects of obfuscation on increasing the security against hardware Trojans for a set of ISCAS-89 benchmark circuits with 20,000 random instances of suspected Trojans, trigger threshold (θ) of 0.2, trigger nodes (q) 2 and 4, respectively. Optimized vector set was generated using N=1000. The same value of $n + S$ applies to both sets of results. The length of the initialization key sequence was 4 ($k = 4$) for all the benchmarks. The effect of obfuscation was estimated by three metrics: (a) the fraction of the total population of structurally justifiable Trojans becoming benign; (b) the difference between the signal probabilities at internal nodes of the obfuscated and original circuit, and (c) the improvement in the *functional Trojan coverage*, i.e. the increase in the percentage of valid Trojans detected by logic testing. Note that the number of structurally justifiable Trojans (as determined by *TetraMax*) decreases with the increase in the number of trigger nodes of the Trojan, and increasing size of the benchmark circuits. From the tables it is evident that the construction of the *obfuscation state space* with even a relatively small number of state elements (i.e. a relatively small value of $n + S$) still makes a significant fraction of the Trojans benign. Moreover, it obfuscates the true signal probabilities of a

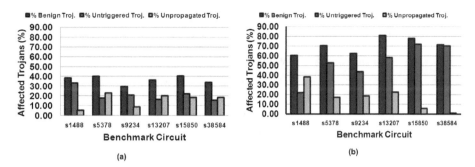

FIGURE 16.7: Effect of obfuscation on Trojans: (a) 2-trigger node Trojans ($q = 2$), and (b) 4-trigger node Trojans ($q = 4$).

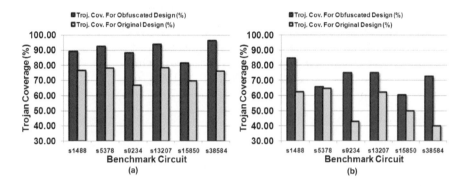

FIGURE 16.8: Improvement of Trojan coverage in obfuscated design compared to the original design for (a) Trojans with 2 trigger nodes ($q = 2$) and (b) Trojans with 4 trigger nodes ($q = 4$).

large number of nodes. The obfuscation scheme is more effective for 4-trigger node Trojans. This is expected since a Trojan with larger q is more likely to select at least one trigger condition from the *obfuscation state space*.

Fig. 16.7 shows the two different effects by which Trojans are rendered benign (as discussed in Section and 16.2.3) - i.e. some of them are triggered only in the *obfuscation state space*, while the effect of some are propagated to the primary output only in the *obfuscation state space*. In these plots, the greater effectiveness of the obfuscation approach for 4-trigger node Trojans is again evident.

Fig. 16.8 shows the improvement in Trojan detection coverage in the obfuscated design compared to the original design for the same number of random vectors. This plot illustrates the net effect of the proposed obfuscation scheme in increasing the level of protection against Trojans, with an average increase of 14.83% for $q = 2$ and 20.24% for $q = 4$. The greater effectiveness for $q = 4$ agrees with the theoretical observation in Section 16.2.4.

Table 16.3 shows the design overheads (at iso-delay) and the run-time for the proposed obfuscation scheme. The proposed scheme incurs modest area and power overheads, and the design overhead decreases with increasing size of the circuit. The results and trends are comparable with the STG modification based watermarking schemes proposed in [276, 426]. As mentioned earlier, the level of protection against Trojan can be increased by choosing a larger $n + S$ value at the cost of greater design overhead. The run-time presented in the table is dominated by *TetraMax*, which takes more than 90% of the total time for sequential justifications.

TABLE 16.3: Design Overhead (at iso-delay) and Run-time[†] for the Proposed Design Flow

Benchmark Circuit	Overhead (%)		Run-time (mins.)
	Area	Power	
s1488	20.09	12.58	31
s5378	13.13	17.66	186
s9234	11.84	15.11	1814
s13207	8.10	10.87	1041
s15850	7.04	9.22	1214
s38584	6.93	2.63	2769

†The run time includes the sequential justification time by Synopsys *Tetramax*, which in most cases was over 90% of the total runtime.

16.4.1　Discussions

16.4.2　Application to Third-party IP Modules and SoCs

Pre-designed third-party hardware IP blocks, which have been supplied either as synthesizable "Register Transfer Level" (RTL) descriptions (also known as "soft macros"), or as synthesized gate-level netlists (also known as "firm macros"), can be modified to implement the proposed methodology. For RTL descriptions, obfuscation of an IP module can be achieved in two ways. In the first, "direct method", the used and unused states of the circuits can be identified by direct analysis of the control and data flow graph (CDFG) of the derived from the RTL, and then additional RTL code can be automatically generated to realize the change in the STG of the circuit. An automated design flow for performing similar key-based control-flow obfuscation for the purpose of IP protection of RTL designs has been previously proposed in [80]. In the second, "indirect method", the RTL description can be synthesized to a gate-level netlist to apply the proposed technique.

The proposed technique can also be extended to multi–IP system-on-chips (SoCs), even in those cases where the communication fabric of the SoC is custom-designed. This is possible since the proposed methodology does not depend on the structure and communication protocols used by the communication fabric of the SoC. A SoC design methodology that employs key-based obfuscation of hardware IP modules has been previously proposed in [77].

16.4.3　Protection against Malicious CAD Tools

Besides protecting a design in foundry, the proposed obfuscation methodology can provide effective defense against malicious modifications (manual or automated) during the IC design steps. As pointed out in Chapter 13, compromised CAD tools and automation scripts can also insert Trojans in a design [107, 335]. Obfuscation can prevent insertion of hard-to-detect Trojans by CAD tools due to similar reasons as applicable in a foundry. It prevents an automatic analysis tool from finding the true rare events, which can be poten-

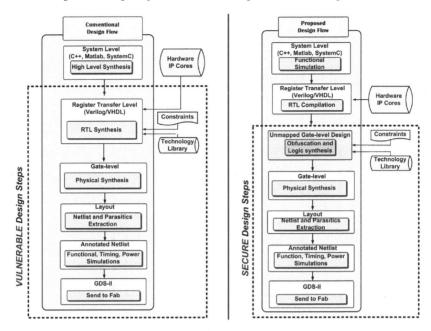

FIGURE 16.9: Comparison of conventional and proposed SoC design flows. In the proposed design flow, protection against malicious modification by untrusted CAD tools can be achieved through obfuscation early in the design cycle.

tially used as Trojan triggers or payloads. Moreover, since large number of states belong to the obfuscation state space, an automation tool is very likely to insert a Trojan randomly that is only effective in the obfuscation mode. Note that since we obfuscate the gate-level netlist, protection against CAD tools can be achieved during the design steps following logic synthesis (e.g. during physical synthesis and layout).

To increase the scope of protection by encompassing the logic synthesis step, we propose a small modification in the obfuscation-based design flow. Fig. 16.9 compares a conventional IP-based SoC design flow with the proposed modified design flow. In the conventional design flow, the RTL is directly synthesized to a technology mapped gate-level netlist, and obfuscation is applied on this netlist. However, in the modified design flow, the RTL is first *compiled* to a technology independent (perhaps unoptimized) gate-level description, and obfuscation is applied on this netlist. Such a practice is quite common in the industry, and many commercial tools support such a compilation as a preliminary step to logic synthesis [374]. The obfuscated netlist is then optimized and technology mapped by a logic synthesis tool. Note that the logic synthesis step now operates on the obfuscated design, which protects the design from potential malicious operations during logic synthesis. Also, the RTL *compilation* (without logic optimization) is a comparatively simpler computational step for which the SoC design house can employ a trusted in-house tool. This option provides an extra level of protection.

This proposed obfuscation methodology also provides protection against malicious CAD tools in Field Programable Gate Array (FPGA) based design flows. As noted in [107], the main threat of Trojan insertion in such a flow comes from the CAD tools which convert the RTL description of a design to the FPGA device specific configuration *bitstream*. Typically, the fabric itself can be assumed to be Trojan-free [107]. Similar to the SoC design flow, we propose a small modification to the FPGA design flow that maximizes the scope of protection against FPGA CAD tools. Fig. 16.10 shows the proposed design flow. The RTL

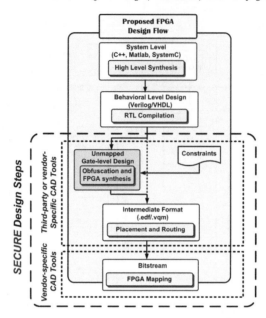

FIGURE 16.10: Proposed FPGA design flow for protection against CAD tools.

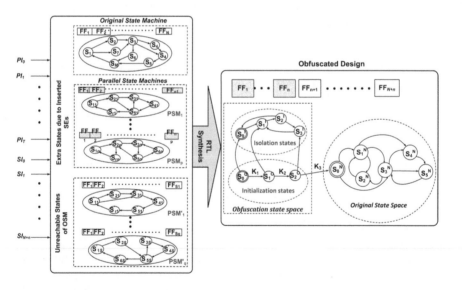

FIGURE 16.11: Obfuscation for large designs can be efficiently realized using multiple parallel state machines which are constructed with new states due to additional state elements as well as unreachable states of original state machine.

corresponding to the circuit can be "compiled" to a unoptimized, technology-independent gate-level netlist. This netlist can then be obfuscated, and the obfuscated design can then be optimized and mapped by either third-party CAD tools or vendor-specific tools to a netlist in an intermediate format. This netlist is then converted to a vendor-specific bitstream format by the FPGA mapping tool to map the circuit to the FPGA. Note that as before, the security against malicious CAD tools propagate to lower levels of design abstraction.

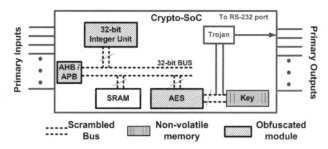

FIGURE 16.12: Functional block diagram of a crypto-SoC showing possible Trojan attack to leak secret key stored inside the chip. Obfuscation coupled with bus scrambling can effectively prevent such attack.

16.4.4 Improving Level of Protection and Design Overhead

Eqn. (16.6) suggests that for large designs with a significantly large *original state space*, to attain satisfactory levels of design obfuscation, it is necessary to have the *obfuscation state space* much larger than the *original state space*. This can be achieved by either: (a) addition of a large number of extra state elements, or (b) using a large number of unreachable states in the *obfuscation state space*. However, finding large number of unreachable states through sequential justification in a complex design is extremely computationally expensive. To keep the problem computationally tractable and reduce the design overhead, we propose a systematic approach to modify the state transition function as shown in Fig. 16.11. The n extra state elements are grouped into p different groups to form parallel FSMs PSM_1 through PSM_p, and RTL code for each of them is generated separately. Similarly, the S existing state elements (corresponding to the unreachable states) used for state encoding in the *obfuscation state space* are grouped in q different groups PSM'_1 through PSM'_q. RTL code for each of the parallel FSMs PSM'_1 through PSM'_q is generated separately based on the unreachable states. Such a scheme of having multiple parallel FSMs to design the *obfuscation state space* achieves similar design obfuscation effects, without incurring high computational complexity and design overhead.

16.4.5 Protection against Information Leakage Trojans

Although in our simulations we considered the Trojans according to the model shown in Fig. 13.5(a), the proposed methodology can also help to protect against Trojan attacks that aim at leaking secret information about internal state of the circuit, either in the form of a data-stream (similar to Fig. 13.5(c)) or as side-channel signature (similar to Fig. 13.5(d)). Such a Trojan is shown in Fig. 16.12, where it transmits out a secret cryptographic key through a covert communication channel by "sniffing" the values on the communication bus. *Bus scrambling* or bus re-ordering is a simple technique to resist against this kind of an attack, so that the data transmitted out by the Trojan is also scrambled. To overcome this defense mechanism, the adversary has to figure out the actual order of bits in the scrambled bus to correctly interpret the collected data. Figuring out the actual order of the bits in a n-bit bus by simulations will require a search among $n!$ possibilities, e.g. $\sim 2 \times 10^{35}$ possibilities for a 32-bit data bus. However, since the attacker has access to the design, he/she is likely to perform structural analysis of the design to determine the order of bits in the bus. If the functional blocks are not obfuscated, one can employ equivalence checking between a functional block in the design and a corresponding reference design to identify the order of bits in both input/output bus for a module. For example, an attacker can perform formal

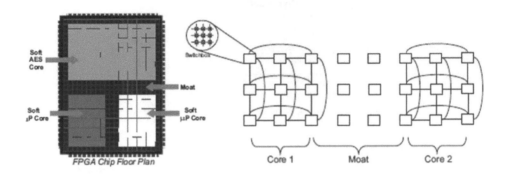

FIGURE 16.13: Module isolation through moats and drawbridges [156].

verification between the integer unit in Fig. 16.12 and a functionally equivalent reference design to find the port association.

However, if all the modules in the given SoC are obfuscated using the proposed approach, it would be practically infeasible for a formal verification tool to establish structural equivalence [77]. The other choice left to the attacker is to simulate the circuit by applying input vectors. For simplicity, assume all modules in the SoC are initialized simultaneously and by the same initialization key sequence. Then, to reach the *normal mode* of operation, the adversary needs to first apply the correct *unknown* initialization vectors in correct order to enable normal operating mode of the IC. Only then the adversary would be able to establish the actual bus order through simulations, the complexity of which has already been shown to be extremely high. The probability of succeeding in reaching the normal mode by the application of random vectors to the primary input of a SoC with M primary inputs and an initialization key sequence length of N is $\frac{1}{2^{M \cdot N}}$. Assuming the SoC shown in Fig. 16.12 has 32 inputs, and assuming the length of the *initialization key sequence* to be 4, the probability of the adversary taking the obfuscated SoC to the *normal mode* is $\sim 10^{-39}$. The width of the data bus for the key is typically 128 or 256, which would increase the complexity exponentially. A similar argument can be presented for Trojans of the type shown in Fig. 13.5(d).

16.5   A FPGA-based Design Technique for Trojan Isolation

A module isolation technique to resist Trojan attacks was proposed in [156]. The main motivation behind the work is that in a multi-core FPGA system, with the cores typically coming from different (potentially untrusted) vendors, it is very difficult to verify whether any of the inserted cores is illegally accessing data that it should not. For example, how can we be sure that a soft microprocessor mapped on a FPGA is not secretly accessing the key being used by an AES encryption circuit on the same FPGA. The solution to this problem as envisioned by the authors is to restrict long communication links between cores, other than those required. This is done by isolating the cores in restricted areas of the FPGA by separation channels, which the authors term as "moats". Communication is only allowed through arbitrated, time-division multiplexed and verifiable communication channels between the cores, which are termed "drawbridges".

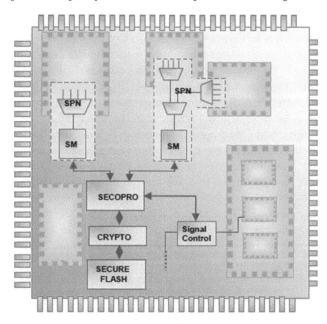

FIGURE 16.14: *DEFENSE* hardware infrastructure for runtime monitoring. [7].

Usually, automatic place-and-route CAD tools for FPGAs do not isolate cores placed on the same FPGA. Hence, it becomes extremely difficult for large designs to verify the connectivity in such overlapped place-and-route situations. The implementation of the moats is done by the authors by performing extensive manual placement of the cores on the FPGA fabric, and the connectivity is verified by custom tools written by the authors.

Fig. 16.13 shows a scenario where several cores on a FPGA are isolated by restricting their placement to different non-overlapping locations of the FPGA. If the interconnects connecting the different "switch-boxes" on the FPGA routing fabric are restricted to a width w, then it is sufficient to separate the modules by a moat of width w while performing placement. Thus, $w = 2$ in the above scenario. However, restricting the interconnect lengths to some limiting values usually results in higher routing-related overhead. For the *Xilinx* FPGA platform, the authors reported 15% average increase in area and 19% average increase in delay.

16.6 A Design Infrastructure Approach to Prevent Circuit Malfunction

This run–time technique [7] is based on the observation that given the widely varying and arbitrarily complex *modus operandi* of hardware Trojans, it might be impractical to devise testing techniques to detect all types of possible hardware Trojans. As we have discussed time and again, all types of Trojan detection techniques suffer from different short-comings which decrease their effectiveness. This problem is especially acute in modern IP–based system development, where complex IPs are procured from different IP vendors. A better option might be to perform in-field, real-time sanity checking during circuit operations, to prevent any disastrous circuit malfunction from happening. Thus, instead of fighting an invisible enemy, the approach is to detect any deviation from the expected circuit operation, and take pro–active preventive measures when such a situation is detected.

Since sometimes it might be difficult to distinguish between a circuit malfunction due to Trojans or circuit defects, these techniques are essentially variants of *fault-tolerant circuit design* techniques, which often use checksums at important internal circuit nodes to detect the state of the circuit. The design is analyzed, and the given HDL code is modified to instantiate special reconfigurable, synthesizable error checking hardware primitives. The authors term such add–on "infrastructure logic" as "DEFENSE" (acronym for "Design–for–Enabling–Security"). The authors describe the features of a commercial CAD software tool to perform the above task, with the user having the liberty to mention the nodes to be monitored.

The checker circuitry periodically performs sanity checking during run-time (without disrupting normal functionality), and reports any deviation from expected behavior on-the-fly. The assertions required to perform the sanity checking, and the comparison of the observed internal logic values with the expected values are performed by re-configurable FSMs called "Security Monitors" (SMs). These FMSs have to be specified by the designer. SMs get their inputs from distributed, pipelined MUX networks termed "Security Probe Networks" (SPNs). SPNs and SMs are configured by a master controller called the "Security and Control Processor" (SECORPRO). The configuration of one SM does not disrupt the normal system operation of the checking activity of another SM. If any deviation from expected behavior is detected, the SECORPRO is informed by the SM that detected the deviation, and this causes the SECORPRO to take remedial measures, such as disabling the misbehaving core. Fig. 16.14 shows the overall scheme. System recovery has to be performed by supervising hardware/software, based on any signal that SECORPRO might generate.

The DEFENSE logic is inserted at the RTL, and then the modified RTL can be subjected to the usual IP–based IC design flow. The SECORPRO is configured by first decrypting an encrypted configuration bitstream stored on a secure flash memory module inaccessible to the chip manufacturer, and any potential attacker. However, the authors do not mention the hardware or performance overhead figures.

Part VI

Physically Unclonable Functions

Chapter 17

Physically Unclonable Functions: a Root-of-Trust for Hardware Security

The chapter is co–written with Durga Prasad Sahoo.

> *"The mantra of any good security engineer is:* **Security is a not a product, but a process.** *It's more than designing strong cryptography into a system; it's designing the entire system such that all security measures, including cryptography, work together."*
>
> Bruce Schneier

17.1   Introduction

The pervasive use of hardware devices makes them vulnerable to physical attacks due to their easy availability to adversaries. To have a secure "digital life", we need to ensure the security of the hardware components along with that of the software. As mentioned in previous chapters, hardware counterfeiting is pervasive in the modern world, and causes great revenue loss to the hardware industry. It also compromises a user's safety and security as she is unsure about the origin of the electronic devices being used, which might carry out surreptitious malicious activities.

Most practical security mechanisms are based on some secret information. In traditional cryptography based solution, this secret information is used as an input(key) to the encryption/decryption algorithm. While cryptographic algorithms are mathematically secure against attack, it is known that digitally-stored secret key in on/off-chip memory can be vulnerable to physical attacks. In security tokens, such as smart cards, the secret key is stored in on-chip non-volatile memory, but FPGAs instead store the key in off-chip memory.

The Physically Unclonable Functions (PUFs) offer an efficient alternative to storing secret keys in on/off-chip memory. They exploit uncontrollable and intrinsic physical characteristic patterns of silicon devices due to physical process variations in manufacturing of integrated circuits (ICs). A PUF maps a set of digital input vectors, known as *challenges*, to a corresponding set of outputs, known as *responses* for use as unique fingerprint after required amount of post-processing. The basic property of a PUF is that the challenge-to-response mapping function is *instance specific*, and cannot be replicated by any known physical mean. Thus, it can be used as a volatile key storage mechanism and deters the invasive attacks for key discovery.

17.2   Physically Unclonable Function

A Physically Unclonable Function (PUF) is the physical embodiment of a function that makes it hard to clone and exhibits an unpredictable challenge-response behavior that is (ideally) hard to characterize or model, but which is otherwise easily and reliably evaluated. In [234], R.Maes et al. explain PUF in a formal setting, by mentioning seven properties that are commonly exhibited by the most PUFs. Those properties are reviewed below using the mapping $\Gamma : \mathcal{C} \to \mathcal{R} : \Gamma(c) = r$ to represent PUF's challenge-response behavior.

TABLE 17.1: PUF Timeline

Year	PUF Type
2000	IC identification using device mismatch [224]
2001	Physically One-way function [293]
2002	Physical Random Function [128]
2004	Arbiter PUF [129], Feed Forward Arbiter PUF [217]
2006	Coating PUF [391]
2007	Ring Oscillator PUF(RO-PUF) [372], SRAM PUF [139], Latch PUF [371], XOR-Arbiter PUF [372, 354]
2008	Butterfly PUF [213], D Flip-Flop PUF [233], Tristate Buffer PUF [283], Lightweight Secure PUF [240]
2009	Power Grid PUF [147]
2010	Glitch PUF [363], SHIC(Super High Information Content)PUF [340]
2011	Mecca PUF [211], Bistable Ring PUF [90], Ultra-low Power Current-Based PUF [239], Current Starved Inverter Chain PUF [212], Logically Reconfigurable PUF [184]
2012	Buskeeper PUF [365], Asynchronous PUF(AsyncPUF/Self-Timed/Clockless) [267], PUF using setup time violation [148]
2013	ClockPUF [423], HELP [5]

1. *Evaluatable*: given Γ and c, it is easy to evaluate $r = \Gamma(c)$.

2. *Unique*: $\Gamma(c)$ contains some information about the identity of the physical entity embedding Γ.

3. *Reproducible*: $y = \Gamma(c)$ is reproducible up to a small (possibly correctable) error.

4. *Unclonable*: given Γ, it is hard to construct a procedure $\Lambda \neq \Gamma$ such that $\forall c \in \mathcal{C}$: $\Lambda(c) \approx \Gamma(c)$ up to a small error.

5. *Unpredictable*: given only a set $\mathcal{Q} = \{(c_i, r_i = \Gamma(c_i)\}$; it is hard to predict $r_u = \Gamma(c_u)$ where $c_u \notin \mathcal{Q}$.

6. *One-way*: given only r and Γ, it is hard to find c such that $\Gamma(c) = r$.

7. *Tamper evident*: altering the physical entity embedding Γ transforms to $\Gamma \to \Gamma'$ such that with high probability $\exists c \in \mathcal{C} : \Gamma(c) \neq \Gamma'(c)$, not even up to a small error.

Research in the field of PUF was started in 2000 by the seminal work of Lofstrom et al. [224] that exploit mismatch in silicon devices for identification of ICs. In 2001, Pappu et al. [293] presented the concept of Physical one-way function which subsequently led to the idea of PUF [128]. Since then, different types of PUFs have been proposed. The type of PUF that soon drew the most attention of the most researchers is Silicon PUF (sPUF). B.Gassend et al. [128] were the first to implement silicon PUF in Commodity Field Programmable Gate Arrays (FPGAs). Table 17.1 shows a chronologic list of progress on PUF design starting from 2000. More detailed study of different type of PUF have been presented in [234]. In the next section we present a detailed classification of PUFs depending on diverse aspects

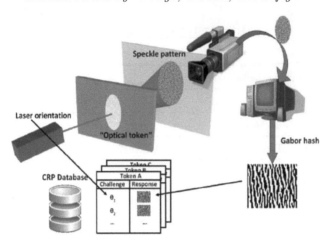

FIGURE 17.1: Basic principle of Optical PUF [234].

such as implementation technology, response collection mechanism, modeling difficulty, and re-configurability.

17.3   Classification of PUFs

17.3.1   Classification based on Technology

All PUFs reported in the literature can be broadly classified into four groups based on the technology used for their physical implementation: Optical PUF, Silicon PUF, Coating PUF, and Acoustic PUF.

- **Optical PUF** (see Fig. 17.1) could be considered as the first proposed PUF [294], although it was originally proposed as the physical embodiment of an (cryptographic) one-way function. The core component of an optical PUF is a transparent token with randomly doped scattering particles. When radiated with a laser a complex image with bright and dark spots arises, a so-called "speckle pattern". A Gabor filter turns out to be a good feature extractor for such a pattern and the filter output is the response of the optical PUF, while the physical parameters of the laser (location, orientation, wave length) constitute the challenge. Due to the complex nature of the interaction of the laser light with the scattering particles, the responses are highly random and unique. The high dependence of the response on the exact microscopic physical details of the optical token causes two equally produced tokens to exhibit different responses to the same challenge, and prevents a particular token from being cloned with high precision.

- **Silicon PUF** exploits uncontrollable CMOS manufacturing variations which are the result of unavoidable imperfections in modern IC fabrication processes. Manufacturing variation of parameters such as dopant concentrations and line widths manifest themselves as differences in timing behavior between instances of the same IC. These timing differences can be measured using a suitable circuit, and if desired, encoded

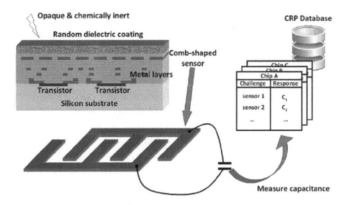

FIGURE 17.2: Basic principle of Coating PUF [234].

to a digital value. Ideally, a silicon PUF should not require a deviation from the normal CMOS processing steps, as well as be implementable using standard EDA design flows. It has been observed that these PUFs are quite sensitive to temperature variations and that compensation schemes for this effect have to be implemented to make the system work properly. More details about silicon PUFs are presented in [234].

- **Coating PUF** (shown in Fig. 17.2) is a PUF where a protective coating of an IC is used as the source of randomness. The opaque coating material is doped with dielectric particles, having random properties concerning their size, shape, and location. Below the coating layer, a comb structure of metal wire sensors is used to measure the local capacitance of the coating. The measured values, which are random due to the randomness present in the coating, form the responses to challenges, each of them specified by a voltage of a certain frequency and amplitude, applied to a region of the sensor array. Due to randomness in the properties of dielectric materials, it is hard to produce two PUFs where all sensors produce same values. The disadvantage of a coating PUF is that it supports limited number of CRPs. The advantage of coating PUFs is that their production price is very low. In addition, a benefit of coating PUF is that they are suitable for detecting a certain level of physical tampering. It is worthwhile to mention that Posch [303] suggested a similar concept to protect a device by embedding a unique signature into the coating material used in smart cards, much before the design of coating PUFs by Tuyls et al. described in [391].

- **Acoustic PUF** was first introduced in [398]. It is based on properties of acoustical wave propagation. An electrical signal (oscillating voltage) is transformed to an identical mechanical vibration by a transducer. This vibration propagates as a sound wave through a solid medium and scatters on the randomly distributed inhomogeneities in the medium. The reflections of those waves are measured by another transducer which converts the vibration back into an electric signal. It turns out that the reflections are unique for each token.

17.3.2   Classification based on Response Collection Mechanism

An alternative classification of PUFs in two categories is based on how the response reader interacts with it: *Intrinsic PUF* and *Controlled PUF*.

- **Intrinsic PUF** is embedded in the hardware it protects without introducing any modification or additions to introduce randomness, and they are read-proof in a sense that a reader can directly interact with it, without affecting its output value. The measurement setup is an inherent part of the PUF, and is integrated on chip. Such PUFs (e.g. most Silicon PUFs) are easy to construct and operate since often they not need any pre-processing and post-processing (other than possibly some error correction for noise), but they have some security vulnerabilities.

- **Controlled PUF** (CPUF) is accessed by an algorithm that is physically linked with the PUF in an inseparable way, such that any attempt to tamper the algorithm will destroy the PUF. This algorithm deters the reader to directly challenge the PUF and limits the information about responses that is seen by the outside world. A controlled PUF makes enumerating PUF responses harder and prevents man-in-the-middle (MITM) attacks. In addition, some PUFs require external or extra logic to explicitly introduce randomness (such as the optical and coating PUF) can also be considered under this category.

17.3.3   Classification based on Difficulty of Modeling

In addition, all PUFs can be classified into two groups based on the level of security they can provide as *Strong PUF* and *Weak PUF*. To be a strong PUF it must have following properties [339]:

- *Challenge-Response Pairs* The number of CRPs must be very large; often it is exponential with respect to some system parameters, for example, number of components used for building the PUF.

- *Practicality and Operability* The CRPs should be sufficiently stable and robust to variations in environmental conditions and multiple readings.

- *Access Mode* Any entity that has access to the Strong PUF can apply multiple challenges to it and can read out the corresponding responses. There is no protected, controlled or restricted access to the PUF's CRPs.

- *Security* Without physically possessing a Strong PUF, neither an adversary nor the PUF's manufacturer can correctly predict the response to a randomly chosen challenge with a high probability.

Weak PUFs possess only a small number of fixed challenges and its responses may remain secret and internal.

It is worth mentioning that meaning of the strong and weak pseudorandom function in classical cryptography are different from the notions of weak and strong PUFs described above. In cryptography, weak does not refer to an amount of CRPs, but to the ability of the adversary to select his queries adaptively.

17.3.4   Classification based on Reconfiguration Technique

The challenge-response behavior of PUFs could be static or dynamic. By dynamic we mean the ability to reconfigure challenge-response space after deployment using some external control. The reconfigurable PUF (rPUF) is a PUF with a mechanism to change the PUF input-output behaviour. Reconfiguration might be performed in two ways: *Logical* and *Physical* reconfiguration. Many practical applications would benefit from reconfigurable

PUFs, for example when rPUF-based wireless access tokens are re-used, the new user would not be able to access privacy-sensitive information of the previous user of the token.

Physical reconfiguration changes the physical structure of PUF. In [214], authors describe that physical reconfiguration of optical PUF by driving the laser at a higher current such that a laser beam of higher intensity is created which melts the polymer locally and enables to the scattering particles to reposition. After a short time the laser beam is removed and the structure cools down such that the particles freeze. Physical reconfiguration of silicon PUFs are possible when they are implemented only on reconfigurable hardware like FPGA. This gives a clear indication of in-applicability of physical reconfiguration for most of the PUF implementation. In [184], the authors present the concept of *Logically Reconfigurable PUF* that can be used as a practical alternative to physically reconfigurable PUFs. LR-PUFs consist of a PUF with a control logic that changes the challenge/response behavior of the LR-PUF according to its logical state, without physically replacing or modifying the underlying PUF.

All reconfigurable PUFs have *forward* and *backward* unpredictability: the former assures that responses measured before the reconfiguration event are invalid thereafter, while the latter assures that an adversary with access to a reconfigured PUF cannot estimate the PUF behavior before reconfiguration.

We now concentrate on silicon PUF designs.

17.4   Realization of Silicon PUFs

Silicon PUFs can be broadly classified into two categories: memory-based PUFs and delay-based PUFs. Memory based PUFs use the characteristics of memory cells such as SRAM-PUFs [139], Butterfly PUF [213], Flip-flop PUF [233] and Latch PUFs (LPUF) [371, 420, 419]. Delay-based PUFs use the characteristics of delay variations such as Arbiter PUF [129], Glitch PUF [363] and Ring Oscillator PUF [372].

17.4.1   Delay-based PUF

17.4.1.1   Ring Oscillator PUF

The ring oscillator (RO) circuit is a classic tool for measuring effects of process variation on gate propagation delay. It is comprised of an odd number of inverters connected in a closed chain to form a combinational loop. The input can have of a 2-input NAND gate that allows external control through a trigger signal. Once triggered, the ring oscillator will run freely at a frequency that is dependent on the propagation delay between the stages, and the number of stages. Average delay of a ring oscillator stage (t_{delay}) is calculated using the following equation when its oscillation frequency (f_{osc}) is given:

$$t_{delay} = \frac{1}{2n_{stages}f_{osc}}$$

where n_{stages} is the number of stages of the ring oscillator.

The propagation delay of gate and interconnection wire are mostly affected by process variation. In [372], the authors designed a so-called "Ring Oscillator PUF" (ROPUF) by exploiting ring oscillator as tool of random noise measurement. The classical ROPUF design, as shown in Fig.17.3, consists of n identically laid-out ring ROs. The challenge of ROPUF

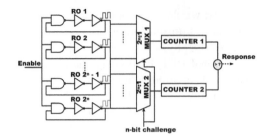

FIGURE 17.3: Ring Oscillator PUF [372].

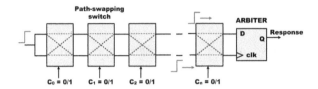

FIGURE 17.4: Arbiter PUF.

selects two distinct ROs, say R_a and R_b, and compare their frequencies to generate response by eqn. (17.1).

$$r = \begin{cases} 1, & \text{if } f_a > f_b \\ 0, & \text{otherwise} \end{cases} \tag{17.1}$$

where f_a and f_b are frequencies of R_a and R_b, respectively.

17.4.1.2   Arbiter PUF

The Arbiter PUF (APUF) is the first silicon PUF that extracts random noise in silicon in terms of the delay difference of two symmetrically designed parallel delay lines. Ideally, delay difference should be zero between two symmetrically laid-out paths, but in practice, it is non-zero due to uncontrollable variation in the IC manufacturing process that introduces random offset between the two delays. Fig. 17.4 depicts the classical APUF design that comprises of n 2×2 path-swapping switches connected serially to build two distinct, but symmetrical paths. The arbiter (usually a simple D flip-flop) at the end of two paths decides which path is faster. The challenge bits are used as the control input of path-swapping switches that eventually selects two paths, over which the an input trigger signal is propagated. The arbiter, at the end, declare which path wins the race in the form of response.

Let, two paths p_1^c and p_2^c are emerged due to challenge $c \in C$, and d_1 and d_2 are propagation delays of trigger pulse through paths p_1^c and p_2^c, respectively. The response of APUF might be defined by Eq. (17.2).

$$r = \begin{cases} 1, & \text{if } d_1 < d_2 \\ 0, & \text{otherwise} \end{cases} \tag{17.2}$$

If the delay offset between the two paths is too small, the *setup time constraint* or *hold time constraint* of the flip-flop arbiter might be violated, and its output will not depend on the outcome of the race any more, but be determined by random noise (as the flip-flop will go to a *metastable* state). The effect of such metastability would be manifested as statistical noise in the PUF responses.

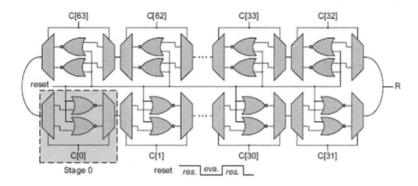

FIGURE 17.5: Bistable Ring PUF.

17.4.1.3 Bistable Ring PUF

Unlike RO, Bistable Ring consists of an even number of inverters connected in a ring. In a loop configuration, an inverter's output is dependent on output of preceding inverter. So, on power up, each inverter enters into one of the two stable states. When all the inverters are in stable states, their outputs generate one of the two sequences: '0101010101...' or '1010101010...'.

In [90], the authors introduce a design principle to modify a bistable ring into a Bistable Ring PUF (BRPUF) with an exponential number of CRPs. Following changes are made to the basic bistable ring:

1. For each stage, the inverter is duplicated, and a pair of multiplexor (MUX) and demultiplexor (DEMUX) is added to select either of the inverters to be connected in the inverter loop, and,

2. All the inverters are replaced with 2-input NOR or NAND gates, and the second inputs of the gates are connected to a reset signal that replaces the power up and power off operations.

Addition of reset signal, as shown in Fig. 17.5, eliminates the power-off operation required before every new measurement. It allows to bring ring into all 0's state by simply applying the reset signal to logic-1; and HIGH-to-LOW transition of the reset signal starts the evaluation of BRPUF for new challenge. Output of any stage can be used as response (1-bit response) and that must be consistently maintained for all challenges. One important point needed to be mentioned is that the *settling time* of BRPUF, the time required by the ring to settle into a stable state, must be estimated accurately. Wrong estimation of this time manifests as random noise in PUF response and reduces the reliability.

17.4.1.4 Loop PUF

The *Loop PUF* [92] consists of N identical delay chains connected in a loop with an inverter on the feedback path. Each delay chain is composed of M controllable delay elements. Fig. 17.6 shows the structure of delay element. The PUF circuit is challenged with the control words generated by the control circuit. Ideally, frequency of a LPUF should remain the same for all permutations of challenge C if the delay chains are perfectly balanced. But in physical devices there is a slight frequency discrepancy because of process variations. The response of the PUF is calculated from frequencies measured after the application of

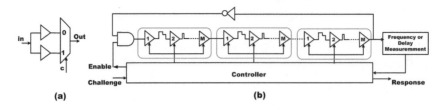

FIGURE 17.6: (a) Basic delay element. (b) Loop PUF structure.

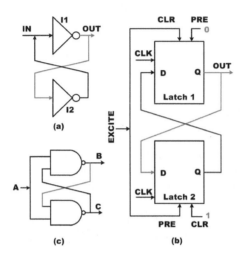

FIGURE 17.7: Memory PUF cell variants: (a) SRAM PUF cell; (b) Butterfly PUF cell; (c) Latch PUF cell.

particular control words. Let, f_X, f_Y and f_Z are frequencies of LPUF due to control words X, Y and Z, respectively. The response generated by the controller might be defined by eqn. (17.3).

$$r = (ID_0, ID_1, ID2) \qquad (17.3)$$

where $ID_0 = sign(f_X - f_Y)$, $ID_1 = sign(f_Y - f_Z)$ and $ID_2 = sign(f_Z - f_X)$.

17.4.2   Memory-based PUF

17.4.2.1   SRAM PUF

The SRAM PUF is a memory-based PUF that employs the initial power-up values of SRAM memory cells as PUF responses. Unlike the previously described Silicon PUFs, it does not receive any challenge. So it could be used to generate device signature. As shown in Fig. 17.7(a), a SRAM cell is built from two cross-coupled inverters that results in two stable states of a cell. Ideally two feedback paths should be symmetric, but due to process variation an offset emerges in the difference of their nominal propagation delays. It has been observed that few cells have tendency of storing logic-0 on power-up, while others store logic-1, and some of the cells have no reference value. But, distribution of these three type cells across SRAM is random and it varies from chip to chip. It should be noted that this PUF cannot be realized in SRAM-based FPGA because in FPGAs, during configuration all unused configuration memory cell are initialized to some predefined values to deter accidental damage like short-circuit.

17.4.2.2 Butterfly PUF

The Butterfly PUF (BPUF) was designed to emulate the behavior of SRAM PUF on FPGA. Unlike SRAM PUF, BPUF cell, as shown in Fig. 17.7(b), consists of two crossed-coupled D latches with clear (CLR) and preset (PRESET) signals. The CLK signal is always set to logic-1 to stimulate the combinational loop. Initially, the EXCITE signal is set to logic-1 to put BPUF cell into an unstable state (as input and output values are opposite for both latches) and subsequently the circuit is allowed to enter one of the stable states by setting EXCITE to logic-0. Final stable state is determined by physical mismatch of constituent latches and cross-coupled interconnection wires. Ideal BPUF design needs symmetric routing of feedback paths to eliminate static delay variation while exploiting random manufacturing variation, which is sometimes challenging on a FPGA design platform.

17.4.2.3 Latch PUF

The core element of latch PUF (LPUF) is latch cell that is a SR latch. SR latch can be implemented using either two cross coupled NAND gates or two cross coupled NOR gates. Whatever be the implementation basic principle of LPUF will be same. Fig. 17.7(b) shows the SR latch implementation using NAND gates. Initially, the LPUF starts from the stable state $(B,C)=(1,1)$ with $A=0$. Subsequently, when signal A transits from 0-to-1, the latch enters into metastable state with the final output settling to either $(B,C)=(0,1)$ or $(B,C)=(1,0)$, and these two states are equally probable (ideally). Due to mismatch in driving capability of two gates, asymmetric routing of feedback wires, or skew input signal A, outputs of most LPUF cells are skewed towards one of the two stable states. The figure shows that the SR latch implementation on FPGA that used delayed versions of the two latch input signals to eliminate input signal skew. Few LPUF cells never enter into stable state that causes the reduction of reliability. The LPUF implementation should employ a technique to identify those random LPUF cells to avoid. Like other memory based PUF, it is also zero-challenge PUF, but locations of LPUF cells could be considered as the challenge. If locations of k-subset of n LPUF cells is treated as the challenge, then there are $\binom{n}{k}$ challenges and each challenge produce k-bits response.

17.4.2.4 Flip-flop PUF

The Flip-flop PUF [233] exploits the initial power-up values of configurable D flip-flops. Fig. 17.8 shows how the configuration memory cells are associated with D flip-flops on Xilinx FPGAs. This cell is used to reset (or preset) flip-flop and read back the flip-flop value. After loading of the configuration data into memory, the "global restore line" (GRESTORE) is asserted to reset (or preset) all flip-flops to their initial values. This action is performed by the configuration controller if the command GRESTORE is present at end of Xilinx configuration file.

To prevent the D flip-flop from being initialized by value provided in configuration data, it is required to remove the GRESTORE command from the configuration file that prevents the controller from performing the flip-flop initialization action. These power-up initial values of flip-flops are used to generate the PUF response. Reading back of these values required following two steps:

- Issue GCAPTURE command to configuration controller. On receiving this command, controller assert global capture line (GCAPTURE) to store current state of flip-flops in their associated configuration memory cells (as shown in Fig. 17.8).

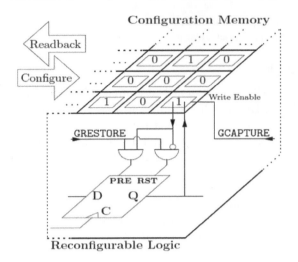

FIGURE 17.8: Configuration memory and its use to initialize D Flip-flop [233].

- If read-back is done after the capture event, then current values of flip-flops, rather that initial values, can be inspected.

The authors of [233] observed that amount of randomness present is power-up values of D flip-flops is limited due to non-uniform distribution of power-up states of flip-flops and it is skewed towards value '0'. This implies the further post-processing of these values is required to make them suitable to be used as random key.

Next, we consider some performance metrics that helps us to quantitatively estimate the quality of a given PUF design.

17.5   PUF Performance Metrics for Quality Evaluation

Design and implementation of a PUF is not the end: evaluation of the designed PUF performance is the most important step of PUF design cycle. There is no unified framework for evaluating PUF's performance, but Hori et al. [151], were the first to develop a framework for performance evaluation, and later Maity et al. [237] provided a compact set of parameters. Brief explanation of the metrics is given below.

17.5.1   Uniqueness

It represents the ability of PUF instance to uniquely distinguish itself among a set of PUF instances of the same PUF type on different chip. Average Hamming Distance (HD) is used to evaluate uniqueness and this value, and ideally it should be close to 50%, which means half the bits are different on average. Let, $R_i^{(C)}$ be the n-bit response of a PUF instance on chip i due challenge set C. The average inter-chip HD among k chips with

TABLE 17.2: List of Metrics Proposed in Literature

Authors	PUF Metrics
Hori et al.	Randomness
	Steadiness
	Correctness
	Diffuseness
	Uniqueness
Maiti et al.	Uniformity
	Bit-aliasing
	Uniqueness
	Reliability
Su et al.	Probability of Misidentification
Majzoobi et al.	Single-bit Probability
	Conditional Probability
Yamamoto et al.	Variety

respect to set of challenge C is defined by eqn. (17.4):

$$\alpha = \frac{2}{k(k-1)}\sum_{i=1}^{k-1}\sum_{j=i+1}^{k}\frac{HD(R_i^C, R_j^C)}{n} \times 100\% \qquad (17.4)$$

It is an estimation of the inter-chip variation in terms of the PUF responses and accuracy of estimation could be improved using large population of PUF instances.

17.5.2 Reliability

The ideal PUF should have perfectly consistent (or reliable) response for a given challenge. But the dynamic noise, due to variation in operating voltage and temperature, affects the different circuit components in a non-uniform manner. As a result, a certain level of inconsistency/instability is introduced in PUF response and is considered as error. A simple estimation of this error can be performed by the deviation of the PUF response from the golden response (ideal response collected on ambient temperature). Average intra-chip Hamming Distance could be used to estimate this deviation. Let, $R_i^{(C)}$ is the golden response of the PUF instance on chip i for challenge set C and it is compared with m n-bit PUF responses collected in m different working environments. Error rate (λ) is defined by eqn. (17.5):

$$\lambda_i = \frac{1}{m}\sum_{t=1}^{m}\frac{HD(R_i^C, R_{i,t})}{n}) \times 100\% \qquad (17.5)$$

The reliability of PUF is defined as $\eta = (1 - \lambda)$.

17.5.3   Uniformity

There should be a uniform distribution of 0's and 1's in a given PUF response r for PUF instance i. For truly random PUF responses, this proportion must be 50%. The uniformity metric can be estimated by eqn. (17.6):

$$\varphi_i = \frac{1}{n} \sum_{l=1}^{n} r_{i,l} \times 100\% \qquad (17.6)$$

where $r_{i,l}$ is the l-th bit of PUF response on chip i.

17.5.4   Bit-aliasing

Bit-aliasing happens when different chips produce nearly identical PUF responses, which is undesirable. We estimate bit-aliasing of l-th bit of PUF responses for a given challenge as the percentage of Hamming Weight (HW) of the l-th bit PUF response across the k devices by eqn. (17.7):

$$\beta_l = \frac{1}{k} \sum_{i=1}^{k} r_{i,l} \times 100\% \qquad (17.7)$$

where $r_{i,l}$ is the l-th bit of PUF response on chip i.

17.5.5   Bit-dependency

The autocorrelation test can be used to detect correlation between bits of a response. Systematic aspect of processes variation may show up as significant correlation at particular intervals. Since the multi-bit responses are extracted from a common fabric it is possible for spatial correlation to appear. This is used to measure the randomness in PUF response. It can be defined by eqn. (17.8):

$$\rho_{xx}(j) = \frac{1}{n} \sum_{i=1}^{n} R_i \oplus R_{i-j} \qquad (17.8)$$

where R_i is the n-bit response being observed, and $\rho_{xx}(j)$ is autocorrelation coefficient with lag j. This value tend toward 0.5 for uncorrelated bit-string and toward 0 or 1 for correlated bit-string.

17.6   Secure PUF: What Makes a PUF Secure?

Two most important security parameter of PUF are: *unclonability* and *unpredictability*. In [34], Armknecht et. al. explain these two parameters in more formal way. Here we review these two properties in brief.

The first, **unclonability** is most desirable property that cannot be achieved using traditional cryptographic techniques. Again, it has two forms: *Physical Unclonability* and *Mathematical Unclonability*. A PUF is physically unclonable if a physical copy of the PUF with similar challenge-response behavior cannot be made, even by the manufacturer. This is also known as *existential unclonabiliy*. In practice this property holds for all known silicon PUFs. On the other hand, a PUF is mathematically unclonable if it is not possible to construct a mathematical approximator which models the original PUF behavior up to some small error. None of the known silicon PUFs is mathematically unclonable.

The second, **unpredictability** states that adversary can't predict response of a new challenge form a known set of CRPs. Classically, the notion of unpredictability of a random function f is formalized by the following security experiment consisting of a *learning* and a *challenge* phase. In the learning phase, the adversary learns the evaluations of f on a set of input challenges $\{x_1, x_2, ..., x_n\}$ (which may be given from outside or chosen by adversary). Then, in the challenge phase, the adversary must return $(x, f(x))$ for some $x \notin \{x_1, x_2, ..., x_n\}$. Usually, unpredictability is measured in terms of entropy(more specifically average min-entropy) of PUF distribution.

We now describe several security applications of PUFs.

17.7   Applications of PUF as a Root-of-Trust

17.7.1   Low-cost Authentication

PUF can be used to authenticate individual ICs without using costly cryptographic primitives. This type of authentication is mostly suitable for resource constrained platforms such as RFIDs where cryptographic operations are too expensive in terms of silicon chip area or power consumption, or off-the-shelf programmable ICs such as FPGAs where the implementation of cryptographic hardware consumes sufficient resources.

As PUF outputs are unique and unpredictable for each chip, it is straightforward to identify ICs with PUF. One can simply record the PUF response (or a set of responses), and compare them with the produced ones when the same challenges are applied. A single CRP is not enough to authenticate a chip because one who has access to the chip can collect the response and build an IC storing the response in memory. Therefore, the authentication mechanism must ensure that adversary does not have access to PUF response. Instead of using a single response, the authentication mechanism always prefers to use a large number of CRPs and each CRP is used only once to prevent *replay attack*.

A trusted party, when in possession of an authentic IC, applies randomly chosen challenges to obtain unpredictable responses. The trusted party stores these challenge-response pairs in a database for future authentication operations. To check the authenticity of an IC later, the trusted party selects a challenge that has been previously recorded but has never been used and obtains the PUF response from the IC. If the response matches (or close enough to) the previously recorded one, the IC is authentic because only the authentic IC and the trusted party should know that challenge-response-pair.

17.7.2   Cryptographic Key Generation

The response of a given PUF instance can not be used directly as a key in cryptograhic primitives, because its responses are likely to be slightly different in each evaluation even for the same challenge, and response is not truly random. This is because in general, a given PUF instance cannot be expected to have perfect reliability. On the other hand, key should be random and each bit of key needs to stay constant. Post-processing is required in that case. "Helper Data Algorithms" (HDA) have been introduced as a primitive for turning fuzzy, non-uniform data into cryptographic keys. The most well-known formulation of the is due to Dodis et al. [112], in the form of "fuzzy extractors". The secure use of fuzzy

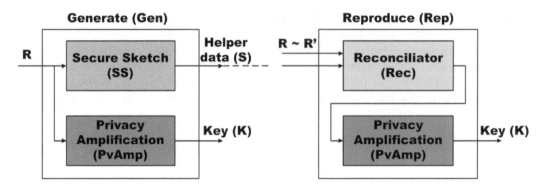

FIGURE 17.9: Overview of the "Helper data" algorithm.

extractors was discussed in [62]. A first efficient hardware implementation of a HDA is given in [61].

Informally, HDA comprises of two phase as shown in Fig. 17.9:

1. **Generation Phase:** It starts with the measurement of the fuzzy secret R, in this context it is PUF response(s). The *Secure Sketch* procedure SS generates (public) helper data $S \leftarrow SS(R)$ that will be used in *reproduction* phase and could be stored in public database. The privacy amplification procedure (Ext) extracts a (secret) key $K \leftarrow Ext(R)$ that could be used in cryptographic primitives as a secret.

2. **Reproduction Phase:** In this phase the same data is measured, but due to the fuzzy nature of the source, the produced response R' will not be exactly the same as R. However, if R' lies sufficiently close to R, the response reconciliator procedure (Rec) is able to reproduce the fuzzy secret $R \leftarrow Rec(R', S)$ with the help of the previously produced helper data S. This is also known as information reconciliation. Like *Generation* phase, privacy amplification procedure (Ext) extracts a (secret) key $K \leftarrow Ext(R)$.

Now, we discuss one implementation of *Gen* and *Rep* using a set of Hash functions (Universal Hash Function) $\mathcal{H}$ and error correcting code $\mathcal{C}$. The parameters $[n, k, d]$ of linear code $\mathcal{C}$ is determined by length of response R and number t of errors to be corrected. Both generation and key reproduction phase are explained below:

1. **Generation Phase:** $(K, W = [W_1, W_2]) \leftarrow Gen(R)$. This phase start with assigning a random code word $C_s \leftarrow \mathcal{C}$ to response R. Then first component of helper data vector $W_1 = S_c \bigoplus R$ is calculated by SS. Next, a hash function h_i is randomly selected from $\mathcal{H}$ by Ext and this sets the $W_2 = i$. The key is calculated by $K = h_i(R)$.

2. **Reproduction Phase:** $K = Rep(R', W)$. The procedure Rec reconstructs key K from the noisy response R' using helper data W. *Rep* performs following two steps:

    (a) *Information Reconciliation (Rec).* Using the helper data W_1, $C' = W_1 \oplus R'$ is computed. Then the decoding algorithm of $\mathcal{C}$ is used to obtain C'. From C', R is reconstructed as $R = W1 \oplus C'$.

    (b) *Privacy Amplification (Ext).* The helper data W_2 is used to select correct hash function $h_i \in \mathcal{H}$ and finally key is reconstructed as $K = h_i(R)$

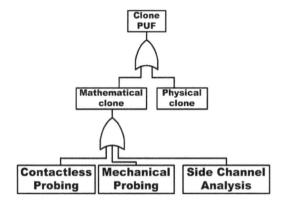

FIGURE 17.10: Types of Cloning Attacks.

17.7.3 IP protection of FPGA Hardware Designs

IP protection of hardware designs is the most important requirement for many FPGA IP vendors. The hardware IPs to be used on SRAM FPGAs are more vulnerable to piracy, as the programming bitstream has to be stored on external non-volatile memory. Hence, the bitstream can be easily copied by an attacker. One accepted solution is the encryption of the bitstream stored in external non-volatile memory. However, this method is not widespread because it rely on battery backed or flash key storage on FPGA that is vulnerable to invasive attack. In [366], Simpson and Schaumont proposed a protocol using a PUF on FPGA that allows to bind a particular IP to a particular FPGA. In [139], authors reduce the computation and communication complexity of the protocols in [366]. All of them developed protocols based on symmetric key primitives. J. Guajardo et al. [140] proposed new protocol for IP protection problem on FPGA based on Public-key (PK) primitives.

17.7.4 Key Zeroization

"Key Zeroization" describes the process of properly deleting certain keys in a system. This might happen by overwriting the entire existing key value with either zeros or a random bit string. This is exactly the point, where PUFs, more precisely reconfigurable PUFs, come into play. With an additional reconfiguration mechanism, this special type of PUFs makes it possible to transform one PUF into another, which then shows completely new CRP behavior.

Assume the keys we manage were generated with the help of a PUF A. When we apply the reconfiguration mechanism, we turn the PUF A into PUF B possessing completely new CRP behavior. In doing so all keys associated with PUF A are corrupted, i.e. they have the same effect as being zeroized.

17.8 Attacks Model: How PUF Security Could Be Compromised?

Introduction of a new security primitive does not only bring new opportunities, but also vulnerabilities and unexpected behaviors. In this section, we review various PUF-specific attacks (see Fig. 17.10) that have significant effects on the security of systems that have used or propose to use PUF as primitives. Till date, researchers have been able (fully or partially) to apply three traditional cryptographic attacks, described next.

17.8.1   Fault Attacks on PUFs and Fuzzy Extractors

Fault attacks aim to introduce an erroneous behavior on device by operating it in extreme environmental condition or forcing it to operate in way to inject fault into it. For example, one may use the device at extreme temperature that will change the PUF's random noise behavior beyond the capabilities of its error correction circuit (the Fuzzy Extractor). Again, although the Fuzzy Extractor's helper data is not private, but security of the Fuzzy extractor holds on the assumption that the helper data cannot be modified by the adversary. So, fault attack on the helper data is another mechanism to compromise the security of PUFs.

17.8.2   Side-channel Attacks on PUFs

Side-channel attack is an implementation-dependent hardware attack that aims to extract secret information (e.g., cryptographic key) from hardware component(s). The adversary observes the behavior (e.g., power consumption) of the component while it is using the secret data to be extracted. Since, the behavior of the component depends on the data being processed by it, so it can leak information about that data. Karakoyunlu et al. [175] and Merli et al. [250] discuss side-channel attacks on typical fuzzy extractor implementations.

17.8.3   Modeling Attacks on Delay-based PUFs

Aim of this attack is to build a mathematical approximator from a certain set of challenge-response pairs, such that subsequently the approximator can be used to predict responses of unknown challenges with relatively small error. If that is possible, then the model, given it is accurate enough, can emulate the input-output behavior of a given PUF instance. This situation creates great vulnerabilities to the proposed applications of PUFs as hardware security primitives, as it makes it difficult to distinguish between an actual PUF instance, and a computer program masquerading as a PUF. If the model is amenable to hardware implementation, then an approximator circuit can be built; if that is not the case, given the ease of fabricating on-chip memory in modern VLSI technologies, a Lookup Table (LUT) based implementation can emulate a PUF (given the set of probable challenges during the authentication phase is known a-priory to an adversary).

Delay-Based PUFs like Arbiter and its variant PUFs are susceptible to modeling attacks due to their linear delay circuits [220]. Two mutually dependent factors that tune the performance of a mathematical model are: (a) the number of CRPs used to build a model, and, (b) the modeling techniques. Supervised Machine Learning (ML) techniques like Support Vector Machine (SVM), Logistic Regression (LR) and Artificial Neural Network (ANN) are mostly used by researcher to model PUFs. B.Gassend et al. [129] first used multi-layer ANN to model FPGA implementation of Arbiter PUF. In [392], authors discussed PUF modeling using ML techniques and Evolutionary Search (ES) in more detailed based on CRPs of simulated PUF. Roel Maes [232] showed successful modeling of ASIC implemented arbiter PUF using SVM.

A number of mitigation have been proposed against modeling attacks, mainly through the introduction of non-linearity in the delay paths, giving rise to designs such as "XOR Arbiter PUFs" and "Feed-forward arbiter PUFs". Unfortunately, all of these have been later shown to be vulnerable to more sophisticated modeling attacks. The "Lightweight Secure PUF" [240], a variant of the arbiter PUF, exhibit most resistance against modeling attacks and it is built following three key principles:(a) mixing multiple delay lines, (b) transformations of the challenge bits, and (c) combination of the outputs from multiple lines.

The relatively ease-to-model problem of delay-Based PUF has a direct implication to its usability as a security primitive. Mitigation of modeling attacks is possible by ensuring that adversary cannot easily challenge the PUF and directly access the response of the PUF. The "Controlled PUF" was introduced to prevent modeling attack. Here, chosen challenge attack is prevented by placing a random hash function at the PUF's input, and a random hash function is also placed at the output of the PUF, to prevent raw responses form being accessed. Clearly, it does not solve the fundamental weakness of delay-based PUFs to modeling attack. So, invasive attacks to collect CRPs is still possible.

We introduce a novel modeling attack on PUFs using ideas of *evolutionary computing* in the next chapter.

17.9 Looking Forward: What Lies Ahead for PUFs?

PUFs have attracted tremendous research attention in the last few years, both from a theoretical perspective, and an implementation perspective. Commercially available VLSI implementations of PUFs have graduated them from being an idealized mathematical novelty, to being an extremely useful hardware security primitives, with wide applications in the security domain. However, the implementations do not always have the same properties that are expected from an ideal PUF, and the non-idealities of PUF implementations create challenges in their usage. The non-idealities also create vulnerabilities such as susceptibilities to modeling attacks, which compromise the security of PUFs. Current and future PUF research is mainly focused on understanding the capabilities and limitations of PUFs, both through novel PUF designs with improved characteristics, and development of potent attacks on them. At the time of writing this book, there is no clear answer to the question of what lies in the future for PUFs – whether or not they would be able to fullfil their promise.

Chapter 18

Genetic Programming-based Model-building Attack on PUFs

Dilbert*: Wow! According to my computer simulation, it should be possible to create new life forms from common household chemicals.*
Dogbert*: This raises some thorny issues.*
Dilbert*: You mean legal, ethical and religious issues?*
Dogbert*: I was thinking about parking spaces.*

Scott Adams
Dilbert Comic strip, 1989.

18.1 Introduction

In the previous chapter, we introduced Physically Unclonable Function (PUF) circuits, discussed some machine learning based attacks on them. In this chapter, we take a different approach to modelling PUF circuits. One of the features of modelling PUF circuits through machine learning techniques is that except for *arbiter PUFs* [220], other PUFs cannot be modelled very satisfactorily in a way to suggest *which* machine learning to apply to model them. Thus, we should concentrate on developing techniques that model an arbitrary given PUF instance accurately and with little computational effort. This observation suggests heuristic techniques which are effective in estimating input–output relationships when the nature of the data is discrete, and the relationship is either unknown or exceedingly complex.

One of the features of modeling PUF circuits through machine learning techniques is that except for *arbiter PUFs* [220], other PUFs cannot be modelled very satisfactorily in a way to suggest *which* machine learning to apply to model them. Thus, we should concentrate on developing techniques that model an arbitrary given PUF instance accurately and with little computational effort, rather than trying to figure out a correlation between a particular modelling technique and the corresponding type of PUF that is amenable to be modelled by it. This suggests heuristic techniques which are effective in estimating input–output relationships when the nature of the data is discrete, and the relationship is either unknown or exceedingly complex.

Evolutionary computation [2] provides algorithms which are often extremely successful in finding patterns in data with the above-mentioned characteristics. Probably the most widely known class of algorithms under this parasol are the so-called *genetic algorithms* [133, 203]. In these, a computer program iteratively solves (or approximately solves) a given problem using biological concepts such as genetic *crossover*, *mutation*, etc., and *Darwinian natural selection*. The characteristic steps of these algorithms are:

1. Set iteration count $i = 0$, and randomly generate a large *initial population* of individuals, where each individual represents a feasible solution to the problem at hand. Often, the characteristics of the individuals are encoded by a binary string called a *chromosome*.

2. Perform *reproduction* among selected members of the population by performing *crossover* among their chromosomes. This process creates new individuals, with potentially better properties. Sometimes, small random changes are performed to the chromosome to abruptly modify the genetic constitution, a process termed *mutation*. Often, some desirable members of the current population are allowed to move unchanged to the next generation. Crossover, mutation and preferential treatment towards desirable members of the previous population constitutes reproduction.

3. Rank the individuals based on a *fitness function*. If a member of the current population seems a good enough solution to the problem, or if the number of generations has reached a pre-defined threshold, STOP. Else, continue and eliminate the members with fitness function values below a pre-decided threshold. This simulates *survival of the fittest*, a basic tenet of Darwinian natural selection.

4. If the number of iterations or the computation time has exceeded pre-decided threshold, STOP and declare the top-ranked member found so far to be the solution. Else, generate a new population, set $i \leftarrow i + 1$ and go back to step (2).

A related class of techniques is *Genetic Programming*, where each individual of a given population is a computer program to solve a given problem [210, 209]. Typically, the computer programs are represented in memory as *tree* data structures, which makes them amenable to iterative structural manipulations with relative ease. In this chapter we use Genetic Programming to model PUFs, in particular, *ring-oscillator PUFs* (RO-PUFs) mapped on FPGAs. We would demonstrate that by having relatively few CRPs, we can derive simple Boolean expressions that approximate the input-output mapping for a given PUF fairly accurately. In addition, the computational effort needed in our scheme (as estimated by the runtime) is also acceptable. The main motivation for our work is the one described in [209], where the author successfully used genetic programming to model an 8:1 multiplexer.

The rest of this chapter is organized as follows. In Section 18.2, we describe the typical steps in the working of genetic programming. In Section 18.3 our experimental methodology is described in detail. Section 18.4 presents the modelling results. We conclude in Section 18.4.2, with hints of future scope of extension of the work.

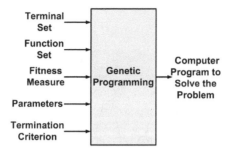

FIGURE 18.1: Model of Genetic Programming.

18.2 Background: Genetic Programming and RO-PUFs

18.2.1 Genetic Programming

The preparatory steps to build genetic model of a problem to be solved using *Genetic Programming* requires identification of and decision about the following [343]:

- The set of *terminals* (i.e., the independent variables of the problem, zero-argument functions, and random constants) for each branch of the to-be-evolved program.

- The set of primitive operators called *functions*, for each branch of the to-be-evolved program.

- Certain parameters for controlling the iterations.

- A way to measure the fitness of a given individual, the "fitness function" (not to be confused with the operator "function").

- Finally, the termination criterion and method for designating the end result of the iterations.

Fig. 18.1 shows genetic programming as an input–output system. Genetic programming starts with an initial population of randomly generated computer programs composed of functions and terminals appropriate to the problem domain. As mentioned previously, usually these computer programs are in the form of *tree* data structures that can be evaluated to yield an expression. The *terminals* denote the terminal nodes, i.e. the leaves of the tree, while the *functions* occupy the non-leaf nodes of the tree. In this work, since the expressions we want to generate are Boolean expressions, we use Boolean operators as the functions.

It should be clear form the above description that we are generating *Binary Expression Trees* with Boolean operators as members of the population, and logic expressions can be generated and/or evaluated by an *in–order* traversal of the expression tree [405]. An example expression tree for the expression $((!a\&b) \mid (c\&d)) \& ((e\&f) \mid (g\&!b))$ is shown in Fig. 18.2(a). *Crossover* in this context implies exchanging sub–trees among two expression trees to generate two new expression trees. *Mutation* in this context as implemented by us is changing the operator at a randomly selected non-leaf node with a different operator. The final objective is to iteratively generate an expression tree that most closely approximates the known CRPs. Figs. 18.2(c) and (d) show the result of crossover and mutation over the expression trees shown in Figs. 18.2(a) and (b).

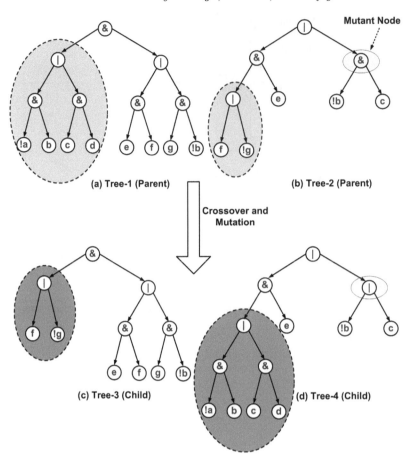

FIGURE 18.2: Example of expression trees and their *crossover*: (a) and (b) parent expression trees; (c) and (d) children expression trees resulting from the crossover of the parent trees.

18.2.2   Ring Oscillator PUF (RO-PUF)

Our FPGA-based RO-PUF (shown in Fig. 18.3 is a variation of the design described in [373, 238]. There are two banks of 128 3-stage ring oscillators; the outputs of each bank of ring oscillators are connected to the input of a 128:1 multiplexer. Through a 7-bit input which acts as the *challenge* here, the i-th ring oscillator outputs are selected from both the banks by the multiplexors, $1 \leq i \leq 128$. The multiplexer outputs are used to drive two counters, and a comparator compares the count values to estimate the oscillation frequencies of the ring oscillators. The output of the comparator (1-bit) is considered to be the *response* for the challenge at the input. Because of device-level process variation effects, the oscillation frequencies of the i-th ring oscillator pairs from the two banks are not identical, potentially resulting in a difference in count between the two counters, and a 0 or 1 value at the comparator output shows whether the selected ring oscillator from bank-1 has a lower or a higher frequency than the selected ring oscillator from bank-2 (a tie in count results in an 0 being output). To eliminate bias due to placement and routing, the i-th ring oscillator pair from the two banks are manually laid out as much symmetrically as possible, and defined to be *hard macros* on the FPGA on which they are to be mapped.

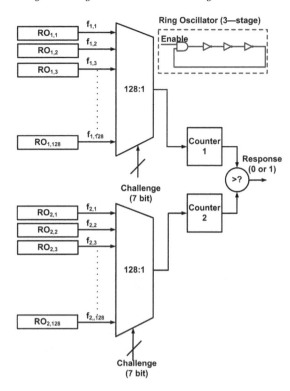

FIGURE 18.3: Ring Oscillator PUF (7–input, 1 output) as implemented by us.

18.3 Methodology

The particulars of the genetic programming scheme implemented by us are:

- The *terminals* are: variables attached to the inputs of the PUF circuit and their logical complements. For example, if $A1$ and $A2$ are the two input variables, the possible terminal nodes are $A1$, $A2$, $!A1$ and $!A2$.

- The *functions* are: AND ("&") and OR ("|"). For simplicity, we consider only a minimal functionally complete set of operators {AND, OR, NOT}. Thus, all our expressions would be Boolean expressions composed of the input variables and their logic complements. Also, we allow each operator to operate on two variables at a time.

- The *parameters* specific to the genetic programming scheme as implemented by us are: (a) initial population size varies from 100 to 1000; (b) two different reproduction schemes (*elitist* and *tournament selection*, described next), (c) total number of leaf nodes (i.e. variables in the Boolean expressions) in each expression tree in the initial population varies between 14 and 32, and total number of non-leaf nodes (i.e. operators in the Boolean expressions) in each expression tree in the initial population varies between 7 and 32, and (d) *mutation probability* of 0.001.

- The *fitness* of an individual is judged: (a) during the *training* (i.e. model building) phase, by the PUF response prediction success rate for 32 arbitrary recorded CRPs of a given PUF, and (b) during the *validation* (i.e. model accuracy estimation) phase, the PUF response prediction success rate for the remaining 96 challenges outside the *training set*, by evaluating the Boolean expression it represents for the same N–bit binary challenge. Note that a given 7–input PUF instance has 128 (=32+96) CRPs.

- The termination criteria are: if the prediction accuracy for the best individuals from two successive generations differ by less than 0.5%, or the number of generations has reached 10, or if the prediction accuracy for the *validation CRP* set is 100%.

18.3.1   Reproduction Schemes

We implemented two different reproduction schemes, *elitist model* and *tournament selection model*. We describe them in brief below.

18.3.1.1   Elitist Model

In this scheme, the top-ranked members of a given generation is allowed to progress unchanged to the next generation. Ensuring the propagation of the elite members to the future generation is termed *elitism* and ensures that not only is an elite member selected, but a copy of it does not become disrupted by crossover or mutation. This is because some parts of the elite member chromosomes often play a very important role in improving the quality of the final solution. In our implementation, the top-ranked 50% members of a given population preferentially progressed to the next generation, and the remaining 50% of the next generation is produced through cross-over among randomly selected parents in the rest of the population, and mutation. Note that we used an elitism fraction (= 50%) higher than the elitist model implementations commonly reported in the literature, where it is usually less than 30% [203, 133], because of superior results we obtained by choosing a slightly higher elitism fraction.

18.3.1.2   Tournament Selection Model

Here, pairs of individuals are chosen at random from a given population set, their prediction accuracies are compared, and the winner among the pair moves to the next generation unaltered. Simultaneously, the algorithm ensures that each member of the population is given only one chance to participate in a tournament selection policy. In this way, half of a given population moves to the next generation unchanged, and the remaining half of the next generation is produced through cross-over among randomly selected parents in the current remaining population, and mutation [203, 133].

18.4   Results

18.4.1   Experimental Setup

The experiments were run on a laptop with a 2.10 GHz CPU and 3 GB of main memory. An *Altera Cyclone-III* FPGA was used to implement six instances of the 7-input RO-PUF (PUF-1 through PUF-6 hereafter) shown in Fig. 18.3, using the *Quartus-II* design environment from Altera. The genetic programming methodology was implemented in C. Each of the two reproduction schemes (*elitist* and *tournament selection*) were executed 100 times for each of the six PUFs. Fig. 18.4 shows the GP methodology implemented by us.

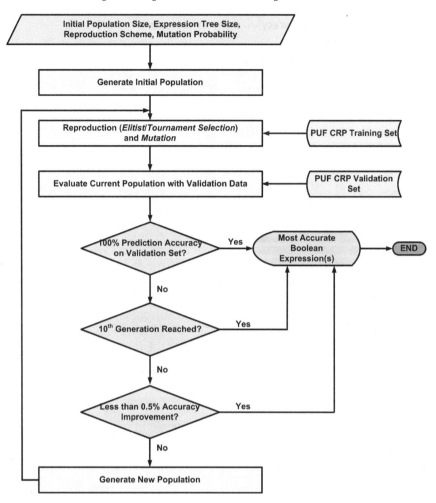

FIGURE 18.4: Flowchart of the proposed Genetic Programming Model.

Fig. 18.5 shows the variation of prediction accuracy over generations for two reproduction schemes - *Tournament Selection Model* and *Elitist Model*, averaged over the results from the six PUF instances. From this plot, it is clear that *Tournament Selection Model* achieves greater prediction accuracy on average than the *Elitist model*, and PUF-6 was most successfully modelled. One interesting feature is that the prediction accuracy shows a slight degradation in some generations compared to the previous generation, but eventually the performance improves. This characteristic of degradation in objective function with subsequent improvement is termed as *genetic drift* in the genetic algorithms literature [203].

Fig. 18.6 shows the variation of the prediction accuracy for the two different reproduction schemes (averaged over the six PUF instances), when the population size varies from 100 to 1000. Table 18.1 shows the execution time of the genetic programming scheme for the same population sizes, again for the two different reproduction schemes (averaged over the six PUF instances). From Fig. 18.6 and Table 18.1, it is apparent that the prediction accuracy is independent of the reproduction scheme for population sizes below 250, and improves at a higher rate in the *tournament selection* scheme. However, this improvement in prediction accuracy comes at a cost of about 40% increase in execution time with respect to the

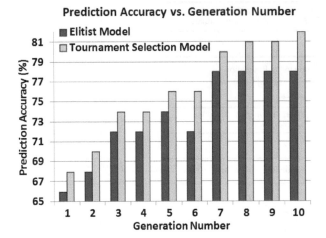

FIGURE 18.5: Variation of prediction accuracy with generation number for two reproduction schemes – *Tournament Selection Model* and *Elitist Model*, averaged over the results from the six PUF instances.

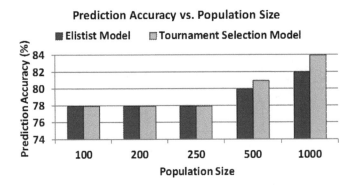

FIGURE 18.6: Impact of population size on prediction accuracy for two reproduction schemes – *Tournament Selection Model* and *Elitist Model*, averaged over the results from the six PUF instances.

elitist model. Table 18.2 shows the best estimator Boolean expressions obtained for the 6 PUFs, considering both the *elitist* and the *tournament selection* models. Here "·" stands for Boolean AND, "+" stands for Boolean OR and "!" stands for Boolean inversion. Fig. 18.7 shows the best prediction accuracy for the *elitist model* for the six PUF instances, for the 100 models built for each. Again, we can observe that the model built for PUF-6 was the most accurate.

18.4.2   Conclusions

Thus we have demonstrated the effectiveness of an evolutionary computation technique, *Genetic Programming* in modelling 7-input RO-PUFs mapped on FPGAs. We envisage a single RO-PUF instance behavior as an unknown 7-input Boolean function, and in 10 generations (iterations), derive a Boolean function based on only $\frac{1}{4}$ of the truth table of

TABLE 18.1: Impact of Population Size on Execution Time

Population Size	Execution Time (sec.)	
	Elitist Model	Tournament Search Model
100	81	110
200	160	220
250	198	267
500	398	546
1000	822	1143

TABLE 18.2: The Best Boolean Expressions Modelling the 6 PUFs

PUF Instance	Best Estimator Boolean Expression
PUF–1	$(a \cdot c + b + d) \cdot (e \cdot f + g) \cdot (((!d + c) \cdot b) + !e)$
PUF–2	$(c \cdot b + (d + a)) \cdot g \cdot e \cdot (f + (((a + b) \cdot c) + d))$
PUF–3	$(b + a) \cdot (d + c) \cdot (e \cdot ((a \cdot b) + (c \cdot d)) + f) \cdot g$
PUF–4	$(c \cdot b + (d + a)) \cdot g \cdot e \cdot (f + (a \cdot c + b + d))$
PUF–5	$(!a \cdot b + !c + d) \cdot ((!c + !d) \cdot (!a \cdot b)) \cdot (e + !f \cdot g)$
PUF–6	$(c \cdot b + (d + a)) \cdot (g \cdot e \cdot (f + ((g \cdot !f) + !e)))$

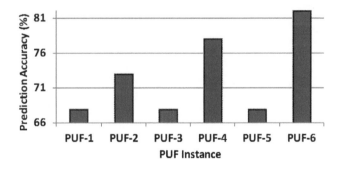

FIGURE 18.7: Best Prediction accuracy for the six different PUF instances across 100 models built through Genetic Programming.

the function, that can accurately predict 84% (in the best case) of the remaining $\frac{3}{4}$ of the truth table. The technique is also computationally inexpensive, and gives satisfactory results at reasonable runtimes. There is scope for future research on this topic to be directed towards modelling other types of PUFs with larger challenge space, and more efficient implementation of the methodology.

Bibliography

[1] *39th International Symposium on Computer Architecture (ISCA 2012), June 9-13, 2012, Portland, OR, USA*. IEEE, 2012.

[2] Evolutionary Computation. Wikipedia, 2012. `http://en.wikipedia.org/wiki/Evolutionary_computation`.

[3] N Mazzocca A. Cilardo, L Coppolino and L Romano. Elliptic Curve Cryptography Engineering. *Proceedings of the IEEE*, 94(2):395–406, Feb 2006.

[4] A. Rudra, P. K. Dubey, C. S. Jutla etal. Efficient Implementation of Rijndael Encryption with Composite Field Arithmetic. In *CHES*, pages 171–184, CHES 2001:Paris, France, May 14-16 2001. Springer.

[5] J. Aarestad, P. Ortiz, D. Acharyya, and J. Plusquellic. HELP: A Hardware-Embedded Delay PUF. *IEEE Design and Test of Computers*, 30(2):17–25, 2013.

[6] Masayuki Abe, editor. *Topics in Cryptology - CT-RSA 2007, The Cryptographers' Track at the RSA Conference 2007, San Francisco, CA, USA, February 5-9, 2007, Proceedings*, volume 4377 of *Lecture Notes in Computer Science*. Springer, 2006.

[7] M. Abramovici and P. L. Levin. Protecting integrated circuits from silicon Trojan horses. Military Embedded Systems, 2009. `http://www.mil-embedded.com/articles/id/?3748`.

[8] Onur Aciiçmez. Yet another MicroArchitectural Attack: : exploiting I-Cache. In Peng Ning and Vijay Atluri, editors, *CSAW*, pages 11–18. ACM, 2007.

[9] Onur Aciiçmez, Billy Bob Brumley, and Philipp Grabher. New Results on Instruction Cache Attacks. In Mangard and Standaert [244], pages 110–124.

[10] Onur Aciiçmez and Çetin Kaya Koç. Trace-Driven Cache Attacks on AES (Short Paper). In Peng Ning, Sihan Qing, and Ninghui Li, editors, *ICICS*, volume 4307 of *Lecture Notes in Computer Science*, pages 112–121. Springer, 2006.

[11] Onur Aciiçmez, Çetin Kaya Koç, and Jean-Pierre Seifert. On the Power of Simple Branch Prediction Analysis. *IACR Cryptology ePrint Archive*, 2006:351, 2006.

[12] Onur Aciiçmez, Çetin Kaya Koç, and Jean-Pierre Seifert. Predicting secret keys via branch prediction. In Abe [6], pages 225–242.

[13] Onur Aciiçmez, Shay Gueron, and Jean-Pierre Seifert. New Branch Prediction Vulnerabilities in OpenSSL and Necessary Software Countermeasures. In Steven D. Galbraith, editor, *IMA Int. Conf.*, volume 4887 of *Lecture Notes in Computer Science*, pages 185–203. Springer, 2007.

[14] Onur Aciiçmez and Werner Schindler. A Vulnerability in RSA Implementations Due to Instruction Cache Analysis and Its Demonstration on OpenSSL. In Tal Malkin, editor, *CT-RSA*, volume 4964 of *Lecture Notes in Computer Science*, pages 256–273. Springer, 2008.

[15] Onur Aciiçmez, Werner Schindler, and Çetin Kaya Koç. Cache Based Remote Timing Attack on the AES. In Abe [6], pages 271–286.

[16] Onur Aciiçmez, Jean-Pierre Seifert, and Çetin Kaya Koç. Micro-Architectural Cryptanalysis. *IEEE Security & Privacy*, 5(4):62–64, 2007.

[17] S. Adee. The hunt for the kill switch. *IEEE Spectrum*, 45(5):34–39, May 2008.

[18] Aes (Rijndael) ip-cores. `http://www.erst.ch/download/aes_standard_cores.pdf`, 2011.

[19] Full datasheet aes-ccm core family for actel fpga. `http://www.actel.com/ipdocs/HelionCore_AES-CCM_8bit_Actel_DS.pdf`, 2011.

[20] M. Agarwal, B. Zhang Paul, M., and S. Mitra. Circuit failure prediction and its application to transistor aging. In *VTS'07: Proceedings of the IEEE VLSI Test Symposium*, pages 277–286, 2007.

[21] Michel Agoyan, Jean-Max Dutertre, Amir-Pasha Mirbaha, David Naccache, Anne-Lise Ribotta, and Assia Tria. How to Flip a Bit? pages 235–239. IOLTS, Jul 2010.

[22] Michel Agoyan, Jean-Max Dutertre, David Naccache, Bruno Robisson, and Assia Tria. When Clocks Fail: On Critical Paths and Clock Faults. pages 182–193. CARDIS, 2010.

[23] D. Agrawal, S. Baktir, D. Karakoyunlu, P. Rohatgi, and B. Sunar. Trojan detection using IC Fingerprinting. In *Proc. IEEE Symposium on Security and Privacy*, pages 296–310, Washington, DC, USA, 2007.

[24] Gregory C. Ahlquist, Brent E. Nelson, and Michael Rice. Optimal Finite Field Multipliers for FPGAs. In *FPL '99: Proceedings of the 9th International Workshop on Field-Programmable Logic and Applications*, pages 51–60, London, UK, 1999. Springer-Verlag.

[25] Monjur Alam, Sonai Ray, Debdeep Mukhopadhyay, Santosh Ghosh, Dipanwita Roy Chowdhury, and Indranil Sengupta. An area optimized reconfigurable encryptor for aes-rijndael. In *DATE*, pages 1116–1121, 2007.

[26] Subidh Ali and Debdeep Mukhopadhyay. A Differential Fault Analysis on AES Key Schedule Using Single Fault. In Breveglieri et al. [63], pages 35–42.

[27] Subidh Ali and Debdeep Mukhopadhyay. An Improved Differential Fault Analysis on AES-256. In Abderrahmane Nitaj and David Pointcheval, editors, *AFRICACRYPT*, volume 6737 of *Lecture Notes in Computer Science*, pages 332–347. Springer, 2011.

[28] Subidh Ali, Debdeep Mukhopadhyay, and Michael Tunstall. Differential Fault Analysis of AES using a Single Multiple-Byte Fault. Cryptology ePrint Archive, Report 2010/636, 2010. `http://eprint.iacr.org/`.

[29] Y. M. Alkabani and F. Koushanfar. Active hardware metering for intellectual property protection and security. In *SS'07: Proceedings of USENIX Security Symposium*, pages 20:1–20:16, 2007.

[30] Y. M. Alkabani, F. Koushanfar, and M. Potkonjak. Remote activation of ICs for piracy prevention and digital right management. In *ICCAD '07: Proceedings of the International Conference on CAD*, pages 674–677, 2007.

[31] M. E. Amyeen, S. Venkataraman, A. Ojha, and S. Lee. Evaluation of the quality of N-detect scan ATPG patterns on a processor. In *ITC'04: Proceedings of the International Test Conference*, pages 669–678, 2004.

[32] D. Anastasakis, R. Damiano, Hi-Keung T. Ma, and T. Stanion. A practical and efficient method for compare-point matching. In *DAC'02: Proceedings of the Design Automation Conference*, pages 305–310, 2002.

[33] B. Ansari and M.A. Hasan. High-performance architecture of elliptic curve scalar multiplication. *Computers, IEEE Transactions on*, 57(11):1443 –1453, November 2008.

[34] Frederik Armknecht, Roel Maes, Ahmad-Reza Sadeghi, Franccois-Xavier Standaert, and Christian Wachsmann. A Formal Foundation for the Security Features of Physical Functions. *IEEE Security and Privacy*, 2011(1):16, 2011.

[35] D. Aucsmith. Tamper resistant software: An implementation. In *IH'96: Proceedings of the International Workshop on Information Hiding*, pages 317–333, 1996.

[36] Australian Government DoD-DSTO. Towards countering the rise of the silicon trojan. `http://dspace.dsto.defence.gov.au/dspace/bitstream/1947/9736/1/DSTO-TR-2220\%20PR.pdf`, 2008.

[37] R. Azarderakhsh and A. Reyhani-Masoleh. Efficient fpga implementations of point multiplication on binary edwards and generalized hessian curves using gaussian normal basis. *Very Large Scale Integration (VLSI) Systems, IEEE Transactions on*, PP(99):1, 2011.

[38] M. Banga and M. S. Hsiao. A region based approach for the identification of hardware Trojans. In *Proc. IEEE International Workshop on Hardware-Oriented Security and Trust (HOST'08)*, pages 40–47, Washington, DC, USA, 2008.

[39] M. Banga and M. S. Hsiao. A novel sustained vector technique for the detection of hardware Trojans. In *VLSID'09: Proceedings of the International Conference on VLSI Design*, pages 327–332, January 2009.

[40] B. Barak, O. Goldreich, R. Impagliazzo, S. Rudich, A. Sahai, S.P. Vadhan, and K. Yang. On the (im)possibility of obfuscating programs. In *CRYPTO '01: Proceedings of the International Cryptology Conference on Advances in Cryptology*, pages 1–18, 2001.

[41] Alessandro Barenghi, Cédric Hocquet, David Bol, François-Xaiver Standaert, Francesco Regazzoni, and Israel Koren. Exploring the Feasibility of Low Cost Fault Injection Attacks on Sub-Threshold Devices through An Example of A 65nm AES Implementation. pages 48–60. in Proc. Workshop RFID Security Privacy, 2011.

[42] Alberto Battistello and Christophe Giraud. Fault Analysis of Infective AES Computations. In Wieland Fischer and Jörn-Marc Schmidt, editors, *Fault Diagnosis and Tolerance in Cryptography – FDTC 2013*, pages 101–107. IEEE Computer Society, 2013.

[43] M. Bednara, M. Daldrup, J. von zur Gathen, J. Shokrollahi, and J. Teich. Reconfigurable Implementation of Elliptic Curve Crypto Algorithms. In *Parallel and Distributed Processing Symposium., Proceedings International, IPDPS 2002, Abstracts and CD-ROM*, pages 157–164, 2002.

[44] Daniel J. Bernstein. Cache-timing Attacks on AES. Technical report, 2005.

[45] Guido Bertoni, Luca Breveglieri, Israel Koren, Paolo Maistri, and Vincenzo Piuri. Error Analysis and Detection Procedures for a Hardware Implementation of the Advanced Encryption Standard. *IEEE Trans. Computers*, 52(4):492–505, 2003.

[46] Guido Bertoni, Vittorio Zaccaria, Luca Breveglieri, Matteo Monchiero, and Gianluca Palermo. AES Power Attack Based on Induced Cache Miss and Countermeasure. In *ITCC (1)*, pages 586–591. IEEE Computer Society, 2005.

[47] Régis Bevan and Erik Knudsen. Ways to Enhance Differential Power Analysis. In *Proceedings of Information Security and Cryptology (ICISC 2002), LNCS Volume 2587*, pages 327–342. Springer-Verlag, 2002.

[48] Eli Biham. A Fast New DES Implementation in Software. In *FSE* [49], pages 260–272.

[49] Eli Biham, editor. *Fast Software Encryption, 4th International Workshop, FSE '97, Haifa, Israel, January 20-22, 1997, Proceedings*, volume 1267 of *Lecture Notes in Computer Science*. Springer, 1997.

[50] Eli Biham and Adi Shamir. Differential Fault Analysis of Secret Key Cryptosystems. *Proceedings of Eurocrypt, Lecture Notes in Computer Science*, 1233:37–51, 1997.

[51] Alex Biryukov and David Wagner. Slide attacks. In *FSE*, pages 245–259, 1999.

[52] Johannes Blömer, Jorge Guajardo, and Volker Krummel. Provably secure masking of aes. In *Proceedings of the 11th international conference on Selected Areas in Cryptography*, SAC'04, pages 69–83, Berlin, Heidelberg, 2005. Springer-Verlag.

[53] Johannes Blömer and Volker Krummel. Analysis of Countermeasures Against Access Driven Cache Attacks on AES. In Carlisle M. Adams, Ali Miri, and Michael J. Wiener, editors, *Selected Areas in Cryptography*, volume 4876 of *Lecture Notes in Computer Science*, pages 96–109. Springer, 2007.

[54] Johannes Blömer and Jean-Pierre Seifert. Fault Based Cryptanalysis of the Advanced Encryption Standard (AES). In *Financial Cryptography*, pages 162–181, 2003.

[55] Kaijjie Wu Bo Yang and R. Karri. Secure scan: A design-for-test architecture for crypto-chips. In *DAC'05: Proceedings of 42nd Design Automation Conference*, pages 135–140, 2005.

[56] Andrey Bogdanov, Thomas Eisenbarth, Christof Paar, and Malte Wienecke. Differential Cache-Collision Timing Attacks on AES with Applications to Embedded CPUs. In Josef Pieprzyk, editor, *CT-RSA*, volume 5985 of *Lecture Notes in Computer Science*, pages 235–251. Springer, 2010.

[57] B. Bollig and I. Wegener. Improving the Variable Ordering of OBDDs is NP-Complete. *IEEE Transactions on Computers*, 45:993–1002, September 1996.

[58] Joseph Bonneau and Ilya Mironov. Cache-Collision Timing Attacks Against AES. In Louis Goubin and Mitsuru Matsui, editors, *CHES*, volume 4249 of *Lecture Notes in Computer Science*, pages 201–215. Springer, 2006.

[59] Giacomo Boracchi and Luca Breveglieri. A Study on the Efficiency of Differential Power Analysis on AES S-Box. *Technical Report*, January 15, 2007.

[60] S. Borkar, T. Karnik, S. Narendra, J. Tschanz, A. Keshavarzi, and V. De. Parameter variations and impact on circuits and microarchitecture. In *DAC'03: Proceedings of the Design Automation Conference*, pages 338–342, 2003.

[61] Christoph Bösch, Jorge Guajardo, Ahmad-Reza Sadeghi, Jamshid Shokrollahi, and Pim Tuyls. Efficient Helper Data Key Extractor on FPGAs. In *Cryptographic Hardware and Embedded Systems (CHES)*, volume 5154 of *Lecture Notes in Computer Science*, pages 181–197. 2008.

[62] X. Boyen. Reusable cryptographic fuzzy extractors. In *Proc. of the 10th ACM conference on Computer and Communications*, pages 82–91, 2004.

[63] Luca Breveglieri, Sylvain Guilley, Israel Koren, David Naccache, and Junko Takahashi, editors. *2011 Workshop on Fault Diagnosis and Tolerance in Cryptography, FDTC 2011, Tokyo, Japan, September 29, 2011*. IEEE, 2011.

[64] Ernie Brickell, Gary Graunke, Michael Neve, and Jean-Pierre Seifert. Software Mitigations to Hedge AES Against Cache-based Software Side Channel Vulnerabilities. Cryptology ePrint Archive, Report 2006/052, 2006.

[65] Billy Bob Brumley and Nicola Tuveri. Remote Timing Attacks are Still Practical. In Vijay Atluri and Claudia Díaz, editors, *ESORICS*, volume 6879 of *Lecture Notes in Computer Science*, pages 355–371. Springer, 2011.

[66] David Brumley and Dan Boneh. Remote Timing Attacks are Practical. *Computer Networks*, 48(5):701–716, 2005.

[67] R.E. Bryant. Graph-based algorithms for boolean function manipulation. *IEEE Transactions on Computers*, 35:677–691, August 1986.

[68] Maciej Brzozowski and Vyacheslav N. Yarmolik. Obfuscation as intellectual rights protection in VHDL language. In *Proceedings of the 6th International Conference on Computer Information Systems and Industrial Management Applications*, pages 337–340, Washington, DC, 2007. IEEE Computer Society.

[69] C. Rebeiro, S. S. Roy, D. S. Reddy and D. Mukhopadhyay. Revisiting the Itoh Tsujii Inversion Algorithm for FPGA Platforms. *IEEE Transactions on VLSI Systems.*, 19(8):1508–1512, 2011.

[70] Methodology for protection and licensing of HDL IP. http://www.us.design-reuse.com/news/?id=12745\&print=yes, 2011.

[71] David Canright. A very compact s-box for aes. In *CHES*, pages 441–455, 2005.

[72] Anne Canteaut, Cédric Lauradoux, and André Seznec. Understanding Cache Attacks. Research Report RR-5881, INRIA, 2006.

[73] E. Castillo, U. Meyer-Baese, A. García, L. Parrilla, and A. Lloris. IPP@HDL: efficient intellectual property protection scheme for IP cores. *IEEE Transactions on VLSI*, 15:578–591, May 2007.

[74] Ç. K. Koç and B. Sunar. An Efficient Optimal Normal Basis Type II Multiplier. *IEEE Trans. Comput.*, 50(1):83–87, 2001.

[75] Çetin K. Koç and Tolga Acar. Montgomery Multiplication in $GF(2^k)$. *DES Codes Cryptography*, 14(1):57–69, 1998.

[76] Çetin Kaya Koç. *Cryptographic Engineering*. Springer, 2009.

[77] R. S. Chakraborty and S. Bhunia. *HARPOON*: a SoC design methodology for hardware protection through netlist level obfuscation. *IEEE Transactions on CAD*, 28(10):1493–1502, October 2009.

[78] R. S. Chakraborty and S. Bhunia. Hardware protection and authentication through netlist level obfuscation. In *ICCAD'08: Proceedings of the IEEE/ACM International Conference on Computer-Aided Design*, pages 674–677, 2009.

[79] R. S. Chakraborty and S. Bhunia. Security against hardware Trojan through a novel application of design obfuscation. In *ICCAD '09: Proceedings of the International Conference on CAD*, pages 113–116, 2009.

[80] R. S. Chakraborty and S. Bhunia. RTL hardware IP protection using key-based control and data flow obfuscation. In *VLSID'10: Proceedings of the International Conference on VLSI Design*, pages 405–410, 2010.

[81] R. S. Chakraborty, F. Wolff, S. Paul, C. Papachristou, and S. Bhunia. *MERO*: a statistical approach for hardware Trojan detection using logic testing. *Lecture Notes on Computer Science*, 5737:396–410, September 2009.

[82] R.S. Chakraborty and S. Bhunia. Security through obscurity: An approach for protecting Register Transfer Level hardware IP. In *HOST'08: Proceedings of the International Workshop on Hardware Oriented Security and Trust*, pages 96–99, 2009.

[83] R.S. Chakraborty and S. Bhunia. RTL hardware IP protection using key-based control and data flow obfuscation. In *VLSID '10: Proceedings of the International Conference on VLSI Design*, pages 405–410, 2010.

[84] H. Chang and M.J. Atallah. Protecting software code by guards. In *DRM '01: Revised Papers from the ACM CCS-8 Workshop on Security and Privacy in Digital Rights Management*, pages 160–175, 2002.

[85] E. Charbon and I. Torunoglu. Watermarking techniques for electronic circuit design. In *IWDW'02: Proceedings of the International Conference on Digital Watermarking*, pages 147–169, 2003.

[86] Suresh Chari, Josyula R. Rao, and Pankaj Rohatgi. Template attacks. In Burton S. Kaliski Jr., Çetin Kaya Koç, and Christof Paar, editors, *CHES*, volume 2523 of *Lecture Notes in Computer Science*, pages 13–28. Springer, 2002.

[87] W. N. Chelton and M. Benaissa. Fast Elliptic Curve Cryptography on FPGA. *IEEE Transactions on Very Large Scale Integration (VLSI) Systems*, 16(2):198–205, February 2008.

[88] Chien-Ning Chen and Sung-Ming Yen. Differential fault analysis on AES key schedule and some countermeasures. In G. Goos, J. Hartmanis, and J. van Leeuwen, editors, *ACISP 2003*, volume 2727 of *LNCS*, pages 118–129. Springer, 2003.

[89] Deming Chen, Jason Cong, and Peichen Pan. FPGA Design Automation: A Survey. *Found. Trends Electron. Des. Autom.*, 1(3):139–169, 2006.

[90] Q. Chen, G. Csaba, P. Lugli, U. Schlichtmann, and U. R ührmair. The Bistable Ring PUF: A new architecture for strong physical unclonable functions. In *Proc. of IEEE International Symposium on Hardware-Oriented Security and Trust (HOST)*, pages 134 –141, 2011.

[91] Z. Chen, X. Guo, R. Nagesh, A. Reddy, M. Gora, and A. Maiti. Hardware Trojan designs on BASYS FPGA board, 2012. http://isis.poly.edu/~vikram/vt.pdf.

[92] Z. Cherif, J. Danger, S. Guilley, and L. Bossuet. An easy-to-design PUF based on a single oscillator: The Loop PUF. In *Proc. of 15th Euromicro Conference on Digital System Design (DSD)*, pages 156–162, 2012.

[93] T. Chou and K. Roy. Accurate power estimation of CMOS sequential circuits. *IEEE Transactions on VLSI*, 4(3):369–380, September 1996.

[94] Christophe Clavier, Jean-Sébastien Coron, and Nora Dabbous. Differential power analysis in the presence of hardware countermeasures. In Çetin Kaya Koç and Christof Paar, editors, *CHES*, volume 1965 of *Lecture Notes in Computer Science*, pages 252–263. Springer, 2000.

[95] Obfuscation by code morphing. http://en.wikipedia.org/wiki/Obfuscated_code#Obfuscation_by_code_morphing, 2011.

[96] C. Collberg, C. Thomborson, and D. Low. Manufacturing cheap, resilient, and stealthy opaque constructs. In *POPL '98: Proceedings of the 25th ACM SIGPLAN-SIGACT symposium on Principles of programming languages*, pages 184–196, 1998.

[97] C.S. Collberg and C. Thomborson. Watermarking, tamper-proofing, and obfuscation: tools for software protection. *IEEE Transactions on Software Engineering*, 28:735–746, August 2002.

[98] Bart Coppens, Ingrid Verbauwhede, Koen De Bosschere, and Bjorn De Sutter. Practical Mitigations for Timing-Based Side-Channel Attacks on Modern x86 Processors. In *IEEE Symposium on Security and Privacy*, pages 45–60. IEEE Computer Society, 2009.

[99] Jean-Sébastien Coron and Ilya Kizhvatov. An Efficient Method for Random Delay Generation in Embedded Software. In Christophe Clavier and Kris Gaj, editors, *CHES*, volume 5747 of *Lecture Notes in Computer Science*, pages 156–170. Springer, 2009.

[100] Jean-Sébastien Coron and Ilya Kizhvatov. Analysis and Improvement of the Random Delay Countermeasure of CHES 2009. In Mangard and Standaert [244], pages 95–109.

[101] Scott A. Crosby, Dan S. Wallach, and Rudolf H. Riedi. Opportunities and Limits of Remote Timing Attacks. *ACM Trans. Inf. Syst. Secur.*, 12(3), 2009.

[102] F. Crowe, A. Daly, and W. Marnane. Optimised Montgomery Domain Inversion on FPGA. In *Circuit Theory and Design, 2005. Proceedings of the 2005 European Conference on*, volume 1, August/September 2005.

[103] J. Daemen and V. Rijmen. *The Design of Rijndael*. Springer-Verlag, 2002.

[104] Joan Daemen and Vincent Rijmen. *The Design of Rijndael: AES - The Advanced Encryption Standard*. Springer, 2002.

[105] Ds2432 1kb protected 1-wire eeprom with sha-1 engine. `http://www.maxim-ic.com/datasheet/index.mvp/id/2914`, 2012.

[106] Ds5002fp secure microprocessor chip. `http://www.maxim-ic.com/datasheet/index.mvp/id/2949`, 2012.

[107] DARPA. TRUST in Integrated Circuits (TIC) - Proposer Information Pamphlet. `http://www.darpa.mil/MTO/solicitations/baa07-24/index.html`, 2007.

[108] Guerric Meurice de Dormale, Philippe Bulens, and Jean-Jacques Quisquater. An Improved Montgomery Modular Inversion Targeted for Efficient Implementation on FPGA. In O. Diessel and J.A. Williams, editors, *International Conference on Field-Programmable Technology - FPT 2004*, pages 441–444, 2004.

[109] Defense Science Board. Task force on high performance microchip supply. `http://www.acq.osd.mil/dsb/reports/200502HPMSReportFinal.pdf`, 2005.

[110] John Demme, Robert Martin, Adam Waksman, and Simha Sethumadhavan. Side-Channel Vulnerability Factor: A Metric for Measuring Information Leakage. In *ISCA* [1], pages 106–117.

[111] W. Diffie and M. Hellman. New Directions in Cryptography. In *IEEE Transactions on Information Theory (22)*, pages 644–654. IEEE, 1976.

[112] Yevgeniy Dodis, Leonid Reyzin, and Adam Smith. Fuzzy Extractors: How to Generate Strong Keys from Biometrics and Other Noisy Data. In C. Cachin and J.L. Camenisch, editors, *Advances in Cryptology – EUROCRYPT 2004*, volume 3027 of *Lecture Notes in Computer Science*, pages 523–540. 2004.

[113] Leonid Domnitser, Aamer Jaleel, Jason Loew, Nael B. Abu-Ghazaleh, and Dmitry Ponomarev. Non-monopolizable caches: Low-complexity Mitigation of Cache Side-Channel Attacks. *TACO*, 8(4):35, 2012.

[114] D. Du, S. Narasimhan, R. S. Chakraborty, and S. Bhunia. Self-referencing: a scalable side-channel approach for hardware Trojan detection. In *Proc. of the International Workshop on Cryptographic Hardware and Embedded Systems (CHES'11)*, pages 173–187, Berlin, Heidelberg, 2010.

[115] Zoya Dyka and Peter Langendoerfer. Area Efficient Hardware Implementation of Elliptic Curve Cryptography by Iteratively Applying Karatsuba's Method. In *DATE '05: Proceedings of the conference on Design, Automation and Test in Europe*, pages 70–75, Washington, DC, USA, 2005. IEEE Computer Society.

[116] Z. Chen *et al.* Hardware Trojan Designs on BASYS FPGA Board. CSAW Embedded Systems Challenge, 2008. `http://isis.poly.edu/~vikram/vt.pdf`.

[117] Federal Information Processing Standards Publication 197. Announcing the Advanced Encryption Standard (AES), 2001.

[118] Federal Information Processing Standards Publication 46-2. Announcing the Standard for Data Encryption Standard (DES), 1993.

[119] H. Feistel. Cryptography and Computer Privacy. *Scientific American*, 228(5):15–23, May 1973.

[120] M. Feldhofer, J. Wolkerstorfer, and V. Rijmen. Aes implementation on a grain of sand. *Information Security, IEE Proceedings*, 152(1):13–20, 2005.

[121] Jacques J. A. Fournier and Michael Tunstall. Cache Based Power Analysis Attacks on AES. In Lynn Margaret Batten and Reihaneh Safavi-Naini, editors, *ACISP*, volume 4058 of *Lecture Notes in Computer Science*, pages 17–28. Springer, 2006.

[122] John B. Fraleigh. *First Course in Abstract Algebra*. Addison-Wesley, Boston, MA, USA, 2002.

[123] W. F. Friedman. The index of coincidence and its application in cryptography. In *Riverbank Publication, Riverbank Labs*. Reprinted by Aegian Park Press, 1920.

[124] Hideo Fujiwara and Marie Engelene J. Obien. Secure and testable scan design using extended de bruijn graphs. In *ASPDAC 10: Proceedings of the 2010 Asia and South Pacific Design Automation Connference*, pages 413–418, 2010.

[125] Katsuya Fujiwara, Hideo Fujiwara, Marie Engelene J. Obien, and Hideo Tamamoto. Sreep: Shift register equivalents enumeration and synthesis program for secure scan design. *Design and Diagnostics of Electronic Circuits and Systems*, 0:193–196, 2010.

[126] G. Piret and J. J. Quisquater. A Differential Fault Attack Technique against SPN Structures, with Application to the AES and Khazad. In *CHES 2003*, pages 77–88. LNCS 2779, 2003.

[127] Jean-François Gallais, Ilya Kizhvatov, and Michael Tunstall. Improved Trace-Driven Cache-Collision Attacks against Embedded AES Implementations. In Yongwha Chung and Moti Yung, editors, *WISA*, volume 6513 of *Lecture Notes in Computer Science*, pages 243–257. Springer, 2010.

[128] Blaise Gassend, Dwaine Clarke, Marten van Dijk, and Srinivas Devadas. Silicon physical random functions. In *Proc. of ACM Conference on Computer and Communications Security*, pages 148–160, 2002.

[129] Blaise Gassend, Daihyun Lim, Dwaine Clarke, Marten van Dijk, and Srinivas Devadas. Identification and authentication of integrated circuits: Research Articles. *Concurrency and Computation: Practice & Experience*, 16(11):1077–1098, 2004.

[130] M. J. Geuzebroek, J. Th. van der Linden, and A. J. van de Goor. Test point insertion that facilitates ATPG in reducing test time and data volume. In *ITC'02: Proceedings of the International Test Conference*, pages 138–147, 2002.

[131] Benedikt Gierlichs, Jörn-Marc Schmidt, and Michael Tunstall. Infective Computation and Dummy Rounds: Fault Protection for Block Ciphers without Check-before-Output. In Alejandro Hevia and Gregory Neven, editors, *Progress in Cryptology – LATINCRYPT 2012*, volume 7533 of *Lecture Notes in Computer Science*, pages 305–321. Springer, 2012.

[132] Christophe Giraud. DFA on AES. In *IACR e-print archive 2003/008*, page 008. http://eprint.iacr.org/2003/008, 2003.

[133] D. E. Goldberg. *Genetic Algorithms in Search, Optimization and Machine Learning*. Addison Wesley, 1989.

[134] O. Goldreich. *Foundations of Cryptography*, volume 2. Cambridge University Press, 2005.

[135] Oded Goldreich and Rafail Ostrovsky. Software Protection and Simulation on Oblivious RAMs. *J. ACM*, 43(3):431–473, 1996.

[136] C. Grabbe, M. Bednara, J. Shokrollahi, J. Teich, and J. von zur Gathen. FPGA Designs of Parallel High Performance $GF(2^{233})$ Multipliers. In *Proc. of the IEEE International Symposium on Circuits and Systems (ISCAS-03)*, volume II, pages 268–271, Bangkok, Thailand, May 2003.

[137] Johann Großschädl and Guy-Armand Kamendje. Instruction Set Extension for Fast Elliptic Curve Cryptography over Binary Finite Fields $GF(2^m)$. In *ASAP*, pages 455–. IEEE Computer Society, 2003.

[138] Johann Großschädl and Erkay Savas. Instruction Set Extensions for Fast Arithmetic in Finite Fields $GF(p)$ and $GF(2^m)$. In Marc Joye and Jean-Jacques Quisquater, editors, *CHES*, volume 3156 of *Lecture Notes in Computer Science*, pages 133–147. Springer, 2004.

[139] Jorge Guajardo, Sandeep S. Kumar, Geert Jan Schrijen, and Pim Tuyls. FPGA intrinsic PUFs and their use for IP protection. In *Proc. of Cryptographic Hardware and Embedded Systems Workshop (CHES)*, volume 4727 of *LNCS*, pages 63–80, 2007.

[140] Jorge Guajardo, Sandeep S. Kumar, Geert Jan Schrijen, and Pim Tuyls. Physical unclonable functions and public-key crypto for FPGA IP protection. In *Field Programmable Logic and Applications*, pages 189–195, August 2007.

[141] Jorge Guajardo and Christof Paar. Itoh-Tsujii Inversion in Standard Basis and Its Application in Cryptography and Codes. *Des. Codes Cryptography*, 25(2):207–216, 2002.

[142] David Gullasch, Endre Bangerter, and Stephan Krenn. Cache Games - Bringing Access-Based Cache Attacks on AES to Practice. In *IEEE Symposium on Security and Privacy*, pages 490–505. IEEE Computer Society, 2011.

[143] Xiaofei Guo and R. Karri. Invariance-based Concurrent Error Detection for Advanced Encryption Standard. In *DAC*, pages 573–578, Jun 2012.

[144] Nils Gura, Sheueling Chang Shantz, Hans Eberle, Sumit Gupta, Vipul Gupta, Daniel Finchelstein, Edouard Goupy, and Douglas Stebila. An End-to-End Systems Approach to Elliptic Curve Cryptography. In *CHES '02: Revised Papers from the 4th International Workshop on Cryptographic Hardware and Embedded Systems*, pages 349–365, London, UK, 2003. Springer-Verlag.

[145] Torben Hagerup and C. Rüb. A guided tour of Chernoff bounds. In *Information Processing Letters, Volume 33, Issue 6*, pages 305–308. Elsevier North-Holland, Inc., 1990.

[146] Shikha Bisht Harshal Tupsamudre and Debdeep Mukhopadhyay. Destroying fault invariant with randomization - a countermeasure for aes against differential fault attacks. In *CHES*, 2014.

[147] Ryan Helinski, Dhruva Acharyya, and Jim Plusquellic. A physical unclonable function defined using power distribution system equivalent resistance variations. In *Proc. of 46th Annual Design Automation Conference(DAC)*, pages 676–681, 2009.

[148] David Hely, Maurin Augagneur, Yves Clauzel, and Jeremy Dubeuf. A physical unclonable function based on setup time violation. In *Proc. of IEEE 30th International Conference on Computer Design (ICCD)*, pages 135–138, 2012.

[149] David Hely, Marie-Lise Flottes, Frederic Bancel, Bruno Rouzeyre, Nicolas Berard, and Michel Renovell. Scan design and secure chip. In *IOLTS '04: Proceedings of the International On-Line Testing Symposium, 10th IEEE*, page 219, Washington, DC, USA, 2004. IEEE Computer Society.

[150] Alireza Hodjat and Ingrid Verbauwhede. Area-throughput trade-offs for fully pipelined 30 to 70 gbits/s aes processors. *IEEE Trans. Comput.*, 55(4):366–372, April 2006.

[151] Y. Hori, T. Yoshida, T. Katashita, and A. Satoh. Quantitative and Statistical Performance Evaluation of Arbiter Physical Unclonable Functions on FPGAs. In *Proceedings of International Conference on Reconfigurable Computing and FPGAs (ReConFig)*, pages 298–303, 2010.

[152] Takashi Horiyama, Masaki Nakanishi, Hirotsugu Kajihara, and Shinji Kimura. Folding of Logic Functions and its Application to Look Up Table Compaction. *ICCAD*, 00:694–697, 2002.

[153] T.W. Hou, H.Y. Chen, and M.H. Tsai. Three control flow obfuscation methods for Java software. *IEE Proceedings on Software*, 153(2):80–86, April 2006.

[154] Wei-Ming Hu. Lattice scheduling and covert channels. In *Research in Security and Privacy, 1992. Proceedings., 1992 IEEE Computer Society Symposium on*, pages 52 –61, may 1992.

[155] Y. L. Huang, F.S. Ho, H.Y. Tsai, and H.M. Kao. A control flow obfuscation method to discourage malicious tampering of software codes. In *ASIACCS '06: Proceedings of the 2006 ACM Symposium on Information, Computer and Communications Security*, pages 362–362, 2006.

[156] T. Huffmire, B. Brotherton, W. Gang, T. Sherwood, R. Kastner, T. Levin, T. Nguyen, and C. Irvine. Moats and Drawbridges: An isolation primitive for reconfigurable hardware based systems. In *SP '07: Proceedings of the IEEE Sympusium on Security and Privacy*, pages 281–295, 2007.

[157] T. Huffmire, C. Irvine, T. D. sand T. Levin Nguyen, R. Kastner, and T. Sherwood. *Handbook of FPGA Design Security*. Springer, Dordrecht, 2010.

[158] Michael Hutton, Jay Schleicher, David M. Lewis, Bruce Pedersen, Richard Yuan, Sinan Kaptanoglu, Gregg Baeckler, Boris Ratchev, Ketan Padalia, Mark Bourgeault, Andy Lee, Henry Kim, and Rahul Saini. Improving FPGA Performance and Area Using an Adaptive Logic Module. In *FPL*, pages 135–144, 2004.

[159] Xilinx Inc. Virtex-II Platform FPGA User Guide (v 2.2). http://www.xilinx.com/support/documentation/virtex-ii.htm, 2012.

[160] Toshiya Itoh and Shigeo Tsujii. A Fast Algorithm For Computing Multiplicative Inverses in $GF(2^m)$ Using Normal Bases. *Inf. Comput.*, 78(3):171–177, 1988.

[161] C. Patel J. Plusquellic J. Lee, M. Tehranipoor. Securing scan design using lock and key technique. In *DFT 05: Proceedings of 20th IEEE International Symposium on Defect and Fault Tolerance in VLSI Systems*, pages 51–62, 2005.

[162] M.H. Jakubowski, C.W. Saw, and R. Venkatesan. Tamper-tolerant software: Modeling and implementation. In *IWSEC '09: Proceedings of the International Workshop on Security: Advances in Information and Computer Security*, pages 125–139, 2009.

[163] K. Järvinen and J. Skytta. On parallelization of high-speed processors for elliptic curve cryptography. *Very Large Scale Integration (VLSI) Systems, IEEE Transactions on*, 16(9):1162 –1175, sept. 2008.

[164] Kimmo Järvinen. On repeated squarings in binary fields. In Michael Jacobson, Vincent Rijmen, and Reihaneh Safavi-Naini, editors, *Selected Areas in Cryptography*, volume 5867 of *Lecture Notes in Computer Science*, pages 331–349. Springer Berlin / Heidelberg, 2009.

[165] D. Jayasinghe, J. Fernando, R. Herath, and R. Ragel. Remote Cache Timing Attack on Advanced Encryption Standard and Countermeasures. In *Information and Automation for Sustainability (ICIAFs), 2010 5th International Conference on*, pages 177 –182, dec. 2010.

[166] Marie-Lise Flottes Jean Da Rolt, Giorgio Di Natale and Bruno Rouzeyre. New security threats against chips containing scan chain structures. In *HOST 11: Proceedings of IEEE Symposium on Hardware-Oriented Security and Trust*, pages 105–110, 2011.

[167] Y. Jin and Y. Makris. Hardware Trojan detection using path delay fingerprint. In *Proc. IEEE International Workshop on Hardware-Oriented Security and Trust (HOST'08)*, pages 51–57, Washington, DC, USA, 2008.

[168] H.G. Joepgen and S. Krauss. Software by means of the protprog method. *Elecktronik*, 42:52–56, August 1993.

[169] D.S. Johnson. The NP-completeness column. *ACM Transactions on Algorithms*, 1:160–176, July 2005.

[170] M. Joye, P. Manet, and JB. Rigaud. Strengthening Hardware AES Implementations against Fault Attack. *IET Information Security*, 1:106–110, 2007.

[171] D. Kahn. The codebreakers: The story of secret writing. New York: Macmillan Publishing Co, 1967.

[172] A.B. Kahng, J. Lach, W.H. Mangione-Smith, S. Mantik, I.L. Markov, M. Potkonjak, P. Tucker, H. Wang, and G. Wolfe. Constraint-based watermarking techniques for design IP protection. *IEEE Transactions on CAD*, 20(10):1236 – 1252, October 2001.

[173] Burton S. Kaliski. The Montgomery Inverse and its Applications. *IEEE Transactions on Computers*, 44(8):1064–1065, 1995.

[174] R. Kapoor. Security vs. test quality: Are they mutually exclusive? In *ITC '04: Proceedings of the International Test Conference*, page 1413, Washington, DC, USA, 2004. IEEE Computer Society.

[175] D. Karakoyunlu and B. Sunar. Differential template attacks on PUF enabled cryptographic devices. In *Proceedings of IEEE International Workshop on Information Forensics and Security (WIFS)*, 2010.

[176] Anatoly A. Karatsuba and Y. Ofman. Multiplication of Multidigit Numbers on Automata. *Soviet Physics Doklady*, 7:595–596, 1963.

[177] Mark Karpovsky, Konrad J. Kulikowski, and Alexander Taubin. Differential Fault Analysis Attack Resistant Architectures for the Advanced Encryption Standard. In *CARDIS*, pages 177–192, Aug 2004.

[178] R. Karri, J. Rajendran, Rosenfeld K., and M. Tehranipoor. Trustworthy hardware: identifying and classifying hardware trojans. *IEEE Computer*, 43(10):39–46, Oct. 2010.

[179] Ramesh Karri, G. Kuznetsov, and M. Goessel. Parity-Based Concurrent Error Detection of Substitution-Permutation Network Block Ciphers. In *CHES*, pages 113–124, Sept 2003.

[180] Ramesh Karri, Kaijie Wu, P. Mishra, and Y. Kim. Concurrent Error Detection Schemes of Fault Based Side-Channel Cryptanalysis of Symmetric Block Ciphers. *IEEE Trans. on Computer-Aided Design*, 21(12):1509–1517, Dec 2002.

[181] Ramesh Karri, Kaijie Wu, Piyush Mishra, and Yongkook Kim. Concurrent Error Detection of Fault-Based Side-Channel Cryptanalysis of 128-Bit Symmetric Block Ciphers. In *DAC*, pages 579–585, 2001.

[182] Ramesh Karri, Kaijie Wu, Piyush Mishra, and Yongkook Kim. Fault-based side-channel cryptanalysis tolerant rijndael symmetric block cipher architecture. In *DFT*, pages 427–435, 2001.

[183] Michael Kasper, Werner Schindler, and Marc Stöttinger. A stochastic method for security evaluation of cryptographic fpga implementations. In *FPT*, pages 146–153, 2010.

[184] Stefan Katzenbeisser, ÃlJnal KocabaÅ§, Vincent Leest, Ahmad-Reza Sadeghi, Geert-Jan Schrijen, and Christian Wachsmann. Recyclable PUFs: logically reconfigurable PUFs. *Journal of Cryptographic Engineering*, 1:177–186, 2011.

[185] John Kelsey, Bruce Schneier, David Wagner, and Chris Hall. Side Channel Cryptanalysis of Product Ciphers. In Jean-Jacques Quisquater, Yves Deswarte, Catherine Meadows, and Dieter Gollmann, editors, *ESORICS*, volume 1485 of *Lecture Notes in Computer Science*, pages 97–110. Springer, 1998.

[186] John Kelsey, Bruce Schneier, David Wagner, and Chris Hall. Side Channel Cryptanalysis of Product Ciphers. *J. Comput. Secur.*, 8(2,3):141–158, 2000.

[187] Mehran Mozaffari Kermani and Arash Reyhani-Masoleh. Parity Prediction of S-Box for AES. In *CCECE*, pages 2357–2360, 2006.

[188] Mehran Mozaffari Kermani and Arash Reyhani-Masoleh. A Low-cost S-box for the Advanced Encryption Standard using Normal Basis. In *EIT*, pages 52–55, 2009.

[189] Mehran Mozaffari Kermani and Arash Reyhani-Masoleh. A High-Performance Fault Diagnosis Approach for the AES SubBytes Utilizing Mixed Bases. In Breveglieri et al. [63], pages 80–87.

[190] Mehran Mozaffari Kermani and Arash Reyhani-Masoleh. A Low-Power High-Performance Concurrent Fault Detection Approach for the Composite Field S-Box and Inverse S-Box. *IEEE Trans. Computers*, 60(9):1327–1340, 2011.

[191] A. Keshavarzi, K. Roy, C. F. Hawkins, and V. De. Multiple-parameter CMOS ic testing with increased sensitivity for i_{DDQ}. *IEEE Transactions on VLSI*, 11(5):863—870, may 2003.

[192] Farouk Khelil, Mohamed Hamdi, Sylvain Guilley, Jean Luc Danger, and Nidhal Selmane. Fault Analysis Attack on an AES FPGA Implementation. pages 1–5. ESRGroups, 2008.

[193] Sagar Khurana, Souvik Kolay, Chester Rebeiro, and Debdeep Mukhopadhyay. Light Weight Cipher Implementations on Embedded Processors. In *Design and Technology of Integrated Systems (DTIS)*. IEEE Computer Society, 2013.

[194] C. Kim. Improved Differential Fault Analysis on AES Key Schedule. *Information Forensics and Security, IEEE Transactions on*, PP(99):1, 2011.

[195] Chang Hoon Kim, Soonhak Kwon, and Chun Pyo Hong. FPGA Implementation of High Performance Elliptic Curve Cryptographic processor over $GF(2^{163})$. *Journal of Systems Architecture - Embedded Systems Design*, 54(10):893–900, 2008.

[196] Chong Hee Kim. Differential fault analysis against AES-192 and AES-256 with minimal faults. In Luca Breveglieri, Marc Joye, Israel Koren, David Naccache, and Ingrid Verbauwhede, editors, *Fault Diagnosis and Tolerance in Cryptography — FDTC 2010*, pages 3–9. IEEE Computer Society, 2010.

[197] Chong Hee KIM. Differential fault analysis of aes: Toward reducing number of faults. Cryptology ePrint Archive, Report 2011/178, 2011. http://eprint.iacr.org/.

[198] Chong Hee Kim and Jean-Jacques Quisquater. New Differential Fault Analysis on AES Key Schedule: Two Faults Are Enough. In Gilles Grimaud and François-Xavier Standaert, editors, *CARDIS*, volume 5189 of *Lecture Notes in Computer Science*, pages 48–60. Springer, 2008.

[199] S. T. King, J. Tucek, A. Cozzie, C. Grier, W. Jiang, and Y. Zhou. Designing and implementing malicious hardware. In *LEET'08: Proceedings of the Usenix Workshop on Large-Scale Exploits and Emergent Threats*, pages 5:1–5:8, 2008.

[200] Alexander Klimov and Adi Shamir. A New Class of Invertible Mappings. In Burton S. Kaliski Jr., Çetin Kaya Koç, and Christof Paar, editors, *CHES*, volume 2523 of *Lecture Notes in Computer Science*, pages 470–483. Springer, 2002.

[201] Donald E. Knuth. *The Art of Computer Programming Volumes 1-3 Boxed Set*. Addison-Wesley Longman Publishing Co., Inc., Boston, MA, USA, 1998.

[202] Paul C. Kocher. Timing Attacks on Implementations of Diffie-Hellman, RSA, DSS, and Other Systems. In Neal Koblitz, editor, *CRYPTO '96: Proceedings of the 16th Annual International Cryptology Conference on Advances in Cryptology*, volume 1109 of *Lecture Notes in Computer Science*, pages 104–113, London, UK, 1996. Springer-Verlag.

[203] D. A. Koley. An introduction to Genetic Algorithms for scientists and engineers. In *Action Report*, pages 42–47. Western Governors Association, Jun. 1995.

[204] Jingfei Kong, Onur Aciiçmez, Jean-Pierre Seifert, and Huiyang Zhou. Deconstructing New Cache Designs for Thwarting Software Cache-based Side Channel Attacks. In Trent Jaeger, editor, *CSAW*, pages 25–34. ACM, 2008.

[205] Jingfei Kong, Onur Aciiçmez, Jean-Pierre Seifert, and Huiyang Zhou. Hardware-Software Integrated Approaches to Defend Against Software Cache-Based Side Channel Attacks. In *HPCA*, pages 393–404. IEEE Computer Society, 2009.

[206] Jingfei Kong, Onur Aciicmez, Jean-Pierre Seifert, and Huiyang Zhou. Architecting Against Software Cache-based Side Channel Attacks. *IEEE Transactions on Computers*, 99(PrePrints), 2012.

[207] I. Koren and C. Mani Krishna. *Fault-Tolerant Systems*. Morgan-Kaufmann, 2007.

[208] F. Koushanfar. Provably secure active IC metering techniques for piracy avoidance and digital rights management. *IEEE Transactions on Information Forensics and Security*, 7(1):51–63, February 2012.

[209] J. R. Koza. A hierarchical approach to learning the Boolean Multiplexer function. In *FOGA'91: Proceedings of the Workshop on the Foundations of Genetic Algorithms and Classifier Systems*, pages 171âĂŞ–192, 1991.

[210] J. R. Koza. *Genetic Programming: On the Programming of Computers by Means of Natural Selection*. MIT Press, 1992.

[211] Aswin Krishna, Seetharam Narasimhan, Xinmu Wang, and Swarup Bhunia. MECCA: A Robust Low-Overhead PUF Using Embedded Memory Array. In *Cryptographic Hardware and Embedded Systems (CHES)*, volume 6917 of *Lecture Notes in Computer Science*, pages 407–420. 2011.

[212] R. Kumar, V.C. Patil, and S. Kundu. Design of Unique and Reliable Physically Unclonable Functions Based on Current Starved Inverter Chain. In *Proc. of IEEE Computer Society Annual Symposium on VLSI (ISVLSI)*, pages 224–229, 2011.

[213] S.S. Kumar, J. Guajardo, R. Maes, G.-J. Schrijen, and P. Tuyls. Extended abstract: The butterfly PUF protecting IP on every FPGA. In *Proc. of IEEE International Workshop on Hardware-Oriented Security and Trust(HOST)*, pages 67–70, 2008.

[214] Klaus Kursawe, Ahmad-Reza Sadeghi, Dries Schellekens, Boris Škorić, and Pim Tuyls. Reconfigurable Physical Unclonable Functions – Enabling Technology for Tamper-Resistant Storage . In *Proc. of 2nd IEEE International Workshop on Hardware-Oriented Security and Trust (HOST)*, pages 22–29, 2009.

[215] J. Lach, W.H. Mangione-Smith, and M. Potkonjak. Robust FPGA intellectual property protection through multiple small watermarks. In *Proceedings of the 36th annual ACM/IEEE Design Automation Conference*, DAC '99, pages 831–836, New York, NY, 1999. ACM.

[216] Cédric Lauradoux. Collision Attacks on Processors with Cache and Countermeasures. In Christopher Wolf, Stefan Lucks, and Po-Wah Yau, editors, *WEWoRC*, volume 74 of *LNI*, pages 76–85. GI, 2005.

[217] Jae W. Lee, Daihyun Lim, Blaise Gassend, G. Edward Suh, Marten van Dijk, and Srinivas Devadas. A technique to build a secret key in integrated circuits for identification and authentication application. In *Proceedings of the Symposium on VLSI Circuits*, pages 176–159, 2004.

[218] Ruby B. Lee, Zhijie Shi, Yiqun Lisa Yin, Ronald L. Rivest, and Matthew J. B. Robshaw. On Permutation Operations in Cipher Design. In *ITCC (2)*, pages 569–577. IEEE Computer Society, 2004.

[219] Wei Li, Dawu Gu, Yong Wang, Juanru Li, and Zhiqiang Liu. An Extension of Differential Fault Analysis on AES. In *Third International Conference on Network and System Security*, pages 443–446. NSS, 2009.

[220] D. Lim. Extracting secret keys from integrated circuits. Master's thesis, Massachusetts Institute of Technology, 2004.

[221] L. Lin, W. Burleson, and C. Parr. *MOLES*: Malicious off-chip leakage enabled by side-channels. In *ICCAD'09: Proceedings of the International Conference on CAD*, pages 117–122, 2009.

[222] L. Lin, M. Kasper, T. GÃijneysu, C. Paar, and W. Burleson. Trojan side-channels: Lightweight Hardware Trojans through side-channel engineering. volume 5747 of *Lecture Notes in Computer Science*, pages 382–395, 2009.

[223] C. Linn and S. Debray. Obfuscation of executable code to improve resistance to static disassembly. In *Proceedings of the ACM Conference on Computer and Communica-tionsSecurity*, pages 290–299, 2003.

[224] Keith Lofstrom, W. Robert Daasch, and Donald Taylor. IC Identification Circuit Using Device Mismatch. In *Proc. of ISSCC*, pages 372–373, 2000.

[225] Victor Lomné, Thomas Roche, and Adrian Thillard. On the Need of Randomness in Fault Attack Countermeasures - Application to AES. In Guido Bertoni and Benedikt Gierlichs, editors, *Fault Diagnosis and Tolerance in Cryptography – FDTC 2012*, pages 85–94. IEEE Computer Society, 2012.

[226] Julio López and Ricardo Dahab. Fast multiplication on elliptic curves over gf(2m) without precomputation. In *Proceedings of the First International Workshop on Cryptographic Hardware and Embedded Systems*, CHES '99, pages 316–327, London, UK, UK, 1999. Springer-Verlag.

[227] Julio López and Ricardo Dahab. Improved Algorithms for Elliptic Curve Arithmetic in $GF(2^n)$. In *SAC '98: Proceedings of the Selected Areas in Cryptography*, pages 201–212, London, UK, 1999. Springer-Verlag.

[228] Jonathan Lutz and Anwarul Hasan. High Performance FPGA based Elliptic Curve Cryptographic Co-Processor. In *ITCC '04: Proceedings of the International Conference on Information Technology: Coding and Computing (ITCC'04) Volume 2*, page 486, Washington, DC, USA, 2004. IEEE Computer Society.

[229] B. Lynn, M. Prabhakaran, and A. Sahai. Positive results and techniques for obfuscation. Cryptology ePrint Archive, Report 2004/060, 2004. http://eprint.iacr.org/.

[230] P. Lysaght. Dynamic reconfiguration of Xilinx FPGAs: enhanced architectures, design methodologies, & CAD tools. Xilinx, Inc., 2012. http://www.xilinx.com/univ/FPL06_Invited_Presentation_PLysaght.pdf.

[231] Chinese firms favoring soft IP over hard cores. http://www.eetasia.com/ART_8800440032_480100_NT_ac94df1c.HTM, 2011.

[232] R. Maes, V. Rozic, I. Verbauwhede, P. Koeberl, E. van der Sluis, and V. van der Leest. Experimental evaluation of Physically Unclonable Functions in 65 nm CMOS. In *Proc. of the ESSCIRC*, pages 486 –489, 2012.

[233] Roel Maes, Pim Tuyls, and Ingrid Verbauwhede. Intrinsic PUFs from Flip-flops on Reconfigurable Devices. In *Proc. of 3rd Benelux Workshop on Information and System Security (WISSec)*, page 17, 2008.

[234] Roel Maes and Ingrid Verbauwhede. Physically Unclonable Functions: A Study on the State of the Art and Future Research Directions. In Ahmad-Reza Sadeghi and David Naccache, editors, *Towards Hardware-Intrinsic Security*, Information Security and Cryptography, pages 3–37. Springer, 2010.

[235] V. Maingot and R. Leveugle. Influence of Error Detecting or Correcting Codes on the Sensitivity to DPA of an AES S-Box. In *ICSES*, pages 1–5, 2009.

[236] P. Maistri and R. Leveugle. Double-Data-Rate Computation as a Countermeasure against Fault Analysis. *IEEE Transactions on Computers*, 57(11):1528–1539, Nov 2008.

[237] Abhranil Maiti, Vikash Gunreddy, and Patrick Schaumont. A Systematic Method to Evaluate and Compare the Performance of Physical Unclonable Functions. *IACR Cryptology ePrint Archive*, 2011:657, 2011.

[238] A. Maity and P. Schaumont. Improving the quality of a Physical Unclonable Function using configurable Ring Oscillators. In *FPL'09: International Conference on Field Programmable Logic and Applications*, pages 703–707, 2009.

[239] Mehrdad Majzoobi, Golsa Ghiaasi, Farinaz Koushanfar, and Sani R. Nassif. Ultra-low power current-based PUF. In *International Symposium on Circuits and Systems (ISCAS)*, pages 2071–2074. 2011.

[240] Mehrdad Majzoobi, Farinaz Koushanfar, and Miodrag Potkonjak. Lightweight secure PUFs. In *Proc. of the 2008 IEEE/ACM International Conference on Computer-Aided Design(ICCAD)*, pages 670–673, 2008.

[241] Stefan Mangard. Hardware Countermeasures against DPA ? A Statistical Analysis of Their Effectiveness. In Tatsuaki Okamoto, editor, *CT-RSA*, volume 2964 of *Lecture Notes in Computer Science*, pages 222–235. Springer, 2004.

[242] Stefan Mangard, Thomas Popp, and Berndt M. Gammel. Side-Channel Leakage of Masked CMOS Gates. In Alfred Menezes, editor, *Topics in Cryptology - CT-RSA 2005, The Cryptographers' Track at the RSA Conference 2005, San Francisco, CA, USA, February 14-18, 2005, Proceedings*, Lecture Notes in Computer Science (LNCS), pages 351 – 365. Springer, 2005.

[243] Stefan Mangard and Kai Schramm. Pinpointing the side-channel leakage of masked aes hardware implementations. In *CHES*, pages 76–90, 2006.

[244] Stefan Mangard and François-Xavier Standaert, editors. *Cryptographic Hardware and Embedded Systems, CHES 2010, 12th International Workshop, Santa Barbara, CA, USA, August 17-20, 2010. Proceedings*, volume 6225 of *Lecture Notes in Computer Science*. Springer, 2010.

[245] Robert Martin, John Demme, and Simha Sethumadhavan. TimeWarp: Rethinking Timekeeping and Performance Monitoring Mechanisms to Mitigate Side-Channel Attacks. In *ISCA* [1], pages 118–129.

[246] B. Mathew and D. G. Saab. Combining multiple DFT schemes with test generation. *IEEE Transactions on CAD*, 18(6):685–696, 1999.

[247] S. Mathew, F. Sheikh, A. Agarwal, M. Kounavis, S. Hsu, H. Kaul, M. Anders, and R. Krishnamurthy. 53Gbps Native $GF(2^4)^2$ Composite-Field AES-Encrypt/Decrypt Accelerator for Content-Protection in 45nm High-Performance Microprocessors. In *VLSI Circuits (VLSIC), 2010 IEEE Symposium on*, pages 169–170, June.

[248] Mitsuru Matsui. New Block Encryption Algorithm MISTY. In Biham [49], pages 54–68.

[249] Alfred J. Menezes, Paul C. van Oorschot, and Scott A. Vanstone. *Handbook of Applied Cryptography.* CRC Press, 2001.

[250] Dominik Merli, Dieter Schuster, Frederic Stumpf, and Georg Sigl. Side-channel analysis of PUFs and Fuzzy extractors. In *Proceedings of the 4th international conference on Trust and trustworthy computing,Pittsburgh, PA*, TRUST'11, pages 33–47, 2011.

[251] Thomas S. Messerges, Ezzat A. Dabbish, and Robert H. Sloan. Examining Smart-Card Security under the Threat of Power Analysis Attacks. *IEEE Trans. Comput.*, 51(5):541–552, 2002.

[252] P. L. Montgomery. Speeding the pollard and elliptic curve methods of factorization. In *Mathematics of Computation*, volume 48, pages 243–264, January 1987.

[253] Peter L. Montgomery. Five, Six, and Seven-Term Karatsuba-Like Formulae. *IEEE Transactions on Computers*, 54(3):362–369, 2005.

[254] W. A. Moore and P. A. Kayfes. US Patent 7213142 - system and method to initialize registers with an EEPROM stored boot sequence. {http://www.patentstorm.us/patents/7213142/description.html}, 2007.

[255] A. Moradi, A. Barenghi, T. Kasper, and C. Paar. On the vulnerability of FPGA bitstream encryption against power analysis attacks: extracting keys from Xilinx Virtex-II FPGAs. In *CCS'11: Proceedings of the ACM Conference on Computer and Communications Security*, pages 111–123, 2011.

[256] Amir Moradi, Mohammad T. Manzuri Shalmani, and Mahmoud Salmasizadeh. A Generalized Method of Differential Fault Attack against AES Cryptosystem. In *CHES*, pages 91–100, 2006.

[257] C.J. Morford. BitMaT – Bitstream Manipulation Tool for Xilinx FPGAs. Master's thesis, Virginia Polytechnic Institute and State University, 2005.

[258] Mehran Mozaffari-Kermani and Arash Reyhani-Masoleh. Parity-Based Fault Detection Architecture of S-box for Advanced Encryption Standard. In *DFT*, pages 572–580, Oct 2006.

[259] Mehran Mozaffari-Kermani and Arash Reyhani-Masoleh. A Lightweight Concurrent Error Detection Scheme for the AES S-boxes Using Normal Basis. *In Proc. CHES*, pages 113–129, Aug 2008.

[260] Mehran Mozaffari-Kermani and Arash Reyhani-Masoleh. A Lightweight High-Performance Fault Detection Scheme for the Advanced Encryption Standard Using Composite Field. *IEEE Trans. VLSI Systems*, 19(1):85–91, 2011.

[261] Dhiman Saha Mukesh Agarwal, Sandip Karmakar and Debdeep Mukhopadhyay. Scan based side channel attacks on stream ciphers and their counter-measures. In *Indocrypt '08: Proceedings of Progress in Cryptology-Indocrypt, LNCS 5365*, pages 226–238, 2008.

[262] D. Mukhopadhyay. An improved fault based attack of the Advanced Encryption Standard. In *AFRICACRYPT'09: Progress in Cryptology*, pages 421–434, 2009.

[263] D. Mukhopadhyay, S. Banerjee, D. RoyChowdhury, and B. B. Bhattacharya. Cryptoscan: A secured scan chain architecture. In *ATS '05: Proceedings of the 14th Asian Test Symposium on Asian Test Symposium*, pages 348–353, Washington, DC, USA, 2005. IEEE Computer Society.

[264] Debdeep Mukhopadhyay. An Improved Fault Based Attack of the Advanced Encryption Standard. In *AFRICACRYPT*, pages 421–434, 2009.

[265] Debdeep Mukhopadhyay. An Improved Fault Based Attack of the Advanced Encryption Standard. In Bart Preneel, editor, *AFRICACRYPT*, volume 5580 of *Lecture Notes in Computer Science*, pages 421–434. Springer, 2009.

[266] Debdeep Mukhopadhyay and Dipanwita Roy Chowdhury. An efficient end to end design of rijndael cryptosystem in 0.18 μ cmos. In *VLSI Design*, pages 405–410, 2005.

[267] Julian Murphy. Clockless physical unclonable functions. In *Proc. of 5th international conference on Trust and Trustworthy Computing*, TRUST'12, pages 110–121, 2012.

[268] F. N. Najm. Transition Density: a new measure of activity in digital circuits. *IEEE Transactions on CAD*, 14(2):310–323, February 1993.

[269] Giogio Di Natale, Marie-Lisa Flottes, and Bruno Rouzeyre. A Novel Parity Bit Scheme for SBox in AES Circuits. In *DDECS*, pages 1–5, Apr 2007.

[270] Giogio Di Natale, Marie-Lisa Flottes, and Bruno Rouzeyre. On-Line Self-Test of AES Hardware Implementation. *WDSN*, 2007.

[271] Michael Neve, Jean pierre Seifert, and Zhenghong Wang. Cache Time-Behavior Analysis on AES, 2006.

[272] Michael Neve and Jean-Pierre Seifert. Advances on Access-Driven Cache Attacks on AES. In Eli Biham and Amr M. Youssef, editors, *Selected Areas in Cryptography*, volume 4356 of *Lecture Notes in Computer Science*, pages 147–162. Springer, 2006.

[273] Michael Neve, Jean-Pierre Seifert, and Zhenghong Wang. A Refined Look at Bernstein's AES Side-Channel Analysis. In Ferng-Ching Lin, Der-Tsai Lee, Bao-Shuh Lin, Shiuhpyng Shieh, and Sushil Jajodia, editors, *ASIACCS*, page 369. ACM, 2006.

[274] J. Note and E. Rannaud. From the bitstream to the netlist. In *FPGA'08: Proceedings of the International ACM/SIGDA Symposium on Field Programmable Gate Arrays*, pages 264–271, 2008.

[275] Kaisa Nyberg. Differentially uniform mappings for cryptography. In *EUROCRYPT*, pages 55–64, 1993.

[276] A. Oliveira. Robust techniques for watermarking sequential circuit designs. In *DAC'99: Proceedings of the ACM/IEEE Design Automation Conference*, pages 837–842, 1999.

[277] A.L. Oliveira. Techniques for the creation of digital watermarks in sequential circuit designs. *IEEE Transactions on CAD*, 20(9):1101 –1117, September 2001.

[278] OpenCores. http://www.opencores.org, 2011.

[279] Gerardo Orlando and Christof Paar. A High Performance Reconfigurable Elliptic Curve Processor for $GF(2^m)$. In *CHES '00: Proceedings of the Second International Workshop on Cryptographic Hardware and Embedded Systems*, pages 41–56, London, UK, 2000. Springer-Verlag.

[280] Dag Arne Osvik, Adi Shamir, and Eran Tromer. Cache attacks and Countermeasures: the Case of AES. Cryptology ePrint Archive, Report 2005/271, 2005.

[281] Dag Arne Osvik, Adi Shamir, and Eran Tromer. Cache Attacks and Countermeasures: The Case of AES. In David Pointcheval, editor, *CT-RSA*, volume 3860 of *Lecture Notes in Computer Science*, pages 1–20. Springer, 2006.

[282] Maria Elisabeth Oswald, Stefan Mangard, Norbert Pramstaller, and Vincent Rijmen. A Side-Channel Analysis Resistant Description of the AES S-box. In *Proceedings of Fast Software Encryption (FSE 2005), LNCS Volume 3557*, pages 413–423. Springer-Verlag, 2005.

[283] E. Ozturk, G. Hammouri, and B. Sunar. Physical unclonable function with tristate buffers. In *Proc. of IEEE International Symposium on Circuits and Systems(ISCAS)*, pages 3194–3197, 2008.

[284] P. C. Kocher. Timing Attacks on Implementation of Diffie-Hellman, RSA, DSS and Other Systems. In *Proceeding of Crypto, LNCS 1109*, pages 104–113, 1996.

[285] G. Letourneux P. Dusart and O. Vivolo. Differential Fault Analysis on AES. In *Cryptology ePrint Archive*, pages 293–306, Oct 2003.

[286] Christof Paar. *Efficient VLSI Architectures for Bit-Parallel Computation in Galois Fields*. PhD thesis, Institute for Experimental Mathematics, Universität Essen, Germany, June 1994.

[287] Christof Paar. A New Architecture for a Parallel Finite Field Multiplier with Low Complexity Based on Composite Fields. *IEEE Transactions on Computers*, 45(7):856–861, 1996.

[288] D. Page. Theoretical Use of Cache Memory as a Cryptanalytic Side-Channel, 2002.

[289] D Page. Defending Against Cache-Based Side-Channel Attacks. *Information Security Technical Report*, 8(1):30 – 44, 2003.

[290] Dan Page. Partitioned Cache Architecture as a Side-Channel Defence Mechanism. *IACR Cryptology ePrint Archive*, 2005:280, 2005.

[291] A. Papoulis and S. U. Pillai. *Probability, Random Variables and Stochastic Processes (4th ed.)*. McGraw–Hill, 2002.

[292] A. Papoulis and S. U. Pillai. Predictive technology model, 2012. `http://www.eas.asu.edu/~ptm/`.

[293] Ravikanth S. Pappu. *Physical one-way functions*. PhD thesis, Massachusetts Institute of Technology, March 2001.

[294] Ravikanth S. Pappu, Ben Recht, Jason Taylor, and Niel Gershenfeld. Physical one-way functions. *Science*, 297:2026–2030, 2002.

[295] S. Paul, H. Mahmoodi, and S. Bhunia. Low-overhead f_{max} calibration at multiple operating points using delay sensitivity based path selection. *ACM Transactions on Design Automation of Electronic Systems*, 15(2):19:1–19:34, February 2010.

[296] Paulo S. L. M. Barreto. The AES Block Cipher in C++.

[297] David Peacham and Byron Thomas. âĂIJA DFA attack against the AES key scheduleâĂÎ. SiVenture White Paper 001, 26 October, 2006.

[298] Colin Percival. Cache Missing for Fun and Profit. In *Proc. of BSDCan 2005*, 2005.

[299] Steffen Peter and Peter Langendörfer. An efficient polynomial multiplier in $GF(2^m)$ and its application to ECC designs. In *DATE '07: Proceedings of the conference on Design, automation and test in Europe*, pages 1253–1258, San Jose, CA, USA, 2007. EDA Consortium.

[300] G. Piret and J.J. Quisquater. A Differential Fault Attack Technique against SPN Structures, with Application to the AES and Khazad. In *CHES*, pages 77–88, Sept 2003.

[301] Rishabh Poddar, Amit Datta, and Chester Rebeiro. A Cache Trace Attack on CAMELLIA. In Marc Joye, Debdeep Mukhopadhyay, and Michael Tunstall, editors, *InfoSecHiComNet*, volume 7011 of *Lecture Notes in Computer Science*, pages 144–156. Springer, 2011.

[302] I. Pomeranz and S. M. Reddy. A measure of quality for n-detection test sets. *IEEE Transactions on Computers*, 53(11):1497–1503, 2004.

[303] Reinhard Posch. Protecting Devices by Active Coating. *Journal of Universal Computer Science*, 4(7):652–668, 1998.

[304] Norbert Pramstaller, Stefan Mangard, Sandra Dominikus, and Johannes Wolkerstorfer. Efficient aes implementations on asics and fpgas. In Hans Dobbertin, Vincent Rijmen, and Aleksandra Sowa, editors, *AES Conference*, volume 3373 of *Lecture Notes in Computer Science*, pages 98–112. Springer, 2004.

[305] Predictive Technology Model (PTM). `http://http://www.eas.asu.edu/$\sim$ptm/`.

[306] Qiong Pu and Jianhua Huang. A Microcoded Elliptic Curve Processor for $GF(2^m)$ Using FPGA Technology. In *Communications, Circuits and Systems Proceedings, 2006 International Conference on*, volume 4, pages 2771–2775, June 2006.

[307] R. Rivest, A. Shamir and L. Adleman. A Method for Obtaining Digital Signatures and Public-Key Cryptosystems. *Communications of the ACM, Previously released as an MIT "Technical Memo" in April 1977*, 21(2):120–126, 1978.

[308] R. Rad, J. Plusquellic, and M. Tehranipoor. A sensitivity analysis of power signal methods for detecting Hardware Trojans under real process and environmental conditions. *IEEE Transactions on Very Large Scale Integration (VLSI) Systems*, 18(12):1735 –1744, December 2010.

[309] R. M. Rad, X. Wang, M. Tehranipoor, and J. Plusquellic. Power supply signal calibration techniques for improving detection resolution to hardware Trojans. In *Proc. IEEE/ACM International Conference on Computer-Aided Design (ICCAD'08)*, pages 632–639, Piscataway, NJ, USA, 2008.

[310] D. Rai and J. Lach. Performance of delay-based Trojan detection techniques under parameter variations. In *Proc. IEEE International Workshop on Hardware-Oriented Security and Trust (HOST'09)*, pages 58–65, Washington, DC, USA, 2009.

[311] J. Rajendran, H. Borad, S. Mantravadi, and R. Karri. SLICED: Slide-based Concurrent Error Detection Technique for Symmetric Block Cipher. In *HOST*, pages 70–75, Jul 2010.

[312] C. Rebeiro and D. Mukhopadhay. Boosting Profiled Cache Timing Attacks with Apriori Analysis. *Information Forensics and Security, IEEE Transactions on*, PP(99):1, 2012.

[313] Chester Rebeiro, Mainack Mondal, and Debdeep Mukhopadhyay. Pinpointing Cache Timing Attacks on AES. In *VLSI Design*, pages 306–311. IEEE Computer Society, 2010.

[314] Chester Rebeiro and Debdeep Mukhopadhyay. High speed compact elliptic curve cryptoprocessor for fpga platforms. In *INDOCRYPT*, pages 376–388, 2008.

[315] Chester Rebeiro and Debdeep Mukhopadhyay. Power attack resistant efficient fpga architecture for karatsuba multiplier. In *VLSI Design*, pages 706–711, 2008.

[316] Chester Rebeiro and Debdeep Mukhopadhyay. Power Attack Resistant Efficient FPGA Architecture for Karatsuba Multiplier. In *VLSID '08: Proceedings of the 21st International Conference on VLSI Design*, pages 706–711, Washington, DC, USA, 2008. IEEE Computer Society.

[317] Chester Rebeiro and Debdeep Mukhopadhyay. Cryptanalysis of CLEFIA Using Differential Methods with Cache Trace Patterns. In Aggelos Kiayias, editor, *CT-RSA*, volume 6558 of *Lecture Notes in Computer Science*, pages 89–103. Springer, 2011.

[318] Chester Rebeiro, Debdeep Mukhopadhyay, Junko Takahashi, and Toshinori Fukunaga. Cache Timing Attacks on CLEFIA. In Bimal Roy and Nicolas Sendrier, editors, *INDOCRYPT*, volume 5922 of *Lecture Notes in Computer Science*, pages 104–118. Springer, 2009.

[319] Chester Rebeiro, Rishabh Poddar, Amit Datta, and Debdeep Mukhopadhyay. An Enhanced Differential Cache Attack on CLEFIA for Large Cache Lines. In Daniel J. Bernstein and Sanjit Chatterjee, editors, *INDOCRYPT*, volume 7107 of *Lecture Notes in Computer Science*, pages 58–75. Springer, 2011.

[320] Chester Rebeiro, Sujoy Sinha Roy, and Debdeep Mukhopadhyay. Pushing the limits of high-speed gf(2 m) elliptic curve scalar multiplication on fpgas. In *CHES*, pages 494–511, 2012.

[321] Chester Rebeiro, Sujoy Sinha Roy, Sankara Reddy, and Debdeep Mukhopadhyay. Revisiting the itoh-tsujii inversion algorithm for fpga platforms. *IEEE Trans. VLSI Syst.*, 19(8):1508–1512, 2011.

[322] Chester Rebeiro, A. David Selvakumar, and A. S. L. Devi. Bitslice Implementation of AES. In David Pointcheval, Yi Mu, and Kefei Chen, editors, *CANS*, volume 4301 of *Lecture Notes in Computer Science*, pages 203–212. Springer, 2006.

[323] Mathieu Renauld, François-Xavier Standaert, and Nicolas Veyrat-Charvillon. Algebraic side-channel attacks on the aes: Why time also matters in dpa. In *Proceedings of the 11th International Workshop on Cryptographic Hardware and Embedded Systems*, CHES '09, pages 97–111, Berlin, Heidelberg, 2009. Springer-Verlag.

[324] H.G. Rice. Classes of recursively enumerable sets and their decision problems. *Trans. Am. Math. Soc,*, 74:358–366, 1953.

[325] V. Rijmen. Efficient Implementation of the Rijndael Sbox. http://www.esat.kuleuven.ac.be/ rijmen/rijndael.

[326] Vincent Rijmen. Efficient Implementation of Rijndael S-Box. http://www.esat.kuleuven.ac.be/ rijmen/rijndael/.

[327] Thomas Ristenpart, Eran Tromer, Hovav Shacham, and Stefan Savage. Hey, you, get off of my cloud: Exploring Information Leakage in Third-Party Compute Clouds. In Ehab Al-Shaer, Somesh Jha, and Angelos D. Keromytis, editors, *ACM Conference on Computer and Communications Security*, pages 199–212. ACM, 2009.

[328] Sabel Mercurio Henríquez Rodríguez and Francisco Rodríguez-Henríquez. An FPGA Arithmetic Logic Unit for Computing Scalar Multiplication using the Half-and-Add Method. In *ReConFig 2005: International Conference on Reconfigurable Computing and FPGAs*, Washington, DC, USA, 2005. IEEE Computer Society.

[329] Francisco Rodríguez-Henríquez and Çetin Kaya Koç. On Fully Parallel Karatsuba Multipliers for $GF(2^m)$. In *Proc. of the International Conference on Computer Science and Technology (CST)*, pages 405–410.

[330] Francisco Rodríguez-Henríquez, Guillermo Morales-Luna, Nazar A. Saqib, and Nareli Cruz-Cortés. Parallel Itoh-Tsujii Multiplicative Inversion Algorithm for a Special Class of Trinomials. *Des. Codes Cryptography*, 45(1):19–37, 2007.

[331] Francisco Rodríguez-Henríquez, N. A. Saqib, A. Díaz-Pèrez, and Çetin Kaya Koc. *Cryptographic Algorithms on Reconfigurable Hardware (Signals and Communication Technology)*. Springer-Verlag New York, Inc., Secaucus, NJ, USA, 2006.

[332] Francisco Rodríguez-Henríquez, N. A. Saqib, A. Díaz-Pèrez, and Cetin Kaya Koc. *Cryptographic Algorithms on Reconfigurable Hardware (Signals and Communication Technology)*. Springer-Verlag New York, Inc., Secaucus, NJ, USA, 2006.

[333] Francisco Rodríguez-Henríquez, Nazar A. Saqib, and Nareli Cruz-Cortés. A Fast Implementation of Multiplicative Inversion Over $GF(2^m)$. In *ITCC '05: Proceedings of the International Conference on Information Technology: Coding and Computing (ITCC'05) - Volume I*, pages 574–579, Washington, DC, USA, 2005. IEEE Computer Society.

[334] A. Roy, F. Koushanfar, and I.L. Markov. Extended abstract: Circuit CAD tools as a security threat. In *HOST'08: Proceedings of the IEEE International Workshop on Hardware Oriented Security and Trust*, pages 65–66, 2008.

[335] J. A. Roy, F. Kaushanfar, and I. L. Markov. Extended abstract: circuit CAD tools as a security threat. In *HOST'08: Proceedings of the International Workshop on Hardware-oriented Security and Trust*, pages 61–62, 2008.

[336] J. A. Roy, F. Koushanfar, and I. L.Markov. *EPIC*: ending piracy of integrated circuits. In *DATE'08: Proceedings of the Conference on Design, Automation and Test in Europe*, pages 1069–1074, 2008.

[337] Sujoy Sinha Roy, Chester Rebeiro, and Debdeep Mukhopadhyay. Theoretical modeling of the itoh-tsujii inversion algorithm for enhanced performance on k-lut based fpgas. In *DATE*, pages 1231–1236, 2011.

[338] Sujoy Sinha Roy, Chester Rebeiro, and Debdeep Mukhopadhyay. Theoretical Modeling of the Itoh-Tsujii Inversion Algorithm for Enhanced Performance on k-LUT based FPGAs. In *Design, Automation, and Test in Europe DATE-2011*, 2011.

[339] U. Rührmair, S. Devadas, and F. Koushanfar. Security based on Physical Unclonability and Disorder. chapter Book Chapter in Introduction to Hardware Security and Trust. Springer, 2011.

[340] U. Rührmair, C. Jaeger, C. Hilgers, M. Algasinger, G. Csaba, and M. Stutzmann. Security Applications of Diodes with Unique Current-Voltage Characteristics. In *Financial Cryptography and Data Security*, volume 6052 of *Lecture Notes in Computer Science*, pages 328–335. 2010.

[341] Dhiman Saha, Debdeep Mukhopadhyay, and Dipanwita Roy Chowdhury. A Diagonal Fault Attack on the Advanced Encryption Standard. *IACR Cryptology ePrint Archive*, page 581, 2009.

[342] Dhiman Saha, Debdeep Mukhopadhyay, and Dipanwita Roy Chowdhury. Pkdpa: An enhanced probabilistic differential power attack methodology. In *INDOCRYPT*, pages 3–21, 2011.

[343] T. Sakurai. Genetic Algorithms: principles of natural selection applied to computation. *Science (New Series)*, 261(5123):872–878, Aug 1993.

[344] T. Sakurai and A. R. Newton. Alpha-power law MOSFET model and its applications to CMOS inverter delay and other formulas. *IEEE Journal of Solid-State Circuits*, 25(2):584–594, apr 1990.

[345] N. A. Saqib, F. Rodríiguez-Henríquez, and A. Diaz-Perez. A Parallel Architecture for Fast Computation of Elliptic Curve Scalar Multiplication Over $GF(2^m)$. In *18th International Parallel and Distributed Processing Symposium, 2004. Proceedings*, April 2004.

[346] sasebo.   Side-channel   Attack   Standard   Evaluation   Board. http://staff.aist.go.jp/akashi.satoh/SASEBO/en/index.html.

[347] Akashi Satoh, Sumio Morioka, Kohji Takano, and Seiji Munetoh. A Compact Rijndael Hardware Architecture with S-Box Optimization. In Colin Boyd, editor, *ASIACRYPT*, volume 2248 of *Lecture Notes in Computer Science*, pages 239–254. Springer, 2001.

[348] Akashi Satoh, Sumio Morioka, Kohji Takano, and Seiji Munetoh. A compact rijndael hardware architecture with s-box optimization. pages 239–254. Springer-Verlag, 2001.

[349] Akashi Satoh, Takeshi Sugawara, Naofumi Homma, and Takafumi Aoki. High-Performance Concurrent Error Detection Scheme for AES Hardware. In *CHES*, pages 100–112, Aug 2008.

[350] Werner Schindler, Kerstin Lemke, and Christof Paar. A stochastic model for differential side channel cryptanalysis. In *CHES*, pages 30–46, 2005.

[351] B. Schneier. *Applied Cryptography: Protocols, Algorithms and Source Code in C*. John Wiley & Sons, 2001.

[352] A. Schulman. Examining the Windows AARD detection code. *Dr. Dobb's Journal*, 18, September 1993.

[353] J. Seberry and J. Pieprzyk. *An Introduction to Computer Security*. Advances in Computer Science Series, 1988.

[354] Frank Sehnke, Christian Osendorfer, Jan Sölter, Jürgen Schmidhuber, and Ulrich Rührmair. Policy Gradients for Cryptanalysis. In *Proc. of 20th International Conference on Artificial Neural Networks (ICANN)*, volume 6354, pages 168–177, 2010.

[355] N. Selmane, S. Guilley, and J. L. Danger. Practical Setup Time Violation Attacks on AES. In *EDCC'08: Proceedings of the European Dependable Computing Conference*, pages 91–96, 2008.

[356] Nidhal Selmane, Sylvain Guilley, and Jean-Luc Danger. Practical Setup Time Violation Attacks on AES. pages 91–96. European Dependable Computing Conference, 2008.

[357] Gaurav Sengar, Debdeep Mukhopadhyay, and Dipanwita Roy Chowdhury. Secured flipped scan-chain model for crypto-architecture. *IEEE Trans. on CAD of Integrated Circuits and Systems*, 26(11):2080–2084, 2007.

[358] R. Sever, A.N. Ismailoglu, Y.C. Tekmen, and M. Askar. A high speed asic implementation of the rijndael algorithm. In *Circuits and Systems, 2004. ISCAS '04. Proceedings of the 2004 International Symposium on*, volume 2, pages II–541–4 Vol.2, 2004.

[359] C. E. Shannon. Communication theory of secrecy systems, vol 28, no 4. In *Bell System Technical Journal*, pages 656–715. Bell, 1949.

[360] Shay Gueron. Intelő Advanced Encryption Standard (AES) Instructions Set (Rev : 3.0), 2010.

[361] Y. Shi, N. Togawa, M. Yanagisawa, and T. Ohtsuki. Design-for-secure-test for crypto cores. In *ITC09: Proceedings of International Test Conference.*, page 1, 2009.

[362] Y. Shi, N. Togawa, M. Yanagisawa, and T. Ohtsuki. Robust secure scan design against scan-based differential cryptanalysis. *Very Large Scale Integration (VLSI) Systems, IEEE Transactions on*, PP(99):1–15, 2011.

[363] Koichi Shimizu, Daisuke Suzuki, and Tomomi Kasuya. Glitch PUF: Extracting Information from Usually Unwanted Glitches. *IEICE Transactions on Fundamentals of Electronics, Communications and Computer Sciences*, E95.A(1):223–233, 2012.

[364] Daniel P. Siewiorek and Robert S. Swarz. Reliable Computer Systems: Design and Evaluation. *A K Peters/CRC Press; 3 edition*, 1998.

[365] P. Simons, E. van der Sluis, and V. van der Leest. Buskeeper PUFs, a promising alternative to D Flip-Flop PUFs. In *Proc. of IEEE International Symposium on Hardware-Oriented Security and Trust (HOST)*, pages 7 –12, 2012.

[366] Eric Simpson and Patrick Schaumont. Offline hardware/software authentication for reconfigurable platforms. In *Proc. of the 8th international conference on Cryptographic Hardware and Embedded Systems (CHES)*, pages 311–323, 2006.

[367] Sergei P. Skorobogatov and Ross J. Anderson. Optical Fault Induction Attacks. In *proceedings of CHES*, pages 2–12, Aug 2002.

[368] William Stallings. *Cryptography and Network Security: Principles and Practice*. Pearson Education, 2002.

[369] William Stallings. *Cryptography and Network Security (4th Edition)*. Prentice-Hall, Inc., Upper Saddle River, NJ, USA, 2005.

[370] Douglas Stinson. *Cryptography: Theory and Practice, Second Edition*, pages 117–154. Chapman & Hall, CRC, London, UK, 2002.

[371] Y. Su, J. Holleman, and B. Otis. A 1.6pJ/bit 96% Stable Chip-ID Generating Circuit using Process Variations. In *Proc. of IEEE International Solid-State Circuits Conference(ISSCC)* , pages 406–611, 2007.

[372] G. Edward Suh and Srinivas Devadas. Physical unclonable functions for device authentication and secret key generation. In *Design Automation Conference*, pages 9–14, 2007.

[373] G.E. Suh and S. Devadas. Physical unclonable functions for device authentication and secret key generation. In *DAC'07: Proceedings of the ACM/IEEE Design Automation Conference*, pages 9–14, 2007.

[374] Interra Systems. Concorde – fast synthesis. `http://www.interrasystems.com/eda/eda_concorde.php`, 2009.

[375] W. Chelton T. Good and M. Benaissa. Review of stream cipher candidates from a low resource hardware perspective.

[376] Junko Takahashi and Toshinori Fukunaga. Differential Fault Analysis on AES with 192 and 256-Bit Keys. Cryptology ePrint Archive, Report 2010/023, 2010. `http://eprint.iacr.org/`.

[377] Junko Takahashi, Toshinori Fukunaga, and Kimihiro Yamakoshi. DFA Mechanism on the AES Key Schedule. In Luca Breveglieri, Shay Gueron, Israel Koren, David Naccache, and Jean-Pierre Seifert, editors, *FDTC*, pages 62–74. IEEE Computer Society, 2007.

[378] M. Tehranipoor and M. Koushanfar. A survey of hardware trojan taxonomy and detection. *IEEE Design and Test of Computers*, 27(1):10–25, Jan. 2010.

[379] Thicket^{TM} family of source code obfuscators. `http://www.semdesigns.com`, 2011.

[380] Kris Tiri, Onur Aciiçmez, Michael Neve, and Flemming Andersen. An analytical model for time-driven cache attacks. In Alex Biryukov, editor, *FSE*, volume 4593 of *Lecture Notes in Computer Science*, pages 399–413. Springer, 2007.

[381] I. Torunoglu and E. Charbon. Watermarking-based copyright protection of sequential functions. *IEEE Journal of Solid–State Circuits*, 35(3):434–440, March 2000.

[382] Elena Trichina. Combinational logic design for aes subbyte transformation on masked data. *IACR Cryptology ePrint Archive*, 2003:236, 2003.

[383] Trivium. http://www.ecrypt.eu.org/stream/triviump3.html.

[384] Eran Tromer, Dag Arne Osvik, and Adi Shamir. Efficient Cache Attacks on AES, and Countermeasures. *Journal of Cryptology*, 23(2):37–71, 2010.

[385] Dan Tsafrir, Yoav Etsion, and Dror G. Feitelson. Secretly Monopolizing the CPU without Superuser Privileges. In *Proceedings of 16th USENIX Security Symposium on USENIX Security Symposium*, SS'07, pages 17:1–17:18, Berkeley, CA, USA, 2007. USENIX Association.

[386] Yukiyasu Tsunoo, Teruo Saito, Tomoyasu Suzaki, Maki Shigeri, and Hiroshi Miyauchi. Cryptanalysis of DES Implemented on Computers with Cache. In Colin D. Walter, Çetin Kaya Koç, and Christof Paar, editors, *CHES*, volume 2779 of *Lecture Notes in Computer Science*, pages 62–76. Springer, 2003.

[387] Yukiyasu Tsunoo, Etsuko Tsujihara, Kazuhiko Minematsu, and Hiroshi Miyauchi. Cryptanalysis of Block Ciphers Implemented on Computers with Cache. In *International Symposium on Information Theory and Its Applications*, pages 803–806, 2002.

[388] Yukiyasu Tsunoo, Etsuko Tsujihara, Maki Shigeri, Hiroyasu Kubo, and Kazuhiko Minematsu. Improving Cache Attacks by Considering Cipher Structure. *Int. J. Inf. Sec.*, 5(3):166–176, 2006.

[389] Michael Tunstall and Olivier Benoît. Efficient Use of Random Delays in Embedded Software. In Damien Sauveron, Constantinos Markantonakis, Angelos Bilas, and Jean-Jacques Quisquater, editors, *WISTP*, volume 4462 of *Lecture Notes in Computer Science*, pages 27–38. Springer, 2007.

[390] Michael Tunstall, Debdeep Mukhopadhyay, and Subidh Ali. Differential Fault Analysis of the Advanced Encryption Standard Using a Single Fault. In *WISTP*, pages 224–233, 2011.

[391] Pim Tuyls, Geert-Jan Schrijen, Boris Škorić, Jan van Geloven, Nynke Verhaegh, and Rob Wolters. Read-proof hardware from protective coatings. In *Proc. of Cryptographic Hardware and Embedded Systems Workshop*, volume 4249 of *LNCS*, pages 369–383, 2006.

[392] Ulrich R ührmair, Frank Sehnke, Jan S "olter, Gideon Dror, Srinivas Devadas, and J "urgen Schmidhuber. Modeling attacks on physical unclonable functions. In *Proc. of 17th ACM conference on Computer and communications security(CCS)*, pages 237–249, 2010.

[393] U.S. Department of Commerce,National Institute of Standards and Technology. Digital signature standard (DSS), 2000.

[394] Bhanu C. Vattikonda, Sambit Das, and Hovav Shacham. Eliminating Fine Grained Timers in Xen. In Christian Cachin and Thomas Ristenpart, editors, *CCSW*, pages 41–46. ACM, 2011.

[395] Tobias Vejda, Dan Page, and Johann Großschädl. Instruction Set Extensions for Pairing-Based Cryptography. In Tsuyoshi Takagi, Tatsuaki Okamoto, Eiji Okamoto, and Takeshi Okamoto, editors, *Pairing*, volume 4575 of *Lecture Notes in Computer Science*, pages 208–224. Springer, 2007.

[396] Ingrid Verbauwhede, Senior Member, Patrick Schaumont, Student Member, and Henry Kuo. Design and performance testing of a 2.29-gb/s rijndael processor. *IEEE Journal of Solid-State Circuits*, 38:569–572, 2003.

[397] Joachim von zur Gathen and Jamshid Shokrollahi. Efficient FPGA-Based Karatsuba Multipliers for Polynomials over F_2. In *Selected Areas in Cryptography*, pages 359–369, 2005.

[398] Serge Vrijaldenhoven. Acoustical Physical Uncloneable Functions. Master's thesis, Technische Universiteit Eindhoven, 2005.

[399] C. Wang, J. Hill, J. C. Knight, and J. W. Davidson. Protection of software-based survivability mechanisms. In *DSN'01: Proceedings of the International Conference on Dependable Systems and Networks*, pages 193—202, 2001.

[400] F. Wang. Formal verification of timed systems. *Proceedings of the IEEE*, 92(8):1283–1305, August 2004.

[401] X. Wang, M. Tehranipoor, and J. Plusquellic. Detecting malicious inclusions in secure hardware: Challenges and solutions. In *HOST'08: Proceedings of the IEEE International Workshop on Hardware-Oriented Security and Trust*, pages 15–19, 2008.

[402] Zhenghong Wang and Ruby B. Lee. New cache designs for thwarting software cache-based side channel attacks. In Dean M. Tullsen and Brad Calder, editors, *ISCA*, pages 494–505. ACM, 2007.

[403] Zhenghong Wang and Ruby B. Lee. A Novel Cache Architecture with Enhanced Performance and Security. In *MICRO*, pages 83–93. IEEE Computer Society, 2008.

[404] André Weimerskirch and Christof Paar. Generalizations of the Karatsuba Algorithm for Efficient Implementations. Cryptology ePrint Archive, Report 2006/224, 2006.

[405] M. A. Weiss. *Data Structures and Algorithm Analysis in C (2nd ed.)*. Pearson Education, 1997.

[406] Michael Weiß, Benedikt Heinz, and Frederic Stumpf. A cache timing attack on aes in virtualization environments. In Angelos D. Keromytis, editor, *Financial Cryptography*, volume 7397 of *Lecture Notes in Computer Science*, pages 314–328. Springer, 2012.

[407] Michael J. Wirthlin and Brian McMurtrey. IP delivery for FPGAs using applets and JHDL. In *Proceedings of the 39th annual Design Automation Conference*, DAC '02, pages 2–7, New York, NY, 2002. ACM.

[408] F. Wolff, C. Papachristou, S. Bhunia, and R. S. Chakraborty. Towards Trojan-free trusted ICs: problem analysis and detection scheme. In *Proc. Conference on Design, Automation and Test in Europe (DATE'08)*, pages 1362–1365, New York, NY, USA, 2008.

[409] Johannes Wolkerstorfer. *Hardware Aspects of Elliptic Curve Cryptography*. PhD thesis, Institute for Applied Information Processing and Communications, Graz University of Technology, 2004.

[410] Johannes Wolkerstorfer, Elisabeth Oswald, and Mario Lamberger. An asic implementation of the aes sboxes. In *Proceedings of the The Cryptographer's Track at the RSA Conference on Topics in Cryptology*, CT-RSA '02, pages 67–78, London, UK, UK, 2002. Springer-Verlag.

[411] J. C. Wray. An Analysis of Covert Timing Channels. In *Research in Security and Privacy, 1991. Proceedings., 1991 IEEE Computer Society Symposium on*, pages 2 –7, may 1991.

[412] Kaijie Wu, Ramesh Karri, G. Kuznetsov, and M. Goessel. Low Cost Concurrent Error Detection for the Advanced Encryption Standard. In *ITC*, pages 1242–1248, Oct 2004.

[413] M. G. Xakellis and F. N. Najm. Statistical estimation of the switching activity in digital circuits. In *DAC '94: Proceedings of the Design Automation Conference*, pages 728–733, 1994.

[414] Chenglu Jin Xiaofei Guo, Debdeep Mukhopadhyay and Ramesh Karri. Nrepo:normal basis recomputing with permuted operands. Cryptology ePrint Archive, Report 2014/497, 2014. `http://eprint.iacr.org/`.

[415] Debdeep Mukhopadhyay Xiaofei Guo and Ramesh Karri. Provably secure concurrent error detection against differential fault analysis. Cryptology ePrint Archive, Report 2012/552, 2012. `http://eprint.iacr.org/`.

[416] Debdeep Mukhopadhyay Xiaofei Guo and Ramesh Karri. Provably secure concurrent error detection against differential fault analysis. Cryptology ePrint Archive, Report 2012/552, 2012. `http://eprint.iacr.org/`.

[417] Xilinx. Using Block RAM in Spartan-3 Generation FPGAs. Application Note, XAPP-463, 2005.

[418] Xilinx. Using Look-Up Tables as Distributed RAM in Spartan-3 Generation FPGAs. Application Note, XAPP-464, 2005.

[419] Dai Yamamoto, Kazuo Sakiyama, Mitsugu Iwamoto, Kazuo Ohta, Takao Ochiai, Masahiko Takenaka, and Kouichi Itoh. Uniqueness Enhancement of PUF Responses Based on the Locations of Random Outputting RS Latches. In *Proc. of 13th International Workshop on Cryptographic Hardware and Embedded Systems (CHES)*, pages 390–406, October 2011.

[420] Dai Yamamoto, Kazuo Sakiyama, Mitsugu Iwamoto, Kazuo Ohta, Masahiko Takenaka, and Kouichi Itoh. Variety enhancement of PUF responses using the locations of random outputting RS latches. In *Journal of Cryptographic Engineering*, pages 1–15, 2012.

[421] B. Yang, K. Wu, and R. Karri. Secure scan: A design-for-test architecture for crypto chips. *Computer-Aided Design of Integrated Circuits and Systems, IEEE Transactions on*, 25(10):2287–2293, Oct. 2006.

[422] Bo Yang, Kaijie Wu, and Ramesh Karri. Scan based side channel attack on dedicated hardware implementations of data encryption standard. In *ITC '04: Proceedings of the International Test Conference*, pages 339–344, Washington, DC, USA, 2004. IEEE Computer Society.

[423] Y. Yao, M. Kim, J. Li, I. L. Markov, and F. Koushanfar. ClockPUF: Physical Unclonable Functions based on Clock Networks. In *Design, Automation & Test in Europe (DATE)*, 2013.

[424] H. Yotsuyanagi and K. Kinoshita. Undetectable fault removal of sequential circuits based on unreachable states. In *VTS'98: Proceedings of the IEEE VLSI Test Symposium*, pages 176–181, 1998.

[425] Pengyuan Yu and Patrick Schaumont. Secure FPGA circuits using controlled placement and routing. In *Proceedings of International Conference on Hardware Software Codesign (CODES+ISSS)*, pages 45–50. ACM, 2007.

[426] L. Yuan and G. Qu. Information hiding in finite state machine. In *IH'04: Proceedings of the International Conference on Information Hiding*, IH'04, pages 340–354, 2004.

[427] Erik Zenner. Cache Timing Analysis of HC-256. In *15th Annual International Workshop, SAC 2008*, 2008.

[428] XinJie Zhao and Tao Wang. Improved Cache Trace Attack on AES and CLEFIA by Considering Cache Miss and S-box Misalignment. Cryptology ePrint Archive, Report 2010/056, 2010.

[429] Zhijie Jerry Shi and Xiao Yang and Ruby B. Lee. Alternative Application-Specific Processor Architectures for Fast Arbitrary Bit Permutations. *IJES*, 3(4):219–228, 2008.

[430] X. Zhuang, T. Zhang, H.S. Lee, and S. Pande. Hardware assisted control flow obfuscation for embedded processors. In *CASES '04: Proceedings of the 2004 International Conference on Compilers, Architecture, and Synthesis for Embedded Systems*, pages 292–302, 2004.

[431] Xiaotong Zhuang, Tao Zhang, Hsien-Hsin S. Lee, and Santosh Pande. Hardware Assisted Control Flow Obfuscation for Embedded Processors. In Mary Jane Irwin, Wei Zhao, Luciano Lavagno, and Scott A. Mahlke, editors, *CASES*, pages 292–302. ACM, 2004.

[432] Xiaotong Zhuang, Tao Zhang, and Santosh Pande. HIDE: an Infrastructure for Efficiently Protecting Information Leakage on the Address Bus. In Shubu Mukherjee and Kathryn S. McKinley, editors, *ASPLOS*, pages 72–84. ACM, 2004.

Index